FPL
REF
X809.1
V.29

Borod'
$105.00

3 1213 01092

P9-DCY-847

DISCARD

FRAMINGHAM PUBLIC LIBRARY

OCT 2 1 2008

DISCARD

POETRY
for Students

Advisors

Susan Allison: Head Librarian, Lewiston High School, Lewiston, Maine. Standards Committee Chairperson for Maine School Library (MASL) Programs. Board member, Julia Adams Morse Memorial Library, Greene, Maine. Advisor to Lewiston Public Library Planning Process.

Jennifer Hood: Young Adult/Reference Librarian, Cumberland Public Library, Cumberland, Rhode Island. Certified teacher, Rhode Island. Member of the New England Library Association, Rhode Island Library Association, and the Rhode Island Educational Media Association.

Ann Kearney: Head Librarian and Media Specialist, Christopher Columbus High School, Miami, Florida, 1982–2002. Thirty-two years as Librarian in various educational institutions ranging from grade schools through graduate programs. Library positions at Miami-Dade Community College, the University of Miami's Medical School Library, and Carrollton School in Coconut Grove, Florida. B.A. from University of Detroit, 1967 (magna cum laude); M.L.S., University of Missouri–Columbia, 1974. Volunteer Project Leader for a school in rural Jamaica; volunteer with Adult Literacy programs.

Laurie St. Laurent: Head of Adult and Children's Services, East Lansing Public Library, East Lansing, Michigan, 1994–. M.L.S. from Western Michigan University. Chair of Michigan Library Association's 1998 Michigan Summer Reading Program; Chair of the Children's Services Division in 2000–2001; and Vice-President of the Association in 2002–2003. Board member of several regional early childhood literacy organizations and member of the Library of Michigan Youth Services Advisory Committee.

Heidi Stohs: Instructor in Language Arts, grades 10–12, Solomon High School, Solomon, Kansas. Received B.S. from Kansas State University; M.A. from Fort Hays State University.

POETRY
for Students

**Presenting Analysis, Context, and Criticism on
Commonly Studied Poetry**

VOLUME 29

GALE
CENGAGE Learning™

Detroit • New York • San Francisco • New Haven, Conn • Waterville, Maine • London

GALE
CENGAGE Learning™

Poetry for Students, Volume 29

Project Editor: Ira Mark Milne

Rights Acquisition and Management: Mollika Basu, Jermaine Bobbitt, Sara Teller, Robyn Young

Composition: Evi Abou-El-Seoud

Manufacturing: Drew Kalasky

Imaging: Lezlie Light

Product Design: Pamela A. E. Galbreath, Jennifer Wahi

Content Conversion: Civie Green, Katrina Coach

Product Manager: Meggin Condino

© 2009 Gale, Cengage Learning

ALL RIGHTS RESERVED. No part of this work covered by the copyright herein may be reproduced, transmitted, stored, or used in any form or by any means graphic, electronic, or mechanical, including but not limited to photocopying, recording, scanning, digitizing, taping, Web distribution, information networks, or information storage and retrieval systems, except as permitted under Section 107 or 108 of the 1976 United States Copyright Act, without the prior written permission of the publisher.

Since this page cannot legibly accommodate all copyright notices, the acknowledgments constitute an extension of the copyright notice.

For product information and technology assistance, contact us at **Gale Customer Support, 1-800-877-4253.**
For permission to use material from this text or product, submit all requests online at **www.cengage.com/permissions.**
Further permissions questions can be emailed to **permissionrequest@cengage.com**

While every effort has been made to ensure the reliability of the information presented in this publication, Gale, a part of Cengage Learning, does not guarantee the accuracy of the data contained herein. Gale accepts no payment for listing; and inclusion in the publication of any organization, agency, institution, publication, service, or individual does not imply endorsement of the editors or publisher. Errors brought to the attention of the publisher and verified to the satisfaction of the publisher will be corrected in future editions.

Gale
27500 Drake Rd.
Farmington Hills, MI, 48331-3535

ISBN-13: 978-0-7876-9893-5
ISBN-10: 0-7876-9893-8

ISSN 1094-7019

This title is also available as an e-book.
ISBN-13: 978-1-4144-3834-4
ISBN-10: 1-4144-3834-6
Contact your Gale, a part of Cengage Learning sales representative for ordering information.

Printed in the United States of America
1 2 3 4 5 6 7 13 12 11 10 09 08

Table of Contents

Just a Few Lines on a Page

I have often thought that poets have the easiest job in the world. A poem, after all, is just a few lines on a page, usually not even extending margin to margin—how long would that take to write, about five minutes? Maybe ten at the most, if you wanted it to rhyme or have a repeating meter. Why, I could start in the morning and produce a book of poetry by dinnertime. But we all know that it isn't that easy. Anyone can come up with enough words, but the poet's job is about writing the *right* ones. The right words will change lives, making people see the world somewhat differently than they saw it just a few minutes earlier. The right words can make a reader who relies on the dictionary for meanings take a greater responsibility for his or her own personal understanding. A poem that is put on the page correctly can bear any amount of analysis, probing, defining, explaining, and interrogating, and something about it will still feel new the next time you read it.

It would be fine with me if I could talk about poetry without using the word "magical," because that word is overused these days to imply "a really good time," often with a certain sweetness about it, and a lot of poetry is neither of these. But if you stop and think about magic—whether it brings to mind sorcery, witchcraft, or bunnies pulled from top hats—it always seems to involve stretching reality to produce a result greater than the sum of its parts and pulling unexpected results out of thin air. This book provides ample cases where a few simple words conjure up whole worlds. We do not actually travel to different times and different cultures, but the poems get into our minds, they find what little we know about the places they are talking about, and then they make that little bit blossom into a bouquet of someone else's life. Poets make us think we are following simple, specific events, but then they leave ideas in our heads that cannot be found on the printed page. Abracadabra.

Sometimes when you finish a poem it doesn't feel as if it has left any supernatural effect on you, like it did not have any more to say beyond the actual words that it used. This happens to everybody, but most often to inexperienced readers: regardless of what is often said about young people's infinite capacity to be amazed, you have to understand what usually does happen, and what could have happened instead, if you are going to be moved by what someone has accomplished. In those cases in which you finish a poem with a "So what?" attitude, the information provided in *Poetry for Students* comes in handy. Readers can feel assured that the poems included here actually are potent magic, not just because a few (or a hundred or ten thousand) professors of literature say they are: they're significant because they can withstand close inspection and still amaze the very same people who have just finished taking them apart and seeing how they work. Turn them inside out, and they will still be able to come alive, again and again. *Poetry for Students* gives readers of any age good practice in feeling the ways poems relate to both the reality of the time and place the poet lived in and the reality of our emotions. Practice is just another word for being a student. The information given here helps you understand the way to read poetry; what to look for, what to expect.

With all of this in mind, I really don't think I would actually like to have a poet's job at all. There are too many skills involved, including precision, honesty, taste, courage, linguistics, passion, compassion, and the ability to keep all sorts of people entertained at once. And that is just what they do with one hand, while the other hand pulls some sort of trick that most of us will never fully understand. I can't even pack all that I need for a weekend into one suitcase, so what would be my chances of stuffing so much life into a few lines? With all that *Poetry for Students* tells us about each poem, I am impressed that any poet can finish three or four poems a year. Read the inside stories of these poems, and you won't be able to approach any poem in the same way you did before.

David J. Kelly
College of Lake County

Introduction

Purpose of the Book

The purpose of *Poetry for Students* (*PfS*) is to provide readers with a guide to understanding, enjoying, and studying poems by giving them easy access to information about the work. Part of Gale's "For Students" Literature line, *PfS* is specifically designed to meet the curricular needs of high school and undergraduate college students and their teachers, as well as the interests of general readers and researchers considering specific poems. While each volume contains entries on "classic" poems frequently studied in classrooms, there are also entries containing hard-to-find information on contemporary poems, including works by multicultural, international, and women poets.

The information covered in each entry includes an introduction to the poem and the poem's author; the actual poem text (if possible); a poem summary, to help readers unravel and understand the meaning of the poem; analysis of important themes in the poem; and an explanation of important literary techniques and movements as they are demonstrated in the poem.

In addition to this material, which helps the readers analyze the poem itself, students are also provided with important information on the literary and historical background informing each work. This includes a historical context essay, a box comparing the time or place the poem was written to modern Western culture, a critical overview essay, and excerpts from critical essays on the poem. A unique feature of *PfS* is a specially commissioned critical essay on each poem, targeted toward the student reader.

To further aid the student in studying and enjoying each poem, information on media adaptations is provided (if available), as well as reading suggestions for works of fiction and nonfiction on similar themes and topics. Classroom aids include ideas for research papers and lists of critical sources that provide additional material on the poem.

Selection Criteria

The titles for each volume of *PfS* were selected by surveying numerous sources on teaching literature and analyzing course curricula for various school districts. Some of the sources surveyed included: literature anthologies; *Reading Lists for College-Bound Students: The Books Most Recommended by America's Top Colleges*; textbooks on teaching the poem; a College Board survey of poems commonly studied in high schools; and a National Council of Teachers of English (NCTE) survey of poems commonly studied in high schools.

Input was also solicited from our advisory board, as well as educators from various areas. From these discussions, it was determined that each volume should have a mix of "classic" poems (those works commonly taught in literature classes) and contemporary poems for which information is often hard to find. Because of the interest in expanding the canon of literature, an emphasis was also placed on including works by international, multicultural, and women poets. Our advisory board members—educational professionals—helped pare down the list for each volume. If a work was not selected for the present volume, it was often noted as a possibility for a future volume. As always, the editor welcomes suggestions for titles to be included in future volumes.

How Each Entry Is Organized

Each entry, or chapter, in *PfS* focuses on one poem. Each entry heading lists the full name of the poem, the author's name, and the date of the poem's publication. The following elements are contained in each entry:

Introduction: a brief overview of the poem which provides information about its first appearance, its literary standing, any controversies surrounding the work, and major conflicts or themes within the work.

Author Biography: this section includes basic facts about the poet's life, and focuses on events and times in the author's life that inspired the poem in question.

Poem Text: when permission has been granted, the poem is reprinted, allowing for quick reference when reading the explication of the following section.

Poem Summary: a description of the major events in the poem. Summaries are broken down with subheads that indicate the lines being discussed.

Themes: a thorough overview of how the major topics, themes, and issues are addressed within the poem. Each theme discussed appears in a separate subhead and is easily accessed through the boldface entries in the Subject/Theme Index.

Style: this section addresses important style elements of the poem, such as form, meter, and rhyme scheme; important literary devices used, such as imagery, foreshadowing, and symbolism; and, if applicable, genres to which the work might have belonged, such as Gothicism or Romanticism. Literary terms are explained within the entry, but can also be found in the Glossary.

Historical Context: this section outlines the social, political, and cultural climate *in which the*

author lived and the poem was created. This section may include descriptions of related historical events, pertinent aspects of daily life in the culture, and the artistic and literary sensibilities of the time in which the work was written. If the poem is a historical work, information regarding the time in which the poem is set is also included. Each section is broken down with helpful subheads.

Critical Overview: this section provides background on the critical reputation of the poem, including bannings or any other public controversies surrounding the work. For older works, this section includes a history of how the poem was first received and how perceptions of it may have changed over the years; for more recent poems, direct quotes from early reviews may also be included.

Criticism: an essay commissioned by *PfS* which specifically deals with the poem and is written specifically for the student audience, as well as excerpts from previously published criticism on the work (if available).

Sources: an alphabetical list of critical material quoted in the entry, with full bibliographical information.

Further Reading: an alphabetical list of other critical sources which may prove useful for the student. Includes full bibliographical information and a brief annotation.

In addition, each entry contains the following highlighted sections, set apart from the main text as sidebars:

Media Adaptations: if available, a list of audio recordings as well as any film or television adaptations of the poem, including source information.

Topics for Further Study: a list of potential study questions or research topics dealing with the poem. This section includes questions related to other disciplines the student may be studying, such as American history, world history, science, math, government, business, geography, economics, psychology, etc.

Compare & Contrast: an "at-a-glance" comparison of the cultural and historical differences between the author's time and culture and late twentieth century or early twenty-first century Western culture. This box includes pertinent parallels between the major scientific, political, and cultural movements of the time or place the poem was written, the time or place the poem was set (if a historical work), and modern Western culture. Works written after 1990 may not have this box.

What Do I Read Next?: a list of works that might complement the featured poem or serve as a contrast to it. This includes works by the same author and others, works of fiction and nonfiction, and works from various genres, cultures, and eras.

Other Features

PfS includes "Just a Few Lines on a Page," a foreword by David J. Kelly, an adjunct professor of English, College of Lake County, Illinois. This essay provides a straightforward, unpretentious explanation of why poetry should be marveled at and how *Poetry for Students* can help teachers show students how to enrich their own reading experiences.

A Cumulative Author/Title Index lists the authors and titles covered in each volume of the *PfS* series.

A Cumulative Nationality/Ethnicity Index breaks down the authors and titles covered in each volume of the *PfS* series by nationality and ethnicity.

A Subject/Theme Index, specific to each volume, provides easy reference for users who may be studying a particular subject or theme rather than a single work. Significant subjects from events to broad themes are included, and the entries pointing to the specific theme discussions in each entry are indicated in **boldface**.

A Cumulative Index of First Lines (beginning in Vol. 10) provides easy reference for users who may be familiar with the first line of a poem but may not remember the actual title.

A Cumulative Index of Last Lines (beginning in Vol. 10) provides easy reference for users who may be familiar with the last line of a poem but may not remember the actual title.

Each entry may include illustrations, including photo of the author and other graphics related to the poem.

Citing Poetry for Students

When writing papers, students who quote directly from any volume of *Poetry for Students* may use the following general forms. These examples are based on MLA style; teachers may request that students adhere to a different style, so the following examples may be adapted as needed.

When citing text from *PfS* that is not attributed to a particular author (i.e., the Themes, Style, Historical Context sections, etc.), the following format should be used in the bibliography section:

> "Angle of Geese." *Poetry for Students.* Ed. Marie Napierkowski and Mary Ruby. Vol. 2. Detroit: Gale, 1998. 8–9.

When quoting the specially commissioned essay from *PfS* (usually the first piece under the "Criticism" subhead), the following format should be used:

> Velie, Alan. Critical Essay on "Angle of Geese." *Poetry for Students.* Ed. Marie Napierkowski and Mary Ruby. Vol. 2. Detroit: Gale, 1998. 7–10.

When quoting a journal or newspaper essay that is reprinted in a volume of *PfS*, the following form may be used:

> Luscher, Robert M. "An Emersonian Context of Dickinson's 'The Soul Selects Her Own Society'." *ESQ: A Journal of American Renaissance* 30.2 (1984): 111–16. Excerpted and reprinted in *Poetry for Students.* Ed. Marie Napierkowski and Mary Ruby. Vol. 1 Detroit: Gale, 1998. 266–69.

When quoting material reprinted from a book that appears in a volume of *PfS*, the following form may be used:

> Mootry, Maria K. "'Tell It Slant': Disguise and Discovery as Revisionist Poetic Discourse in 'The Bean Eaters'." *A Life Distilled: Gwendolyn Brooks, Her Poetry and Fiction.* Ed. Maria K. Mootry and Gary Smith. Urbana: University of Illinois Press, 1987. 177–80, 191. Excerpted and reprinted in *Poetry for Students.* Ed. Marie Napierkowski and Mary Ruby. Vol. 2. Detroit: Gale, 1998. 22–24.

We Welcome Your Suggestions

The editorial staff of *Poetry for Students* welcomes your comments and ideas. Readers who wish to suggest poems to appear in future volumes, or who have other suggestions, are cordially invited to contact the editor. You may contact the editor via E-mail at: **ForStudentsEditors@cengage.com.** Or write to the editor at:

Editor, Poetry for Students
Gale
27500 Drake Road
Farmington Hills, MI 48331-3535

Literary Chronology

1591: Robert Herrick is baptized on August 24 in London, England.

1648: Robert Herrick's "The Night-Piece: To Julia" is published .

1674: Robert Herrick dies in October in Devon, England.

c. 1753: Phillis Wheatley is born in West Africa.

1773: Phillis Wheatley's "On Being Brought from Africa to America" is published.

1784: Phillis Wheatley dies on December 5 in Boston, Massachusetts.

1788: George Gordon Byron (later Lord Byron) is born on January 22 in London.

1816: Lord George Gordon Byron's "When We Two Parted" is published.

1824: Lord George Gordon Byron succumbs to a fever and dies on April 19 in Mesolonghi, Greece.

1892: Marina Tsvetaeva is born on October 9 in Moscow, Russia.

1911: Czeslaw Milosz is born on June 30 in Szetejnie, Lithuania.

1921: Richard Wilbur is born on March 1 in New York City.

1926: W. D. Snodgrass is born on January 5 in Wilkinsburg, Pennsylvania.

1926: Allen Ginsberg is born on June 23 in Newark, New Jersey.

1928: Marina Tsvetaeva's "An Attempt at Jealousy" is published.

1929: Adrienne Rich is born on May 26 in Baltimore, Maryland.

1933: Yevgeny Yevtushenko is born on July 18 in Stantzia Zima, Siberia.

1934: Saadi Youssef is born in Abulkhasib, near Basra, Iraq.

1935: Kathleen Fraser is born on March 22 in Tulsa, Oklahoma.

1936: Lucille Clifton is born on June 27 in Depew, New York.

1937: Muriel Rukeyser is born on December 15 in New York City.

1941: Marina Tsvetaeva dies of suicide by hanging on August 31 in Elabuga, USSR.

1944: Shirley Geok-lin Lim is born on December 27 in Malacca, Malaysia.

1956: Allen Ginsberg's "Howl" is published.

1956: Richard Wilbur's "Love Calls Us to the Things of This World" is published.

1957: Richard Wilbur is awarded the Pulitzer Prize in Poetry for *Things of This World: Poems*.

1959: W. D. Snodgrass's "Heart's Needle" is published.

1960: W. D. Snodgrass is awarded the Pulitzer Prize for Poetry for *Heart's Needle*.

1961: Yevgeny Yevtushenko's "Babii Yar" is published.

1966: Natasha Trethewey is born in Gulf Port, Mississippi.

1968: Kathleen Fraser's "Poem in Which My Legs Are Accepted" is published.

1973: Adrienne Rich's "Diving into the Wreck" is published.

1974: Czeslaw Milosz's "From the Rising of the Sun" is published.

1976: Muriel Rukeyser's "St. Roach" is published.

1980: Muriel Rukeyser dies in New York City on February 12 after a series of strokes.

1980: Lucille Clifton's "homage to my hips" is published.

1980: Czeslaw Milosz is awarded the Nobel Prize for Literature.

1985: Shirley Geok-lin Lim's "Pantoun for Chinese Women" is published.

1989: Richard Wilbur is awarded the Pulitzer Prize in Poetry for *New and Collected Poems*.

1997: Allen Ginsberg dies on April 5 from a heart attack brought on by complications of liver cancer, in New York City.

2002: Saadi Youssef's "America, America" is published.

2004: Czeslaw Milosz dies of undisclosed causes on August 14 in Krakow, Poland.

2006: Natasha Trethewey's "Native Guard" is published.

2007: Natasha Trethewey wins the Pulitzer Prize for Poetry for *Native Guard*.

Acknowledgments

The editors wish to thank the copyright holders of the excerpted criticism included in this volume and the permissions managers of many book and magazine publishing companies for assisting us in securing reproduction rights. We are also grateful to the staffs of the Detroit Public Library, the Library of Congress, the University of Detroit Mercy Library, Wayne State University Purdy/ Kresge Library Complex, and the University of Michigan Libraries for making their resources available to us. Following is a list of the copyright holders who have granted us permission to reproduce material in this volume of *PFS*. Every effort has been made to trace copyright, but if omissions have been made, please let us know.

COPYRIGHTED EXCERPTS IN *PFS*, VOLUME 29, WERE REPRODUCED FROM THE FOLLOWING PERIODICALS:

African American Review, v. 36, 2002. Copyright © 2002 Mary McAleer Balkun. Reproduced by permission.—*Al-Ahram Weekly Online*, April 17–23, 2003. Reproduced by permission.—*America*, May 12, 1990. Copyright © 1990 www.americamagazine.org. All rights reserved. Reproduced by permission of America Press. For subscription information, visit www.america magazine.org.—*American Poetry Review*, v. 35, March-April, 2006 for "Wild at Heart," by Vivian Gornick. Reproduced by permission of the author.—*Antioch Review*, v. 58, summer, 2000.

Copyright © 2000 by the Antioch Review Inc. Reproduced by permission of the editors.—*Arab Studies Quarterly*, v. 19, fall, 1997. Copyright © 1997 Association of Arab American University Graduates and Institute of Arab Studies. Reproduced by permission of *Arab Studies Quarterly*.— *Ariel: A Review of International English Literature*, v. 30, October, 1999 for "An Interview with Shirley Geok-lin Lim," by Kirpal Singh. Copyright © 1999 The Board of Governors, The University of Calgary. Reproduced by permission of the publisher and the author.—*Callaloo*, v. 22, winter, 1999. Copyright © 1999 The Johns Hopkins University Press. Reproduced by permission.—*Christian Science Monitor*, March 8, 1991. Reproduced by permission.—*College Literature*, v. 33, spring, 2006. Copyright © 2006 by West Chester University. Reproduced by permission.—*Commonweal*, v. 119, November 6, 1992. Copyright © 1992 Commonweal Publishing Co., Inc. Reproduced by permission of Commonweal Foundation.— *differences: A Journal of Feminist Cultural Studies*, v. 12, 2001. Copyright © 2001 Brown University and *differences: A Journal of Feminist Cultural Studies*. All rights reserved. Used by permission of the publisher.—*Early American Literature*, v. 27, 1992 for "Phillis Wheatley's Appropriation of Isaiah," by William J. Scheick. Copyright © 1992 by the University of North Carolina Press. Used by permission.—*Explicator*, v. 40, spring, 1982; v. 62, fall, 2003. Copyright © 1982, 2003 by Helen

Dwight Reid Educational Foundation. Both reproduced with permission of the Helen Dwight Reid Educational Foundation, published by Heldref Publications, 1319 18th Street, NW, Washington, DC 20036-1802.—*Five Points: A Journal of Literature and Art*, v. 11, September, 2007. Reproduced by permission.—*MELUS*, v. 28, winter, 2003. Copyright © *MELUS: The Society for the Study of Multi-Ethnic Literature of the United States*, 2003. Reproduced by permission.—*Nation*, March 8, 1980. Copyright © 1980 by The Nation Magazine/The Nation Company, Inc. Reproduced by permission.—*New England Review*, v. 21, winter, 2000 for "A Conversation with W. D. Snodgrass," by Roy Scheele. Reproduced by permission of the author.—*New Republic*, May 6, 1991. Copyright © 1991 by The New Republic, Inc. Reproduced by permission of *The New Republic.—Poetry*, v. 191, October, 2007 for Review of "Native Guard," by Ange Mlinko. Reproduced by permission of the author.—*Prairie Schooner*, v. 80, winter, 2006. Copyright © 2006 by University of Nebraska Press. Reproduced by permission of the University of Nebraska Press.—*Progressive*, v. 58, January, 1994. Copyright © 1994 by The Progressive, Inc. Reproduced by permission of *The Progressive*, 409 East Main Street, Madison, WI 53703, www.progressive.org.—*Renascence*, v. 45, September 1992. Copyright © 1992 Marquette University Press. Reproduced by permission.—*Slavic and East European Journal*, v. 38, summer, 1994; v. 38, autumn, 1994. Copyright © 1994 by AATSEEL of the U.S., Inc. Both reproduced by permission.—*Southern Review*, vol. 42, autumn, 2006, for "Shocking, Surprising Snodgrass," by Jay Rogoff. Copyright © 2006 Louisiana State University. Reproduced by permission of the author.—*Studies in Romanticism*, v. 39, summer 2000. Copyright © 2000 by the Trustees of Boston University. Reproduced by permission.—*Texas Studies in Literature and Language*, v. 49, summer, 2007 for "Robert Herrick and the Ambiguities of Gender," by David Landrum. Copyright © 2007 by the University of Texas Press. Reproduced by permission of the publisher and author.—*Tricycle*, v. 16, spring, 2007. Reproduced by permission.—*World Literature Today*, v. 66, winter, 1992; v. 70, fall, 1996. Copyright © 1992, 1996 by *World Literature Today*. Both reproduced by permission of the publisher.

COPYRIGHTED EXCERPTS IN *PFS*, VOLUME 29, WERE REPRODUCED FROM THE FOLLOWING BOOKS:

Byron, George Gordon. From "When We Two Parted," in *The Poetical Works of Byron*. Edited by Robert F. Gleckner. Houghton Mifflin, 1975. Copyright © 1975 by Houghton Mifflin Company. All rights reserved. Reproduced by permission of Houghton Mifflin Company.—Calhoun, Richard J. From "Richard Wilbur," in *Dictionary of Literary Biography, Vol. 169, American Poets Since World War II, Fifth Series*. Edited by Joseph Conte, State University of New York at Buffalo. Gale Research, 1996. Copyright © 1996 State University of New York at Buffalo. Reproduced by permission of Gale, a part of Cengage Learning.—Fraser, Kathleen. From *Change of Address*. Harper & Row, 1974. Copyright © 1974 by Kathleen Fraser. All rights reserved. Used by permission of Marian Reiner for the author.—Herrick, Robert. From "The Night-Piece, to Julia," in *Seventeenth-Century Prose and Poetry*. Edited by Alexander M. Witherspoon and Frank J. Warnke. Harcourt, Brace, 1963. Copyright © 1963 by Verso. Reproduced by permission of Cengage Learning.—Lim, Shirley Geok-lin. From "Pantoun for Chinese Women," in *The Forbidden Stitch: An Asian American Women's Anthology*. Edited by Shirley Geok-lin Lim, Mayumi Tsutakawa, Margarita Donnelly. Calyx Books, 1988. Copyright © 1989 by Calyx Inc. All rights reserved. Reproduced by permission.—Quartermain, Peter. From "Kathleen Fraser," in *Dictionary of Literary Biography, Vol. 169, American Poets Since World War II, Fifth Series*. Edited by Joseph Conte. State University of New York at Buffalo. The Gale Group, 1996. Copyright © 1996 State University of New York at Buffalo. Reproduced by permission of Gale, a part of Cengage Learning.—Trethewey, Natasha. From "Native Guard," in *Native Guard*. Houghton Mifflin, 2006. Copyright © 2006 by Natasha Tretheway. All rights reserved. Reprinted by permission of Houghton Mifflin Company.—Tsvetayeva, Marina. From *Selected Poems*. Translated by Elaine Feinstein. Carcanet Press, 1999. Copyright © 1971, 1981, 1986, 1993, 1999 Elaine Feinstein. Reproduced by permission of Carcanet Press Limited.—Wheatley, Phillis. From "On Being Brought from Africa to America," in *The Poems of Phillis Wheatley*. Edited with an Introduction by Julian D. Mason Jr. University of North Carolina

Press, 1966. Copyright © 1966 by the University of North Carolina Press. Copyright © renewed 1989. All rights reserved. Used by permission of the publisher, www.uncpress.unc.edu.—Yevtushenko, Yevgeny. From "Babii Yar," in *Early Poems*. Edited and translated by George Reavey. Marion Boyars, 1989. Copyright © 1966, 1989 Marion Boyars Publishers. All rights reserved. Reproduced by permission.—Youssef, Saadi. From *Without an Alphabet, Without a Face*. Translated by Khaled Mattawa. Graywolf Press, 2002. Copyright © 2002 by Saadi Youssef. Reprinted with the permission of Graywolf Press, Saint Paul, Minnesota.

Contributors

Susan Andersen: Andersen holds a PhD in literature and teaches literature and writing. Entry on *On Being Brought from Africa to America*. Original essay on *On Being Brought from Africa to America*.

Bryan Aubrey: Aubrey holds a PhD in English. Entry on *Diving into the Wreck*. Original essay on *Diving into the Wreck*.

Jennifer Bussey: Bussey is an independent writer specializing in literature. Entry on *America, America*. Original essay on *America, America*.

Catherine Dominic: Dominic is a novelist and freelance writer and editor. Entries on *From the Rising of the Sun* and *When We Two Parted*. Original essays on *From the Rising of the Sun* and *When We Two Parted*.

Sheldon Goldfarb: Goldfarb has a PhD in English, specializing in the literature of Victorian England. Entry on *An Attempt at Jealousy*. Original essay on *An Attempt at Jealousy*.

Joyce Hart: Hart is a published author of more than twenty books. Entry on *Native Guard*. Original essay on *Native Guard*.

Neil Heims: Heims is a writer and teacher living in Paris. Entry on *The Night Piece: To Julia*. Original essay on *The Night Piece: To Julia*.

Diane Andrews Henningfeld: Henningfeld is a professor of literature who writes widely for educational publishers. Entry on *homage to my hips*. Original essay on *homage to my hips*.

Sheri Metzger Karmiol: Karmiol has a doctorate in English Renaissance literature and teaches literature and drama at the University of New Mexico, where she is a lecturer in the university honors program. She is also a professional writer and the author of several reference texts on poetry and drama. Entries on *Babii Yar* and *Pantoun for Chinese Women*. Original essays on *Babii Yar* and *Pantoun for Chinese Women*.

David Kelly: Kelly is a writer and an instructor of creative writing and literature at two colleges in Illinois. Entries on *Heart's Needle*, *Love Calls Us to the Things of This World*, and *St. Roach*. Original essays on *Heart's Needle*, *Love Calls Us to the Things of This World*, and *St. Roach*.

Claire Robinson: Robinson has an MA in English. She is a teacher of English literature and creative writing and a freelance writer and editor. Entry on *Howl*. Original essay on *Howl*.

Carol Ullmann: Ullmann is a freelance writer and editor. Entry on *Poem in Which My Legs Are Accepted*. Original essay on *Poem in Which My Legs Are Accepted*.

America, America

SAADI YOUSSEF

2002

Published in 2002 in *Without an Alphabet, Without a Face*, Saadi Youssef's poem "America, America" is a complex work driven by imagery and emotion. It was originally written in 1995 to describe the life of the Iraqi people as their country endured United Nations-led sanctions. The poem describes war and politics, but at a human level. Youssef's voice in the work is that of the common Iraqi man or woman rendered powerless to change the nation's current regime or the world's reaction to it.

The dominant themes of "America, America" are war, struggle, cultural identity, and the individual's experience in history. The style is free verse featuring a steady flow of images. Like most of Youssef's poetry, it is personal and based on experience. As of the poem's writing, Youssef had been creating verse for four decades. This work reflects his maturity as a poet and his broad experience in the world.

AUTHOR BIOGRAPHY

Saadi Youssef was born in 1934 in Abulkhasib, near Basra, Iraq. He began writing poetry at the age of seventeen. By then, young writers had begun to write free verse in Arabic, breaking with tradition and bringing modernity to Arabic poetry. After Youssef joined this movement, he became one of the most celebrated and prolific

Saadi Youssef (Pascal Le Segretain / Getty Images)

Arabic poets of the modern age. He attended school in Basra and Baghdad, earning a degree in Arabic from Baghdad University, before beginning his career as an educator and journalist. Meanwhile, he continued to write poetry and to develop his style and voice. In the 1950s and 1960s, he primarily wrote political poetry, striving to be a voice of his people. In the 1970s, his poetry began to shift to include subjects from everyday life. Youssef's first major volume of poetry translated into English was *Without an Alphabet, Without a Face* (2002), in which "America, America" appears. The volume won the 2003 PEN Award for Poetry in Translation.

It was in 1957 that Youssef experienced his first exile: After taking an unauthorized trip to Moscow, he was forced to stay in Kuwait until a revolution occurred in Iraq a year later. In the 1960s, Youssef had a brief stay in jail, followed by a job teaching and writing (journalism) in Algeria. In 1971 he returned to Iraq to take a job with the Ministry of Culture, but when Saddam Hussein ascended to power in 1979, Youssef left his native Iraq permanently. Under Hussein's increasingly dominant regime, Youssef was under intense pressure to join the leader's Baath Party, even to the point of threats. His exile took him to various parts of the world, including Syria, Lebanon, Yugoslavia, Yemen, Jordan, Algeria, France, and finally London, where he made a permanent home.

In the literary world, Youssef has made a name for himself with more than thirty volumes of poetry, in addition to fiction, essays, and translations. In fact, he has translated into Arabic the works of such luminaries as Walt Whitman (who is mentioned in "America, America"), George Orwell, Federico García Lorca, Wole Soyinka, and V. S. Naipaul. As of 2008, Youssef was living in London.

POEM TEXT

> *God save America,*
> *My home, sweet home!*
>
> The French general who raised his tricolor
> over Nuqrat al-Salman where I was a prisoner
> thirty years ago ...   5
> in the middle of that U-turn
> that split the back of the Iraqi army,
> the general who loved Saint Emilion wines
> called Nuqrat al-Salman a fort...
> Of the surface of the earth, generals know only
>   two dimensions: 10
> whatever rises is a fort,
> whatever spreads is a battlefield.
> How ignorant the general was!
> But *Liberation* was better versed in topography.
> The Iraqi boy who conquered her front page   15
> sat carbonized behind a steering wheel
> on the Kuwait-Safwan highway
> while television cameras
> (the booty of the defeated and their identity)
> were safe in a truck like a storefront   20
> on Rivoli Street.
> The neutron bomb is highly intelligent.
> It distinguishes between
> an "I" and an "Identity."
>
> > *God save America,*   25
> > *My home, sweet home!*
> >
> > *Blues*
> > How long must I walk to Sacramento?
> > How long must I walk to Sacramento?
> > How long will I walk to reach my home?   30
> > How long will I walk to reach my girl?
> > How long must I walk to Sacramento?
> > For two days, no boat has sailed this stream,
> > Two days, two days, two days.
> >
> > Honey, how can I ride?   35
> > I know this stream,
> > But, O but, O but,
> > For two days, no boat has sailed this stream.

La Li La La Li La
La Li La La Li La   40
A stranger becomes afraid.
Have no fear, dear horse.
No fear of the wolves of the wild,
No fear, for the land is my land.
La Li La La Li La   45
La Li La La Li La
A stranger becomes afraid.

    God save America,
    My home, sweet home!

I too love jeans and jazz and *Treasure Island*   50
and John Silver's parrot and the balconies of
    New Orleans.
I love Mark Twain and the Mississippi steam-
    boats and Abraham Lincoln's dogs.
I love the fields of wheat and corn and the smell
    of Virginia tobacco.
But I am not American.
Is that enough for the Phantom pilot to turn me
    back to the Stone Age?   55
I need neither oil nor America herself, neither
    the elephant nor the donkey.
Leave me, pilot, leave my house roofed with
    palm fronds and this wooden bridge.
I need neither your Golden Gate nor your
    skyscrapers.
I need the village, not New York.
Why did you come to me from your Nevada
    desert, soldier armed to the teeth?   60
Why did you come all the way to distant Basra,
    where fish used to swim by our doorsteps?
Pigs do not forage here.
I only have these water buffaloes lazily chewing
    on water lilies.
Leave me alone, soldier.
Leave me my floating cane hut and my fishing
    spear.   65
Leave me my migrating birds and the green
    plumes.
Take your roaring iron birds and your Toma-
    hawk missiles. I am not your foe.
I am the one who wades up to the knees in rice
    paddies.
Leave me to my curse.
I do not need your day of doom.   70

    God save America,
    My home, sweet home!

America:
let's exchange gifts.
Take your smuggled cigarettes   75
and give us potatoes.
Take James Bond's golden pistol
and give us Marilyn Monroe's giggle.
Take the heroin syringe under the tree
and give us vaccines.   80
Take your blueprints for model penitentiaries
and give us village homes.
Take the books of your missionaries
and give us paper for poems to defame you.

Take what you do not have   85
and give us what we have.
Take the stripes of your flag
and give us the stars.
Take the Afghani mujahideen beard
and give us Walt Whitman's beard filled with
    butterflies.   90
Take Saddam Hussein
and give us Abraham Lincoln
or give us no one.

Now as I look across the balcony,
across the summer sky, the summery summer,   95
Damascus spins, dizzied among television
    aerials,
then it sinks, deeply, in the stones of the forts,
    in towers,
    in the arabesques of ivory,
and sinks, deeply, far from Rukn el-Din   100
and disappears far from the balcony.

And now
I remember trees:
the date palm of our mosque in Basra, at the
    end of Basra
a bird's beak,   105
a child's secret,
a summer feast.
I remember the date palm.
I touch it. I become it, when it falls black
without fronds,   110
when a dam fell, hewn by lightning.
And I remember the mighty mulberry
when it rumbled, butchered with an axe . . .
to fill the stream with leaves
and birds   115
and angels
and green blood.
I remember when pomegranate blossoms cov-
    ered the sidewalks.
The students were leading the workers
    parade . . .

The trees die   120
pummeled.
Dizzied,
not standing, the trees die.

    God save America,
    My home, sweet home!   125

We are not hostages, America,
and your soldiers are not God's soldiers . . .
We are the poor ones, ours is the earth of the
    drowned gods,
the gods of bulls,
the gods of fires,   130
the gods of sorrows that intertwine clay and
    blood in a song . . .
We are the poor, ours is the god of the
    poor,
who emerges out of farmers' ribs,
hungry
and bright,   135
and raises heads up high . . .

America, we are the dead.
Let your soldiers come.
Whoever kills a man, let him resurrect him.
We are the drowned ones, dear lady.   140
We are the drowned.
Let the water come.

POEM SUMMARY

Each section of "America, America" is set off by
the poem's refrain, a slight variation on the last
lines of the song "God Bless America."

Section 1
The first section begins with the poem's refrain
and then describes the leadership of a general in
command of Nuqrat al-Salman, a notorious
prison in the Iraqi desert. The speaker claims
that military generals interpret the landscape as
either forts (if they rise) or battlefields (if they are
flat). The speaker then boldly declares the ignorance of such a general.

The speaker's attention then shifts to *Liberation*, a French newspaper. He describes the front
page as displaying an Iraqi bomb victim, while
the media trucks are at a safe distance. The
speaker declares that the neutron bomb is intelligent enough to distinguish between forms of ego.

Section 2
The second section begins with the refrain and
then offers the words to a blues song. Based on
the reference to the Californian city of Sacramento, the singer is understood to be American.
His worries relate to walking to Sacramento to
see his girl. The singer seems to reassure a
stranger that there is nothing to fear in this
land, but he then reiterates the stranger's fear
at the end of the stanza.

Section 3
The speaker now tells the reader all of the American things that he loves, just as his readers (or
other Americans) love. He mentions jeans,
American music, New Orleans, Mark Twain,
and Abraham Lincoln. He refers to *Treasure
Island*, a renowned adventure novel by Robert
Louis Stevenson. Stevenson was Scottish, and
the novel is in the canon of English literature.

After listing the things that he loves, the
speaker lets the reader know that he is not an

American. He then asks if the fact that he is not
American is reason enough to send a bomber to
destroy him. His point may be that he and Americans are not so different at a human, or individual, level, but their differences in nationality
seem to be all that is required to bring on military
hostility. He adds that he does not need oil,
America, or American political parties, asking
that the bomber leave his humble home alone.
The speaker says that he does not need the
Golden Gate Bridge or city skyscrapers or New
York City, all symbols of the bustling accomplishment of urban America. He asks why the
American soldiers came heavily armed to otherwise peaceful villages and hopes to be left alone.
He tells the soldier to take back his missiles and
aircraft because he (the speaker) is not an enemy.

Section 4
After the refrain, the speaker again begins a dialogue of sorts with America. This time, he proposes a series of trades. In each case, the speaker
tells America to take away something destructive
that has been imported into Iraqi culture (like
cigarettes and Bibles). In return, the Americans
are to give things that help nourish Iraqi society
(like potatoes, vaccines, and paper for poetry to
insult Americans). He instructs America to take
what it does not already have and to let the
speaker's people take what is already theirs. In
one line, the speaker asks for Abraham Lincoln
or nobody at all. In the context of the poem, the
speaker is asking for a leader seeking to provide
unity and freedom rather than a dictator like
Hussein—or, perhaps, rather than the soldiers
described in the previous section.

The speaker's attention then turns to the
landscape and cityscape. He sees Damascus
spinning and then sinking into oblivion. The
speaker then turns to his own memories of
Basra and the mosque there. He describes a series of sense memories, including things he saw,
touched, and heard. After describing natural
elements, he recalls a memory of political activism. The section concludes with simple statements about trees dying after being beaten and
dizzied, imagery that recalls the description of
Damascus spinning away to nothing.

Section 5
In the last section, the speaker boldly addresses
America. He says that he and his people are not
hostages and that the American military is not
God's army. He then iterates that he and his

people are poor, indicating that even their gods are poor. He goes on to declare that his people are dead and drowned.

THEMES

War

Throughout "America, America," the speaker addresses war both in general terms and in terms of what is happening to his people and his country. The speaker does not think highly of war as a solution to the problems faced by his country.

The poem opens with images of a military leader who oversaw a prison in the desert, with the speaker viewing the general as a simpleton who is unable to see the cruelty and reality of the prison because he is only capable of seeing forts and battlefields in the world. Since the camp is a building, or something that rises up from the ground, he sees it only as a fort. In the same section, the speaker blasts the foreign press for exploiting the tragedy brought on by the military. A French newspaper features prominently on its front page a photograph of a bomb victim. The media's awareness of the war prompts them to find a safe place to park their trucks (say, away from the threat of neutron bombs), such that the media does not connect with the real tragedy suffered by the Iraqi people.

In section three, the speaker bemoans the presence of bomber planes and heavily equipped soldiers. To him, these things represent not hope and peacemaking but destruction and fear. He tries to impress upon the Americans that he and his people are the ones who suffer, even though they are not the enemy, as their villages are compromised and their way of life is disrupted by the presence of the military. In the last section, the speaker again implores the Americans to understand that the Iraqi people should not be treated as hostages; their lives have been destroyed, and their situation seems utterly hopeless.

Peoplehood

"America, America" is an expression of the voice of Youssef's people. *Peoplehood* refers to the collective identity and experience of a community of people, often as bound together by ethnicity. This concept is a strong element in "America, America." The voice of the poem reads like the

TOPICS FOR FURTHER STUDY

- Choose two other poems from the *Damascus/Amman* section of *Without an Alphabet, Without a Face* to compare and contrast with "America, America." Create a chart that reflects your findings.

- Research the sanctions imposed against Iraq in the 1990s. What events led to the decision to establish these sanctions? What was the outcome supposed to be? What was the eventual outcome? What were the major arguments for and against the sanctions? Write a report discussing your findings.

- Read about the work and character of the Iraqi poets Badr Shakir al-Sayyab and Nazik al-Malaika, who were influences on Youssef and other modern poets. What were the traditional forms of Arabic poetry prior to their careers? What changes did they spearhead? Write a poem in the traditional Arabic form, then write about the same topic in the style of Youssef and his predecessors.

- Find at least five examples of traditional Arabic art and at least five examples of modern Arabic art. Architecture may be used for one or two examples. Then find at least three examples of traditional Arabic poetry. What shifts do you notice in the evolution of art in Arabic culture? Give a class presentation in which you draw parallels (or contrasts) between art and literature. Lead a discussion on what may account for these changes.

voice of a common Iraqi man or woman. It is not a voice specific to Youssef but one that expresses the frustrations, fears, and hostility of the average Iraqi. The speaker is not a soldier, a politician, or a government leader. He is merely a man crying out in the midst of the destruction and chaos brought on by the Americans.

When the speaker talks, he often frames his ideas in terms of the Iraqi culture and way of life. He is moved to speak on behalf of Iraqis

Iraqis live in squalor in former air force base (Chris Hondros / Getty Images)

collectively. In section three, the speaker lists many of the things he loves that Americans also love, punctuating his list with a reminder that he is not American. His identity as an Iraqi is important, especially in the context of what he and Americans have in common, as he refuses to compromise his identity as a member of the Iraqi community. Although there are many things about America that he loves, he has no need for many elements of its culture, such as its impressive city skylines and its political parties. During Saddam Hussein's reign, of course, there was really only one political party operating in Iraq; still, the speaker does not have any use for the two American parties. In a communal voice, the speaker declares that what he does need is his village, a place to fish nearby, native flora and fauna, and peace. The memories that bring him contentment are those that are uniquely Iraqi, including those of the date palms and the mosque in Basra. Such memories are probably shared among the Iraqi people. In the last section, when the speaker refers to the gods of his people, it is with notes of loyalty if not of victory.

STYLE

Free Verse

"America, America" is written in free verse, a form that inspired Youssef as a young poet, and one that he has refined and claimed as a legitimate form of Arabic poetry. Traditional Arabic poetry is not written in free verse, but Youssef and others have shown that modern readers of Arabic can relate to free verse in a meaningful way. It should be mentioned that Youssef is known for his rhyming abilities, a poetic trait that is lost in translation. In "America, America," Youssef uses the form to present the past and present Iraq in a series of images and declarations that lend insight into the everyday Iraqi's feelings toward the Americans. Free verse reads as more conversational and spontaneous than highly structured poetry, and it gives the poet the freedom to present descriptions, thoughts, memories, and emotions without the confines of rhyme, foot, or meter. This form is well suited to "America, America," in which emotions ranging from passion to surrender are central to the speaker's expression. Youssef's use of free verse allows him to distinctly focus on memories, the blues, lists, and trades, endowing each section with its own unique character.

Figurative Language

"America, America" is rich with figurative language, making it accessible to readers who have no experiential way to relate to the material. In the first and last sections, the speaker utilizes flashback to relate his memories to the reader. In the first section, the memory is of his time three decades ago in a prison called Nuqrat al-Salman, a harsh prison in the Iraqi desert. Along with the memories of the prison, the speaker recalls a specific newspaper cover page that reminds him of the separation between the media and the horrors of war. In the last section, the speaker's flashback is of his childhood, and the tone and descriptions indicate a peaceful, pleasant upbringing. The second flashback is a counterpoint to the first and a clever way of telling the reader how his country has experienced both contentment and upheaval.

The predominant figurative device in "America, America" is imagery. From start to finish, the speaker relates rich images that evoke a wide range of emotion in the reader. There is sorrow and horror in the image of the bomb victim, and there is nostalgia in the images of Mark Twain and Marilyn Monroe. In fact, the third section is almost like a series of snapshots reflecting American culture and history, as followed by a series of images reflecting how everyday, humble life once was in Iraq. In the fourth section, the speaker again goes through a series of images, but here, the imagery is intimately tied to symbolism. The image of the heroin syringe, for example, may symbolize self-destruction and indulgence, whereas the vaccines represent the opposite use of syringes—for health and progress. Similarly, the speaker juxtaposes an image of an Afghani beard with one of Walt Whitman's, as followed by the image of Saddam Hussein against the image of Abraham Lincoln. The symbolism is rich and clear, and Youssef manages it without much detail or explanation.

Other figurative language in the poem includes metaphor, such as with the Iraqi army's back and the bombers described as birds; simile, as with the media truck; irony, as with the bomb victim depicted as conquering the front page; repetition and anaphora, as in the blues section; synecdoche and metonymy, as in the naming of elements of American and Iraqi life in section three; and oxymoron, as when the speaker asks the soldiers who kill to also resurrect. Readers should remember that wherever alliteration appears, it occurs only in translation.

Blues Lyrics

Youssef devotes an entire section of his poem to blues lyrics. This section adds to the overall collage effect, as the poem contains memories, arguments, snapshot imagery, and song lyrics. Blues is a distinctly American style of music, so it is fitting that Youssef included this style in his poem about America. Blues songs came out of the African American folk song tradition in the South, which included work songs and spirituals. Such songs are characteristically repetitious, sorrowful or longing, personal, and structured in short stanzas. In Youssef's blues song, these characteristics are evident. He uses partial and whole repetition within and between lines, and the song is about the speaker's desire to see his girl. Youssef takes the blues lyrics out of their tradition when he introduces the segment about the stranger being afraid. This section is vaguer and more symbolic—and thus less purely the blues.

HISTORICAL CONTEXT

United Nations Sanctions against Iraq

After Saddam Hussein sent his Iraqi military to invade the small, oil-rich nation of Kuwait, the United Nations demanded Iraq's disarmament. Any facilities involved in producing weapons of mass destruction were to be destroyed; the sanctions were also originally intended to force Iraq to help rebuild Kuwait. Iraq had proven itself to be aggressive, and there were suspicions that the nation's government was already using weapons of mass destruction against some of its own people (the Kurds). When Iraq insisted that it would rule itself without supervision from the rest of the world, the United Nations implemented economic sanctions against the country in hopes that the ensuing hardship would force it to comply with inspections and disarmament. Without cash from international trade, Iraq would be rendered unable to wage war. The United Nations specified that Iraq could sell only enough oil to cover food and medicine for its people (part of the "oil for food" program).

Violation of the rules would lead to the total disallowance of international trade.

In reality, the sanctions hurt only the Iraqi people, not Hussein or his regime. Hussein firmly prioritized his military, such that the people suffered for lack of provisions. For various reasons, including Hussein's control of the media, the Iraqi people grew angry at the United Nations, especially at member countries from the West (and especially at the United States), instead of being angry at Hussein's regime for not taking care of the people first and itself second.

Even with limited reliable information about Iraq at the time, vocal critics of the sanctions believed that they were only hurting the Iraqi public. The critics further argued that the sanctions did not seem to be having an effect on Hussein's regime, its military strength, or its willingness to comply with inspections. Despite the fact that the United Nations handled Iraq's money and purchased supplies to be delivered to its borders, the regime was left in charge of distribution. Estimates in 2001 placed the number of people dead because of the sanctions at between 500,000 and 1 million. David Cortright, writing in the *Nation*, called the sanctions a "humanitarian disaster." The health care system suffered tremendously, spiking the mortality rates of infants and children. Basic supplies like clean syringes and water filtration systems were scant.

Saddam Hussein

In 1968, the powerful Baath Party ascended to power in Iraq, destroying government officials who disagreed with its politics. In 1979, Saddam Hussein took control of the party. Harsher and more dictatorial than his predecessor (who was sent into exile), Hussein quickly established his iron-fisted regime. He understood that anything less than absolute power would render him vulnerable to the kind of overthrow that had typified politics in the Middle East. He himself had been ruthless in his rise to the top, so he knew how dangerous it was to be there. He had a hunger for power, and he had a vision of Iraq as a present-day Babylon. He wanted to make Iraq a military stronghold as well as a modernized, culturally energized nation.

In addition to having no tolerance for disloyalty among those close to him in leadership, Hussein put the People's Army in place. The People's Army was a paramilitary group known for brutality that included torture and execution. Many who believed that they and their families were or would soon be in serious danger fled Iraq early in Hussein's regime, while they could still get out of the country.

Free Verse Movement in Arabic Poetry

Traditionally, Arabic poetry was extremely disciplined and structured. Not only were the lines, meter, and rhyme strictly governed by convention, but even the way the poems were collected and grouped followed a system. In the mid-twentieth century, a few new poets began trying their hands at writing Arabic poetry in free verse and in prose poems. A woman named Nazik al-Malaika graduated from the College of Arts in Baghdad in 1944 and then earned a master's degree from the University of Wisconsin. Her first book of poetry was published in 1947. She taught Arabic and literature in Iraq until fleeing in 1970 under the oppressive Baath regime. Badr Shakir al-Sayyab wrote free verse, too, but he set out to write poetry that challenged traditional verse in terms of both structure and content. He wrote about humanity as a whole, social issues, and personal feelings and experiences. At the same time, he drew on classic myths and symbols unique to his cultural background. These two poets were on the cutting edge of the movement to bring free verse to Arabic poetry, and they were great influences on Youssef.

CRITICAL OVERVIEW

Critical reception of Youssef's *Without an Alphabet, Without a Face* has been overwhelmingly positive. Critics and readers alike are drawn to the poet's unique perspective; after residing in Iraq and enduring hardship because of his beliefs, he then lived in exile all over the world before settling in the West. In this collection, the poems are organized by location to assist the reader in understanding the poet's changing perspective and subjects. In *Publishers Weekly*, a reviewer of the collection remarks on Youssef's use of the many places he has lived in his writing: "The poems work brilliantly through their differing times and places, pushing unflinching description through a steady determination to foment a more just world." Khaled Mattawa (the translator of *Without an Alphabet, Without a Face*) notes in his introduction to the collection that "as the poet continued to travel

Walt Whitman (The Library of Congress)

from one country to another, a pattern emerged: a series of short, imagistic poems where the poet assumes a neutral voice are then followed by a longer, much more complicated poem."

Having been a poet for four decades, Youssef is a writer who knows his voice and knows how to express his experience, feelings, insights, desires, memories, and hopes. He is also intriguing because he writes in free verse, a form that is familiar to Western readers. However, Youssef is not out to win over a Western readership; in fact, he writes in Arabic and pulls no punches with his words. Commenting on a French-language edition of *Without an Alphabet, Without a Face*, Marilyn Booth, in *World Literature Today*, notes that Youssef's "new collection . . . puts more focus on the longer poetic reflections that trace journeys across space and time." She adds that the poet "has been fearless in privileging the language and the cultural forms of everyday life, as well as mundane images, in complexly structured polyphonic poems. He anchors his poetic journey in geographies of exile, memory, and history." Mattawa writes, "Youssef's greatest contribution to contemporary Arabic poetry lies in his consistent effort

to preserve the dignity of personal experience, despite and within a context of difficult socio-political realities in his native Iraq and in the Arab world at large."

In *Books & Culture*, Laurance Wieder encourages the reader to enjoy Youssef's writing, noting, "Even in translation, an honest intelligence shines through." Wieder later adds, "One poetry that travels well is the voice of an honest man, talking perhaps to himself." Perhaps that is why Mattawa finds that in "America, America" in particular, "we experience the culmination of Youssef's experimentation with surprise and discovery." Wieder furthermore sees parallels with Western free verse poets, specifically in reference to "America, America." Wieder comments, "Saadi Youssef's 1995 Damascus poem, 'America, America,' has a kinship with Whitman and Allen Ginsberg, and a sharp eye for the balance of trade."

CRITICISM

Jennifer Bussey

Bussey is an independent writer specializing in literature. In the following essay, she compares Saadi Youssef's depiction of the United States in "America, America" to the ways American poets, such as Walt Whitman, Allen Ginsberg, Carl Sandburg, and Marilyn Chin, have depicted America in their works.

Saadi Youssef is a renowned expatriate Iraqi poet who is recognized as one of the preeminent modern poets writing in Arabic. His verse draws deeply from his many varied experiences in Iraq and all over the world. While his experiences give him vast material for his poetry, his skills with imagery and expression invite the reader into his past and present. The context of "America, America" is the period in the 1990s when sanctions were imposed against Iraq by the United Nations. The Iraqi people knew that these sanctions were spearheaded by the West, and they particularly blamed the United States. In Youssef's poem, the speaker rails against America for its violence and destruction against Iraq. Although the speaker loves some things about American culture, he wants the United States to leave his country alone. Youssef is not vague or subtle in his expressions of frustration and anger toward America.

WHAT DO I READ NEXT?

- Edited and compiled by Mounah Abdallah Khouri, *An Anthology of Modern Arabic Poetry* (1974) allows English-speaking readers a glimpse into the writing of Arabic poets in the late twentieth century.
- *Post-Gibran Anthology of New Arab American Writing* (1999), edited by Munir Akash and Khaled Mattawa, contains the work of more than forty Arab American writers. The anthology features previously unpublished works in all genres, including fiction, nonfiction, essays, drama, and poetry.
- Nuha al-Radi is an Iraqi woman who lived in Iraq during the Persian Gulf War and was directly affected by the United Nations' sanctions. She relates her experiences and her opinions in *Baghdad Diaries: A Woman's Chronicle of War and Exile* (2003). American readers are often unnerved by her anti-American feelings, but her story brings history to life.
- Phebe Marr's *The Modern History of Iraq* (2004) sets out to explain the nation's complicated and dramatic history, beginning with the British mandate in 1921 and bringing the reader to the twenty-first century. Politics, culture, war, economics, tribes, nationalization, and other topics are covered.

Given Youssef's depiction of America, what do other poets say about it? Youssef's work has been compared to that of Walt Whitman (whom Youssef names as an influence and who is referenced in "America, America") and Allen Ginsberg, both of whom have offered unique depictions of their native country. Other interesting perspectives on America can be found in the work of Carl Sandburg, considered by many to be the quintessential American poet, and the Chinese-American poet Marilyn Chin. Some poets embrace America and romanticize it, others criticize it, and still others express more

> SOME POETS EMBRACE AMERICA AND ROMANTICIZE IT, OTHERS CRITICIZE IT, AND STILL OTHERS EXPRESS MORE AMBIGUOUS SENTIMENTS STEMMING FROM DIVIDED CULTURAL IDENTITIES. SUCH PERSPECTIVES VIEWED IN COMPARISON TO YOUSSEF'S RENDER AN INTERESTING VIEW OF AMERICA."

ambiguous sentiments stemming from divided cultural identities. Such perspectives viewed in comparison to Youssef's render an interesting view of America.

Youssef, as well as other free verse Arabic poets, consider Walt Whitman an influence on their work, and he and his famous beard are mentioned in Youssef's poem. Although Youssef and Whitman have much in common in terms of their craft, their views of America are very different. In "I Hear America Singing," Whitman describes a variety of Americans going about their daily business. He hears their singing and regards them as strong melodies that inspire him to write the poem. The songs are metaphorical, representing the business of daily life. The poem describes each song as suitable for each person; among the people are a mechanic, a carpenter, a mason, a boatman with his deckhand, a shoemaker, a hatter, a wood-cutter, a farmer, a mother and wife, a girl doing chores, and a party of young men. All of these are everyday people embracing their roles and their tasks. Whitman's depiction of America is of an energetic country full of all kinds of people, all happily going about their lives. The tone of the poem is carefree and uplifting. This overall depiction is in marked contrast to Youssef's, in which America is hostile and uncaring. Youssef sees America as represented by its military, not as a nation of the same kind of everyday people who move him to compassion in Iraq. Both poets use imagery to the hilt, and both make the most of the free verse form, but beyond that, they have little in common besides love of home country.

Youssef has also been compared to the Beat poet Allen Ginsberg, whose sharp and often controversial poetry exemplifies to many the

American spirit of free expression and individualism. Ginsberg also wrote in free verse, with dependence on imagery and direct language—and in fact, Ginsberg shared Youssef's admiration for Whitman. In "A Supermarket in California," Ginsberg introduces Whitman as a character with whom he interacts. The speaker of the poem begins by addressing Whitman and telling him that he was thinking of him. The speaker also self-referentially says that he was walking down the street in search of images. The speaker is in an urban setting at night, and the images are of shopping, neon, streets, cars, and a grocery store. Toward the end of the poem, the speaker asks Whitman if they will dream of America, describing it as lost. He even asks Whitman (with a nickname that refers to his beard, just as Youssef referred to Whitman's beard in "America, America") about the America he once knew. In this poem, Ginsberg describes America as filled with superficial things, such as the items in a grocery store and neon signs. He seems to be searching and even longing for a stronger sense of America. He feels that America is lost and reaches out to someone he admires to ask about America in the past.

Ginsberg's most famous—and most controversial—poem is probably "Howl," in which he lashes out against the craziness that he claims has destroyed the great minds of his generation. The poem is chaotic and filled with images, many disturbing. The America described in this poem is one that is not at all peaceful, being filled with drugs, alcohol, censorship, and violence. The landscape of the poem is urban, but not the peaceful setting of "A Supermarket in California." Here, it is harsh, imposing, and overwhelming. Ginsberg describes tenement roofs, subways, hotels, cemeteries, bridges, meat trucks, and skyscrapers. In the second part of the poem, there is one question mark after the first statement, and exclamation points follow for the rest of the poem. The effect is unnerving and frantic. Although this poem is not specifically about America, there are numerous references to the New York City setting (the Brooklyn Bridge, the Empire State Building, Chinatown) throughout the poem. Because the speaker refers so often to the external world, and because specific references are made to an American city, the reader cannot help but conclude that a lot of the madness is American-made. The speaker sees America as claustrophobic, chaotic, permissive, and stifling. Although Ginsberg's speaker is not criticizing the military or politics of America, he is very critical of the culture and people of America.

Carl Sandburg is regarded as a uniquely American poet who wrote from an American perspective as an observer of his land. Unlike Ginsberg or Youssef, Sandburg is not a critical voice against America but a respectful observer of it. In "Hope Is a Tattered Flag," Sandburg writes a series of metaphors to describe hope. Like Youssef, Whitman, and Ginsberg, he is writing in free verse, but the structure is held together by each line's being a new metaphor. While Ginsberg depicted in "Howl" a landscape that was very urban and stressful, Sandburg creates one that is more sweeping and comforting. He describes a rainbow, the evening star, the coal mines and steelworks, blue hills, a car salesroom, a radio bringing music from all over the world, the Salvation Army, spring, and a skyscraper that is empty and therefore peaceful. Sandburg's America is first and foremost hopeful; irrespective of the geography, he sees hope everywhere. His depiction is of a nation where people are content in their daily lives, similar to Whitman's depiction. However, Sandburg focuses on the landscape and the external world, whereas Whitman focuses on the people who populate and bring life to that world. All of this stands in contrast to Youssef's depiction of America; on the other hand, parallels can definitely be found between the way Sandburg perceives America and the way Youssef perceives pre-sanctions Iraq. Particularly in Youssef's last section, the tone echoes that of Sandburg.

Aside from a foreigner's view of America and several native views, what might an immigrant's view of America be? Marilyn Chin's family came to America from Hong Kong, led a humble existence, and tried to make the opportunities of America available for their younger generation. Chin became a poet who grapples with issues of dual identity and self-exploration. In "How I Got That Name," she writes openly about her identity as an American and as a Chinese. She tells the reader outright that the poem is about assimilation. Her birth name was Mei Ling Chin, but her father's obsession with Marilyn Monroe led him to rename his daughter on the way to America. He not only bought into American popular culture but even wanted his daughter to begin assimilating right away. While this assimilation is to a degree necessary and makes life easier, it also complicates identity issues. In her poem, Chin strikes back at stereotypes and imagines a deity seeing her as in-between. In the end, the speaker decides to move forward and live life even though it is often complicated and difficult. Chin sees America as a place where she has the freedom to write poetry and choose which culture she will embrace in different parts of her life, but it is also the place where she is stereotyped and where her father degenerated to gambling and thuggery. In the end, the opportunity of living in America is not so simple a blessing, creating its own complexities. Still, Chin has the freedom in adulthood to stay in America, go to China, or go somewhere else entirely, and she chooses to stay in America.

Youssef's portrayal of the United States in "America, America" is critical and harsh. Yet that is the reflection of his personal experience and the history of his people, just as Whitman, Ginsberg, Sandburg, and Chin depict America according to their own personal experiences. Comparing and contrasting these poems, then, is an exercise in context. When reading a poem it is important to keep in mind that each poem has its own context, and that the poem itself also exists in a larger context of poetry as a whole. Some poems praise the wonders of love, for example, while others reject it and want no part of it. Similarly, Youssef and Ginsberg write about America in derogatory terms, while Whitman and Sandburg write about it in positive terms and Chin seems to write about it in neutral tones. Thus, the truth of human experience is that everyone experiences and perceives things differently, based on history, location, upbringing, culture, and personality. Just as it is enlightening to see the differences among poems, it is equally enlightening to see the similarities. There are stylistic and structural similarities that transcend time and location, as exemplified in the use of free verse and imagery in the poems discussed here. There are also similarities in how the poets grapple with identity (Youssef and Chin) and how they love their cultures (Youssef, Whitman, Sandburg, and Chin). It is also intriguing to realize that poets are often influenced by poets with whom they have little in common. Youssef claims Whitman as an influence in terms of style and form, which means that he is able to set aside his philosophical differences with Whitman about America. All of these factors are important both in writing poetry and in studying and learning from it.

Source: Jennifer Bussey, Critical Essay on "America, America," in *Poetry for Students*, Gale, Cengage Learning, 2009.

Ferial J. Ghazoul

In the following excerpt from a review of Without an Alphabet, Without a Face: Selected Poems, *Ghazoul writes that the book is "a work for all seasons and for all readers."*

For a poetic chronicle of modern Iraqi life, one could not find better than the works of renowned Iraqi poet Saadi Youssef. Not only does he capture the tragedies within tragedies in the unfolding of contemporary Iraqi history, but also the hope against hope in Iraqi experience. Born in 1934 near Basra, and reared in rural Abul-Khasib by his grandfather, he continues to retain a fascination with the rustic nature of southern Iraq—its palm trees and sunsets, its marshes and migratory birds. His poetry, written regularly since his teenage years, is a record of a collective experience, albeit one expressed in highly personal lyrics. Educated in Basra and Baghdad, and a long-time resident of several Arab and European capitals, the voracious reader Saadi Youssef has assimilated world literature as well as lived the struggles and plights of cities like Aden and Beirut. He has translated major Western poets—Walt Whitman, Constantine Cavafy, Yannis Ritsos, Giuseppe Ungaretti, and Frederico Garcia Lorca—and several African novelists. He is thoroughly acquainted with the great historians, Thucydides and Ibn Khaldun, as well as radical thinkers from Marx to Angela Davies [*sic*]. His encyclopaedic knowledge does not appear on the surface of his poetry, but functions as a solid foundation for his deceptively simple lyrics.

Though Saadi Youssef has been translated into English before and published in anthologies, journals, and literary supplements, *Without an Alphabet, Without a Face*, is the first book-length collection of his poetry. The translator, Khaled Mattawa, has selected poems from the various collections of Saadi Youssef and arranged them in chronological order, covering more than four decades, from 1955 to 1997. As an experimental poet, Saadi Youssef covers several themes and partakes in varied styles: shorter imagist poems and longer epic poems, political poems and nature poems. Regretfully, the translator did not include samples of Saadi Youssef's erotic poetry, published in a collection illustrated by an Iraqi artist Jabr 'Alwan, entitled, *Erotica*. Not only is this collection significant because it shows another aspect of Saadi's

HAVING LIVED IN MORE THAN [A] DOZEN CITIES IN THE ARAB WORLD AND EUROPE WITHOUT SETTLING ANYWHERE PERMANENTLY, SAADI EXEMPLIFIES THE EXILIC CONDITION."

poetry and poetics, but it also contains powerful and universally accessible poems.

The Libyan translator, Khaled Mattawa, is himself an Anglophone poet who has authored a fascinating collection, *Ismailia Eclipse*. He has also translated other Iraqi poetry, including Hatif Janabi's *Questions and Their Retinue* and Fadhil Al Azzawi's *In Every Well a Joseph Is Weeping*. Khaled Mattawa was educated in Libya, Egypt, and the United States. He teaches creative writing in the Department of English at the University of Texas at Austin. This collection is published in the prestigious Lannan Translation Series by an independent, non-profit, publisher. The translator's 14-page introduction is a brilliant critical essay that introduces the poet and his poetics while avoiding the pitfalls of academic jargon. The notes at the end of the book are short and to the point; they help explain the allusions in the poems as well as the places and proper names, thus contextualising the poems. Poetic traces of past moments reel and converge to sketch the quest of an Iraqi poet for that elusive dream of happiness for his people and freedom for his homeland.

The most successful poems in the collection are the shorter ones. The longer ones use a variety of strategies to extend the lyric outpouring: narrative strategy or cyclical structure. Saadi Youssef's poetry is written in the *taf'ila* mode, akin to *vers libre*, which has dominated new poetry since the metrical revolution that was initiated in Iraq in the late 1940s. What constitutes the distinctive feature of Saadi's poetics is his avoidance of rhetorical flares and ornate diction, so typical of Arabic poetry. His poetics is based on figures of thought rather than figures of speech, on surprising while understating, rather than moving his readers by resorting to hyperbole. His voice is fresh and strives after the right word and the precise image. His thorough

grounding in classical poetry allows him to be in touch with the works of the past while able to branch out into new venues. In an interview with critic Majid Al-Samirra'i, the poet expressed his attitude towards innovation and tradition: "I consider the poetic tradition to be a root that should not be cut. The Arabic word is not abstract, though it has a potential for abstraction. I use traditional artistic values in a new way, a way that is related to this age. Formal opposition, which is revealed in antithesis (*tibaq*), may be developed into dialectical opposition, just as comparison by simile may be transformed into expression by images." Saadi's attitude to tradition is critical but not hostile; his poetics is that of transformation, not rupture.

Many of his poems are autobiographical fragments presented in lyrical flashes. Having been detained, he presents the experience of captivity in his short poem "In Their Hands" (1956)...

This short poem condenses the political philosophy of the poet, which can be paraphrased as when you are repressed (thrown and roughly handled) think of the noble cause (Basra). The poet's city is a synecdoche for the homeland, and the homeland is associated with "sun, bread, and love". The diction is made up of everyday vocabulary and familiar words (rib, blue, night, sing, etc.). The poetic effect comes from the syntactical play in the poem: the move from "think of Basra" to "think with Basra." Basra changes from being an object to becoming a subject, and thus it is implicitly personified. By resorting to the concrete, the poet points to the abstract. Another short poem that represents the poet's social philosophy, is condensed in "Attention" (1993), where he distinguishes between two types of people—those to recall and those to dismiss from memory. The perfect balance between the first stanza and the second, between the statement and the imagery, captures the symbolic economy in Saadi's poetics...

The subtle music and internal rhythms of Saadi's poetry are delicately rendered by the translator as in the finale of a poem entitled "Spanish Plaza" (1965)...

Saadi's poetry avoids declamation and resounding statements. It is as if the poet is engaged in an intimate conversation and we—as readers—overhear him. Even his political poems have a subdued tone. They do not lend themselves to recital on a platform, nor can his verse be borrowed for a slogan. In a sequence of poems written in besieged Beirut in 1982, Saadi describes life at the edge in haiku-like minimalism. In "A Raid," the most dramatic of sounds—an explosion—is described in a gentle manner, as if whispering:

> *The room shivers*
> *from distant explosions.*
> *The curtains shiver.*
> *Then the heart shivers.*
> *Why are you in the midst of this shivering?*

This sequence of miniature poems constitutes the diaries of the poet in West Beirut when he was living under the bombardment of Israeli war planes, with water and electricity cut off by the invading army. The telegraphic style seems appropriate for this precarious existence. The short, abrupt sentences and the rationed diction reproduce aesthetically the ascetic conditions of life in a war zone. The repetition of "shiver" in the poem recreates the convulsive motion of shuddering.

Many of the poems of Saadi are shots of a scene or even shots of a detail in a scene. Such scenes, which Saadi encapsulates in his poems, are perfectly ordinary, if not down right familiar and mundane. The poet makes us see beauty in small things and sense the poetry of everyday scenes. The poetic is not sought in the distant and elevated, in the transcendent or fantastic, but in the here and now. Thus Saadi teaches us his aesthetic philosophy: beauty is lying there in front of us in the street, in the market place, in our sitting rooms and bedrooms. All we have to do is see it.

The Iraqi critic, Tarrad Al-Kubaisy, has called Saadi: "He who saw"—a locution often reserved for Gilgamesh, the hero of the ancient Mesopotamian epic. Seeing is then not simply observing but also penetrating what is beneath the surface. Saadi is the lucid one who sees the inner core of things and who makes his readers see the invisible beneath—not beyond—the visible. He makes us see the harmony, the beauty, and the poetry of the quotidian, of the passing moment. His aim is not to immortalise but to retrieve and preserve. In this sense he is, like Cavafy, fully aware of the passage of time and the urgency to record special moments. Because Saadi has been a wandering poet, a modern-day troubadour constantly on the move, his fugitive existence makes him more prepared to snatch the moment from our disjointed times. The

tavern, the bar, the café, and the hotel recur as settings in his poems. They point to transitory existence, a life on the go, in which companionship is based on free spirit and individual choice rather than on settled and conventional considerations. "The Chalets Bar" (1984) is a poem that points to the thriving fellowship of people from different races and nationalities, drinking together in a Yemeni bar. Memory also plays an important role in Saadi's poetry. Having been imprisoned, he recalls in his cell what he could not see and partake in. Living away from his homeland, he remembers the sites of his country. As he grows older, reminiscences of childhood unfold in his poetry, as in this extract:

> *And now*
> *I remember trees:*
> *the date palm of our mosque in Basra, at the*
>   *end of Basra*
> *a bird's beak,*
> *a child's secret,*
> *a summer feast.*

> I remember the date palm.
> I touch it. I become it, when it falls black
> without fronds,
> when a dam fell, hewn by lightning.

> *And I remember the mighty mulberry*
> *when it rumbled, butchered with an axe.*

In his poem "A Woman" (1984), the title suggests a woman, but she turns out to be *the* woman. It is one of several poems by Saadi where the closure explains the rest of the text and pushes the reader to read the poem retrospectively...

Having lived in more than [a] dozen cities in the Arab world and Europe without settling anywhere permanently, Saadi exemplifies the exilic condition. This dispersion, translated poetically into fragmentation, leaves for the poet the task of reconstructing the self, of making the shards into a whole. Poetry becomes the medium by which a face is given to this defaced existence. In his poem entitled "Poetry" (1985), Saadi refers to the task of the poet by referring to himself through the persona of *L'Akhdar*, a poetic double who figures in more than one poem...

In the longer poems, such as "The Trees of Ithaca" (1989), Saadi narrates the exodus of the Palestinians from Beirut. The classical journey of Odysseus, and its re-interpretation by the poet Cavafy, is a subtext in this poem. One displacement recalls another and is linked to it, "We turn in the earth the way a shepherd wraps his cloak around him." In another long poem, written in 1995 and addressing the US which led the war against Iraq in 1991, entitled "America, America", Saadi uses different voices in his polyphonic poem. The words of an Iraqi poetic persona is juxtaposed to the song by an American soldier, probably an African-American as his lyric is entitled "Blues". The soldier longs to go back to his home town, Sacramento, and suggests his unhappiness with the war and his anxiety as a stranger in a country that is not his.

The Iraqi voice wonders whether it is his identity that has made him a target: "But I am not American./ Is that enough for the Phantom pilot to turn me back to the Stone Age?" The poem sarcastically uses the refrain, "God save America,/My home, sweet home!"

... The title of this rich collection, *Without an Alphabet, Without a Face*, is taken from a verse line in a poem entitled "The Ends of the African North" (1971). It focuses on the image of a child weeping, the violation of innocence that has become a recurring motif in the age of global imperialism:

> In the neighbourhoods of Tunis and their winter cafés
> at the gates of Africa's spread thighs
> I saw a girl weep
> without an alphabet, without a face.
> Snow was falling and a girl wept under it.

The richness and accessibility, as well as the breadth and depth, of this collection turn this book into a work for all seasons and for all readers.

Source: Ferial J. Ghazoul, "Spiral of Iraqi Memory," in *Al–Ahram Weekly On-line*, No. 634, April 17–23, 2003, 7 pp.

Saadi A. Simawe
In the following excerpt, Simawe demonstrates the way that Youssef uses southern Iraqi vernacular within traditional Arabic poetic forms.

When Irish poet seamus Justin Heaney was awarded the Nobel Prize for Literature in 1995, the Academy praised him for "works of lyrical beauty and ethical depth, which exalt everyday life and the living past" (Schlessinger 93). Though having no power to grant a Nobel Prize, many critics, students of literature, and general readers have noted with fascination the

> A MAJOR ASPECT OF YUSUF'S POETRY THAT HAS BEEN TOUCHED UPON, BUT NOT SUFFICIENTLY EXPLORED, BY CRITICS IS HIS REMARKABLE BLEND OF STANDARD ARABIC (AL-LUGHA AL-FUSHA) WITH THE IRAQI VERNACULAR (AL-LAHJA AL-'AMMIYYA)."

magical power of Sa'di Yusuf's unassuming, short, and subtle poems that exalt the heroism and the epical perseverance of everyday life in the Arab World, particularly in Iraq where the very act of surviving with some form of dignity becomes in itself heroic. Yusuf's poetry since the early 1950s has become an epic song of survival in the face of both fascism and Western intervention.

A major aspect of Yusuf's poetry that has been touched upon, but not sufficiently explored, by critics is his remarkable blend of standard Arabic (al-Lugha al-Fusha) with the Iraqi vernacular (al-Lahja al-'Ammiyya). In this essay I will argue that Yusuf's talent for "poetization of the familiar and the quotidian," as Ghazoul aptly put it ("The Poetics of the Political Poem," 117), lies largely in his capability of creating a poetic diction of his own—a linguistic synthesis that blends al-Fusha and al-'Ammiyya. Yusuf's new poetic diction reflects on the one hand his Marxist politics and on the other his poetics. Though most of the time a fellow traveler, his esthetics asserts itself with occasional rebellion against the ideological dictates of the Iraqi Communist Party. Yet his loyalty to his esthetics and to the ordinary, vulnerable individual never wavered throughout his long journey.

Born in 1934 (the year the Iraqi Communist Party was founded) in a village near Basra, Iraq, Sa'di Yusuf began writing poetry when he was about fifteen years old. Upon graduating from high school, he went to Dar al-Mu'allimeen al-'Allia in Baghdad (Higher Teachers' Training Institute), where he earned a B.A. in Arabic with a teaching certificate. His life in Iraq, from the early 1950s to 1964 and then from 1973 to 1978, was spent between teaching at various high schools, working with progressive or Communist journalism, and serving political prison terms. Like the majority of Iraqi writers, educators, and intellectuals, Yusuf was forced to leave Iraq in 1978, when Saddam Hussein assumed absolute power. After several years in Algeria, Lebanon, and Yemen, Yusuf settled in Damascus, Syria, where now he works as journalist with the Palestinians and with the Iraqi opposition groups.

Since 1952, Yusuf has published more than twenty volumes of poetry. He has also published fiction, essays, and translated the Nineteenth Century American poet Walt Whitman and contemporary Kenyan novelist Ngugi wa'Thionga, as well as works by European authors. Yusuf learned English and French on his own, taking advantage of the periods of exile he was forced into due to his involvement, like most Iraqi writers, with the Iraqi Communist Party since his college years in Baghdad (probably even before that when he was in Basra). Although he demonstrated remarkable versatility in most literary genres, Yusuf is primarily considered a towering figure in Iraqi modernist poetry, Jama'at al-Ruwwad (The Group of Pioneers) established in the early 1950s.

From the beginning of his career Yusuf was interested not only in registering the poetic glow in the ordinary and the common, but also in portraying the seemingly insignificant. The majority of his characters are below even ordinary people; they are the marginalized and on the fringes of the society: children attempting to survive their vulnerability, women caught in the double plight of sexism and classism, the poorest farmers and menial laborers. Scenes and moments that inspire his best poetry are frequently the invisible and the unnoticed. This vision of the ordinary seems to account for Yusuf's language a language that suggests rather than oppresses or stifles the poetry of the ordinary. As many critics have observed, when we read Yusuf's poetry, we cannot help but notice the closeness of his standard Arabic to the vernacular.

In her *Modern Arabic Poetry* (1987) poet and critic Salma Khadia Jayyusi characterizes Yusuf's greatness as "his capacity to speak in direct and simple yet highly poetic terms about life's constant routine and day-to-day experiences, subjects which so many Arab poets shun" (480). Other critics point more specifically to Yusuf's talent for capturing the ordinary and

the obvious in a kaleidoscopic poetic medium. "It seems to me," al-Saggar states, "that Sa'di is keenly aware of his environment, and he deals with it on the basis that it is a reality that demands his recognition without imposing on it any kind of logic that does not sound at any rate apropos. He is a hunter of the first moment—which is no doubt the essential stuff of poetry. Once it is in his hand, he does not allow it to escape by reflection and much analysis" (143). More specifically, Ghazoul in her essay titled "Saadi Yusuf: Qasa'id Aqalu Samtan" focuses on what she terms Yusuf's "poetization of the familiar and the quotidian" (23).

Textual evidence from Yusuf's poetic work supports the critics' understanding of the crux of his poetic vision and the source of his inspiration. In one of his poems of 1976 titled "How Did al-Akhdhar bin Yusuf Write His New Poem," Yusuf, who had already made al-Akhdhar bin Yusuf his poetic persona or double (Ghazoul, "The Poetics of the Political Poem," 117) or a mask (Abbas, 73–74) reflects on his own process of writing:

> Well, here is al-Akhdhar bin Yusuf facing a problem more complicated than he initially thought.
> It's true that when he writes the poem he rarely thinks of its destiny. But usually writing becomes easier when he can focus on a thing, a moment, a vibration, a leaf of grass.
> Whereas now he is in front of Ten Commandments, he does not know which one he should choose. More importantly: How to begin?
> Endings are always open. And beginnings are closed (Yusuf, *al-'Amal al-Kamila*, 62).

The Ten Commandments, arguably a metaphor for ideology, seem to block the poet's vision from focusing on one thing, whether human or natural. Poetry flows naturally, Yusuf seems to suggest, when it is free from rigid thought, when it captures the rhythm within a scene or a moment.

Before the July Revolution of 1958, Yusuf's experiments with the vernacular by incorporating slang words and phrases and even sentences in the standard Arabic were considered audacious, even blasphemous by the mainstream critics. What made Yusuf's experiments possible, it seems to me, is the fact that he was one of a group of young poets working independently to break the traditional poetic styles, what is usually called 'Amud al-Sh'ir (the pillar of poetry). Like Yusuf, Badr Shakir al-Sayyab (1926–1964),

Nazik al-Mala'ika (1923-), Buland al-Haydari (1926–1996), and Abdul Wahab al-Bayaati (1926-), among others, were experimenting with new techniques in search of a language that expressed their new vision of reality. Significantly, all of these young poets were more or less progressive in their political views. Despite their nationalism, Marxism, or Communism, they were united in their opposition to the status quo in literature and life.

More than any of them, Yusuf has been interested in quietness in poetry as well as in politics. It seems that he believes that whispering is more effective than declaiming, suggesting is more convincing than stating, and portraying the ordinary is more enduring than portraying the extreme. Significantly, all three qualities are essential parts of folklore and vernacular literature. In a poem published in 1971, appropriately titled "Tanwima" (Nursery Song), Yusuf demonstrates his mature experimentation with the poetics of the ordinary ...

The poetic diction is so simple that it is almost colloquial in its idiom and the choice of words. Any reader can relate to the poem; even the illiterate listener would not find it difficult to understand the general theme and the narrative line. In order to capture the situation suggested by the title, the speaker, a tired and sleepy young mother, wearily sings to put her baby to sleep. Similar to folkloric songs, the poem relies on the magic created by repetition of words and phrases. The repetition actuates the hypnotizing rhythm, which is the most effective aspect of the poem. The meaning of specific lines is vague and elusive, even as obscure and unlimited as the setting of the poem, the wilderness. The young mother, weary and sleepy, glows in the middle of the wilderness with yellow light intensified by the yellow light coming from her restless baby, whose face and hair are also yellow. The two faces, the mother's and the baby's, circled with yellow halos definitely evoke the Madonna, thus elevating the ordinary scene to a mythical level. No change happens in the situation until one star falls, indicating the coming of the dawn: the baby's face changes from yellow to red. At this point another speaker, apparently the poet, intrudes to urge the young mother to sleep.

Actually, in this poem there are two nursery songs being sung simultaneously: one by the young mother to her baby and another by the poet to the beautiful young mother in the

wilderness. The poem tries to capture the anxiety of the anonymous young mother, lonely in the middle of the dark universe. The experience is not really unique; it is an ordinary every-night experience. The poetry in it arises from the poet's ability to make the agony of the young mother unique through imagery and rhythm. By both repetition and austere minimalism, Yusuf creates what he later calls al-qasida al-mutaqashifa, that is, the ascetic poem (Yusuf, "Letter," 1994). Because of the intensity of his language, its self-consciousness, its playfulness, and its ultimate defamiliarizing of the familiar, Yusuf's poetry would be the delight of the New Critic and the Russian Formalist. In a crucial passage from his Russian Formalism: History, Doctrine (1955), Victor Erlich identifies the technique by which the poet is able to transform ordinary language into poetry:

> If in informative 'prose,' a metaphor aims to bring the subject closer to the audience or drive a point home, in 'poetry' it serves as a means of intensifying the intended aesthetic effect. Rather than translating the unfamiliar into the terms of the familiar, the poetic image 'makes strange' the habitual by presenting it in a novel light, by placing it in unexpected context. (150)

But like any good poetry, Yusuf's poetry both satisfies and disturbs poetic theory. As the Russian Formalist would like to see, language in Yusuf's poetry becomes, like a child, happily aware of itself. But when Yusuf liberates the language and makes it self-conscious, he inadvertently gives voice to new, even revolutionary, realities—realities that are relegated to the margins or made insignificant. As Derrida's deconstructionism has demonstrated—though poets and writers are always ahead of philosophers—to highlight the insignificant or the fringe or the margin naturally threatens the center, which is by definition a political act (Culler, 193–4).

Another poem titled "Ilhah" (Insistence) written in 1956 utilizes techniques from folklore and diction from the vernacular. These include magical repetition of words and phrases, entrapment of the vulnerable speaker/protagonist that immediately appeals to the reader and entices his or her identification, and the exposition of the elemental level of the desire. An ordinary individual, who seems to be a farmer or a shepherd, desperately tries to cross the river to meet his young wife, who is taking care of her sick father on the other side of the river. The speaker, who is the farmer, tries to beg a ride from a boat owner, Salim al-Murzuq...

For the traditional school of poetry the theme of this poem is unthinkable because of its apparent vulgarity. But what is the source of poetry in this experience? The conflict between the speaker's desperate desire to meet his wife and Salim al-Murzuq's desire to have sex with him as the only acceptable price for taking him on the boat seems both comic and sad. Again this unfortunate moment is elevated to a memorable folkloric level primarily by rhythm, repetition, and what might be called the vernacularization of the standard Arabic. Phrases such as "take my eye as a price," "and you are a man of courage," and "she is pretty" are as close as the standard Arabic can be brought to the southern Iraqi dialect. In the twenty lean lines of the poems, the name Salim al-Murzuq is repeated six times. Repetition of words and phrases, which can be seen as symptoms of entrapment, is the only way to express an elemental desperate desire, as is evident in the repetitive lyrical intensity of African American blues and spirituals. Also repetition gives the poem a child-like quality. By making the speaker repeat phrases and words, the poet captures his child-like character and his vulnerability. Specifically, the intensity of the desire expressed through repetition lends the entire moment an intimate lyricism—a prominent feature in most of Yusuf's poetry.

In both poems discussed above, "Tanwima" and "Ilhah," the poet does not seem interested in a closure: he captures the individual's vulnerability in a highly lyrical simple language, only to leave it jarring in our imagination. It is in this ability to depict the persistence and perseverance of the vulnerable that Yusuf seems to whisper and quietly celebrate the ordinary individual's heroism.

Further, by using vernacular or near-vernacular yfulness of the popular rhythms and the innocence of language (i.e. not traditional standard Arabic, the official literary language), Yusuf is able to construct near-folkloric song poems.

In Yusuf's near-vernacular poetic diction, the narrator frequently indulges in intimate play with words, like a child fascinated with colorful balls. In this immersion in language, meaning or theme becomes secondary, conceding the foreground to the innocence of the language that is just liberated from the tyranny of rational thinking and suffocation of ideologies. Let us look at the function of language in the following examples:

> Do you remember? (When the action becomes a memory, the question is immediately lost) O sir, what a flavor does this evening have? In a cabaret in Rabbat we saw the bottles empty and the bottles were twenty, and empty in the evening and empty are the women eyes and empty are all those bottles ("Hiwar ma'a al-Akhdhar bin Yusuf"), (A Dialogue with al-Akhdar Bin Yusuf), (*Al-'Amal al-Kamila*, 101)

"Empty" is repeated four times, and "bottles," three times. There is no logic or rhetorical rationale to the repetition, but merely association. On the sensory level the reader enjoys the repetition of the words without having time to think about their meaning. What the lines seem to convey is a kind of verbal music that seduces the emotions and suspends the reasoning. The language's capability to suspend reason and stir emotion is usually best achieved in religious sermons and in folklore, and in both traditions meaning is subdued by rhythm and the magical impact of language on the unconscious, as Lacan has demonstrated in his analysis of the unconscious as inseparable from language (Lacan, 147). More specifically, Robert Hass in "Listening and Making" has identified the naturally subversive politics of rhythm:

> Because rhythm has direct access to the unconscious because it can hypnotize us, enter our bodies and make us move, it is power. And power is political. That is why rhythm is always revolutionary ground. It is always the place where the organic rises to abolish the mechanical and where energy announces the abolition of tradition. New rhythms are new perceptions. (Hass, 147)

Another example of the poet's gratuitous play with words can be seen in a poem titled "Khatawat," (Steps):

> Of the mirrors of the gardens I can be satisfied with the slim woman and the burning thirst that I had and the meagerness that became mine and the dialogue that naturally harmonizes in a slender woman (*Al-'Amal al-Kamila*, 91)

In the first line the word "mirrors" conjures up "woman" primarily because of the sound affinity between the two words: in Arabic "mirrors" is marayah and "woman" is mar'ah. Logically there is no connection between the two words, but linguistically linkage makes solid sense in terms of the verbal pleasure it provides to the reader. The play with words becomes more intense in the next line, further subordinating the meaning of the lines to the linguistic quality. "Burning thirst" and "meagerness" are in Arabic ghalil and qalil. They not only make a perfect rhyme, but through consonance and assonance, they resonate in our imagination. The last line is heavily charged with emotion, announcing the climax through lyrical intensity:

and the dialogue that naturally harmonizes in a
slender woman

The word "dialogue," which is hiwar in Arabic, seems to exude an erotic glow before it collapses in the harmony with the slender woman. Actually, the Arabic verb yatajanas, which means "harmonize," has a definite sexual pun that transforms the word dialogue from its literal level to a symbolic level of sexual intercourse. Yet, one cannot resist feeling that the speaker's sensual, even erotic, pleasure shines not only through his harmony with the slender woman, but also through his child-like excitement at seeing his words linguistically harmonize in a slender poem. The poem gains its integrity not from its reasoning or its intellectual content. Rather it gathers force and focus from its emotional unity, which is expressed in a linguistic harmony that seems to liberate the language from reason, logic, and other symptoms of ideology. A reader familiar with Iraqi vernacular poetry, especially the folkloric part of it, can easily appreciate Yusuf's experimentation with the vernacularization of standard Arabic.

In 1973, upon his return to Baghdad from a seven-year exile in Algeria, Sa'di Yusuf published "Fi Tilka Al-Ayyam" (In Those Days), his most impressive poetic collage of the vernacular and standard Arabic. The poem is a celebration of survival and safe homecoming, but it is also a glorification of the poet's involvement with the Iraqi Communist Party. On one level the poem is a tribute to the Iraqi people and their struggle against colonialism and fascism; on the other, it is the poet's tribute to himself and the pride he derives from the sacrifices he made in belonging to the Party and to the people. Significantly, the poem is dated 31 March, the birth-date of the Iraqi Communist Party in 1934. To express these layers of emotions, Yusuf chose the most popular and most folkloric of Iraqi vernacular poetry, the abudhiyia. It is a quatrain in which the first three lines rhyme; the fourth line usually has a different rhyme, typically presenting a resolution to the problem stated in the first three lines. Because the poem epitomizes Yusuf's main poetic characteristics, it is worth translating in its entirety:

On May 1, I was officially imprisoned And the royal officers registered me as a Communist I was charged—as usual in those days—and My shirt was black, my tie was yellow. I left the court, with the guards' beatings And the judge's ridicule. I have a wife Whom I love, and a book made of date-palms in which I learned the first names. I have been to some jails full of lice, and others full of sands, and others vacant, except for my face.

That day when we ended up in the prison that never ends I assured myself that the ultimate end is not ended O you who get to my people, tell them I am not ended Tonight we stayed here, the morning we will be in Baghdad.

Tonight I celebrate the moon that visits me through the bars, the Guard has slept, and the breaths of Siba are heavy with the humidity of Shat al-Arab, The visiting moon turned toward me, I was humming in the corner of my cell: What are you carrying for me in your eyes? Air I can touch? Greetings from her? The visiting moon used to enter my cell through the bars and sit with me, sharing the black blanket. When he left me I found a silver key in my hand.

All the songs have vanished but the people's songs. And when the voice is salable, the people will never buy. Deliberately I forgot what [went wrong] between me and the people For I belong to them, I am like them, and the voice comes from them.

On the third of May, I saw the six walls cracked up. And from them a man I know comes out, wearing a proletariat fatigue, and a hat of black leather. I asked him, I thought you left … wasn't your name among the first names? Haven't you volunteered to fight in Madrid? Haven't you fought behind the revolutionary bunkers in Petrograd? Haven't you been killed in the oil strike? Haven't I seen you in the marshes [among the reeds] with your machine gun? Haven't you hoisted your red flag for [Paris] Commune? Weren't you organized in the people's army in Sumatra? Take my hand. For the six walls could close up any moment … take my hand.

O Neighbor, I have believed in the homeless star. O Neighbor, the nights of my age announced: you are the home. We have traveled all ways, but the heart stays at home. O Neighbor, do not go farther, my destination is Baghdad. (*al-'Amal al-Kamila*, 132–134)

The underlined quatrains are written in the traditional abudhiyya of the vernacular poetry of southern Iraq. Their poetic intensity, coming from their high pitch, enhances the dramatic sense in the poem by counterpointing the standard Arabic, which sounds more meditative and therefore prosaic. What gives the entire poem its distinct poetic quality is its surprising hybrid quality and the folkloric depiction of the popular Communist hero, who is given an archetypal dimension; that is, he is capable of transcending places and times in order to inspire the international revolution. While the peaks of emotion are expressed with highly lyrical intensity in the vernacular quatrains, the standard Arabic, al-fusha, is employed to capture historical moments of epic heroism. The folkloric element is deftly used to enhance that epic or mythical quality of the Communist hero. In lines 15–20, the moon collaborates with the hero in prison, bringing him good news from his faraway beloved and giving him a silver key. In southern Iraqi folklore, a silver key is supposed to have magical qualities that help one to open all kinds of doors, including prison doors.

Significantly, the three quatrains are devoted to celebrating the people, and the speaker in them becomes a collective voice of the popular masses, punctuating the three movements of the poem. The element of repetition, which is part of the structure of al-abudhiyya, is effectively utilized. As a quatrain, al-abudhiyya requires that the first three lines end in exact (or perfect) rhymes, that is, the same word with the condition that each time it suggest a different meaning. In the first quatrain, lines 11–14, the word intaha ("ended" or "vanished") has three different meanings. In the first line it means the prison "has not ended yet," in the second, our aspiration "has not vanished," and in the third, the speaker/hero has not, despite prison and torture, been defeated.

Repetition is one of Yusuf's favorite and most effective poetic techniques. It links his poetic discourse with the traditional poetic forms of the southern Iraqi vernacular. Furthermore, as Ferial J. Ghazoul has insightfully noticed, repetition in Yusuf's poetry becomes a means of resistance and defiance ("Qasa'id Aqalu Samtan," p. 247). In other words, Yusuf employs repetition as a means of political resistance. A good example of the defiant repetition is found in a poem titled "The Night of Hamra," written, as Ghazoul, who translated the poem into English ("The Poetics of The Political Poem," 113–114), notes, "in the summer of 1982 in West Beirut under siege by Israeli forces" (113–114) . . .

In addition to the incantatory force the repetition of the word "candle" establishes, as Ghazoul notes, the ascetic slimness of the poem renders the poem itself into a candle that the entire Israeli blackout could not extinguish. Actually the last line, "A candle in my hand," transforms the poet, amidst the ruins of civilization in Beirut, into a Diogenes still for centuries carrying his lamp in the middle of the day, searching for meaning and truth in the absurdity of the human condition.

Sa'di Yusuf's fascination with and aspiration to the condition of vernacular and folkloric poetry are evident in the majority of his poetry. In fact one is tempted to say that Yusuf achieves his best poetry when he is closest to the vernacular and the folkloric. Significantly, in 1956, very early in his career, Yusuf declared his fascination with the vernacular when he discovered and introduced Muzaffer al-Nawwab, the most prominent Iraqi vernacular poet. In his article on al-Nawwab's first published poem, "Li al-rail wa Hammad," (For the Train and Hamad), Yusuf is reported to have said he would put all his poetry at the feet of that beautiful poem. This love for the ordinary and the simple and the sonic as the natural attributes of the vernacular inspired Yusuf to creatively appropriate for his own poetic purposes both the vernacular and the classical Arabic forms. Whereas the other pioneers and practitioners in the free verse, such as al-Sayyab and al-Mala'ika, were liberating the Arabic poem from the traditional unity of the line and the mandatory use of the two-hemistich form, Yusuf's achievement primarily lies in creating what might be called a hybrid poetic form that collapses the traditional Arabic poetic forms into a synthesis of the Iraqi southern vernacular, folklore, and popular songs. Evidently, Yusuf's politics and his poetics, which inform each other, coincide and blend into a highly distinctive poetic style that influenced and has been influencing younger poets since the 1956s.

Source: Saadi A. Simawe, "The Politics and Poetics of Sa'di Yusef: The Use of the Vernacular," in *Arab Studies Quarterly*, Vol. 19, No. 4, Fall 1997, 10 pp.

SOURCES

Booth, Marilyn, Review of *Loin du premier ciel*, in *World Literature Today*, Vol. 74, No. 4, Autumn 2000, p. 904.

Chin, Marilyn, "How I Got That Name," in *The Phoenix Gone, the Terrace Empty*, Milkweed, 1994, pp. 16–18.

Cortright, David, "A Hard Look at Iraq Sanctions," in *Nation*, December 3, 2001, pp. 20–24.

Ginsberg, Allen, "Howl," in *Howl, and Other Poems*, City Lights Books, 1996, pp. 9–27.

———, "A Supermarket in California," in *Howl, and Other Poems*, City Lights Books, 1996, p. 29.

Mattawa, Khaled, Introduction, in *Without an Alphabet, Without a Face: Selected Poems*, translated by Khaled Mattawa, Graywolf Press, 2002, pp. xi, xviii–xix.

Review of *Without an Alphabet, Without a Face: Selected Poems*, by Saadi Youssef, in *Publishers Weekly*, Vol. 249, No. 47, November 25, 2002, p. 59.

Sandburg, Carl, "Hope Is a Tattered Flag," in *The Complete Poems of Carl Sandburg*, Harcourt, 2003, p. 455.

Whitman, Walt, "I Hear America Singing," in *The Portable Walt Whitman*, edited by Michael Warner, Penguin Books, 2004, p. 182.

Wieder, Laurance, "After Babel: Two Arab Poets—One Palestinian, the Other Iraqi—and the Vicissitudes of Exile and Translation," in *Books & Culture*, Vol. 9, No. 5, September–October 2003, pp. 8–9.

Youssef, Saadi, "America, America," in *Without an Alphabet, Without a Face: Selected Poems*, translated by Khaled Mattawa, Graywolf Press, 2002, pp. 172–76.

FURTHER READING

Darwish, Mahmoud, *Unfortunately, It Was Paradise: Selected Poems*, translated and edited by Munir Akash and Carolyn Forché, University of California Press, 2003.
> Darwish is a Palestinian writer whose poetry reflects his sense of loss at being exiled from his country for more than two decades. Like Youssef, he writes in Arabic and is one of the dominant poetic voices of the Middle East in translation today.

Handal, Nathalie, ed., *The Poetry of Arab Women: A Contemporary Anthology*, Interlink Books, 2001.
> A woman was one of the first free-verse Arabic writers to blaze the trail for writers like Youssef, yet women's voices in Arabic poetry have remained largely obscured. Here, Handal offers a wide range of women's voices that reflect the unique experiences and emotions of Arab women.

Lewis, Adrian R., *The American Culture of War: The History of U.S. Military Force from World War II to Operation Iraqi Freedom*, Routledge, 2007.
> Lewis provides an in-depth look into the United States military culture as it relates to politics, technology, media, economics, and values. By covering events from the 1940s to the present, Lewis portrays consistent themes and strategies present in the American military.

Simawe, Saadi, and Daniel Weissbort, eds., *Iraqi Poetry Today*, Modern Poetry in Translation, 2003.
> The years of war in Iraq in the 1980s and 1990s produced Iraqi literary voices describing cultural changes, survival experiences, and quests for national identity. These voices are collected in this anthology, allowing readers from other parts of the world insight into the uniquely Iraqi experience.

Whitman, Walt, *Leaves of Grass and Other Writings: Authoritative Texts, Other Poetry and Prose, Criticism*, edited by Michael Moon, Norton, 2002.
> Whitman has influenced writers of free verse all over the world. This edition presents his most famous and beloved poetic work, complete with articles and notes for deeper study.

An Attempt at Jealousy

MARINA TSVETAEVA

1928

"An Attempt at Jealousy," by Marina Tsvetaeva (sometimes spelled Tsvetayeva or Cvetaeva), is a poem about disappointment in love. Tsvetaeva, a celebrated Russian poet writing in the early twentieth century, was known for her poems about love, loneliness, and alienation. This poem is usually said to have been inspired by one or more of her actual failed romances, of which she had many, and it is notable for its nostalgic contrast of an ideal mythologized love in the past with a present full of commonness, vulgarity, and ill health.

"An Attempt at Jealousy" was first published in Russian under the title "Popytka revnosti" in 1928 in a collection of Tsvetaeva's poems called *Posle Rossii*. The collection was translated into English in a 1992 edition as *After Russia*. The book was published in Paris, as Tsvetaeva was living there in exile at the time, having left her native Russia in 1922 after the Bolshevik Revolution and subsequent civil war.

The poem is available in a number of English editions, including a selection of Tsvetaeva's poems translated by Elaine Feinstein under the title *Selected Poems* (first published in 1971 and revised in 1999).

AUTHOR BIOGRAPHY

Born in Moscow on October 9, 1892, Marina Tsvetaeva was the child of a pianist mother and a father who was a professor of art history at Moscow University. Though well off as a child and adolescent, Tsvetaeva felt alienated and lonely. She had an especially difficult relationship with her mother, who wanted her to pursue a musical career when she much preferred literature.

After her mother died of tuberculosis in 1906, Tsvetaeva was able to concentrate on writing poetry, and she published her first collection of poems, *Vechernii al'bom* (Evening Album) in 1910 to much acclaim. She was beginning to develop a reputation as an important poet when the Russian Revolution broke out in 1917. Feeling herself part of the cultural elite threatened by the revolution, Tsvetaeva left Russia in 1922, joining many other Russian intellectuals in exile first in Berlin, then in Prague and Paris.

Though she married another writer, Sergei Efron, in 1912, Tsvetaeva pursued numerous romances with other men and women throughout her life. She did this when separated from her husband during the civil war that followed the revolution as well as when they were reunited in exile. Her lovers and would-be lovers were generally writers, painters, or actors and included the poet and novelist Boris Pasternak, although the romantic connection with him consisted almost entirely of letters.

While in Prague in 1923 Tsvetaeva began an affair with another émigré, Konstantin Rodzevich. Like all her affairs, it ended badly, and she felt devastated. Soon after she became infatuated with the literary critic Mark Slonim, who, however, did not return her interest. According to some commentators, it was one or both of these experiences that inspired "An Attempt at Jealousy," which she wrote in Russian in November 1924 as "Popytka revnosti" and later published in her collection *Posle Rossii* (1928). The collection was translated into English in a 1992 edition as *After Russia*.

Although he had fought in the White Army against the Communists in the civil war, Tsvetaeva's husband came to sympathize with the Soviet Union and eventually became a Soviet agent. After his involvement in a political assassination became known, he fled France for the Soviet Union in 1937. Tsvetaeva followed him reluctantly in 1939, knowing that the Soviet Union would not be a congenial place for her. However, she was finding herself increasingly alienated in the emigré community in Paris and also had remained close to her husband despite their political differences and her many affairs.

In 1939, both Tsvetaeva's husband and her daughter were arrested by the Soviet authorities. Her husband was later executed. Tsvetaeva meanwhile could not publish her works in the Soviet Union and was seen as a dangerous person to associate with. In her last days she was reduced to seeking work as a dishwasher to support herself and her son.

On August 31, 1941, she committed suicide by hanging. She died in the town of Elabuga, Russia, to which she had been evacuated after the German invasion of the Soviet Union earlier that summer.

POEM TEXT

How is your life with the other one,
    simpler, isn't it? One   stroke of the oar
then a long coastline, and soon
    even the memory of me

will be a floating island   5
    (in the sky, not on the waters):
spirits, spirits, you will be
    sisters, and never lovers.

How is your life with an ordinary
    woman?   without godhead?   10
Now that your sovereign has
    been deposed (and you have stepped down).

How is your life? Are you fussing?
    flinching? How   do you get up?
The tax of deathless vulgarity   15
    can you cope with it, poor man?

'Scenes and hysterics   I've had
    enough! I'll rent my own house.'
How is your life with the other one
    now, you that I chose for my own?   20

More to your taste, more delicious
    is it, your food? Don't moan if you sicken.
How is your life with an *image*
    you, who walked on Sinai?

How is your life with a stranger   25
    from this world? Can you (be frank)
love her? Or do you   feel shame
    like Zeus' reins on your forehead?

How is your life? Are you
    healthy? How do you   sing?   30
How do you deal with the pain
    of an undying conscience, poor man?

How is your life with a piece of market
    stuff, at a steep price.
After Carrara marble;   35
    how is your life with the dust of

plaster now? (God was hewn from
    stone, but he is smashed to bits.)
How do you live with one of a
    thousand women after   Lilith?   40

Sated with newness, are you?
    Now you are grown cold to magic,
how is your life with an
    earthly woman, without a sixth

sense? Tell me: are you happy?   45
    Not? In a shallow pit How is
your life, my love? Is it as
    hard as mine with another man?

POEM SUMMARY

The title is interesting for its suggestion that the poem is merely an attempt at jealousy, as if the speaker is not really jealous but has to try to appear jealous for some reason. Perhaps that is the point: the speaker is trying to appear indifferent or nonchalant, as if not caring about her rival, trying to make it seem that her rival is not worth being jealous over.

Stanza 1
After suggesting that her ex-lover's life must be simpler now with another woman, the speaker conjures up an image of rowing, as if the ex-lover is rowing away, gliding on the water, away from the speaker, who is represented as both an island and a coastline. There is a calmness here that belies the storminess to come, perhaps suggesting how easy it was for the ex-lover to leave.

Stanza 2
The speaker at this point seems merely curious to know how long it took the memory of her to disappear, as if this were merely an idle inquiry. At the same time she describes herself as a floating island, floating in the sky, not on the water. Perhaps the significance of the island here is that the speaker is somehow high above, not down below with her ex-lover.

Sarcasm now emerges in the poem, as the speaker suggests that her ex-lover and his new woman will be not lovers but sisters. This seems a jab at her ex-lover's masculinity and also perhaps an expression of hope that what goes on between him and the new woman will not be sexual love but something platonic. The

references to them as spirits or souls may also suggest that any love between them will be nonphysical.

Stanza 3
In the third stanza the speaker's feelings become more intense. She describes her rival as ordinary and herself as a sort of god or monarch. Her former lover has abandoned the divine or royal life with her and has gone down to something lower. There is an image of revolution here, of a sovereign being forced from the throne, just as the Russian tsar was forced from his, resulting in a sort of descent not only by the sovereign but by those who overthrew the sovereign; the tsar or queen or spurned woman has been hurt, but the one doing the spurning has been hurt as well, at least in the speaker's view.

Stanza 4
The nature of the hurt is elaborated on in the fourth stanza. The former lover, it seems, must deal with endless banality and commonplaceness with the new woman. The speaker even affects to feel sorry for him. The poem's aim has quickly become to make the former lover feel the speaker's contempt and also to feel that he is paying a tax or a high price for abandoning the speaker.

Stanza 5
The fifth stanza begins by varying the pattern whereby the speaker has been asking more and more insistent and belittling questions. For its first two lines, the speaker allows the ex-lover to speak, though of course it is really the speaker remembering something the ex-lover said, namely, his explanation for leaving, which is that life with the speaker had contained too many emotional upheavals.

Interestingly, the speaker does not dispute the characterization of life with her as one involving emotional upheavals or, to follow another translation, anxiety and discomfort. That perhaps is the price to pay for being with the speaker, a price that she thinks is well worth it, because she after all is goddess-like and her rival is a nobody.

Stanza 6
The rest of the poem builds on this contrast between divinity and commonplaceness, offering a variety of references to divinities from different traditions. These divinities are mostly ways of describing the speaker. For instance,

stanza 6 contains a reference to Sinai, which no doubt means Mount Sinai, the place where Moses encounters God in the Bible. The suggestion seems to be that the ex-lover was Moses and the speaker was his God; the speaker even refers to him as the one she chose, just as God chose the children of Israel as his special people.

Yet the ex-lover has turned his back on his God and is making do with an image or an imitation, a delusion perhaps, someone who makes bad food, food that may have seemed more to the ex-lover's taste originally but which now threatens to sicken him. In fact, the speaker suggests that her ex-lover's health in general is threatened; she speaks of a wound or ulcer or pain that he must suffer. The imagery conjures up a sense of actual physical illness. The speaker is perhaps trying to make her ex-lover feel ill.

Stanza 7
Besides illness, the ex-lover is suffering also, so the speaker suggests, from shame. It is just a suggestion, of course, as is everything the speaker says about her former lover. In fact, the things she says are technically not even suggestions, just questions—but every question is heavy with the weight of accusation. In the seventh stanza, the speaker first asks the lover if he loves the new woman and then provides an alternative, wondering if instead he feels shame. The idea here is that someone who mingled with gods should feel shame to have lowered himself to an ordinary woman.

The shame is compared to the reins of Zeus in this stanza, again a reference to a deity, this time one from ancient Greece. The image conjured up is one of Zeus as a charioteer lashing the poor lover, who must be some sort of horse. It is as if the speaker has acquired the power of the sorceress Circe, who is able to turn a man into a beast. This perhaps is part of her revenge, part of her jealousy.

Stanza 8
The speaker here suggests that the ex-lover must be suffering from a bad conscience, presumably for abandoning her. In this stanza she also wonders if he still sings, which may really be a suggestion that he no longer does anything joyful, singing being an example of the joyful things the two of them used to do when they were still together.

Stanza 9
The speaker returns to the notion of price again in the ninth stanza, referring to the new woman as goods from the market which cost too high a price, the price presumably being the vulgarity referred to in stanza 4. The speaker also calls the other woman mere plaster of Paris, whereas she, the speaker, is Carrara marble, a type of marble considered to be of high quality. During the Renaissance Michelangelo used Carrara marble for his famous sculpture of David. This double metaphor, therefore, once again compares the new woman unfavorably with the speaker; the new woman is like some ordinary plaster, as opposed to the fine marble that best describes the speaker.

Stanza 10
The metaphor in the ninth stanza about marble leads into a slight digression in the tenth stanza, in which the speaker talks of a god made from a block, presumably a block of marble; this is a statue she is talking about, one that has been destroyed. It is as if a god once existed, in this case perhaps meaning the whole relationship rather than just the speaker, or perhaps the speaker again is the god. The destruction of the god thus may mean the destruction of the relationship, the divine relationship between the speaker and the ex-lover; or it may mean the destruction of the speaker herself, who is unable to live without her worshipful ex-lover. In a way, both interpretations come to the same thing, for without a worshipper, how can there be a god? It is as if the speaker's whole existence was bound up with that of her worshipful lover, and now that he is gone, she has been smashed to pieces— or at least their relationship has.

The speaker goes on to compare herself to Lilith, in Babylonian mythology a seductive demon and in Jewish folklore Adam's first wife, before Eve. Being like Lilith might not seem entirely positive, but the demonic aspect of the woman seems, at least the way the speaker puts it, a small price to pay for the magic and divinity of a relationship with her. Or perhaps demonic power is something the speaker thinks should be thought appealing.

Stanza 11
In this stanza the speaker again compares her rival to a market commodity or someone of the earth, as opposed to someone with a sixth sense, like the speaker presumably. There is also talk of

magic, in most of the translations as associated with the speaker, which again draws a contrast with the supposedly more ordinary woman that the ex-lover is now with.

Stanza 12

The lover, however, has renounced Lilith and her powers and now, according to the speaker, must content himself with a bottomless pit, which sounds like Hell. As the poem draws to a close, the speaker seems almost to feel bad over this possibility, that her former lover may be in a hellish relationship; she uses an endearment in asking her second-to-last question. And her last question suggests that if life is hard for the ex-lover, it is also hard for her. For a moment it seems that the speaker has put aside the vengefulness and spite that seems to be motivating her and is expressing empathy for her old lover's plight.

But then the last phrase of the poem seems an attempt to reestablish the speaker's superiority and distance from her former love. After suggesting that life is hard for both of them, she turns the final question into a statement that she is with another man. This is a hard life perhaps, because she would prefer to be with her ex-lover, but she has moved on and found someone new and thus does not need her ex-lover. It is a dismissive statement, suggesting that the speaker has no need for jealousy because she has turned her eyes in a new direction—and yet of course she has written a whole poem about her ex-lover, such that she may not really be over him. Life must still be hard for her; her new man must not be consolation enough.

THEMES

Jealousy and Abandonment

As the title suggests, the whole poem is about the speaker's jealousy over the ex-lover's abandonment of her for another woman. It is not an entirely original theme for a poem; in Victorian England, Alfred Tennyson, for one, built one of his famous poems, "Locksley Hall," on the basis of his speaker's unhappiness over a romantic rejection. However, whereas Tennyson uses his speaker's jealousy as a jumping-off point leading into discussions of the social and political state of England, Tsvetaeva's poem stays resolutely fixed on the notion of jealousy and abandonment and in stanza after stanza conveys the

TOPICS FOR FURTHER STUDY

- Write a poem about feelings of jealousy and abandonment in the wake of a failed romance.

- Research the different political movements competing in Russia on the eve of the revolutions in 1917. What happened to them? Did any of them survive outside of Russia? Write a paper detailing your findings, including whether any political movements from before 1917 have followers in Russia today.

- Research the different literary movements in Russia in the early decades of the twentieth century. What happened to them? Did any of them influence literary movements outside of Russia? Write a paper detailing your findings, including whether any literary movements from before 1917 exist in Russia today.

- Research the mythological figure of Lilith. Find out if she appeared in any other literary works of the era of Tsvetaeva's poem. Write a paper detailing your findings, including the different ways Lilith has been portrayed.

speaker's feelings of hurt and pain over the situation, feelings only slightly masked by a surface layer of contempt and indifference. Over and over she suggests that she is highly superior to her rival, as if not understanding how her lover could have left her for such a rival. And as a form of revenge for her abandonment, she imagines her lover suffering almost physically and certainly paying an emotional price for choosing another over her.

Nostalgia

By implication, Tsvetaeva's poem is a celebration of the past, of a time of majesty, grandeur, and divinity. Her speaker conjures up numerous images of what the relationship of that time used to be like for the departed lover. It was like walking on Mount Sinai with a divinity or being in the presence of royalty; it was like living with the finest marble instead of a cheap imitation or experiencing a time of magic. The present that the speaker imagines for her lover is immeasurably inferior to the divine time to which she keeps referring.

Tsvetaeva's nostalgia, it is noteworthy, does not stem just from the passage of time but from a specific and misguided action. It was the lover's deliberate decision to leave her for an unworthy rival that destroyed the paradise that they had together. Just as Adam and Eve forfeited paradise by an act of disobedience, thus did the dethronement of the sovereign in Tsvetaeva's poem mean the destruction of a past so nostalgically remembered.

Revolution

"An Attempt at Jealousy" is not on the surface a political poem, but it contains political implications especially relevant to Tsvetaeva's own life. The third stanza, with its reference to the overthrow of a monarch, though on the surface referring to the speaker as the monarch, also conjures up thoughts of the Russian tsar, overthrown in Tsvetaeva's lifetime. This poem thus fits in with Tsvetaeva's political nostalgia for a time before the Russian Revolution, in her view a superior time of artistic achievement before the revolutionaries subjected Russia to rule by the masses. It can thus be seen as a poem opposed perhaps to revolution in general but more pointedly to the Russian Revolution in particular.

Commercialism

Indirectly, Tsvetaeva's poem is an indictment of commercialism and ordinary life. She refers to her rival as something bought in the market and speaks of the price or tax her ex-lover must now pay. The life of money and commerce, the life of everyday things, is contrasted with a life of divine magic. Tsvetaeva in real life devoted little time to moneymaking and other mundane activities, as she sought to devote herself to art; this poem expresses the notion that there is a sphere far superior to the everyday world of market goods, ordinary food, taxes, and vulgarity. In this respect the poem is reminiscent of the Romantic poet William Wordsworth's work titled "The World Is Too Much with Us."

Love as Magic and Miracle

Finally, the poem is a celebration of the magic and miracles associated with the speaker and with love. The speaker is able to float in the air; she is or has been a deity or a queen; she had a sixth sense and demonic powers; and the relationship with her was like a walk with God upon Mount Sinai or like a statue of a god. It is not entirely clear whether the speaker is suggesting that she was divine or that the relationship between her and the lover was divine; perhaps both are implied. In any case, the idea is that love with the speaker involved something magical, divine, and perhaps demonic all at the same time. This is perhaps meant to suggest something about the nature of true love or just something about the speaker.

STYLE

Repetition

Tsvetaeva's most obvious poetic device in this poem is repetition. Over and over again, eleven times altogether, the speaker asks the same question of her departed lover: How is your life now with the other woman? The force of the repetition becomes like hammer blows attacking the old lover, building from a fairly innocuous reference to the rival simply as the other woman to more insulting references calling her ordinary or simple or a piece of merchandise from the market or a piece of plaster dust. The movement of the poem is from the asking of neutral questions to the asking of loaded ones. But the point of the matter is not just that the questions become insulting; the very number of questions, the repetition of the questions, becomes an attack in itself, expressing the intense emotions of the speaker by means of a relentless interrogation.

Imagery in Opposition

The poem conjures up a number of images, not all apparently consistent with one another but most tending to depict a glorious, divine past, as contrasted with a mundane, vulgar present; or to put it another way, contrasting the glorious, divine speaker with her mundane, vulgar rival. The floating island in the sky suggests a superior past, with the speaker hovering above; the image of a sovereign being dethroned suggests the royal nature of the speaker and of the relationship with her; walking on Sinai suggests God and a divine experience; Carrara marble suggests a grand work of art, contrasting with cheap plaster; and references to the marketplace create an image of the vulgar hustle and bustle of vendors—the life the lover has chosen in contrast to the more glorious one suggested by the imagery about Sinai and a throne.

The image of the reins of Zeus on the lover's forehead and the reference to an ulcer or wound are somewhat different but still fit in with the theme of jealousy and revenge. They suggest pain and suffering for the lover, something the speaker seems to wish on him.

Only one image in the poem neither glorifies the speaker and the old relationship nor casts aspersions on the rival nor depicts pain for the lover: the opening image about rowing, which seems such a neutral, peaceful image of the lover pulling away from the coastline that is the speaker. Perhaps this neutrality is meant to suggest that the rupture with the old world can seem to be quite peaceful, yet, as the rest of the poem suggests, it may in fact be something catastrophic. Or this image can simply represent the speaker warming up, speaking in neutral tones until her emotions overtake her and lead her into more intense images.

And yet even that opening image of rowing away contains something violent in it, for it is described by referring to the stroke of an oar. The use of the word *stroke*, found in at least four published translations, though in context just what an oar does in the peaceful act of rowing, does suggest a striking or a blow. Thus, even at the beginning there is a hint of the anger that is to come.

Pointed Metaphors and Allusions

Most of Tsvetaeva's uses of imagery in her poem also serve as examples of her use of metaphor and allusion. To mention Sinai is to allude to the biblical story of Moses and God on Mount Sinai. To speak of the reins of Zeus is to allude to the king of the Greek deities, and the mention of Zeus's reins on the lover's forehead is a metaphorical description of him as some sort of animal, perhaps a horse, pulling a chariot. Similarly, the mention of Carrara marble is both an allusion to a famous building material and also a metaphor in which the speaker becomes this famous and superior building material, while her rival metaphorically becomes much less valuable plaster dust. To call oneself a

queen or sovereign is also to use metaphor, as it is to implicitly compare bad conscience to an ulcer or wound.

A special type of metaphor called *synecdoche* may be at work in stanza 8, when the speaker asks the lover if he still sings. This may simply be a literal question, but singing, which she implies he is no longer doing, could represent something more. In asking if he still sings, she may be asking if his whole relationship is joyful and exultant. The singing, or lack thereof, is thus seen as representing the whole relationship.

Enjambment

More than once in her poem, Tsvetaeva uses enjambment, running a sentence from one stanza into the next. This is not so uncommon a practice in modern poetry, in contrast with more traditional works, in which thoughts and sentences more often end and remain in one stanza. In Tsvetaeva's case, the enjambment may reflect the passion of the poem, which leads to the thoughts overflowing the bounds of the stanzas.

HISTORICAL CONTEXT

Prerevolutionary Russia

Tsvetaeva lived through difficult times in her native Russia and abroad. During her childhood and adolescence, protests against tsarist rule in Russia culminated first in the failed revolution of 1905 and then in the two revolutions of 1917, the February revolution, in which the tsar was overthrown and replaced with a liberal provisional government, and the October revolution, in which the Bolsheviks or Communists took power, leading to the civil war between the Red Army of the Bolsheviks and the White Army of their opponents.

Before the 1917 revolutions Russia had been a place of ferment in both the political and literary spheres. New political parties sprang up, and the government experimented with representative government, while in the literary sphere the conventional realism of the nineteenth century was challenged by a number of modernist movements, including symbolism, acmeism, and futurism.

COMPARE
&
CONTRAST

- **1920s:** Russia is in turmoil, having just endured a revolution and civil war, and is beginning to pose a threat to the West because it is led by a Communist Party dedicated to the destruction of capitalism.

  Today: Iraq is in turmoil, suffering through an ongoing war, and extremist elements now based there pose a threat to the West.

- **1920s:** The Soviet Union establishes a closed society, censoring literature and other works.

  Today: With the rise of the Internet, information and literature flow much more freely, though attempts to block the flow of information are still seen in places like China.

- **1920s:** In the wake of World War I, the collapse of empires, and revolution in Russia, intellectuals like Tsvetaeva experiment with new ideas and attitudes and are much freer in their personal relationships.

  Today: The freedom that began a hundred years before continues to lead to new experimentation of various sorts in the arts and in personal relationships.

Bolshevik Rule

Tsvetaeva did not participate in any political or literary movements, but she did use the freedom provided by the times to experiment with new forms of poetry, making innovative use of words and rhythms. However, after the triumph of the Bolsheviks, literary experimentation was gradually suppressed in favor of socialist realism, one of the reasons Tsvetaeva felt herself to be out of tune with the new Soviet Union created by the Bolsheviks.

The first few years of Bolshevik rule, called "War Communism," were also a time of starvation and poverty for many, including Tsvetaeva, her property having been confiscated. Members of the elite like Tsvetaeva, unless they joined the Bolsheviks, were denounced as bourgeois, in a way a totally inappropriate term for Tsvetaeva, who had no interest in money or material possessions.

Russian Émigrés

Many Russian intellectuals and aristocrats fled the country after the revolution and civil war, establishing émigré communities in Paris, Prague, and Berlin in the 1920s. These communities contained representatives of various prerevolutionary movements and schools of thought, from monarchists and conservatives to liberals and non-Communist socialists. Tsvetaeva found she did not fit in well with such thinkers because she was not inclined to adhere to any movement and would even praise Soviet poets if she admired their poetic abilities, much to the dismay of her fellow Russian exiles.

Russia under Stalin

In consolidating their power, the Bolsheviks, especially under Joseph Stalin, repressed dissent and resorted to mass arrests of those labelled counterrevolutionary. They also established a secret police force called first the Cheka and then the NKVD (later to be called the KGB). Tsvetaeva's husband became an agent of the NKVD, but this did not save him when he returned to the Soviet Union, where he was quickly arrested and executed. Upon returning to the Soviet Union herself in 1939, Tsvetaeva found a society filled with fear, even in the arts allowing no deviation from the rules set down by the Communist Party, which essentially meant that Tsvetaeva could no longer publish her works, because she would not conform to the rules. When Nazi Germany invaded the Soviet Union in June 1941 as part of World War II, she felt that the situation had indeed worsened, as she now had German bombs to fear in addition to her other hardships, and she also worried that her son would be exposed to danger in the army; he did in fact die in the war.

Prerevolutionary Nostalgia

Tsvetaeva was not a political poet, so much of her work ignores the political upheavals of her day, though she did write sympathetically about the deposed tsar and the White Army and generally expressed support for the prerevolutionary world that vanished after 1917. When it refers to the dethroning of a sovereign, "An Attempt at Jealousy" may be drawing on these feelings of nostalgia for the prerevolutionary era, and in its dismissiveness of vulgarity and ordinariness it may be expressing some of Tsvetaeva's distaste for the idea of rule by the masses advocated by the Bolsheviks. At the same time, Tsvetaeva was no friend to Western commercialism either, another notion that emerges in the poem. However, this work, like many of her poems, is primarily about personal relations rather than historical context or political events.

CRITICAL OVERVIEW

Lily Feiler, in her biography *Marina Tsvetaeva: The Double Beat of Heaven and Hell*, calls the poet "one of the major Russian poets" of the twentieth century. Elaine Feinstein, in her introduction to her translation of Tsvetaeva's *Selected Poems*, follows the poet Anna Akhmatova in grouping Tsvetaeva with Boris Pasternak, Osip Mandelstam, and Akhmatova herself as the four leading non-Soviet Russian poets during the Soviet era. Tsvetaeva also won praise from famous commentators like Joseph Brodsky and Susan Sontag, and with the fall of the Soviet Union, she became an object of study and celebration in Russia, as she had already become in the West.

According to Feiler, from her biography, Pasternak called Tsvetaeva "the greatest and most innovative of our living poets," and even her earliest book of poems was hailed as doing something new in exploring personal, intimate experiences—the sort of approach she takes in "An Attempt at Jealousy" and many other poems. She later won praise from the exiled Russian writer Aleksandr Solzhenitsyn.

On the other hand, Soviet commentators often condemned Tsvetaeva. In the early days of the revolution, the Bolshevik political leader Leon Trotsky denounced her for being preoccupied with love and religion, and later the Soviet poet Vladimir Mayakovsky denounced her as a counterrevolutionary. By this time she was in exile, however, and winning great acclaim in the Russian émigré community, where she gave readings and found publishers for her books and poetry. However, she managed to antagonize the émigré community by issuing a critical work of her own, "A Poet on Criticism," in which she criticized émigré commentators. She also alienated anti-Soviet circles by praising the work of some Soviet poets like Mayakovsky, while the more conservative critics were put off by some of her literary innovations.

Posle Rossii, the 1928 collection of poetry in which "An Attempt at Jealousy" first appeared in Russian, did not have the success Tsvetaeva would have liked, and it was the last book she published in her lifetime. After her death, her reputation declined in the 1940s but began to recover in the 1950s, even in the Soviet Union. The relaxation of literary controls after the death of Stalin led to the publication of another book of her poems in 1961, with a larger edition coming out in 1965. Meanwhile, poems of hers that were still not permitted to be published openly circulated through underground samizdat, or clandestine literary press operations.

According to Maria Razumovsky in *Marina Tsvetaeva: A Critical Biography*, Soviet commentators on "An Attempt at Jealousy" debated the identity of the man that Tsvetaeva addresses in the poem. Victoria Schweitzer comments in her biography, *Tsvetaeva*, that it may in fact not be addressed to a single man but to all past and future lovers, and Razumovsky notes that Tsvetaeva actually sent the poem to several different men with whom she had been involved.

Aside from debating the addressee of the poem, critics have not devoted much attention to "An Attempt at Jealousy." The *Modern Language Review* critic Barbara Heldt has pointed to the poem as one that "gives us poetic models for female experience" and also provides a "highly disciplined and crafted poetic response to a painful emotion of love irretrievably ended."

CRITICISM

Sheldon Goldfarb

Goldfarb has a PhD in English, specializing in the literature of Victorian England. In this essay, he seeks out the underlying dynamic beneath the surface jealousy, pain, and fantasizing in "An Attempt at Jealousy."

At the end of her analysis of "An Attempt at Jealousy" in *Modern Language Review*, Barbara Heldt seeks to explain the poem's odd title by saying that the attempt at jealousy fails at the end because the other woman does not really exist for the speaker. This is an odd conclusion to reach, for if Tsvetaeva's poem expresses anything, it expresses jealousy.

Over and over again, Tsvetaeva's speaker attacks the other woman and imagines a horrible plight for her ex-lover. The other woman is ordinary, says the speaker, and like plaster of Paris, not fine Carrara marble or a deity or a queen like the speaker. The ex-lover must be suffering ulcers or wounds and paying a high price in living with this other woman, the speaker says. She wonders if he can be happy; he must be sick of the other woman's cooking, and his forehead must be lashed by the reins of Zeus.

All this speaks of a jealous mind, and indeed the historical record suggests that Tsvetaeva was an extremely jealous person, sensitive to the slightest slight, so it would not be surprising if her poetry reflected this attitude. Indeed, in *Marina Tsvetaeva: The Woman, Her World and Her Poetry*, Simon Karlinsky goes so far as to suggest that Tsvetaeva almost deliberately set herself up to be slighted and rejected so as to produce material for her poetry. She would frequently idealize men she was interested in (and women too), attributing to them qualities they did not have. According to Karlinsky, her husband understood the pattern well, calling Tsvetaeva "a creature of passions" who liked to "plunge headlong into a self-created hurricane" of attraction for almost anyone. The passion would then end, and Tsvetaeva would plunge into "an equally hurricane-like despair," followed by ridicule of the former object of desire.

The one twist on this pattern that is seen in "An Attempt at Jealousy" is that the ridicule in this poem is directed less at the former lover than at the rival woman. In the failed romance described in this poem, the focus is less on the wrongdoing of the departed lover than on the

WHAT DO I READ NEXT?

- Other poems by Tsvetaeva can be found in *Selected Poems* (1999), translated by Elaine Feinstein. The volume provides a comprehensive overview of Tsvetaeva's work.

- Tsvetaeva's writings on poetry have been collected and translated under the title *Art in the Light of Conscience: Eight Essays on Poetry* (1992). The essays are translated by Angela Livingstone.

- For a much older poetic treatment of a relationship's end, see Michael Drayton's poem "Since There's No Help, Come Let Us Kiss and Part" (1619). The poem's speaker seeks to be calm and not jealous or resentful.

- For an eighteenth-century novel about disappointment in love, see Johann Wolfgang von Goethe's *The Sorrows of Young Werther* (1774).

- For William Shakespeare's classic work on jealousy, see *Othello*, written around 1604 and published in quarto form in 1622.

- For a fictionalized account of the Russian Revolution by one of Tsvetaeva's friends, see Boris Pasternak's, *Doctor Zhivago* (1957).

- For an enthusiastic account of the Russian Revolution by an American sympathizer, see John Reed's *Ten Days That Shook the World* (1919).

- For a highly critical account of the Russian Revolution written on the eve of the collapse of the Soviet Union, see Richard Pipe's *The Russian Revolution* (1991).

shortcomings of the romantic rival. It is in fact a poem all about jealousy, making the title highly ironic.

Taken literally, the title would suggest that the speaker feels no jealousy and is having to make an attempt to display some—pretending

> BUT PERHAPS THE TRUE MESSAGE TO TAKE AWAY FROM 'AN ATTEMPT AT JEALOUSY' IS NOT TO TRUST SUCH IDEALIZED PORTRAYALS OF LOVE. LOVE SO PORTRAYED MUST ALMOST CERTAINLY LEAD TO DISAPPOINTMENT."

to be jealous, in other words. But since the speaker is in fact clearly jealous, what she is doing is pretending to pretend. It is not a failure to be jealous, as Heldt suggests, but a disguise of indifference covering up very real jealousy.

Since the poem is permeated by jealousy, it may also be fruitful to consider what balances the jealousy. The corollary to the feelings of rejection and hurt is the nostalgia in the poem for a time when there was no hurt, when there was in fact the opposite of hurt—a time when the lovers walked on Sinai, and there was a god of marble in their lives, a time of magic and perhaps demonic possession, a time of godliness and majesty. Did such a time ever exist? It is interesting that Tsvetaeva's speaker describes this time only in retrospect, after it is gone. One could imagine another sort of poem in which such a paradise of love could first be described while it is happening, but that is not how this poem is written.

For a poem in which such a paradise is indeed described as it seems to happen, one can turn to Alfred Tennyson's "Locksley Hall." In the first part of this poem, the speaker remembers the love he shared with his cousin Amy. He does not simply describe it to contrast it with a time when the love has gone but instead lets it run forward as if it were happening in the present without any shadow of a parting over it. Thus, for at least a few lines the speaker loses himself in a description of love in springtime, with lovers kissing and looking out to sea together.

After a few lines of this in Tennyson's poem the speaker sinks into bitter gloominess, denouncing Amy as false for leaving him for another and sounding much like the speaker in Tsvetaeva's poem. The difference between the two poems, then, is that in Tennyson's it is

more possible to believe in a time of love between the speaker and the object of affection; that love is presented as actually happening. In Tsvetaeva's poem, not even a few lines are devoted to the time of paradise; there are just brief allusions to a better time, all harnessed to the service of showing that the present is not as good as the mythical past—mythical in the sense of deriving from old myths, such as those of Lilith and Zeus and the traditions of the Bible, but also mythical in the sense of being of dubious validity. In Tsvetaeva's poem it is hard to believe in the time of true love.

Here, then, is the intersection of Tsvetaeva's life with this poem, and no doubt with other poems by her: In her life, according to her husband and Karlinsky and other commentators, she was constantly falling in love and then having to deal with one failed romance after another. Karlinsky reports that she herself expressed, perhaps with some exaggeration, that she could be in ten relationships at a time and make each lover feel special, but at the same time, as she wrote, "I cannot tolerate the slightest turning of the head away from me. I HURT, do you understand? I am a person skinned alive, while all the rest of you have armor."

It is perhaps fair to say that Tsvetaeva is a poet of hurt, at least in this poem and in many others. As Karlinsky suggests, Tsvetaeva almost sought out hurt so as to have material for her poems. And thus, in trying to understand "An Attempt at Jealousy," it is important not to take the poem entirely at face value. In addition to being a poet of hurt, Tsvetaeva seems to be a poet of idealized fantasy. The reader may wonder how real the paradise was that her speaker alludes to in "An Attempt at Jealousy." In her biography, Feiler notes that when she was in Prague, Tsvetaeva wished she was back in Berlin; when she was in Paris, she wished she was back in Prague. She never wished she was back in Russia, but of course the Russia she might have wanted to return to no longer existed. She seems to have been one of those people ever unhappy with where she is and always imagining that where she used to be was better.

Before leaving Moscow at the end of the civil war, Tsvetaeva met the Communist poet Vladimir Mayakovsky, who would later denounce her as a counterrevolutionary. Despite their diametrically opposed political views, however, they got along—perhaps because of their commitment to poetry and perhaps because of something similar in their temperaments. What that similarity was may have been a desire to find a paradise in some time other than the present. Mayakovsky, described by Feiler as a "romantic hooligan poet" who yearned to be a Communist, looked to the future to the better society he had convinced himself could be built through Communism. Tsvetaeva, in contrast, looked to the past, generally yearning for the prerevolutionary past and for places she used to live; in "An Attempt at Jealousy" she has her speaker look back to an idealized romance that for some reason is no more.

There is of course a third alternative to the past and the future, and that is the present. In "An Attempt at Jealousy," however, this is not a pleasant alternative. Whereas the past is a time of paradise, the present is a time of vulgarity, illness, shame, and guilt for the departed lover (at least, the speaker hopes that that is what his present is like); and for the speaker the present is a time of remembering a better past and issuing bitter vituperations toward her former love. The present, in other words, is unbearable, and the past is like a refuge. But the past is gone and the speaker can conjure it up only in fragments.

Now, these fragments are very appealing fragments. They speak of grandeur and divinity. They make love seem like paradise. But perhaps the true message to take away from "An Attempt at Jealousy" is not to trust such idealized portrayals of love. Love so portrayed must almost certainly lead to disappointment. The opposition in this poem is between the majestic and divine love of the past and the rejection and abandonment of the present. Tsvetaeva's speaker is mired in this hopeless present with only a probably mythical past to console her. It is perhaps the yearning for myths and paradise that is her problem, combined, one might add, with an excessively admiring view of herself. Seeing oneself as a sort of deity or queen is perhaps not the best way to maintain a relationship with a mere mortal.

One can say that the attitude expressed in "An Attempt at Jealousy" is perhaps not the healthiest one. It is a mixture of hurt, jealousy, and fantasizing. This does not, however, detract from the power of the poem. It is a poem about love, and in love people are prone to feelings of hurt and jealousy, along with fantasizing. This is a poem in the end that perhaps springs from a deeper hurt than is found on the surface—not

the hurt of some passing love affair but some earlier pain. In Tsvetaeva's early life, she suffered from an unsympathetic mother and a distant father. She later lived through the privations of the Bolshevik Revolution and War Communism. And throughout, though this may have been a subjective feeling or a situation she helped provoke, she felt alienated and alone, friendless, unsupported. In such a situation, what is more natural than to imagine a perfect love? And what is more natural than to be disappointed in the search for it?

In the Greek myth of Zeus and Semele, Semele, a young maiden, is burnt to a crisp when her lover, Zeus, appears to her in all his true glory. Such are the dangers of loving a deity. Tsvetaeva, according to the reports of her biographers, was something like Zeus in relation to her lovers. She burned them up with her intensity; she was too passionate for them. Bereft of love, suffering and alone, the alienated one seeks much too intensely for love, dooming herself over and over to disappointment and rejection. It is a cycle not peculiar to Tsvetaeva, which explains the power of this poem about doomed love.

Source: Sheldon Goldfarb, Critical Essay on "An Attempt at Jealousy," in *Poetry for Students*, Gale, Cengage Learning, 2009.

Pamela Chester

In the following review of a collection including "An Attempt at Jealousy," Chester comments on the difficulties of translating Tsvetaeva's poetry.

One of the welcome effects of last year's Cvetaeva centennial celebration is the appearance of several new volumes on the poet and her work. Michael Naydan, with Slava Yastremski as his native informant, has produced a complete translation of *Posle Rossii*, the last, best, and most difficult of Cvetaeva's poetry collections. The volume includes side-by-side Russian and English versions of the verse as well as notes, commentary, and afterword.

Cvetaeva's lyrics are notoriously complex and obscure, even for the native speaker of Russian. A bi-lingual edition of her poetry is a welcome aid not only for the student of Russian approaching Cvetaeva for the first time, but for the graduate student or researcher probing the rich ambiguities of these poems. As Naydan points out at the outset (xii), some of these poems present almost insuperable difficulties for the translator. A translation of a poem is by necessity an act of interpretation, and by its nature Cvetaeva's verse tends to defy any single interpretation. Naydan's solution is to supply ten pages of annotation, indicating other possible translations, and clarifying some of the many mythological, literary and Biblical allusions.

This combination of translation, Russian text, and notes is ingeniously calculated to draw the bilingual reader into a dialogue with poet and translator. Inevitably there are places where another reader of Cvetaeva will remain unsatisfied; one early example is the translation "a hand/Rustling over silk" (9) for Cvetaeva's phrase "шелка/Разбрасывающая рука" (8), where the sense of the hand spreading or casting aside the silks (and the contrast with the lips smoothing the silks in the following two lines) is lost, and with it much of the erotic charge of the stanza.

At times, the English translation over-exaggerates the difficulty of the Russian diction: Naydan's neologism "exerted freneticality" (7) renders the standard Russian of "в трудной судорожности" (6) (Ожегов, *СΩоварь русскоsо языка*, 10th ed., M., 1973, 715). By contrast, his invented words "transorally" and "transvisually" (161), if not entirely successful, are certainly motivated by Cvetaeva's neologisms "заустно" and "заглазно" (160). One might also quibble with some of his decisions about word order, stanza structure, and enjambment, but on the whole the shape of Cvetaeva's verse is changed remarkably little.

One stated goal of the translation is to make Cvetaeva accessible to non-Russian speakers (xii). Here the translator may have misjudged his audience. His refusal to overinterpret the verse, as some earlier translators have done, honors what he calls Cvetaeva's "telegraphic terseness" (xii), but it results at times in translations so bare that they may be quite misleading to the reader with no knowledge of Russian. "—Sky!—like the sea I color myself into you," a word-for-word translation of "—Небо!— морем в тебя окрашиваюсь" (228–229), may convey less than "*with* the sea I color myself [to look] *like* you"; admittedly, this loses the exact parallelism with the following stanza. A more informative translation of "на сон крестил" might be "blessed for the night" or even "put to bed" rather than "baptized the earth into a dream" (66–67). An exotic word like "yataghan" (211) surely merits a note of explanation. Some

phrases appear to be simply mistaken, like the translation of "простоволосые мои" as "My straight-haired ones" (42–43); oddly enough, "bareheaded" does occur in the translation of "Здравствуй! Не стрела ..." (17). In "An Attempt at Jealousy," Cvetaeva's faithless lover is told, "You don't have yourself to blame" and her hyperbolic 100,000th woman is scaled back to a mere "one-thousandth."

The problem of reconciling the different gender systems in Russian and English, exemplified in this last phrase, could be solved with a reference in the notes. Often Naydan's translation elides the gender of the Russian. For example, the four words "Не тот.—Ушло./Ушла." (8) play on all three genders, but Naydan offers only "Wrong one. Gone./I left." (9). Similarly, a notable shift occurs when the phrase "Каждая из нас—Синай/Ночью ..." (174) is rendered (by a male translator) simply, "Each of us is Sinai" (175). A refreshingly frank discussion of Cvetaeva's affair with Parnok is included in the afterword. It seems odd, then, that Sappho's sexuality is misrepresented in Note 101 (241); Sumerkin at least notes that this heterosexual Sappho is the stuff of legends (Cvetaeva, *Стихотворения и поэмы*, t. 3, NY: Russica, 1983, 456). In this case, as in a number of others, the reader is left wishing for more detailed commentary.

In many instances, Naydan finds economical, highly expressive solutions for nearly insoluble translation problems: the chime of "alive," "a lie" for "zhivu", "lzhivo" (220–221) and the laconic "God/Is gratis" for "Besplaten/Bog" (174–175) are among the rewards of reading this collection.

The Afterword is somewhat uneven. The first section begins with an error of fact, minor but misleading: Naydan repeats the common misconception that "Varvara Ilovaisky died prematurely of tuberculosis in 1890" (245) when Cvetaeva's own account in "House at Old Pimen" refers to a blood clot in early postpartum (*проза, M.*, 1989, 131).

It seems that perhaps Naydan was not well served by his editors at Ardis. Misprints such as, "In a letter to Vera Bunina dated March 20, 1928, Cvetaeva announced that the book would soon appear [. . .]. Two months later on March 23 [. . .]" (261), and typographic errors like those in the verse at the bottom of 271 (struchkoi and

Vremia; ty menia obmanesh'!), mar the volume unnecessarily.

The Afterword concludes with an excellent discussion of the publication history and a very interesting section on structural and thematic features of *Posle Rossii*; some points are arguable, but Naydan's discussion of time and space, Biblical and historical themes, and Cvetaeva's exploration of the chronicle structure is insightful and stimulating.

This monumental fruit of the translator's labor belongs in every library which serves undergraduate students of Russian, and offers a thought-provoking reference for the scholar.

Source: Pamela Chester, Review of *After Russia*, in *Slavic and East European Journal*, Vol. 38, No. 2, Summer 1994, pp. 382–86.

SOURCES

Feiler, Lily, *Marina Tsvetaeva: The Double Beat of Heaven and Hell*, Duke University Press, 1994, pp. 1, 118, 135, 190, 198.

Feinstein, Elaine, "Introduction," in *Selected Poems*, 5th ed., by Marina Tsvetaeva, translated by Elaine Feinstein, Carcanet, 1999, p. XIV.

Heldt, Barbara, "Two Poems by Marina Tsvetayeva from 'Posle Rossii,'" in *Modern Language Review*, Vol. 77, No. 3, July 1982, pp. 679, 686–87.

Karlinsky, Simon, *Marina Tsvetaeva: The Woman, Her World, and Her Poetry*, Cambridge University Press, 1985, pp. 119–20, 129–30, 135, 192.

Razumovsky, Maria, *Marina Tsvetayeva: A Critical Biography*, translated by Aleksey Gibson, Bloodaxe Books, 1994, pp. 1, 177.

Schweitzer, Viktoria, *Tsvetaeva*, translated by Robert Chandler and H. T. Willetts, Harvill, 1992, p. 246.

Tennyson, Alfred, Lord, "Locksley Hall," in *English Victorian Poetry: An Anthology*, edited by Paul Negri, Dover, 1999, pp. 16–21.

Tsvetaeva, Marina, "An Attempt at Jealousy," in *Selected Poems*, 5th ed., translated by Elaine Feinstein, Carcanet, 1999, pp. 92–93.

Wordsworth, William, "The World Is Too Much with Us," in *Romanticism: An Anthology*, 3rd ed., edited by Duncan Wu, Blackwell, 2006, p. 534.

FURTHER READING

Chamberlain, Lesley, *The Philosophy Steamer: Lenin and the Exile of the Intelligentsia*, Atlantic Books, 2006.
> Chamberlain provides an account of an expulsion of 160 intellectuals from Russia that occurred at the same time Tsvetaeva was leaving the country.

Smith, S. A., *The Russian Revolution: A Very Short Introduction*, Oxford University Press, 2002.
> In this volume, Smith provides a history of Russia between 1917 and 1936.

Walker, Barbara, *Maximilian Voloshin and the Russian Literary Circle: Culture and Survival in Revolutionary Times*, Indiana University Press, 2005.
> Walker discusses the literary circle surrounding Voloshin, which included Tsvetaeva.

Williams, Robert C., *Culture in Exile: Russian Emigrés in Germany, 1881–1941*, Cornell University Press, 1972.
> Williams explores the situation of Russian intellectuals outside Russia, focusing especially on "Russian Berlin" in the 1920s, the time when Tsvetaeva resided there.

Babii Yar

YEVGENY YEVTUSHENKO

1961

Yevgeny Yevtushenko composed "Babii Yar" in September 1961. The first public reading of the poem took place at Oktober Hall in Kiev, Ukraine, the following month. The opening lines of "Babii Yar" are a lament that there is no public monument to remind visitors that more than 33,700 Kiev Jews were massacred at Babi Yar in September 1941. In his poem, Yevtushenko uses the less common Russian spelling for Babii Yar; however, the more common and customary spelling for the location itself is Babi Yar, which is how the massacre there is most often referenced. Much of Yevtushenko's focus throughout "Babii Yar" is then directed toward the anti-Semitism that was so prevalent in the Soviet Union after the end of World War II. To illustrate the damage caused by anti-Semitism, he explores the long history of anti-Semitism from the ancient Greeks to the Holocaust.

"Babii Yar" was first published in *Literaturnaya Gazeta*, a Soviet magazine, in 1961. After the poem's publication, Dmitri Shostakovich telephoned Yevtushenko and asked if he could set the poem to music. The result is Shostakovich's *Symphony No. 13*, in which, during the first movement, a male chorus sings Yevtushenko's poem. The Soviet Communist government would not permit Shostakovich's symphony to be performed, however, unless Yevtushenko changed the words to focus on the Ukrainian and Russian victims who were also killed at Babi Yar rather than on the Jewish victims.

Yevtushenko made the changes, as requested; after the fall of Communism, the original text was reinserted in performances outside of Russia. It is the original text that appears in anthologies of Yevtushenko's poetry, such as *Early Poems* (1966), which was published in the United Kingdom, and *The Collected Poems* (1992), published in the United States. The former was the first printing of "Babii Yar" in one of Yevtushenko's books. "Babii Yar" is also included in *Holocaust Poetry* (1995), compiled by Hilda Schiff.

AUTHOR BIOGRAPHY

Yevgeny Aleksandrovich Yevtushenko was born at a small settlement, Stantzia Zima (Winter Station), along the Trans-Siberian Railway, on July 18, 1933. Yevtushenko's father, Gangus, was a geologist; he was also a Latvian intellectual who read poetry and other literature and who made sure that his son also read literature. Yevtushenko's mother, Zinaida, also a geologist, was a Ukrainian whose family had lived in Siberia for many generations. Zinaida took Yevtushenko and his sister, Yelena, to live in Moscow in the late 1930s. Because of the war, Yevtushenko and his sister were evacuated from Moscow in 1941 and returned to Zima to live with their grandmother. Their parents divorced shortly afterwards, and their father remarried and moved to Kazakhstan. In 1944, Yevtushenko returned to Moscow and to school. He was expelled from school and joined his father in Kazakhstan, where he found a job with a geological expedition. For a while Yevtushenko thought about a career playing soccer, but then in 1949 his first poem was published in *Soviet Sport*. Yevtushenko was soon encouraged to become a writer and enrolled at the Gorky Literary Institute in Moscow, where he studied from 1951 to 1954.

Yevtushenko's first book of poetry, *The Prospectors of the Future*, was published in 1952. He followed this with another collection of poems, *Third Snow*, in 1955. Additional collections of poetry quickly followed, including *Highway of the Enthusiasts* in 1956 and *Promises* in 1957. In 1959 Yevtushenko had two collections of poetry published, *The Bow and the Lyre* and *Poems of Several Years*, which was a retrospective anthology of some of his earlier poetry.

Yevgeny Yevtushenko (*The Library of Congress*)

Yevtushenko began traveling outside the Soviet Union in 1961. By this time he was quite well known, and his poem "Babii Yar" had added to his notoriety. He attracted large crowds wherever he went. In 1962 he published an unauthorized autobiography (by Soviet Union standards) in Germany, titled *A Precocious Autobiography*, in which he criticizes Soviet society. He was then denounced by the Soviet government, and his works were heavily criticized. The book was published in English in 1963.

After Yevtushenko's 1965 collection of poetry *Bratskaya GES* was published to critical acclaim, he was once again in the good graces of Soviet authorities. "Babii Yar" was first included in a dual Russian and English edition of his poetry titled *Early Poems*. This work was issued in 1966 and reissued in 1989. The edition of Yevtushenko's poetry most frequently discussed is *The Collected Poems*, issued in 1991. At more than 600 pages, this volume, which contains much of the author's poetry, is considered one of his major works. Also in 1991, Yevtushenko published a collection of political speeches and essays titled *Fatal Half Measures: The Culture of Democracy in the Soviet Union*. Yevtushenko is a prolific writer. Over the course of his career he has published dozens of books of poetry, both in Russian and in English, as well as plays and novels. He also wrote a documentary, in which he starred. While Yevtushenko was frequently critical of the Soviet government throughout his career, he was honored by that government many times. As of 2008, Yevtushenko lived in both the United States and in Russia. In the United States, he has taught poetry and cinema at Queen's College in New York and at the University of Oklahoma in Tulsa. Yevtushenko has been married four times and has had five children.

POEM TEXT

No monument stands over Babii Yar.
A drop sheer as a crude gravestone.
I am afraid.
    Today I am as old in years
as all the Jewish people.   5
Now I seem to be
    a Jew.
Here I plod through ancient Egypt.
Here I perish crucified, on the cross,
and to this day I bear the scars of nails.   10
I seem to be
    Dreyfus.
The Philistine
    is both informer and judge.
I am behind bars.   15
    Beset on every side.
Hounded,
    spat on,
        slandered.
Squealing, dainty ladies in flounced Brussels lace   20
stick their parasols into my face.
I seem to be then
    a young boy in Byelostok.
Blood runs, spilling over the floors.
The bar-room rabble-rousers   25
give off a stench of vodka and onion.
A boot kicks me aside, helpless.
In vain I plead with these pogrom bullies.
While they jeer and shout,
    "Beat the Yids. Save Russia!"   30
some grain-marketeer beats up my mother.
O my Russian people!
    I know
        you
are international to the core.   35
But those with unclean hands
have often made a jingle of your purest name.
I know the goodness of my land.
How vile these antisemites—
    without a qualm   40
they pompously called themselves
"The Union of the Russian People"!
I seem to be
    Anne Frank
transparent   45
    as a branch in April.

And I love.
    And have no need of phrases.
My need
    is that we gaze into each other.   50
How little we can see
    or smell!
We are denied the leaves,
    we are denied the sky.
Yet we can do so much—   55
    tenderly
embrace each other in a dark room.
They're coming here?
    Be not afraid. Those are the booming
sounds of spring: 60
    spring is coming here.
Come then to me.
    Quick, give me your lips.
Are they smashing down the door?
    No, it's the ice breaking ...   65
The wild grasses rustle over Babii Yar.
The trees look ominous,
    like judges.
Here all things scream silently,
    and, baring my head,   70
slowly I feel myself
    turning gray.
And I myself
    am one massive, soundless scream
above the thousand thousand buried here.   75
I am
    each old man
        here shot dead.
I am
    every child   80
        here shot dead.
Nothing in me
    shall ever forget!
The "Internationale", let it
    thunder   85
when the last antisemite on earth
is buried forever.
In my blood there is no Jewish blood.
In their callous rage, all antisemites
must hate me now as a Jew.   90
For that reason
    I am a true Russian!

POEM SUMMARY

Lines 1–21

The opening lines of Yevtushenko's poem "Babii Yar" present a lament that there is no public monument to commemorate the massacre of Kiev Jews that occurred at that site in September 1941. Yevtushenko's speaker begins with a geographical image of the site of the massacre,

MEDIA ADAPTATIONS

- A recording of Yevtushenko reading "Babii Yar" in Russian (with the actor Alan Bates reading the poem in English) was released by Caedmon in 1967.

- A recording of Dmitri Shostakovich's *Symphony No. 13*, in which "Babii Yar" is sung by a men's chorus, was released by Everest in 1967. The album was recorded during a live performance in Moscow on November 20, 1965.

---

describing a sheer cliff hanging over a ravine that became a mass grave. This site creates fear, which can be understood in two ways. The fear might certainly be the fear associated with an event so terrible that even the location seems to be haunted. In this case the fear that the victims felt at the moment of their death still pervades the location. A second possible fear is the concern that such an event might happen again— that there could once again be a time when people's lives could have so little value that many thousands could die in a brutal fashion in such a short period of time.

After referring to the event and briefly describing the location, the speaker begins a section in which he refers to the history of anti-Semitism. He identifies himself as Jewish. It is important to know that Yevtushenko is not Jewish; instead, his speaker assumes this identity in a rhetorical strategy allowing Yevtushenko to place himself historically into the Jewish experience. He writes that he is as old as the anti-Semitism that Jews have encountered throughout the ages, beginning with the enslavement of Jews by ancient Egyptians. The speaker understands the suffering of each one of the many Jews who have faced oppression during the past several thousand years. He imagines that he is one of the Jewish slaves who were used by the Egyptians to make their ancient land great. The speaker next imagines that he is Jesus, a Jew who was crucified for his religious beliefs. The speaker envisions himself with the scars from the wounds that Jesus suffered at the hands of his tormenters.

The speaker also sees himself as Alfred Dreyfus, a French military officer who, though innocent, was tried and convicted of treason in 1894. Dreyfus endured a public shaming ceremony in which he was stripped of his military rank and was then exiled to Devil's Island, a penal colony off the coast of South America, where he was sentenced to spend the rest of his life. Dreyfus was a Jew, and his unjust conviction and imprisonment were the result of anti-Semitism in France at the end of the nineteenth century. Dreyfus is yet another example of the injustice caused by anti-Semitism. He was accused and secretly tried and never permitted to see the contrived evidence used against him. Yevtushenko refers to those who persecuted Dreyfus as Philistines, the ancient biblical enemy of the Jews, who in this case acted as accuser, prosecutor, and judge. In Yevtushenko's poem, Dreyfus's reputation is destroyed and he is subjected to public attacks. He is jailed, an outcast from society.

Lines 22–42

In the first few lines of this section, Yevtushenko continues to personally identify with Jewish victims of anti-Semitism. He recalls the pogroms of Byelostok, known in English as Bialystok, in what is now Poland. Pogroms were violent riots directed against Jewish inhabitants. The 1906 pogrom in Bialystok killed more than a hundred people. Yevtushenko envisions himself as a young Jewish boy who has been kicked and beaten and who lies covered with blood on the floor. The boy must watch his mother being beaten by drunken men. The smell of vodka helps to define the men, who use alcohol to fuel their violent attack. Perhaps Yevtushenko is suggesting that they need the alcohol to give them the gall to beat up a child and his mother. The setting for the beating is a bar, and the bully who beats the woman is a grain clerk. He is just an ordinary man, not a soldier, and so the violence is not a result of a military action of some kind. These violent men scream that the beating of the boy's mother is a patriotic act. To beat up the Jews glorifies Russia.

In the next lines, Yevtushenko moves from the list of anti-Semitic atrocities to call upon his fellow Russians to join the international community and condemn those whose actions denigrate their

Russian heritage. He reminds the people that most Russians are good at heart. Yevtushenko argues that people who are kind and good are being abused by those people, whose hands have been dirtied by their crimes. According to Yevtushenko, the actions of those who use anti-Semitism to persecute their fellow Russians have debased all Russians. Russia cannot unite as one people with these criminals in their midst.

Lines 43–63

Yevtushenko opens this section by recalling the story of Anne Frank, a young girl who hid with her family in an attic until someone betrayed the family's hiding place. She later died at the Bergen-Belsen concentration camp, in Poland. Yevtushenko again casts himself as the Jew, vulnerable as the starving girl, who died in April 1945. He imagines that he is Anne, longing to share love with Peter van Pels, the teenage boy who shared Anne's hiding place in the secret attic annex. Yevtushenko imagines the two lovers wordlessly exchanging glances. Although they are imprisoned in their hiding place and cannot experience the world outside, they can still share an embrace. This tender embrace helps them forget the sky that they are not permitted to see or the leaves on the tree that they cannot touch. Then suddenly the lovers' tender embrace is interrupted by the loud noises of the Nazis, who have come to arrest them. But Anne's lover seeks to reassure her and tells her that the noises that she hears are just the sounds of spring coming, of the ice in the river breaking up. He tells Anne not to be afraid, that his embrace and kiss will keep the danger away.

Lines 64–84

Anne's story is resolved in the following lines, with her fearful worry that the door is being broken down, but her lover provides one last reassurance that the pounding at the door is only the ice breaking on the river. Yevtushenko does not mention that the Frank family was captured in October 1944. It was not spring but fall, and even a lover's embrace could not protect the fifteen-year-old Anne from the Nazi extermination camps. The mindless hatred of anti-Semitism resulted in the deaths of all but one of the eight people who hid in that attic; only Anne's father, Otto, survived their time in the extermination camps.

In the next line, Yevtushenko moves from Anne and the stories of destruction caused by anti-Semitism and returns to Babi Yar, where even the grass cannot rest at the site of so much slaughter. Even the physical location has become representative of the massacre that occurred there. The trees remain as witnesses to the events of 1941, standing as if they judge those who committed this atrocity. The trees also judge those who allowed it to happen and those who have forgotten to honor this massacre. All of nature silently cries out in protest, according to the speaker, who joins in the silent cries of the hundred thousand who died at Babi Yar. He removes his hat in acknowledgment of the events that occurred twenty years earlier and stands at the precipice of death. Slowly the speaker's hair turns gray, and he is each old man who stood in this same place, facing his executioners. At the same time, he is every child who faced the executioners' guns. The speaker recognizes that standing at this place has changed him, and he will remember with every fiber of his being the events that took place at Babi Yar.

Lines 85–92

In this last section of the poem, the speaker claims that the "Internationale," the official song of the Soviet Union, will be shouted loudly to acclaim the moment when the last anti-Semite is buried and forgotten. Yevtushenko ends his poem by stating that while he is not Jewish, those who are anti-Semitic now rage against him and hate him as if he is Jewish. The anti-Semites who hate Jews are not true Russians. In contrast, Yevtushenko's speaker's hatred of anti-Semitism makes him a true Russian.

THEMES

Anti-Semitism

An important theme of "Babii Yar" is the destruction caused by anti-Semitism. Anti-Semitism was responsible for the killing of nearly all European Jewry during World War II, and anti-Semitism at other times in other countries, such as Ukraine and Poland, also caused many Jewish deaths. In his poem, Yevtushenko recalls many of the acts of anti-Semitism that predated the events of Babi Yar and the Holocaust. He recalls the slavery of Jews in Egypt, the crucifixion of Jesus, and the anti-Semitism in France that resulted in Dreyfus being persecuted and jailed. In his final example, Yevtushenko turns to the Holocaust and to Anne

TOPICS FOR FURTHER STUDY

- Half of all the Jews who died during the Holocaust died along the war's eastern front, which spanned Ukraine, Lithuania, Latvia, Belorussia, and other countries bordering Poland and the Soviet Union. Many of these Jews died at the hands of the Einsatzgruppen, mobile killing squads. Investigate the Einsatzgruppen and then write a paper in which you discuss their formation, how they were used, and the events that led to their being demobilized.

- Anatoly Kuznetsov's documentary novel *Babi Yar* is the story of what he observed there as a sixteen-year-old. Locate a copy of his book, and after you have read it, write an essay in which you compare the novel's depiction of the events at Babi Yar to Yevtushenko's poem. What do you see as the essential differences? In what ways do they capture the emotional impact of Babi Yar? Cite specific lines from both texts to support your findings.

- Unfortunately, Babi Yar was neither the first nor the last massacre of its kind. Choose another massacre either from World War II or from any other period of time. Thoroughly research the events of this massacre and then give a class presentation on your findings.

- With a group of classmates, research the history of anti-Semitism, beginning in the ancient world, as Yevtushenko does in his poem. Assign each member of your group a specific century or two to research and then create a timeline and poster presentation that traces this history. Collectively analyze the eras that you have researched and discuss what can be learned from this history.

Frank, whose death then becomes representative of the suffering endured by all the children whose lives were destroyed because of anti-Semitism.

Death

Death permeates the ravine at Babi Yar. Yevtushenko describes the physical location as emotionally representative of the massacre that occurred on that site. The grass cannot rest, and even the trees stand in judgment of the murders that occurred in that place. The dead are the hundred thousand and more people who continue to scream out in anguish; their silent screams dispel any idea that Babi Yar is a restful cemetery. Traditionally, people think of death as the inevitable end of life, but mass murder is not the natural end of life, and thus so many unjust deaths cannot have left the site untouched. These were not peaceful deaths but lives ended in great fear and pain. When Yevtushenko's speaker imagines that he is each of the old men and children who were slaughtered at that site, he does so to put on the mantle of their suffering and to keep their suffering alive, even beyond their death. Yevtushenko makes sure that these deaths will not be forgotten.

Genocide

Although genocides occurred before the Holocaust, the word was not used to describe such mass killings until 1944, when a Jewish lawyer combined two classical root words—the Greek *geno* and the Latin *cide*—to create a word to describe the deliberate killing of a race or tribe of people. The word was first used at the Nuremberg trials, held after the end of World War II. The word *genocide* is now used to describe very violent crimes directed against a specific group of people with the intent to destroy that group in its entirety. In his poem, Yevtushenko identifies with the victims of a massacre, the Jews of Kiev, who were destroyed because they were Jewish. Their murder fits the description of a genocide, since the killings at Babi Yar were an attempt to erase all evidence of Jewish life in Kiev.

Identity

Throughout the poem, the speaker's identity continues to shift from one person to another. The speaker assumes the personas of those who have suffered for their religion, beginning with the ancient Jews, who were slaves of the Egyptians. Another identity is that of Jesus. In this guise, Yevtushenko's speaker is crucified and bears the scars of his suffering. Later in the poem, he is the unjustly persecuted Dreyfus, the beaten boy in Bialystok who watches his mother being battered, and Anne Frank, who never grew up to experience a life shared with a man she loved. The speaker does not identify himself as a poet or even as a Russian. His own identity is obscured by the suffering of the Jews and cannot resurface until all anti-Semites in the Soviet Union are dead and forgotten. Only then can his own identity as a Russian once again be the role he assumes.

Remembering

The opening line of Yevtushenko's poem is about remembering the massacre that occurred at Babi Yar. When he visited Babi Yar twenty years after the events took place, Yevtushenko was dismayed to see that the area was a refuse dump. There was no monument to the nearly 34,000 Jews who were slaughtered at that place in September 1941; there was also no memorial to the many thousands, including additional Jews, Gypsies, Communists, and Soviet prisoners of war, who were also slaughtered at Babi Yar in the following months and years. Although Yevtushenko uses his poem to remember Jewish victims from throughout the centuries, his main theme is that those who died at Babi Yar should not be forgotten. Although monuments help to memorialize the Jews and other victims who died, they can be vandalized or even destroyed. In contrast, Yevtushenko's poem will be a more lasting memorial to those who perished.

STYLE

Historical Allusion

In "Babii Yar," Yevtushenko alludes to a number of events and people, trusting that his readers will understand or determine what he means. When he alludes to the Jews in ancient Egypt, he trusts his readers to know that the Jews were slaves under the reign of the pharaohs. The reference to Dreyfus is also an indirect allusion that relies upon the reader's having or gaining awareness of the events that occurred in late nineteenth-century France. Dreyfus's name suggests anti-Semitism, just as Anne Frank's name suggests the events of the Holocaust. Yevtushenko refers to notable events and people with whom his readers can identify, and thus he does not need to provide the complete stories. Allusions serve as a kind of shorthand for the poet; they require some effort on the part of the reader to fill in the gaps, but understanding the allusions makes the poem more enjoyable.

Human Rights Poetry

Although this poem might be considered a poem of political protest, it is really more a call to civic responsibility or to human rights and justice. Human rights poetry is concerned about the rights of the individual, including freedom of expression, such as through religion, and the right to live free of oppression. Poets and poetry are often focused on the individual, since the creation of poetry is a very individual occupation. Concern about human rights formed a significant movement for twentieth-century poets, including Yevtushenko, who uses his poetry to call attention to injustice, in this case the anti-Semitism of the Soviet Union, which intensified after World War II ended. For Yevtushenko, equality is a human right for all Russians, which he makes clear in the final lines of the poem when he reminds his readers that they will all be true Russians when the last anti-Semite is dead and buried. That will be the moment when all Russians can sing the "Internationale," the song of the Soviet Union.

Free Verse and Split Lines

There is no pattern of rhyme or meter to "Babii Yar," and in fact, there is no division into stanzas. Instead, the irregular line breaks give the poem more of a sing-song rhythm that is best appreciated by reading it aloud. For many poets, the practice of splitting lines is simply an aesthetic choice, with no function. Yevtushenko, however, splits lines of poetry to emphasize the concluding thoughts. If the reader reads the poem aloud, the emphases on the second parts of lines becomes clearer. Splitting the lines simply highlights this importance.

HISTORICAL CONTEXT

The Soviet Union, Communism, and the Nazis

The Russian Soviet Federative Socialist Republic was the largest and most populated of the fifteen countries that comprised the Soviet Union, which collapsed in 1991. Russia became an established country in 1917 and part of the Soviet Union in 1922. Moscow, the capital of Russia, then became the capital of the Soviet

COMPARE
&
CONTRAST

- **1940s:** The Einsatzgruppen begin systematically rounding up and killing the Jews of eastern Europe and the Soviet Union. It is estimated that the Einsatzgruppen squads kill 1.3 million Jews, about one-quarter of the total number of Jews killed during the Holocaust.

  1960s: In Nigeria, an estimated 3.1 million people are killed during the uprisings of 1966. There are also reports of genocide taking place in Indonesia and Uganda in the early 1960s.

  Today: In Darfur, Sudan, it is estimated that more than 400,000 civilians have been killed and 2.5 million people have been displaced through genocidal acts.

- **1940s:** During Germany's six-month occupation of Krasnodar, Russia, every member of the Jewish community in the city is murdered. After the Germans are driven out in February 1943, Soviet authorities convict eleven Russian collaborators for their involvement in the killings. Three are sentenced to twenty years' imprisonment; eight of the eleven are executed in July 1943.

  1960s: From 1963 to 1964, a group of former officials at the Belzec extermination camp, near the Ukrainian border, are tried in West Germany. Only one of the seven officials is found guilty, to receive a sentence of less than five years.

Today: In 2005, ten former Nazis are convicted for taking part in the 1944 massacre of more than 500 villagers at Sant'Anna di Stazzema, Italy. The convicted men are not present at their trial, which was held in Italy, because Germany does not extradite its citizens to stand trial in other countries.

- **1940s:** Anti-Semitism exists in the Soviet Union, but it is not a significant aspect of Soviet life through the early part of the decade.

  1960s: After the end of World War II, anti-Semitism begins to increase, culminating in the dismantling of the Jewish community structure and the destruction of all Jewish cultural institutions. By the early 1960s, Jews have become the scapegoat for the economic problems faced by the Soviet Union. Nearly half of all executions from 1961 to 1964 are of Jewish citizens.

  Today: State sponsored anti-Semitism no longer exists in Russia, but anti-Semitism is still a problem in Russian society. In the twenty-first century, the number of attacks against Jews has not increased, but they have become more violent. Neo-Nazi skinheads have become a stronger presence in Russia, and there are increasing reports of vandalism of Jewish institutions and cemeteries as well as of Holocaust memorials.

Union. Communism had been the dominant political party in the Soviet Union beginning in 1912 and had also dominated Russian politics since its formation in 1917. During most of the twentieth century, the Communist Party was the only political group tolerated by the Soviet government. Communism was the antithesis of Adolf Hitler's belief in the superiority of all things German. Communism promoted equality, especially the equal distribution of rewards for all those who worked. In contrast, Hitler promoted German superiority. For him, the idea that non-Germans, whom he thought subhuman, should be rewarded equally for equal work was intolerable. Hitler simply did not believe that non-Germans could accomplish as much as Germans.

Karl Marx, who founded Communism, was a Jew, which added to Hitler's dislike of the ideology. It did not matter to the Nazis that Marx had renounced Judaism and had become a Lutheran. His Jewish background worked well for the Nazi goal of attacking Communism, which became indelibly associated with Jewish thought and Jewish Bolshevism and was thus seen as part of the Jewish conspiracy to destroy Germany. Hitler emphasized this purported Jewish Communist conspiracy in speeches that were designed to create more support for his planned invasion of the Soviet Union. Hitler claimed that Moscow and the Communists would invade Germany. Hitler also pointed out that the reason that the Soviets had become Communists was because they were Slavs, a peasant group with no real culture or sophistication. Hitler thought that an invasion of the Soviet Union would be easily accomplished and that the rich fertile lands of the Soviet Union would quickly become available for German expansion. The German invasion of the Soviet Union, labeled Operation Barbarossa, began in June 1941. It is estimated that more than 20 million Soviets died before the Germans were driven out of the Soviet Union, after Hitler's army was defeated in Leningrad in January 1944.

The Massacre at Babi Yar

Before the city of Kiev fell into German hands in September 1941, there were an estimated 175,000 Jewish citizens among the nearly 875,000 residents. When the threat of invasion became certain, the Soviets evacuated factory workers, whom the Soviets considered important to the war effort; among these factory workers were an estimated 20,000–30,000 Jews. The remaining Jewish population was captured by the German army when they invaded. Although some Jews were killed during the initial invasion, there was no organized action directed against the Jewish population. Then on September 24, several bombs were detonated in the city, destroying buildings occupied by the German army and killing hundreds of German soldiers and officers. The bombs had been placed by Soviet partisans, but the blame was placed on the Jewish population. Several German military commanders stationed in that area quickly decided that all Jews in Kiev must be killed as punishment for the sabotage. The large ravine at Babi Yar was chosen as the location, and on September 28, 1941, an order was issued compelling all Jews in Kiev to assemble at the designated location on September 29 at 8 a.m. The date was Yom Kippur, the Jewish Day of Atonement. The Jewish population was told to bring all valuables and warm clothing, since they were to be relocated to labor camps. The order stipulated that any Jews not complying would be shot immediately.

Thousands of Jews complied with the orders and assembled as directed. They were marched in groups of one hundred to a Jewish cemetery near the ravine at Babi Yar. The area was cordoned off with barbed wire. The people were ordered to undress and leave their belongings neatly sorted and stacked. Many were then beaten with sticks as they awaited their fate. The people were taken in groups of ten to the ravine, where they were ordered to march to the bottom and lie down, often on top of those who had already been killed. They were then shot. The remaining Jews watched their family and neighbors being shot but were unable to escape, since the barbed wire enclosure was heavily guarded. There was not enough ammunition to kill everyone separately, and so in some cases two people were placed together and killed by one bullet. Many small children were thrown in the ravine alive and buried under all of the bodies. The massacre took two days, and by the end of the second day more than 33,700 Jews had been killed. The killing of Kiev's Jews did not end on the second day, however, as this first wave of killings continued at least until October 3, 1941. It is estimated that over the next several months more than 100,000 and perhaps as many as 200,000 people were killed at Babi Yar before the Soviets liberated the area in 1943. The number of dead included nearly all of the remaining Jews of Kiev as well as Gypsies, Communists, Ukrainian civilians, and Soviet prisoners of war. A few Jews survived because they were hidden by their non-Jewish neighbors, and a very few survived the killings because the bullets missed them or because they fell into the ravine just before the shot was fired. These few survivors provided witness testimony to the events that occurred at Babi Yar.

Memorials at Babi Yar

Several efforts were made to clean up the massacre site at Babi Yar. Before leaving Kiev, the German army tried to eradicate any evidence of what they had done; thus, they burned as many corpses as possible before their retreat in 1943. After the war ended, the Soviets burned many of the remaining corpses as well. In the early 1950s a dam was built in that area, and the ravine was flooded. After the dam failed, the ravine was used as a garbage dump. Eventually a park and soccer stadium were built on the site, and in time a television station and factory were also built there. However, no memorial was erected, which Yevtushenko noted in the poem that he wrote immediately after he visited the site in the fall of 1961. Yevtushenko's poem and Shostakovich's symphony created enough government embarrassment that a monument was at last built in 1976. This bronze monument is fifty feet tall, but its inscription does not specifically mention the Jews who died. Instead, it simply states that at this location more than 100,000 citizens of Kiev and Soviet prisoners of war were killed between 1941 and 1943. Finally, in 1991, Jewish groups erected a large bronze menorah away from the ravine and over the site where the bodies had been burned and the ashes buried. The menorah was vandalized in 2006, when the inscription at the base was badly damaged. Jewish leaders remain unhappy that children play soccer on the site of the massacre, but since the site is a popular park, there are no plans to change its use. Yevtushenko's poem "Babii Yar" is considered by many to be the most fitting and enduring memorial to the Jews who died there.

CRITICAL OVERVIEW

Yevgeny Yevtushenko's "Babii Yar" is controversial and has accordingly attracted critical attention. In 1961, in an essay published in the *New York Times*, Harry Schwartz reported that the Russian reception of "Babii Yar" was decidedly negative. Schwartz notes that Yevtushenko's reading of his poem resulted in two articles appearing in the Soviet literary journal *Literatura i Zhizn*. Both articles "bitterly denounced Mr. Yevtushenko for allegedly slandering the Russian people in his poem and for ignoring the Communist party's alleged opposition to anti-Semitism." Schwartz does not deal with the technical or aesthetic virtues of "Babii Yar"; instead, his focus is on the political ramifications of the poem. Indeed, the political ramifications of Yevtushenko's poetry have long been an issue for critics reviewing his work. In a 1966 critique of *The Poetry of Yevgeny Yevtushenko, 1953–1965* in the *Russian Review*, Louis J. Shein remarked on the success that Yevtushenko had experienced. According to Shein, "Yevtushenko's fame is not due so much to the high quality of his poetry as to his

outspoken criticism of Soviet bureaucracy." Shein argues that Yevtushenko should be judged "solely on the quality of his poetry and not on his 'political' views."

In a lengthy 1973 *New York Times Magazine* profile of the poet, Robert Conquest notes Yevtushenko's personal popularity with audiences who attend his readings. In the early 1960s, his audiences at times numbered ten thousand or more, and "his poems were printed in editions of 100,000." This is a number unheard of for most American poets, whose books might sell anywhere from 500 to 2,500 copies. In speaking specifically about "Babii Yar," Conquest notes that Yevtushenko "yielded to pressure on this poem, eliminated two lines and added two others to include Russian and Ukrainian victims of the massacre." In doing so, according to Conquest, Yevtushenko elected to "play down the theme of anti-Semitism" for which the poem is best known. In a 1991 *New Republic* article, the critic Tomas Venclova devotes most of his attention to criticizing Yevtushenko's more controversial reputation in Russia, especially his perceived betrayal of dissident poets, which benefited his own status and allowed him to travel more extensively outside the Soviet Union. Venclova also singles out a couple of Yevtushenko's poems for closer criticism, including "Babii Yar," which he calls "poetically feeble, and full of sentimental clichés." Regardless of whether critics admire Yevtushenko or his poetry—and clearly many critics are not fans of either the poet or his work—the importance of "Babii Yar" remains. It acts as a memorial to the Jewish victims of the massacre at Babi Yar and as a reminder of the dangers that anti-Semitism presents.

CRITICISM

Sheri Metzger Karmiol

Karmiol has a doctorate in English Renaissance literature and teaches literature and drama at the University of New Mexico, where she is a lecturer in the university honors program. She is also a professional writer and the author of several reference texts on poetry and drama. In this essay, Karmiol discusses how "Babii Yar" functions within the tradition of Holocaust poetry that gives voice to the unspeakable.

WHAT DO I READ NEXT?

- *The Collected Poems, 1952–1990* was published in 1991 and contains more than 660 pages of Yevtushenko's vast collection of poetry.

- Yevtushenko's *Fatal Half Measures: The Culture of Democracy in the Soviet Union* (1991) is a collection of essays, speeches, and articles that the author has written on a variety of subjects, including the unequal status of Soviet women, racism, and anti-Semitism.

- *The Cambridge Introduction to Russian Poetry* (2004), by Michael Wachtel, is a discussion of the last three centuries of Russian poetry. Included is information about concepts and the different styles of poetry most often used by Russian poets, such as love poetry and patriotic verse.

- Lawrence Langer's *Art from the Ashes: A Holocaust Anthology* (1995) contains a large selection of Holocaust poetry as well as excerpts from memoirs, diaries, and short fiction.

- Nelly Sachs's collection of poetry *The Seeker, and Other Poems* (1970) focuses on different aspects of the Holocaust and includes several poems that deal with death.

- *Anti-Semitism: A History* (2002), by Dan Cohn-Sherbok, provides a 3,000-year history of anti-Semitism and explores why anti-Semitism has played such an important role in history.

In the years immediately after the end of World War II, little Holocaust literature was produced. Many Jewish survivors of the Holocaust were intent on rebuilding their lives, by establishing careers, marrying and having children—by recreating what had been destroyed by the Nazis. As the events receded into the past and the population of survivors aged, many began writing memoirs, and these memoirs became a

> YEVTUSHENKO DID NOT EXPERIENCE THE HOLOCAUST. HE IS NOT JEWISH, AND 'BABII YAR' IS NOT THE POETRY OF EXPERIENCE. NEVERTHELESS, YEVTUSHENKO'S POETRY CAPTURES THE TRUTH OF THAT EXPERIENCE."

way for Holocaust survivors to bear witness. Poetry about the Holocaust is different, however. The role of Holocaust poetry is not clearly defined, nor perhaps is it clearly definable. Holocaust poetry can be, as Susan Gubar suggests in her book *Poetry after Auschwitz*, "a therapeutic response to the catastrophe." Holocaust poetry can also function as a warning or as a way to teach through verse. This last point is the argument that Sir Philip Sidney makes in his lengthy prose work *The Defence of Poesy*, in which he claims that the role of literature in a civilized society is to educate and to inspire those who read to ethical and virtuous actions. Sidney's argument for poetry's purpose is one that can be used to help understand poetry written about the Holocaust.

When Holocaust literature is published, the expectation is that readers will buy it. Whether the output is a memoir, fiction, a screenplay, or poetry, the selling of the Holocaust has become a business. There are now a number of excellent documentaries about the Holocaust, and even fictional accounts, whether novels or films, have become somewhat commonplace. Still, there remains an expectation that using the Holocaust will result in a product that educates but does not exploit. The expectation that writing about the Holocaust will result in a treatment that dignifies and honors the victims depends a great deal on perception. For example, in a *New York Times* review of the 1978 NBC miniseries *Holocaust*, the Auschwitz survivor and Nobel Peace Prize winner Elie Wiesel objects to the use of the Holocaust to promote spectacle and to the blending of the facts of the Holocaust with the fiction of television. In his review, Wiesel asserts that "the Holocaust is unique, not just another event." The screenwriter who wrote this miniseries no doubt felt that he was honoring the victims and educating the public about these events. In a sense, his goal was probably not much different than Yevtushenko's. The difference is that when Yevtushenko created "Babii Yar," he did not create fictional victims, as did the screenwriter. There was no need to do so; instead, the poet sought to remember those who died by campaigning against the anti-Semitism that fed the hate that killed them.

The ethical issue of how the Holocaust can and should be used as a literary subject is astutely captured by Wiesel's questions: "How is one to tell a tale that cannot be—but must be—told? How is one to protect the memory of the victims?" Wiesel's demand that Holocaust literature not be used to trivialize the event presents a concern that Naomi Mandel considers in an article in the journal *boundary 2*. Mandel notes that the Holocaust is "commonly referred to as unspeakable, unthinkable, inconceivable, incomprehensible, and challenging." The Holocaust is an event that forces us "to reestablish, or to rethink, or to acknowledge" the limits of representation. Speech is too limited to describe the indescribable. The Holocaust is filled with examples of human cruelty beyond simple explanation or description. Words cannot adequately express the unspeakable—which is why Yevtushenko does not try to do so. "Babii Yar" does not describe the details of genocide. Instead Yevtushenko uses a few calculated words and phrases to capture certain images, like that of the small boy bleeding from a kick delivered by the well-placed boot of a drunken anti-Semite. The poet relies upon the imagination of the reader to visualize Anne Frank being pulled from the arms of those she loved, a teenager—a child still—sent to her death. Just as Wiesel worries about the appropriation of the Holocaust, Mandel also worries that using the event, even for poetry, violates the victims, since "to speak their experience would run the risk of understanding that experience, with its concurrent possibilities of trivializing or betraying it."

Yevtushenko uses "Babii Yar" to force his readers to recognize the truth about the injustice of the past. The expectation is that past injustices will be recognized and not repeated. Gubar recognizes that there are stereotypes about Jews, and as a result, she declares that the poetry of the Holocaust must be completely honest, not "too theatrical or too theoretical, too glib or too sanctimonious," but instead it must "make the present see the past." Yevtushenko did not

experience the Holocaust. He is not Jewish, and "Babii Yar" is not the poetry of experience. Nevertheless, Yevtushenko's poetry captures the truth of that experience. James Finn Cotter remarks in the *Hudson Review* that "the truth of poetry is not in reciting facts but in creating veracity." Poetry must create the truth, and this is even more important for Holocaust poetry. Cotter explains that he asks "a poem to be true to itself, to convince me and to capture my attention with its thought, emotion, imagery, and language." In the long sequence of "Babii Yar" in which Yevtushenko imagines that he is each old man or young child facing death there, the imagery fulfills Cotter's requirement that poetry must convince the reader of an essential truth. According to Cotter, Yevtushenko has stood for "poetry as a voice that rallies public consciousness." Yevtushenko demands the "freedom to speak out in protest against human rights violations." His is a worldview, according to Cotter, "that transcends nationalist boundaries" and represents "the power of the individual against bureaucracy and oppression." When Yevtushenko, a non-Jew, imagines himself a Jew, he does so not in a search for sympathy but in an expectation of justice. His poem demands that the Soviet bureaucracy acknowledge the destruction of Kiev Jewry at Babi Yar in 1941.

Wiesel adamantly states that "the Holocaust *must* be remembered." Yevtushenko's choice to speak of certain Holocaust events through poetry is one way to remember. It is also a way to honor those who died, as with his demand for a memorial at Babi Yar. Poetry is also a way to remind readers of the destructiveness of hate, as Yevtushenko does when he recalls the long history of anti-Semitism. In the introduction to the anthology of Holocaust literature *Art from the Ashes*, Lawrence L. Langer suggests, "If the Holocaust has ceased to seem an event and become instead a theme of prose narrative, fiction, or verse, this is not to diminish its importance, but to alter the route by which we approach it." Yevtushenko chooses to call attention to an event that had been covered up and ignored. His route is to remind readers of the past. Literature, regardless of the form that it takes, cannot offer a complete picture of the Holocaust, because as Wiesel observes, "You may think you know how the victims lived and died, but you do not." Each experience of having lived through the Holocaust is unique. The picture created by literature, or even by film, cannot create a complete picture, as Langer admits, but it can create a composite of that experience, which he suggests can illuminate the event and help readers decipher it. This is the function of poetry that Gubar argues is essential; what happened at Babi Yar is the kind of moment that when "rendered in writing allows authors and readers to grapple with the consequences of traumatic pain without being silenced by it." There is no way that Yevtushenko or any other poet can make the events at Babi Yar comprehensible, but Yevtushenko's approach in dealing with anti-Semitism and the need for remembrance is one way to allow readers to have a voice in preventing genocide. If poetry is to have the role that Sidney envisioned it having more than three hundred years ago, the ability to teach lessons is even more important for Holocaust poetry.

Yevtushenko wrote "Babii Yar" to change the world. When he found it incomprehensible that no memorial marked the place of such a massive act of genocide, his poem became that memorial. In his text *A Defense of Poetry*, written in 1821, Percy Bysshe Shelley argues that poetry does not simply reflect the world; it changes the world. Poetry makes things happen. According to Shelley, poets "are the institutors of laws, and the founders of civil society." He emphasizes the social importance of poetry, which plays upon the subconscious and thus can transcend ideology and "creates anew the universe." Poetry is more than beauty; it is useful and beneficial to society because it removes distinctions of class and gender and, by extension, differences of religion. Shelley, of course, could never have predicted an event such as the Holocaust, just as those who now know of it find it difficult to accept that such inhumanity could have ever been directed toward other human beings.

What was missing from the events that took place at Babi Yar, or Auschwitz, or Treblinka, or any of the other sites of mass annihilation of the Jewish population was empathy for those who were being murdered. The perpetrators at Babi Yar did not see Jewish infants and children as human beings. When Yevtushenko places himself at Babi Yar on September 29, 1941, he does what those who committed the murders did not do. He envisions himself as a gray-haired old man or as a young child. Yevtushenko does as Shelley mandates in asserting that "a man, to be greatly good, must imagine intensely and comprehensively." According to Shelley, a man must possess the ability to imagine the pain of others, to "put himself in the place of another and of many others; the pains and pleasures of his species must become his own." Shelley's words found little application in the actions of the Nazis or even in the actions of the ordinary civilians who collaborated with the Nazis. The poet, as defined by Shelley, not only "beholds intensely the present as it is," or as it should be according to moral laws, but also holds forth the promise of "the future in the present." It took a poet such as Yevtushenko to look at the neglected ravine at Babi Yar and see beyond the garbage-strewn site to witness the humanity of those who lost their lives at that place. It was a poet who looked at that site and saw what bureaucrats did not see—the absolute need to remember the tragedy that occurred there.

The importance of poetry is, as Shelley claims, "never more to be desired than at periods when . . . an excess of the selfish and calculating principle" exceeds the "laws of human nature." Holocaust poetry can illuminate the injustice of tyranny, the inhumanity of mankind, and the unfathomable suffering of those whose only offense was to have existed. It remains the imperative of poets to illuminate what is unspeakable. As Yevtushenko illustrates with "Babii Yar," poets can change the world. And as Shelley notes at the end of his argument, "Poets are the unacknowledged legislators of the world."

Source: Sheri Metzger Karmiol, Critical Essay on "Babii Yar," in *Poetry for Students*, Gale, Cengage Learning, 2009.

Jonathan Z. Ludwig

In the following review, Ludwig discusses the political importance of Yevtushenko's poetry.

Yevgeny Yevtushenko notes in the opening line of "Bratsk Hydroelectric Station" that "a poet in Russia is more than a poet" (160). Throughout history, poets have used their poetry to call for societal, governmental, and political changes within their country. It is Russian poets, perhaps, who have acted in this political role most openly. In the last forty years, few poets in Russia have been as prolific a writer and as major a political player as Yevtushenko has been. It is fitting, therefore, that this collection of poems, a collection which includes selections

THE SECOND [SECTION], CONSISTING OF POEMS
WRITTEN BETWEEN 1956 AND 1962 AND INCLUDING
POEMS SUCH AS 'BABI YAR' AND 'THE HEIRS OF STALIN,'
IS APTLY INTRODUCED BY THE LINES 'THAT TIME SO
STRANGE WHEN SIMPLE / HONESTY LOOKED LIKE
COURAGE.' ... "

spanning his entire career, shows Yevtushenko
both as a poet and as a politician. Indeed, as
anyone who has followed his career can note,
with Yevtushenko, poetry and politics are
never far apart.

The book opens with an introduction by
Albert C. Todd which demonstrates exactly
how true this statement is. Although this introduction is not an orderly examination of Yevtushenko's life and career, it does highlight the
points which are significant and defining for his
career as a poet and as a politician. In addition, it
discusses several poems which are clearly political and gives the history behind them and their
publication. Just as important for this collection
as a whole, however, the introduction also
presents Yevtushenko's personal philosophy, a
love for nature, life, and the living which was
instilled in him by his grandmother while growing up in Zima Junction, not far from Lake
Baikal.

The poems in this collection, which were
translated by a number of well-known writers
and poets including James Dickey, Ted Hughes,
John Updike, and Richard Wilbur, are organized chronologically and divided into nine sections. Each section contains poems written in a
specific period, ranging in length from two to six
years, and is introduced by a line from one of the
poems in that section. Often this epigraph signifies the overriding theme of the section. Of the
nine sections into which this collection is divided, four are closely tied thematically to their
epigraph. The first section which includes poems
written between 1952 and 1955 is introduced by
the line "People are really talking now" (1). It
includes several poems which indicate the air of
freedom which began to be felt after Stalin's

death. The second, consisting of poems written
between 1956 and 1962 and including poems
such as "Babi Yar" and "The Heirs of Stalin,"
is aptly introduced by the lines "that time so
strange when simple/honesty looked like courage" (59). The sixth section of poems are those
which were written between 1973 and 1975. It is
introduced by the lines "A poet is always in
danger/when he lives too safely" (367) and notably contains a number of poems less politically
controversial than several others in this collection. The ninth and final section, introduced
with the exclamation "We can't go on this
way!" (595), includes "Requiem for *Challenger*,"
"We Can't Go On," "Half Measures," and other
poems penned between 1986 and 1990, all of
which plaintively wonder where the world is
heading and where its future lies.

Although the remaining five sections do not
tie in closely with their respective epigraphs, they
are, nevertheless, no less significant. The third
section, introduced by the lines "The sea was
what I breathed/it was sorrow I exhaled ..."
(117), includes poems such as "Nefertiti,"
"Wounded Bird," and "The City of Yes and the
City of No," written in 1963 and 1964. The
fourth section includes very solemn poems written between 1965 and 1967 such as "Yelabuga
Nail," "Monologue of a Blue Fox," and "Cemetery of Whales." It is introduced by a statement
of Yevtushenko's views on the power of poetry
on the self: "It acts kind of crazy, flutteringly,/
when it chooses us" (177). The fifth section,
comprised of poems written between 1968 and
1972 and introduced by the lines " ... I'll come
seeping through/these rainy bits of slipperiness/
between the toes of barefoot urchins" (273), is a
selection of rather somber poems which concludes with the very upbeat "I Would Like."
The seventh section, introduced by the lines
"Hunger has the speed of sound,/when beginning as a moan, it becomes a scream" (437),
contains another selection of very somber
poems written between 1976 and 1978. The
eighth section, introduced by the lines "A half
blade of grass in the teeth—/there's my whole
secret" (519) and containing poetry written
between 1979 and 1985, is comprised of several
of the most openly politically controversial
poems written by Yevtushenko since the late
1950s and the early 1960s.

Throughout the collection, significant events,
individuals, places, and cultural motifs are explained

in notes, thus allowing a reader not thoroughly versed in Russian and Soviet history, politics, culture, and current events to more readily understand these pieces. Also useful to readers and scholars of this poetry are the four appendices with which the book concludes. The first two are listings of writers, historical figures, rivers, and geographic names frequently referred to in the poems. The third identifies smaller collections of Yevtushenko's poetry which have been published in English translation, and the fourth lists bibliographic data for each of the poems in the collection. In this final appendix, each poem is listed both in English translation and in transcription and is followed by the place and date of first publication, generally in a journal or newspaper; an indication of the first book publication of the poem; and a notation of where it is located in Yevtushenko's three-volume collected works.

Yevtushenko scholars, obviously, will find the bibliographic data in the final appendix useful, especially in order to locate a copy of the poem in the original Russian or to compare the book publication version(s) with the original published version. Those who study Russian and Soviet culture will also find much of interest in this collection, since Yevtushenko quite often integrates a number of literary and cultural allusions into his poetry. Finally, historians and political scientists, who normally might not use poetry as a source of information, will find many poems in this collection of use, especially in a study of the last four decades of Soviet and Russian history.

Since the appearance of this collection, Yevtushenko has published two other works of note. The first work appears in the collection *20th Century Russian Poetry: Silver and Steel* (Doubleday: New York, 1993) which Yevtushenko himself edited and introduced. Included among the several poems of his own which he placed in this collection is the 1991 poem "Loss," a poem previously unpublished in English. This poem is particularly timely, for it poses several political questions, including "Is it true that we Russians have only one unhappy choice?/The ghost of Tsar Ivan the Terrible?/Or the Ghost of Tsar Chaos?" (820), questions which are surely on the mind of nearly every Russian yet today.

The second work, the novel *Don't Die Before Your Death: A Russian Tale* (Liberty Publishing House: New York, 1993) is set during the attempted 1991 coup. It is not only an historical novel, but it is also a detective story, a sentimental romance, a satire, and a philosophical treatise in which the author himself is the hero. Above all, however, it represents a serious look at everyday life in contemporary Russia. The publication of this novel and the aforementioned poem demonstrates that Yevtushenko is continuing to write in the way that made him well-known both in Russia and in the West: critical of that which he considers wrong, yet continuing to affirm nature, life, and the living.

Source: Jonathan Z. Ludwig, Review of *The Collected Poems: 1952–1990* and *Don't Die before Your Death*, in *Slavic and East European Journal*, Vol. 38, No. 3, Autumn 1994, pp. 515–17.

Patricia Pollock Brodsky
In the following review, Brodsky evaluates a collection of Yevtushenko's poetry that includes the poem "Babii Yar."

The new *Collected Poems 1952–1990* reflects Yevgeny Yevtushenko's poetic career in microcosm: vast and uneven, sometimes irritating, often appealing, and ever astonishing in its variety. The title is somewhat misleading, since the volume offers only a selection from Yevtushenko's extensive oeuvre, and in addition, several long poems are represented in excerpts only. Yevtushenko's allusiveness can be a problem for Western readers; a few names and terms are explained in footnotes, but this practice could profitably have been expanded. A helpful feature is the chronological list of poems with their Russian titles, date and place of first publication, and location, if any, in the 1983 *Sobranie sochinenii* (see *WLT* 59:4).

Like the poems themselves, the translations by twenty-five translators vary in quality. A few are revisions of earlier versions. Most of Yevtushenko's poems use slant rhyme relying heavily on assonance, a practice so closely associated with him as to be called "Yevtushenkean rhyme" (*evtushenkovskaia rifma*). Russian's rich phonetic structure allows almost limitless use of this kind of rhyme; a master of the form and clearly one of Yevtushenko's teachers was the poet Marina Tsvetaeva. Wisely, few attempts are made to retain this feature in the English translations, or indeed to use rhyme at all.

From the beginning of his prolific career in the early 1950s, Yevtushenko's poetry has been characterized by strong stances on political issues. He praises Allende and Che Guevara, condemns the Vietnam War, and deplores the situation in Northern Ireland. His criticism is not limited to the West, however. A popular and privileged poet whose readings at one time filled football stadiums and who was given unprecedented freedom to travel abroad, he nevertheless warned against abuses at home, castigating militarists, dishonest bureaucrats, and toadies of all kinds. These critical poems range from "The Heirs of Stalin" and "Babi Yar" in the early 1960s to "Momma and the Neutron Bomb" and poems about the dissident Andrei Sakharov and the Afghanistan war in the 1980s. The roots of his ferocious morality are to be found in his love for Russia, and in his stubborn belief in the ideals of the revolution.

Even the semiofficial poet was not immune from censorship, however. Included in the new collection are a number of poems that were written during the sixties but for political reasons could not be published until many years later. Among them are verses to fellow poets Tsvetaeva (1967/1987) and Esenin (1965/1988), "Russian Tanks in Prague" (1968/1990), and "The Ballad of the Big Stamp," a bawdy tale about castration for the good of the party (1966/1989).

Yevtushenko is at his best when he is specific and detailed, and this happens most frequently in poems dealing with his native Siberia, its nature and history, its sailors, whalers, berry pickers. These include the long poem "Zima Junction" (1955) and a series written in 1964 about life on the northern frontier. Yevtushenko has a strong visual sense (he is an accomplished photographer), and color often plays an important role in his works. In the fairy-tale-like "Snow in Tokyo: A Japanese Poem" (1974), for example, a proper and repressed Japanese matron discovers the wonders of painting and finds the courage to rebel against her stultifying life through the world of color.

A thread running through Yevtushenko's work is the importance of poetry and the responsibility of the poet to mankind. He constantly questions his own talent and mission, thus continuing the Russian tradition of meta-poetry. Likewise very Russian is the dialogue between writers living and dead that Yevtushenko carries on, in poems addressed to or evoking Pushkin, Pasternak, Neruda, and Jack London, along with numerous others.

> 'BABII YAR' (1961) TREATED ANTI-SEMITIC TENDENCIES IN RUSSIAN LIFE, AND PROVOKED A RABID REACTION IN FASCIST AND FASCISTOID CIRCLES."

Finally, Yevtushenko's poetry is a kind of personal diary which details his extensive travels and especially his many love affairs and marriages. Remarkable love poems follow the poet from first love, to the birth of his sons, to the sadness of falling out of love again. The poems contain a rich fabric of quarrels, memories, farewells, even a conversation with his dog, who shares the poet's grief that his woman has gone. Perhaps the most attractive thing about Yevtushenko is his human breadth, his willingness to lay himself open to our reactions. *The Collected Poems* provides the reader with numerous opportunities to become acquainted with this engaged and engaging poet, one of the important, questioning voices of our age.

Source: Patricia Pollock Brodsky, Review of *The Collected Poems 1952–1990*, in *World Literature Today*, Vol. 66, No. 1, Winter 1992, pp. 156–57.

Tomas Venclova

In the following appraisal of Yevtushenko's poetry, Venclova calls "Babii Yar" the "high point of Yevtushenko's personal and political career."

An interesting article by Yevgeny Yevtushenko, part essay, part memoir, recently appeared in *Literaturnaya Gazeta* in Moscow, in which the poet dwells at length on his skirmishes with Soviet reactionaries. The title of the article is "Fencing with a Pile of Dung," which is meant to be a bold metaphor. Among other tales, Yevtushenko tells the story of his visit to the pre-perestroika Kremlin, where he was to be honored with the Order of the Red Banner:

> The Order was presented by a vice-chairman of the Presidium of the Supreme Soviet, an Azerbaijani whose last name I cannot, for the life of me, recall. Pinning the order to the lapel of my jacket and inviting me to a hunting party in Azerbaijan, he awkwardly pierced my jacket, my shirt, and even pricked me. It was rather painful. The Kremlin people hurt me often enough. They hurt others, too.

The next story deals with the presentation of a State Prize to Yevtushenko in 1984 for his long poem "Momma and the Neutron Bomb." "The censorship office attempted to ban the poem," he writes, "but it did not succeed." Yevtushenko took his medal and his certificate (and his money). According to the requirements of Soviet protocol, he was expected to express his gratitude to the Party at the ceremony. His wrath was so impossible to contain, however, that he neglected etiquette and returned to his seat without breaking his proud silence. His bravery, he tells us, inspired several other recipients of the prize, who also refused to say thanks.

Now, there is something fundamentally wrong about this picture. You are pampered by a totalitarian government, or you are persecuted by it. You are given honors and awards by party functionaries, or you are not. You are invited to their hunting parties, or you are their open enemy. But both cannot happen to you at the same time. Andrei Sakharov received perks similar to Yevtushenko's while he was busy with the Soviet nuclear program; but later his moral rectitude led him to the camp of the dissidents, and the world knows what followed. You see, you cannot fence with a pile of dung. You either sink into it or you leave it. To pretend otherwise requires extraordinary cynicism, extraordinary naïveté, or both. When Yevtushenko implicitly compares the pain caused by that pricking pin to the sufferings of Sakharov, Pasternak, and many, many others, he goes beyond the limits of naïveté, and even of cynicism. He approaches the obscene.

The case of Yevtushenko is one of the most unusual cases of our times. (Stanislaw Baranczak recently listed it, in *Newsday*, among the top ten hoaxes of the twentieth century.) Two large books by Yevtushenko, which just appeared in English, provide an opportunity to study it more closely. The first is a volume of verse [*The Collected Poems*] put into English by many translators, including some of the masters of the language. The second is a collection of political speeches, essays, travelogues, and divagations on Russian writers [*Fatal Half Measures*]. Both books are provided with rapturous introductions and blurbs: the author is "the legendary Russian literary leader," "a people's poet in the tradition of Walt Whitman," "a seeker of Truth like all great writers," and so on. It seems that many members in good standing of the American literary establishment consider these descriptions to be true, or at least partly true. Unfortunately, they are false.

One thing has to be admitted: Yevtushenko is an incredibly prolific writer who is endowed with a buoyant personality. He is not only a versifier and an essayist, but also a scriptwriter, a film director, an actor, a photographer, a novelist, a political figure, and a world traveler—a Soviet cultural emissary in virtually all parts of the globe, which is a function that he inherited from Vladimir Mayakovsky and Ilya Erenburg, who played the same role on a less extensive scale. In his tender years, Yevtushenko was also a goalkeeper and a folk dancer of repute.

The amount of energy, the sheer labor, devoted to all these enterprises cannot fail to impress. Yevtushenko says about himself, without false modesty but not without reason: "my fate is supernatural, / my destiny astonishing." Sixty-four countries visited by 1976 (by now the number is larger) and forty-six books of original poetry so far—this certainly is supernatural, if we recall that permission to travel abroad once or twice was the sweetest dream of almost any Soviet writer before the Gorbachev era, and that many good poets of the USSR considered themselves lucky if they managed to publish a slim and heavily blue-penciled volume once in a decade. On top of all that, we learn (from his editor Antonina W. Bouis) that Yevtushenko "has been banned, threatened, censored, and punished," though he has not been imprisoned.

The tales of Yevtushenko's tribulations are not totally unfounded. In the beginning, he did not fit snugly into the Procrustean bed of Stalinist literature, and he was attacked by some of the worst hacks of the period, not least by the anti-Semites. (Yevtushenko has no Jewish background, but his Latvian father's last name, Gangnus, looked suspicious.) Yet the controversy about Yevtushenko was always a quarrel *within* the Soviet literary framework. Yevtushenko never displayed the slightest inclination to work outside it.

A fight within the Soviet establishment, even if it is conducted for a liberal cause, is bound to degenerate into a fight for the benevolence of the authorities. In this regard, Yevtushenko happened to be more skillful, and incomparably more successful, than his dull opponents. And so they never forgave him. Yevtushenko is still denounced by the lunatic fringe, by the Pamyat people and their supporters. (Pamyat has done him a great favor: its opposition has been adduced as proof of his credentials as a humanist and a fighter for freedom.) Much less publicized is the fact that democratic and dissident Soviet critics exposed Yevtushenko's literary weaknesses and moral vacillations long ago and mercilessly. Today hardly anyone in that literary community considers his work worthy of serious study.

He started out, in 1949, at the age of 16, as an average if precocious maker of Soviet-style poems. His first book appeared at the very nadir of Stalinism, in 1952, and suited the time rather nicely: it was optimistic, full of clichés, and boring. But after coming from his native Siberia to the Moscow Literary Institute, Yevtushenko felt the first timid stirrings of the post-Stalin mood and expressed them, too, in his verses. This stage of his poetry is amply represented in the new English collection. In the era of glasnost, it looks antediluvian. Still, there is something attractive in it: youthful sentimentality, straightforward intonation, impetuous imagery.

Yevtushenko was among the first writers of the period to introduce into his work a slice of real Soviet life—of the so-called *byt*, the daily grind of tedium, hardship, and deprivation. Here and there he mentioned queues, dirty staircases, bedbugs, fences with obscene inscriptions, and so on. (Later even such taboo subjects as condoms and drinking eau de cologne appeared in his lyrics.) He also wrote about love and its betrayals; and though they are essentially Victorian, those poems provoked attacks on Yevtushenko as an advocate of promiscuity.

His early verses can be read as an anthology of modes and fads of the bygone days. Some of his heroes (including the narrator) were *stilyagas*, the scornful name for a member of the Soviet "golden youth" who were fond of Western clothes, dances, and so on—a sort of mixture of hippie and yuppie; and the message of Yevtushenko's poetry was that they were good Soviet people who would bravely fight for their socialist fatherland. Yevtushenko played up his Siberian heritage, moreover, and employed all the trivial mythology of Siberia—not the land of the Gulag, but the magnificent wilderness inhabited by rough and honest men. And he emphasized his manifestly difficult childhood ("I started out as a lonely wolf cub"). All these traits were at their most obvious in the long poem

"Zima Junction," which appeared in 1955. It made Yevtushenko's reputation.

"Zima Junction," a narrative poem about Yevtushenko's visit to his native Siberia, very cautiously touched the political sensitivities of its era: the so-called Doctors' Plot, Stalin's death, the fall of Beria. On the whole, it was full of the usual stuff—decent Chekists, naive but nice Red cavalrymen, upright but flawed Russian peasants, and the author himself, a young lad in search of a way to serve his country. It was attacked by literary conservatives, but it was also instrumental in generating strong support for Yevtushenko in some circles of the Party, among people whose background and experience were similar to his own. There is a persistent rumor that Mikhail Gorbachev was one of them.

Today Yevtushenko states that "in 1953 it seemed I was all the dissidents rolled up into one." And "the early poetry of my generation is the cradle of glasnost." Such revelations are less than modest. In addition, they are untrue. There were many thousands of dissidents in 1953. Most of them were in prison camps or in internal exile. Some of them, like Pasternak, Akhmatova, and Nadezhda Mandelshtam, were still at large, but they were totally cut off from their readers and from the general public. Glasnost—to be more precise, the revolution taking place in the Soviet Union today—was the fruit of their untold suffering, and their incredibly stubborn efforts to maintain moral and cultural standards during that era of contempt. Yevtushenko and his ilk, in other words, took the place that rightfully belonged to others. They promoted literature and ideology that was adapted to their totalitarian milieu, into which they introduced a measure of half truth and half decency.

Many Western critics are fond of uncovering the influences of Mayakovsky, Yesenin, Pasternak, and Blok in Yevtushenko's poetry, thereby suggesting that he is a rightful heir to the giants. The poet himself never tires of invoking their shades, although he does not transcend the level of schoolboyish clichés when he talks about their heritage. His real mentors, however, were second-rate, incurably Soviet, and largely obscure poets such as Stepan Shchipachev, Mikhail Svetlov, Aleksandr Mezhirov, and Konstantin Vanshenkin. (Numerous dedications to them can be found throughout *The Collected Poems*.)

For a time their heir Yevtushenko surpassed them, since he became genuinely popular. His popularity might have been owed in part to his great histrionic gifts. As Andrei Sinyavsky has observed, Yevtushenko managed to revive the theatrical concept of a poet's destiny (rejected by Pasternak, but characteristic of Mayakovsky and Tsvetaeva), according to which a poet's biography had to become an integral part, even the principal part, of his or her work. Readers and audiences had to be well acquainted with a poet's personal life, with his or her everyday dramas. For Mayakovsky and Tsvetaeva, the theatrics were genuinely tragic. For Yevtushenko, in accordance with the worn Marxist dictum, they tended to be farcical.

He succeeded in creating an image of a nice guy, an old chap, a macho simpleton who matter-of-factly recounts his family problems, his sexual exploits, his daily chores and daily doubts. Yevtushenko's audience of Soviet youths, immature and disoriented after several decades of Stalinist isolation, longing for a touch of sincerity, hungrily gulped down anything "Western" and "modern," and adopted Yevtushenko (together with Voznesensky and several others) as their idol. This did not last too long; the more sophisticated part of the audience found real, previously suppressed Russian poetry, and the other and larger part became rather apathetic to all poetry, including Yevtushenko's.

I should acknowledge that two early poems by Yevtushenko made history. Politically, if not poetically, they have a lasting place in the annals of Soviet liberalism. "Babii Yar" (1961) treated anti-Semitic tendencies in Russian life, and provoked a rabid reaction in fascist and fascistoid circles. It was a noble public act, perhaps the high point of Yevtushenko's personal and political career. And it differs favorably from Voznesensky's poems on the same topic; it is more measured, discreet, and restrained, and it avoids formal experimentation and the homespun surrealism that is decidedly out of place when one speaks about the Holocaust. Still, it is poetically feeble, and full of sentimental clichés ("Anne Frank / transparent as a branch in April"). But perhaps these weaknesses may be overlooked.

The other famous poem is "The Heirs of Stalin" (1962). In its case, the situation is different. Most likely "Babii Yar" was a spontaneous outpouring. "The Heirs of Stalin" was a calculated gamble, a move in the intra-Party game of old fashioned Stalinists and Khrushchevian liberals. It did not avoid dubious statements, like "prison camps are empty." (In 1962 they were not.) "The Heirs of Stalin" impressed Khrushchev and was printed in *Pravda*. Yevtushenko had managed to place his bet on the winning horse. In his memoirs of the time, the poet portrays himself as a virtual outcast, but the scene that follows in his telling leaves the reader a bit doubtful about the depth of his predicament. At a reception in Havana, presumably in Castro's residence, where Mikoyan also is present, Yevtushenko picks up the issue of *Pravda* with his provocative poem. "[Mikoyan] handed Castro the newspaper. Mikoyan apparently thought that I knew all about it and was rather shocked to see me practically tear the newspaper out of Castro's hands." Hardly an episode in the life of a freedom fighter.

Of course the world traveler did not confine himself to Cuba. Travelogues in verse and prose, including long and not terribly interesting poems on Chile, Japan, the United States, and other places, make up a very considerable part of his creative output. The Western establishment, eager for reassuring signs of moral and cultural revival in Russia, was encouraged by the sight of an audacious person who seemed enlightened and tractable compared with the typical Soviet *nyet* people. And the advertising tricks usually reserved for movie stars were trotted out on the poet's behalf, which increased his already appreciable vanity. (Yevtushenko proudly recounts instances when a Western cultural figure called him "Mayakovsky's son.")

Some misunderstandings with the authorities ensued. Some credit must be given to Yevtushenko, since he behaved with dignity even when he was assaulted by Khrushchev himself. (At his famous meeting with the intelligentsia, Khrushchev delivered himself of the Russian proverb that "hunchbacks are corrected by the grave," at which Yevtushenko retorted: "The time when people were corrected by the grave has passed.") Still, it was as clear as the noon sun that he remained totally loyal to the Party, even if he was a bit heterodox in secondary matters. Thus the campaign against him fizzled. In 1964 he expiated his sins by writing the long poem "Bratsk Hydroelectric Station." The poem, long selections of which are included in the English volume, marked a new stage in Yevtushenko's development: an era of resourceful compromises, cheating moves, and clever adaptations to existing conditions (which became more and more stifling after Khrushchev's removal in October 1964). The poet himself pictured his rushing about as a wise stratagem serving the liberal cause. But not many Russian and non-Russian intellectuals agreed with him; the dissident movement virtually discarded Yevtushenko as an ally. And that was irreversible.

"Bratsk Hydroelectric Station" is a paean to one of the typical Soviet industrial projects in Siberia. (Today such projects, usually unprofitable and fraught with ecological disasters, are repudiated by public opinion, and even by the government itself.) The central part of the poem consists of an argument between an Egyptian pyramid and the Siberian powerhouse: the former symbolizes all the conservative and enslaving tendencies of history (Stalinism supposedly included), while the latter defends the cause of idealist faith and human emancipation. Yevtushenko overlooked the fact that the opposition is far from perfect: slave labor or near-slave labor played an approximately identical part in building both monuments. And the forces of freedom are represented in the poem by rather dubious figures. One of them is Stenka Razin, leader of a savage peasant revolt in the seventeenth century, whose confessions sound chilling ("No, it is not in this I have sinned, my people, / for hanging boyars from the towers. / I have sinned in my own eyes in this, / that I hanged too few of them"). There is also a scene where young Lenin (never named but perfectly recognizable) guides a drunken woman (supposedly Mother Russia) by the elbow, and she blesses him as her true son. This transformation of Lenin into a Christ-like figure insulted equally the followers of Lenin and the followers of Christ.

Virtually the same applies to many of Yevtushenko's later poetic works. The long poem "Kazan University" (1970) described czarist Russia with some wit and verve. Reactionary tendencies of the nineteenth century brought to mind Brezhnevian stagnation, and the liberal scholar Lesgaft, harassed by the authorities, might be easily interpreted as a forebear of Sakharov. But the university of Kazan was also the breeding ground for Lenin, who, according to the author (and to the Soviet textbooks), was the crown prince of Russian democracy. Never mind that Lenin was the very opposite of democracy—and that he never attempted to conceal it. Transforming him into a

prophet of human rights, of brotherhood and justice, into a Gandhi or a Sakharov *avant la lettre*, is nauseating. (It is also un-Marxist.)

Many of Yevtushenko's poems on Western topics are characterized by the same double-think. Harangues against the "doltish regime" of Salazar, against the Chilean murderers or American bureaucrats ("Under the Skin of the Statue of Liberty," 1968) can be construed as transparent allegories: in fact, the poet is attacking native Soviet deficiencies. But at the same time the attacks perfectly conform to the general tenor of the Party's propaganda; Salazar, Pinochet, the FBI, and the Pentagon always were convenient bugaboos, and in that capacity helped the Party to keep the people silent and loyal. Moreover, the general picture of the West in these poems is usually touristy and superficial. Fascinated by material standards and the ever changing fashions of the First World, Yevtushenko nevertheless mythologizes his role as "the ambassador of all the oppressed" and a Russian (and Soviet) patriot. There are also endless exhortations for peaceful coexistence and friendship of peoples ("Russia and America, / Swim closer!"), essentially noble, but less than irreproachable in the era of détente.

The poet's editors and promoters tend to emphasize his heroic gestures during the crisis periods in the USSR. It is true that he sent a telegram to Brezhnev protesting the Czech invasion. It is also said that he phoned Andropov to express his intention to die on the barricades if Solzhenitsyn was imprisoned. But his protests were incomparably more cautious, and much less resonant, than the protests of real dissenters, who paid with their freedom. And the telegram to Brezhnev has the air of an intimate exchange of views between allies: Yevtushenko speaks in it about "our action," which is a damaging mistake, "a great gift to all the reactionary forces in the world." The poem "Russian Tanks in Prague," moreover, was circulated secretly and reached a very limited circle, so as to avoid doing any harm to the poet's career.

A poet's dubious moral and political stance does not always preclude good poetry. In Yevtushenko's case, though, it does. His verses, as a role, do not belong to the realm of poetry at all. They are made up of middlebrow journalism and an interminable flow of didactic chatter; they have virtually nothing in common with the true problems of modern (or any) poetics. For all his declarations of ardor and fervor, Yevtushenko is hackneyed, kitschy, and lukewarm. On almost every page you stumble on something like "eyelashes laden / with tears and storms," or "eyes half-shut with ecstasy and pain." Melodramatic effusions ("My love is a demolished church / above the turbid river of memories") alternate with revelations worthy of a sex manual ("When we love, / nothing is base or tasteless. / When we love, / nothing is shameful.").

I am trying not to be unfair. There are some concessions I must make in Yevtushenko's favor. He is usually free of Voznesensky's pretentiousness. You can find in his books good similes, successful vignettes of daily life, touching characters, and hair-raising stories that may, alas, be true. And his weaknesses become more obvious in translation. I would be inclined to praise such poems as "Handrolled Cigarettes" or "The Ballad of the Big Stamp" (the latter is hilarious, though it suffers in translation since it lacks a factual commentary about Russian religious sects). And of course Yevtushenko is a figure to reckon with because of his inexhaustible energy. But all these attractive traits are deeply tainted by his taste for comfort and accommodation, by his eagerness to play humiliating games with the censors, by the mixture of self-admiration, self-pity, and coquettish self-deprecation that have become his indelible mark.

Today Yevtushenko is a member—by no means the leader—of the liberal wing of the perestroika establishment. His book of journalistic prose, *Fatal Half Measures*, from which I have quoted extensively, traces his political career between 1962, when *A Precocious Autobiography*, published in the West, caused a passing commotion, and 1990, when his speeches resounded, rather hollowly, in several public forums. The book is preceded by a poem in which Yevtushenko seems to be admonishing Gorbachev: "Don't half recoil, / lost in broad daylight, / half rebel, / half suppressor / of the half insurrection / you gave birth to!"

But the book's title perfectly applies to the poet's own style of action. Fatal half measures, indeed. Yevtushenko lags desperately behind events. The gap between his wordy, complacent prose and the Soviet public mood became unbridgeable long ago. In the book, Yevtushenko launches crusades against nuclear war, against the monopoly of the Party, against

HE KNEW WHAT MATTERED MOST TO HIM. HE WANTED A ROLE IN SOCIETY; HE WANTED TO BE ACCEPTED AS A POET."

Russian chauvinism, against cruelty to animals, and lots of other unsavory phenomena. Most of his thoughts on these topics are with the angels. But they are still wrapped in the old Soviet discourse, and that discourse is finally as dead as nails. He strives to improve his fatherland without rejecting the main part of the ideology that makes such a project hopeless. He is what he always was, a man of fatal half-truths, of fatal half measures. In this way, he is the counterpart of his presumably avid reader Gorbachev. Both attempt to promote something like totalitarianism with a human face. It never worked. It never will.

Source: Tomas Venclova, "Making It," in *New Republic*, May 6, 1991, pp. 33–37.

Thomas D'Evelyn

In the following article, D'Evelyn discusses several of Yevtushenko's most famous poems, including "Babii Yar."

For about 30 years now, Yevgeny Yevtushenko has lit up the international scene with his unique fireworks, a blend of chutzpah, charm, and sheer gall. His most recent coup—a teaching stint at the University of Pennsylvania—brings the career of this Soviet poet to a pinnacle of success. Now the publication of his complete poems in English [*The Complete Poems*] will provide opportunities for a long look at the basis of his career, a large body of poems of diverse kinds that is at once accessible and beguilingly obscure.

Yevtushenko was 20 when Stalin died. He rode the anti-Stalin wave to prominence, reading in front of thousands and selling tens of thousands of his books of poetry. Even when the inevitable swerve came and Khrushchev attacked modern art, Yevtushenko kept baiting dogmatic bureaucrats and those he would call "comradwhatifers" in a poem. He also spoke in solidarity with Jews. In 1963, the great hammer fell. Yevtushenko was forced to confess his irreparable error. While others, like Solzhenitsyn, chose silence, Yevtushenko got a second wind and was praised by party organs for his civic-mindedness.

This patriot, who has achieved extraordinary freedom of movement, uses the word "international" as a term of highest praise. In one of his earliest and most publicized poems, "Babii Yar," he addresses his audience: "O my Russian people! / I know / you / are international to the core." While this cannot be taken literally, it does confirm usage elsewhere. For Yevtushenko, patriotism and internationalism do not conflict.

Yet the springs of Yevtushenko's art appear to well up from the same source that fed the great Russian novelists of the 19th century. In his introduction to *The Collected Poems, 1952–1990*, Albert C. Todd says, "Confession, grappling with self-understanding, is the impetus behind most of the poems that are mistakenly understood to be merely social or political. His sharpest attacks on moral cowardice begin with a struggle within his own conscience."

Yevtushenko wrote in 1965: "The first presentiment of a poem / in a true poet / is the feeling of sin / committed somewhere, sometime." His experience in the '60s gave him many opportunities for his brand of poetry. In 1964 he published the big patriotic poem "Bratsk Hydroelectric Station." Although he's silent about the cruel slave labor used to erect the station, in a section entitled "Monologue of the Egyptian Pyramid," he does mention the whip under which the Egyptian slaves labored. The comparison seems obvious and intentional.

Yevtushenko often uses the monologue to speak indirectly about himself. In "Monologue of an Actress," he speaks as an actress from Broadway who can't find a suitable role. "Without some sort of role, life / is simply slow rot," she says.

This throws light on the public nature of Yevtushenko's calling as a poet, as well as on his passivity toward events. Despite the confessional nature of much of his poetry, he needs public events—including his own feelings, which he makes public—to become inspired.

In "Monologue of a Loser" (1978), he voices the moral ambiguity of one who has played the game of moral dice, the game into which every poet in a closed society must buy if he wishes a big public. "My modest loss was this: / dozens of tons of verses, / the whole globe, / my country, / my friends, / my wife,/ I myself—/ but on that account, however, / I'm not very upset. / Such trifles / as honor / I forgot to consider."

Other poems put his difficulties more objectively.

In "My Handwriting," he symbolizes the Soviet ship of state as a "pugnacious coastal freighter." The lurch and list of the freighter makes it difficult for the poet to write neatly. Besides that, it's very cold. "Here—/ fingers simply grew numb. / Here—/ the swell slyly tormented. / Here—/ the pen jerked with uncertainty / away from some mean shoal." Nevertheless, sometimes "an idea breaks through the way a freighter on the Lena / breaks through to the arctic shore—." Most poets wouldn't shift the metaphor this way, using it first as a narrative idea, then using it to point to a specific experience.

Todd suggests in the introduction that "ultimately Yevtushenko will be judged as a poet, a popular people's poet in the tradition of Walt Whitman." But Yevtushenko himself uses the uncompromising standards of art to illuminate his moral life. In "Verbosity," he confesses, "I am verbose both in my daily life / and in my verse— that's your bad luck—/ but I am cunning: I realize / that there's no lack of will / behind this endless drivel, / rather my strong ill will!" In the end, though, he admits that "Eternal verities rest on the precise; / precision, though, consists in sacrifice. / Not for nothing does the bard get scared—/ the price of brevity is blood. / Like fear of prophecies contained in dreams, / the fear of writing down eternal words / is the real reason for verbosity." Writing this clearly about the moral intersection of poetry and precision is no mean achievement.

It helps to read Yevtushenko literally. Doubtless Yevtushenko felt he was speaking for thousands like him. In "The Art of Ingratiating," he seems to speak for the whole country. "Who among us has not become a stutterer, / when, like someone dying of hunger / begging from ladies on the porch steps, / we mealymouth: / 'I want to call long-distance . . .' / How petty authorities / propagate themselves! / How they embody / the supreme insolence!" Then he reports a prophetic dream: "By breeding / bulldogs / from mutts, / we ourselves / have fostered / our own boors. / I have a nightmare / that in the Volga / our groveling / has begotten / a crocodile." The well wisher who now contemplates the self-destruction of perestroika may well hear in Yevtushenko's words the feelings of Gorbachev himself. Bulldogs and crocodiles indeed!

On the other hand, it's tempting to simply say of Yevtushenko's collected poems, "how they embody the supreme insolence!" For all his clarity, Yevtushenko does not seem to anticipate certain cruel ironies. He writes "To Incomprehensible Poets," and confesses, "My guilt is in my simplicity. / My crime is my clarity. / I am the most comprehensible of worms," he may not hear his audiences silently agreeing. When he says to the incomprehensible poets (he has in mind some of the main lines of modern Russian poetry), "No restraint frightens you. / No one has bridled you with clear ideas." But he may not realize that the kinds of "restraint" he accepts as a public poet are child's play compared with the restraints accepted by Pasternak and Joseph Brodsky, restraints that originate in the subtlety of their analysis and the purity of their taste. Finally, when he says, "All the same it is frightening / to be understood like me / in the wrong way, / all of my life / to write comprehensibly / and depart / so hopelessly uncomprehended," one cannot be too sympathetic.

Long ago he stuck up for the Jews and recited his poem "Babii Yar" one too many times. Khrushchev exploded at him. This was the turning point of his career and his life. He knew what mattered most to him. He wanted a role in society; he wanted to be accepted as a poet.

In his own eyes, on his own terms, Yevtushenko has been highly successful. If he does not go down as a great Russian poet, it's because choosing to be what he has become meant he could not travel the higher road of art.

Source: Thomas D'Evelyn, "A Soviet Whitman," in *Christian Science Monitor*, March 8, 1991, p. 10.

SOURCES

Braham, Randolph L., ed., *Contemporary Views on the Holocaust*, Springer, 1983, pp. 154–55.

Conquest, Robert, "The Sad Case of Yevgeny Yevtushenko: The Politics of Poetry," in *New York Times Magazine*, September 30, 1973, pp. 16–7, 56, 58–60, 62, 64, 69–70.

Cotter, James Finn, "The Truth of Poetry," in *Hudson Review*, Vol. 44, No. 2, Summer 1991, pp. 343–48, 350–51.

Gitelman, Zvi Y., ed., *Bitter Legacy: Confronting the Holocaust in the USSR*, Indiana University Press, 1997, pp. 20–1.

Gubar, Susan, *Poetry after Auschwitz: Remembering What One Never Knew*, Indiana University Press, 2003, pp. xvii, 7–8.

Khiterer, Victoria, "Babi Yar, the Tragedy of Kiev's Jews," in *Brandeis Graduate Journal*, Vol. 2, 2004, http://www.brandeis.edu/gsa/gradjournal/2004/khiterer2004.pdf (accessed February 8, 2008).

Korey, William, "The Origins and Development of Soviet Anti-Semitism: An Analysis," in *Slavic Review*, Vol. 31, No. 1, March 1972, pp. 111–35.

Langer, Lawrence L., ed., *Art from the Ashes: A Holocaust Anthology*, Oxford University Press, 1995, p. 3.

Mandel, Naomi, "Rethinking 'After Auschwitz': Against a Rhetoric of the Unspeakable in Holocaust Writing," in *boundary 2*, Vol. 28, No. 2, 2001, pp. 203–28.

Reydt, Peter, "British Government Does Not Prosecute Nazi War Criminal," January 5, 2000, http://www.wsws.org/articles/2000/jan2000/nazi-j05.shtml (accessed January 4, 2008).

Schwartz, Harry, "Popular Poet Is Accused of Slandering Russians by Hint That Bigotry Continues in Soviet Union," in *New York Times*, September 28, 1961, p. 22.

Shein, Louis J., Review of *The Poetry of Yevgeny Yevtushenko, 1953–1965*, translated by George Reavey, in *Russian Review*, Vol. 25, No. 2, April 1966, p. 210.

Shelley, Percy Bysshe, *A Defense of Poetry*, 1821, reprinted in *Critical Theory since Plato*, edited by Hazard Adams, Harcourt Brace Jovanovich, 1971, pp. 500–13.

Sidney, Sir Philip, *The Defence of Poesy*, 1595, reprinted in *Sidney's "The Defence of Poesy" and Selected Renaissance Literary Criticism*, edited by Gavin Alexander, Penguin, 2004, pp. 1–54.

Sosland, Benjamin, "A Premiere Recalls the Horror of Babi Yar," in *Juilliard Journal*, Vol. 22, No. 4, December 2006.

Van Biema, David, "Yevgeny Yevtushenko: Nagged by Mortality and Accusations of Compromise, the Aging Boy Wonder Hungers to Leave an Indelible Legacy," in *People Weekly*, March 31, 1986, pp. 70–4.

Venclova, Tomas, "Making It," in *New Republic*, May 6, 1991, pp. 33–7.

Wiesel, Elie, "Trivializing the Holocaust: Semi-Fact and Semi-Fiction," in *New York Times*, April 16, 1978.

Yevtushenko, Yevgeny, "Babii Yar," in *Early Poems*, edited and translated by George Reavey, Marion Boyars, 1966; reprinted, 1989, pp. 144–49.

FURTHER READING

Bergen, Doris L., *War & Genocide: A Concise History of the Holocaust*, Rowman & Littlefield, 2003.

As the title of this book makes clear, this short text provides an easy to read and understand introduction to the events that occurred during the period that came to be called the Holocaust.

Duffy, Peter, *The Bielski Brothers: The True Story of Three Men Who Defied the Nazis, Saved 1,200 Jews, and Built a Village in the Forest*, HarperCollins, 2003.

This book is a very readable and true story of three brothers who hid in the forest while the Nazis murdered their parents, siblings, and the rest of the villagers in their small Belorussian town. The brothers formed a guerilla fighting unit that successfully waged war against the Nazis.

Figes, Orlando, *The Whisperers: Private Life in Stalin's Russia*, Metropolitan Books, 2007.

This book presents personal stories of life in a repressive regime, with almost every family facing reprisals, the gulag, or forced resettlement during Stalin's years as dictator.

Megargee, Geoffrey P., *War of Annihilation: Combat and Genocide on the Eastern Front, 1941*, Rowman & Littlefield, 2006.

Megargee provides a concise history of the German army's initial campaign as it invaded the Soviet Union in 1941. Much of the focus of this book is on the brutality of the Germany military officers, who historically blamed the genocide that occurred on the Eastern Front on the Nazis and not the army.

Wiesenthal, Simon, *The Sunflower: On the Possibilities and Limits of Forgiveness*, rev. ed., Schocken Books, 1998.

In the first section of this book, Wiesenthal relates a story of how, as a prisoner of war in a concentration camp, he was brought in to see a dying SS officer who asked the prisoner to forgive him for what had happened to the Jewish people. In the second part of the book, Wiesenthal asks a number of well-known intellectuals whether he should have offered forgiveness to the soldier.

Diving into the Wreck

ADRIENNE RICH

1973

"Diving into the Wreck," by the American poet Adrienne Rich, was first published as the title poem in her collection *Diving into the Wreck* in 1973. The book is still in print, and the poem also appears in the 2002 *Norton Anthology of American Literature*. The early 1970s was a time when the women's movement was having a significant influence on American society, and Rich's poem reflects her interest in feminism, taking the form of a heroic quest. The poet/speaker presents herself as a deep-sea diver who plunges into the ocean to examine the remains of an old sailing ship. The wreck she examines has different levels of meaning, referring to the neglected, unexamined inner lives of women, or perhaps to civilization itself, ruined by false ideas and stereotypes about gender and gender roles. The poet hopes to discard these falsehoods. "Diving into the Wreck" has had a prominent place in Rich's oeuvre ever since its publication. It expresses her search for the truth about women's lives and also represents an important landmark in the literature of second-wave feminism.

AUTHOR BIOGRAPHY

One of America's leading contemporary poets, Adrienne Rich was born on May 16, 1929, in Baltimore, Maryland. Her father, Arnold Rich, was a professor of pathology at Johns Hopkins University, and her mother, Helen Jones Rich,

Adrienne Rich (AP Images)

was a pianist and composer. Rich attended Radcliffe College, graduating in 1951 with an AB (cum laude). That same year she published her first book of poetry, *A Change of World*, for which she was awarded the Yale Younger Poets Prize. Two years later, Rich married Alfred Conrad, a Harvard economist, and moved to Cambridge, Massachusetts. The couple had three sons over the next five years.

Rich found her true poetic voice in the 1960s, beginning in 1963 with the publication of *Snapshots of a Daughter-in-Law*, her third book of poetry, in which she first expressed her emerging feminist ideas. Rich and her family moved to New York in 1966, where she taught a remedial English program at City College. This was during the period when the feminist, civil rights, and anti-Vietnam War movements were growing in strength, and Rich became deeply engaged in these social issues. Her beliefs were reflected in her books, *Necessities of Life* (1966), *Leaflets* (1969), and *Will to Change* (1971). In 1969 she separated from her husband, who committed suicide a year later.

"Diving into the Wreck" was first published as the title poem in her 1973 collection. *Diving into the Wreck* received lavish praise from critics

and won the National Book Award for Poetry, but Rich refused to accept the award for herself. Instead, she joined with two other female poets and accepted it on behalf of all women whose voices had been silenced.

Many other poetry volumes followed, including *Twenty-One Love Poems* (1976), *A Wild Patience Has Taken Me This Far* (1981), *The Fact of a Doorframe* (1984), *Your Native Land, Your Life* (1986), *Time's Power* (1989), *An Atlas of the Difficult World* (1991), *Dark Fields of the Republic* (1995), *Midnight Salvage* (1999), and *Fox* (2000). Her collection *The School among the Ruins: Poems, 2000–2004* (2004), won the National Book Critics Circle Award. This was one of many literary awards Rich has received, including the first Ruth Lilly Poetry Prize, the Brandeis Creative Arts Medal, the Common Wealth Award, the William Whitehead Award for Lifetime Achievement, and the National Poetry Association Award for Distinguished Service to the Art of Poetry. In 1997 Rich refused the National Medal of Arts because she disagreed with the policies of the Clinton administration. Rich has also written many volumes of prose, including *Of Woman Born: Motherhood as Experience and Institution* (1976), *On Lies, Secrets, and Silence* (1979), *Blood, Bread, and Poetry* (1986), *What Is Found There: Notebooks on Poetry and Politics* (1993), and *Arts of the Possible: Essays and Conversations* (2001).

Rich has taught at many colleges and universities, including Swarthmore, Columbia, Brandeis, Rutgers, Cornell, San Jose State, and Stanford University. She was a professor of English and feminist studies at Stanford University from 1986 to 1992. Since 1976, Rich has lived with Michelle Cliff, her partner, a writer and editor.

POEM SUMMARY

Stanzas 1–3
At the literal level of the poem, the speaker of "Diving into the Wreck," who could be either male or female, is in a schooner out at sea, preparing to dive into the ocean in search of a wreck. The journey she (assuming a female speaker) is about to take is both external and internal, since she is also journeying into the depths of her own psyche and, symbolically, into history and society. Taking with her a camera and a knife, she

MEDIA ADAPTATIONS

- *Adrienne Rich Reading at Stanford* was produced by the Stanford Program for Recordings in Sound in 1973. Rich reads fourteen of her poems on the recording, including "Diving into the Wreck."

puts on her rubber diving outfit, including mask and flippers. Then she comments that unlike Jacques Cousteau, the famous twentieth-century French marine explorer, she has no team of helpers to assist her; she is going to dive alone. There is a ladder hanging from the side of the schooner, and the speaker descends. As she begins her descent she is very conscious of the daylight and the air, the normal, familiar environment in which humans live. Her flippers make her feel uncomfortable as she descends the ladder with difficulty, conscious of the fact that she is alone, with no one to guide her.

Stanzas 4–6
She reaches the water and descends into it, conscious of how her visual environment has changed from the blue of the sky to the green of the water, which quickly turns to black. She is grateful for her mask and now has to learn how to move underwater, which is much different from moving about on land and requires a new set of skills. As she surveys the scene underwater, observing the teeming marine life, she realizes that she must focus her mind on the purpose of her dive and not forget it. The speaker reminds herself that she has come to explore the remains of a sunken ship. She wants to examine the extent of the damage the wreck has suffered and also to find what valuables remain.

Stanzas 7–10
The speaker explains that what she really wants is to find out the true condition of the ship, which may not be the same as what she has read or heard about it. The conventional wisdom about the ship may only be a myth. Just before she

arrives at the wreck, she pictures to herself the effigy of a female face that was carved on the prow of the old sailing ship, which always looked upward, and she thinks of the damage the wreck has undergone in all the years it has spent underwater, with just a skeleton of its form remaining. She finally arrives at the wreck in stanza 8 and imagines herself as a mermaid that can take both male and female form. In this kind of imaginative androgynous form she swims all around the wreck and enters its hold. She refers again to the female face on the prow and then appears to find the ship's cargo of precious metals inside rotting barrels. She also discovers the messy, worn-away remnants of other parts of the ship's equipment, including its log and compass. The poem ends with an affirmation of the importance of making such a journey, whatever the motivation for undertaking it. The allusion here is clearly to the journey as one of inner exploration in search of the truth, the real truth as opposed to what others may have said.

THEMES

The Search for Truth
Although the poem can be read at the literal level, it is really about the exploration of the areas of the speaker's mind, heart, and experience of life that have, for whatever reason, not been examined before. It relates a journey from the conscious, surface levels of the mind, the everyday reality of life, to the deeper subconscious levels that have been ignored, repressed, or distorted by self and others. The schooner on which the poet stands is the metaphoric equivalent of the everyday world: it exists in the daylight and the sunlight. The water into which the poet dives represents the deeper levels of the mind, and the ship discovered there represents the parts of the psyche that have not been consciously acknowledged. The poet is determined to discover the truth about these murky, unexplored regions, which is why she takes with her a knife (to dissect what she finds and to distinguish truth from falsehood) and a camera, which will record with absolute fidelity and without distortion what is truly present. There will be no convenient distortions to make life more superficially comfortable: the truth must be faced.

That this is a difficult undertaking is made abundantly clear, because the speaker has to don

TOPICS FOR FURTHER STUDY

- Other than anatomical differences, are there any other innate differences between men and women? Are all psychological and emotional differences the result of cultural influence and gender stereotyping? Are some roles in society more appropriate for one gender than for the other? Why do conservatives and liberals differ in their responses to these questions? Write an essay in which you discuss these issues.

- Write a report describing some of the gains made by second-wave feminism from the 1960s to the early 1990s. Given this progress, conclude your report by discussing what you think feminism has yet to accomplish.

- Bearing in mind that "Diving into the Wreck" advocates truthful inquiry into difficult situations, write a free verse poem in which the speaker faces up to an uncomfortable truth about his or her life, perhaps a situation or an inner conflict that he or she has been reluctant to acknowledge or deal with for some time.

- Read several other poems in *Diving into the Wreck* and conduct a class presentation in which you compare them to the title poem. Are the other poems more or less overtly feminist? What attitude does the poet show toward men, and how does that compare to the attitude shown in "Diving into the Wreck"?

uncomfortable clothing, complete with mask, rubber diving suit, and flippers, and get used to exploring unfamiliar regions. Different skills are called for than those that equip a person to succeed in everyday life, in which people may be compelled to adopt surface personas that are far from the truth of who they really are. And yet these subconscious regions of the mind, including desires, feelings, and hopes that have been repressed perhaps since childhood because the conscious mind decided that they were unacceptable, contain vital elements that are necessary for the person's psyche to be whole. This is clear from the fact that the cargo of the wreck contained precious metals, many of which remain within the shell of the sunken ship, waiting to be rediscovered by the intrepid explorer. This section of the poem (the penultimate stanza) also suggests the wisdom inherent in the deeper, unconscious levels of the psyche, since it refers to the instruments that once kept the ship on course. Getting in touch with those forgotten instruments (the authentic self rather than the socially acceptable self) is essential if the speaker is to live a life true to herself rather than to the standards and expectations of others.

Exploring Gender Roles and Their Meaning

The poem has a social as well as a personal dimension. Written by a female poet in the early 1970s, it is a plea for the voices of women to be heard by society. The collective rather than individual element in the poem is clear from the reference that the poet makes to the book in the first and last lines of the poem. This is probably a reference to the patriarchal nature of American society at the time, in which men determined what was important and what was true; in doing so they left women out of the discourse and tried to shape women's lives as they thought they ought to be, without reference to what women might actually want or be capable of achieving. This is why the book is referred to as a myth, since it does not record the truth and, as the last line suggests, often ignores the lives of women altogether. In this sense the poem can be read as a kind of feminist manifesto, according to which women must learn to understand the truth of their own lives and maintain that truth in the face of male ignorance and prejudice. However, the feminist interpretation does not exclude other interpretations, since the poet is careful to show the diver as an androgynous figure as he/she swims around the wreck. The implication is that both men and women need to be liberated from restrictive gender roles. It is in the interests of men as much as women that a more equitable society should be created, one in which women are as free as men have always been to achieve their goals and ambitions.

STYLE

Free Verse

The poem is written in free verse, which does not conform to traditional patterns of meter and rhyme. It became a popular form of verse during the 1960s, when it represented, as it does in this poem, a rebellion against traditional form that paralleled the spirit of political and social upheaval and rebellion that characterized the decade. Thus, "Diving into the Wreck," a poem that has a feminist theme, is not restricted by any formal rhyme or meter but follows its own individual shape and rhythm. The poem is arranged in ten stanzas, ranging in length from seven to twelve lines. The lines are of many different lengths, as short as two syllables and as long as twelve. Thus the poem breaks with traditional form in the same way that it calls for a breaking with tradition in terms of women's place in society. Form and theme complement each other.

Metaphor

The controlling metaphors are those of the deep-sea diver and the sunken wreck. Almost every image in the poem belongs in one or other of these categories, creating a broadly unified effect. The first metaphor, of the diver, represents the individual speaker. The speaker is on a quest to explore the crushed, buried aspects of the mind and heart; she probably represents all women who have been forced to suppress their deepest desires, longings, and ambitions because they were dominated by men, both individually and collectively, who arranged society for their own benefit rather than in an equitable manner. The sunken wreck represents everything that has been forgotten, devalued, and suppressed, all of which could have been of enormous value to the individual and to society had it been used properly. Instead, it has been left to rot.

HISTORICAL CONTEXT

The Beginnings of the Modern Women's Movement

The opening line of "Diving into the Wreck," about a female speaker who has read a book of myths, might be interpreted to mean the ways in which American culture viewed women and the role they were expected to play in society before the feminist movement arose. This would be America in the 1950s, when Rich was a young mother married to a Harvard professor and raising her three sons. In those days this was considered the ideal role for women: They stayed at home and raised the children while their husband was the breadwinner. According to statistics cited by William Chafe in *The Road to Equality: American Women since 1962*, in 1960, only one married woman in four held a paid job. If women did join the workforce, certain jobs, such as secretary, nurse, receptionist, bank teller, and clerk, were considered women's jobs, while only the unusual woman was given the opportunity to become a lawyer or a doctor, and even more rarely did women occupy senior positions in corporations. In 1960, women earned only 59 percent of what men received. This was a world in which men had all the power and privilege, a situation that was justified by the notion that this was a natural division of the sexes, sanctioned by tradition and even religious scriptures. It was presented as the truth of how things had to be, but emerging feminists understood it to be only a culturally generated myth.

The status quo between the genders began to change in the 1960s, a decade of immense social upheaval that included the civil rights movement. A landmark year for feminism was 1963, which coincidentally was also the year when Rich began to find her own authentic poetic voice. In that year the Presidential Commission on the Status of Women, created by President John F. Kennedy, reported that there was significant discrimination against women in employment and recommended improvements in the areas of fair hiring, training and promotion, paid maternity leave, and child care. Also in 1963 Congress passed the Equal Pay Act, which banned discrimination on the basis of gender and established the principle of equal pay for equal work and responsibility. And that same year Betty Friedan published her book *The Feminine Mystique*, which is widely credited with launching what is known as the second-wave feminist movement. The book was an eloquent and passionate protest against the restricted roles that society imposed on women, especially middle-class women.

In 1964, the Civil Rights Act banned discrimination in employment on the basis of gender or race. Two years later, feminists including Friedan founded the National Organization of

COMPARE
&
CONTRAST

- **1970s:** Female poets such as Alice Walker, Marilyn Hacker, Marge Piercy, Linda Hogan, and Sharon Olds begin to make their mark on American poetry. Feminist writers argue their case in influential books such as *Sexual Politics* (1970), by Kate Millett, and *The Female Eunuch* (1971), by Germaine Greer. Publishing houses such as Feminist Press and Virago Press are established solely to publish work by women. *Ms.* magazine is founded in 1972 by Gloria Steinem and her associates to espouse the goals of the women's movement and challenge the images of women presented in traditional women's magazines.

  Today: Women's publishing houses continue to flourish, although they face challenges due to the rising costs of publishing and the advent of alternative sources of information for readers, such as the Internet. However, the market for feminist writings now extends to mainstream publishing houses, which are eager to publish books with feminist themes. The popularity of books by and about women may partly be due to the continuing growth of women's studies at universities, which indicates that feminist thought is no longer a minority interest but is part of the cultural mainstream.

- **1970s:** As second-wave feminism develops, it produces different kinds of approaches to ending discrimination against women. Organizations such as NOW take a liberal approach, emphasizing the need to expand opportunities for women at the individual level. More radical feminists take a collective approach in which they oppose the entire patriarchal system in all its aspects—social, political, economic, and cultural.

  Many such feminists see their struggle in terms of class warfare. Other feminist groups include socialist feminists and lesbian feminists.

  Today: The newest generation of feminists are part of what is known as third-wave feminism, which began in the 1990s among women who came of age in the 1980s and who had grown up with an awareness of feminist issues. One prominent third-wave feminist is Rebecca Walker. In her introduction to a collection of essays titled *To Be Real: Telling the Truth and Changing the Face of Feminism* (1995), Walker criticizes earlier feminism because it sought to apply a new orthodoxy about how women were supposed to be.

- **1970s:** According to statistics supplied by the U.S. Department of Labor, in 1970, more women are employed in the labor force than ever before in U.S. history. Mothers are more likely to work outside the home than ever before. However, the earnings gap between men and women is considerable; families headed by a woman who works are more likely to live in poverty than those headed by a man; and women tend to work in low-income occupations that do not reflect their educational achievements.

  Today: According to NOW, women who work full time still earn only 77 percent of what men are paid. Although women have more opportunities to succeed in professions such as medicine, law, and business, the "glass ceiling," which prevents them from reaching their field's most senior positions, remains firmly in place.

Women (NOW). The goals of NOW included the passing of the Equal Rights Amendment to the Constitution, guarantees of equal employment opportunity, the right to paid maternity leave, publicly provided child-care facilities, equality in education, job training and housing for women living in poverty, and the legal right to abortion. NOW grew rapidly, from 300 members in 1966 to 48,000 in 1974 (as cited in Judith Papachristou's *Women Together: A History of the Women's Movement in the United States*).

While this political action was taking place to improve the lot of women, feminist writers were analyzing the psychological and sociological bases of the new movement. As Judith Hole and Ellen Levine state in their book *Rebirth of Feminism*, there were two aspects to this process. First, feminists had to counter the "biological differences" argument: "The single most important assumption of feminist analysis is that there are no inherent emotional, intellectual, or psychological differences between men and women. All differences that are considered to be rooted in 'nature' are ... a reflection of socially-imposed values." The second aspect of the feminist argument of the era was a "social critique" in which the differences between men's and women's social values and institutions were viewed as the result of "sex-role stereotyping."

Feminism in the Early 1970s

Although gains had been made, in 1970 women still represented a substantially disadvantaged portion of the population in terms of economic opportunity. According to statistics issued by the Women's Bureau of the U.S. Department of Labor in 1970, as cited in *Rebirth of Feminism*, women were significantly underrepresented in the leading professions. Women made up only 9 percent of scientists, 7 percent of physicians, 3 percent of lawyers, and 1 percent of engineers and federal judges. Starting salaries for college graduates in every field from accounting to liberal arts were considerably lower for women than they were for men.

However, during the 1970s the women's movement continued to make a huge impact on American culture and society. In 1972 the Equal Rights Amendment (ERA) was passed by Congress and sent to the states for ratification, a goal of feminist activists for fifty years. (In 1982 the ERA perished because it was not ratified by the minimum thirty-eight states required under the Constitution.) Also in 1972, Title IX of the Education Amendments Act banned gender discrimination in colleges and universities receiving federal aid. The result was a dramatic increase in the number of college sports programs available to women. A major landmark in the achievement of feminist goals came in 1973,

when the Supreme Court ruled in *Roe v. Wade* that a woman's right to abortion was enshrined in the Constitution because of inherent privacy rights. Before this, abortion had been illegal in many states.

During the early 1970s the new opportunities for women were reflected in an upsurge of political participation. According to Chafe in *The Road to Equality*, from 1972 to 1974 the number of women candidates for state legislatures increased by 300 percent; participation by women in party political conventions also showed dramatic increases.

Along with these social and political changes, feminists set out to change the images of women presented in the media that reinforced the traditional notion that a woman's place was in the home. Feminists also mounted crusades against pornography, which they believed exploited women and contributed to sexual violence against women. The women's movement also opposed beauty pageants, arguing that such contests treated women as sexualized objects rather than as people.

CRITICAL OVERVIEW

Since its publication in 1973, "Diving into the Wreck" has been held in high esteem by scholars of Rich's poetry. The poem is considered central to her life's work as a whole. In an interpretation of the poem in *Adrienne Rich's Poetry*, Wendy Martin comments that "the poet returns alone to the sea, the origin of life, to explore 'the wreck' of civilization in an effort to determine what went wrong." Once she arrives at the wreck, "she accepts the wreck and learns what she can from it as a necessary prelude to beginning again." Erica Jong, in her essay in the same volume, asserts that "the old myths of patriarchy ... that split male and female irreconcilably into two warring factions" must yield to Rich's "image of the androgyne" with "its idea that we must write new myths, create new definitions of humanity which will not glorify this angry chasm but heal it." Judith McDaniel, in *Reconstituting the World: The Poetry and Vision of Adrienne Rich*, notes that the poem "is Rich's most complex use of an image of rebirth." The wreck itself is "the history of all women submerged in a patriarchal culture; it is that source of myths about male and female sexuality which shape our lives and roles today." McDaniel also notes

Scuba diver moving toward shipwreck on seabed,
Bermuda *(Stephen Frink / Digital Vision /Getty Images)*

that the reader is "given no explanation for why the wreck occurred. Nor is there any account of the swimmer's return, the use to which she puts this new information." For Cheri Colby Langdell, author of *Adrienne Rich: The Moment of Change*, the poem "embodies a true epic quest, with hero, mission, myth, epic locale." Langdell notes the originality of the poet's "focus on androgyny" and describes the epic quest as a journey that "becomes both a spiritual quest and a recollection of alienated parts of the hero's—or rather heroine's—self, a reconciliation or restitution of what is lost."

CRITICISM

Bryan Aubrey

Aubrey holds a PhD in English. In this essay on "Diving into the Wreck," he discusses the images of women that were presented in American culture during the 1950s and 1960s and how such stereotypes impacted the poem.

No reader of Adrienne Rich's "Diving into the Wreck" will be left in any doubt about the difficulty of the underwater journey that the speaker undertakes. Simply to make the metaphorical dive itself is an act of courage, a refusal to accept the status quo, an affirmation of the duty of the individual to investigate for herself what is true and what is false, even if society as a whole seems satisfied with the version of truth that it has decided upon. Throughout the poem the perilous nature of the journey is emphasized; it involves a completely different way of being in the world, a different way of moving, a different way even of breathing, and certainly a different way of examining evidence. Also emphasized is the isolation of the speaker. There is no support along the way, no advisors or guides to help the underwater traveler. She is on her own. This is a journey away from the group mind, which is easily satisfied with lazy generalizations, in the direction of the power of the individual to discern the real nature of things for herself, if she can keep her nerve and trust the truths she uncovers.

The poem might be considered pessimistic. After all, the speaker descends in search of a wreck. The wreck might refer to the inner, true lives of all women, which have been undervalued and suppressed to the point where they barely exist anymore, worn away by the constant pressure from a male-dominated society that is not interested in acknowledging the reality of women's selves. The wreck is far gone and seems unsalvageable, and the speaker proposes no plan of rescue. Can any woman, given this wreckage, still find the lost things of value deep within herself? And, bearing in mind that the speaker is depicted at the end of stanza 8 as being androgynous—both male and female—can men also somehow liberate themselves from this same wreck? Just as women have been presented with a false image of themselves, so men have accepted a view of their own roles that is equally limiting.

Set against the rather pessimistic feelings generated by the poem is the striking, twice-mentioned image of the female face carved on the prow of the ship, which appears to have survived intact. The eyes are open and look up to the sun, an image that suggests the tenacity and will to survive of women in general, which seems to be

WHAT DO I READ NEXT?

- *The Fact of a Doorframe: Poems Selected and New, 1950–1984* (1984), by Adrienne Rich, is a collection largely culled from the poet's first nine books of poetry. Arranged in chronological order, the selection gives a good overview of how Rich's poetry developed over the period of more than thirty years.

- *No More Masks! An Anthology of Twentieth-Century American Women Poets* (1993), edited and with an introduction by Florence Howe, is an expanded and updated edition of an anthology first published in 1973. The anthology features over 400 poems by 104 poets from many different cultures and periods and includes a generous selection by second-wave feminist writers.

- *Strike Sparks: Selected Poems, 1980–2002* (2004), by Sharon Olds, is a representative selection from Olds's seven published volumes of poetry. Olds is one of America's leading female poets, popular with readers and hailed by critics. Her work covers many vital areas of human experience—including childhood, marriage and children, sexuality, and domestic and political violence—with candor and unwavering insight.

- *The Beauty Myth: How Images of Beauty Are Used against Women* (2002), by Naomi Wolf, was first published in 1992. It shows the persistence, even after decades of the women's movement, of the supposedly ideal images of women that appear in popular culture. Wolf argues that women should accept their own natural beauty, even if it does not conform to an ideal imposed by society.

- *Faces of Feminism: An Activist's Reflections on the Women's Movement* (1997), by Sheila Tobias, is largely a history of the women's movement in the United States from the 1960s to the 1980s. Tobias documents the successes and failures of the movement and also offers personal reflections about her own involvement.

---

confirmed by the fact that when the diver arrives at the scene he/she indeed discovers the precious metals that remain. It is as if the essence, the gem-like quality of the inner self remains, even in the midst of all the destruction that time and culture have wrought on both men and women.

Other significant images, of knife and camera, suggest an optimism, too. Culturally disadvantaged they may be, but women still possess the tools they need to reexamine themselves and their fate, and the same tools are possessed also by men, should they decide to use them for a similarly ruthless self-examination. The knife will cut through everything that is false, and the camera can record with photographic realism the truth. As the saying goes, the camera does not lie.

One of the central ideas of "Diving into the Wreck" is of a prevailing myth. The poem begins and ends with reference to a book of myths, which the speaker admits to having read; at the end of the poem she claims to have not found his/her name in it. The book of myths refers to the reality that has been created by society, which distorts both men's and women's understandings of themselves. Their true natures are not allowed to appear in this book, recording as it does a false history and a false culture that boys and girls are nonetheless raised to believe in without question, and which most adult men and women do not challenge. In creating myths about women, men have also created myths about themselves, which means that both sexes are equally trapped in a web of illusions about gender and identity.

But what exactly were those myths that operated in American society during the 1950s and 1960s, when Adrienne Rich was herself a

> IN CREATING MYTHS ABOUT WOMEN, MEN HAVE ALSO CREATED MYTHS ABOUT THEMSELVES, WHICH MEANS THAT BOTH SEXES ARE EQUALLY TRAPPED IN A WEB OF ILLUSIONS ABOUT GENDER AND IDENTITY."

young woman, a wife and mother raising three sons? Times have changed greatly since those decades, and young Americans today live in a culture that is fundamentally different in terms of how women's roles in society are perceived. Women today do not have to undertake the ruthless stripping away of misleading cultural stereotypes that Rich and the women of her generation were forced to undertake.

In her seminal book *The Feminine Mystique* (1963), Betty Friedan refers precisely to this cultural myth as "the feminine mystique," a set of ideas about women's nature and correct role in life that had been universally adopted, even by women themselves, during the two decades following the end of World War II. According to the underlying premise of the feminine mystique, there are innate differences between men and women not only in biology but also in emotional and psychological make up. A woman finds her fulfillment in being a wife and a mother. This is her preordained "feminine" role. As Friedan puts it, as long as this view prevails, "there is no other way for a woman to dream of creation or of the future. There is no way she can even dream about herself, except as her children's mother, her husband's wife." A woman's task is to make sure that her husband is happy, and this will also ensure that she keeps him. Her job is to clean the house, cook the meals, and raise the children while her husband pursues his career, earns all the money, and makes all the important decisions. Belief in the feminine mystique created a situation, Friedan points out, in which the drudgery, the endless repetitive routine of housework, was the only "career" available to women. This meant that a woman's mental horizons were necessarily narrow. Women were not interested in the wider world, the world of politics and social issues, which was the domain of men. In *The Feminine*

Mystique Friedan tells a story about when she sat in on a meeting of mostly male magazine writers and editors. One editor of a women's magazine explained that his readers were not interested in national or international affairs; they were only interested in reading about family and home. After a guest speaker had talked about the nascent civil rights movement and how it might affect the upcoming presidential election, one editor remarked, "Too bad I can't run that story. But you just can't link it to woman's world."

The cultural myth of the feminine mystique was thus relentlessly reinforced by the mass media. A year after the publication of her groundbreaking work, Friedan was commissioned by *TV Guide* to write an article about how women were represented on television. For two weeks, Friedan watched television, morning, afternoon, and evening. After watching women in commercials, soap operas, situation comedies, and game shows and noting their almost complete absence in serious dramas or documentaries, she concluded in her essay that "television's image of the American woman, 1964, is a stupid, unattractive, insecure little household drudge who spends her martyred, mindless days dreaming of love—and plotting nasty revenge against her husband." In the article, which was later included in her collection *It Changed My Life: Writings on the Women's Movement*, Friedan calls for radical change: "Television badly needs some heroines. It needs more images of real women to help girls and women take themselves seriously and grow and love and be loved by men again."

Over forty years later, many of the changes in the media's presentation of women that feminists such as Friedan called for have taken place. Today, one can switch on the television and see any number of series about successful women lawyers, doctors, forensic scientists, athletes, and even action heroines who dish out violence to the bad guys as efficiently as any man. In the sphere of current events, there may be as many female news anchors as men, and women TV journalists regularly file reports from dangerous war zones. But in those far-off days in the 1950s and early 1960s, millions of American women, if they had time to watch any television at all (after spending so many hours scrubbing and waxing floors, running the washing machine, and trying to make themselves beautiful so that their husbands wouldn't leave them), would have seen this uniform, thoroughly impoverished image of women appear on the screen night after night.

This is the all-pervasive myth, or at least one aspect of it, that Rich's diver in "Diving into the Wreck" is determined to confront. The presence of the myth, which was affirmed and reinforced in every aspect of American culture, explains why the diver's journey is so perilous and difficult. How does one find truth when there are no cultural models to base it on? Such is the challenge taken up by Rich's diver.

Source: Bryan Aubrey, Critical Essay on "Diving into the Wreck," in *Poetry for Students*, Gale, Cengage Learning, 2009.

Matthew Rothschild

In the following interview, Rothschild speaks with Rich about poetry, feminism, and politics.

Adrienne Rich is one of the leading American poets of our century. For forty years, her distinguished writings have brought accolades, including the National Book Award, the Fellowship of American Poets, and the Poet's Prize. But as she puts it in her early 1980s poem "Sources," she is a "woman with a mission, not to win prizes/but to change the laws of history."

It is this mission that sets Rich apart, for she has forsaken the easy path of academic poetry and hurled herself into the political fray. An early feminist and an outspoken lesbian, she has served as a role model for a whole generation of political poets and activists. Consciously she has fused politics and poetry, and in so doing, she—along with Audre Lorde, June Jordan, and a small handful of colleagues—rediscovered and rejuvenated the lost American tradition of political poetry.

Her latest work, *What Is Found There: Notebooks on Poetry and Politics*, takes its title from a stanza of William Carlos Williams: "It is difficult/to get the news from poems/yet men die miserably every day for lack/of what is found there." This ambitious, sweeping work contains an elaborate defense of political poety, an intricate reading of three of her great predecessors (Walt Whitman, Emily Dickinson, and Muriel Rukeyser), and generous introductions to dozens of contemporary political poets. It also is a trenchant indictment of American society today and a turbulent coming-to-grips with her own citizenship. In this regard, it is a prose continuation of *An Atlas of the Difficult World: Poems 1988–1991*.

> OTHER PEOPLE'S POETRY HAS MADE A HUGE DIFFERENCE IN MY LIFE. IT HAS CHANGED THE WAY I SAW THE WORLD. IT HAS CHANGED THE WAY I FELT THE WORLD."

I spoke with her one cool sunny September afternoon on the patio of her modest home on the outskirts of Santa Cruz, California, which she shares with her partner, the novelist Michelle Cliff. When it became too cold, we went inside and finished the interview in her living room. Works by June Jordan and Audre Lorde rested on a nearby coffee table.

Q: In What Is Found There *you write that "poetry is banned in the United States," that it is "under house arrest." What do you mean?*

Adrienne Rich: When you think about almost any other country, any other culture, it's been taken for granted that poets would take part in the government, that they would be sent here and there as ambassadors by the state proudly, that their being poets was part of why they were considered valuable citizens—Yeats in Ireland, Neruda in Chile, St.-John Perse in France. At the same time, poets like Hikmet in Turkey, Mandelstam in the Soviet Union, Ritsos in Greece, and hundreds of others have been severely penalized for their writings, severely penalized for a single poem. But here it's the censorship of "who wants to listen to you, anyway?"—of carrying on this art in a country where it is perceived as so elite or effete or marginal that it has nothing to do with the hard core of things. That goes hand in hand with an attitude about politics, which is that the average citizen, the regular American, can't understand poetry and also can't understand politics, that both are somehow the realms of experts, that we are spectators of politics, rather than active subjects. I don't believe either is true.

Q: How did American poetry come to be viewed as so marginal?

Rich: Poetry in America became either answerable to a certain ideology—as it was, Puritanism—focusing on certain themes, expressive of certain attitudes, or it became identified in the Nineteenth Century with a certain femininity, the feminization of literature, what Nathaniel Hawthorne called "that horde of scribbling women." In *What Is Found There*, I suggest that in carrying out the genocide of the indigenous people, you had to destroy the indigenous poetry. The mainstream American tradition depends on the extirpation of memory and the inability of so many white American poets to deal with what it meant to be a North American poet—Whitman, of course, the great exception in his way, and in her own way Dickinson, so different but so parallel. And yet that still doesn't altogether explain it.

Q: What more is there?

Rich: I think there's been a great denial of the kinds of poets and poetries that could speak to a lot more people. Poetry has been kind of hoarded inside the schools, inside the universities. The activity of writing about poems and poetry the activity of making it available and accessible became the property of scholars and academics and became dependent on a certain kind of academic training, education, class background.

Q: Is that why people say, "I just don't get it. I don't understand poetry"?

Rich: It's something people say in reaction to feeling, "I don't know much about it. I haven't been exposed to a lot of it." It may also be a defense against what Muriel Rukeyser calls "the fear of poetry"—which she calls a disease of our schools.

Q: But a lot of contemporary political poetry is extremely clear and accessible, isn't it?

Rich: Instead of political poetry, we might want to say poetry of witness, poetry of dissent, poetry that is the voice of those and on behalf of those who are generally unheard. I'm reading poetry all the time that is enormously accessible in its language. And I don't mean by that using the smallest possible vocabulary. We're living in a country now where the range of articulateness has really diminished down to almost a TV level, where to hear people speaking with rich figures of speech, which used to be the property of everybody, is increasingly rare.

Q: What you call "the bleached language" of our era?

Rich: Yes. But I'm seeing a lot of poetry that is new, that is political in the broadest and richest sense. Fewer people would feel the "fear of poetry" if they heard it aloud as well as read it on the page. There are enormous poetry scenes now—poetry slams or competitions—they have the flavor of something that is still macho, but certainly lots of people go to them, and there are some remarkable women participants, like Patricia Smith. Throughout this country, there are readings that have nothing to do with academic sponsorship.

Q: The macho-ness, the turning of poetry into a competitive sport, does that trouble you at all?

Rich: For people to have a good time with it is wonderful. But in the past twenty years I have participated in and gone to so many women's poetry readings where the sense of building a voice, communally, was the thing rather than individuals trying to compete against each other to be the best, the winner. That sense of poetry as a communal art feels crucial to me. It's certainly something that has prevailed in other movements, as well. It was present in the antiwar movement, it was present certainly in the black liberation struggle of the 1960s, it's certainly present in the community activities and the community building of other groups in this country. So for poetry to operate as a community-building and community-enhancing project—rather than something for the glory of the poet—would be a tremendous opening up.

Q: Did it bother you earlier in your career when your critics dismissed your political poetry as angry, or bitter, or merely political?

Rich: Well, yeah, it bothered me when I was younger a lot. It bothers me a lot less now.

When I was putting together the manuscript of my third book, which was called *Snapshots of a Daughter-in-Law* and which contains what I think of as my first overtly feminist poem, called "Snapshots of a Daughter-in-Law," some friends of mine looked at the manuscript and said, "Now don't give it this title. People will think it's some sort of female diatribe or complaint." I wanted that title, and I wanted that poem. And it was true: Critics said that book was too personal, too bitter (I don't think the word "shrill" was being used then). But I knew this was material that would have to find a place in my poetry, in my work, that it was probably central to it—as indeed it came to be.

Recently, I was sent a clipping from the *Irish Times* in which the Irish poet, Derek Mayhon, refers to me as "cold, dishonest, and wicked." He deplores the "victimology" of my ideas, which he says have seduced younger women poets. When I read that, I was sort of astounded, because we are in 1993. But then I thought, what this man is afraid of is the growing feminism in Ireland and the growing energy and strength of Irish women poets. It's easier for him to criticize a North American woman poet than to address what's going on in his own country—that might be very threatening to him as a male and in a country where poetry has been so predominantly a male turf. Anyway, those kinds of attacks have come all along, and you do expect them.

Q: It's just a standard put-down for you now, isn't it?

Rich: I don't really see it directed at me. I see it directed at a larger phenomenon. It's not just about me and my work. It's about movements of which I am a part. It's about a whole social structure that is threatened or feeling itself threatened.

Q: Are you saying it's an attack on the women's movement or the lesbian movement?

Rich: Well, yes. I suppose if you attack one writer, you think then others will have less temerity. But there are such wonderful younger women writers coming along who are creating out of their anger, their fury, their sense of the world. Nothing's going to stop that.

Q: There does seem to be a lot of energy left in the women's-liberation movement, and the lesbian and gay-rights movement, two movements you've been closely associated with. Do you share that assessment?

Rich: Partly because of economic conditions, and partly because of work that has gone on in the women's movement and the lesbian-gay movement, we're realizing there can be no single-issue campaigns. We're realizing we can work in one area or another but we need to be constantly conscious of ourselves as part of a network with others. I see the women's movement as a much more multicultural movement than it has ever been, which I think is a tremendous strength. It's also a question of providing for the needs—just basically that—providing shelters for battered women, providing the rape-crisis hot line, and providing food and shelter a lot of the time.

We're talking about something really large: How does change come about at the end of this century, at this particular time that we're finding ourselves in? I still believe very strongly that there isn't going to be any kind of movement joined, any mass movement, that does not involve leadership by women—I don't mean only leadership by women or leadership by only women but leadership by women. This is the only way that I see major change approaching. And I think one of the things that we're seen [*sic*] over the last few years in some of the spectacles that have been served up on television such as the Anita Hill hearings is the way the system has revealed itself as a white man's system.

Q: You say somewhere that it was not until 1970 that you saw yourself fully as a feminist.

Rich: I think it was then that I first used the word about myself. It's odd because there's so much discussion now about whether young women want to be labeled feminist or not. And I remember thinking I didn't want to be labeled as a feminist. Feminists were these funny creatures like Susan B. Anthony, you know. She was a laughingstock when I was growing up. Or Carrie Nation. They were caricatured.

Q: Why the current resistance?

Rich: Names, labels get kind of lodged in a certain point of time and appear to contain only a certain content, and they lose their fluidity, they lose their openness, and then the new generation comes along and wants to register its own experience in its own way. That doesn't really bother me that much. I myself have gotten tired of the word feminism and am going back to the old phrase, women's liberation.

Q: Why is that?

Rich: Women's liberation is a very beautiful phrase; feminism sounds a little purse-mouthed. It's also become sort of meaningless. If we use the phrase women's liberation, the question immediately arises, "Liberation from what? Liberation for what?" Liberation is a very serious word, as far as I'm concerned.

Q: You make great claims for women's liberation as a democratizing force.

Rich: I see it as potentially the ultimate democratizing force. It is fundamentally anti-hierarchical, and that involves justice on so many levels because of the way women interpenetrate every-where. And the places we don't interpenetrate—the higher levels of power—are bent on retaining power, retaining hierarchy, and the exclusion of many kinds of peoples.

Q: What do you make of the current attacks on feminism, which seem to be on two tracks right now: that it is a cult of victimization, and the other, that women's studies is peripheral or unrigorous intellectually?

Rich: Women's studies and feminism have always been attacked. I think it was in 1970 that I remember seeing an article in Harper's called "Requiem for the Women's Movement," when the women's movement was just beginning to show its face. Its death is being constantly announced. But it's an unquenchable and unkillable movement that has come and gone or come and submerged throughout the world in many different places in many different times. At this point, I think we live in an era of such global communications that that cannot happen again.

Q: Sometimes in your description of the United States the task of changing our society seems so awesome, so daunting. One of the recurring metaphors in your book What Is Found There *is that the United States is in depression, mental depression, a clinical depression, a depressive state. What do you mean by that?*

Rich: I was writing that in 1990, and I was trying to look at what I saw around me: a shared mood, a shared emotional crisis, that people—battered by a more-than-ever indifferent and arrogant distribution of resources—felt themselves to blame for the fact that they couldn't manage, that they couldn't survive, that they couldn't support their families, that they couldn't keep a job, the enormous proliferation of weaponry . . .

Q: You have an arresting image when you write that "war is the electroshock treatment" for this depression.

Rich: Which was part of the purpose of the Persian Gulf war—to distract from the domestic anger and despair. And to some extent it worked. But it was very ephemeral. It's not that I feel that the depression is only psychological, but we do have to take note of the psychological effects of an economic system. Capitalism, as we know it, leads to this kind of despair and self-blame, stagnation of the will. It's really important to look at that, and move through it.

Q: One of the manifestations of that depressiveness is the proliferation of pop therapies. You seem to take those on and lash out at them in What Is Found There. *What bothers you so much about them?*

Rich: It's not that I don't believe in introspection, in the recovery of buried memory, in the things that therapy is supposed to do, but—and I saw this most vividly in the women's movement—therapy, twelve-step groups, support groups so-called, seemed to be the only kind of organization going on in small groups, in communities; they seemed to be the only thing that people were doing. I compared this to the early consciousness-raising of the women's liberation movement where, yes, women met in groups to speak about their experience as women but with the purpose of going out and taking action. It was not enough simply to put everything in the pot and let it sizzle. The solutions in these therapy groups are purely personal. It's not that I haven't seen activists who became ineffectual because of the failure to attend to their feelings. I'm not saying write all that off. But therapy, self-help became the great American pastime. It also became an industry.

Q: The fatuousness of the language that came along with these therapies seemed to rankle you?

Rich: Yes, because it sells us—and what we're going through—so completely short. And it keeps us in one place; it keeps us stagnating.

Q: Is that fad fading?

Rich: It's hard to say in a place like Santa Cruz. It's also been largely but not entirely a middle class preoccupation.

Q: In your last two works, you seem to be wrestling with what it means to be a citizen of the United States.

Rich: To a certain extent in *Atlas*, I was trying to talk about the location, the privileges, the complexity of loving my country and hating the ways our national interest is being defined for us. In this book, *What Is Found There*, I've been coming out as a poet, a poet who is a citizen, a citizen who is a poet. How do those two identities come together in a country with the particular traditions and attitudes regarding poetry that ours has?

Q: This claiming of your citizenship marks a departure from universal brotherhood or sisterhood, or could be viewed as that. You talk of the Virginia Woolf lines . . .

Rich: "As a woman, I have no country. As a woman, I want no country. As a woman, my country is the whole world."

Q: You write that at one point you embraced that view but now in a sense you are rejecting it. How did you change your mind?

Rich: Through recoginzing that I was, among other things, a white and middle-class citizen of the United States, not only a woman. I had been to Nicaragua when the whole issue of what it means to be a citizen of a large and powerful country that is making it impossible for the people of small adjacent countries to have a decent or secure life was uppermost.

Q: But isn't that an unusual time to claim your citizenship in the United States, since you recognized yourself as part of that "raised boot" of oppression in Nicaragua and Latin America?

Rich: Well, it's not simply a joyful claiming. It has its pain. A couple of friends of mine who come from Latin America and the Caribbean have described some of the things they have gone through when they were coming off a plane to enter the United States—what it means to travel with a certain passport. Their experience is different from mine, traveling around the world with an American passport: I have never been taken off to detention; I have never been questioned; I have generally been told to go ahead in line. Small but very large experiences like that—real differences in what this piece of paper brings you—the benefits, the privileges. Overall in my life it has been a privileged passport behind which stands a lot of power that has been placed on the side of some of the worst regimes in the world. So I'm trying to make sense of that, to come to grips with it— but not to deny it and not to float beyond it and say I transcend this because I'm a woman, I'm a feminist, and I'm against imperialism.

Q: Since the Right is so much more powerful than the Left or the movements on the Left in this country, don't you fear it's more likely that the Right will ascend as things get tighter?

Rich: I certainly feel the Right's enormous power to control the media. Sometimes I ask myself if we don't need to reconceptualize ourselves in this country. We—something broadly defined as the Left, which has maybe got to have a different nomenclature altogether—really need to consider ourselves as a resistance movement. We have to see ourselves as keeping certain kinds of currents flowing below the surface—the "secret stream" that Vaclav Havel talks about. He writes in his essay "The Power of the Powerless" about the small things that people have done and do all the time—just small acts of resistance all the time—that are like signals to other people that you can resist just a little bit perhaps here, just a little bit perhaps there. This isn't something sweeping yet, but these things can interconnect—these gestures, these messages, these signals. Sometimes I feel we need to be conceptualizing ourselves more that way—as a resistance movement.

Q: At times you seem to be waging an internal battle about the value of revolutionary poetry, the value of the word versus political action. You almost seem to ask yourself whether writing poetry of witness is adequate to the task at hand or even a good use of your time.

Rich: I wouldn't say it isn't a good use of my time because it's really at the very core of who I am. I have to do this. This is really how I know and how I probe the world. I think that some of those voices come from still residual ideas about poetry not making a difference. I happen to think it makes a huge difference. Other people's poetry has made a huge difference in my life. It has changed the way I saw the world. It has changed the way I felt the world. It has changed the way I have understood another human being. So I really don't have basic doubts about that. And I'm also fortunate to be able to participate with my writing in activism. But still there are voices in my head. The other thing is that at the age I am now and the relative amount of visibility that I have, that gives you a certain kind of power, and it's really important to keep thinking about how to use that power. So I just try to keep that internal dialogue going. I would never want it to end. Having listened to so many women whose lives and the necessity of whose lives have made it very, very difficult for them to become the writers they might have become or to have fulfilled all that they wanted to fulfill as writers makes it feel like a huge privilege to have been able to do my work. So that's a responsibility.

Q: You must get reinforcement from readers. Do you have readers who come up to you and say, "You've changed my life?"

Rich: Yes, I do, and I usually say to them— which I also believe to be true—"You were changing your life and you read my book or you read that poem at a point where you could use it, and I'm really glad, but you were changing your life." Somehow when we are in the process of making some kind of self-transformation—

pushing ourselves out there further, maybe taking some risk that we never believed we would take before—sometimes a poem will come to us by some sort of magnetic attraction.

Q: That reminds me of the one time I heard Audre Lorde speak. She was quite defiant to her audience when they started to clap. She really wasn't interested in applause at all. And she said, "Applause is easy. Go out and do something." I'd never seen anything like it. Most people who speak like to give a performance and bask in the glow of the applause. She really didn't want any of it.

Rich: Well, Audre had a strong sense of the energy that can be generated by poetry, that poetry is a source of power, as you know if you read an essay like "Poetry Is Not a Luxury." And she resisted being turned into some kind of mascot or token—which is something that happens in the women's movement as it does anywhere else—an artist comes along and people try to capture her and take their own latent power and hand it over to someone who is viewed as stronger, braver, more powerful. She wanted people to keep their energy and keep their power, touch it through her poetry, but then go out and use it, seriously. We used to talk about this a lot—there was this phrase, I don't know if I found it or she found it, but it was "assent without credence," where people are applauding you but they don't make what you're saying part of their life, their living. She was very, very aware of it and concerned. And she was resisting like hell being made into some token black goddess in some largely white women's gathering, as so often would be the case.

Q: Is it a question of resisting being a leader, or resisting playing the role of the leader?

Rich: I think she was ambivalent about that because she knew she was a leader, for better or worse. And she was no shrinking violet: She liked being up there, but I think she had a real conscience about it, too.

Q: Like Audre Lorde, you suggest that poetry has revolutionary power. How does poetry have such power?

Rich: It's such a portable art, for one thing; it travels. And it is made of this common medium, language. Through its very being, poetry expresses messages beyond the words it is contained in; it speaks of our desire; it reminds us of what we lack, of our need, and of our hungers. It keeps us dissatisfied. In that sense, it can be very, very subversive.

Q: You have a line, "poetry is the liquid voice that can wear through stone."

Rich: It's an ever growing current that's being fed by all these rivulets that were themselves underground. I think we're producing a magnificent body of poetry in this country today, most of which unfortunately isn't enough known about. But it's out there, and some people know about it.

Q: June Jordan has this great remark in one of her poems, "I lust for justice." You have that, too. Where does it come from?

Rich: Sometimes I think it's in all of us. It gets repressed. It gets squashed. Very often by fear. For me, I know it's been pushed down by fear at various times.

Q: Fear of what?

Rich: Fear of punishment. Fear of reprisal. Fear of not being taken seriously. Fear of being marginalized. And that's why I think it's so difficult for people on their own and in isolated situations to be as brave as they can be because it's by others' example that we learn how to do this. I really believe that justice and creativity have something intrinsically in common. The effort to make justice and the creative impulse are deeply aligned, and when you feel the necessity of a creative life, of coming to use your own creativity, I think you also become aware of what's lacking, that not everyone has this potentiality available to them, that it is being withheld from so many.

Q: Do you ever get totally depressed about the possibility of change in this country?

Rich: I find the conditions of life in this country often very, very depressing. The work that I choose to do is very much in part to not get lost and paralyzed. The activism I choose to do, the kind of writing I choose to do has a lot to do with that, with going to the point where I feel there is some energy. And there is a lot of energy in this country—but it's diffused, it's scattered, it's localized. And it's not in the mainstream media; you can get totally zonked there. What is so notably absent from there is the very thing that poetry embodies, which is passion, which is desire, real desire—I'm not talking about sex and violence. And what I feel among my friends who are activists, who are making things happen, however locally and on however limited a scale—there is an energy there.

We're in this for the long haul. That just cannot be said too often. I mean, there's not going to be some miracle in the year 2001. It seems to me our thinking is much less naive than when I started out—about what it's going to take to make real human possibility happen, to make a democracy that will really be for us all.

Q: You write in What Is Found There, *"You're tired of these lists; so am I"—these lists being sexism, racism, homophobia, etc. Do you ever get so tired that you just don't want to do politics for a while?*

Rich: No, I'm not tired of the issues; I'm tired of the lists—the litany. We're forced to keep naming these abstractions, but the realities behind them are not abstract. The writer's job is to keep the concreteness behind the abstractions visible and alive. How can I be tired of the issues? The issues are our lives.

Source: Matthew Rothschild, "Interview with Adrienne Rich," in *Progressive*, Vol. 58, January 1994, pp. 31–35.

SOURCES

Chafe, William H., *The Road to Equality: American Women since 1962*, Vol. 10 of *Young Oxford History of Women in the United States*, Oxford University Press, 1994.

Friedan, Betty, *The Feminine Mystique*, Norton, 1963, pp. 37, 62.

——, "Television and the Feminine Mystique," in *It Changed My Life: Writings on the Women's Movement*, Random House, 1976, pp. 48, 56.

Hole, Judith, and Ellen Levine, *Rebirth of Feminism*, Quadrangle Books, 1971, p. 170.

Jong, Erica, "Visionary Anger," in *Adrienne Rich's Poetry*, edited by Barbara Charlesworth Gelpi and Albert Gelpi, Norton, 1975, p. 174; originally published in *Ms.*, July 1973, pp. 31–33.

Langdell, Cheri Colby, *Adrienne Rich: The Moment of Change*, Praeger, 2004, pp. 118–19.

Martin, Wendy, "From Patriarchy to the Female Principle: A Chronological Reading of Adrienne Rich's Poems," in *Adrienne Rich's Poetry*, edited by Barbara Charlesworth Gelpi and Albert Gelpi, Norton, 1975, p. 185.

McDaniel, Judith, *Reconstituting the World: The Poetry and Vision of Adrienne Rich*, Spinsters, Ink, 1978, pp. 15–16.

Papachristou, Judith, *Women Together: A History in Documents of the Women's Movement in the United States*, Knopf, 1976, p. 220.

Rich, Adrienne, "Diving into the Wreck," in *Diving into the Wreck: Poems, 1971–1972*, Norton, 1973, pp. 22–24.

FURTHER READING

Freedman, Estelle, *No Turning Back: The History of Feminism and the Future of Women*, Ballantine, 2002.
    In a global historical context, Freedman examines how patriarchy and gender segregation first emerged and the history of women's resistance to it. Taking an interdisciplinary approach, she discusses subjects including politics, economics, race, and violence in relation to feminism.

Keyes, Claire, *The Aesthetics of Power: The Poetry of Adrienne Rich*, University of Georgia Press, 1986.
    In a brief excerpt in this work regarding "Diving into the Wreck," Keyes analyzes the poem as a heroic quest, emphasizing the idea of androgyny.

Schneir, Miriam, ed., *Feminism: The Essential Historical Writings*, Vintage, 1994.
    This is a collection of more than forty historical feminist writings, covering a period from the American Revolution to the early twentieth century. The collection includes excerpts from books, essays, speeches, letters, poetry, and fiction.

Templeton, Alice, *The Dream and the Dialogue: Adrienne Rich's Feminist Poetics*, University of Tennessee Press, 1994.
    Templeton discusses the poems in *Diving into the Wreck* in terms of Rich's growing feminist vision. She notes that in "Diving into the Wreck," Rich pays more attention to the process of exploring the wreck than the nature of the wreck itself.

From the Rising of the Sun

CZESLAW MILOSZ

1974

Czeslaw Milosz's poem bearing the Polish title "Gdzie wschodzi słońce i kedy zapada," later translated as "From the Rising of the Sun," was published in 1974 in a collection titled with the name of the same poem. An English translation of "From the Rising of the Sun" is available in Milosz's *New and Collected Poems (1931–2001)* (2001). Milosz was born in Lithuania, which at the time, in 1911, was a part of the Russian Empire. (Following the Russian Revolution in 1917 and the subsequent Russian Civil War, which lasted from 1918 until 1921, the region known as the Russian Empire would become the Soviet Union.) Milosz was educated in an area of the Lithuanian region that after World War I had become a part of Poland; hence the language in which he wrote the majority of his works was Polish.

"From the Rising of the Sun" is a lengthy poem featuring a combination of verse and prose and is considered by some critics to be among Milosz's greatest works, although in his lifetime Milosz's poetry was somewhat overshadowed by his political and philosophical essays. The poem is a work of great thematic and stylistic complexity. Like many of Milosz's works, poetic and otherwise, it explores issues that were dear to him throughout his life, including those pertaining to religion and theology, the relationship between faith and reason, and the natural world. The work also reflects the poet's longing for his native Lithuania, in part through

reminiscences of the neighborhoods he recalls from his childhood there. A survivor of both World Wars I and II, Milosz is one of the best-known Polish writers in the West, and he was awarded the Nobel Prize in Literature in 1980.

AUTHOR BIOGRAPHY

Czeslaw Milosz was born to Weronika Kunat Milosz and Aleksander Milosz on June 30, 1911, at Szetejnie, in Lithuania, which was then part of the Russian Empire. His father, a civil engineer, served in the Imperial Russian Army from 1914 through 1918, during World War I. From 1921 through 1929, Milosz attended secondary school in Wilno (now known as Vilnius), which was the historical capital of Lithuania but after the war had become part of Poland. He then began studying law at Stefan Batory University, also in Wilno. There he published his first poems in the university newspaper. In 1933, Milosz published his first volume of poetry, *Poemat o czasie zastyglym* (A Poem on Frozen Time). Upon completion of his law studies in 1934, Milosz left Poland to study in France. He returned to Wilno in 1936 and that same year published his second book of poems, *Trzy zimy* (Three Winters).

In 1940 Milosz left Wilno, which was then occupied by the Soviet army, and arrived in Nazi-occupied Warsaw, procuring a position as a janitor in a university library. He married Janina Dluska in 1944; the couple would eventually have two sons. In 1945 Milosz and his wife left Poland, which was once again under Soviet rule, in order for Milosz to take a diplomatic position in the United States, working in the service of the Polish Communist government. During this time Milosz translated the work of American poets into Polish. Soon disillusioned by the Communist Party, Milosz defected from Communist Poland, and in 1951 he made a request to the French government for political asylum; he accepted a diplomatic position in Paris that same year. He published *Zniewolony umsyl*, translated as *The Captive Mind*, in 1953. The English and French translations were both published at the same time. This political work explores the power of totalitarianism in Eastern Europe. During his years in Paris, Milosz published two novels, a collection of poems, and an autobiography, among other works.

Czeslaw Milosz *(Keystone | Getty Images)*

In 1960 Milosz was offered a position as a lecturer in Polish literature at the University of California, Berkeley. He was soon offered tenure, and he settled in Berkeley. Meanwhile he continued to write and publish poetry and essays in Polish. In 1973 Milosz's first volume of poetry in English was published, titled *Selected Poems*. The following year he published the volume of poetry *Gdzie wschodzi słońce i kedy zapada* in Polish, a work for which he received the I. Wandycz Award. The slim collection was later translated by Milosz himself, along with Lillian Vallee and Robert Hass (who publishes poetry under the name Robert Hass), as *From the Rising of the Sun* and was included in its entirety in his larger collection *The Collected Poems: 1931–1987*. The collection *From the Rising of the Sun* contains the poem by the same name. Milosz's second collection of poetry in English, *Bells in Winter*, was published in 1978.

When Milosz was seventy years old, in 1980, he won the Nobel Prize for Literature. At about the same time the Solidarity worker protest movement in Poland was emerging in opposition to Communist rule, a development Milosz followed closely. Several years later, in 1986, Milosz's wife,

Janina, died. He published *Collected Poems, 1931–1987* in 1988, giving American critics and audiences the most comprehensive selection of his work available in English to date; Milosz translated much of this work himself. While his works often treat the difficulties inherent in integrating faith and reason, and while his faith was often challenged by the cruelties he witnessed during the two world wars and years of Communist oppression in Poland, much of his poetry retains a consistently Christian tone. In 1989 Milosz returned to Poland for the first time after decades of exile. In 1992 he married Carol Thigpen. The couple made a home in Crakow, spending their summer months there, while Milosz continued to publish essays and poetry in English and Polish. His work during this time period included *Piesek przydrozny* (1997), a collection of poems translated and published as *Roadside Dog* (1998). Milosz's second wife died in 2002. At the age of ninety-three, Milosz died in Crakow, on August 14, 2004.

POEM SUMMARY

Section 1: The Unveiling

In the first section of "From the Rising of the Sun," the poet speaks of being moved to write, regardless of where he is or what he is doing. He reveals how on this occasion, of beginning to write again, he is fearful. The cause of this frightened state appears to be a combination of his feeling that language itself is not up to the task of conveying truth, yet he feels at the same time that he is compelled to write, he is unable to stop. At the same time, the poet makes several references to a red horse. (A red horse, associated with war, figures prominently in the biblical book of Revelation, which deals with the apocalypse. As apocalyptical themes are explored in the poem, some critics have suggested that this image of the red horse is an allusion to the horse of Revelation.) The poet additionally describes his feelings of loss and longing for a native land that he believes he will never see again. This lament will continue throughout the work, taking various forms in the course of the poem. In this first section, the lament takes the form of a chorus, as in a song of sorrow, as the poet describes dark cities and old people full of hopes that will never be fulfilled. After mentioning once again the red horse, the poet states that he is able, however

dimly, to see the past, and that as an unnamed other speaks for him, he is able to write in a state described in spiritual terms.

Section 2: Diary of a Naturalist

In this lengthy section, Milosz combines verse and prose and recounts experiences in which the dream of a unity with nature is sought but is never achieved. Discussions of the natural world yield to the lament of a lost generation, lost cities, and Milosz's lost past that cannot be regained. The poet then describes a pilgrimage undertaken when he turned from his hopes of being a traveler and a naturalist to other endeavors. The pilgrimage ends with the poet viewing an image of a wooden Madonna with the infant Jesus along with a throng of art lovers. He reflects on his inability to identify and connect with a sense of holiness.

Section 3: Lauda

The sense of yearning for something almost indefinable is carried over in the third section of the poem, in which Milosz reflects on his native region in Lithuania, describing the place he was baptized and the character of the people of the region. The verse portion of this section gives way to a prose selection in which the poet discusses, among other things, the etymology of the title of the section, "Lauda,"; the noble family of the region of Liauda, a noble line of which he is a descendant; he also provides a medieval inventory of the possessions of a magistrate of the region. The prose shifts once again to verse. Milosz reflects on the futility of words, of language, to capture meaning but simultaneously expresses his urgent need to use language as a tool to construct order out of the chaos of experience. This section additionally includes a poem by the Lithuanian poet Teodor Bujnicki and an extended prose commentary on the work of a Lithuanian ethnographer, Father Jucewicz, who collected traditional songs and folk legends.

Section 4: Over Cities

This section begins, in verse, with the poet's denial of responsibility. He states that if he does bear responsibility, he does not bear it for everything. The verse in this section quickly switches to prose in which the poet describes himself presenting a lecture to students on the Christian monk and theologian Maximus the Confessor. The students are informed that Maximus warned against the temptation offered by the truth of reason, underscoring the struggle the poet has been facing in different forms throughout the course of the poem, the struggle to hold on to faith despite the lessons of loss taught by reason and experience. Milosz once again turns to verse, recalling his mother and the faith she offered him. The section concludes with the poet's expression of a sense of being disoriented, isolated. He is once again lost, asking where he has gone.

Section 5: A Short Recess

Milosz envisions a different life in this section, one distinct from the one he lives now. He imagines what his life would have been like if his early dreams had come true, if he had remained in his native land. But, as he explains, he realized that he wanted more, including fame and power. Yet after he began to travel to far off countries to seek his desires, he learned that the goal was an empty one, that he had been deluded. The section ends with an emphasis on the poet's sense of isolation and his pain and shame at trying to behave as he believed he was supposed to, trying to be like other people while knowing that truly he was not like them. He wonders in the last lines of this section whether or not one's life ever ends up meaning much.

Section 6: The Accuser

In this section, the poet addresses what he describes as sins: his vanity, his self-willfulness, his interest in the poison of faiths that contradict the church history he has learned. In particular he mentions Manicheanism and Gnosticism, two philosophies that deny the benevolence and omnipotence of God. The poet also makes reference to Marcionism, which holds that the vengeful Hebrew God of the Old Testament was a separate and lesser being than the all-forgiving deity of the New Testament. The movement of the poem carries the reader with the poet on a journey in which he chooses a difficult path over an easy one, with the goal being a serene castle in the clouds where he will find communion with those who know and love him. But what the poet finds is that the castle never existed. What follows is a list of horrors he has witnessed, a stark description of human suffering. The ending of the section features the hope offered by a ritual for the purposes of purification.

Section 7: Bells in Winter

Milosz begins the final section of the poem with a description of a dream-vision in which he is told by a messenger of God that the Lord's mercy will save us. The poet then informs the reader that the incident he has just recounted, of traveling from Transylvania and having this vision, never happened, yet it could have, he insists. He promises that the next portion of the poem is not an invention, and he describes a street in a village, and the home he had there, along Literary Lane. While he speaks of the place fondly, he states that there is no reason for him to try to re-create such a place in the here and now. He acknowledges now a sense of connection that has eluded him in various ways throughout the course of the poem. Stating that he belongs to those people who believe in *apokatastasis*, he explains what the word means to him: movement in reverse, backward toward a state of unity. It means, he tells us, restoration, in the spiritual sense. The poet explains that everything possesses a dual existence, as everything exists in time as well as when time itself shall no longer exist. From this explanation, Milosz moves to a description of a frigid winter morning. The sound of the bells jingling nearby gives way to the more persistent and insistent pealing of church bells at various churches (nine of which he lists by name). He returns once again to the old servant, Lisabeth, whom he described in the section on Literary Lane. Now she hears the bells and is urged to Mass. He identifies himself with her now, now that he too is old. Lisabeth is also identified as a member of the communion of saints, and Milosz lists others who are members of that group, specifically other women-witches forced to confess their wickedness, women used by men for pleasure, and wives who have been divorced. He imagines the song of the choirmaster, imagines the cleansing away of sins with the proper rituals. Asking what year it is and answering himself, that it is easy to remember, Milosz brings the reader back to the present, where he can see San Francisco through the fog. He suggests that maybe his reverence will save him after all from the apocalypse he describes in the last lines of the poem, the end of days that may be far off or may occur next week. He speaks again of the hope of the spiritual restoration he discussed earlier, yet the last line grimly states that he was judged for his despair, for he has been unable to understand the truth of such a restoration.

THEMES

Alienation

The theme of alienation is a pervasive one in "From the Rising of the Sun," and Milosz explores it in all its variations. The poet underscores the extreme isolation he experiences from mankind, focusing on the religious, social, temporal, and geographic sources of this sense of disconnection. Throughout the poem he makes reference to his sense of alienation from faithful Christians. He fears that his investigations into alternative philosophies and faiths have isolated him from the his religious peers. He despairs that he will be excluded from the final restoration of mankind to its original glory with God due to his inabilities to fully embrace his faith, due to his difficulty in believing what he cannot rationally understand. The poem also depicts the poet's yearning for the home he left behind in Lithuania. He longs for the people and places he remembers from long ago. Trying to capture a sense of what he left behind, of the history of his homeland, he constructs elaborately detailed and lengthy lists, designed to offer at least a glimpse into the lives of his native people. He identifies in many ways with the people of Lithuania and Poland, as shown by his verses on the old servant woman, Lisabeth. Yet he nevertheless is fully aware of his distance from them, in terms of time and geography. In the last section of the poem, Milosz emphasizes this distance by reminding the reader that while much of the poem depicts his onetime home in Eastern Europe and how it existed years ago, he is in fact writing from present-day California. He furthermore implies that he is even isolated from himself when he speaks of the unchanging consciousness, which we may assume is *his*, that will not forgive.

Judgment and the Apocalypse

A number of religious issues are treated in "From the Rising of the Sun," including sin and the nature of God. The title of the poem itself is taken from a line from the biblical book of Psalms. The full verse is an urging to praise God's name from sunrise to sunset. One of the most prominent of the poem's religious features is its repeated reference to both individual judgment (God's personal judgment against the poet) and the final judgment of mankind, the end of days, the apocalypse. While Milosz expresses his quest for faith throughout the

TOPICS FOR FURTHER STUDY

- In "From the Rising of the Sun," Milosz refers to several faiths or philosophies that deviate from the teachings of Christianity. Research one of these systems of thought and write an essay comparing it to the teachings of modern-day Christianity.

- Milosz speaks lovingly of the Lithuanian people in his depictions of their lives, their homes, their villages and towns, and their countryside. Focusing on one or two aspects of Lithuanian life and culture, create a presentation about Lithuanians, incorporating visual elements, music, or food, for example.

- A variety of political forces shaped the development of the Lithuania that Milosz describes in "From the Rising of the Sun." Write a report on the twentieth-century wars and occupations that plagued the country, being sure to include a discussion of the nation's struggle for independence.

- Milosz employs both verse and prose in "From the Rising of the Sun." Write a poem that emulates this unique structure. Like Milosz's poem, it may reflect on the past and provide conjecture on the future. Select themes that are representative of your interests and concerns.

course of the poem, he returns with some regularity to the question of his ultimate fate, seeming to doubt that he has been faithful enough to achieve the ultimate union with God he claims to believe in.

In the opening stanza of the poem, Milosz refers to a red horse, a symbol taken from the book of Revelation in its depiction of the apocalypse. (One of four horses mentioned in Revelation, the red horse and its rider are associated with war, one of the indicators of the coming apocalypse.) Also in the first section of the poem, he speaks of the challenges that the man who has lived a long life will face in being forgiven for his sins. In the third section of the poem, Milosz makes reference again to the apocalypse, commenting on what might exist when the world no longer does. Once again, he speaks of the judgment he will face at the end of his life, observing that we are all of us alone at this dark trial. The fifth section similarly meditates on death, what might come after, and the purpose of our lives. Milosz, in the sixth section of the poem, expresses his fears that his questioning of faith, and his explorations into philosophies that conflict with his church's teachings have perhaps poisoned him. He speaks of these inquiries in terms of sin and the resultant guilt. He wonders whether purification before the final judgment is possible. The final stanza of the final section closes the poem with the same grim tones that opened it, with references to the apocalypse. The poet wonders when it might come; he knows that it is inevitable and that a silence that cannot be imagined will follow. While Milosz speaks of the restoration of all to God's glory, he ends the poem with the comment that his final judgment will stem from his despair at not being able to comprehend the possibility of this restoration.

STYLE

Verse and Prose

Milosz's approach to "From the Rising of the Sun" is extremely complex in terms of structure and voice. In combining verse and prose, Milosz constructs a work whose narrative often feels jarring and disjointed. The Milosz scholars Leonard Nathan and Arthur Quinn, in *The Poet's Work: An Introduction to Czeslaw Milosz*, comment on this poem's structure, stating that "the effort needed to follow the movement of the poem from section to section is staggering." In fact, the disorienting effect of the stops and starts in verse, with the interruptions by long sections of prose, is challenging but underscores the painful themes of the poem, which focus on alienation and judgment, fear and longing. The prose is sometimes used as a mini-lecture, conveying instruction by Milosz crafted to help the reader understand the import of the verse, as when the poet discourses on the origins of the word "lauda," which is the title of the poem's third section. The prose supports the verse in other ways as well. In a prose portion of the poem's third section Milosz incorporates medieval

family histories, along with a household inventory of a magistrate. The exhaustively detailed tracts of prose highlight the poet's longing for what has passed, for a sense of family and history that has been left behind. The prose sections are often attempts to order the feelings he possesses regarding his isolation from his native land, feelings he explores in a more lyrical manner in the verse sections of the poem.

Multiple Voices

In addition to the complex structure, "From the Rising of the Sun" also makes use of different points of view, giving the effect that there are a variety of speakers in the poem. Milosz at times speaks in the third person, at other times in the first, and some sections in the poem are structured in a question-and-answer format, although it appears as though Milosz is doing both the asking and the answering. He describes scenes as though recalling things that happened to him and then informs the reader that such things never actually happened to him; he thus provides voices from the past that never existed. At the same time, he introduces us to other individuals whom he recalls vividly, who he affirms are real, and in telling their stories, he gives them a voice. By occupying these various identities, by voicing his thoughts and feelings through a multiplicity of individuals both real and imagined, Milosz again underscores his yearning for connection as well as his isolation.

HISTORICAL CONTEXT

Lithuania and Poland in the 1940s

Although "From the Rising of the Sun" was not written during the 1940s, nor is it specifically about that time period in Lithuanian and Polish history, lengthy sections of the poem contain Milosz's reminiscences about the home he left. The turmoil in his homeland, which Milosz had escaped in the mid-1940s, would haunt his prose and poetry for years to come; the longing Milosz expresses, generated at least in part by his separation from the land of his birth, textures much of the poem. Warfare in the regions of Lithuania and Poland from before World War I, in the years between World Wars I and II, and during World War II resulted in a shifting in borders. The land Milosz called home, the Vilnius region in what is now Lithuania, was alternately

COMPARE & CONTRAST

- **1970s:** Milosz, working as a professor at the University of California, Berkeley, writes poetry and publishes it in Polish. However, Polish readers are unable to read his poetry; Milosz's works are banned in Poland by the Soviet Communist party.

  Today: Milosz's poetry has been read in Poland since the ban on his works was lifted in 1980, the year Milosz won the Nobel Prize in Literature. His work is now respected and emulated by Polish poets.

- **1970s:** In "From the Rising of the Sun," Milosz comments on the dangers that wildlife and the environment face from mankind. His focus reflects a growing interest in America on the environment. In April 1970, the United States celebrates its first Earth Day.

  Today: With the release of Al Gore's book and film titled *An Inconvenient Truth* in 2006, a renewed interest in the effects of global warming on the environment is witnessed in America. Gore's work in this area wins him the Nobel Peace Prize in 2007.

- **1970s:** American poetry undergoes a surrealist revival during the decade, with an increased focus on the freeing of the mind and the imagination. Poetry is also an increasingly academic endeavor, with creative writing programs growing in many colleges and universities.

  Today: Contemporary poetry is engaged in an ongoing debate regarding whether it has become too academic in nature, with some poets maintaining that the academic setting has fostered poetry that is formulaic in its attempts to challenge conventional forms.

---

possessed by imperialist Russia and later, from 1920 through 1938, by Poland. It was during these years that Milosz attended secondary school and then law school in Wilno, the Polish name for Vilnius. For a brief time, following a Soviet invasion of Poland, all of Poland and Lithuania were under Soviet control. In October 1939 a portion of the region, including Vilnius, was given to Lithuania by the Soviet Union. In 1941, Lithuania was occupied by Nazis. Following World War II, in 1944, both Poland and Lithuania were once again entirely dominated by Soviet control. Having escaped Soviet-controlled Wilno in 1940, Milosz landed in Warsaw (in Poland), which was then occupied by the Nazis, as per the Nazi-Soviet Pact of 1939. Milosz and his wife left Poland in 1945 for the United States. By this time the Soviets had driven out the Germans, and Poland and Lithuania were once again both under Soviet rule. Milosz lived in exile for the next several decades, first in the United States and then for a time in France before his return to America.

Soviet Communism in the 1970s

Milosz's painful emotional response to his estrangement from his countrymen, and to the suffering that decades of Soviet rule inflicted on the residents of Poland and Lithuania, colors portions of "From the Rising of the Sun." When Milosz wrote the poem in 1974, Lithuania and Poland were both still ruled by the Soviet Union. The 1970s in Communist Poland and Lithuania were years characterized by government attempts to prop up failing economies. Attempts to modernize the industries of the countries and to rejuvenate the economic structure met with some success, yet the efforts resulted in massive debts. With Lithuanian and Polish writers and artists pushing for greater freedom of expression, opposition to the Soviet government often took the form of underground publications, the creators of which had to avoid detection by the Soviet secret police. Other Poles and Lithuanians sought to work within the system rather than against it and subsequently joined the Communist party in an attempt to transform the country from within the established form of government. Milosz himself, as evidenced by his writings in such works as *The Captive Mind*, viewed Communism as a dehumanizing system; he wrote about its dangerous allure in Europe. Having spoken out through his political writings against Communism, Milosz, who by now had settled in Berkeley, California, found his works banned in his native land by the Soviet Communist party. Soviet control of Poland and Lithuania was finally relinquished in 1990, with independence being gained the following year.

CRITICAL OVERVIEW

"From the Rising of the Sun" has the reputation of being a complex, challenging work. According to the Russian poet Joseph Brodsky (as quoted by George Gomori in the *Independent* in a 2004 obituary of Milosz), "From the Rising of the Sun" was "perhaps the *magnum opus*" of Milosz. Milosz's Berkeley colleagues Leonard Nathan and Arthur Quinn, in *The Poet's Work: An Introduction to Czeslaw Milosz*, regard "From the Rising of the Sun" as "a deliberately obscure initiation into a final wisdom, in which the poet occupies the role of priest, of mystagogue." What appears to be confusion and disorder becomes clear and coherent when the poem is understood in this way, Nathan and Quinn state. The critics then take the approach of dissecting the poem section by section and analyzing the way the themes and techniques of each section dovetail. The effect produced, they argue, is one in which harmony of the "multi-vocal clash of voices" is elusive but nevertheless offers "tentative, personal hope."

While the work is not often examined separately from Milosz's poetic oeuvre (body of work) as a whole, when it is studied alone a thematic approach is often used. Aleksander Fiut, in a 1987 study of Milosz's poetry titled *The Eternal Moment: The Poetry of Czeslaw Milosz*, explores portions of "From the Rising of the Sun." Fiut focuses on the themes Milosz develops in the work and maintains that Milosz posits the imagination and the "cult of the particular" against the pull of nihilism and the temptation toward impiety. For Milosz, Fiut maintains, Lithuania is a spiritual homeland to which the poet longs to return. Fiut additionally explores elements of Milosz's nature poetry through an examination of the "Diary of a Naturalist" section of "From

Coffin with the body of Czeslaw Milosz (*AFP | Getty Images*)

the Rising of the Sun." In this section, Fiut identifies a sense of disillusionment that he argues the hero of the poem experiences in his encounter with nature.

Other critics have commented more generally on the overarching themes of Milosz's work. Jaroslaw Anders, writing in a 2005 introduction to *Legends of Modernity: Essays and Letters from Occupied Poland, 1942–1943* (a collection of essays by Milosz), observes that Milosz's writings were shaped by a "sense of Europe's spiritual crisis, and his own crisis of faith." This understanding, Anders states, led to Milosz's "lifelong preoccupation with religious and metaphysical subjects." Similarly, Edward Mozejko, in an essay on Milosz's writings from the 1988 collection of essays *Between Anxiety and Hope: The Poetry and Writing of Czeslaw Milosz*, stresses that throughout Milosz's works there exists "a surprising continuity and a consistency rarely found among writers." Yet the critic also observes that despite this harmony and the consistent exploration of metaphysical themes, Milosz's poetry is characterized by a complex intermingling of voices, times, places, and cultures. "Polyphony" is a "creative principle" for Milosz, Mozejko contends, and it is "one of the foremost characteristics of Milosz's poetry." Certainly these statements regarding Milosz's themes and stylistic approach apply to "From the Rising of the Sun."

CRITICISM

Catherine Dominic

Dominic is a novelist and freelance writer and editor. In the following essay, Dominic contends that while "From the Rising of the Sun" features several points of view or different voices, a structure that randomly incorporates verse and prose, and a style that ranges from lyrical to instructional, the poem possesses a distinct unity in its persistent longing for the comfort of faith.

Descriptors such as "multivocal" and "polyphony" are often used in discussing the style of Milosz's "From the Rising of the Sun." In fact, the effect in question pervades every aspect of the poem. "From the Rising of the Sun" is characterized by a startling multiplicity in terms of voice, form, style, and content. Stunning lyricism, for example, gives way to historical essays or lists of facts, just as the first-person point of view shifts to the third person. Yet despite the dissonance that these transitions create, the poem is unified by the sense of yearning that pervades the poem, a yearning specifically for faith and comfort in it. In a sense, to the extent that the poem can be said to be *about* any one thing, "From the Rising of the Sun" is about the poet's longing for faith as compensation for the deep sense of isolation and alienation he feels so viscerally. It is about the interplay between despair and hope—the despair that experience teaches and the hope that faith offers.

From the opening of the first section the relationship between despair and hope is outlined, underscoring the poet's sense of longing to transition from one state to the other. He speaks in the second stanza of the first section of his fear, his weakness, and about the need to at least imagine oneself brave in order to brace oneself for the spiritual restoration, symbolized by the light of day, with which the repentant sinner will be rewarded at the end of the world, symbolized by the red horse, a reference to one of the biblical book of Revelation's four horses and horsemen that initiate the apocalypse. The

WHAT DO I READ NEXT?

- *Zniewolony umsyl*, translated as *The Captive Mind* and published in 1953, is Milosz's political examination of totalitarianism and is counted among Milosz's best-known works.

- *Native Realm: A Search for Self-Definition*, originally published in 1959 in Polish as *Rodzinna Europa*, is Milosz'a autobiography. The English translation was originally published in 1968.

- *Lithuania: The Rebel Nation* (1996), by Vytas Stanley Vardys and Judith B. Sedaitis, offers a history of Lithuania's struggle against Soviet oppression and provides a thorough exploration of the effects of the Soviet occupation on Lithuanian culture.

- *Contemporary East European Poetry: An Anthology*, edited by Emery George, was originally published in 1983 and then reprinted in an expanded form in 1993. The collection contains representative twentieth-century poetry from Eastern European countries, including Lithuania. The section on Lithuania allows one to compare Milosz's poetry to that of his countrymen.

poet goes on to speak of the unfulfilled hopes of old people who await glory and power. This opening section sets the stage for the rest of the poem, in which dark images and sentiments are juxtaposed with references to faith and the glory of God.

In the second section of the poem, after outlining the struggles inherent in the natural world, the poet speaks of the losses he has witnessed—a lost generation, lost cities, lost nations. Descriptions of death and destruction are offered in a lamenting tone before the poet turns to the pilgrimage he embarked upon. He sets off, seeking and yearning, pursuing faith and true belief, but he finds only an idol, an image of religion (a

"

THE SPEAKER'S LONGING FOR HIS HOMELAND
IS A MAJOR THEME IN THE POEM IN ITS OWN RIGHT, YET
IT SERVES ADDITIONALLY AS A METAPHOR FOR HIS
YEARNING FOR TRUE FAITH AND THE SPIRITUAL SUSTE-
NANCE SUCH BELIEF CAN PROVIDE."

Madonna and child carved out of wood), rather than faith itself. This section emphasizes the undulations of hope and despair throughout the poem; hope is perpetually sought as a salve to the poet's sense of despair, but these dreams are never fulfilled.

The lengthy third section of the poem, "Lauda," features the longest prose portions to be found in the poem. In the verse portion that opens the section, the poet speaks lovingly about his native land, the Liauda region in Lithuania. He recalls simple times, yet the juxtaposition of despair and spiritual hope remains. After commenting that he has been baptized and has renounced evil, he refers, several stanzas later, to a devil that has not been sufficiently baptized. What follows is a prose section featuring a thoroughly detailed discussion of the etymology, or word origin, of the title of this section of the poem and its relation to both his native region and an Italian term for a song of praise. He gives an account of the nobility of the region, an account that includes reference to his ancestors and details regarding Lithuanians killed in battle. The prose section continues with an account of the household items of a particular magistrate and the subsequent fate of his belongings. The details seem random, but their exhaustive nature and their focus to some degree on the domestic underscore the depth of the poet's longing for a place he left long ago, for a sense of home. This yearning for something that feels like home to him is transmuted into a striving toward faithfulness, as the poem shifts from prose to verse once again. The focus shifts to a song described as a song of the Catholic season of Lent. In it, the poet speaks of the grief and despair he feels at being unable to understand his faith; he speaks of words that produce no light inside him.

The beginning of the shorter fourth section of "From the Rising of the Sun" is laden with references to religious holidays and images. Waking from this parade of imagery, the poet strives to understand its meaning. Later, he speaks of entering a monastery, seeking a moment of comprehension. He is constantly hoping for clarity, for true knowledge that would justify faith. Near the end of this section, having wondered what use he has been in his life, the poet observes that at the end our days, when we are judged, we stand alone for our trial, waiting in the dark for our fate. In this way the poet emphasizes the relation between his yearning for faith and his fears in having questioned too much for too long. The poem is colored by the poet's apprehension that in seeking rational understanding of faith—something that others accept without question—he will be judged unfavorably by God.

This apprehension is taken up again by the poet in the fifth section. Throughout this section he speaks of his shortcomings. While others forgave each other and were forgiven, he sought fame and power and earthly glory. He comments on his sense of isolation from others, on the pain that reminded him of the foolishness of trying to be like other people. By the end of this section he is once again expressing his despair over whether or not he, or anyone, can live a life that truly means anything. This section offers little sense of hope. Futility, despair, and alienation take center stage. Similarly, the next section focuses on sin and guilt. These stem largely from the poet's desire for knowledge of faith, a desire that led him to explore ideas about God that ran contrary to church teachings. He speaks of living in a void, and he relays images of human suffering. Yet the section ends with the poet's now-familiar thirst for faith, this time for the release offered through a purification ritual.

In the poem's final section, the exchange between despair and hope, which characterizes the poet's longing for faith and which has played itself out throughout the often jarring course of the poem, is examined repeatedly, almost stanza by stanza. The poet opens with a vision of God's mercy, a dream that the poet recounts having had on his travels. Almost immediately thereafter he denies having had this experience, although he insists that he could have. His desire to accept his faith without skepticism is strong, but it is not stronger than his skepticism. Each of the poet's efforts to connect with faith is somehow negated. The poet's longing for his native Lithuania, for a sense of home and community, has been a stand-in throughout the poem for the poet's longing for the comfort offered by faith. In the poem's final section, the home of his past makes an appearance once again as the poet remembers an old servant named Lisabeth, with whom he now identifies. He remembers Lisabeth going to morning Mass and thinks how long ago that was. The poet recognizes that he, too, is now old, just as he remembers Lisabeth to be. Emphasizing his affinity with her, he notes that they are the same, and the implication is that it is not just in their ages that they are similar. Perhaps he, too, longs for the solace offered by morning Mass. The poet then draws the reader back to the present time and place in which he is writing the poem and suggests that maybe his reverence will offer him salvation after all; perhaps his respect for the faith will be enough. Yet his hope for the final peace that faith promises is undercut by the sentiments of the poem's final line. In this line the poet acknowledges that judgment will befall him for his despair, for his inability to accept the glory of God on faith. In this ultimate line, the poet suggests that his desire for faith will not be sufficient in the end, for he has been unable to accept without question the tenets of his faith despite his deep desire to do so.

Throughout "From the Rising of the Sun," the poet demonstrates his inability to approach faith without question, using various methods to accomplish this. The speaker's longing for his homeland is a major theme in the poem in its own right, yet it serves additionally as a metaphor for his yearning for true faith and the spiritual sustenance such belief can provide. His sense of alienation from both his countrymen and the faithful highlights his pain and his despair. Although affirming Milosz's essential Catholicism in an essay published in the religion-oriented journal *First Things* following Milosz's death in 2004, Jeremy Driscoll writes that "Milosz often sensed a lack in his own faith." In "From the Rising of the Sun," this deficiency and its ramifications are thoroughly explored; for the poet, hoping for the ability to accept faith without question yields not comfort but alienation and despair.

Source: Catherine Dominic, Critical Essay on "From the Rising of the Sun," in *Poetry for Students*, Gale, Cengage Learning, 2009.

> IN HIS NOBEL LECTURE, WHICH CLOSES *BEGINNING WITH MY STREETS*, MILOSZ ASKS HIS AUDIENCE'S FORGIVENESS FOR 'LAYING BARE A MEMORY LIKE A WOUND.'"

Suzanne Keen

In the following excerpt, Keen comments on Milosz's Collected Poems: 1931–1987, *including "From the Rising of the Sun." Keen draws upon Milosz's essays in order to interpret his poetic work.*

This fall, Ecco Press reissues one of the essential books of our time, *The Collected Poems* of 1980 Nobel laureate Czeslaw Milosz. Born in Lithuania in 1911, educated in Wilno (Vilnius), a city with overlapping Polish and Lithuanian identities, Milosz has written in Polish while living in France, Poland, and, since 1961, California. He does not regret the decision to write in the language in which he is the best poet, nor should he, for his translators convey his vivid particularity and his range of tones with such success that I must remind myself to think of what I'm missing. Despite the loss of the Polish sounds, rhythms, formal structures, and idiomatic and cultural resonances, Milosz's poetry in translation is the real thing.

The poet Robert Hass has frequently collaborated with Milosz in translating himself, most recently in *Provinces: Poems 1987–1991*. From that volume, the poem "The Thistle, the Nettle" demonstrates how superbly these poets make English poetry from Milosz's original.

... The desolate music of the lines defies the "earth without grammar" that the aging poet faces. The poet reanimates his cousin Oscar Milosz's catalog of weeds, quoted in the epigraph to the poem, making continuity out of arranged words even as he disbelieves in the efficacy of poetry's claim on the future. My own experience of vacant lots and the accidental meadows of the postindustrial landscape, not to mention the prospect of the end of the poet's vocation, is whipped into shape by this rigorous lyric.

Writing of his own translations of Robinson Jeffers in an essay collected in the new volume, *Beginning with My Streets,* Milosz concludes that "the translator sees a sort of 'empty space' in his own home, in his home of sounds and intonations that he has known since childhood, and desires that it not remain empty." It is our good fortune to have not only the works that reveal and occupy this space in excellent English versions, but also Milosz's own guide to his personal and intellectual geography. A collection of essays, interviews, reviews, and addresses, *Beginning with My Streets* makes a fascinating companion to *The Collected Poems* and to *Provinces.*

Milosz's poetry draws our attention to the amnesia of recent history regarding Central Eastern Europe, although most of the poems are invested with a piercing personal vision that is not always obviously political. The meditations on places, people and concepts in *Beginning with My Streets* paradoxically awaken us to the knowledge lost to the world during the half century of Milosz's experience as a writer. Always painfully aware of the partiality and incompleteness of an individual witness's account, Milosz nonetheless invests these diverse writings with a compassionate and encompassing spirit. In his Nobel Lecture, which closes *Beginning with My Streets,* Milosz asks his audience's forgiveness for "laying bare a memory like a wound." Of his responsibility to reveal the "hidden reality" that drives and eludes human reckoning, he writes, "There are moments when it seems to me that I decipher the meaning of afflictions which befell the nations of the 'other Europe,' and that meaning is to make them the bearers of memory—at the time when Europe, without an adjective, and America possess it less and less with every generation." The poet's characteristic irony tings through a statement in another essay, "On Nationalism": "It is difficult to forget what happened in Catholic Croatia during the last war, when crimes of genocide were committed in the name of religion as the only distinctive mark separating the Croats from the Orthodox Serbs." The empty space lies exposed; it was all too easy for us to forget, until we were recently reminded.

The opening essay takes off from the twelfth section of the poem "City without a Name," reprinted in its entirety in the *Collected Poems.* In the essay, Milosz compiles details of architecture, geography, and persons in a digressive map of his original territory, the city Wilno. The dialogue with Tomas Venclova brings home the importance of such remembering, for Venclova's Vilnius, "having experienced the twentieth century" is Wilno no more. The contesting claims of Poland and Lithuania and, of course, the former Soviet Union to this city result in a double or triple naming that threatens to obliterate meaning. In the poetic sequence "From the Rising of the Sun," Milosz writes, "Everything would be fine if language did not deceive us by finding different names for the same thing in different times and places." The failure of the Platonic ideal to exist immanently in all objects threatens poetry, as well:

> A word should be contained in every single
> thing
> But it is not. So what then of my vocation?

A permanent sense of being rooted in a specific point on the globe governs and legitimates Milosz's vocation: "Even if I were gathering images of the earth from many countries on two continents, my imagination could cope with them only by assigning them to positions to the south, north, east, or west of the trees and hills of one district."

The phrase, "a sense of place," so often applied to poetry, takes on new meaning in Milosz's moral geography. In an essay on Stanislaw Vincenz's *On the Side of Memory,* Milosz concurs with the author's polemic: "The godless man can travel for many hundreds or thousands of kilometers in a single day without noticing anything that might move him, and just as space loses the value of the particular to him, so, too, does time lose value; for him, the past is obscured by a cloud of gray dust, it is reduced to vectors of motion, 'lines of development'; no inn, in which it would be pleasant to stop and rest, attracts him." Yet Milosz insists on addressing the hazards of creating, in imagination and poetry, a substitute world out of the particularities noticed by the alert person. In "The Costs of Zealousness," Milosz describes the poet's reaction to life: "Then the substitute world, which originally was a separate island, occupies more and more territory within us and the zealousness that it exacts . . . generates a further skewing of our day-to-day obligations toward people."

An intriguing essay called "Saligia" reveals more of the poet's self-examination, arranged around the meanings in Latin and in Polish, in youth and in adulthood, of the seven deadly sins.

Here as elsewhere in Milosz's essays, he scrutinizes himself: "It is easy to understand the anger of the oppressed, the anger of slaves," he writes in the section on ire, "particularly if you yourself have lived for several years inside the skin of a subhuman. In my century, however, the anger of the privileged who are ashamed of their privilege was even louder. I am fairly well acquainted with this anger." Therein lies the sin of the successful, he warns, as "well-fed, rosycheeked [*sic*] people have often gotten entangled in duplicity when they pretended they were suffering."

A reader unfamiliar with Milosz's lively, tender, wry, self-deprecating, and often hilarious poetry might come away with a false impression of the poet from this brief description of *Beginning with My Streets,* or indeed from the volume itself. For this reason I recommend that a reading of the essays accompany an excursion into the poems, which are luckily available in both *The Collected Poems* and in *Provinces....*

Source: Suzanne Keen, Review of *The Collected Poems: 1931–1987,* in *Commonweal,* Vol. 119, No. 19, November 6, 1992, 3 pp.

William Lach

In the following interview, Milosz talks about his upbringing in Lithuania and the spiritual underpinning of his poetry.

In a small club room at the Ritz-Carlton Hotel, Czeslaw Milosz is seated on a sofa having tea, surrounded by several academics from universities in the Boston area and a representative of the City Council. The Polish Nobel Prize-winning poet is in town today to give a poetry reading in the Lowell Lectures at Boston College. A short, but not slight, older man, Mr. Milosz sits quietly while the others discuss the political events in Eastern Europe: the collapse of the Berlin Wall a few weeks earlier and the lifting of travel restrictions for Czech citizens that very morning. When I enter the room, Milosz lets me know that he will speak to me in a few minutes' time. For a moment there's an awkward pause, a shuffling of chairs and places as everyone suddenly realizes Milosz's presence. I'm reminded of a passage by Milosz himself on the social awkwardness of the artist, "ill at ease in one place, ill at ease in the other—always and everywhere ill at ease—who managed to distance himself by spinning, cocoon-like, his incomprehensible language."

Born in 1911 in Wilno (Vilnius), Lithuania, to Polish and Lithuanian parents, Czeslaw

> I HAVE BEEN OBSERVING SO MANY DESTRUCTIONS, SO MANY RUINS, NOT ONLY IN THE PHYSICAL SENSE, BUT IN THE SPIRITUAL SENSE, AND I NOTICED THAT RUINS IN THE HUMAN MIND PRECEDED PHYSICAL RUINS."

Milosz's reticence during the morning's discussion reveals the experience of one familiar enough with the unpredictability of the political situation in Eastern Europe to be wary of making definitive comments about it. After receiving a degree in law at the age of 23, Milosz became involved in underground circles in Warsaw with the coming of the Nazis to Poland in 1939. When the war ended, he served in the Polish Foreign Service, eventually leaving his post in Paris in 1951 to reside in the West thereafter. He established his literary reputation through the publication of political and literary essays, several semi-autobiographical novels and, most notably, several volumes of poetry, his most recent being *The Collected Poems 1931–1987,* published by Penguin Books in 1988.

This most recent selection of Milosz's poems is an especially revelatory selection in its representation of both the devastating and hopeful in his work. "Proof," a poem written in Berkeley, Calif., in 1975 begins, "And yet you experienced the flames of Hell./You can even say what they were like: real,/Ending in sharp hooks so that they tear up flesh/Piece by piece, to the bone." On the facing page, also written in Berkeley in the same year, is "Amazement," which reveals a different tone entirely, opening with lines whose detailed simplicity is characteristic of Milosz's work, "O what daybreak in the windows! Cannons salute. The basket boat of Moses floats down the green Nile./Standing immobile in the air, we fly over flowers:/Lovely carnations and tulips placed in long low tables."

Milosz's depictions of an earthly hell and a present-day paradise reveal, in their coexistence within his creative scheme, a sense of traditional Judeo-Christian morality often shunned in the work of many modern artists. I ask Milosz how he retained this traditional sense of ethics in a world where existentialism has long prompted many of his contemporaries to discount the ethical duality of good and evil altogether. "Sometimes one discovers the value of elementary attachment to the notion of good and evil, and my faith is rooted in my childhood," responds Milosz, in slow, thoughtful tones whose color reflects his Eastern European background. "One discovers the value of certain basic notions: of catechism, of the notions of good and evil inculcated by our parents in childhood. So that's a sort of an indication of simple tools against highfalutin and complicated things of philosophy, and very often ominous philosophies of the 20th century.

"I have been observing so many destructions, so many ruins, not only in the physical sense, but in the spiritual sense, and I noticed that ruins in the human mind preceded physical ruins. I know to what extent catastrophes of the 20th century were determined by a kind of erosion that was going on during the 19th century. I should say that if I preserved faith, it was largely empirical, through seeing diabolical forces at work."

I'm struck by his unpretentiousness. Milosz has written *The History of Polish Literature,* a massive, scholarly work, and is Professor Emeritus of Slavic and Eastern European languages at the University of California at Berkeley. But he possesses an ingenuous wisdom one would expect to find in someone removed from the academic world. It is this wisdom that takes over when I press him about the possibility for someone of today's generation to possess strong religious faith when the notion of "the banality of evil" itself has become banal.

"You may see a contradiction because I said that because of experiences of the 20th century, one appreciates naïve notions inculcated in childhood. I do not see any contradiction because this is not a naïve approach, but through a religious upbringing one can appreciate naïve attitudes. That is not identical with being naïve, you see. It's looking from another angle. You understand what I mean?"

I assure him that I do. His tremendous faith in his traditional religious upbringing seemed as intuitive in his speech as it does in his poetry. Indeed, his major literary influences include English Romantic poet William Blake, and he has lectured extensively on the Russian novelist Fyodor Dostoyevsky. I recall one of Dostoyevsky's more oft-quoted statements, "If I had to

choose between Christ and truth, I would choose Christ," and ask if he agrees.

"This is specific of Dostoyevsky. Simone Weil said that when confronted with such a choice, 'I would always choose truth, because I am convinced that what is really true cannot be against Christ.' Dostoyevsky meant scientific truth, truth of science of the 19th century versus Christ. And Simone Weil was fanatically attached to science and even to the notion of determinism in the 19th century because she considered that this didn't interfere with her faith.

"As everybody in the 20th century, I have been under a very strong influence of science and technology, pervading all our lives. But because of that influence, I believe that faith in the 20th century is something very different from naïve faith of the past, of medieval man, for instance. So if I have faith, it is seasoned with irony, with humor, with various elements that are unavoidable once we are confronted with the scientific world inherited from the 19th century."

Then what is it that attracts him to Dostoyevsky, if not simply his faith? "I was interested primarily in Dostoyevsky as a spokesman of the Russian intelligentsia in the 19th century, and as a prophet of the Russian Revolution. Undoubtedly, such novels—*The Possessed,* for instance—are prophetic books. And, for Dostoyevsky, the erosion of Christianity, the erosion of religious imagination, inevitably led his characters to a Promethean revolutionary hope. *The Possessed* is a novel about a revolutionary group that is like a body of the Bolsheviks in the Russian Communist Party. And Russians themselves recognize the prophetic character of Dostoyevsky's writings. The Russian Revolution was not only a social and historical phenomenon, it was a profound metaphysical phenomenon."

I ask how he saw this metaphysics today, in light of the political revolution that has recently taken place throughout virtually all of Eastern Europe. "External changes are very important, but even more important is the complete end of Marxism as a doctrine, as a philosophy. Still we can expect many turns and turns, but one is certain that Marxist philosophy is dead, it's all over. And that's a fact of tremendous importance for the world, more important, perhaps, than political changes that have made the reversals that we see. In China we saw a reversal and it doesn't matter, for there is no messianic feeling, and no messianic faith, no philosophy as a substitute for religion, which it was, for several decades of the century.

"It is very, very hard to predict," he says when I ask if he believes that this messianic faith will return to religion in Eastern Europe. "In Western societies undoubtedly, especially in Western Europe, there is the loss of the feeling of the sacred and the sort of transformation of the churches into clubs of social activity. Why, excluding the former Communist countries, we don't know. We are before such a tumultuous and such a bleak situation that it is hard to tell what will emerge. But undoubtedly, there is a need for basic spiritual values in all those countries, much stronger than in the West."

Perhaps art itself will fill this spiritual gap? "That's something that occurred in the 19th century already. Obviously, the slogan 'art for art's sake' was a kind of substitute of religion. And if you observe today's scene, you will observe the names of artists, of great painters like van Gogh, like Matisse, like Goya and so on—we see a kind of religious cult of art. They take the figure of spiritual heroes, the place of saints, or even gods. And this is taken over by mass media. There is a cult of art—in America, for instance. In Western Europe, also. Museums are now a kind of temple."

Although he speaks passionately about his own religious views, Milosz is generally reserved. When I ask who his favorite contemporary poets are, he laughs politely and replies that he wouldn't drop names. However, as fair alternative to the previous question, he does offer advice to aspiring poets. "Read good poetry. And among good poetry, I place old Chinese poetry, of the T'ang dynasty, for instance." Although he cannot read in Chinese, he believes that, "reading in translation is legitimate. I have been acting as a translator of the Bible from the original Hebrew and Greek. I translated the Book of Psalms, and the Book of Job. And from Greek I translated the Gospel according to Mark.

"I have written one poem in my life in English, the rest in Polish. I translate myself with the help of my American friends; mostly translations are a corporate effort."

In his critical work *The Land of Ulro,* Milosz writes, "A work condemned never to leave the artist's workshop has the same power as a work of lasting significance for the public." I asked him why he believed in this, what he calls the "magical intervention through unseen communion."

"I can now say here, quoting French poet Charles Baudelaire, who said in one place, 'Every form, even one created by man, is immortal.' Interpret it as you like.

"Of course in the material sense, it makes a great difference" for the public if a work of art is displayed in a museum, Milosz admitted. "But what Baudelaire meant is probably on another spiritual level, that energies that are drawn into creating a work, a painting, for instance, that is not known to the public at all, that [these] energies somehow act, turn in the human sphere."

This spiritual, personal view of his work reflects Milosz's desire to be a hermetic poet, an intensely private artist with a small but loyal following. "My adventure was very strange because I started as a hermetic poet and because of various circumstances, including literary prizes and the situation in Poland, and so on, I became a kind of spokesman for people, for many people; and it happened practically against my own will. I have written a certain number of poems during the war that were anti-Nazi poems, and after the war I wrote poems connected with the situation in Poland, and those poems brought me a response, as I said, practically against my will.

"In 1950 I wrote a short poem, 'You who harmed a simple man.' It waited for some 30 years and that poem was placed on the monument for workers killed in Gdansk by the police; it is there, on the monument. So those are adventures of a hermetic poet!"

Throughout the interview, Milosz's responses are often serious, yet undercut by his gentle wit. When I suggest that perhaps the artist owes a debt to the general public, he replies without hesitation. "I am for an artist going after his business, and his business is, as Auden said, 'To praise the world, praise everything which is in being,' but I have been taught by history, if you are completely cornered, if you have no way out except to give vent to your moral indignation, then you write poems—committed poems, in a way."

Source: William Lach, "A Conversation with Czeslaw Milosz," in *America,* May 12, 1990, pp. 472–75.

SOURCES

Anders, Jaroslaw, Introduction, in *Legends of Modernity: Essays and Letters from Occupied Poland, 1942–1943,* by Czeslaw Milosz, Farrar, Straus and Giroux, 2005, pp. ix–xvi.

Czaykowski, Bogdan, "Czeslaw Milosz," in *Dictionary of Literary Biography*, Vol. 215, *Twentieth-Century Eastern European Writers*, First Series, edited by Steven Serafin, The Gale Group, 1999, pp. 236–49.

Driscoll, Jeremy, "The Witness of Czeslaw Milosz," in *First Things: A Monthly Journal of Religion and Public Life*, Vol. 147, November 2004, pp. 28–33.

Fiut, Aleksander, *The Eternal Moment: The Poetry of Czeslaw Milosz*, translated by Theodosia S. Robertson, University of California Press, 1990, pp. 6–36, 37–62.

Gomori, George, Obituary of Czeslaw Milosz, in *Independent*, August 16, 2004, http://news.independent.co.uk/people/obituaries/article39034.ece (accessed February 14, 2008).

Milosz, Czeslaw, "From the Rising of the Sun," in *New and Collected Poems, 1931–2001*, Ecco, 2001, pp. 278–331.

Mozejko, Edward, "Between the Universals of Moral Sensibility and Historical Consciousness: Notes on the Writings of Czeslaw Milosz," in *Between Anxiety and Hope: The Poetry and Writing of Czeslaw Milosz*, edited by Edward Mozejko, University of Alberta Press, 1988, pp. 1–29.

Nathan, Leonard, and Arthur Quinn, *The Poet's Work: An Introduction to Czeslaw Milosz*, Harvard University Press, 1991, pp. 99–154.

FURTHER READING

Maciuszko, Jerry J., "The Moral Aspect of Czeslaw Milosz's Creativity," in *World Literature Today*, Vol. 73, No. 4, Autumn 1999, p. 675.

Much of Milosz's poetry, including "From the Rising of the Sun," is concerned with crisis, such as a crisis of faith or the crises inflicted on Milosz's homeland by warfare. Maciuszko explores the moral attitude that informs the catastrophism (the focus on crises) of Milosz's work.

Royal, Robert, "The Ecstatic Pessimist," in *Wilson Quarterly*, Vol. 29, No. 1, Winter 2005, pp. 72–83.

Royal contends that in his poetry, Milosz does not retreat from the horrors he witnessed in his life, but neither does he express an attitude of bleakness. Rather, Royal argues, Milosz uses his painful experiences as a source of insight.

Smoley, Richard, *Forbidden Faith: The Secret History of Gnosticism*, HarperOne, 2006.

Gnosticism intrigued Milosz, and he mentions in "From the Rising of the Sun" how the temptation of this school of thought, along with those of similar faiths, perhaps poisoned him against his Catholic faith. Smoley traces the roots of Gnosticism from its origins and describes its modern depiction in books and film.

Wat, Aleksander, *My Century: The Odyssey of a Polish Intellectual*, translated by Richard Lourie and introduced by Czeslaw Milosz, New York Review Books, 2003.

Wat, a contemporary of Milosz, was an acclaimed Polish poet who lived in Poland during the Nazi and Soviet occupations; he remained in Poland longer than Milosz and experienced to a more extensive degree the Soviet oppression that possessed Poland following World War II. His recollections of the Nazi and Soviet occupations offer a detailed historical framework for understanding what Milosz endured as well as what he escaped. Portions of the work are based on interviews between Wat and Milosz.

Heart's Needle

W. D. SNODGRASS
1959

When it was published in 1959, in a poetry collection of the same name, W. D. Snodgrass's poem "Heart's Needle" was a sensation. Snodgrass won a Pulitzer Prize, and the poem came to be recognized as one of the very first examples of confessional poetry, a term coined that year to describe poetry that deals straightforwardly with autobiographical material. Snodgrass's talent was immediately viewed as equal to that of such luminaries as John Berryman, Allen Ginsberg, Robert Lowell, and Sylvia Plath. Indeed, "Heart's Needle" is almost universally acclaimed, whether as an example of a particular style of poetry or for its own potent message.

The poem itself concerns the poet's relationship with his daughter after he divorced her mother (when his daughter was three years old). Told over a series of ten sections, each written in a distinct style, "Heart's Needle" reflects on the poet's weakening bond with his daughter. "Heart's Needle" can now be found in Snodgrass's 2006 collection *Not for Specialists: New and Selected Poems.*

AUTHOR BIOGRAPHY

W. D. Snodgrass was born William De Witt Snodgrass on January 5, 1926, in Wilkinsburg, Pennsylvania. His father was an accountant and his mother was a homemaker. After high school

W. D. Snodgrass *(Joan Liffring / Pix Inc. / Time & Life Pictures / Getty Images)*

he enrolled in Geneva College, now called Hobert College, in Beaver Falls, Pennsylvania. His studies there were interrupted when he was drafted during World War II. He went into the U.S. Navy and served in the Pacific. After his discharge from the navy in 1946, he continued his education at the University of Iowa, where he enrolled in the college's internationally famous Writers' Workshop program. He earned a master's degree in fine arts from Iowa in 1953. He married the first of his four wives, Lila Jean Hank, in 1946; their divorce in 1953, and Snodgrass's subsequent losses in the battle for custody of their daughter, Cynthia Jean, were frequent subjects of his poetry during that period, which was one of the reasons why he came to be categorized in the confessional school of poetry.

Snodgrass started publishing poetry in the 1950s, appearing in the most prestigious literary magazines of the time, including the *New Yorker*, *Partisan Review*, and the *Hudson Review*. In 1957 he established himself as one of the most important rising stars on the American poetry scene when a long section of "Heart's

Needle" was published in an anthology called *New Poets of England and America*, edited by Donald Hall, Louis Simpson, and Robert Pack. Snodgrass won several prestigious awards before his first book of poetry was published, including the Ingram Merrill Foundation Award in 1958, the Longview Foundation Literary Award for 1959, and the Hudson Review Fellowship in Poetry for 1958–1959. His first published poetry collection, *Heart's Needle*, was published in 1959 and received a citation from the Poetry Society of America, a grant from the National Institute of Arts, the 1960 Pulitzer Prize for Poetry, and the British Guinness Award in 1961.

After the success of *Heart's Needle*, Snodgrass published his next book, *Remains*, under the pen name S. S. Gardons. This alternate identity was one that he did not try very hard to keep a secret, and later, after the deaths of both of his parents (whom the book was about), he talked about his pseudonymous work openly and reissued *Remains* under his own name.

In the following decades, Snodgrass taught at several colleges and universities. His longest-lasting association was with the University of Delaware, Newark, where he was a distinguished visiting professor from 1979 to 1980 and a distinguished professor of creative writing and contemporary poetry from 1980 to 1994; since then he has been a distinguished professor emeritus. He has published numerous books of poetry, several plays, and several collections of literary essays. He has been awarded some of the most prestigious fellowships available to poets, including fellowships from the Academy of American Poets, the Ford Foundation, the Guggenheim Foundation, the National Institute of Arts and Letters, and the National Endowment for the Arts. As of 2008, Snodgrass was retired, splitting his time between Erieville, New York, and San Miguel de Allende, Mexico. His most recent publication was *Not for Specialists: New and Selected Poems* (2006).

POEM SUMMARY

Epigraph

After dedicating "Heart's Needle" to his daughter, Snodgrass begins with a passage from the Irish legend of Suibhne. Suibhne, a Gaelic version of the name Sweeney, was a king of Ulster

MEDIA ADAPTATIONS

- Snodgrass reads from "Heart's Needle" on *Nine Pulitzer Prize Poets Read Their Own Poems*, an LP recording by the Library of Congress Recordings Laboratory that was released in 1963 as part of its *Twentieth Century Poetry in English* series.

- As read by the author, sections 7 and 9 of this poem are available on a cassette tape titled *Calling from the Woods' Edge*, released in 1986 by Watershed Tapes.

who was driven insane by a curse that was placed on him by a bishop he had attacked. In the section of the story that Snodgrass relates, Suibhne has left society and is living in a tree. He gradually comes to his senses when a noble, Loingseachan, tells him of the deaths of his mother, his sister, his daughter, and his son, and he drops out of the tree, only to be arrested. In the midst of this discussion, he refers to an only daughter as being a needle of the heart, which can imply both the pain of a needle puncture and the sense of direction given by a compass needle.

Section 1

Snodgrass begins the poem by comparing his feelings for his daughter to those felt by a farmer toward his field that is covered by winter snow. His daughter was born in the winter, and, like a field in winter, she represented pure, unsullied potential. As Snodgrass depicts the situation, the daughter's life, like the coming summer for the farmer's fields, will be full of work and suffering before there is any rest to be had.

The marriage that the child is born into is not portrayed as a happy one. The poet describes himself as being torn by love and as silenced by his fears. Although the birth of the child is a happy occasion, it is also one that is fraught with uncertainty.

Section 2

The poem's second section takes place when the child is three. The time of year is also moved forward, from the dead of winter to April, a pattern that the poem follows throughout.

The central image of this section is a garden that the father is helping his child plant. The perimeter of the garden is defined by strings, which are said, a little jokingly, to pose a defense against animals that might crawl or tunnel into it. The father advises his daughter to watch over it, to water the seeds, and to keep her garden free of weeds. In the end, he admits that she will be responsible for looking after her garden because he will not be living at that house any more in a few months, when the plants come up.

Section 3

Section 3 is about the tension in the speaker's household that precedes the family's breakup. Snodgrass draws a comparison between the unhappy household and the political situation known as the cold war. The main similarity presented here is that the soldiers of the cold war were kept in a constant state of anxiety, prepared to fight but always kept waiting for actual combat to break out, just as the people in a bad marriage might spend much of their time wondering when all of the pent-up hostility might turn into actual fighting.

The first image in this section, in the first stanza, is that of a child walking along the street with two parents and being lifted up over a puddle, with each parent taking one hand. The child is not the daughter that Snodgrass talks about throughout most of the poem but a boy, mentioned with the masculine pronoun. In this stanza, all three members of the family are presented as one homogenous unit, working together smoothly, but once the child is swung over the puddle they separate from each other.

At the end of this section, the speaker of the poem once again addresses his daughter. He recalls a time when, playing with her, he pulled too hard on her arm and dislocated her wrist. Writing from a distance, as someone who now lives apart from her, he wishes that some twist of fate, as in a Chinese play, would tell the girl that he was wholly responsible for her, that he was as much her mother as her father.

Section 4

The fourth section of this poem takes place after the father has already moved out of the house. It starts with a mention of the time when he told her that he must leave, but most of the stanza takes place during a visit in the autumn, just as the cold weather is arriving. Snodgrass describes the plants and flowers that they see as they walk together and the ways that the change in the weather affects them. He specifically mentions that these are not the flowers that the father and daughter were planting in section 2 but municipal flowers planted by the city.

In the sixth stanza of this section, the poet compares the vines that are hardened and ruined by the cold to the lines of poetry that he cannot complete, showing how the emotional complexity of his divorce and separation from his child affects his life as an artist. In the last stanza of section 4, he relates the story of a different child, the daughter of a friend, who became so attached to the sound of a cricket outside her window that she cried when it died. This image connects the coming of winter with a child's emotional state, conveying the sadness of the child who has to deal with changes that are natural and unavoidable.

Section 5

This section takes place in the middle of winter. The daughter is still three years old, as she was in the section about spring planting, section 2. Although she is still in the same year of her life, much has changed: She has new friends, and she has learned new songs. She has forgotten songs that her father used to sing to her and she is no longer familiar with his routines or habits, such as singing to her before going out for a nighttime walk. The poem illustrates this situation with the image of Snodgrass's footprints in the snow filling up with new snow over time.

At the end of this section, the poet uses the image of an injured fox to show how he feels. The fox is missing one leg, having chewed his own leg off in order to free himself from a trap. The fox returns to the place where the trap is and, staring at his own paw, is aware that he cannot feel it anymore.

Section 6

In section 6, the setting is Easter, which is traditionally thought of as marking the beginning of the spring season. The daughter comes to visit, and they go to the river; the river's waters are high, as rivers usually are in the spring, which brings to mind the killdeers that were displaced from their nests another time the river overflowed. This brings back other memories associated with birds.

The daughter remembers a time that a blackbird attacked her father for coming near its nest. They also recall starlings whose nests were destroyed when workers cut down branches that had been weakened by a wind storm and a pigeon that the father tried to catch but had to let go when she flapped her wings in panic. About the last, Snodgrass notes that there are some things that his daughter reminds him of that he is not proud of.

In the last two stanzas of this section, the poet recalls a time when he came to his daughter's bed when she was sick and could not breathe, comparing that feeling to how disabled he felt after his divorce. He ends this section by noting that he now has a new wife and an adopted child to care for.

Section 7

Section 7 offers a brief look at the father and daughter playing on a July day. The father pushes his daughter on a swing, and every time he pushes her away she comes back to him with even more force. This very action can be seen as a symbol for their difficult relationship, which has by this point reached a sense of balance.

Section 8

In section 8, Snodgrass compares the relatively easy relationship that the father and daughter had when she was young with the strained relationship they have when she comes to visit him at his new house. He recalls that as a baby she would not eat unless her milk had some lemon juice put in it and that as a toddler she would chew the white clover in the yard. He recalls taking her to the zoo and feeding the animals from the bag lunches they brought with them. After the divorce, he could not afford to have her visit often and had to cut back on the times that he could see her.

The second half of this section takes place at Halloween. The daughter comes to visit for a week. She dresses as a fox, but when the neighbors ask who she is and she takes off her mask, they still do not recognize her and ask whose child she is, being unfamiliar with that part of the poet's life. The daughter has a terrible time during her visit; she quits eating, and the father leaves her untouched plate in her room until she will eat it. When she leaves to return home, it is November, and there is snow on the ground again. The father has a terrible appetite for candy when she has gone, even though he is very aware of how harmful it is to his teeth.

Section 9

In this section, it has been three months since the daughter's last visit. The speaker, who has not been in communication with his child in that time, wanders through a natural history museum, where the carcasses of birds and animals have been preserved and are displayed in glass cases. He recalls being there a year earlier with his daughter and her stepsister, his daughter in his new marriage, and how the girls ran around and had fun with one another before having their first argument. Some of the animals are big and ferocious, but they are frozen still now, unable to attack—just as the father's relationship with his daughter is in a state of suspended animation.

In the second half of this section, the speaker goes from listing the museum's stuffed animals to listing the odd medical specimens preserved in liquids in jars, including a kitten, a two-headed goat, and a tiny horse with no limbs. The sights of these animals, which died before they were born, makes him even more aware of the fact that he has a living, healthy daughter that he has not talked to for three months.

Section 10

It is springtime again. The poem brings up images of renewal, of plants growing and new-born animals, such as colts and piglets. The daughter has come to visit her father once again, just as the seasons come around regularly. Any bitterness that has built up is melted like the winter snow, and they are at the park again, feeding the animals as they did in years gone by.

THEMES

Separation and Its Effects on the Parent-Child Relationship

The most obvious and powerful theme covered in this poem is the relationship between the poem's speaker and his daughter. From the first line to the last, Snodgrass explores

TOPICS FOR FURTHER STUDY

- Snodgrass varies the rhyme scheme over the different sections of this poem. Choose two sections of "Heart's Needle" and consider their differing rhymes and rhythms. Write an essay on the topic.

- Research the cognitive abilities of three-year-old children. Choose some of the daughter's actions described in the poem and write a report that explains them in terms of standard developmental phases and abilities.

- In section 3, the speaker describes dislocating the child's wrist when he pulled it while playing. Contact a social worker and find out about the frequency of unintended injuries caused by well-meaning parents, and write a report on your findings. In your report, be sure to propose steps that could help curtail the problem.

- Make a list of all of the species of birds mentioned in this poem. Research the behaviors of each, and then write a brief interpretation of what those behaviors might symbolize in "Heart's Needle."

the unique relationship that occurs when a father and his daughter are separated from one another by divorce when the girl is very young. The separation itself causes its share of problems, introducing a sense of strangeness and unfamiliarity that puts a strain on the naturally occurring bond between parent and child. Added to that is the hostility that often occurs when two parents decide to go their separate ways—not only the hostility between the parents that caused the breakup in the first place but the lingering resentment that the child can feel at being in a certain sense abandoned. In this case, the tension of the situation is made even more pronounced by the fact that the daughter has to deal with the father's new family when she comes to visit.

For most of the poem, the speaker and his daughter maintain a solid relationship, given the circumstances. He recalls pleasant activities that they have shared in together, like planting her garden, going out to neighbors' homes for Halloween, helping an injured bird, and going through the wildlife museum with her stepsister. Their relationship throughout these activities is, however, strained by their growing unfamiliarity with one another.

The greatest strain on their relationship comes from a disagreement that is almost trivial in nature. At the end of section 5, the speaker recalls how, during the Halloween visit, his daughter refused to eat her dinner. Not willing to let her flaunt the law of his household, he left her uneaten food in her room for days, which created resentment in her, so that they parted at the end of the trip angry at one another. This fight eventually settles itself by her next visit, but the speaker nonetheless agonizes over the emotional distance that has grown between himself and his daughter. Looking back, he seems to understand that his response to his daughter's attitude was as much a cause of the problem as her attitude itself; in being separated from her, meanwhile raising a stepdaughter who was presumably already more mature when he arrived, he has missed out on the opportunity to develop his sense of fatherhood gradually, and he is therefore bound to make mistakes along the way.

Time and Its Passage

Snodgrass adds an element to the reader's understanding of the relationship between father and daughter by focusing on a particular time of her youth. Specifically, he follows how their relationship progresses in relation to the progression of the seasons. In doing this, he juxtaposes the natural measurement of time with the unnatural changes that occurred in his and his daughter's emotional lives as their family came apart. Moving from winter at the beginning to springtime at the end, the poem never talks about any events in the speaker's life without telling readers what time of year it was when they occurred.

Time is of course an important part of this relationship for several reasons. The most obvious one relates to the father's sense of the child growing up quickly. In one section she is a newborn, and then almost immediately they are playing together in the yard, and then she has become rebellious, and her father seems to be caught unprepared for each new development. This is true of many relationships between parents and children, but it is especially true of the estranged circumstances described in this poem. After the breakup of their family, their time is not continuous together. They see each other for specific lengths of time that occur irregularly, and they have to make the best of that. While the changing seasons will be roughly the same each year, each meeting between father and daughter draws attention to the differences that time has brought.

Shame and Remorse

There is a sense of shame and remorse in "Heart's Needle," as the speaker comes just short of apologizing to his daughter for the circumstances that made their lives more difficult than they might otherwise have been. The whole poem takes the form of an explanation, such that his daughter can, at some time in the future, see how his behavior was at least well-intentioned. The complexity of their social situation is laid out in the first section, where Snodgrass compares his first thoughts about fatherhood to the sense a farmer has before his fields have grown, to establish how his daughter's birth filled him with anticipation; the ominous imagery of a frozen, snow-covered field lets readers feel the sadness that lies behind that anticipation. The poem goes on to chronicle missteps that the father took in his relationship with his daughter, including pulling her arm too hard when she was an infant and allowing himself to be distracted from her by his new family. Going into the poem's final section, it seems that he does not think much of himself as a father. In the end, however, the relationship between father and daughter rights itself through no particular effort of his own, much to his relief.

STYLE

Varying Rhyme Scheme

Snodgrass gives this poem a comforting sense of familiarity by using a strong, recognizable rhyme scheme. While using rhyming patterns that are easily recognized, though, he also changes the rhyming patterns frequently, such that the structure of the poem always feels new. For instance, the first section follows an *abba* pattern, with the words at the ends of the first and fourth line rhyming and the words at the ends of the second and third lines rhyming. The second section has an *abacbc* pattern, as line 1 rhymes with line 3, line 2 with line 5, and line 4 with line 6. Section 3 is *aabccb*, section 4 is *ababb*, and so forth. The most disorderly part of the poem is section 8, which is the only one where the rhyme schemes changes within the section: the first stanza of this section follows an *abacb* pattern, the second stanza is *ababb*, the third stanza is *abbac*, and so on. This irregularity is appropriate for this part of the poem, as this is the section that deals with the most emotional confusion; still, Snodgrass retains some rhyming structure even as he alters it, giving the poem a strong sense of control.

Distinct Sections

"Heart's Needle" is organized into ten distinct sections that tell a comprehensive story when they are put together but which can also be read independently. In fact, individual sections have sometimes been published separately in anthologies, where readers can appreciate them for their own internal logic. The sections are not equal in length, and they have differences in stanza length and rhyme schemes, but they all have similarities in their structures and, of course, they share similar subject matter. Although this poem can be examined in terms of its individual parts, the overall effect when the ten sections are read together is greater than the sum of those parts.

HISTORICAL CONTEXT

The Confessional Poetry Movement

"Heart's Needle" is often identified as one of the first confessional poems, ushering in a trend in poetry that was prevalent in the 1950s and 1960s. Confessional poetry is generally characterized as poetry that looks deeply into aspects of the poet's life that might be considered embarrassing. Among those who were considered to be practitioners of the confessional school of poetry were Snodgrass, Sylvia Plath, John Berryman, Anne Sexton, and Robert Lowell.

By the late 1950s poetry had come to be viewed as having strayed too far from actual, lived experience. After World War II, the government's G.I. Bill provided financial assistance to veterans who wanted to attend college. A great number of aspiring writers took advantage of this opportunity, as evidenced by a swelling of enrollment in creative writing programs. While this seemed to offer training to common people who might never have been able to hone their writing skills, some writers felt that it led to a trend toward poetry that focused on technical, impersonal aspects that could be taught in the classroom. One response was the poetry of the Beat generation, a group of writers, including William S. Burroughs, Allen Ginsberg, and Jack Kerouac, who sought deeper understanding of existence by living life to its fullest and who wrote poetry, prose, and fiction based on their experiences, recorded in a stream-of-consciousness style that made the writing seem spontaneous and unpolished.

The confessional poets, by contrast, did not reject formal poetic techniques, and they did not seek out intense experiences to write about. Instead, they looked inward, at the aspects of common life that are worth examination but that often are seldom discussed. Plath wrote about her damaged relationship with her father and how that affected her ability to function as an adult; Lowell wrote about his family and his personal life; Snodgrass wrote about the dissolution of his family and his feelings of loss after losing custody of his daughter; and Sexton wrote about infidelity and abortion.

The phrase "confessional poetry" was coined in 1959, when the critic M. L. Rosenthal was reviewing Lowell's collection *Life Studies* in the *Nation*. Although similarities could be seen in the works of certain poets writing at the time, few of them, including Snodgrass, cared to have their works categorized as confessional. For most, they were simply seeking to do what poetry has always done: unveil truths. Still, there is a distinct trend in poetry written in the late 1950s and early 1960s toward the revelation of personal details often considered too embarrassing to discuss publicly.

The Cold War

Snodgrass refers to the cold war several times in this poem, using it as a metaphor for the unspoken tension between him and the mother of their daughter after their divorce. It is an apt metaphor, as the cold war was a time of hostility between the world's two superpowers that never grew into an actual war.

When World War II ended in 1945, most of the countries of Europe, Africa, and Asia had suffered. Manufacturing capacity had been damaged in countries that had been involved in the fighting, and populations of skilled workers

COMPARE
&
CONTRAST

- **1950s:** In the event of a divorce, the custody of any children is almost automatically granted to the mother.

  Today: Courts take many factors into consideration in determining which of two divorced parents should have primary custody.

- **1950s:** A parent living across the country from his child has to rely upon letters and expensive long-distance phone calls to keep in touch.

  Today: Written messages and photos can be sent instantly by e-mail or can be posted to Web pages. Most cell phones have plans that include unlimited long-distance calls.

- **1950s:** The United States is in competition with the Soviet Union. People live in fear that nuclear war might erupt at any moment, destroying whole civilizations.

  Today: The fear of nuclear war is less immediate than the fear of terrorist attacks.

had been diminished. The two countries that were left in the strongest positions were the United States and the Soviet Union, which were run under opposing political ideologies: The Soviet Union, which came into existence in 1917, practiced and supported the spread of communism, while the United States was a democracy with a capitalistic economic structure. Though both countries were allies during the war, they disagreed immediately after about the political structure Europe was to have.

What followed for both nations were decades of suspicion, hostility, and covert operations aimed at undermining each other's power. The two sides often gave support to opposing factions in smaller countries, as in the Korean War and the Vietnam War, rather than instigating direct U.S.-Soviet combat. Though crises often threatened to bring about direct fighting, such as with the Cuban Missile Crisis in 1962, tensions were always calmed through diplomacy. The cold war managed to remain an abstract, theoretical war through the collapse and dissolution of the Soviet Union in 1991.

CRITICAL OVERVIEW

When it was first published in 1959, "Heart's Needle" was viewed as a groundbreaking work, setting the tone for a generation of poetry. The book that bears the poem's title won the Pulitzer Prize for Poetry the year that it was released, as well as the Guinness Award in England the following year. Although some critics characterized the poet's style as being too academic, these critics were themselves often dismissed as being too infatuated with the antiestablishment aesthetics of the Beat generation. M. L. Rosenthal, the critic who coined the term "confessional poetry" (the style that Snodgrass was to become most closely associated with), reviewed *Heart's Needle* in the *Nation* in 1959. In his review, Rosenthal speaks of the power of the title poem: "The undramatic misery of the troubled father anxious to create common memories ... has great authority." Rosenthal adds that Snodgrass gains this authority "through a gift of understatement that is yet saturated with feeling." Later in his review, the critic states that "the poem remains true to its germinating feeling of quiet suffering, and to its author's special talents."

As the years passed, Snodgrass's reputation as a major poet did not persist. Nothing that he has written since his first volume has made such an impact on the literary world. By the 1990s, the release of a new collection was not met with enthusiasm. This can be seen in William Pratt's review in *World Literature Today* of Snodgrass's 1994 collection *Each in His Season*. "Sadly," Pratt remarks, "Snodgrass is a poet who found his voice early but who has not been able to sustain it into his later years."

Egg in nest (*Pat Powers and Cherryl Schafer / Phototdisc / Getty Images*)

Some critics attribute Snodgrass's waning reputation to the tremendous impact "Heart's Needle" had when it was first published. Writing in the *Southern Review* in 2006, Jay Rogoff recalled a discussion he had with another poet who, in the 1980s, had recently reread *Heart's Needle* and had failed to understand the enthusiasm she had once had for it and for confessional poetry in general. Rogoff explains, "Our difficulty today in seeing Snodgrass's special quality actually derives from his success and his influence, as well as the influence of Lowell, John Berryman, Sylvia Plath, and others: What looked forbidden in his poetry, what made it new and startling at the time, has become the norm." Nevertheless, Rogoff goes on to praise *Heart's Needle* for its "impeccable craft," noting that "its technical mastery still compels us and argues for its enduring power."

CRITICISM

David Kelly

Kelly is a writer and an instructor of creative writing and literature at two colleges in Illinois. In the following essay, he explores the implications of the

WHAT DO I READ NEXT?

- The poet Seamus Heaney wrote a modern translation of the traditional Irish legend *Buile Suibhne*, the myth that Snodgrass quotes at the beginning of "Heart's Needle." Heaney's modernized version, titled *Sweeney Astray*, was published in 1984.

- In section 9 of "Heart's Needle," Snodgrass gives a detailed description of a visit to a museum, tucked away in a university building, that has display cases full of animals that have been stuffed and posed. The sociological aspect of such museums is explored in Stephen T. Asma's 2003 study *Stuffed Animals and Pickled Heads: The Culture and Evolution of Natural History Museums*.

- While "Heart's Needle" is often considered the first poem to be categorized as confessional, Sylvia Plath's "Daddy," in which an adult daughter voices her resentment toward her father, is considered one of the most powerful examples of confessional poetry. It was published in 1965, shortly after Plath's death, in her collection *Ariel*.

- The term "confessional poetry" was coined to describe Robert Lowell's *Life Studies*. The collection was published in 1959, the same year as *Heart's Needle*.

- Snodgrass uses "Heart's Needle" to demonstrate how a writer begins a work in his essay "Finding a Poem." The essay is included in his book *In Radical Pursuit: Critical Essays and Lectures* (1975).

label *"confessional poetry" and how the label relates to "Heart's Needle."*

In the nearly half a century since it was first published, W. D. Snodgrass's poem "Heart's Needle" has been referred to as one of the earliest examples of the burgeoning confessional poetry movement. It is a label that Snodgrass has tried

" THE SEARCH FOR CONFESSIONS IN
CONFESSIONAL POETRY BECOMES LIKE SORTING
SALT FROM SAND WITH TWEEZERS, A JOB SO LABOR-
INTENSIVE THAT IT CAN NEVER END UP BEING
WORTH ITS WHILE."

to distance himself from, and for good reason. For one thing, the description is counterproductive in regards to understanding an individual poem. Labels explain little, and at the same time they limit a work's possibilities. Labels may make readers feel that a poem is only relevant to a particular place and time. Because of this, readers may study a poem as a historical curiosity rather than as a work of art that is relevant to the world they live in today.

Besides the ways in which labeling can limit how readers view a poem, there is the broader issue in this case of whether the label even provides an accurate description. Confessional poetry describes a poetry that reveals secrets of the author's that most people would rather keep hidden. There does not seem to be any need for confession, after all, if there is not some secret involved.

It simply is not clear whether "Heart's Needle" is any more revealing of the secrets of the human soul than any other well-written poem. Certainly, its subject matter, concerning the changes that come between a man and his growing daughter after his divorce, seems like pretty tame stuff today when compared to some of the therapeutic childhood stories and poems that are routinely published concerning abandonment, incest, and mental disease. The ordinariness of Snodgrass's poem, though, should not be a consideration here. It just would not be right to judge the poem by the standards of today, given that the confessional poets worked against different social standards, breaking barriers of taste and propriety that modern readers can only imagine. Writers of Snodgrass's generation—Lowell, Berryman, Plath, and the rest—made the personal poetry that is now commonly published possible. What makes a poem confessional or not is a matter

not of how embarrassing the reader might find the relationships it describes so much as what the events in the poem mean to the speaker.

Here, the evidence about whether this poem is actually a confession is unclear. At times, it seems as if "Heart's Needle" is telling readers details of the poet's personal life that he would just barely be able to whisper among the closest of friends. More often, though, the poem reads as if the poet is standing up to announce his declaration, a justification of what he did as being what he had to do. A justification is quite a different thing than a confession.

The uncertainty about this poem's tone starts in the epigraph and follows through from there. Snodgrass starts by providing a section of the ancient Gaelic story *The Frenzy of Suibhne*. This brief vignette provides the poem's title, as Suibhne states upon hearing that his daughter has died that an only daughter is like a needle in the heart. Just what this story is supposed to mean is ambiguous, and that ambiguity carries into the rest of the poem. On the one hand, it could be read that the father is saying that his overwhelming love for his daughter makes him vulnerable to news of her bad fortune. On the other hand, Suibhne does not seem to be suffering too much over his daughter's death; a needle is a much smaller thing than, say, a dagger. He might as well call his daughter's death a minor, though sharp, pain.

Even more perplexing is the question of how readers are to apply Suibhne's story to "Heart's Needle." Snodgrass does not stop at Suibhne's line about his daughter and a needle in the heart but carries on, including the response Suibhne then gives upon hearing of the death of his son. Whatever this means to the overall story of *The Frenzy of Suibhne*, it is almost offensively dismissive in relation to "Heart's Needle." Snodgrass does not mention a son anywhere in his poem. The passage as used in this epigraph seems to make an even more radical point than the suggestion that a son's fate is more important to a father than a daughter's: Snodgrass's use of it gives the impression that he may think even a theoretical son is more important to him than his real daughter. By including the lines that give Suibhne's reaction to the death of his son, Snodgrass goes out of his way to put the focus on a character who does not even correspond to one in his poem, thus taking the spotlight off his daughter.

If this is true, then the poem might indeed well deserve its categorization as confessional. The speaker is perhaps confessing to a much dimmer level of concern for his daughter than is socially expected. The divorcing father should be lavishing affection on his daughter, but the use of this epigraph implies that he is dismissing her as an inconvenience. There is a sense of shame implied in the lines the poet has chosen from Suibhne's story. If Snodgrass actually is admitting, confessing, this as the reality of his relationship with his daughter, he is taking a gamble that he might embarrass his readers.

Throughout the poem itself, however, the poet's sense of shame is not so clear. Just when he seems to be confessing to loving his daughter too little, new evidence arises to show that he feels he has loved her the best he could. Examples of this can be found from the very first image of the poem. Snodgrass starts by referring to his daughter as the child of his winter. In other circumstances, the mention of one's winter would mean the later years of one's life, when growth is past and one is facing the cold of death, as in the title of Shakespeare's play *A Winter's Tale*. In this case, though, the poet was still a relatively young man when his daughter was born. Later references to soldiers and the cold war indicate that the winter he means is an emotionally cold and dead period that he went through. The reference to his cold, frozen emotions could be read as a confession, as a way of saying that he was more inaccessible to her than a father should be. But it could just as much be read as the poet accepting what life has dealt him, as if his coldness, like the cycle of the world's climate, is just something that recurs now and then. One might confess if they looked back and saw that they had turned aloof, shutting out wife and child, but one would hardly confess for being cold because the temperature dropped. Observing a natural occurrence is not a confession.

And that is the problem overall with calling this poem, or any poem, confessional. Poets do what they can to look at their subject matter and find meaning in it, but the word *confession* distracts readers from precisely what is being said. The focus ends up being on what the situation described means to the poet, on whether he is discussing or confessing. The possibility of confession invites the reader to pass judgment; these judgments will usually be favorable, but if the

poet seems to be trying too hard for a favorable judgment—if he is twisting his description of the circumstance to make his actions look at all favorable—then his "confession" lacks sincerity. The search for confessions in confessional poetry becomes like sorting salt from sand with tweezers, a job so labor-intensive that it can never end up being worth its while.

The task of the artist is to look at life and present it with all of its flaws. "Heart's Needle" tells a story that is emotionally true. The truth of what it has to say remains unchanged, regardless of where the ideas came from or how much Snodgrass felt shame about the details he shares within the poem. The label "confessional" can make readers overlook that fact. There may indeed be such a thing as the confessional poetry movement, and critics and historians can argue about who and what the term applies to. Still, segregating these poets because they happened to use their lives as subjects does little to further one's understanding and appreciation of their works; by the time one finishes sorting through the confessional elements, the poem's other splendors have lost their allure.

Source: David Kelly, Critical Essay on "Heart's Needle," in *Poetry for Students*, Gale, Cengage Learning, 2009.

Jay Rogoff

In the following excerpt, Rogoff reviews Snodgrass's collection Not for Specialists: New and Selected Poems, *along with specific discussion of "Heart's Needle." Rogoff praises the collection, noting its "technical mastery."*

Almost two decades ago, when W. D. Snodgrass's last *Selected Poems* appeared, another poet told me how different she felt revisiting his *Heart's Needle* sequence after many years. Back in the 1960s, she said, those poems had shocked her—had shocked everyone—with their subject matter: the guilt and anger of the speaker's divorce and the anxious difficulty of maintaining a loving relationship with his estranged young daughter. But the poetry now seemed tame, decorous in its formal restraint, and she had difficulty perceiving what had created such a fuss. And truly, it was quite a fuss: The 1959 *Heart's Needle*, Snodgrass's first collection, took the Pulitzer Prize over, among others, *Life Studies*, the now-iconic book by Snodgrass's teacher Robert Lowell that, together with *Heart's Needle*, brought family trauma and psychological disturbance out of the closet and made them

> IF *HEART'S NEEDLE*'S SUBJECT NO LONGER PIQUES OUR LUST FOR GOSSIP OR SCANDAL, ITS TECHNICAL MASTERY STILL COMPELS US AND ARGUES FOR THE SEQUENCE'S ENDURING POWER."

fair game for verse, inspiring M. L. Rosenthal to create the label "confessional poetry." These books shocked readers in 1959 precisely because Snodgrass and Lowell presented themselves not as wild-man outsiders like Allen Ginsberg, who, guided by Blakean vision and elegiac Whitmania, ran naked through America, but strong traditionalists who clothed disturbing personal dramas in technical beauty, so the rawness of the wounds they examined seeped through the gold tissue of their poems' finery.

Our difficulty today in seeing Snodgrass's special quality actually derives from his success and his influence, as well as the influence of Lowell, John Berryman, Sylvia Plath, and others: What looked forbidden in his poetry, what made it new and startling at the time, has become the norm. The wrong turns that in the 1950s counted as dirty secrets of private life—divorce, adultery, and the emotional snarls they make of parent-child relationships—have become common American experiences and, therefore, common poetic subjects. The culture has caught up with Snodgrass and Lowell, and poetry, as always, has pushed beyond the culture, outing all of its skeletons from the closet into cold print.

If *Heart's Needle*'s subject no longer piques our lust for gossip or scandal, its technical mastery still compels us and argues for the sequence's enduring power. Snodgrass has included all ten sections of the title sequence in his new book of selected poems, *Not for Specialists,* and they demonstrate how, early on, he had achieved an impeccable craft.

... The poem's complex grammar unrolls in a single sentence whose long parenthetical phrases interrupt his address to the child, suggesting the constant interruptions in their love. It embodies the difficult balancing act the speaker has assigned himself: to salvage some harvest in his emotional winter, to control his sometimes violent feelings (the sequence's third poem describes how he "tugged your hand, once" so hard he "dislocated/The radius of your wrist"), and to establish a lasting bond with his daughter (the same poem boasts that "Solomon himself might say/I am your real mother" since he has surrendered her to his rival parent rather than tearing her in half like "Love's wishbone"). If the movement from the Korean War to the divorced couple's "cold war" seems presumptuous, the development of the snow metaphor for the child's mind resonates richly. The "new snow," her *tabula rasa,* presents a comforting purity but also induces anxiety, implicit in the preceding image of Asian snows "fouled" by death, in the guise of "fallen soldiers," "new" in both their youth and their sacrifice. By turns, her "new snow" recalls the trauma "Of birth or pain," offers itself "spotless as paper" for the poet-father to make his mark upon, and demands protection from "the weasel tracking, the thick trapper's boot," and other predatory dangers.

Yet the speaker also feels temporary and helpless, like "the chilled tenant-farmer" who neither owns the land nor can, in the dead of winter, cultivate "His fields asleep." His lack of rights eliminates any certainty in his life with her: He has "planned" only to leave much between them to chance, realizing that any paternal protection he can provide must be hit or miss. The poem's stanza, swelling to four beats in the third line before dwindling to two at the end, plays out his swelling love and shrinking hope, while the language details his restrained and terrible acceptance. Later, in poem seven, set in summer, the rhythm of a playground swing enacts precisely his combined love and despair in their periodic relationship, ending, as she returns through the air to him, with an emblem of their tentative love: "Once more now, this second,/ I hold you in my hands." That the subject matter of "Heart's Needle" has grown commonplace reflects on us, not on the poetry, which still succeeds in its skillful designs.

In his letters from the late 1950s, Lowell repeatedly judges Snodgrass "better than anyone [of the new poets] except [Philip] Larkin," and his best early poems warrant the comparison. Snodgrass is more flamboyant than his English contemporary, as in this stanza I often quote to my students from "Mementos, 1," from his second book, *After Experience* (1968), a poem unfortunately left out of *Not for Specialists*:

> Sorting out letters and piles of my old
> Canceled checks, old clippings, and yellow
>   note cards
> That meant something once, I happened to
>   find
> Your picture. *That* picture. I stopped there
>   cold,
> Like a man raking piles of dead leaves in his
>   yard
> Who has turned up a severed hand.

Here is the sense of shock my poet friend missed on rereading *Heart's Needle,* a rancid memory instantly transforming domestic life into gothic horror. Snodgrass comes closer to Larkin, however, in presenting the accumulated disappointments of modern daily emotional life, cast into formal structures that keep them art, as in "Leaving the Motel," whose mildly despondent, postcoital mood highlights the tawdry side of adultery.

. . . Yet Snodgrass's particularly American confessionalism—his lack of reticence in appropriating his own life and family for poetry—also distinguishes his early work from Larkin's. *Not for Specialists* includes six poems from his 1970 chapbook *Remains,* a bitter exposé of unhappy family life centering on the early death of a hopelessly mousy wallflower sister, a sequence apparently so personal that he first issued it under the anagrammatic pseudonym S. S. Gardons.

. . . This poem, "Disposal," also describes how "One lace/Nightthing lies in the chest, unsoiled/By wear, untouched by human hands," and notes "those cancelled patterns/ And markdowns that she actually wore,/Yet who do we know so poor/ They'd take them?" That "actually" serves a vital role, not just filling out the meter, but expressing quiet amazement at her impoverished taste and acceptance of her shriveled emotional circumstances. As in Donne's elegy "Going to Bed," clothing becomes a synecdoche for the woman who wears it, but here creating a scenario of isolation and misery rather than erotic play.

As a student I loved Snodgrass's poetry, especially how its formal elegance domesticated the worst shocks of our emotional lives, intensifying them by ironically pretending they participated in an orderly universe we could endure. I chose Syracuse University's writing program expressly to study with him, and found a man as boisterously outspoken as his poems were movingly restrained. He attended intensively to detail, the minutiae of rhythm, rhyme, and sound, as you would expect from a poet with such an impeccable ear, but he also encouraged a tendency to sarcasm I wished, at the time, to exorcise from my work. He would declaim poetry to us each week, and if his exuberant performances of "Frankie and Johnnie," Wyatt, Wordsworth, and Whitman, designed for a thousand-seat hall with no amplification, felt overbearing at the seminar table, they offered an antidote to 1970s poetry-reading syndrome—a monotonous delivery distanced from expressiveness, punctuated by a rising inflection at the ends of lines or sentences. Snodgrass helped me learn to read aloud by demonstrating that, yes, poetry could stand dramatic emotion in oral delivery, and I borrowed from his approach while softening it by several decibels. When I tested my new style one Sunday, reading at the local art museum, Snodgrass joined our quiet chatter afterwards to congratulate me in his booming voice: "That was WONderful! That was deLISHious! And YOU used to read SO BADly!"

With the first installment of his next poetic cycle, *The Fuehrer Bunker* (1977) [originally titled *The Führer Bunker*], the first book ever published by BOA Editions, Snodgrass's subject shocked us all—interior monologues in the voices of Hitler and his circle during the war's final days—as did its explosive, often obscene language: "if any foe rejects us,/We'll broil their liver for our breakfast/And fry their balls like bacon!" ("Chorus: Old Lady Barkeep"). It showed an encyclopedic understanding of form—ballads, tetrameter couplets for Goebbels, envelope sextets for Goering, a pantoum for Magda Goebbels—in addition to experiments in free verse, especially for Hitler. (Snodgrass had used free verse in *After Experience* for some of his poems based on paintings. "Van Gogh: 'The Starry Night,'" the lone example included in *Not for Specialists,* is unfortunately rather slack; I prefer the psychological drama of his Vuillard poem, on "The Mother and Sister of the Artist," which harmonizes chillingly with the tensions of Snodgrass's other family poems.)

As a sequence, a gesture toward a long poem, *The Fuehrer Bunker,* which Snodgrass kept expanding and revising until the complete cycle appeared in 1995, fails for all the reasons that his other work succeeds: The monstrous nature of many of the characters resists his attempts to humanize them, and we don't feel the force of poetic revelation; a more sympathetic Hitler and company might have created a literary sensation. In Snodgrass's bunker, the most successful poems belong to the women. The pantoum's repetitions circle around Magda Goebbels's mind as she meditates on how to save her children—"Now Joseph's sister's offered us the chance/To send the children somewhere farther West/Into the path of the Americans/To let them live. It might be for the best"—several days before she and her husband will hit on the final family solution of poisoning them all. In contrast, Eva Braun flounces about the bunker, ecstatic at the new life she has defined for herself and Hitler: "Today He ordered me to leave,/To go back to the mountain. I refused./I have refused to save my own life and He,/In public, He kissed me on the mouth."

In the 1980s Snodgrass began a series of collaborations with the painter DeLoss McGraw, resulting in humorously sinister books with titles like *The Death of Cock Robin* and *W. D.'s Midnight Carnival.* If Nazi history moved Snodgrass toward the prosaic, McGraw's paintings helped him discover a new musicality, mixed with grotesquely comic intimations of mortality, in a set of nursery rhymes for adults.

... Snodgrass jumbles into this vaudeville an open embrace of all his favorite traditions, alluding more obviously than before to writers ranging from the seventeenth-century cavalier poets, to the troubadours (he has ably translated Provençal poetry), to modern masters like Wallace Stevens ("They say, 'Your songs do not compute./ Your music's mixed; your moral's moot") and W. H. Auden ("In the perspective of the heart/Those dearly loved, when they depart,/Take so much of us when they go/That, like no thing on earth, they grow/Larger ... "). Working with McGraw relieved Snodgrass of the overbearing obligation to seriousness with which *The Fuehrer Bunker* saddled him, and by letting himself have more fun, he created more interesting and important poetry. In their try-anything, on-with-the-show, shuck-and-jive spirit, Snodgrass's McGraw poems owe something to John Berryman, and while they do not possess *The Dream Songs'* wild, manic power, they constitute a significant accomplishment.

Not for Specialists concludes with forty new poems, written over the past decade or so, which provide many satisfying symmetries with the early work. Snodgrass has always acknowledged the comical nature of his name ("poor ill-named one," sympathized Randall Jarrell): His early "These Trees Stand ...," which opens the book, notes, "Your name's absurd," and turns on a delightfully ludicrous refrain, "Snodgrass is walking through the universe." The recent poem "Who Steals My Good Name" returns to the name blame game: It casts spells upon a Snodgrass masquerader "who obtained my debit card number and spent $11,000 in five days," after beginning with a complaint from "My pale stepdaughter": "Well, that's the last time I say my name's/Snodgrass!" Even better, his homage to Marvell, "Chasing Fireflies," exploits his name's literal sense, since "to snod" means "to make smooth, trim, or neat."

... The *Heart's Needle* sequence also earns a reprise, in "For the Third Marriage of My First Ex-Wife," which speaks once more of the woes of wedlocks past—

> not once in twelve years had we laid
> each other right. What we *had* made
> were two nerve-wracked, unreconciled,
> spoiled children parenting a child.

—in order to look benignly ahead and wish everyone well. This moving gesture acknowledges all the hearts badly in need of repair, including that of the daughter, as well as providing some comic and benevolent surprises:

> Our daughter, still recovering from
> her own divorce, but who's become
> a father, in her call at least
> as an Episcopalian priest,
> will fly down there to officiate
> in linking you to your third mate;
> only some twenty years ago
> that daughter married me also
> to the last of my four wives.

"Also, save the best for last," the poem ends. Not all the new poems that end *Not for Specialists* rank with Snodgrass's best, but several decidedly do. All told, they provide a delightful and absorbing range of subjects and moods: splenetic political poems denouncing the Bush administration's war in Iraq, satiric Ben Jonson-like epigrams on a contemporary literary culture designed (his book's title implies) increasingly *for* specialists, wry observations on the foibles of advancing age, and generous accounts of love for wife, children, and friends. Through it all, Snodgrass remains undiminished in his technical skill and unapologetic about his formalism, the secret subject of "Warning," a poem ostensibly about "rumors that Richard Wilbur has had a hip replacement so he could go on playing tennis":

> Wilbur's ball and ceramic socket
> Propel him like a racing sprocket
> To where his artful serve and volley
> Dole out love games and melancholy.
> Tremble, opponents: learn by this
> What power's secured through artifice.

The poem is not just a charming tribute to his important fellow poet, but a witty manifesto, recalling Robert Frost's quip that writing free verse is like playing tennis with the net down. After more than fifty years refining his "love game," Snodgrass keeps mindful of the rules, and the rules have enabled him continually to surprise and delight us. If his poems dare to commit the occasional fault, they can still move and enchant us with the power artifice can secure.

Source: Jay Rogoff, "Shocking, Surprising Snodgrass," in *Southern Review*, September 22, 2006, pp. 885–92.

Roy Scheele

In the following excerpt from an interview, Snodgrass gives a conversational retrospective of his poetic career.

... *[INTERVIEWER:]* Heart's Needle *was published in 1959 and won the Pulitzer Prize for Poetry in 1960. It is an amazing first book, made even more so, perhaps, by the fact that it was partly written while you were a student. It is difficult now to speak of the book outside its importance in contemporary literary history—its influence on Robert Lowell's* Life Studies, *for example. Yet the title poem seems to me one of the major American lyrics of the past fifty years, and I would like to talk a bit about the poem itself. Did you conceive of such a long sequence when you began ...?*

SNODGRASS: ... Somebody suggested to me a cycle of short poems rather than a long single poem, but I don't remember who that was. That was long ago, of course; I've changed every molecule seven times since then. I started making the first notes for that at a concert, and I still have the concert program. I don't think I had any idea how many poems it might come to, whether it would be several poems, or one, or what. The writing stretched out over about two and a half years, which is the amount of time that

> BUT I ALSO SUSPECT—RIGHTLY OR WRONGLY—THAT I CAN'T WRITE POEMS NOW.... I DO FEEL THAT IF I COULD INVENT A NEW KIND OF POEM, THAT WOULD BE WORTH THE EFFORT. BUT THAT'S NEVER GUARANTEED."

the poem covers, season by season. I don't believe the writing exactly followed that pattern, but it took roughly the same amount of time.

INT: Several of the poems in the book—"At the Park Dance," "The Marsh," "September in the Park," the two "Songs"—have the centered lines, and something of the tone, of certain sections in the title poem. "The Marsh" especially suggests the subject matter and imagery of "Heart's Needle." Was "The Marsh" origininally a draft section of the longer poem?

SNODGRASS: No. No, it wasn't. I suspect it was written first, but I am not positive. Oh, wait a minute: I remember how I wrote it. Good heavens, I haven't thought of this in a long time! I'd been out tromping around in the woods, wandered into a marsh and saw the things that come up in the poem. And I'd been trying to write a poem about it, but it didn't seem to work. I had to monitor an exam for a friend, and I thought, I've been stuck with the same phrases, etc. for months. Since I have to get up and put the time on the blackboard every five minutes, I'll write a line and if it doesn't work within that five minutes, I'll cross it out and write another. At the end of the two-hour exam, I had [a] poem, which amazed me, because I usually take weeks, months, years. I think this showed me something about being more ruthless with my first phrasings.

INT: Some sections of "Heart's Needle" have stanzas in which the lines are all flush left, with capitalized first letters, while in other sections the lines are centered and only the first letter of sentences is capitalized. Was there a design to that?

SNODGRASS: No, only that I decided that if I was going to make a series of shorter poems I would want a slightly different form for each of them.

INT: You wanted a different visual form.

SNODGRASS: Yeah. And each one would also have a different sound, I would hope. I don't mean that you necessarily pause at the end of a line. But if you don't have capital letters I assume that the lines are "rove over," as Hopkins says.

INT: A leitmotif in the poem is the speaker's feeling that he cannot write. It is introduced in Section 1 when he envisions the farmer's snowy fields as being "spotless as paper spread/For me to write," continues in Section 4 where he compares the frost-shriveled morning-glory vines to "broken lines/of verses I can't make," is alluded to again in Section 5 when he remembers singing songs to his daughter at bedtime "Before I went for walks/And did not write," and then seems to be resolved in Section 9 with his statement that "I write you only the bitter poems/that you can't read." These references seem a kind of objective correlative of the speaker's emotional limbo at the beginning of the poem, and of his growing acceptance of the divorce and separation at poem's end. Did the writing of "Heart's Needle" represent an overcoming on your part of a period of silence in our work?

SNODGRASS: Your inference is correct, though perhaps the cause and effect weren't quite so direct. I see the passage in Section 1 as more about the promise of what those fields could produce, though I do recall that I often talked about one's terror of the blank page; the other passages seem to me just as you suggest.

When my first marriage was breaking up I had been blocked for about two years and did go into therapy at the University Hospital in Iowa City. Both problems rose at least partly from my own passivity, and the therapy did help. The doctor, by the way, was R. M. Powell, to whom "MHTIS ... OU TIS" is addressed.

INT: The fox is an image which recurs several times in the poem. Is there any special reason for that?

SNODGRASS: I'm not sure. I always did sing my daughter the song "Fox Went Out on a Chilly Night," from that old Burl Ives recording. I tended to think of myself as being a fox type as opposed to a hedgehog. I'd been reading Isaiah Berlin, and I thought, OK, I wish desperately to be a hedgehog, and I can't; I've got to try to play foxy. So I tended to identify with that kind of critter.

INT: In your recently published After-Images: Autobiographical Sketches *(BOA Editions, 1999), you speak of your conviction that*

"one of the most important developments in our poetry has been the polyvoiced poem," and among other examples you cite Eliot's The Waste Land *and Henry Reed's "Naming of Parts." Why in your view has the polyvoiced poem been so important?*

SNODGRASS: Generally, I suspect that this is related to the loss of religious faith and surrendering the hope of finding some universal philosophical system, some one formula or formulation to sum up our fragmented experience.

For myself, I was very much moved by the poems you mention, but also by Theodore Weiss's *Gunsight* and especially by Henri Coulette's *War of the Secret Agents.* (I was on a jury that gave the latter the Lamont Poetry Prize.) Poems of this type, I thought, offer something like the oppositions of sonata form in music, pitting theme against theme and building that into a larger structure. Everybody then was looking for ways to reproduce musical forms in poetry; this seemed to work for me first in a poem called "After Experience Taught Me...," which pits two voices I'd discovered at the same time (Spinoza and a hand-to-hand combat instructor) against each other. In terms of idea, of course, they're saying the same thing (whatever you do to protect your life is justified), but in actuality it means something far different according to the personality of the speakers. I'd been trying ever since the war to write about those combat instructions, so when I liked the result of this voice-collision, that made a large impression on me.

INT: When viewed as a cycle of poems, the monologues of The Führer Bunker *are polyvoiced. This seems to me a perfect way of presenting the Nazi hierarchy: from their own points of view, in their own voices. And yet I wonder whether much of the negative critical reaction to the book doesn't spring from a basic failure of aesthetic distance, i.e., the failure of many critics to separate the speaker of a given monologue from the author himself. Haven't such critics in fact identified you with the speakers of the cycle and thereby associated you with the Nazis' own evil?*

SNODGRASS: That depends on what you mean by "identify." To do those poems, I did have to find those characters in myself—and they were there, at least as potentials, though I suspect I'm less liable to violence and direct cruelty than to the self-deceptions of people like Himmler and Bormann. Someone once called these my really confessional poems. Some critics would like to accuse me of somehow approving the Nazis, but the poems won't justify that. I've shown those characters as more wicked than any historian has. But I was careful not to imply that I am, or we are, or that those critics are, immune to such wickedness. When I was young, people still said, "The only good Indian is a dead Indian"; later they said, "Better dead than red," and in many places we saw to it that people became dead instead. Only a month or two ago, a man in my post office said, "Hitler should have killed them all, right?" Sadly, we can understand such persons since we have not always been above such actions and sentiments. And I do not believe that to understand is to forgive. That we did not commit all the same vicious actions may be more a matter of luck than of some inherent moral superiority.

INT: There is no easy view of morality in The Führer Bunker, *no comfortable equation of Us vs. Them. Rather, the book sees humanity as being universally capable of such evil. Why do you think so many readers have insisted on the more simplistic moral view?*

SNODGRASS: People find it lots nicer to abominate others' evil than to examine their own. They'd like to believe, for example, that we fought World War II to free the Jews. We fought the war to preserve our markets. The Jews' salvation was a byproduct which many here did not welcome—anti-Semitism was widespread (and still is, in places).

My views on evil were stated perfectly by Simone Weil: "I suggest that barbarism be considered a permanent and universal human characteristic which becomes more or less pronounced according to the play of circumstances." If we haven't all confirmed that since the war, I must be reading the wrong papers.

INT: One of the most telling of the monologues is "Dr. Joseph Goebbels, Minister for Propaganda—20 April 1945." In the last four stanzas there you contrast lines from Goebbels's radio speech of 19 April celebrating Hitler's birthday with Goebbels's real thoughts about Hitler, which are cynical and derisive. This contrast is heightened by your use of rhyming couplets, each first line giving the public rhetoric and each second line giving Goebbels's own thoughts. Are such contrapuntal devices, which occur frequently in The Führer Bunker, *meant to point out the moral chasm*

between the Nazis' rhetoric and the sometimes bestial realities underlying that rhetoric?

SNODGRASS: Oh, sure. And there are other devices that are meant to do that. Bormann's idealistic letters to his wife and his real aims and operations, for example. That's meant to be happening all the time there.

INT: Blank verse, of course, is the traditional medium for the dramatic monologue, and I find it intriguing that you have written the Führer Bunker *monologues in lyrical forms such as the triolet, sestina, and villanelle and in the nonce forms you chose for such speakers as Speer and Himmler. I'm wondering whether you were consciously trying to rebel against the expectations of the form or were simply trying to match the form to the character of each speaker.*

SNODGRASS: I don't believe I consciously intended to rebel against traditional forms of dramatic monologue, though I suppose one always wants to do something different from what others have done. As you suggest, I was conscious of trying to match form to personality. Those fancy French forms I used for Magda Goebbels were traditionally part of the romantic love paraphernalia. She had always used such things for unscrupulous advantage, and I thought her repetitive lies very similar to those of her husband. I think I've said elsewhere that if it's true, you only need say it once.

INT: I'd like to ask some random questions now. Your poem "Seasoning Barn" employs a very wide line, carefully controlled and modulated. How would you describe that line? Is it loose blank verse, or free verse? Or does it split the difference between the two?

SNODGRASS: It isn't one that I often read …[*Studies text of poem for a moment.*] Yeah, I think you're right: I am splitting the difference between blank verse and free verse there… I remember the event. My third wife and I had been at an early music collegium up in New England, and we were driving back from there and saw this sign on a big barn that said, "Fantastic tables!" We were tired of driving and said, "Let's go see what's in there." And here was this amazing scene that I describe in the poem. This man, whose name is Roy Sheldon, had been a painter. He had gone with the expatriates to Paris and painted there. And he had commissions for four or five big jobs back in the States. While he was at sea on the way home the market crashed, and of course the commissions didn't come through. He became an economist and the government sent him around to different places to work. When he got to retirement age he decided he'd go back into the arts, or at least into crafts, and he started making tables. And he had people shipping him chunks of wood from all over the world. We ordered a cherry dining room table and a walnut coffee table from a tree that came out of Pennsylvania; it had some kind of rot that made very interesting patterns in the wood. My present wife and I still use the cherry table and we love it. It has a certain amount of sapwood in it, and tiny black dots in places, and some knots. I wanted all those, I didn't want the pure straight stuff. Anyway, it seemed like a long line fit that subject somehow. And I thought, as I wrote it (though I don't think I started out with that idea), that that was the way I'd like to write poems: take material and let it season for ten or fifteen years until it's hardened, and then try to make something out of it.

INT: Has Edwin Arlington Robinson, with his disposition to write narrative lyrics, been an important poet to you?

SNODGRASS: Yes indeed. I'm very fond of "Mr. Flood's Party," which is just marvelous, and quite a few of the others. But I haven't read him very extensively. There's a couple of his very long poems which I read years ago and admired a lot but haven't gone back to for some reason. The same way with Browning. It's been a long time since I read "Mr. Sludge, 'The Medium,'" although I loved it. Then there's "Bishop Blougram's Apology" and poems like that that must have had a pretty strong influence on me, but I haven't looked at them in so long I don't really know.

INT: What contact did you have with John Crowe Ransom?

SNODGRASS: He used to come to Iowa and give lectures, and he was the sweetest man that ever lived. I sort of thought of him as my grandfather, because his immediate children were Lowell and Jarrell and those people, and I felt like their baby. He did like one poem of mine, much to my surprise; mostly he didn't like my stuff. He was so fond of indirection, whereas I tended to be much more direct, and I think that jarred him a little bit. But he was wonderful, and I loved to hear him read. I just wonder if his poems will ever seem so good to people who haven't heard him read. He had a marvelous voice: very Southern, soft and charming but, underneath, affectionately knowing and skeptical.

INT: You have a great admiration for the work of Walt Whitman. What do you value most in his work?

SNODGRASS: Oh, I suppose breadth of emotion and breadth of identification.

INT: His ability to include almost everything.

SNODGRASS: Exactly. As a matter of fact, at the end of this tour I'm doing a reading of *Song of Myself*—well, of selections from—a reading of the whole poem would be three hours long! But that's the kind of reading I most like to do. It's just wonderful to read that poem out loud. Whitman really had an ear. A lot of people that you're supposed to like who are said to be like him don't seem to me to be like him at all.

INT: I don't think there's anyone like him.

SNODGRASS: No, there isn't. He's just incredibly gifted—above all, in the musical sense.

INT: The music of a poem is really important, isn't it?

SNODGRASS: Absolutely. I'm inclined to think that reading silently cannot really approximate the poem's full power. For me it is an aural experience: no music, no poem. Some of Cummings's poems, the typographical doodles, for instance, can't be read out loud, and if you can't read it out loud I don't think it's a poem. I think the voice and speech and sound go very deep: even while you're in the womb you're hearing people say things and you're responding to that, and you're surely responding to your mother's heartbeat. For me, when that goes out of the poem, the poem itself is gone.

*INT: In your lecture "Tact and the Poet's Force" (*In Radical Pursuit: Critical Essays and Lectures, *Harper & Row, 1975), you say that the poet "takes some idea, ordinary enough in itself, and represses it from conscious assertion, so that it can spread into the details, the style, the formal techniques" of the poem. And in "Finding a Poem" you observe how necessary it is for the poet to write what he or she really thinks or feels in a given situation. It's very difficult, isn't it, to achieve a balance between tact and honest expression?*

SNODGRASS: It is indeed. There was a great problem of that for Whitman, for instance.

I mean, you get all those violent sexual scenes, dealing with touch, in *Song of Myself*—I forget which section it is—that turn into what I think is a description of a gang rape. Bloom said it was masturbation, somebody else said it was something else, but Whitman's very careful not to tell you exactly who's doing what to whom, with what, and yet you know there's some kind of wild sexual thing happening. Well, of course he had to get it printed, and he couldn't have if he had been more specific. And of course he got it printed partly because everybody was very careful not to understand. But he tells you everything you need to know.

INT: You've remarked that your typical way of revising a poem is not to pare or tighten it but to expand it, to write a longer version of the original. You do this, I take it, in order to allow your own voice, your real thoughts and feelings, freer play. But does your sense of poetic tact also assert itself as you revise?

SNODGRASS: I don't know. I don't think I approach it that consciously. I just ask, "Does this sound better?" I don't usually ask in what way is it better. I do know this: if the poem is working, as you revise it it gets to seeming more and more tossed off, freehand, whereas the initial drafts often seem very midnight-oil-covered—labored. If you're any good at revising, as you work at it the poem gets to seeming more spontaneous.

INT: A good deal of your work in recent years—the Cock Robin *poems, for example—is in light verse. What freedom and/or restrictions do you experience in writing light verse?*

SNODGRASS: I enjoy writing comic and/or light verse but for many years didn't dare indulge myself—we all had to be so serious. DeLoss McGraw's paintings helped spring me. And, like almost nothing else I've written, these came very quickly and without my usual endless revisions. Also causal was a sense of relief and celebration when I found that I could, after all, finish *The Führer Bunker*. I thought that was the major commitment of my career; if I couldn't finish it, I'd die a failure. When I was sure I could finish, I found an example in Rilke's *Duino Elegies*. (I'm not suggesting that I rose to those heights.) Before he was quite finished but knew he could, Rilke started the *Sonnets to Orpheus* and wrote fifty-six of them in eighteen days. They, of course, aren't light verse, but they are elective and gratuitous—not, like the *Elegies,* mandatory.

INT: Given the hard work of drafting and revising, is the writing of poems fun for you?

SNODGRASS: Except perhaps for those poems based on McGraw, I don't think writing poetry has ever been fun for me. It's just that I feel so much worse if I don't write poems.

Since I've finished *The Führer Bunker,* I've only written six or eight poems. That's partly because I'm writing prose pieces: first, the autobiographical sketches; now, a book of critical essays; next, a book of what I call de/compositions. These were my favorite teaching device: I'd take a fine poem and make revisions which destroyed its excellences, then ask the students what I'd lost from the original. Handling the poems that closely, they had to experience how little of a poem's greatness lay in its dictionary sense, in the literal, translatable meaning. Of course these projects have taken much more time and effort than I expected—most pages have probably been revised twenty times or so. Maybe I need a classroom full of students taking an exam!

But I also suspect—rightly or wrongly—that I can't write poems now. I have puzzled over this and come up with four or five possible causes; I've no idea which is (or are) actually the case. I don't even know whether it's good or bad—perhaps anything I wrote at my age would be weaker. I do feel that if I could invent a new kind of poem, that would be worth the effort. But that's never guaranteed. We'll see what happens when I finish these books.

Source: Roy Scheele, "A Conversation with W. D. Snodgrass," in *New England Review*, Vol. 21, No. 1, Winter 2000, pp. 56–66.

SOURCES

Pratt, William, Review of *Each in His Season*, by W.D. Snodgrass, in *World Literature Today*, Vol. 68, No. 2, Spring 1994, p. 375.

Rogoff, Jay, "Shocking, Surprising Snodgrass," in *Southern Review*, Vol. 42, No. 4, Autumn 2006, pp. 885–86.

Rosenthal, M. L., "Notes From the Future: Two Poets," in *Nation*, October 24, 1959, pp. 257–58.

Snodgrass, W. D., "Heart's Needle," in *Not for Specialists: New and Selected Poems*, BOA Editions, 2006, pp. 19–34.

FURTHER READING

Egan, Catherine, "A Cycle of Identity: W. D. Snodgrass' Pseudonym S. S. Gardons," in *Journal of Undergraduate Research*, University of Rochester, Vol. 1, No. 1, Fall 2002, pp. 11–13.

Egan examines the factors that drove Snodgrass, after the resounding success of *Heart's Needle*, to publish his next volume, *Remains*, under a pen name.

Royko, David, *Voices of Children of Divorce*, Golden Books, 1999.

Royko includes dozens of interviews with children of divorced parents, showing the range of emotions that children can experience as a result.

Snodgrass, W. D., *W. D. Snodgrass in Conversation with Philip Hoy*, Between the Lines, 1998.

This eighty-page book is full of the poet's anecdotes and reflections on other poets.

Turco, Lewis, "The Poetics of W. D. Snodgrass," in *Hollins Critic*, June 1993, pp. 1–10.

This overview of Snodgrass's work includes thorough analyses of a few of his poems and helps readers understand his overall style.

homage to my hips

LUCILLE CLIFTON

1980

Lucille Clifton's "homage to my hips" first appeared in the book *Two-Headed Woman* (1980), a collection of poems written between 1960 and 1980. Although Clifton was publishing both poetry and children's books during this period, *Two-Headed Woman*, nominated for the Pulitzer Prize, established her as a major American poet. Clifton calls the opening section "Homage to Mine" and includes several "homage" poems; "homage to my hair" is the poem that immediately precedes "homage to my hips." In both cases, the poet is celebrating a part of her body that has traditionally been demeaned.

In "homage to my hips," Clifton provides a sometimes playful (but always mighty) expression of African American womanhood. In just seventy-eight words, she frees herself from both the dominance of Caucasian ideals of beauty and from masculine notions of femininity. The poem has been widely anthologized in collections such as *Twentieth-Century American Poetry* (1994), and it is also available in Clifton's important collection *Good Woman: Poems and a Memoir, 1969–1980* (1987).

AUTHOR BIOGRAPHY

Lucille Clifton was born Thelma Lucille Sayles in Depew, New York, on June 27, 1936. Her parents were Samuel and Thelma Moore Sayles.

Her father was a steelworker, her mother a laundress and homemaker. Clifton was born with six fingers on each hand, a trait she shared with her mother and later with her daughter. This trait becomes a significant motif in Clifton's poetry.

Neither of Clifton's parents finished elementary school; although her father could read, he never learned to write. Her mother, on the other hand, was a poet herself, producing verses in traditional iambic pentameter. Life was not pleasant in the Sayles household, even after their move to Buffalo, New York, when Lucille was seven years old. Her father was a womanizer and was cruel to her mother, who also suffered from epilepsy. In addition to Lucille, her parents, and her younger brother, Sammy, the family also included a daughter, Josie, from Samuel Sayles's first marriage and a daughter, Elaine, born to Sayles and a neighbor woman a few months after Lucille's birth. Money was tight, and Sayles drank, at times heavily. He sexually molested Lucille, and this early abuse is reflected in many of her later poems.

In 1953, Lucille left home to begin study at Howard University as the recipient of a prestigious scholarship. While at Howard, she encountered some of the finest minds of her generation. Her professor, the noted poet Sterling A. Brown, invited her to join a writers' group that included James Baldwin, Owen Dodson, and Joe Walker, as well as Lucille's friend LeRoi Jones (later known as Amiri Baraka). She also became friends with fellow students Toni Morrison, who would later win a Nobel Prize in Literature, and Roberta Flack, who would become a famous singer and composer.

Lucille left Howard in 1955 and attended Fredonia State Teachers College briefly. While at Fredonia, her friend Ishmael Reed introduced her to a Buffalo State University student named Fred James Clifton, an educator who later helped to found the department of African American studies at Harvard University. In 1958, the young couple began a marriage that would flourish through the births of six children in the first seven years and last until Fred Clifton's death of cancer at age forty-nine in 1984. Sadly, Lucille Clifton's mother died in 1959 at age forty-four.

In 1967, the Clifton family moved to Baltimore, Maryland, where Fred Clifton worked on educational reform in the city's schools. Meanwhile, Clifton herself continued to write poetry and children's books, just as she had during the years in Buffalo. She longed to have a wider audience for her work, however, and thus sent some of her poems to Langston Hughes and Robert Hayden, both highly regarded African American poets. Hayden in turn showed the poems to another important poet, Carolyn Kizer, who in turn showed the poems to some friends at the 92nd Street YMCA in New York City, which sponsored one of the most prestigious writing contests in the country; as a result of poets sharing Clifton's work with other poets, she ended up receiving the 1969 New York Young Women's and Young Men's Poetry Discovery Award. This award led to a reading in New York attended by an editor from Random House who asked Clifton to submit a manuscript. The book became *Good Times*, published in 1969. In addition, Clifton also began her long career as a writer of illustrated children's books with *Some of the Days of Everett Horton*.

During the next two decades, Clifton continued to produce both poetry and picture books, and her work was included in several prominent anthologies. She served as the poet laureate of Maryland from 1975 to 1985. *Generations*, Clifton's memoir, appeared in 1976. In 1980, her poetry collection *Two-Headed Woman*, published by the University of Massachusetts Press, won the Juniper Prize and was nominated for the Pulitzer Prize. It was in this collection that "homage to my hips" was first published.

In 1984, with the death of her beloved husband, Clifton wrote the children's book *Everett Anderson's Goodbye*, a volume that won the American Library Association's Coretta Scott King Award. Her 1987 publications, *Next* and *Good Woman: Poems and a Memoir, 1969–1980* (including "homage to my hips"), netted her another Pulitzer nomination, as did her 1991 work *Quilting*. Clifton was named a Maryland "Living Treasure" in 1993; she was finalist for the National Book Award, the Lenore Marshall Prize, and the Los Angeles Times Book Award, all in 1996; and she won the Lifetime Achievement Award for Excellence from the Lannan Foundation in 1996. She was also elected to the Board of Chancellors of the Academy of American Poets and named a fellow of the American Academy of Arts and Sciences in 1999. Clifton won the National Book Award for Poetry for *Blessing the Boats* in 2000 and the Anisfield-Wolf Lifetime Achievement Award from the Cleveland Foundation in 2004.

Following the death of her husband, Clifton endured breast cancer in 1994 and kidney failure in 1997. She received a kidney transplant from her daughter Alexia. Clifton lost her daughter Frederica to a brain tumor in 2000 and her son Channing to heart failure in 2004.

Throughout her life, Clifton has continued to teach creative writing across the country at small and large universities alike. Although she retired in 2005 from St. Mary's College of Maryland, where she held the Hilda C. Landers Chair in the Liberal Arts, as of 2007 she still returned to teach for at least part of each subsequent year. She counts among her friends some of the most important writers of the twentieth century, including Toni Morrison, Gwendolyn Brooks, and Ishmael Reed. Her name is familiar to children, students, adult readers, and scholars alike.

POEM SUMMARY

Lines 1–5

In lines 1 through 3, Clifton asserts that her hips are large and that they must have adequate room for movement. From the start, the sounds and rhythms employed by Clifton mimic the swaying of hips. In line 4, Clifton says that her hips cannot squeeze into small spaces. Perhaps the expansiveness of her hips transcends the narrowness of the culture—as if white American culture in particular, with its obsessive concerns with women's weight, is too constraining for the magnificent hips Clifton pays homage to. Clifton places a comma in the middle of line 5, signaling a turn to a new thought. In the second half of line 5, Clifton attaches the notion of freedom to her hips.

Lines 6–10

The notion begun in the second part of line 5 continues through line 10. She touches on the topic of slavery in this section, asserting that her hips are not slaves. Her hips have the freedom to be where they will and to do whatever she would like them to do. Her hips, then, become symbolic of emancipation, a word that resonates with both racial and gender inequalities of the past. Emancipation, on the one hand, describes the freeing of slaves during the American Civil War; the Emancipation Proclamation is an

MEDIA ADAPTATIONS

- The Academy of American Poets maintains an audio clip of Clifton reading "homage to my hips" on their website at http://www.poets.org/poet.php/prmPID/79.

- A video recording of Clifton reading "homage to my hips" and other poems was made on March 17, 1988. The Library of Congress website has posted this recording as a webcast at http://www.loc.gov/today/cyberlc/feature_wdesc.php?rec=3656.

important and significant national document. In addition, the term *emancipation* can also refer to voting rights. African American men were given the right to vote in 1870 with the ratification of the Fifteenth Amendment to the Constitution. Women, both black and white, on the other hand, did not become enfranchised until much later with the passage of the Nineteenth Amendment in 1920.

Lines 11–15

Line 12 is nearly identical to line 11, with only one word different between them. In addition, the two differing words begin with the same initial sound. The similarity of the lines draws attention to the differing words while at the same time creating the effect of an incantation. That is, the words of these lines, when read aloud, sound like words of magic, designed to enchant. Indeed, as the poem continues, Clifton ascribes supernatural qualities to her hips. She also speaks of her hips as if they have existence independent from her. She says that in the past, her hips have enchanted a male and completely confused him. The final five lines of "homage to my hips" move the poem from one in which the speaker's concern is with claiming space for her hips (and by extension, her whole body) to one in which the hips are powerful tools of supernatural strength.

TOPICS FOR FURTHER STUDY

- In addition to "homage to my hips," Clifton wrote several other poems about her body including "homage to my hair," "i was born with twelve fingers," and "what the mirror said." Read a wide selection of these poems, then write several poems to various parts of your own body. What would you like to celebrate? Why? How is your celebration of your own body different from or similar to commonly held cultural views? Write a brief essay addressing these questions.

- Clifton counted among her friends some of the most important writers of the black arts movement. Research the movement, and find representative pieces of art, music, and literature. Using what you learn and collect, develop a multimedia presentation on the black arts movement and present it to your class.

- Gwendolyn Brooks, a close friend of Clifton and the first African American to win a Pulitzer Prize, wrote a very famous poem called "the mother." This poem is often compared and contrasted with Clifton's "the lost baby poem." Read both poems carefully, along with interviews with both writers, then write an essay comparing and contrasting the position the two poems seem to take on the subject of abortion.

- The poet Sharon Olds published a volume of poems about her father called *The Father* in 1992. Likewise, one of Sylvia Plath's most famous poems, "Daddy," is about the poet's relationship with her father. Read these poems along with Clifton's many poems that concern her father and write an essay comparing and contrasting the poets' views of fatherhood.

- Ideals of feminine beauty change across time and across culture. Collect copies of paintings and photographs of women from a wide variety of time periods and countries. Can you make a list of what features were considered beautiful in each time period and in each culture? Make a collage of these images and write a report about the changing perceptions of feminine beauty.

THEMES

Cultural Notions of Beauty

In "homage to my hips," Clifton makes a statement about culturally held notions of beauty. For decades, majority American culture has prized slender hips and overall thinness. Top models such as Twiggy, from the 1960s, and more recently Kate Moss have provided the iconic waif-like look found on the covers of fashion magazines. The bodies of these models resemble that of a young boy rather than that of a fully developed woman. In addition, the excessively thin women who grace the covers of women's magazines typically have little in common with the women who read the magazines.

Clifton asserts in her poem that her large hips have much more power than do small hips. By extension, she calls for women to free themselves from the self-limiting notions of beauty foisted upon them by media and culture. Rather than worrying about dieting and trying to make her body conform to some impossible, externally imposed idea about beauty, she celebrates her own large hips, equating their largeness with the largeness of the life she wants to live. Moreover, she seems to be saying that her choice to have large hips frees her from all limitations. Culture enslaves women by requiring that they look a particular way in order to be deemed attractive; Clifton, on the other hand, asserts that her hips have always been free. As such, they belong to no one but herself.

In "homage to my hips" Clifton is also associating herself with the "Black Is Beautiful" movement of the 1960s and 1970s, the period when this poem was written. This movement urged African Americans to reject western European notions of beauty and to instead embrace Afrocentric features as their standard of beauty. As the poet Alicia Ostriker notes in the *American Poetry Review*, "Clifton began writing during the explosive Black Arts movement of the late 1960's and early 1970's," and she "records her womanly conversion from bleaching cream and 'whiteful ways' to the love of blackness."

Liberation from Expectation

Ajuan Maria Mance, writing in a chapter from *Recovering the Black Female Body: Self-Representations by African American Women*, argues, "In 'homage to my hips,' Clifton continues her pursuit of a new and emancipatory vision of the black female corpus." The word *emancipate* means to free from slavery or other restraint; an emancipationist is someone who favors or advocates emancipation from some legal, social, or other restraint. Another term for an emancipationist is a liberationist. In "homage to my hips," Clifton foremost plays the role of a women's liberationist. She remarks on the pettiness and narrowness imposed by patriarchal and societal expectations of women. She demands space— space to move her large hips in a dance to her own expansive soul. She also asserts that her hips have more strength than a man's. Revealing a second role, Clifton's assertion that her hips are free, never having been contained by slavery, reminds the reader that Clifton is not just a woman but a woman of color, a woman whose own great-great-grandmother was captured in Africa and brought to North America. She celebrates her freedom in making a negating reference to an institution that turned proud people into chattel by depriving them of the most fundamental of all human rights, the ownership of their own bodies. Her statement that her hips have freedom of movement and freedom of intention embodies the abstraction of liberty itself. Nothing will impede the forward progress of these powerful hips, and by extension, the progress of a powerful people.

Transformation from the Mundane to the Supernatural

By the end of "homage to my hips," Clifton's hips have assumed more than just the power of a free, individual woman of color. They have grown to large and supernatural proportions, capable of overpowering and confusing a man. Clifton refers directly to her hips being capable of casting magical enchantments over a man. The reference to magic suggests that Clifton may be referring to juju, the magic of an object or fetish believed by West Africans to hold supernatural power. Clifton's hips, with their freedom and their strength, have not only natural human power but also the juju power of the supernatural and of Clifton's female ancestors. In this brief poem, then, Clifton invokes the spirits of the women who went before her, women who were under the cruel reign of slavery as well as those who were free in Africa, to endow her hips with supernatural power.

STYLE

Alliteration and Repetition

The poem "homage to my hips" consists of only seventy-eight words organized into fifteen lines. As with many of Clifton's poems, "homage to my hips" does not have capital letters, although it is punctuated. The poem does not have regular rhyme or meter, but strong sound and rhythmic qualities are created by the use of repetition, both of whole words and of sounds. The repetition of initial sounds is called alliteration, and Clifton uses this device throughout the poem. The repetition of sounds and words serves to emphasize Clifton's themes. In addition, through the repeated sounds and words, the poem itself takes on the rhythm of an incantation or magic spell. Thus, both the meanings of the selected words and the sounds of the words work dynamically to convey the sense that the speaker is a woman of power and possibility.

Synecdoche

Synecdoche is a literary figure of speech in which one part signifies the whole. For example, when a sailing captain calls out, "All hands on deck!" he or she does not literally mean that everyone on board should place their hands on the boat deck. Rather, the captain is using the term "hand" to represent the whole sailor. For a synecdoche to work well, it should use an important part of the whole, and it should be a part that is directly connected to the topic. Thus, in the above example, "hands" is a good choice as a synecdoche for sailors for two reasons: first, sailors perform most of their work with their hands, and second, when a captain calls for all hands to come on deck, there is work to be done. If the captain wanted the sailors to be on the lookout for an enemy vessel, on the other hand, he or she might instead call out, "All eyes to starboard!" A bad or unclear synecdoche would be if the captain called out, "All elbows down below!" The appropriateness of the synecdoche contributes to the clarity of the figure of speech.

Mark Bernard White, in an article in the *CLA Journal*, asserts that Clifton's use of hips in "homage to my hips" is a form of synecdoche. He writes, "Hips become a synecdoche, even a theme or motif, in Clifton, to suggest her own womanliness, the power of the feminine form, and especially to celebrate the aesthetics of black women's bodies." The rightness of White's statement is obvious on reflection. When Clifton argues that her hips are free and do not belong to anyone else, she of course also means that her whole body is free. It would be a logical impossibility for it to be otherwise. In addition, the synecdoche is clear for the two important reasons noted above: first, hips are an essential part of a woman's body, and second, hips are directly related to the topic under discussion, a woman's beauty and sense of self. Clifton, therefore, uses the literary device of synecdoche to provide a concrete visual image in the form of her hips to stand in for the abstraction of the free female body.

Minimalism

Minimalism is a movement in visual, architectural, and literary arts characterized by a striving to reach the essence of an idea with a minimum of words or detail. In minimalist literature, each word resonates with significance, such that only a few words can carry the theme. Well-known minimalist writers include Raymond Carver and Anne Beattie. An examination of Clifton's poetry as well reveals this aesthetic function. Alicia Ostriker, in the *American Poetry Review*, comments on why this is such an effective technique for Clifton: "The work of a minimalist artist like Clifton makes empty space resonate. A spacious silence is not mere absence of noise, but locates us as it were on a cosmic stage." That is, the carving away of words to reveal the essence of a poem results in space in which the poem can move, in much the same way that Clifton revels in space for her hips. Writing in

Black Women Writers (1950–1980): A Critical Evaluation, Haki Madhubuti likewise praises Clifton for being "an economist with words" who "is effective because, despite consciously limiting her vocabulary, she has defined her audience.... She is communicating ideas and concepts." Thus, Clifton's minimalist style focuses attention on her ideas and concepts rather than on a large or academic vocabulary. By using language common among her audience, she writes poetry that speaks directly to those she wishes to address.

HISTORICAL CONTEXT

Civil Rights and the Black Power Movement

Clifton was born in 1936, a time when African Americans were excluded from many of the amenities of American life. Particularly in the southern states, African Americans were legally segregated into their own schools, neighborhoods, and recreational facilities. So-called Jim Crow laws established that segregation was legal so long as facilities were separate but equal. Conditions, however, were scarcely ever equal, and generations of young African Americans struggled with inferior schools and education.

The return of African American soldiers from World War II in 1945 began a decades-long struggle to achieve civil rights for African American citizens. In 1954, while Clifton was a student at Howard University, in Washington, D.C., the U.S. Supreme Court ruled in *Brown v. Board of Education* that it was the right of African American children to attend school with all other children. Over the next few years, civil disorder broke out as schools began the long process of desegregation.

Throughout the late 1950s and early 1960s, African Americans and their white allies worked tirelessly to establish equal rights for all citizens. Led by leaders such as Dr. Martin Luther King, Jr., civil rights activists engaged in voter registration drives and civil disobedience, sometimes at the cost of their own safety. In spite of the successes the civil rights leaders achieved in securing legal civil rights, discrimination in many forms continued to plague the country.

By 1966, the tenor of the civil rights movement began to change. Groups of militant African Americans, such as the Black Panthers and

COMPARE
&
CONTRAST

- **1970s:** Anorexia nervosa, a potentially deadly eating disorder in which victims starve themselves to become thin (sometimes resulting in death), comes to public attention.

  Today: Some researchers estimate that the incidence of anorexia has doubled in the United States since 1970, yet at the same time an ever-growing segment of the population has become obese.

- **1970s:** Women struggle to attain equal status with men in all segments of society, including the workplace.

  Today: Although women still find it difficult to break through the "glass ceiling" (a term indicating the limitations in career advancement for women), many more women serve as presidents and executives of large companies than ever before.

- **1970s:** Through the black arts movement, the artistic corollary to the black power movement, writers such as Amiri Baraka and Ishmael Reed argue that art, particularly among African Americans, must not be just art for art's sake but rather should have a moral, ethical, and political purpose.

  Today: African American writers and artists produce work in all genres of art; while their work often reflects African American experience, their audiences include all segments of the culture.

---

the followers of Malcolm X, rejected King's nonviolent approach to integration, preferring to focus on African American self-sufficiency and self-determination. Leaders such as Stokely Carmichael and Robert Williams called for a new racial consciousness represented by the slogan "Black Power." The black power movement asserted that self-esteem and self-determined standards of beauty were necessary to bring the imbalance of power between African Americans and whites into line. A subsidiary of the black power movement was the "Black Is Beautiful" initiative. African Americans were encouraged to embrace a new appreciation for their own physical characteristics and for their own artistic creations, rather than use cosmetic products such as hair straighteners and skin bleach or adopt literary genres and styles borrowed from European writers.

Clifton's poems in *Two-Headed Woman* were composed between 1969 and 1980. The poem "homage to my hips" in particular demonstrates the celebration of African American beauty and womanhood growing out of the black power movement.

The Black Arts Movement

The black arts movement was the cultural corollary to the more political black power movement. The black arts movement called for a black aesthetic that would connect the worlds of art and literature with the world of African Americans. The purpose of such an aesthetic would be to use black experience as a vital and necessary component of art. Only through the celebration and valuing of black experience could African Americans reforge a common culture from those that had been nearly destroyed over the centuries among the black diaspora after African peoples were kidnapped and sold into slavery all over the globe.

The black arts movement found expression with writers such as Clifton's friend, Amiri Baraka, who founded the Black Arts Repertory Theatre/School (BART/S). Baraka believed that artists are by necessity political activists. Members of Baraka's school performed plays on street corners and wherever they could find an audience. Other important writers of the period included Larry Neal, Gwendolyn Brooks, Sonia Sanchez, Betye Saar, Jeff Donaldson,

Ishmael Reed, and Haki Madhubuti, among many others. The literature of the movement was often written in black vernacular and addressed issues such as interracial tension, the African diaspora, and politics. Clifton was well acquainted with many of these writers, and she and her husband were also deeply involved in issues concerning African Americans. Written between 1969 and 1980, poems such as "homage to my hips" and others of *Two-Headed Woman* demonstrate many of the aesthetic qualities called for by the movement.

Literary historians and critics vary in their assessment of the importance of the black arts movement. An increasing number of studies, however, suggest that the movement not only was revolutionary for African American artists but also shifted the course of American literature.

The Feminist Movement

At the same time that African American citizens were growing increasingly vocal about their civil rights, women of the United States also began to reexamine their roles in American society. Simone de Beauvoir's *The Second Sex* (1948; translated 1953), Betty Friedan's *The Feminist Mystique* (1963), and Kate Millet's *Sexual Politics* (1970) were all important texts that led to women asserting civil, political, and social equality. Like the writers of the black arts movement, feminist writers called for women artists to write their experiences as women rather than imitate the genres and styles of male writers. Indeed, one of the central tensions of the feminist movement was one of similarity or difference: Should women be judged against the same criteria as men, since as people they should be inherently equal? Or, on the other hand, should women be judged as women, determining for themselves what criteria constitute success?

During this period, feminists called for equal pay for equal work and fought against the unspoken assumptions about women that kept women from achieving success in their careers. For Clifton, a wife and mother of six children, the demands of running a house while attempting a full-time career as a professor and writer illustrated the very issues feminists were attempting to highlight. Many of Clifton's poems from the 1960s and 1970s illustrate her growing need to value her womanhood in addition to valuing her blackness.

CRITICAL OVERVIEW

Clifton's 1980 poetry collection *Two-Headed Woman* won the Juniper Prize, sponsored by the University of Massachusetts Press, and was nominated for the Pulitzer Prize. Poems from this collection such as "homage to my hips" received special mention. The poet Marilyn Nelson Waniek (who is mostly known as Marilyn Nelson), for example, writing a 1983 review of *Two-Headed Woman* in *Callaloo*, calls Clifton "a visionary poet. Her vision, however, is one of sanity, connectedness, light. She can write poems which are bright little gems of perceptive observation." Likewise, Haki Madhubuti, writing an early critical evaluation of Clifton's work in *Black Women Writers (1950–1980): A Critical Evaluation*, comments on the poems of *Two-Headed Woman*. Madhubuti states that Clifton "understands that precise communication is not an easy undertaking; language, at its root, seeks to express emotion, thought, action."

By the mid-1990s, critics were noting Clifton's particular ability to write about the body. Jean Anaporte-Easton, for example, writing in the *Mid-American Review*, comments, "The distinctive quality of Clifton's voice comes from her ability to ground her art in an imagery of the body and physical reality." Likewise, a few years later, in a chapter from *Recovering the Black Female Body: Self Representations by African American Women*, Ajuan Maria Mance comments, "In many ways Clifton's *Two-Headed Woman* ... marks the beginning of her interest in depicting the transgressive black body."

Other critics, such as Mary Jane Lupton in *Lucille Clifton: Her Life and Letters*, began to compare Clifton to a variety of writers such as Gwendolyn Brooks, Ann Sexton, and Sylvia Plath. Hilary Holladay, writing about Clifton in the essay collection titled *The Furious Flowering of African American Poetry*, argues that Clifton's "mastery of the lyric recalls the stylistic pleasures of imagism and the visceral emotion of confessional poetry. Like William Carlos Williams, Ezra Pound, H.D., and Wallace Stevens, Clifton is capable of the stunning miniature." That Holladay connects Clifton with such highly regarded modernist poets suggests that by the mid-1990s, Clifton's work was transcending narrow categorization as work by a woman of color. A few years later, in one of the first book-length studies of Clifton's oeuvre, *Wild Blessings: The*

Poetry of Lucille Clifton, Holladay argues that Clifton's focus on female uniqueness places her "in the long tradition of poets mythologizing womanhood."

Clifton's reputation seems likely to increase in the coming years. Mark Bernard White asserts in the *CLA Journal*, "That Lucille Clifton is one of the most engaging, gifted, and significant of contemporary poets is a critical evaluation more and more commonly held." Equally complimentary about Clifton's work is her biographer Lupton, who writes that "Lucille Clifton is a major figure in contemporary American poetry, a woman whose intense exploration of her body and psyche has helped make possible a new honesty, a new perspective." The first full-length critical studies of Clifton's work appeared in the early years of the twenty-first century, some twenty years after the publication of "homage to my hips." It is likely that more will follow.

CRITICISM

Diane Andrews Henningfeld

Henningfeld is a professor of literature who writes widely for educational publishers. In the following essay on "homage to my hips," she analyzes Clifton's undermining of traditionally held assumptions about racial and patriarchal power.

The poem "homage to my hips" appears in Lucille Clifton's 1980 collection *Two-Headed Woman*, in a segment titled "Homage to Mine." This collection is an important one for Clifton; it garnered her first Pulitzer Prize nomination, and she chose to include the entire collection of poems in the 1987 volume *Good Woman: Poems and a Memoir, 1969–1980*. Many readers will recognize "homage to my hips" as well as its sister poem, "homage to my hair," as two of Clifton's most frequently anthologized works. In her biographical work *Lucille Clifton: Her Life and Letters*, Mary Jane Lupton asserts that it is Clifton's "intense exploration of her body" in poems such as these that has led to "a new honesty, a new perspective" in poetry. Certainly, "homage to my hips" offers a new and honest perspective on the sources of feminine power.

In this poem (as well as in the other poems from *Two-Headed Woman*), Clifton asserts her right to speak of her own body and to claim her own physical nature. Such a claim might seem unnecessary; everyone is, after all, embodied. No

WHAT DO I READ NEXT?

- Gwendolyn Brooks's *Blacks* (1987) is a comprehensive collection of the Pulitzer Prize–winning writer's best work. Brooks was a close personal friend and role model to Clifton.

- Maya Angelou's *I Know Why the Caged Bird Sings* (1970) is a memoir of a young African-American woman who was sexually abused as a child. Her memoir complements the autobiographical detail of Clifton's poetry.

- Clifton's *Good Woman: Poems and a Memoir, 1969–1980* (1987) remains the essential text for any student wishing to become better acquainted with Clifton's work. The volume includes all of the poems of *Two-Headed Woman* as well as Clifton's memoir *Generations*.

- *The Black Arts Movement: Literary Nationalism in the 1960s and 1970s* (2005), by James Edward Smethurst, offers a historical assessment of the movement that nurtured writers like Clifton. Smethurst traces the connections between the black arts movement and the black power movement and argues that the black arts movement changed the way that Americans viewed the connection between art and popular culture.

mind can live independently from the physical body. Moreover, few contemporary readers would doubt that each person owns his or her own body.

However, for Clifton, the great-great-granddaughter of a woman taken from Africa and brought to North America as a slave, such an assertion cannot be taken lightly. Her own genetic and ancestral histories demonstrate that the ownership of one's body is something that must be guarded and proclaimed. Further, as a woman, she has inherited long histories of

WITH THE INTRODUCTION OF MAGIC IN THE
LAST FOUR LINES OF 'HOMAGE TO MY HIPS,' CLIFTON
ASSOCIATES HERSELF WITH AFRICAN, FEMININE,
INTUITIVE, SUPERNATURAL POWER, AND WITH A LONG
LINE OF SPELL CASTERS."

misogynistic law, medical theory, and religion that have complicated the female body. As Lupton notes, "Like many of her metaphors, the idea of enslavement refers both to woman's bondage and to racial bondage." In the fifteen lines of "homage to my hips," Clifton undertakes nothing less than the recapture of the inherent strength of her race and of her womanhood, to thus free herself from white ideas about black bodies and from patriarchal assertions about female weakness.

Ajuan Maria Mance, in a chapter in *Recovering the Black Female Body: Self-Representations by African American Women*, argues that "homage to my hips" offers an "emancipatory vision of the black female corpus," a vision that allows Clifton to free herself from conventional assumptions about beauty, a project she continues in "homage to my hair." The blue-eyed, blond-haired princess of Euro-American fairy tales does not hold a candle to the hip-swinging, wild-haired enchantress of these two poems. Rather than succumbing to white standards of beauty requiring the African American woman to imitate Caucasian features, Clifton defines her own criteria of beauty in these two poems, locating these standards in features that are stereotypically black physical attributes. She rejoices in her hair and revels in her hips. As Mance asserts, "Clifton reinterprets the outrageousness and excess associated with the African American female body as a source of power and a point of pride."

Likewise, Clifton unravels centuries of Western patriarchal misogyny, or hatred of women, as it has been codified in the teachings of law, medicine, and religion. Legally, women were typically under the control of first their fathers and then their husbands until very recent history. In the Middle Ages and the Renaissance, for example, laws regarding rape were located not in criminal codes but rather in property law. A rape, therefore, was a crime against the man to whom the woman "belonged," not against the woman. In addition, women were not granted the right to vote in the United States until 1920 (some fifty years after African American men were granted the same right). Before that time, virtually all legal decisions concerning women were handled by men. If a woman was charged with a crime, for example, she could not expect a jury of her peers, since women were prohibited from sitting on juries.

Similarly, medical texts and traditions from Aristotle onward through the early twentieth century perpetuated a construction of the female body that suggested that women were inferior members of the species. In fact, many medieval medical writers argued that women were perhaps not even of the same species as men. Aristotle's influential teachings perpetuated the notion that all fetuses start out male, but then because of some error in development, some fetuses become female.

Clifton clearly rejects both legal and medical traditions, claiming that her hips are her own, not her father's, nor her husband's, and that her strength is even greater than that of a man. She is perfection in her own right, both as a woman and as an African American; she is neither an imperfect male nor an imperfect human being.

Clifton also takes on masculine, patriarchal preaching about the dangers and lewdness of the female body. As far back as the early Middle Ages, Christian church fathers taught women to hide and be ashamed of their bodies. After all, Eve's transgression in the Garden of Eden, according to early biblical interpretations, led to the downfall of all mankind. Clifton vehemently rejects this construction. At the same time, she also rejects the Western religious and philosophical position of binary opposition. That is, Western thought has traditionally and conventionally divided reality into pairs of opposites, such as man/woman, right/left, white/black, mind/body, religion/magic, Christian/pagan. In each of these pairs, the first term is in a position of privilege in relation to the second, such that the second term is often defined by negation. For example, a woman can be defined as not a man. Thus, in a discussion of the differences between men's and women's sports, for example, women are often deemed inferior because they do not have the size or strength of some men; they are judged by what they do *not* have rather than by what they do have. Put another way, the unspoken assumption is that the first term in each pair above is the normative term, while the second can be defined by its deviation from the norm. Western thought has traditionally privileged logic, science, and authority over intuition, magic, and experience.

Clifton's project, then, constitutes nothing less than an overturning of this entire tradition. Instead of allowing herself to be defined by what she is not, Clifton asserts what she is: a woman of fair proportions, a woman who can destroy both racial and patriarchal injustice through the power of her words. She does this in part through the invocation of magic. According to Mance:

> When Clifton assigns to her black female subjects fantastic traits and mythical capabilities that exceed the boundaries of traditional womanhood, their flagrant disregard for the roles that would limit their function and meaning challenges the positionality of those institutions and identity groups whose visibility depends upon the preservation of blackness and womanhood as opposing categories.

The "positionality" that Clifton challenges is the position of privilege. Without the ability to impose rules or standards on Clifton's magical women, privileged groups can no longer sustain the myth that their position of privilege is inherent in their being. Rather, it becomes clear that their position of privilege has been maintained only through the acquiescence of those who accept their power. Once women accept their own magical nature, they can emancipate themselves from those who would bind them. With the introduction of magic in the last four lines of "homage to my hips," Clifton associates herself with African, feminine, intuitive, supernatural power, and with a long line of spell casters. She is capable of directing her magic at a man and utterly confusing him, setting his head and his body spinning.

Clifton also defeats the powers that would bind her by turning their own language against them. A closer examination of the title of the poem reveals that Clifton has engaged in a linguistic pun. In contemporary English, the word "homage" means respect and reverence. This is a generalization, however, of a term that had a very specific meaning in the Middle Ages: *homage* was the term used for the acknowledgment by a vassal that he owed his lord loyalty and service. Indeed, the vassal pledged his very

body to his lord. This was not an abstract concept but rather the very real and very concrete promise of one man to another that he accepted the lord's superiority and that he would die for the lord. In exchange, the vassal could expect protection and provisions from the lord. The word *homage* itself can be traced back to the Latin word for man.

Thus, the title of Clifton's poem can be read in two ways: In the first and most common reading, the poet herself pays respect and reverence to her hips in a playful, alliterative gesture. That she uses a word associated with men renders the title even more clever. In the second reading, Clifton demands homage to her magical hips, and by extension to her magical body, and by even further extension to the magical bodies of all women of color—and even further, to all women. The homage she demands is not that of a vassal to a lord or that of a slave to a slaveholder. Rather, the homage she demands is the free acknowledgment from human brothers that she and her hips have assumed their rightful position in the family of humankind. Clifton's "homage to my hips" is an expression of liberation and empowerment.

Source: Diane Andrews Henningfeld, Critical Essay on "homage to my hips," in *Poetry for Students*, Gale, Cengage Learning, 2009.

Michael S. Glaser

In the following excerpt from an interview, Clifton talks about her memories and the role her memories play in her writing.

... Michael Glaser: Lucille, you often state that writing for you is linked to being human, to your own staying awake and your desire that the world stay awake. Would you talk a little bit about that? Why do you write?

Lucille Clifton: Well, it always seemed to be something that came very naturally to me, to

> IF YOU BEAR WITNESS, YOU REMAIN ROOTED IN SOME WAY. YOU CONTINUE TO FEEL WHAT YOU SEE MATTERS. WHAT YOU HEAR MATTERS. IT'S A WAY TO CONNECT FULLY, INSTEAD OF JUST INTELLECTUALLY."

write things down. I like words a lot, as you know. I have always been very fond of words, and the different sounds they make. But, for me, I think the real question is, Why do I continue to write? Because, for me, I think that writing is a way of continuing to hope. When things sometimes feel as if they're not going to get any better, writing offers a way of trying to connect with something beyond that obvious feeling ... because you know, there is hope in connecting, and so perhaps for me it is a way of remembering I am not alone. And the writing may be sending tentacles out to see if there is a response to that.

Michael: So writing is a way of being connected?

Lucille: Yes.

Michael: But part of that connectedness for you is also bearing witness, isn't it?

Lucille: Yes. If you bear witness, you remain rooted in some way. You continue to feel what you see matters. What you hear matters. It's a way to connect fully, instead of just intellectually.

See, I believe in energy. I believe there is energy. It exists, and it continues to exist. And I believe it exists in humans, and it's sort of like if someone says, "Oh, everything is going to hell, I have seen it." Well, *I* have seen something other, and if that first message is out there, then the other message should be out there too.

You know, I have seen other. The *worst* has *never* happened to me. Because even in my imagination, even when it seems like something really, really bad has happened, I can imagine something worse than that. And it's not an either/or. What it means is that even in the face of this madness, there still is, "it *could have* been even beyond that," but it wasn't.

Michael: Do you feel that writing toward that positive energy is a necessary thing to counterbalance the negative?

Lucille: I think that you recognize the negative. You have to mention it when you see it. I believe in mentioning that which is negative.

Michael: But if we didn't acknowledge it, if we didn't mention it, if we didn't write over against it, that would create more space for ...

Lucille: For IT. Right. For its energy to expand.

Michael: So part of the act of writing is a way of keeping back the darkness?

Lucille: Yes.

Michael: When you talk to your students about writing, what do you encourage them to do?

Lucille: Well, one does not write to be famous, you know? First of all, how famous is a writer, when you think about it? And I don't write because I have a mission to heal the world. My mission is to heal Lucille if I can, as much as I can. What I know is that I am not the only one who has felt the things I feel. And so, if what I write helps to heal others, that's excellent, but my main thing is for me not to fall into despair, which I have done on occasion and could do at any time.

Michael: So, your sense for young people is to write because ...

Lucille: To write because you need it. It will somehow help you get through a difficult life. Don't just accept the surface as the reality. You know, there is form and there is substance. Choose substance, mostly. You can't do it all the time, I suppose. I certainly don't. But at least be aware of the difference. Pay attention.

Michael: You do an awful lot, Lucille, probably too much: you write regularly, you teach, you give way too many readings, you sit on boards and panels, you serve as a major competition judge once or twice a year. You work too hard. You don't have *to do all these things you do. So what's that about? Is it compulsive, are you a missionary in your own way? Every time you're in front of an audience, every time you're in front of the classroom, you are trying to not just be a good woman but to encourage other people to be good. What's involved there?*

Lucille: I don't know. I think that I would have been a good preacher [*laughs*]. I think that sometimes some of it is feeling that I have to prove that I am a good person. But also I have always been someone who was very affected by injustice, by what seems unfair. And sometimes I feel that maybe I can help.

Michael: Whatever it is that causes that, it's what I see as a calling of yours. You call others forth to be their best selves, and you inspire others toward that. I hope you realize what a gift that is to your students. They don't see many professors in front of them who are sharing their own struggle to be their best self, to fight against injustice, to fight against discrimination without becoming bitter.

Lucille: And I think, I really do think, that one of the things people ought to do in classrooms is model being a whole human. And you have to allow yourself to be vulnerable ... to pain, to hurt, so that you can love. Otherwise ...

Michael: We don't take those risks?

Lucille: No! We use the word, but we don't take the risks.

Michael: A while ago, you told me that someone had mumbled that you had played the race card when you read the poem about James Byrd, the black man who was dragged to his death by the truck in Texas. And you said you were happy to know that people respond that way. Why is that?

Lucille: Because it made clear to me what I suspect sometimes: that for me, who has to some degree been accepted in the world, people don't expect me to talk about race or think about it. Except in a positive kind of way.

Michael: That's your dues for being accepted?

Lucille: Yes, yes. It's like, because I can speak about race, and because I have friends who are not African American, it must be that I think everything is OK, that I don't feel racism because, after all, I'm OK. But I've got a cousin who's not OK, you know what I mean? And I have friends who are of my race who are not OK, and I am not always OK.

Michael: You're also part of a human family.

Lucille: Exactly.

Michael: Which is something that poetry, and your poetry especially, is about.

Lucille: Absolutely. My poetry is not about "how does it look." It's about "how does it feel." You know?

Michael: Talk about that ...

Lucille: Well, it's not about the surface of things. I hope it's more than that. I hope it is about humans who are deeper than that. And it's certainly not about forgetting—it's about remembering, because memory is what we have. I've started writing a poem about what so often happens with memories. I was thinking about that because I was beginning to forget some things about my mother. Now, she's been dead forty years, and I'm forgetting some things about how it felt when her hand touched my hair. I know that she touched it, I've seen the pictures of it, you know what I mean?

Michael: You don't remember how it felt?

Lucille: Once the sensation of it, the feeling of it goes, the photo becomes the memory. And that's not good because the photo isn't the memory.

Michael: I was thinking about your mother the other day and the poem that you wrote about her burning her poems. I've heard you talk about your father forbidding her to publish, and how you watched your mother go to the basement and burn her poems in the furnace, but I've never heard you talk about how that felt and how that impacted on you, watching that. You were sitting on the steps ...

Lucille: I was standing on the steps of the basement, and I don't even know if she knew I was there. I was a young girl, and to me this was just another strange thing that was happening in that house. You know?

Michael: Did you hear what your father had said to her?

Lucille: Yes. Well, I don't remember that conversation, but I had heard that, "Ain't no wife of mine going to be no poetry writer." And I think that it did impact on me. I think it had something to do with the reason I never stopped writing, and I've been writing since I was a little girl. I think maybe that's where that came from, as I think back.

Michael: And your mother knew that you wrote?

Lucille: Oh yes. She would ...

Michael: She encouraged that?

Lucille: Oh yes. Well, they both encouraged me, believe it or not, to do whatever I wanted to. They thought I could do whatever I wanted to. Clearly, that wasn't true [*laughter*]. And I knew that it wasn't true. But it was very nice of them.

Michael: They believed in you.

Lucille: They did, very much.

Michael: So here's your mother burning her poems, and your context is, this house is always crazy ...

Lucille: I knew that she was an unhappy woman. I used to think that she was the most unhappy person I had ever seen in my life. But I'm not that sure now ... What was it Camus said? "In the midst of winter I found myself in a wonderful summer," something like that. There are moments of great joy. I have known those moments too.

Michael: Moments of happiness?

Lucille: And perhaps if we allow them to be, they'll be enough, you know? Why do we think that we need to be so favored in the universe that we are guaranteed tremendous happiness at all costs?

Michael: Lucille, when I think back over the last several years, I'm really astonished by what you have been through and how well you have survived.

Lucille: You know, sometimes I think that too!

Michael: You have come through cancer and chemotherapy, kidney failure, dialysis, kidney transplant—you've been looking at death for five years. How do you deal with that?

Lucille: Well, I think about death a fair amount. But what I'm saying to myself is, I'm not going to go out like this. And I'm beginning to do things that I used to do when I was younger, like listening to jazz, going to the Blue Note. I haven't done something like that in so many years. All those things, and suddenly I think, "I enjoyed life very much as a young woman." I just enjoyed fun, and I want to enjoy it again.

Michael: You never really had a chance to get back to that...

Lucille: No, no.

Michael: After Fred died you were too busy being a mother and a poet?

Lucille: I think it wasn't until I went to the book fair in L.A. last year that I found myself suddenly feeling like I was doing things that Lucille did. I'm really enjoying doing these things again...

Source: Michael S. Glaser, "I'd Like Not to Be a Stranger in the World: A Conversation/Interview with Lucille Clifton," in *Antioch Review*, Vol. 58, No. 3, Summer 2000, pp. 310–28.

Charles H. Rowell

In the following excerpt from an interview, Clifton discusses her life and her poetry.

ROWELL: I want to make a confession to you.

CLIFTON: Okay.

ROWELL: And it has to do with one of your early poems, "miss rosie."

CLIFTON: Oh, uh-huh.

ROWELL: I have carried Miss Rosie in my head all of these years. She personally represents

> **BUT THE FIRST POEM I EVER WROTE THAT I REMEMBER—I THOUGHT 'NOW, I DON'T KNOW IF THIS IS A POEM OR NOT BUT THIS IS WHAT I SOUND LIKE....'"**

our ancestors, our common past. When I think of her, I am given strength to move forward on the shoulders of those who went before us, those who prepared the way for us—the ancestors who struggled, survived, and prevailed. I want to read the complete poem.

... I think Miss Rosie's is one of those "terrible stories" that you referred to earlier. And our standing on her shoulders—and those of so many of the ancestors like her—signifies many more of those "terrible stories."

CLIFTON: It is terrible...

ROWELL: Throughout your collections, you've been telling these terrible stories. Yes, I want to confess to you that I have carried Miss Rosie with me all of these years and that she has been very important to me.

CLIFTON: But she is important to us all. You know, the whole idea that, "Look, I'm where I am because somebody was before me, and that somebody suffered so that I might get here. And whether or not they suffered so I could be here is irrelevant. The fact that that happened is what has helped me to be here." It seems important for us to remember that. Well, for me it's important to remember that I never in my life have worked as hard as my mother did. Never. And my mother did not work as hard as her mother did. A lot of people have said to me in the early years that they thought I didn't like Miss Rosie; and I can't understand why they would think such a thing, when I honor her and recognize my debt. And there was a lady who was Miss Rosie. There're a lot of ladies who are or were. And I honor them. Because I can't drive, when I was in Baltimore, I had a man who drove me around all the time. He was in his 70s. He wasn't a very good driver, but he was so interesting. He would drive me and my kids. One time he said, "You know what I don't understand?" and I said, "What?" and he said, "I don't understand why these young kids"—this is in the

1960s—"are so mad. I'm the one what took the stuff." And I thought, "Now that's really interesting, isn't it?" That he was mad but he didn't feel himself enraged in the same way. What he also felt was that they ["these young kids"] weren't mad about him. They were mad about themselves. And he saw them as having it better than he did.

ROWELL: Will you talk about the 1960s? You also wrote during that period.

CLIFTON: Yes, I did.

ROWELL: And yet you, as far as I can tell, did not subscribe to what, at that time, was referred to as the Black Aesthetic. Neither did you subscribe to the politics of the Black Power Movement. I was never convinced that your poetry was part of the Black Arts Movement.

CLIFTON: It did not reflect it. At the time I didn't even know what that was.

ROWELL: You are right. Your poetry does not reflect the mainstream of that movement. But we were all influenced by the new concept that "Black is beautiful," which suggested possibilities and self-affirmation.

CLIFTON: Let me tell you what I think. Well, during the 1960s, I was pretty much pregnant. I have six kids, and they're six and a half years apart in age, from the oldest to the youngest. The Black Aesthetic. I am a black person; everything I write is a black thing. How could I not? But, on the other hand, it's always struck me as strange that all of a sudden people discovered that when somebody said "nigger" they were talking about them. Charles, I've been knowing that. Do you know what I mean? I had known that a long time. The inequities and all of that! I knew that. So what was new? At that time, I thought, well this must have to do with going to college. [*Laughter*] That's terrible. But I'm talking about my young self. I had not done that. I had come from poor folks in Buffalo, New York, which was not an interesting city at the time, and had seen that my parents were not even elementary school graduates. My grandparents—I don't know if they'd seen a school. So the kind of struggles and things that were happening were not things that I had suddenly discovered involved me too; I had *been* knowing that. I also think that in trying to see things wholly—which I've done all my life, tried to see what is whole—I could see some possible repercussions of some of the things that were said

and that happened that were not positive for our race. That was for me something I had to think about. In those days, I lived a very regular life, the life of a poor black person. I'm the only poet I know who's been evicted twice in her life. In my family we have some of everything, even a lot of relatives in jail. So these things people were talking about were not new to me. But I was trying, I think, to see if I could live a life of courage—which I admire greatly—and a life that did not fill my head with white people, positively or negatively, so I could go on, because my family's quite short-lived. My mother died at 44. My father was a youngish man; he was in his early 60s. My husband died at 49. Somebody had to remember. I also thought that there had been in history some people who were positive people. I thought that there had been some black people that I knew were negative. And I didn't see why I should pretend that was not so. But that doesn't mean I did not notice and that I do not notice what goes on in the world, because I do. I know what the person looks like who has *generally* offended people who look like me; I know what that person looks like. I am not crazy. I don't know if that explains it or not. I also am not a person to pretend. Well, I talk about being human all the time. But I'm not a person who does not notice that I'm a black person; that would be ridiculous. My children, for instance, because they've never got anything about black history in school, got it at home. I know that black is beautiful; they know it too. I knew I was cool. [*Laughter*] My mother was beautiful. Even though I know he was a challenging and difficult man, I saw my father's strengths, many of which I inherited.

ROWELL: Will you look back for a moment and think about the Black Arts Movement, which was a part of the Black Power Movement? What did the Black Arts Movement do for our literature?

CLIFTON: Well, I think it brought to American literature a long missing part of itself. I think it made a gateway for younger non-white people to come into American poetry, into American literature. And I think that's important. When I was young, I didn't see a gate through which I could come, so it didn't occur to me that I could be a part of American literature, or part of what is read, etc. But I think the Black Arts Movement ... to tell the truth, when I was a young woman I didn't even know what that was. I didn't know what was meant. One day, I got a letter from Hoyt Fuller who was editing *Negro Digest* (you know it latter [*sic*] became *Black World*). He told me that he was grateful that when I mention when I was first published, I always said it was in *Negro Digest*. He said some people forget. [*Laughter*] I didn't forget. I think that allowed there to be a gate through which I could come, certainly, though I was a little older than some. But people have a tendency, I think, to believe that if you don't say "black" in every other line, you must be somehow not wishing to be part of Black. But as Gwendolyn Brooks has said, "Every time I walk out of my house, it is a political decision." And I think that's true.

What was the effect of the Black Arts Movement on our literature? Given the above, how can we know? What I do understand is that it is better to speak our stories than to keep silence. It is better to try and define ourselves than to remain defined by others. A better question might be this: What was the effect of the movement on our lives? There is a tendency in our literature, in the American tongue, to write with an eye on how the critics and intellectuals receive us. Are we writing for them? Poetry is a human art. It is about being human, whatever gender or color or class. My cousins have never heard of any movements much. Do we not write for them also?

ROWELL: Good Times, *your first book of poems, was published in 1969, and others followed.* Good Woman: New and Selected Poems *was published in 1987.* The Terrible Stories *followed in 1997. Why did you omit* Ten Oxherding Pictures: A Meditation *from the list of your volumes of poems?*

CLIFTON: Ten Oxherding Pictures—because it's a different kind of thing. *Ten Oxherding Pictures* is twelve poems. It was privately printed in Santa Cruz, California. It's based on a series of pictures done as a Buddhist Meditation aid in the 12th century. I've always had a kind of—well, I say I'm not religious—I've always had a spiritual dimension in my life. When I saw the names of the pictures, I had been reading something about children's books, and this one author had these pictures in her house. The last one of the pictures is called "Entering the City with Bliss Bestowing Hands." When I heard that, something just sparked in me, and I quickly wrote, just based

on the caption of these pictures—which I had not seen at the time—poems about this spiritual search. The ox is metaphorized as the spiritual goal. That was different. So I didn't think it'd fit in the regular bibliography. The book is handmade of handpaper and a leather binding. It is an expensive book, and it's still around. It must cost a lot now, quite a lot.

ROWELL: What do you think of Ten Oxherding Pictures? *I like it very much. It is an extraordinary text.*

CLIFTON: I like it. As I said, it's just different from most of my books. But I like it. It's part of who I am. I do a lot of things with the Christian Bible people, Biblical things, which I know well. But I've always had a kind sixth sense—especially when somebody talks about hands. Yes, a sixth sense—if you want to call it that—that deals with spirituality and with the sacred. These are poems that came from that part of me. But remember that it's not either/or for me. That's part of who I am too. I am one who can feel the sacred, sometimes, and the one who's profane at other times—[*Laughter*] I like Bach. Everybody knows I like Bach a lot—and I also think that Levi Stubbs and the Four Tops is really fabulous. I also love Aretha [Franklin]. I am that kind of person: complex, like other people. I have some other poems that deal with the sacred, not with religion but with the sacred. Some have not been published.

ROWELL: Will you talk about your new work, that which follows The Terrible Stories? *I heard you read some of your new poems last January [1998] at Xavier University in New Orleans. Like* Ten Oxherding Pictures, *the new work you read there was different from the work in* Good Woman. *I heard a different Lucille Clifton in them.*

CLIFTON: Well, I think that people have said these poems seem darker, but you know, I've had cancer, I've had kidney failure, I've been on dialysis, I had a kidney transplant. I've had many losses, and in those new poems I'm exploring some of the more obviously terrible things. I also feel a kind of urgency in our culture, in the United States, to—what the old people say—"get right or get left," a feeling of great need to balance itself. I feel that strongly. And writing about some of the signs—I think this book is going to be called *Signs*—some of the feelings of negativity, and self-servingness, and greed, etc. All of these I feel in the air. I think somebody needs to write about that. And I may as well since I'm one of the ones, I'm sure, who can feel that.

I don't think that critics, and perhaps readers as well, have ever quite known where to put me. [*Laughter*] I suppose I'm not sure where to put myself. [*Laughter*] But I know that I write poems, and I also know, Charles—this is true, I know—that what I'm doing is what I'm supposed to be doing. Whatever it is, whatever is next. I have a poem that says "What is coming next? I don't know." But I know that I accept what is coming next, and I will try to do it.

ROWELL: It's interesting that people say they don't know where to put you. That is probably a good thing. You don't sound like any of your contemporaries that I have read. But some of your poems remind me of Langston Hughes.

CLIFTON: Now, people have said that. I don't think I sound like Langston Hughes. I read him more after I started writing than before.

But I did at one point know him, and in fact I received a letter from him about a week before he died, because he had gone to Paris—they were doing a thing from Hughes' Semple stories, and he was going to come to the house when he came back. But he had died. I think maybe the idea of language in that I always wanted to use language to its fullest possibility. And so I think of my poetry as many-layered. You know, that you can understand it on a lot of layers, and I certainly, purposefully, wish to be read and understood in some way by literary critics and theoreticians, and also by my Aunt Timmy and my Uncle Buddy. [*Laughter*] I always wanted to be understood and to speak to and for, if possible, people in a whole lot of levels—I guess you'd say, of whom we all are. I have been told that I have been compared to so many people: Langston [Hughes], quite a lot, but often to Langston because of our color; Emily Dickinson, and that's often because we write short poems. Who else? H.D., somebody said, which I didn't see at all, but somebody said that I wrote like the French something and the African griots. I've been compared to a lot of people. But I think I sound pretty much like myself. And somebody said they could always tell a poem of mine; they said because it's musical. Some people are triggered by the eye. I am triggered by the ear. I need to hear a poem, and I do read them aloud and hear them in my head. But maybe it's because I had to learn and to learn my own voice. This is

what I sound like. Now who else sounds like that, I don't really know. I give honor to Gwendolyn Brooks for many things, and one of them is her poem "the mother" because it is after reading that poem that I could write the poem called. "The Lost Baby Poem." I give honor to Gwendolyn Brooks not only for her wonderfulness but for that poem, which allowed me to write a poem.

ROWELL: What do you mean when you say "I had to learn my own voice"?

CLIFTON: Well, I had to learn that poetry could sound like me. When I was a girl writing, I wrote sonnets. [*Laughter*] Isn't that great? That's sort of the kind of poems I read in books. And that was form, that sort of thing. But the first poem I ever wrote that I remember—I thought "Now, I don't know if this is a poem or not but this is what I sound like"—was a poem that—I don't think it has a title—the poem that opens my first book, the first poem in *Good Times*.

... And I thought "Now that's what I want to say in the way I would say it. That's what I'm going to do. I don't know if it's going to be a poem or not. I don't know if others will call it that. But I know that's what I'm supposed to do."

ROWELL: People have commented also on the deceptive simplicity of your lines. Take that very ending, for example, of the poem you just read: "like we call it / home." Simplicity, yes, but so much history, so much meaning. One reality implied against another . . .

Source: Charles H. Rowell, "An Interview with Lucille Clifton," in *Callaloo*, Vol. 22, No. 1, Winter 1999, pp. 56–72.

SOURCES

Anaporte-Easton, Jean, "Healing Our Wounds: The Direction of Difference in the Poetry of Lucille Clifton and Judith Johnson," in *Mid-American Review*, Vol. 14, No. 2, 1994, pp. 78–82.

Clifton, Lucille, "homage to my hips," in *Twentieth-Century American Poetry*, edited by Dana Gioia, David Mason, and Meg Schoerke, McGraw-Hill, 1994, p. 874.

Holladay, Hilary, "Song of Herself: Lucille Clifton's Poems about Womanhood," in *The Furious Flowering of African American Poetry*, edited by Joanne V. Gabbin, University Press of Virginia, 1999, p. 281.

————, *Wild Blessings: The Poetry of Lucille Clifton*, Louisiana State University Press, 2004, p. 65.

Lupton, Mary Jane, *Lucille Clifton: Her Life and Letters*, Praeger, 2006, pp. 1–3, 7, 87.

Madhubuti, Haki, "Lucille Clifton: Warm Water, Greased Legs, and Dangerous Poetry," in *Black Women Writers (1950–1980): A Critical Evaluation*, edited by Mari Evans, Anchor Press/Doubleday, 1984, pp. 150–60.

Mance, Ajuan Maria, "Re-locating the Black Female Subject: The Landscape of the Body in the Poems of Lucille Clifton," in *Recovering the Black Female Body: Self Representations by African American Women*, edited by Michael Bennett and Vanessa D. Dickerson, Rutgers University Press, 2001, pp. 123–34.

Ostriker, Alicia, "Kin and Kin: The Poetry of Lucille Clifton," in *American Poetry Review*, Vol. 22, No. 6, November/December 1993, pp. 41–48.

Waniek, Marilyn Nelson, Review of *Two-Headed Woman*, by Lucille Clifton, in *Callaloo*, Vol. 6, No. 1, 1983, pp. 160–62.

White, Mark Bernard, "Sharing the Living Light: Rhetorical, Poetic, and Social Identity in Lucille Clifton," in *CLA Journal*, Vol. 40, No. 3, March 1997, pp. 288–304.

FURTHER READING

Brownmiller, Susan, *Femininity*, Ballantine Books, 1985.
    Brownmiller's book offers a historical look at the features that have been used to define femininity. In accessible language, she articulates how women have responded to various definitions of beauty across time.

Collins, Lisa Gail, and Margo Natalie Crawford, eds., *New Thoughts on the Black Arts Movement*, Rutgers University Press, 2006.
    The essays in this well-illustrated collection cover the important figures of the black arts movement and provide additional information concerning the political and artistic concerns of the generation.

Harper, Michael, and Anthony Walton, eds., *Every Shut Eye Ain't Asleep: An Anthology of Poetry by African Americans since 1945*, Little, Brown, 1994.
    This volume includes chapters on thirty-five important contemporary African American poets, including Lucille Clifton, Gwendolyn Brooks, Amiri Baraka, and Robert Hayden.

hooks, bell, *Feminism Is for Everybody: Passionate Politics*, South End Press, 2000.
    An important African American critic and essayist, hooks examines the history of gender oppression in patriarchal society and follows the development of the women's movement.

Howl

ALLEN GINSBERG
1956

Allen Ginsberg's "Howl" was first introduced to the public at a poetry reading on October 13, 1955 (some sources say October 7), at the Six Gallery in San Francisco. Ginsberg's passionate performance of the poem established him as an important figure in the antiestablishment Beat movement. The Beats were a group of American writers who came to prominence in the mid-1950s and early 1960s. They rebelled against conventional post-World War II morality, materialism, consumerism, and war, and embraced spontaneous expression, sexual freedom, alternative lifestyles, spiritual search, and experimentation with drugs. "Howl" was published in the 1956 collection *Howl, and Other Poems*. In 1957, the poem became the target of a landmark obscenity trial.

The poem is an outcry of anguish against all that Ginsberg felt was unjust, repressive, and harmful to the individual in American society: consumerism, mechanization, and intellectual conformity. At the same time, it is a celebration of the emerging counterculture and an expression of sympathy for its pioneers. It is written in the long-line style of Walt Whitman, a nineteenth-century American poet who was an important influence on Ginsberg. "Howl" has a strong autobiographical aspect and also contains sociopolitical critique, as well as some sexual imagery. Over fifty years after its initial publication, the poem retains its power to shock and stands as one of the most influential poems of the modern era.

Allen Ginsberg *(The Library of Congress)*

"Howl" is now available in Ginsberg's *Collected Poems, 1947–1997* (2006). This edition also contains the poet William Carlos Williams's famous introduction to the poem.

AUTHOR BIOGRAPHY

Allen Ginsberg was born on June 3, 1926, in Newark, New Jersey. His mother, Naomi, was a Russian émigré. She supported the Communist Party in her adopted country of the United States and took the young Ginsberg and his older brother Eugene to meetings. She suffered from paranoid schizophrenia and was periodically institutionalized in the Greystone State Mental Hospital. Ginsberg's father, Louis, was a poet and teacher.

Ginsberg's adolescence was troubled and complicated by a growing awareness of his homosexuality. He attended Paterson High School and in 1943 enrolled at Columbia University, in New York City. His literary influences there included his teachers Lionel Trilling and Mark Van Doren and his fellow students Jack Kerouac, William S. Burroughs, and Neal Cassady. Kerouac, Burroughs, Cassady, and Ginsberg would later form the core of the Beat movement of writers. In 1945 Ginsberg was suspended from the university in the aftermath of a murder committed by his friend Lucien Carr. The immediate causes for Ginsberg's suspension were his writing obscenities on a window and his being discovered in bed in his university hall of residence with Jack Kerouac, who no longer attended the university. Although the university authorities may have believed that there was a homosexual aspect to this incident, Kerouac had apparently spent a chaste night with Ginsberg because he had visited to talk and stayed too late to go home. In 1948 Ginsberg resumed his studies at Columbia and graduated the same year.

From 1948 to 1949 Ginsberg had a series of mystical visions of the eighteenth-century English poet William Blake, one of his poetic influences. Ginsberg heard Blake's voice speaking to him. Barry Miles, in *Ginsberg: A Biography*, cites Ginsberg as saying, "The peculiar quality of the voice was something unforgettable because it was like God had a human voice, with all the infinite tenderness and mortal gravity of a living Creator speaking to his son." These experiences prompted Ginsberg to experiment with psychoactive drugs.

In 1949 Ginsberg was arrested after some acquaintances used his apartment to store goods stolen in a robbery. Lionel Trilling and other staff at Columbia University, together with Ginsberg's father, persuaded Ginsberg to commit himself voluntarily to Columbia Presbyterian Psychiatric Institute in New York as a way of avoiding prison. Ginsberg agreed, convinced that he had become insane like his mother. He remained there for eight months while doctors attempted to make him conform to their idea of normality. There he met fellow patient Carl Solomon, who provided inspiration for "Howl"; Ginsberg dedicated the poem to him.

Ginsberg did various jobs in New York City until 1954, when he moved to San Francisco and met Peter Orlovsky, who became his lover and lifelong companion. San Francisco was the center of the countercultural Beat movement, led by such poets as Kenneth Rexroth and Lawrence Ferlinghetti. On the advice of his therapist, Ginsberg gave up his job as a market research analyst to focus on writing poetry full time. He first came to public notice in October 1955 at what has come to be known as an iconic poetry reading at the Six Gallery in San Francisco, hosted by Kenneth Rexroth. Also reading their work were the now-famous poets Philip Lamantia, Michael McClure, Gary Snyder, and Philip Whalen. Ginsberg read "Howl," which was published the following year by Lawrence Ferlinghetti, through his City Lights imprint, in *Howl, and Other Poems* (1956).

In 1962 Ginsberg traveled to India, where he was introduced to yoga and meditation. He became convinced that these spiritual techniques were superior to drugs in raising consciousness; the trip marked the beginning of a lifetime's study of Eastern religions. Ginsberg was particularly interested in mantras, mystical sounds used for certain effects. He incorporated mantras into some of his poems, and often began poetry readings by chanting a mantra. In the early 1970s Ginsberg took classes in Buddhist thought and practice at the Naropa Institute in Colorado, which was founded by the Venerable Chögyam Trungpa Rinpoche, a Buddhist monk from Tibet. In 1972 Ginsberg took vows formally committing himself to Buddhism.

Throughout the 1960s and 1970s Ginsberg became an iconic figure of political dissidence, addressing in his poetry such themes as the McCarthy red hunts and union struggles. He became associated with the antiwar movement that opposed American military involvement in Vietnam and with the philosophy of peace and love promoted by the hippie movement. He was also active in antinuclear protest. Though Ginsberg was a critic of capitalism, he did not consider himself a Communist. He did, however, speak of his admiration for certain Communist and labor leaders in the United States, especially those who were active during the McCarthy red hunt years.

Ginsberg's next important poem after "Howl" was "Kaddish" (published by City Lights Books in 1961 in *Kaddish, and Other Poems*), an elegy to his mother, who died in a mental hospital in 1956. A Kaddish is a traditional Jewish prayer for the dead. Ginsberg's next major work was *The Fall of America: Poems of These States, 1965–1971* (1972), which takes the reader on a cross-country journey, with stops in various places to comment on the spiritual decline of the United States. The collection won the National Book Award in 1974. The poems collected in *Mind Breaths: Poems, 1972–1977* (1977) reflect Ginsberg's interest in meditation and spirituality. Ginsberg's last poems, including those written after he learned he had liver cancer, appear in *Death and Fame: Poems, 1993–1997* (1999).

In the spring of 1997, Ginsberg, who already suffered from diabetes and hepatitis, was diagnosed with liver cancer. He continued to write during his final illness, composing his last poem, "Things I'll Not Do (Nostalgias)," on March 30. He died of a heart attack brought on by complications of liver cancer on April 5, 1997, in New York City.

Ginsberg has received many honors, including a Guggenheim Fellowship (1965), a grant from the National Endowment for the Arts (1966), a National Institute of Arts and Letters Award (1969), membership in the American Institute of Arts and Letters (1974), a National Arts Club Gold Medal (1979), a Poetry Society of America Gold Medal (1986), a Golden Wreath from Yugoslavia's Struga Poetry Festival (1986), a Before Columbus Foundation Award for Lifetime Achievement (1990), a Harriet Monroe Poetry Award from the University of Chicago (1991), an American Academy of Arts and Sciences Fellowship (1992), and a medal of Chevalier de l'Ordre des Arts et des Lettres from the French government (1993).

POEM SUMMARY

Part I

LINES 1–11

In his essay "Notes Written on Finally Recording 'Howl'" (in *Deliberate Prose: Selected Essays, 1952–1995*), Ginsberg describes part I as "a lament for the Lamb in America with instances of remarkable lamblike youths." Jesus Christ is known as the Lamb of God; the name connotes innocence and mercy.

"Howl" opens with Ginsberg's affirmation that he has seen the greatest talents of his generation ruined by madness. He paints a picture of these people and their lives, drawn from his own experiences and those of artists, writers, intellectuals, musicians, and psychiatric patients whom he encountered. The poem shows them as outcasts from conventional society and details the abuses they have suffered.

Desperate, the people he has seen stagger along the city streets looking for drugs in an attempt to use them to make a connection to a spiritual reality. They are starving both materially and spiritually. Poor and exhausted, they live in apartments lacking hot running water. They are described as hipsters, a Beat term for people who felt alienated from conventional society and who were "hip," or in tune with the latest ideas and fashions. Terms opposite to *hip* included *straight* and *square*, which were used by Beats to describe those people who supported conventional society and all that it stood for: the military-industrial complex, mechanization, consumerism, and moral repression.

The El mentioned in line 5 is the elevated railway in Manhattan. The reference to Mohammed connects the Muslim prophet Mohammed's spiritual status to the people

MEDIA ADAPTATIONS

- *Howls, Raps & Roars: Recordings from the San Francisco Poetry Renaissance* (1993), produced by Fantasy, is a boxed set of four audio CDs of some of the best-known poets of the Beat movement reading their own work. The compilation includes a recording of Ginsberg reading "Howl."

- *Howl, and Other Poems* (1998), produced by Fantasy, is an audio CD of Ginsberg reading "Howl" and "Footnote to 'Howl'" as well as other well-known works.

- "Howl" and "Footnote to 'Howl'" (1997) are available as MP3 downloadable recordings of Ginsberg reading his poems.

of the counterculture. The hipsters seek understanding by studying in the universities, which, however, are populated by scholars of war. In an annotation to a later edition of "Howl," Ginsberg writes that while he was at Columbia University, Columbia scientists helped to make the atom bombs that the United States dropped on the Japanese cities of Hiroshima and Nagasaki in 1945.

The allusion to Blake refers to the eighteenth-century English visionary poet William Blake, who was an important influence on Ginsberg. The hipster students are expelled from academe for wild behavior and obscene writings (as Ginsberg was). The Terror in line 8 implies a threatening world beyond these people's rooms. Hipsters have been caught running marijuana from Mexico into the United States.

LINES 12–22

Lines 12 to 15 describe enhanced perceptions experienced under the influence of peyote, Benzedrine (amphetamine), and alcohol. The allusion to hydrogen refers to the hydrogen bomb, a nuclear bomb even more destructive than the atomic bomb.

In their wanderings around New York, the hipsters talk of hospitals, jails, and wars, the destructive institutions of straight society. Line 20 refers to post-college career failures who suffer the tortures of drug withdrawal.

LINES 23–33

The post-college career failures stow away in the boxcars of trains on nighttime journeys to their families' farms. Inspired by spiritual experience, they study mystical authors and psychic phenomena and set out on vision quests to resolve their crises. Lines 27 to 33 describe the fates of people in Ginsberg's circle: some, hungry and lonely, wander through Houston, seeking jazz, sex, or mere sustenance. Others vanish in the wilds of Mexico or, driven by pacifist convictions, launch investigations into the Federal Bureau of Investigation, which they consider to be a tool of repression.

Some hipsters distribute Communist leaflets. Los Alamos is the U.S. government laboratory in New Mexico where the atomic bomb was developed. Protestors (line 32) are pursued by police who are trying to suppress their antiwar activities. The reference to naked victims implies that protestors are interrogated and tortured by a repressive state.

LINES 34–44

Line 34 describes protestors who are arrested but fight back by attacking police. Ginsberg insists that these hipsters have committed no crimes but indulgence in homosexual and drug-related adventures. Line 40 laments the loss of homosexual lovers to conventional heterosexual relationships, married respectability, and mainstream careers. These fates are seen as hostile to creativity.

LINES 45–55

This section describes people walking all night to reach an opium den. Others make suicide attempts on the banks of the Hudson River. Lines 48 to 52 salute the homeless and dispossessed people who sit in boxes under a bridge, suffer from tuberculosis in Harlem apartments, and adapt crates as furniture. One person, desperate for food, plunges under a meat truck in pursuit of an egg.

Hipsters throw their watches off the roof as an act of protest against the straight world of time constraints: they ally themselves with timelessness and eternity. These actions are futile, however, as they are condemned to be woken by an alarm clock each day, presumably to get to a job forced upon them by straight society.

LINES 56–66

This section salutes those innocents who have been destroyed by the prevailing poor taste in literature and the demands of consumerism. A would-be suicide jumps off Brooklyn Bridge but miraculously lives to walk away into the oblivion of Chinatown. Lines 58 through 62 chronicle wild, drunken escapades, including dancing barefoot on broken wineglasses and driving cross-country to talk to a friend about a vision of eternity. Hipsters pray for each other's souls in cathedrals, but the cathedrals seem devoid of hope, suggesting the spiritual bankruptcy of organized religion.

Line 63 describes jail visits, perhaps to Ginsberg's acquaintances who were imprisoned for drug offenses, robberies, or homosexual acts. Line 64 refers to William Burroughs, who (according to Ginsberg's annotation to the facsimile edition of "Howl") retired to Mexico and to Tangiers, Morocco. There is also a reference to Jack Kerouac, who retired to Rocky Mount, North Carolina, and who followed Buddhist teachings. The hypnotic power of the radio in line 65 alludes to Naomi Ginsberg's paranoid belief that doctors had implanted radio receivers in her body through which she received messages. The mention of sanity trials is possibly an oblique satirical comment on obscenity trials, which were a tool of the political establishment against rebels such as the Beats. Obscenity trials, Ginsberg suggests, should be abandoned in favor of sanity trials in which the establishment would stand accused of insanity.

Line 66 (according to Ginsberg's annotated edition) refers to an incident in which Carl Solomon threw potato salad at a college lecturer as a Dadaist statement. (Dadaism is a branch of the artistic movement of surrealism.) Solomon subsequently turned up at a psychiatric institution requesting a lobotomy.

LINES 67–78

Ginsberg describes Carl Solomon being given psychiatric therapies, including electric shock treatment, and overturning a Ping-Pong table in protest. Rockland refers to Rockland

State Hospital, a psychiatric hospital in Orangeburg, New York, where Solomon spent time as a patient. The poet's sympathy with Solomon is expressed in line 72.

Lines 73 and 74 focus on the poet as inspired visionary. The Latin reference translates as "Father Omnipotent Eternal God": the implication is that poetry gives a person the sense of being close to God. Line 75 portrays the poet as shamed and rejected by society, conforming only to the force of creativity. Line 76 links images of an insane tramp and an angel, suggesting that they are both aspects of the same poet, outcast yet divinely inspired. Ginsberg states that poetry deals with eternal values that outlive any individual. The subject of line 77 may be the spirit of poetry, reincarnate in the modern jazz music that expresses the suffering of an America in which love is denied. He likens the saxophone's lament to Christ's words on the cross, which translate as "My God, my God, why hast thou forsaken me?" (Mark 15:34). Collecting together in line 78 the heroes of "Howl," Ginsberg sees their lives as poems, which are, however, cut brutally from their bodies, suggesting that the poets are sacrificed by a cruel society. The sacrificial imagery foreshadows the figure of Moloch in part II. Nevertheless, long after they themselves are gone, the life-poems of the poets and artists live on to sustain others.

Part II

LINES 1–7

In his essay "Notes Written on Finally Recording 'Howl,'" Ginsberg writes that part II "names the monster of mental consciousness that preys on the Lamb." He identifies this monster as Moloch, who was the sun god of the Canaanites. Between the eighth and sixth centuries B.C.E., the Israelites living near Jerusalem sacrificed their firstborn children to him. Representations of the god showed him eating the children. The inspiration for part II came to Ginsberg after he had taken peyote. He "saw an image of the robot skullface of Moloch in the upper stories of a big hotel glaring into my window" ("Notes"). Moloch is thus symbolically identified with a mechanized, dehumanized society that denies sexuality, creativity, and life itself.

This section opens with Ginsberg asking which monster consumed the minds and creativity of the poets and artists commemorated in part I. The monster is made of hard, industrially produced aluminum and cement, linking him with a mechanized, dehumanized society. Ginsberg answers his own question: the monster is Moloch. Moloch is identified with loneliness, the futile pursuit of wealth that underlies capitalism, and human suffering. He is the harsh judge of men, the maker of prisons and of wars. Ginsberg sees the very buildings (perhaps among them, the skyscraper that carried the vision of Moloch) as an expression of Moloch's judgmental nature. This is a reference to William Blake's character of the warlike, repressive, and harshly judgmental Jehovah figure Urizen, who was (according to Ginsberg in his annotated edition) the lawgiver as well as the "creator of spiritual disorder and political chaos." Urizen was portrayed with the calipers of the architect of creation, which, Ginsberg notes, "limit the infinite universe to his egoic horizon" and "oppress physical body, feelings and imagination."

The windows in line 6 are unseeing because they do not see humanity's suffering. Again, the skyscrapers are identified with a harsh, judgmental god, this time the Jehovah or God of the Old Testament, on whom Blake modeled his Urizen. Moloch has engendered the dehumanizing factories of the industrialized society and the radio antennae through which this society broadcasts its version of reality. In line 7, Moloch is identified as a lover of oil, which drives the American economy. Moloch sees artistic genius as mere poverty. The conclusion of his aspirations is the hydrogen bomb. The destruction that such bombs would wreak would purify the world of the peculiarities chronicled in part I, but at the price of extinguishing life. The poet emphasizes that Moloch is merely a mental construct to which man has sacrificed his soul.

LINES 8–15

The poet blames Moloch for his current lonely and insane state and for denying him the joy of the body. He asserts that he will abandon Moloch, and he has a vision of light streaming from the sky.

At line 10, the poet lists the products of Moloch: dehumanized apartments, insane asylums, and bombs. The people sacrifice themselves in service of Moloch, while spiritual values have vanished from America. The inspirations and passions that form the basis of a truly human society are gone. The poet imagines the souls of suicides who jumped into the river. Now that their souls are in eternity, they see from a detached point of view the grim progress of Moloch's world, and so they are laughing.

Part III

LINES 1–19

In his essay "Notes Written on Finally Recording 'Howl,'" Ginsberg writes that part III is "a litany of affirmation of the Lamb in its glory." The poet addresses Carl Solomon directly and makes a recurring statement of solidarity with Solomon in this section. In line 3, Ginsberg states that Solomon reminds him of his mother, who was also institutionalized for mental illness. Line 8 may refer to the dehumanizing treatments given to Solomon, which close down his formerly acute senses. The spinsters whose breasts produce tea may represent a conventional respectability divorced from the natural female body, which would generate nourishing milk. Solomon's nurses are identified with harpies, winged death-spirits in Greek mythology.

Line 12 links the psychiatric hospital with the insanity of the militarized United States at the time of the cold war with Communist Russia. Ginsberg notes that the soul is pure and should not die in a place such as this, divorced from divine grace. In line 13, Ginsberg criticizes the electric shock treatment given to patients such as Solomon and implies that the treatment has separated his soul from his body. He links Solomon with Christ through the image of the cross, thus giving Solomon (and, by extension, his fellow hipsters) the status of a martyr. In line 14, Solomon, who is considered by straight society to be the mad one, rebels by accusing his doctors of insanity and plotting political revolution. Golgotha is the biblical name for the place where Christ was crucified. The poet predicts that Solomon will rise again from this spiritual death, as Christ did.

The poet imagines himself, Solomon, and insane comrades singing the "Internationale," the international socialist and Communist anthem. He envisages himself and Solomon caressing a pure version of their homeland, the United States, surreptitiously, under the bedsheets. This image connotes illicit, secret love. This United States is at the same time likened to a sick person who has not given up on life and who keeps them awake with coughing. Symbolically, the coughing can be construed as reminders to their conscience that their nation is in a critical state.

The climax of the poem is an image of the poet and his companions awakening out of their coma (induced in them by a brutalizing society) to the sound of their own souls, which are likened to airplanes dropping angelic bombs on the hospital. The building is lit up, and the imprisoning walls, the figments of man's perverted mind, collapse. The patients run outside to greet the new world. Line 18 unites the "star-spangled banner" that is the American flag with the mercy of the Lamb of God. The eternal war is the divine counterpart of the dehumanizing manmade wars that the poet has criticized earlier in the poem; it can be seen as the war waged by the light against darkness and ignorance. Now, the poet and his fellows can forget their underwear (line 18), as in this new freedom there is no longer any need to feel shame at their nakedness. Ginsberg ends part III with a vision of Solomon as a modern version of the ancient Greek hero Odysseus, walking along dripping water, as if from an epic sea journey, and arriving at Ginsberg's cottage.

Footnote to "Howl"

LINES 1–15

The "Footnote to 'Howl'" is generally considered to be part of the poem. It is a reply to the abuses chronicled in the earlier parts of the poem, an antithesis to part II, and an affirmation of the sacredness of all life. This includes the humblest parts of the human body that, in Ginsberg's view, have been wrongly shamed by conventional morality and antihomosexual attitudes. These are hailed as being as holy as the angels. Line 5 affirms the holiness of the poetic process. Line 6 names several of Ginsberg's circle and declares them holy: Peter Orlovsky, Ginsberg himself, Carl Solomon, Lucien Carr (a key figure in the Beat movement), Jack Kerouac, Herbert Huncke (a subculture icon and writer who was openly homosexual), William S. Burroughs, and Neal Cassady. Ginsberg includes in his affirmation those people who are rejected by conventional society.

In line 7 Ginsberg affirms the holiness of his insane mother. Line 8 hails the modern jazz music (including the form known as bebop). The image in the second phrase of this line, according to Ginsberg's annotated edition, refers to the ancient Greek philosopher Pythagoras's statement, "When the mode of the music changes the walls of the city shake." The idea is that a change in musical fashion not only reflects but also can cause a societal change.

Even skyscrapers, accused in part II of being creations of Moloch, are welcomed into Ginsberg's fold of sacredness (line 9). A juggernaut (line 10) is any unstoppable force; Ginsberg explains in his annotations that the word refers to the growing military-industrial complex. The places named in line 11 are significant to Ginsberg and the Beats. Moscow is the capital of Russia, which was projected as America's enemy during the cold war. Istanbul, the capital of Turkey, is probably introduced as a cosmopolitan city in contrast to what the Beats saw as the white Anglo-Saxon isolationism of mainstream America. Ginsberg embraces all these places, from the straightest to the hippest, as equally holy.

Line 5 refers to the International Workingmen's Association, which first met in London in 1864, under the leadership of the founders of Communism, Karl Marx and Friedrich Engels. When Ginsberg wrote "Howl," four meetings of the association had taken place, and he is putting forward the notion that it is time for the fifth.

Lines 13 and 14 unite products of industrialization (the railroad and the locomotive) with spiritual qualities: Ginsberg affirms that all are sacred. The conclusion to the footnote hails the inherent kindness of the soul as sacred; it alone can resolve the suffering catalogued in "Howl."

THEMES

The Birth of the Beat Movement

The overriding theme of "Howl" is the emergence of the Beat movement and the conflict between its values and the values of conformist or "straight" American society. Part I captures the essence of the Beat movement by chronicling events from the lives of some of its key figures, including Jack Kerouac, William S. Burroughs, Herbert Huncke, Neal Cassady, Carl Solomon, and Ginsberg himself. These events are characterized by spontaneous expression, sexual freedom, rebellion against convention, experimental drug use, and spiritual search. These people make up the counterculture

TOPICS FOR FURTHER STUDY

- Research the work of any three Beat writers. Identify the similarities in ideas, themes, and stylistic elements that you find. Then identify any differences between the writers: What makes them unique or gives them their own distinctive voices? Write an essay on your findings.

- Trace the development of the Beat movement in music, literature, visual art, and philosophy from its beginnings to the present day. Make a CD or write an essay detailing your findings. You may use illustrations as appropriate.

- Read William Blake's *The Marriage of Heaven and Hell*. In what ways does "Howl" expand on and comment on Blake's work? What similarities and differences are there between the social critique of these two works? Write an essay on your findings.

- In his introduction to "Howl," the poet William Carlos Williams remarks that the poem is a trip into hell. In what way does "Howl" portray the United States as a hell? Lead a class debate on the topic.

- Research the political and social climate of the United States in the 1950s, when Ginsberg wrote "Howl." Identify some of the factors that influenced the poem, taking into consideration both the established "straight" society and the emerging "hip" counterculture. Write a report on your findings.

of hipsters, those at the forefront of change in the direction of freedom and spirituality. They are implicitly contrasted with their opposites, known in Beat parlance as "squares." Square culture was considered to be founded on conformism, materialism, consumerism, moral repression, fear, war, and divisiveness. The deity of the otherwise godless square culture in the poem is Moloch, who symbolizes all that is repressive and destructive to the spirit.

When it first gained colloquial usage in 1948 the term *beat* meant beaten down by conventional society and derelict. Later, Jack Kerouac gave the term the additional meanings of upbeat, beatific, and on the beat musically—and Kerouac and his companions, as well as the hipster culture they inspired, became known as the Beat generation. Both meanings are expressed in "Howl," in which Ginsberg and his friends are presented as dragging themselves through dark streets naked, starving, and abused by society, but also as divinely inspired, angelic, and Christlike figures. Thus, the first part of the poem is both a lament for and a celebration of the lives of the Beat figures. These people put into practice William Blake's aphorism from the "Proverbs of Hell," in *The Marriage of Heaven and Hell* (1794), to the effect that the pursuit of excess leads to wisdom. They tried to follow their desires for love, freedom, and spiritual experience. In their rebellion against conventional authority and their determination to maintain the integrity of their souls whatever the price, they reflect another aphorism from the "Proverbs of Hell," which states that the spontaneous passion of wrath contains more wisdom than the voice of reasoned authority.

Individualism

Part of the Beats' rebellion against conventional 1950s morality was their enthusiastic pursuit of two taboo activities, sexual freedom and experimental drug taking. The former included homosexuality. In the United States in the 1950s, sexual acts between men were illegal in most states under sodomy laws. However, in "Howl," Ginsberg celebrates homosexuality. In reality, Ginsberg is arguing for the freedom of an individual to be as he or she is, and not to be defined or constrained by social conventions.

Madness

The theme of madness permeates the poem and reflects its prominence in Ginsberg's own life: his mother spent years in a psychiatric institution, and Ginsberg himself was institutionalized for eight months. Part III of the poem describes Ginsberg's experience of being institutionalized for mental illness along with Carl Solomon. The poet's attitude is one of sympathy with Solomon. In an ironic reversal in line 14, Solomon accuses his doctors of insanity.

Ginsberg treats his own madness, and that of Carl Solomon, as a badge of honor in an insane world dominated by fear, the cold war, government secrecy, anti-Communist scares, and the ever-present threat of annihilation by the atomic or hydrogen bomb. The poem asks the question, in an insane world such as this, who is truly mad? Ginsberg suggests that those branded as mad are, in fact, the sane ones. Thus, images of madness are connected with images of divinity and Christlike martyrdom.

Nakedness

There are many references to nakedness and bareness in the poem in the descriptions of Ginsberg and his fellow Beats. Examples are part I, lines 1, 5, 8, and 33. In line 1, nakedness connotes madness, poverty, and vulnerability. In line 5, the notion of baring the brain to heaven connotes a direct connection with the divine. In line 33, the vulnerability of nakedness is taken to extreme lengths in an image suggestive of a torture chamber. Generally in the poem, nakedness and bareness suggest honesty and directness on the part of the Beats as set against the hypocrisy and secrecy of mainstream society. Newborn babies come into the world naked, so nakedness suggests innocence and guilelessness.

There is also a suggestion of the prelapsarian (before the Fall) state of man in the biblical Garden of Eden. When Adam and Eve are first created, they are at one with God and do his will. At this point, they are naked and unashamed. But they lose their innocence through giving into Satan's temptation to eat the fruit of the tree of knowledge of good and evil. Immediately, they feel ashamed of their nakedness and cover themselves with clothes. When God sees this, he knows that they have disobeyed him; they have fallen from divine grace. Thus, clothes are a symbol of loss of innocence, of shame about the body, and of division from the divine. Ginsberg's naked and bareheaded Beats are shown as being close to God and as holy prophets.

STYLE

Spontaneous Expression

In "Notes Written on Finally Recording 'Howl,'" (in *Deliberate Prose: Selected Essays, 1952–1995*), Ginsberg explains that when he sat down to write the poem, he intended it to mark a new phase in his poetic development, characterized by complete freedom of expression. He writes:

I thought I wouldn't write a *poem*, but just write what I wanted to without fear, let my imagination go, open secrecy, and scribble magic lines from my real mind—sum up my life—something I wouldn't be able to show anybody, writ for my own soul's ear and a few other golden ears.

The poem, Ginsberg continues, was, "typed out madly in one afternoon, a tragic custard-pie comedy of wild phrasing, meaningless images." The resulting stream-of-consciousness style may indicate that in much of the poem it is futile to look for intentionally logical connections of ideas. The very title of the poem suggests that it is a howl of anguish and other spontaneous feelings.

Transcendentalist Poetry and Philosophy

Ginsberg considered himself the poetic heir to the nineteenth-century American transcendentalist poets and writers, including Henry David Thoreau, Ralph Waldo Emerson, and, in particular, Walt Whitman. The transcendentalists posited the existence of a pure state of spirituality that transcends the material world and that is outside of time. They believed that this state could be accessed through direct mystical experience rather than by following the doctrines of established religions. The transcendentalists shared with Ginsberg and the Beat movement a rejection of materialism and external authority as well as a conviction of the vital importance of the subjective experience of reality.

Confessional Poetry

"Howl" has strong elements of confessional poetry, the poetry of the self. This genre emerged in the United States in the late 1950s and early 1960s with the work of such poets as Sylvia Plath, Robert Lowell, and Anne Sexton. It is characterized by the poet's revelations of raw, intimate, and often unflattering information about himself or herself. While Ginsberg's "Howl" fits this definition, it rises above the genre in its humor about the excesses of his hipsters and in its transcendence of the personal through its rare combination of social critique and prophetic vision.

Density

"Howl" is written in an extremely condensed style. For example, in part I, lines 2 and 15, Ginsberg abandoned normal syntax and the rules of grammar in order to achieve a close juxtaposition of evocative images. Often these images can be unraveled to reveal a number of possible associations and resonances. In other cases, the meaning is enigmatic or ambiguous. This style, which defies grammatical convention, perfectly reflects the rebellious attitude expressed in the poem.

Symbolism

The antithesis of the Beat movement is symbolically represented in the poem by the demonic and robotic figure of Moloch, which represents the evil that grips American society and the fallen state of mind of the individuals that make up that society. The psychiatric institution featured in the poem has a real-life correlate and literal significance, but it also has symbolic significance, representing attempts by conformist society to repress rebels like Solomon, Ginsberg, and (to some degree) Naomi Ginsberg.

Irony

There are many ironic reversals in the poem. Conventional society is portrayed as pathologically insane, while people who have been institutionalized as mentally ill are portrayed as sane, wise, and divinely inspired. Criminals are shown as angelic (part I, line 63), and the homosexual acts that are stigmatized by conventional society are celebrated as holy (perhaps because Ginsberg sees all forms of sex as a part of love).

In part I, line 30, Ginsberg refers to hipster heroes investigating the Federal Bureau of Investigation—an ironic reversal of the expected roles, as Ginsberg and many of his associates were investigated by the bureau for alleged Communist sympathies and drug offenses. Ginsberg's reversal suggests that morally, he believes that the authorities are the ones who deserve to be investigated for crimes.

Ginsberg also points out the ironies and inconsistencies of capitalism, which is described as a narcotic haze. Although the capitalist system of the United States has criminalized the use of many narcotic drugs favored by the Beat generation, it has encouraged addiction to the narcotic drug tobacco, from which tobacco companies make huge profits, as Ginsberg points out in his annotated edition.

Further levels of irony can be found. Ginsberg is saying that capitalism is itself a drug. This may be (in Ginsberg's view) because of the dependence on money and consumerism that capitalism causes members of a society to develop. This dependence may be described as a narcotic or sleep-inducing haze because it can be argued that capitalism must keep people in an unawakened, trancelike state in order to persuade them to consume more and maximize the profits that drive the economy. There is an additional ironic and self-deprecatingly humorous twist in the fact that many of the hipsters who are protesting the capitalist abuses of the tobacco industry are themselves addicted to cigarettes.

Religious Imagery

Images of tortured, suffering, endangered, and wounded bodies abound in the poem, for example, in part I, lines 9, 10, 45, 53, 58, and 69, and part III, line 11. This imagery reinforces the notion that the hipsters are persecuted by conventional society, lending them the aura of martyrs. More specifically, some of the images of suffering link the hipsters to Christ. Examples include the images at part I, line 77, and part III, line 13. The effect of invoking Christ is to lend the hipsters his spiritual authority and status as persecuted innocent. It is important to recall that in his "Notes Written on Finally Recording 'Howl,'" Ginsberg describes part I as "a lament for the Lamb in America with instances of remarkable lamblike youths," with the Lamb referring to Christ's mercy and innocence.

HISTORICAL CONTEXT

The Beat Movement

Jack Kerouac is thought to have introduced the term "Beat generation" around 1948. The term is generally understood to describe a group of American writers who reached prominence from the mid-1950s to the early 1960s. Kerouac introduced the term to John Clellon Holmes, who published a novel about the Beat Generation, *Go*, in 1952 and a manifesto in the *New York Times Magazine* titled "This Is the Beat Generation" (published November 16, 1952).

The adjective *beat* is believed to have been first used by Herbert Huncke to describe someone living roughly without money or prospects. In its early usage, *beat* came to mean beaten down by conformist society, but Kerouac later insisted that it had the positive connotations of upbeat, beatific, and on the beat musically.

The Beats rejected post-World War II conventional social values and embraced Eastern philosophy and religion, drug use, free love, interracial relationships, and nontraditional literary and artistic forms. They were critics of materialism, consumerism, militarism, the cold war, industrialization, mechanization, dehumanizing institutions such as prisons, hospitals and psychiatric institutions, repressive morality, and racial prejudice.

The Beat movement was a twentieth-century expression of romanticism, being antiestablishment and pro-self. Like earlier romantics, the Beats emphasized the spontaneous expression of the individual's vital energies and the validity of subjective experience in the search for truth. They turned their backs on literary convention, using experimental forms and informal styles based on spontaneous speech or streams of consciousness. In subject matter, too, they were rebels, drawing on their own adventurous lives and the lives of people of the counterculture. It could be argued that "Howl" was the first work to bring Beat culture and values to the notice of the general public. With its form based on spontaneous (if extraordinarily voluble) speech patterns, its references to sexuality and drugs, and its passionate and rebellious authorial stance, the poem itself became a manifesto of the Beat movement.

The Cold War

The cold war was a period of tension and rivalry between the United States and the Soviet Union from the end of World War II in 1945 until the early 1990s, when the Communist Soviet Union collapsed. The period was characterized by massive military spending, the involvement of both superpowers in proxy wars around the globe, and a nuclear and conventional arms race. No direct military action occurred between the United States and the Soviet Union, which is why the conflict was called the cold war. Nevertheless, many people in the United States and Europe lived in fear of annihilation or devastation by a nuclear bomb, and the period saw the rapid rise of antinuclear "ban the bomb" demonstrations.

A reference to the nuclear issue occurs in "Howl" in part I, line 15. The militarization of the United States is referenced in part I, line 56, where it is linked with atrocities wreaked upon the innocent, consumerism, and the prevailing

COMPARE
&
CONTRAST

- **1950s:** In the United States, sexual acts between men are illegal in most states under sodomy laws. Homosexuals are stigmatized as threats to national security and are often viewed as diseased.

  Today: While stigmatization continues in some regions, antihomosexual laws are invalidated. In 2007, the U.S. House of Representatives approves the Employment Nondiscrimination Act, outlawing discrimination against employees because of sexual orientation.

- **1950s:** In 1955, Ginsberg's public reading of "Howl" brings the cultural phenomenon of the Beats to public notice. Two years later the work becomes the target of an obscenity trial.

  Today: In 2007, fifty years after a court ruled that the poem is not obscene, the New York radio station WBAI decides not to broadcast the poem, fearing that the Federal Communications Commission would judge it obscene and fine the station.

- **1950s:** Beats and other cultural rebels oppose escalation of the cold war between the United States and the Soviet Union. They also demonstrate against the ongoing development of atomic and hydrogen bombs.

  Today: The *Socialist Worker* reports that according to the French political scientist Dominique Reynié, about 36 million people took part in protests around the world against the war in Iraq between January 3 and April 12, 2003.

---

bad taste in literature. Part I, line 6, critiques the involvement of Columbia University scholars in the research and development of atomic bombs.

The cold war spread across the world as the United States sought to contain Communism and enlisted other countries as its allies. One of the best-known examples of this spread was the Vietnam War (1959–1975), in which the United States supported the Republic of Vietnam (South Vietnam) against the Democratic Republic of Vietnam (North Vietnam), which was Communist. Many American writers, artists, and intellectuals, including Ginsberg, opposed their country's involvement in the Vietnam War.

McCarthyism

McCarthyism is a term describing a period of American history from the late 1940s to the late 1950s characterized by intense anti-Communist suspicion. The period is sometimes called the Second Red Scare (the first being immediately after the birth of the Soviet Union in 1917). Fears of Communist influence on American institutions and of Soviet espionage abounded.

McCarthyism took its name from Senator Joseph McCarthy, who between 1947 and 1957 investigated a large number of politicians, artists, writers, actors, intellectuals, government employees, and other Americans for alleged Communist sympathies. The term McCarthyism later came to refer more generally to any aggressive anti-Communist activities, whoever pursued them. Ginsberg refers to the Communist sympathies of hipsters in part I, line 32, of "Howl."

The Sexual Revolution

The United States in the 1950s was characterized by a morality that disapproved of sex outside marriage, interracial sex, and homosexuality. Homosexual men were persecuted and were in danger of losing their jobs if their sexual orientation was revealed. (Lesbians largely escaped such attention because of a relative lack of awareness of their existence.) From 1947 to 1957, Senator Joseph McCarthy used accusations of homosexuality as a smear tactic in his anti-Communist crusade, combining the Red

People waiting at the bus stop outside City Lights Bookstore, an important place for Beat poets in San Francisco, California (*Panoramic Images / Getty Images*)

Scare against alleged Communists with the so-called Lavender Scare against homosexuals.

Many states had in place sodomy laws that made homosexual acts illegal. Most of these laws were only repealed during the last half of the twentieth century, from the 1960s onward. All remaining antihomosexual laws were invalidated by the 2003 Supreme Court decision *Lawrence v. Texas.*

In the 1960s, the so-called sexual revolution overturned many hitherto accepted conventions. Sex outside of marriage, between people of different races, and between same-sex couples became more widely accepted. Ginsberg was ahead of his time in challenging these taboos; as William S. Burroughs remarked after his death (as cited in Wilborn Hampton's obituary for Ginsberg in the *New York Times*), "He stood for freedom of expression and for coming out of all the closets long before others did." This is, of course, reflected in "Howl."

CRITICAL OVERVIEW

"Howl" first came to public notice in October 1955, when Ginsberg gave an impassioned performance of the poem at the Six Gallery in San Francisco to a rapturous and cheering audience. Among the audience was a drunken Jack Kerouac, who (as cited in Barry Miles's *Ginsberg: A Biography*) shouted "Go!" at the end of some of the lines. The event established Ginsberg as an important, unconventional poet and as a pioneer of the Beat movement.

As was perhaps predictable, when the poem was first published in *Howl, and Other Poems* in 1956, mainstream or "straight" society did not share the Six Gallery audience's enthusiasm. Shock and disapproval was widespread. In 1957, U.S. customs seized 520 copies of the volume arriving in the United States from the printer in England, citing the poem's obscene content. The intervention of the American Civil Liberties Union resulted in a temporary reprieve for "Howl." However, two months later, San Francisco police officers bought a copy of *Howl, and Other Poems* in the City Lights bookstore owned by Ginsberg's publisher and fellow Beat poet Lawrence Ferlinghetti. They returned to arrest Ferlinghetti on obscenity charges. The authorities objected to the poem's references to sex.

At the ensuing obscenity trial, in a landmark decision for literary freedom, Judge Clayton W. Horn ruled that the poem was not obscene. In the *Evergreen Review*, Lawrence Ferlinghetti makes a comment on the case showing the schism between "hip" and "straight" society: "It is not the poet but what he observes which is revealed as obscene. The great obscene wastes of 'Howl' are the sad wastes of the mechanized world, lost among atom bombs and insane nationalisms." The trial helped put Ferlinghetti's City Lights publishing company and bookstore at the center of San Francisco's poetry renaissance of the 1950s and made "Howl" a manifesto for the Beat movement. Since then, the poem has become part of the canon of American literature.

That is not to say, however, that Ginsberg's poem has lost its ability to shock. In 2007, fifty years after Judge Horn's ruling that the poem was not obscene, the New York radio station WBAI decided not to broadcast a recording of "Howl," fearing that the Federal Communications Commission would judge it obscene and fine the station $325,000 for each word deemed offensive.

From the late 1970s, Ginsberg's own status has risen from young outsider of the Beat generation to major American poet, and "Howl" has increasingly been considered one of the most influential and innovative poems of the modern era. Part I has been included in its uncensored form in the *Norton Anthology of American Literature* since 1979.

Nevertheless, critics are divided in their estimation of "Howl" and of Ginsberg. Some accuse Ginsberg of having achieved fame by virtue of his charismatic persona and political activism, as opposed to his poetic talent. John Hollander, in his 1957 review of *Howl, and Other Poems* in the *Partisan Review* (reprinted in the facsimile edition of the poem) is contemptuous of the "utter lack of decorum of any kind in [Ginsberg's] dreadful little volume," which the poet and critic terms "very tiresome." He adds that "Howl" "[sponges] on one's toleration, for pages and pages." Nevertheless, Hollander concedes that Ginsberg has "a real talent and a marvelous ear."

Paul Zweig, on the other hand, writing well after the onset of the Beat phenomenon in a 1969 *Nation* article, recognizes the breakthrough achieved by the poem's frankness: "What Ginsberg forced us to understand in 'Howl' ... was that nothing is safe from poetry." Calling Ginsberg a "shaman" (in tribal culture, a person who acts as an intermediary between the natural and supernatural worlds), Zweig says that Ginsberg has learned, in his psychic journeys, the "demanding truth" expressed by the sixteenth-century French writer Michel de Montaigne: "I am a man, and nothing human is foreign to me."

Related to Ginsberg's humane inclusiveness, perhaps, is that quality of "kindness, or lovingkindness," identified in his poetry, as well as in his character, by the poet and critic Alicia Ostriker in her *American Poetry Review* essay titled "'Howl' Revisited: The Poet as Jew." (Notably, Ginsberg was raised in a secular Jewish family.) Ostriker points out in her essay that this quality of "lovingkindness," known as *chesed* in Hebrew, is one of the thirteen features of God according to the twelfth-century Jewish philosopher Moses Maimonides. Indeed, at the end of the "Footnote to 'Howl,'" Ginsberg hails the kindness of the soul as the quality that redeems humanity from the hell imposed by Moloch. Ostriker further argues in her essay that the power and virtue of the dispossessed and injured are the great themes both of Yiddish literature and of "Howl."

When Ginsberg died in 1997, Wilborn Hampton noted in his *New York Times* obituary that the poet "provided a bridge between the Underground and the Transcendental." Hampton cites J. D. McClatchy, a poet and the editor of the *Yale Review* as saying of Ginsberg that he was "as much a social force as a literary phenomenon." Likening Ginsberg to Walt Whitman, McClatchy says, "He was a bard in the old manner—outsized, darkly prophetic, part exuberance, part prayer, part rant. His work is finally a history of our era's psyche, with all its contradictory urges."

CRITICISM

Claire Robinson

Robinson has an MA in English. She is a teacher of English literature and creative writing and a freelance writer and editor. In the following essay, Robinson explores how Ginsberg's "Howl" embodies spiritual values.

Allen Ginsberg wrote in the tradition of nineteenth-century American transcendentalist poets and writers such as Henry David Thoreau, Ralph Waldo Emerson, and Walt Whitman. Transcendentalism began as a protest against the rationalism and materialism that dominated the universities and mainstream society of the day and against the doctrines of organized religion. At the center of transcendentalist philosophy was a pure state of spirituality that transcends the material world and that is accessible only through the direct mystical experience of the individual, rather than through the doctrines of established religions. The movement had much in common with the Beat movement, including rebellion against conventional society and a conviction regarding the centrality of personal spiritual experience.

Whitman's poetry collection *Leaves of Grass* (1855) was a major influence on "Howl," both in its long-line, free-verse form and in its uninhibited joy in the senses at a time when such

WHAT DO I READ NEXT?

- Ginsberg's poem "Sunflower Sutra" (written in 1955 and published in *Howl, and Other Poems* in 1956) is closely related thematically to "Howl," in that it explores the redemption of fallen aspects of earthly existence through the poet's transformative vision.

- John Clellon Holmes's *New York Times Magazine* article "This Is the Beat Generation" (November 16, 1952) is available online. It is an excellent introduction to Beat philosophy and the response to the Beat movement by mainstream society.

- *The Portable Beat Reader* (2003), edited by Ann Charters, is a thorough study of the Beat movement. The volume includes essays on the major prose and poetry writers of the movement, including Allen Ginsberg.

- The Beat writer William S. Burroughs is best known for his experimental novel *Naked Lunch* (1959). The novel was the target of a 1966 obscenity trial and effectively brought about the demise of America's obscenity laws. The novel is primarily known today for its biting satire of the United States.

- *The Cold War* (2001), by Mike Sewell, examines many aspects of the cold war, including its origins, its spread across the world through events in Europe and Asia, the Cuban Missile Crisis, and its conclusion in the 1980s. This accessible book offers an ideal overview for students.

- *Sexual Politics, Sexual Communities: The Making of a Homosexual Minority in the United States, 1940–1970* (1998), by John D'Emilio, explores the history of homosexual culture from its repressed state in 1940 to its emergence as a widely accepted phenomenon by 1970. Among the topics covered is the persecution of homosexuals during the McCarthy era.

> FOR ALL THE GRIMY DETAILS OF THE HIPSTERS' EVERYDAY LIVES—THE BLOODY TOILETS, THE SLASHED WRISTS, THE CIGARETTE-BURNED ARMS—THEY ARE ANGELIC FIGURES, IN TOUCH WITH A DIVINE LEVEL OF TRUTH."

frankness was considered immoral. Whitman's poetry praises nature and the human body as part of nature but equally emphasizes the role of the mind and spirit, elevating the human body to the level of the spirit. "Howl" is similarly suffused with spiritual values. Ginsberg begins the poem with the claim of having seen a reality beyond that which is immediately visible to the earthly eye. He speaks from the privileged point of view of the prophet and the messianic bard, as a witness to the lives of his hipsters from their most humble and human aspects to their highest spiritual aspects. He frequently uses antithetical (contrasting) imagery to reinforce this godlike vision. For example, in part I, line 49, the same tramp-like figure that sits in boxes in the darkness under bridges rises up to build harpsichords in lofts. This line contrasts lowness (under bridges) with height (lofts), darkness with light, the stygian with the angelic; but the same hipster encompasses both aspects. In the eyes of conventional society, he could sink no lower, but in Ginsberg's bardic vision, he is a blessed angel—with a dirty face, but an angel nonetheless.

For all the grimy details of the hipsters' everyday lives—the bloody toilets, the slashed wrists, the cigarette-burned arms—they are angelic figures, in touch with a divine level of truth. They tread barefoot on broken wineglasses (part I, line 58), but they dance as they do so, recalling the Hindu portrayal of the god Shiva, treading out the dance of creation on the body of a demon. In part III, Carl Solomon appears in a banal light, banging on an old typewriter or a piano, but also as a Christlike figure who suffers torture in the psychiatric institution. In part I, line 77, Ginsberg portrays the jazz musicians of the Beat culture as expressing Christ's suffering through the notes of the saxophone. On the wider canvas, Ginsberg sees the delusion that grips America in a spiritual form, personified in the child-eating malevolent god Moloch. It is a cliché of politicians that children are a society's future, but Ginsberg brings the cliché to life in this shocking symbol of innocent children willfully sacrificed in exchange for power.

These elements, as well as fitting into the transcendentalist tradition, are also characteristic of visionary poetry in the tradition of Ginsberg's spiritual mentor William Blake. Visionary poetry expresses spiritual landscapes discovered through inner journeys undertaken through intuition, meditation, dreams, and psychedelic drugs.

The hipsters' vision of reality is differentiated from the "straight" vision of reality in part by attitudes toward time. The theme of time permeates all parts of the poem, simultaneously pointing to the importance of the theme and lending this disparate poem some unity. The poem implies that straight society is governed by time constraints represented by material clocks and watches. This time is seen as antithetical to spiritual values. The hipsters obey only eternal time, the clocks in space of the "Footnote" (line 12). Thus in part I, line 54, they throw their watches off the roof to cast their vote for eternity, which exists outside of time. The gesture is heroic yet futile, as alarm clocks fall on their heads every day for the next ten years, implying, perhaps, that the hipsters are forced to conform and get conventional jobs in order to survive. At this point in the poem, Moloch is winning the battle between the sacred and the profane, yet the hipsters continue to hurl themselves headlong into the fray, sustained by their knowledge of the rightness of their passion.

The spiritual content of Ginsberg's poem is reflected in its form. It does not have rhyme or regular meter but is arranged in long lines in the style of Walt Whitman. In "Notes Written on Finally Recording 'Howl,'" Ginsberg calls his lines "bardic breath." Both elements in this phrase—bard and breath—can be analyzed in order to throw light on "Howl."

A bard is a reciter of poetry from the ancient oral traditions in which poetry was not written down but passed down through the generations from bard to bard. "Howl" is certainly a poem that demands to be read aloud, and it is fitting that its first public appearance was not as a written publication but as a reading. The experience of hearing these long lines read aloud is of a cascade of words and phrases tumbling over one another in an outpouring of passion, as befits spontaneous expression. This effect is reinforced by the fact that the whole of part I of the poem is one 78-line sentence. The poem is given a unity and coherence by the repetition of the word *who* at the beginning of most of these lines.

Ginsberg explains in his "Notes Written on Finally Recording 'Howl'" that he intends each line of the poem to be spoken as a single breath unit. This mode of organizing his verse may stem from his interest in Eastern religions, which emphasize control over the breath as a way of quieting the mind and increasing subjective awareness of the individual's eternal nature that exists beyond time and change. Later in life, Ginsberg was to practice *shamatha*, a form of Buddhist breath meditation that he learned from his Tibetan teacher, Chögyam Trungpa Rinpoche. Ginsberg's book *Mind Breaths: Poems, 1972–1977* (1977), dedicated to Trungpa, contains poems written with the help of *shamatha* meditation.

Ginsberg's repetition of the word "who" at the beginning of his lines in part I and his repetition of the word "holy" in the "Footnote" are examples of a rhetorical device known as *anaphora*. Anaphora is a literary device whereby certain words are emphasized through their repetition at the beginnings of clauses or lines. In this poem, the repetitions reflect the use of a mantra in meditation. The mantra is a sound that is repeated in order to quiet the mind in a similar way to the breath control in *shamatha* meditation. In the case of the word *holy*, the meaning of the word reflects the intended spiritual effects of the mantra-style repetition. Ginsberg's use of repeated words in a mantra-like way combines with his use of the single-line breath unit to lend his poem an incantatory spiritual power that is calculated to alter the awareness of the poet-bard and the listener alike. This appears to have happened at the first reading of "Howl," when, according to Barry Miles's *Ginsberg: A Biography*, "Allen was completely transported," while the audience was "cheering him wildly at every line."

In choosing the word *holy* for his anaphoric pattern, Ginsberg is consciously echoing the final line of William Blake's *The Marriage of Heaven and Hell*. In the section "A Song of Liberty," after castigating religious hypocrites for claiming that the failure to act on their desires is a virtuous virginity, Blake concludes with the statement that every living thing is holy. Ginsberg, in the "Footnote," makes the same point through imagery. He closely juxtaposes the lowly and (in conventional morality) the profane with the divine, all under the umbrella of holiness. The tramp is elevated to the same level as the angels; the rhythms of bebop are equated in their transformative power with the apocalypse, the end of creation itself. Perhaps, Ginsberg seems to suggest, the new Beat culture will mark the end of Moloch's creation.

Part II and the "Footnote" have a parallel anaphoric structure, in that each part mirrors the other with the repetition of a key word, respectively, "Moloch" and "holy." These two concepts are antithetical, or in opposition, to each other. Ginsberg subverts this antithesis when the same skyscrapers that are condemned as the machinery of Moloch in part II, are carried over to the "Footnote," where they are declared holy. Because the "Footnote" has the last word, the poem ends in an ecstatic redemption achieved not by any change in external circumstances but by the poet's transformative vision.

Source: Claire Robinson, Critical Essay on "Howl," in *Poetry for Students*, Gale, Cengage Learning, 2009.

Michael Schumacher

In the following essay, Ginsberg biographer Schumacher traces Ginsberg's growth as a poet and his journey toward writing "Howl."

Twenty-five years ago, while explaining his method of spontaneous composition, Allen Ginsberg stated that "it [was] possible to get in a state of inspiration while improvising." He often improvised during poetry readings, using an already published poem such as "America" as the framework for lengthy new improvisations, similar to the way jazz musicians used a song as the framework for extended solos. It was much more difficult, Ginsberg allowed, to accomplish this when he was actually writing. Longer works such as "Howl" or *Kaddish,* two masterworks generally acknowledged as towering examples of Ginsberg's skills in spontaneous composition, required a lot of ingredients coming together at once.

"You have to be inspired to write something like that," he said. "It's not something you can very easily do just by pressing a button. You have to have the right historical and physical combination, the right mental formation, the right courage, the right sense of prophecy, and the right information, intentions, and ambition."

> THE YOUTHFUL GINSBERG WAS A HOLY MESS OF PSYCHOLOGICAL, INTELLECTUAL, AND ARTISTIC CHARACTERISTICS AND AMBITIONS, OFTEN IN CONFLICT YET ALWAYS SEEKING THE CORRECT (AS OPPOSED TO PROPER) FORM OF EXPRESSION."

A handful of recently published books, released to commemorate the fiftieth anniversary of the writing and publishing of "Howl," provide fresh and welcome insight into this crucial combination of factors behind one of the great achievements of American literature. The story of the writing of "Howl" has been told and retold by Ginsberg, most notably in his recently reissued annotated edition of "Howl," but all too often a very important fact is lost in the telling: while Ginsberg did indeed sit down at his typewriter and, in a single extended work session, compose the massive main body of one of the most influential poems of the twentieth century, he did not do so by simply pressing a button and unleashing what his friend and mentor William S. Burroughs called a "word horde." Ginsberg was twenty-nine in 1955 when he wrote "Howl," and every one of those twenty-nine years seems to have acted as an unwritten preamble to the poem.

The author of "Howl" was not the same Allen Ginsberg that the public came to know later in his life after he'd reached his iconic level of fame. He wasn't the confident, long-haired, politically-charged and savvy figure depicted in Fred McDarrah's famous "Uncle Sam top hat" photo, or the suited, professorial Ginsberg captured by Robert Frank for later book jackets. The youthful Ginsberg was a holy mess of psychological, intellectual, and artistic characteristics and ambitions, often in conflict yet always seeking the correct (as opposed to proper) form of expression.

"I'm writing to satisfy my egotism," he wrote in 1941, shortly before his fifteenth birthday. "If some future historian or biographer wants to know what the genius thought and did in his tender years, here it is. I'll be a genius of some kind of other, probably in literature, I really believe it. (Not naively, as whoever reads this is thinking.) I have a fair degree of confidence in myself. Either I'm a genius, I'm egocentric, or I'm slightly schizophrenic. Probably the first two."

Not surprisingly, this and similar entries embarrassed the adult Ginsberg to such a degree that he refused to allow his youthful journals to be published until after his death. Bill Morgan and Juanita Lieberman-Plimpton started compiling and editing Ginsberg's *The Book of Martyrdom and Artifice* nearly two decades ago, and these journals, along with Morgan's excellent new biography, *I Celebrate Myself: The Somewhat Private Life of Allen Ginsberg,* ultimately serve as guides to the long, painstaking, and often painful journey leading to the composition of "Howl."

Ginsberg's childhood and adolescence, recalled in excruciating detail in *Kaddish* other later poems, and recounted in Morgan's biography, caused William Carlos Williams to marvel that Ginsberg had survived long enough to write "Howl." As a boy, Ginsberg watched his mother, Naomi, a Russian immigrant, drop deeper and deeper into an abyss of paranoid schizophrenia; she would be in and out of mental institutions for much of her adult life, and even today it's hard to tell which was more difficult on her youngest son. His father, Louis Ginsberg, a teacher and moderately successful poet, labored to raise a family on a modest salary while trying to fulfill his own poetic aspirations. It wasn't easy, to say the least. It grew even more difficult for the young Allen Ginsberg when he became aware of his homosexuality and suffered the psychological penalties for trying to hide it from an intolerant society. When he enrolled at Columbia, Ginsberg had just turned seventeen, and while he might have been intellectually capable of taking on formal university studies, he was emotionally lagging behind his peers. He desperately needed love, but he didn't dare pursue it. He wanted to write poetry, but he couldn't even discuss it with his own father, since Louis Ginsberg had always joked that poets weren't normal.

Three Columbia professors—Lionel Trilling, Mark Van Doren, and Raymond Weaver—recognized Ginsberg's potential and offered encouragement, albeit in the traditional academic sense. More important, Ginsberg met Lucien Carr, Jack Kerouac, and William Burroughs, each bright but unconventional thinkers, each filling his head with attitudes and ideas completely alien to anything he had witnessed or experienced while growing up in Paterson, New Jersey.

Ginsberg's formal and informal educations clashed. He didn't dress (or care to dress) like his well-outfitted Ivy League classmates; he hung out with all the wrong people. Kerouac was persona non grata at Columbia, and when Ginsberg was caught housing him overnight in his dorm room, Columbia officials suspected the worst and drummed him off the campus. Ginsberg and Carr had tried to come up with what they called a "new vision" for literature—a form that, in an apocalyptic world, addressed real people in real situations in real language, literary models of the day be damned—but all Ginsberg knew, from his father and his studies, were existing literary models. His early poems, now published for the first time in *Martyrdom and Artifice,* indicated an undeveloped poet with great command of form, but with only the vaguest clue as to how to marry it to content. Ginsberg loved Whitman, but since Whitman was out of favor in the poetry establishment, he chose to imitate Marvell and Donne. It didn't work.

His life became still more complicated when he met Neal Cassady, the street-smart, self-educated, hyperkinetic, sexually supercharged "Western hero" who so enthralled Kerouac that he eventually devoted two major novels to him. Ginsberg saw him in a different light. He fell in love with the man first and the mind later, and, as would be the case throughout Ginsberg's sexually confused life, the man he was intensely drawn to happened to be (mostly) heterosexual.

Ginsberg's pursuit of Cassady, presented at great length in *Martyrdom and Artifice,* was both pathethic and heartbreaking. Here was a young man, pining like a teenage kid over his newfound love, hoping against all that he knew to be true that he would actually be able to find some miraculous solution to his homosexual yearnings. After arranging meetings under the guise of writing lessons, Ginsberg would sit alone in his room waiting for Cassady to arrive, only to learn that Cassady was jumping from woman to woman while he was keeping his lonely vigil. By the time Ginsberg was capable of accepting the truth, he was so psychologically and emotionally depleted that he had lost almost all of his self-respect—and he wasn't all that far from losing his mind as well.

His friends and mentors weren't faring well, either. Lucien Carr was behind bars, imprisoned for murdering David Kammerer, another Ginsberg acquaintance, who had been stalking Carr with the hopes of forcing him into a relationship. Kerouac, who had helped Carr dispose of evidence, had avoided a jail sentence by marrying and moving to Michigan. Burroughs, fed up with the New York scene, had relocated to Texas. And if all that wasn't taxing enough on Ginsberg's frail state of mind, his parents had split up and Naomi Ginsberg was gradually sliding into such a mental decline that Allen would eventually be asked to sign papers authorizing his mother's lobotomy.

Ginsberg teetered at the edge of his limits. He continued to write poetry with remarkable self-discipline, even as his daily existence crumbled and he himself began to question his sanity. His friends began to wonder as well, especially when, in 1948, Ginsberg announced to anyone who would listen that he'd had a series of "visions" rooted in William Blake's poetry, visions that convinced him that he had a sacred vocation to pursue poetry and pass along the minute particulars of his life and experiences to future generations, just as Blake's voice had been handed down through the ages.

At this point, a feature in Morgan's biography becomes especially useful. HarperCollins has recently published a massive, 1,189-page, updated edition of Ginsberg's *Collected Poems,* encompassing all of Ginsberg's published poetry, and Morgan has included, in the margins of his biography, the titles of poems and their page numbers in *Collected Poems* corresponding with the events of Ginsberg's life. Ginsberg always insisted that his poetry was a "graph" of his mind, and this feature in Morgan's biography shows just how precisely this was so. The poems written immediately following Ginsberg's "Blake visions" ("The Eye Altering Alters All," "On Reading William Blake's 'The Sick Rose,'" "Vision 1948") are two wrapped up in Ginsberg's efforts to reproduce and analyze his visions to be effective as poems, whereas, a decade later, in "The Lion for Real," he managed to be much more successful when he was not so self-conscious.

Ginsberg's artistic development accelerated as his personal life dipped into a purgatory that would supply him with the grist for an epic poem. He was arrested after he allowed a group of petty thieves to use his apartment as a storehouse for stolen goods, and in a plea bargain with prosecutors, he chose time in a sanitarium [*sic*] over time in jail. While undergoing psychiatric evaluation, Ginsberg met Carl Solomon, the brilliant yet pathologically unconventional figure to whom "Howl" is dedicated. He also met and was befriended by William Carlos Williams, an acclaimed local poet well connected with the publishing world and much more suited to act as a Ginsberg tutor than anyone at Columbia. Williams encouraged Ginsberg to use American language and idiom in his poetry, and Ginsberg took the advice to heart.

The poetry written shortly after Ginsberg's introduction to Williams, eventually published in 1961 in a volume of early poems, *Empty Mirror,* now published along with additional, previously unpublished poems in *Martyrdom and Artifice,* represent nothing less than a chrysalis between the derivative young Ginsberg and the fully realized poet he would become. Some of the work is still too self-consciously clever to represent anything other than an interesting exercise, but there are diamonds to be found as well, intimations that, for Ginsberg, content and form were finally coming together. The discovery was purely accidental. When Ginsberg tried to impress Williams by breaking lines from his journals into short poems similar to those written by Williams, the elder poet responded enthusiastically. He praised the work and promised to see it published. Ginsberg, like any eager young pupil beaming from his teacher's praise, proceeded to break his journals down into a hefty volume's worth of poems.

During this same period, Ginsberg's spiritual growth took an unexpected turn when Jack Kerouac "discovered" Buddhism and suggested that his friend look into it. Ginsberg would always credit Kerouac for being the force behind his lifelong devotion to and study of Buddhism, but in reality Kerouac was far too preoccupied with his travels and writing for an in-depth study. Ginsberg, true to character, took a more scholarly approach, and while two decades would pass before Ginsberg would meet the Tibetan master Chögyam Trungpa and formally dedicate himself to Trungpa's teachings, the initial studies proved significant, especially when he moved to San Francisco and met Gary Snyder and Philip Whalen, two poets who used Buddhism and Eastern thought as anchors in their work.

Ginsberg fled New York and an unsatisfactory attempt at a relationship with William Burroughs in 1953, and after spending nearly half a year in Mexico, exploring the Mayan ruins and writing *Siesta in Xbalba* (his first successful long poem) he returned to the States with the intention of reuniting with Neal Cassady, who had married and moved to San José. The reunion was short-lived. After Carolyn Cassady walked in on the two men in the midst of a sexual encounter, she loaded Ginsberg into the family car and dumped him off in San Francisco.

The city and its poetry community, as it turned out, were the final crucial ingredients necessary for the composition of "Howl."

Beat generation historians tend to employ a kind of shorthand in delineating Ginsberg's early days in San Francisco: Ginsberg arrives in town; meets a psychologist who recommends that he give up his day job for poetry; begins a lifelong relationship with Peter Orlovsky; writes "Howl" and reads it at the legendary Six Gallery reading; and rockets to the forefront of a new generation of poets. As Morgan shows, it wasn't really a quick, simple path from one point to the next. In fact, "Howl" might not have been written at all if Ginsberg hadn't again backed himself into a corner. After Carolyn Cassady dropped him off in San Francisco, Ginsberg made a half-hearted attempt at living a "normal" life, taking up with a girlfriend and working a job, with predictable results. He *was* encouraged by a psychiatrist to drop the job and live an openly gay lifestyle if that would ease his mind, but it didn't—not at first, at least. Peter Orlovsky, like Neil Cassady, was essentially heterosexual, and while he and Ginsberg agreed to maintain a mutually exclusive gay relationship, there were all kinds of troubles on the horizon.

Unhappy with the direction his life with Ginsberg was taking, Orlovsky left Ginsberg in the summer of 1955. Emotionally distraught, uncertain where his life was going, geographically removed from his closest friends and family, and discouraged by his own inability to get his work published, Ginsberg was again at a personal crossroads. Rather than lapse into another extended period of self-pity, he pondered the plights of those he knew to be in similar or worse condition—"best minds" that had been beaten down by society and circumstance, friends who had died (or, worse, were walking dead);

friends who had suffered, people scarred by the marks of woe, as Blake would have it.

His life had led him to this moment. The long lines of the poem, which he initially entitled "Stropes" but then renamed "Howl," were torrential outpourings, one leading easily to the next, devoted to actual events in his and his friends' lives. Since he had no intention of ever publishing the work—it was too personal, as well as being far too sexually explicit for the times—he improvised as he went along, becoming more inspired with each line. Instead of writing something bathetic, as he might have done just a few years earlier, he chose to celebrate the lives he was depicting in the poem. The tone of his new work, oratorical and angry at first glance, was actually cathartic, almost ecstatic—proof that sympathy could unburden the spirit.

"I saw the best minds of my generation, destroyed by madness . . . " He was thinking of all the others. He was thinking of his former self.

Source: Michael Schumacher, "Prelude to a Poem," in *Tricycle*, Vol. 16, No. 3, Spring 2007, pp. 96–103.

Vivian Gornick

In the following article, Gornick reflects on the resemblances between Ginsberg's poetry and poetry by Walt Whitman.

In 1947 Saul Bellow published a novel called *The Victim,* in which a derelict character named Kirby Allbee haunts another named Asa Leventhal, claiming that Leventhal is responsible for his downfall. Kirby, one of Bellow's fabled fast talkers—all feverish self-abasement and joking insult—repeatedly baits Leventhal, and at one point, when Leventhal murmurs something about Walt Whitman, says to him, "Whitman? You people like Whitman? What does Whitman mean to you people?" Who could ever have dreamed that less than a decade after the publication of *The Victim* not only would "you people" be announcing out loud that they liked Whitman but it would appear that they themselves had reincarnated him. The day after Allen Ginsberg's celebrated 1955 reading of "Howl" in San Francisco, Lawrence Ferlinghetti sent Ginsberg a telegram that read, "I greet you at the beginning of a great career"—the sentence Emerson had used writing to Whitman upon the publication, exactly a hundred years earlier, of *Leaves of Grass.*

Fifty years later, I think it can safely be agreed that Allen Ginsberg *is* the poet who,

" "

LIKE *LEAVES OF GRASS,* IT IS AN INGENIOUS
EXPERIMENT WITH THE AMERICAN LANGUAGE THAT
DID WHAT EZRA POUND SAID A GREAT POEM SHOULD
DO: MAKE THE LANGUAGE NEW."

within living memory, most legitimately resembles Whitman. He, like Whitman, wrote an emblematic American poem that became world famous; was experienced preeminently as a poet of the people, at home among the democratic masses; developed a public persona to match the one in his writing—hugely free-spirited and self-promoting, an open-hearted exhibitionist. And he, again like Whitman, is remembered as a man in possession of an extraordinary sweetness that, throughout his life, welled up repeatedly to astonish the hearts of all who encountered him.

I met Ginsberg only twice, the first time at Jack Kerouac's funeral in 1969. I was there for *The Village Voice.* It was my very first assignment as a working journalist. Here is the scene as I remember it:

At the head of the viewing room stood the casket with Kerouac, hideously made up, lying in it. In the mourners' seats sat Kerouac's middle-class French-Canadian relatives—eyes narrowed, faces florid, arms crossed on their disapproving breasts. Around the casket—dipping, weaving, chanting *Om*—were Allen Ginsberg, Peter Orlovsky, and Gregory Corso. Then there was Kerouac's final, caretaker wife, a woman old enough to be his mother, weeping bitterly and looking strangely isolated. I sat mesmerized, staring in all directions. Suddenly Ginsberg was sitting beside me. "And who are you?" he asked quietly. I told him who I was. He nodded and wondered if I was talking to people. Especially the wife. I must be sure to talk to her. "Oh, no," I said quickly. "I couldn't do *that*." Ginsberg nodded into space for a moment. "You must," he murmured. Then he looked directly into my eyes. "It's your job," he said softly. "You must do your job."

The second time we met, nearly twenty years later, was at an infamous meeting of the PEN board called to debate a letter (drafted by Ginsberg) that the Freedom-to-Write Committee had sent to Israel's premier, taking his government to task for censoring Palestinian and Israeli journalists. I sat in my seat, listening to Ginsberg read his letter aloud to a packed room. He was now in his sixties, his head bald, his beard trim, wearing an ill-fitting black suit, the voice as gentle as I remembered it and twice as dignified. Although the letter had been signed by Susan Sontag, William Styron, and Grace Paley among others, it was Ginsberg himself who drew fire from the opposition. In a communiqué that had been sent earlier to the committee, Cynthia Ozick had practically accused him of being an agent for the PLO; and now, the essence of the charge coming from the floor seemed to be "It's people like you who are destroying Israel." I remember Ginsberg standing there, his glasses shining, nodding in all directions, urging people toward compassionate reason. He never raised his voice, never spoke with heat or animosity, never stopped sounding thoughtful and judicious while all about him were losing their heads. When he stepped from the microphone and was making his way through the crowd, I pressed his hand as he passed me and thanked him for the excellence of the letter's prose. He stopped, closed his other hand over mine, and looking directly into my eyes, said softly, "I know you. Don't I know you? I *know* you."

Allen Ginsberg was born in Newark, New Jersey, in 1926 to Louis and Naomi Ginsberg; the father was a published poet, a high school teacher, and a socialist; the mother, an enchanting free spirit, a passionate communist, and a woman who lost her mental stability in her thirties (ultimately, she was placed in an institution and lobotomized). Allen and his brother grew up inside a chaotic mixture of striving respectability, left-wing bohemianism, and certifiable madness in the living room. It all felt *large* to the complicated, oversensitive boy who, discovering that he lusted after boys, began to feel mad himself and, like his paranoid parents, threatened by, yet defiant of, the America beyond the front door.

None of this accounts for Allen Ginsberg; it only describes the raw material that, when the time was right, would convert into a poetic vision of mythic proportion that merged brilliantly with its moment: the complicated aftermath of the

Second World War, characterized by anxiety about the atomic bomb, a manipulated terror of godless Communism, the strange pathos of the Man in the Gray Flannel Suit, and the subterranean currents of romanticized lawlessness into which the men and women ultimately known as the Beats would funnel an old American devotion to the idea of revolutionary individualism.

When Ginsberg entered Columbia University in 1942, he was already possessed of a presentation of self, shall we say, that would make it impossible for him to gain the love of the teachers he most admired, namely, Lionel Trilling and Mark Van Doren. (Trilling memorialized Ginsberg in his short story "Of This Time, of That Place" as the brilliant student whom the narrating academic can experience only as mad.) Emulating these men would mean going into a kind of internal exile that Allen, even then, knew he could not sustain. His dilemma seemed profound. Then he met Jack Kerouac, also a student at Columbia. Through Kerouac he met William Burroughs; together they picked up a Times Square junkie poet named Herbert Huncke; and after that Neal Cassady, the wild man of all their dreams: a handsome, grown-up delinquent who drank, stole, read Nietzsche, fucked like a machine, and drove great distances at great speeds for the sake of movement itself. As Burroughs put it, "Wife and child may starve, friends exist only to exploit for gas money ... Neal must move." (Cassady became Dean Moriarty in *On the Road* and the Adonis of Denver in "Howl.")

For Ginsberg, these friends came to constitute a sacred company of inspired madmen destined to convert the poisoned atmosphere of America's Cold War politics into one of restored beauty—through their writing. The conviction among them of literary destiny was powerful. And why not? People like Ginsberg, Kerouac, and Cassady are born every hour on the hour: how often do their lives intersect with a political moment that endows their timeless hungers with the echoing response of millions, thereby persuading them that they are, indeed, emissaries of social salvation? What is remarkable among this bunch—considering how much they drank, got stoned, and flung themselves across the country in search of heavenly despair—is how well they sustained one another throughout their faltering twenties, when life was all worldly rejection and self-dramatizing desperation.

In 1949, now twenty-three years old, depressed, and at loose ends, Ginsberg let Herbert Huncke—a true criminal—crash at his apartment, where Huncke proceeded to stash an ever-increasing amount of stolen goods. Inevitably, the police appeared at the door, and everyone was arrested. Rescued from a prison sentence by friends, family, and his Columbia teachers, Ginsberg was sent to the New York State Psychiatric Institute, where he spent eight months that did, indeed, change his life. Here he met the man to whom he would dedicate "Howl."

Carl Solomon was Allen's double—a Bronx-born bisexual self-dramatizing left-wing intellectual. They saw themselves in each other almost immediately. Solomon held out his hand and said, "I'm Kirilov" (a character in Dostoevsky's *The Possessed*). Allen responded, "I'm Myshkin" (Dostoevsky's fabled idiot). There was, however, one important difference between them. Solomon had lived in Paris, was soaked in existentialist politics and literature; and here, at New York State Psychiatric, he introduced Allen to the work of Genet, Artaud, and Céline, the mad writers with whom he instantly felt at one. Ginsberg marveled at Solomon's melancholy brilliance and proceeded to mythicize it. If Carl was mad, it could only be that Amerika had driven him mad. When Ginsberg emerged from the institution, he had his metaphor in place:

> I saw the best minds of my generation destroyed by madness, starving hysterical naked,
> dragging themselves through the negro streets at dawn looking for an angry fix.

For the next few years he wandered, all over the country and halfway around the world, becoming a practicing Buddhist along the way. Arrived at last in San Francisco in 1954 (with Kerouac, Cassady, and Corso dancing about him), here and now, in the American city experienced as most open (that is, farthest from the seats of eastern power), he wrote his great poem, read it aloud one night in October 1955—and awoke to find himself famous.

While thousands of young people responded to "Howl" as though they'd been waiting *years* to hear this voice speaking these words, the literary establishment promptly vilified it. Lionel Trilling hated the poem, John Hollander hated it, James Dickey hated it, and Norman Podhoretz hated it. Podhoretz hated it so much that he wrote about it twice, once in *The New Republic* and then again in *Partisan Review.* By the time these pieces were being written, *On the Road* had been published, as well as *Naked Lunch,* and for Podhoretz the American sky was falling. The Beats, he said, were the barbarians at the gate, rabble-rousers who "embraced homosexuality, jazz, dope-addiction and vagrancy" (he got that part right), at one with "the young savages in leather jackets who have been running amuck in the last few years with their switch-blades and zip guns." Jack Kerouac was cut to the quick and wrote to complain that the Beats were about *beatitude,* not criminalism; they were here to *rescue* America (from corporate death and atomic bomb politics), not destroy her.

In the summer of 1957, "Howl" was brought to trial in San Francisco on charges of obscenity, with a wealth of writers testifying on behalf of the poem's literary value. In retrospect, the trial can be seen as an opening shot in a culture war destined to throw long shadows across American life. And indeed, throughout the sixties, both the poem and its author were celebrated, the former as a manifesto of the counterculture, the latter as one of its emblematic figures.

Today, nearly fifty years after it was written, "Howl" is never out of print, is read all over the world (it's been translated into more than two dozen languages), and by most standards is considered a literary classic. Like *Leaves of Grass,* it is an ingenious experiment with the American language that did what Ezra Pound said a great poem should do: make the language new. Its staccato phrasing, its mad juxtapositions and compacted images, its remarkable combining of the vernacular with the formal—obscene, slangy, religious, transcendent, speaking now in the voice of the poet, now in that of the hipster—is simply an astonishment. The effect of all this on the reader? "Even today," as Jonah Raskin, one of Ginsberg's biographers, says, "reading the poem yields a feeling of intoxication. The words produce an electrical charge that is exhilarating."

That charge is actually the *dis*charge of a man and a time well met. There is a feverish hunger for poetry and glory in Ginsberg as he moves through the late forties that is absolutely at one with his political and cultural moment. Prowling the streets of New York as if it were Dostoevsky's Petersburg; rising in an English class at Columbia to terrify students and teachers alike with some brilliant, unpunctuated rant;

looking for sex in Times Square; seeing Blake in a vision in his own kitchen; nodding wordlessly when the cops ask him if he is a homosexual—we have a vivid figure standing squarely in the foreground of significant disconnect.

Yet, we also see why Ginsberg could survive his own youth to become an emblematic figure of growth and change while Kerouac and Cassady could not. Neal Cassady was a drifter through and through. To read his letters—although the ones to his writer friends are richly literate—is to see a man perpetually on the run from himself. It was all drugs, drink, women, and motion without a stop. He is forever in the car hurtling toward New York, Denver, or California. If he stops, it's to get one woman pregnant, marry a second, start an affair with a third, all in what feels like the space of a month; then it's back in the car, writing to each one, "I'll be home in a week, babe, ten days at the latest." Kerouac, except for the books, was not so very different. Neither of these men could inhabit the space he actually occupied at any given moment. Each had a leak somewhere in the middle of himself that made experience drain exhaustingly away (both were dead in their forties).

Ginsberg, by contrast, was remarkably heart-whole: it made all the difference. His experience nourished him, gave him the strength to complete the self-transformation he had been bent on from the beginning. I don't think it an exaggeration to say that when he died at seventy his life had given new meaning to the word "self-created." For the formal poets and critics of his own generation, Ginsberg would remain only an original: the gifted, problematic amateur (in 1963 Robert Lowell wrote to Elizabeth Bishop "the beats have blown away, the professionals have returned"). For the American culture, however, Ginsberg (indeed, like Walt Whitman) had become an inspirited incarnation: the authentic made-in-America holy fool.

Source: Vivian Gornick, "Wild at Heart," in *American Poetry Review*, Vol. 35, No. 2, March–April 2006, pp. 4–6.

David E. Pozen

In the following critique, Pozen examines the significance of Ping-Pong in "Howl."

Though typically linked with such benign associations as rec-room leisure and adolescent camaraderie, the game of Ping-Pong takes on much deeper and darker meanings in Allen

" ALTHOUGH THE AGGRESSIVE TREATMENTS OF

MENTAL HOSPITALS, SUCH AS FORCED DRUG INJEC-

TIONS AND ELECTRIC SHOCKS TEND TO PROVOKE THE

LOUDEST PUBLIC OBJECTIONS, GINSBERG LOCATES THE

EMPTY MONOTONY OF 'PINGPONG' AT THE CORE OF

THE CONCRETE VOID'S SUFFOCATING DARKNESS."

Ginsberg's poem "Howl." At two key junctures in the poem, Ginsberg incorporates the image of a Ping-Pong game into descriptions of his lover Carl Solomon. In part 1, Ginsberg uses Ping-Pong to satirize the medical treatments administered to Solomon in a mental asylum and to dramatize the human struggle for self-expression. By evoking the repetitive, almost mindless nature of the game and its frivolity as a pastime, Ginsberg illuminates the moral and spiritual emptiness of Solomon's hospital experiences. Then, in part 3, he returns to the metaphor of Ping-Pong to explore the forces of love and death that operate on Solomon. At the end of "Howl," Ginsberg's destabilizing images of Ping-Pong have transformed the seemingly innocuous word into a round, complex symbol that speaks to his relationship with his lover, his project as a poet, and his notion of death; Ginsberg may be the game-playing type, but he makes Ping-Pong a very serious affair.

When he equates the modern treatment methods of mental hospitals with Ping-Pong, Ginsberg mocks the methods' effectiveness by implicitly reducing them to the level of a mere game. He writes, "and who were given instead the concrete void of insulin Metrazol electricity hydrotherapy psychotherapy occupational therapy pingpong & amnesia," when he first describes the "madhouse" that Carl Solomon inhabits in part 1. As Ginsberg goes down the line of treatments, they become increasingly more obscure and less physical, from intravenous drugs (insulin and Metrazol), to shock treatment (electricity hydrotherapy), to mental conditioning (psychotherapy and occupational therapy), and finally to Ping-Pong. Ironically, all of the zealous, invasive treatment methods of modern medicine resolve

into the child's game of Ping-Pong, the stereotypical form of amusement allowed hospital patients. The unfeeling doctors may have victimized his lover Solomon and countless others at the mental ward, but Ginsberg turns the tables of power by denigrating their work in his poetry.

Although it ridicules the practices of the madhouse, Ping-Pong's inclusion in the list of treatments also extends Ginsberg's image of the "concrete void" at the heart of mental hospitals. Through his elision of the commas that would normally separate the different treatments in prose, Ginsberg casts them as a single entity, impossibly unified like "concrete" and "void." As a result, each item in the laundry list of treatments loses its individual meaning, just as each recipient of these treatments risks losing his individual personality. "Amnesia"—the ultimate detachment from and erasure of one's own self—awaits the mental patient at the end of the day. By not differentiating the items in his catalogue of treatments, Ginsberg thus personifies their dehumanizing effects. The banality of Ping-Pong (which one imagines most patients playing just to pass the time) and its apparent disjunction from the other items in the list further extend this sense of dehumanization, of meaninglessness. Ping-Pong may be a symbol for Ginsberg's power as a writer, but it also serves as a symbol for his helplessness to protect his lover Solomon from the tortures of the asylum.

Beyond its symbolic implications for Solomon's treatment and his personal plight, the repetitions that Ginsberg creates around "pingpong" also engage the image in a deeper, more abstract dialogue on the human condition. Entering the poem after three consecutive uses of "therapy," the word "pingpong" has its own internal rhyming quality. Though "Ping-Pong" is the correct spelling, Ginsberg marks the significance of the word and highlights its internal rhyme by omitting the dash. Embedded in the external repetitions of the catalogue of treatments, the internal repetition of sounds in "pingpong" places the word at the core of the concrete void, a point driven home by Solomon's decision in the next stanza to overturn "one symbolic pingpong table." Although the aggressive treatments of mental hospitals, such as forced drug injections and electric shocks tend to provoke the loudest public objections, Ginsberg locates the empty monotony of "pingpong" at the core of the concrete void's suffocating darkness.

As a result, when Carl overturns the Ping-Pong table, he not only protests his treatment at the asylum, but he also makes a profound statement about the human need to resist the concrete void. In line with its repetitive, childish name (note that Ginsberg could have used the more stately synonym "table tennis"), the game of Ping-Pong is itself a repetitive, rather childish endeavor, demanding little in the way of creativity. Along with his mentor Jack Kerouac, Ginsberg embraces spontaneity and improvisation as core values, both for living and for writing. Because Ping-Pong fundamentally conflicts with his value system, Ginsberg celebrates Solomon's overturning of the table as a positive act of self-actualization, not simply as a negative act against his oppression.

Yet like Ginsberg's writing, Solomon's act does not present a pure example of improvisation; "humorless protest" requires an element of premeditation. Ginsberg's choice of a Ping-Pong table—his second reference to "pingpong" in as many stanzas—for Solomon's object of protest reflects the tension Ginsberg feels between the goal of spontaneity and the human need for order (repetition being a defining element of order). Both Ginsberg and Solomon want to assert their individuality but can only do so within the context and restrictions of their environment. For Solomon in the asylum, those restrictions are quite literal; for Ginsberg, they are figurative: as a poet, he must frame his message with enough clarity and logic for readers to grasp it. Ginsberg challenges the strictures of classical, iamb-based poetry in "Howl" by taking liberties with line and meter (and, in the case of "pingpong," with spelling), but he cannot disregard the basic need for poetic order. In the very next stanza after Solomon overturns the Ping-Pong table, Ginsberg begins with a word other than "who" for the first time in the poem. Taking a cue from his friend in the asylum, Ginsberg the poet overturns his own symbolic Ping-Pong table and affirms his artistic independence.

When Ping-Pong returns in part 3 of the poem, Ginsberg further develops its symbolic reach by offering "pingpong" as a metaphor for both death and love. In Rockland, Solomon appears seriously ill, perhaps mortally ill, "losing the game of the actual pingpong of the abyss." Not surprisingly, the medical treatments he received in part 1 do not seem to have worked so well. Ping-Pong here comes to represent not the concrete void of the asylum but the ultimate

concrete void for humankind—death. Above and beyond the monotony and triteness we struggle against in life, Ginsberg tells us that the "actual" Ping-Pong game exists at a cosmic level. As Solomon knows, to fight for one's individuality against the emptiness of ping-pong is to fight for one's soul.

Yet at the same time that he plays Ping-Pong with death, Solomon also plays ping-pong with Ginsberg's love in the poem. The structure of part 3 mirrors a Ping-Pong game: Ginsberg serves up an opening statement ("Carl Solomon!"), followed by a back-and-forth between Ginsberg the steady companion ("I'm with you in Rockland") and his descriptions of Solomon. Love appears as a game of call and response, the repetition possessing a unity unto itself. For a single person, the loss of individuality entailed by this repetition creates a sort of spiritual and emotional death; for a couple, the loss of individuality creates love as two fuse into one. Through the shared metaphor of Ping-Pong, Ginsberg expresses this essential entwinement of death and love, and he claims his place as Solomon's eternal partner in the transcendent game.

Source: David E. Pozen, "Ginsberg's *Howl*," in *Explicator*, Vol. 62, No. 1, Fall 2003, pp. 54–57.

SOURCES

Blake, William, "Proverbs of Hell," in *The Marriage of Heaven and Hell*, Oxford University Press, 1975, pp. xviii–xix.

———, "A Song of Liberty," in *The Marriage of Heaven and Hell*, Oxford University Press, 1975, p. xxviii.

Callinicos, Alex, "Anti-War Protests Do Make a Difference," in *Socialist Worker*, Vol. 1943, March 19, 2005.

Ferlinghetti, Lawrence, "Horn on 'Howl,'" in *Evergreen Review*, Vol. 1, No. 4, Winter 1957, pp. 145–58.

Garofoli, Joe, "'Howl' Too Hot to Hear: 50 Years after Poem Ruled Not Obscene, Radio Fears to Air It," in *San Francisco Chronicle*, October 3, 2007, p. A-1.

Ginsberg, Allen, "Footnote to 'Howl,'" in *Collected Poems, 1947–1997*, HarperCollins, 2006, pp. 134–42.

———, "Howl," in *Collected Poems, 1947–1997*, HarperCollins, 2006, pp. 134–42.

———, *Howl: Original Draft Facsimile, Transcript, and Variant Versions, Fully Annotated by Author, with Contemporaneous Correspondence, Account of First Public Reading, Legal Skirmishes, Precursor Texts, and Bibliography*, edited by Barry Miles, HarperCollins, 2006, pp. 125–26, 129–31, 133–34, 139, 146.

———, "Notes Written on Finally Recording 'Howl,'" in *Deliberate Prose: Selected Essays, 1952–1995*, edited by Bill Morgan, HarperCollins, 2000, pp. 229–30.

Hampton, Wilborn, Obituary of Allen Ginsberg, in *New York Times*, April 6, 1997, pp. A1, A42.

Hollander, John, Review of *Howl, and Other Poems*, in *Howl: Original Draft Facsimile, Transcript, and Variant Versions, Fully Annotated by Author, with Contemporaneous Correspondence, Account of First Public Reading, Legal Skirmishes, Precursor Texts, and Bibliography*, by Allen Ginsberg, edited by Barry Miles, HarperCollins, 2006, p. 161.

Holmes, John Clellon, "This Is the Beat Generation," in *New York Times Magazine*, November 16, 1952, p. SM10.

Lawrence v. Texas, 539 U.S. 558 (2003), http://www.law.cornell.edu/supct/html/02-102.ZS.html (accessed July 30, 2007).

Merrill, Thomas F., *Allen Ginsberg*, Twayne, 1969. p. 89.

Miles, Barry, *Ginsberg: A Biography*, Simon and Schuster, 1989, pp. 99, 196.

Ostriker, Alicia, "'Howl' Revisited: The Poet as Jew," in *American Poetry Review*, Vol. 26, No. 4, July–August 1997, pp. 28–31.

Ower, John, "Allen Ginsberg," in *Dictionary of Literary Biography*, Vol. 5, *American Poets since World War II*, First Series, edited by Donald J. Greiner, Gale Research, 1980, pp. 269–86.

Perlman, David, "How Captain Hanrahan Made 'Howl' a Best-Seller," in *Howl: Original Draft Facsimile, Transcript, and Variant Versions, Fully Annotated by Author, with Contemporaneous Correspondence, Account of First Public Reading, Legal Skirmishes, Precursor Texts, and Bibliography*, by Allen Ginsberg, edited by Barry Miles, HarperCollins, 2006, p. 171.

Williams, William Carlos, Introduction to "Howl," in *Collected Poems, 1947–1997*, HarperCollins, 2006, p. 820.

Zweig, Paul, "A Music of Angels," in *Nation*, Vol. 208, No. 10, March 10, 1969, pp. 311–13.

FURTHER READING

Abele, Robert P., *A User's Guide to the USA Patriot Act and Beyond*, University Press of America, 2005.

> This book examines the controversial Patriot Act, which passed into law six weeks after the events of September 11, 2001, and which some critics view as an attack on free speech and civil liberties comparable to the McCarthyism referenced in "Howl."

Fried, Albert, *McCarthyism: The Great American Red Scare; A Documentary History*, Oxford University Press, 1997.

> This book draws upon contemporary documents to explore the period of McCarthyism, from the late 1940s to the mid-1960s. It describes the routine persecution of Americans on the grounds of their being allegedly unpatriotic or sympathetic to Communism.

Raskin, Jonah, *American Scream: Allen Ginsberg's "Howl" and the Making of the Beat Generation*, University of California Press, 2004.

> Raskin investigates the cold war, the Beat movement, and those aspects of Ginsberg's life and ideas that led him to write "Howl."

Whitman, Walt, *Leaves of Grass*, Dover Publications, 2007.

> No study of "Howl" would be complete without a reading of at least some of the poetry of Whitman, one of Ginsberg's major influences. This collection, first published in 1855, is Whitman's great free-verse hymn of praise to the self, the body, the spirit, and nature.

Love Calls Us to the Things of This World

RICHARD WILBUR

1956

Richard Wilbur's poem "Love Calls Us to the Things of This World" is one of the most frequently anthologized poems in the English language. The title refers to a passage from St. Augustine's *Confessions*, written in the fourth century, in which the saint laments that the beautiful things of the world have created distance between him and God. St. Augustine is responding to the gospel of St. John, who advises humans to "Love not the world, neither the things that are in the world." In this poem, Wilbur presents a person waking up in the morning and looking outside at laundry that has just been hung on the clothesline and imaging, in a half-aware slumber, that the clothes and sheets hung there are moved by angels, not the wind. He examines the balance between the material world and the spiritual world. This poem's central image, of laundry waving on a line, opens up the poem to issues of existence, morality and religion.

Since its first publication in Wilbur's 1956 collection *Things of This World*, this poem has been considered a masterful achievement for its clear style, its authorial control of form and symbol as well as its clarity of meaning. Most recently, the poem has become available with all of Wilbur's most significant works in his Pulitzer Prize-winning 1988 collection *New and Collected Poems*.

AUTHOR BIOGRAPHY

Richard Wilbur was born in New York City on March 1, 1921. His father was a commercial portrait artist and his mother came from a line of newspaper publishers, which led him, when he was in his teens, toward a career in newspaper cartooning. When he was very young, the family moved to a remote, rural area of New Jersey, where Wilbur spent his childhood wandering the countryside. After high school, he went off to Amherst College in Massachusetts, majoring in English. In college, he met Charlotte Ward, who was attending nearby Smith, and they fell in love. They were married in 1942 after he graduated, but very soon after that he was drafted to serve in World War II.

After the end of the war, Wilbur took advantage of the G. I. Bill, which paid college tuition for veterans, and attended Harvard University. As a scholar in English, he met the poet Robert Frost and, despite nearly a fifty-year difference in their ages, the two became close friends after Frost discovered that Wilbur's wife was the granddaughter of the first publisher to print his poetry. Though he had been writing poetry for some time, Wilbur started to consider publishing his works. He gave a few poems to a friend who was an editor, and the friend returned a few hours later with a proposal for a book. In September of 1947, Wilbur's first poetry collection, *The Beautiful Changes*, was published. Wilbur was only twenty-seven years old at the time.

Wilbur's next book of poetry, *Ceremony And Other Poems*, was published to critical acclaim in 1950. It was followed in 1956 by *Things of This World: Poems* (which includes "Love Calls Us to the Things of This World"); this collection won the Pulitzer Prize and the National Book Award. With his reputation as one of America's most important poets established, Wilbur took a position at Wesleyan University in Middletown, Connecticut, where he was to teach for the next twenty years.

In addition to his fame as a poet, Wilbur has proven to be one of the great translators of drama into the English language. His translation of French playwright Molière's *The Misanthrope*, published in 1953, set standards for the use of poetic sensibilities in translation. Wilbur went on to publish translations of all of Molière's comedies, to great acclaim.

Richard Wilbur (Nancy Palmieri | AP Images)

Wilbur retired from teaching in 1986. He served as the Poet Laureate of the United States from 1987–1988, and won a second Pulitzer Prize in 1989 for *New and Collected Poems*, making him the only poet to ever win that award twice. Over the course of his life he has won most of the important prizes given to poets, including the Wallace Stevens Award, the Frost Medal, the Gold Medal for Poetry from the American Academy of Arts and Letters, two PEN translation awards, two Bollingen Prizes, the T. S. Eliot Award, a Ford Foundation Award, the Edna St. Vincent Millay Memorial Award, the Harriet Monroe Poetry Award, the Prix de Rome Fellowship, and the Shelley Memorial Award.

POEM SUMMARY

Stanza 1

The first stanza of "Love Calls Us to the Things of This World" introduces readers to the poem's

MEDIA ADAPTATIONS

- "Love Calls Us To The Things of This World" is read by the author on *The Caedmon Poetry Collection*, a three-disc collection released by Caedmon in 2000.

- Wilbur also can be heard reading "Love Calls Us To The Things of This World" on *Poetry on Record: 98 Poets Read Their Work, 1888–2006*, a four-disc collection edited by Rebekah Presson Mosby and released by the Shout! Factory in 2006.

situation: a person waking up and, being acutely aware at that moment of the division between the spiritual and physical realities, sees the laundry on the clothes line outside of the window animated by wind, moving as if inhabited by otherworldly powers. In the first two lines, the waking person is "spirited from sleep" by the "cry of pulleys," which are used in a high-rise building to feed clothesline out between two buildings. The wet clothes on the line hang limp for a short time, "bodiless and simple / As false dawn."

In lines 4 and 5, the laundry comes alive with motion, lifted by the breeze. The spectral motion of the linens makes them look like angels, flapping as angels do with their wings. The poem retains the image of hanging laundry while talking about angels by using the word "awash" to describe the way the sky is filled with angels.

Stanza 2

The poem goes on to describe the visual effect of the laundry items that are hanging on the clothesline. Wilbur lists "bed-sheets" and various items of clothes that move with the wind, rising and falling, as if they are alive. The motion that they make is described as being calm, first with the word "calm" itself to describe a wave-like movement and then with the word "halcyon," a synonym for "calm."

In the second stanza, the idea that the laundry is inhabited by angels is continued. In lines 7

and 10, the poem refers to the angels with the pronoun "they," granting them human identities. In line 10, they are given even more human personality with mentions of emotion, their "joy," and even a reference to the physical act of basic respiration as the angels that inhabit the clothes are said to be "breathing."

Stanza 3

The third stanza is the last one focused on the motion of the laundry on the line. Wilbur indicates a change in the look of the things hanging there with the first word of line 11 ("now"), indicating that what he is describing is a new situation. While the previous stanza presented the laundry as swaying calmly in the breeze, this one opens with it swirling rapidly, with motions that make it look like it is "flying." Continuing the conceit that the laundry is moving due to the presence of angels, Wilbur attributes the speed with which it is whirling around to the angels' "omnipresence," their supernatural ability to be in all places at the same time.

In the middle of stanza 3, the tone of the poem slows down. This begins with the image of the laundry as water, which is said to be "moving" at the end of line 12 and then "staying" in line 13. After that, the clothes and bed sheets quiet down, lose their kinetic energy, and droop. After attributing their motion to the angels that inhabit them, the poet expresses surprise at this sudden immobility, stating, as if it is impossible to believe, that "nobody seems to be there."

At the same time that the laundry on the line quiets down, the poem's mood also becomes more quiet and reflective. Line 15 announces that "the soul shrinks," a foreshadow of the tone that is to pervade in the second half of the poem.

Stanza 4

The second half of "Love Calls Us to the Things of This World" is marked by a somber mood that contrasts markedly from the thrill and wonderment that dominated the first half. In stanza 4, the speaker of the poem outlines the ways that humans use to avoid awareness of the physical world that surrounds them. The statement that ended stanza 3 continues, so that the word "shrinks," which on its own would denote a shriveling or loss of size, is linked with "from" to mean that it turns from or retreats from things that it finds upsetting. In line 17, waking, the new encounter with the physical world each morning, is characterized negatively as "the punctual rape of every blessèd day": the implication is that the day would be much better off if left alone from the sudden appearance of human consciousness.

The last half of stanza 4 represents the soul speaking, personifying the general attitude of the human situation. It gives a cry begging for simplicity in life, for the physical world to be nothing but physical motion, without any spiritual involvement. The mention of "the sight of heaven" in line 20 shows that the human spirit does not wish to believe that the supernatural beings do not exist, but is only uncomfortable with the idea of heavenly powers being involved in life on earth, interacting with and affecting the natural processes in the form of angels.

Stanza 5

Stanza 5 acknowledges the complexity of the human situation. While the previous stanza showed how afraid the soul was of facing the physical world, this stanza reverses that equation, looking at what is heartening and inviting about the physical world. It starts with the sun, warm and bright, showing the shapes of physical objects (described, plainly but not negatively, as "hunks") and their colors.

In the middle of this stanza, the soul, which has been the observer since the end of stanza 3, is united with the body as it awakens. This union is described as being a common event, happening regularly. The mood of the union between soul and body is said to be one of "bitter love," a description that captures the entire poem's point about the begrudging alliance between the physical world and spiritual awareness.

In line 25, the poem refers to the observer who has been feeling all of these mixed emotions as "the man." In holding back this particular wording, Wilbur makes his point about the soul and body being separate, distinct entities, and the human being, the combination of the two, being a separate, third entity unto itself.

Stanza 6

The entire last stanza of "Love Calls Us to the Things of This World" is a quote that reflects the new attitude of the observer who has been brought to reconsider the moral nature of the world around him. A parallel is drawn between thieves who are on the gallows to be executed and angels, as the man thinks that the condemned criminals deserve linens just as much as

the heavenly spirits. Lovers, who often represent a moral contradiction as they balance between the transcendent aspects of romance and the baseness of carnal relationships, are acknowledged to be simultaneously "fresh and sweet" and also "undone." Nuns, who are traditionally thought of for their spirituality, are at the same time considered "heav[y,]" with an emphasis on their physical presence.

The last line of the poem refers to the "difficult balance" that all of these people, from varied walks of life, need to strike in order to survive. Throughout its entire length, "Love Calls Us to the Things of This World" calls attention to how very different the physical world is from the spiritual world. In the end, it points to how that difference does not have to be a problem, how it can be accepted and celebrated, if it is handled with the right amount of care.

THEMES

Flesh versus Spirit

Even a casual reading of "Love Calls Us to the Things of This World" will lead one to conclude that the central point the poem is investigating is the basic distinction between the physical world that can be experienced by the five senses and the spiritual world that can only be experienced through intuition. Wilbur uses two basic symbols to characterize these two aspects: laundry and angels.

When philosophers and theologians discuss the contrast between these two spheres of reality, they often use phrases like "flesh versus spirit" or "mind versus body." These common expressions reflect the most basic and personal cases in which most people face this issue. Everyone has a body and everyone has thoughts, but, though the two always exist together, there is no clear, definitive relationship between them. The mind seems to influence the body and the body, particularly the brain, seems to affect the mind, but no scientist has ever shown exactly how they are connected.

Instead of referring to the human body to represent the physical world, Wilbur starts the poem using laundry as the poem's central image. For one thing, making readers think about laundry removes the emotional attachment that comes with talking about being human: it is easier to think objectively about laundry because

TOPICS FOR FURTHER STUDY

- Richard Wilbur is well known for his translations of classic plays. Adapt this poem and rewrite it as a play, and then perform it for your class.

- The branch of theology that studies the different types of angels is called "angelology." Do some research in angelology, and write an essay in which you explore possible theological roots that inspire the angelic imagery in "Love Calls Us to the Things of This World."

- This poem presents waking up as a process of the soul joining the body. Narrate a video of someone waking up, with a voice-over to explain the scientific processes that are taking place at each step of the way.

- When this poem was published, Wilbur was considered to be one of a wave of Metaphysical Poets publishing in America, a group of poets in the mid-twentieth century emulating the original Metaphysical Poets of the seventeenth century. Their works appealed to the intellect over emotion, incorporating witty wordplay and extended metaphors. Read about the political and social history of the 1950s, and produce a chart that shows both the characteristics of the times and the corresponding characteristics of Metaphysical Poetry.

laundry is just not that important in most people's lives. On the other hand, the use of laundry can be telling about the dichotomy between flesh and spirit because it allows the poet to allude to moral judgments such as those commonly associated with thieves, lovers, and nuns, who are brought in later as examples. Laundry is a useful metaphor to raise such issues because, as a category, laundry is always considered as being some degree of "dirty" or "clean."

Wilbur removes the human identification from the "spirit" part of the equation by using angels to represent the nonphysical part of the world. These angels represent the forces that cannot be measured or experienced directly, but that are usually recognized as existing. While the existence of angels can be debated, they are used in this poem to stand for such commonly accepted ideas as "soul" or "personality."

After establishing the relationship between the physical and spiritual worlds with the image of the laundry's phantom motion, the poem eventually introduces a human soul in line 15, its exact center. Two stanzas later, that soul is united with a physical body in the process of awakening. The combination of the two is referred to as a man, and the experience of their coming together, having been separated during sleep, leads the man to reflect on how he often pays too little attention to the distinction between flesh and spirit.

Revelation through Imagination

The revelation that comes to the man in this poem after imagining that the clothes and shirts are moved by angels is important. It changes the way he looks at the world to an uncomfortable degree. In stanza 4, he begs for his old perspective back, to be able to view reality as a world of mechanical motion that has no interaction with the spiritual world, where angels are in heaven and merely observe what humans do on earth. Having imagined the laundry filled with angels and then made the leap of imagination to the way the soul fills a body, the man is forced to reevaluate assumptions with which he had been comfortable. Imagination is not just a tool for entertainment, it is a force for expanding one's relationship to reality.

Spirituality and Dignity

At the end of "Love Calls Us to the Things of This World," the character being described draws some conclusions about social roles. For one thing, he recognizes the rights of thieves sentenced to hang on the gallows, calling for them to be comforted with clean linens. The linens, reminiscent of the laundry that led him to view the world in a new way, reflects his new realization that even thieves are blessed with the same spiritual force that animates everyone else, and should therefore be shown the same dignity that anyone else deserves.

A more simplistic world view might reverse the dignity accorded to the thief by taking away some of the nun's dignity, judging her to be too honored for her spiritualism. Although Wilbur does emphasize the nun's physical nature by pointing out the darkness and heaviness of her clothing, he also calls for her to be able to float, in spite of the gravity of her presence. After offering lightness to the criminal, he does not go to the extreme of characterizing the nun as lacking angelic qualities. Rather than favor one side or another, the poem's point is that all sides of the social spectrum struggle equally to reach a balance that is, admittedly, difficult.

STYLE

Conceit

A "conceit" is the word used to describe the poetic technique of using one extended metaphor that serves as a touchstone for the entire poem's logic and sensibility. In "Love Calls Us to the Things of This World," the main conceit is that of waking up and encountering the world anew. This situation is not only the poem's opening situation, it is continued through to the last stanza, adapting its significance in different parts of the poem: waking is used to suggest wide-eyed amazement in one place, a violent rape in another, and a descent into bitterness in still another. Similarly, laundry is used to remind readers of different things throughout the poem, from angels dancing in midair to the laborers who work over the washtubs to the "clean linen for the backs of thieves."

Imagery

Poets use imagery when they invoke an emotion by referring to the experiences of the five senses. In this poem, Wilbur does not tell readers what they should think of the situation that he presents, but instead he provides images, such as laundry hanging on a line, steam, nuns, and colors. When poets choose their images carefully and place them with other poems that give them a context, readers will understand what the writer feels about a subject, even if ideas are never explicitly discussed.

Alliteration

Alliteration is the use of words that begin with the same consonant sound in close proximity to each other, with the end result that the reader feels, consciously or not, the cumulative effect.

Often, alliteration makes use of soft sounds, like "f" or "s," to give the poem a quiet tone, while a cluster of harder sounds like "k" or "t" give the poem a machine gun-like staccato feeling.

In "Love Calls Us to the Things of This World" Richard Wilbur uses alliteration freely to enhance the poem's musical qualities. In the second and third lines, for instance, there are four words starting with the letter *s*. These, in addition to the pronounced *s* sounds in the words "astounded," "bodiless," and "false," make this part of the poem flow by with a hushed smoothness. The build up of the alliterative words beginning with "s" is repeated in stanza 3, with "staying," "sudden," "swoon," and "seems," cumulating with the final words: "soul shrinks." This softness is reinforced in the middle of the stanza with the alliterative "white water." There are other uses of alliteration, such as "feeling, filling" in line 9 and "let lovers" in line 28, fulfilling the same function.

Assonance

The term "assonance" refers to the repeated use of vowel sounds in a work. Assonance is usually considered to mean the sounds within words, like when Wilbur uses "steam" two words away from "clear" or the repetition of the "o" sound, slightly different but basically the same, in "swoon down into so." The definition of assonance accounts for vowel sounds within words, but that is because vowel sounds usually do appear within words. In the first stanza of this poem, though, Wilbur combines assonance and alliteration, presenting a cluster of words that start with the same vowel sound. Line 4 is broken at the words "outside the open," and line 5 ends with "air is all awash with angels," giving this part of the poem a particularly light, airy feeling that is appropriate for its discussion of angels. Though assonance in the first letters of words is rare, it fits well in a poem like this, which is dedicated to the contrast between the hardness of reality and the untouchable nature of the soul.

HISTORICAL CONTEXT

Metaphysical Poetry

The phrase Metaphysical Poets originally referred to a group of poets in England in the seventeenth century. These poets, including John Donne, George Herbert, Thomas Traherne, Abraham

COMPARE
&
CONTRAST

- **1950s:** Catholic nuns wear the traditional habit that covers the entire body and head.

  Today: Since the Second Vatican Council of 1962, nuns have been allowed to opt for more casual attire that makes it easier for them to fit in socially with their parishioners.

- **1950s:** In the wake of World War II, the United States becomes an economic juggernaut. As a result, theologians and philosophers fear that the country's growing obsession with material goods will undercut spirituality.

  Today: The United States, spurred on by a booming consumer economy, has become increasingly secular (nonreligious).

- **1950s:** The gallows that Wilbur mentions in the poem are used less and less frequently. Public support for the death penalty in the United States is starting to decline. Mercy for criminals who have been sentenced to die is considered a sign of human compassion.

  Today: The death penalty is becoming more and more uncommon worldwide, though its popularity in America has risen steadily since the 1970s.

Cowley, Richard Crashaw, and Andrew Marvell, concerned themselves with understanding reality, and in particular how ideas manifest themselves in the physical world. Their works were characterized by clever wordplay that was intended to make readers think about the ways that the poet's words, and, in particular, the mechanical structure of the poem, reflected the complex mechanical workings of the observable reality. The use of wit in their poems, and particularly the use of the metaphor that was often extended to such a degree that its logic could strain the reader's reasoning faculties (referred to as a "metaphysical conceit"), helped to identify a writer as a metaphysical poet more than any particular declaration of artistic theory.

Historically, those who have been called Metaphysical Poets were not intimately associated with each other. The name was given to them by Samuel Johnson, who used the phrase "metaphysical poets" in his 1744 study *The Lives of the Poets*. While Johnson was referring to the philosophical connection between writers, this does not necessarily mean that the writers themselves read each other's works, let alone that they would have planned to participate in a school of poetry with one another.

In the early twentieth century, interest in Metaphysical Poetry was revived. Especially influential in this renewed interest was that literary criticism written by the poet T. S. Eliot, whose 1923 essay, "The Metaphysical Poets," along with other critical works, helped people see that the poets who were put in this general category were more than just clever, but actually based their witty conceits and wording on deep philosophical underpinnings. Many twentieth-century poets show the influence of metaphysical poetry in the way that they merge a poem's form with its ideas. Richard Wilbur, in particular, is often referred to as a twentieth-century metaphysical poet for his wit and his use of the metaphysical conceit: not only does the apparent lightheartedness of his approach belie a seriousness about existence, but he also is prone to use one extended metaphor in a poem in order to make readers think about a phenomenon from different angles.

Religion in the 1950s

American society during the 1950s is usually characterized as conformist, and in many ways this attitude applies to religious beliefs in social life. While America has always been considered a country that values religious freedom, the social forces at play during the 1950s steered religious practice toward collective thinking and away from individualism.

One of the most significant factors influencing American society during that decade was the fear of Communism. After World War II ended in 1945, the world was left with two major countries, or superpowers, with opposing social orders. The Soviet Union had a Communist social order, based roughly on the social principles first laid out by economist Karl Marx in his book *The Communist Manifesto*, published in 1841. While Communism is basically an economic theory, the Soviet empire was a totalitarian state that controlled many aspects of daily life, including religion. The Communist Party of the Soviet Union officially supported atheism, opposing belief in any God. American atheists therefore were suspected of being sympathetic to the Soviets at the least, and possibly even of being active supporters of America's Cold War opponents. Americans who did not want to fall under a cloud of suspicion were more likely to participate in organized religion: membership in a church or synagogue was the overwhelming standard for religious life.

This tendency toward a socially recognizable religious life was augmented in the 1950s by the postwar advent of television. Almost as soon as television became a popular consumer commodity in the late 1940s, ministers realized its usefulness as a way to reach nationwide congregations. Bishop Fulton Sheen, of Rochester, New York, is recognized as the first television preacher with a national audience, with programs that started in 1951 and continued, in various forms and on different networks, through to the late 1960s. Other ministers followed, expanding the homogenizing effect of television, which brings one shared experience to millions at a time, to religion.

It was within this context that Wilbur was writing about angels and one person's individual musings about them. While most of society was moving toward a religious hierarchy, listening to the words of specialists about the existence and order of angels and how unknown spirits affect daily life, Wilbur's poem represents the unmediated experience of an individual trying to understand religious significance in his own terms.

CRITICAL OVERVIEW

The poem "Love Calls Us to the Things of This World" inspires the title of Richard Wilbur's 1956 collection *Things of This World*, which was awarded both the Pulitzer Prize and the National Book Award. This was the same year that Wilbur became a familiar name among people who do not read poetry, as his translation of Voltaire's comedy *Candide*, with music by Leonard Bernstein, appeared on Broadway. Indeed, Wilbur's fame was lasting. In a 1996 survey by Jed Rasula, "Love Calls Us to the Things of This World" was found to be the most often anthologized American poem between 1940 and 1990.

The poet Marjorie Perloff, writing in *Poetry On & Off the Page*, reports that the poem was given serious examination in a discussion by three poets in Anthony Ostroff's 1964 work *The Contemporary Poet as Artist and Critic*. In the course of this discussion, Richard Eberhart considers the most important thing about "Love Calls Us to the Things of This World" to be the way "it celebrates the immanence of spirit in spite of the 'punctual rape of every blessèd day.'" May Swenson, in the same volume, concentrates on Wilbur's balance of the physical and spiritual, concluding that "the whole poem . . . is in fact an epitome of relative weight and equipoise," or counterbalance. Perloff, who provides these quotes from Eberhart and Swenson, has a more complicated view of the poem. Writing in the 1990s, Perloff is able to look back several decades to review the poem and its reputation over time; she concludes that the poem stands out from all the metaphysical poetry that was in vogue at the time of its publication.

While other critics have found flaws in the poem, the overall consensus has always been positive. Donald L. Hill, writing in *Richard Wilbur*, applauds Wilbur's lightheartedness in "Love Calls Us to the Things of This World." "It is good to follow this free and playful excursion of the mind," Hill says at the end of his discussion of the poem: "so unbound by anxiety, so unhurried, serene, and good-humored. Good humor—once again, let it be said—is one of the primary aspects of Wilbur's charm." Bruce Michelson, in his book *Wilbur's Poetry: Music in a Scattering Time*, echoes the emphasis on the poem's lighthearted demeanor: "People who apparently enjoy little else in Wilbur's work delight in 'Love Calls Us' for its gusto and its

The poem suggests that laundry on a clothesline sometimes looks like anglels (*Jodi Cobb | National Geographic | Getty Images*)

easy, spontaneous air ... The poem marks an important development in Wilbur's relationship with words, for here he succeeds as never before in making wordplay look easy."

CRITICISM

David Kelly

Kelly is a professor of literature and creative writing. In this essay on "Love Calls Us to the Things of This World," he explores the poem's structure, focusing on the particular function of the fourth and fifth stanzas.

Richard Wilbur's "Love Calls Us to the Things of This World" is not only one of Wilbur's most admired poems, it is one of the most admired and reprinted poems of the twentieth century, and for good reason: it has something for everybody. The poem satisfies realists with its style—it is calibrated to almost mathematical precision—but its overall theme is a testimony to the transcendent spirit.

For readers who view the universe as basically a series of mechanical processes, Wilber offers not only praise for the things of this world (as opposed to the view of, say, the gospel of St. John, which warns that worldly objects are a distraction) but also the poem's mechanical regularity: its consistent five-line stanzas, its easily understood metaphors, its even progression from talking about a "soul" to talking about a "man."

For those who view the world as a phantom place, the imagined realm of the spirit, the poem acknowledges that unseen forces control the physical nature of the world with its supposition of the intangible angels. The poem's structure reflects its freedom from strict form in several ways. The most obvious of these is, of course, the use of the split line. Not only does this serve to obscure the strict consistency of the five-line stanzas, but Wilbur uses the split line in no regular pattern throughout the poem—fourth line of stanza 1, fifth line of stanza 3, third line of stanza 4 and the last line of the last stanza. This throws any sense the reader might have of the

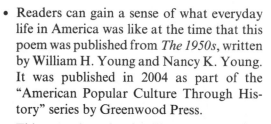

WHAT DO I READ NEXT?

- Readers can gain a sense of what everyday life in America was like at the time that this poem was published from *The 1950s*, written by William H. Young and Nancy K. Young. It was published in 2004 as part of the "American Popular Culture Through History" series by Greenwood Press.

- This poem is such a familiar piece of American literature that writer Sherman Alexie uses it as a springboard for his own poem entitled "Grief Calls Us to the Things of This World." The poem is included in Alexie's collection *Thrash*, which was published in 2007.

- Wilbur is often associated with the poet Anthony Hecht, his contemporary. Hecht's poem "Late Afternoon: The Onslaught of Love" has quite a few similarities in form and subject matter to "Love Calls Us to the Things of This World." It can be found in Hecht's collection *The Light* (2001).

- *Conversations with Richard Wilbur* (1990) contains a dozen interviews with the poet. Subjects discussed range from poetic form to current events.

- Richard Wilbur is as famous for his translations of plays as he is for his poetry. In particular, his translations of the works of the comedies of the French writers Molière and Voltaire are considered definitive. Most notable among his many exceptional accomplishments in translation is his version of Molière's *Tartuffe* (1963).

---

poem being strictly regulated off track. In the same way, the lines do not seem as if they are mostly written in the ten-syllable, five-foot pentameter standard (though they are). This is because Wilbur is not strict, allowing the lines to swell to twelve or thirteen syllables at times. And the meter, predominantly iambic, is riddled

> "THROUGHOUT THESE LINES, VISUAL IMAGERY OF SHEETS AND SHIRTS WAVING IN THE BREEZE, MILDLY THEN WILDLY, IMPRESSES UPON READERS THE RELATIONSHIP BETWEEN THAT WHICH CAN BE OBSERVED AND THAT WHICH CAN ONLY BE KNOWN THROUGH SPECULATION."

---

with exceptions as well. As much as the poem seems to support the idea of a physical world, it also undermines that idea by allowing the poetic style to swing freely. Everyone can be happy with this poem because form and freedom, body and soul, are all presented with equal, balanced attention.

Examples of how well order is balanced against mystery in this poem are nearly countless, starting with the obvious, the central metaphor of the mundane laundry being animated by the heavenly hosts and going on to the personalization of angels ("filling whatever they wear") and the final image of nuns, who balance their heavy habits on their heads in exactly the same way they balance their transcendent spirits against the physical requirements of their worldly bodies. One aspect of the poem that reflects this balance, but does so in such a subtle way that it would be easy to overlook, is the work's overall structure.

Wilbur's use of six stanzas, along with the line-by-line consistency of shape, invites readers to look for patterns, since six divides evenly into segments of two or three. In fact, such a pattern emerges when studying "Love Calls Us to the Things of This World." The first three stanzas concern themselves with the central metaphor, laundry on a clothesline. Throughout these lines, visual imagery of sheets and shirts waving in the breeze, mildly then wildly, impresses upon readers the relationship between that which can be observed and that which can only be known through speculation. As much as this image is drawn with specificity, however, it stops at the end of line 15. Wilbur uses a full half of the poem to set up his idea without comment, and does not even begin to touch upon what all of this action means until the second half.

The second half of the poem can be read as two different styles. The most obvious one is the style used in the sixth and final stanza. As the conclusion of the poem, this stanza carries the weight of announcing its moral message to its readers, a task that it completes with logic and clarity. As a result of the preceding meditations on how physical and spiritual aspects interact, condemned criminals are put on the same level as lovers and nuns, all of them accorded the upbeat comforts of clean linen, pure, floating walking, and the sanctity to "go fresh and sweet." While some of the language of this stanza can be obscure, such as the meaning of how, exactly, the lovers are going to be "undone," most of it shows a return to a level of concrete imagery that marked the poem's first half. One final stylistic element that sets stanza 6 off from the ones that precede it is the fact that it is made from one single long quote. Even though the poem has used a quotation before, in stanza 4, this one is different because of its length and because, coming at the end, it represents the culmination of how the events of this poem have affected the character in it. Though not a return to the style of the first half, and certainly far from it in subject matter, stanza 6 still has more in common with the first three stanzas than it does with the two that precede it.

The two remaining stanzas are the traditional ones, bridging the event that motivates raised awareness and the heightened awareness that ensues. It is in this part of the poem that understanding is born, and it is a difficult birth. Thematically, what is notable about stanzas 4 and 5 is how much darker they are than the others. Stylistically, what is most notable is how much they resemble each other, almost to the point of redundancy.

The first half of the poem is mostly characterized by the sense of wonderment that comes from seeing things in a new way when the conscious mind is disoriented by sleep. This buoyant feeling only fades in the third stanza, when the angels' speed, which could be exhilarating to them, is described negatively as "terrible." At the end of the third stanza, as it segues into the next phase of the poem's inquiry, stands the phrase "the soul shrinks": darker but still not very threatening, it is a harbinger of the mood to come, standing apart from line 15 in a neutral zone. Nothing in the first half of the poem prepares the reader for the use of the phrase "punctual rape" to describe the mechanical regularity of the rising sun, or the sourness of "bitter love" to explain the soul's reluctance to join its body after a night of sleep. This is more than the resentment of someone who is not a morning person: in using such strong wording, Wilbur presents the basic division between mind and body as being overtly hostile. The gentle tone that is to follow in stanza 6 is not just the result of someone following his observations of the laundry moving to its logical conclusions, it is the synthesis that comes out of a battle by two conflicting forces.

Taking stanzas 4 and 5 as an independent unit, the parallels between them jumps out. Some phrases are repeated, others are mirrored with their opposites, but all show a special bond between these two stanzas that does not connect them with any others. In the first line of stanza 4, for instance, the soul does "remember," and in the first line of stanza 5 the sun does "acknowledge." The sun's acknowledgement "with a warm look" of the world is paralleled, in its placement in the stanza, to its "punctual rape of every blessèd day" in the stanza before. In stanza 4, the steam is "rising," while in stanza 5 the soul "descends." The "clear dances done in the sight of heaven" could easily be seen as an idealization of how speaking "in a changed voice as the man yawns and rises." In all, the theme that is explored throughout the poem, of the similarities and differences between the real and ideal, is magnified within the space of these two stanzas.

Readers who look only at the subject matter of a poem are missing much of its message, obviously: the way the author organizes ideas on the page is used to magnify what the author is trying to say. Ideally, every detail should be working to make the poem's point. In the case of a poem like "Love Calls Us to the Things of This World," readers can understand the main idea easily enough from one quick reading: the imagery is striking enough to identify the dichotomy (or contrast) between the physical and spiritual worlds. The poem's conclusion, regarding the equality of all, seems reasonable enough. These basic concepts become even clearer, though, as one reads deeper. In this poem, the fourth and fifth stanzas seem like they could represent a lull in the case that Wilbur is putting

> IF THE IMAGINATION DOES CREATE A WORLD INDEPENDENT OF OBJECTS, IT IS MADE CLEAR IN 'LOVE CALLS US TO THE THINGS OF THIS WORLD' THAT LOVE ALWAYS BRINGS ONE BACK TO THE WORLD OF OBJECTS."

forth: instead, they represent the refinement of his ideas.

Source: David Kelly, Critical Essay on "Love Calls Us to the Things of This World," in *Poetry for Students*, Gale, Cengage Learning, 2009.

Richard J. Calhoun

In the following essay, Calhoun gives a critical analysis of Wilbur's work.

Richard Wilbur has always been recognized as a major literary talent and as an important man of letters—poet, critic, translator, editor—but he has never quite been ranked as one of the two or three best contemporary American poets. Early in his career he was overshadowed as a poet by Robert Lowell, who won the Pulitzer Prize for *Lord Weary's Castle* in 1947 (the year Wilbur's first book of poems, *The Beautiful Changes and Other Poems*, was published) and whose *Life Studies* (1959) was given principal credit for important new directions in poetry that Wilbur chose not to take. In the 1960s comparisons between Lowell and Wilbur as important new poets became comparisons between Lowell and James Dickey as the country's most important poets. Since the 1970s more critical attention has been given to such poets as John Ashbery, A.R. Ammons, James Wright, W.S. Merwin, and James Merrill than to Wilbur.

For more than four decades Wilbur's poetry has remained much as it has always been—skilled, sophisticated, witty, and impersonal. In 1949 when Philip Rahv in *Image and Idea* divided American writers into two camps—"Palefaces," elegant and controlled, and "Redskins," intense and spontaneous—Richard Wilbur was clearly a "Paleface." After Lowell made his break in 1959 with modernist impersonality in poetry, he revised Rahv's distinction in his National Book

Award comments by specifying American poets as either "cooked" or "raw." Wilbur's "marvelously expert" poetry was undeniably one of the choice examples of "cooked" poetry. In *Waiting for the End* (1964), at a time when poetic styles were moving away from impersonality, Leslie A. Fiedler, one of the advocates of the reemergence of the "I" at the center of the poem and of a neo-Whitmanesque rejection of objectivity, found the influence of T.S. Eliot's formalistic theories especially strong on Wilbur: "There is no personal source anywhere, as there is no passion and no insanity; the insistent 'I,' the asserting of sex, and the flaunting of madness considered apparently in equally bad taste."

Wilbur has seldom likened his poetry to that of his contemporaries. Instead, in "On My Own Work," an essay collected in *Responses, Prose Pieces: 1953-1976* (1976), he described his art as "a public quarrel with the aesthetics of E.A. Poe," a writer on whom he has written some significant literary criticism. In Wilbur's view, Poe believed that the imagination must utterly repudiate the things of "this diseased earth." In contrast, Wilbur contends it is within the province of poems to make some order in the world while not allowing the reader to forget that there is a reality of things. Poets are not philosophers: "What poetry does with ideas is to redeem them from abstraction and submerge them in sensibility." Consequently, Wilbur's main concern is to maintain a difficult balance between the intellectual and the emotive, between an appreciation of the particulars of the world and their spiritual essence. If he is explicit in his prose about his quarrel with Poe, it might also be said that he had an implicit quarrel with the "raw" poetry in Donald Allen's *New American Poetry 1945-60*, an anthology recognized in the 1960s as a manifesto against the "academy," and also with the extremely personal, seemingly confessional poetry of Lowell, W. D. Snodgrass, and Anne Sexton. Wilbur as a poet clearly accepts the modernist doctrine of impersonality and does not advertise his personal life in his poetry. "I vote for obliquity and distancing in the use of one's own life, because I am a bit reserved and because I think these produce a more honest and usable poetry," he commented in a 1967 questionnaire in *Conversations with Richard Wilbur* (1990).

Richard Purdy Wilbur was born in New York City, one of two children of Lawrence L. and Helen Purdy Wilbur. His father was a portrait painter. When Wilbur was two years old, the family moved into a pre-Revolutionary War stone house in North Caldwell, New Jersey. Although not far from New York City, he and his brother, Lawrence, grew up in rural surroundings, which, Wilbur later speculated, led to his love of nature.

Wilbur showed an early interest in writing, which he has attributed to his mother's family because her father was an editor of the *Baltimore Sun* and her grandfather was both an editor and a publisher of small papers aligned with the Democratic Party. At Montclair High School, from which he graduated in 1938, Wilbur wrote editorials for the school newspaper. At Amherst College he was editor of the campus newspaper, the *Amherst Student*. He also contributed stories and poems to the Amherst student magazine, the *Touchstone*, and considered a career in journalism.

Immediately after his college graduation in June 1942, Wilbur married Mary Charlotte Hayes Ward of Boston, an alumna of Smith College. Having joined the Enlisted Reserve Corps in 1942, he went on active duty in the army in 1943 in the midst of World War II. He served with the Thirty-sixth "Texas" Division in Italy at Monte Cassino and Anzio and then in Germany along the Siegfried Line. It was during the war that he began writing poems, intending, as he said in a 1964 interview with *The Amherst Literary Magazine* (borrowing Robert Frost's phrase), "a momentary stay against confusion" in a time of world disorder. When the war ended he found himself with a drawer full of poems, only one of which had been published.

Wilbur went to Harvard for graduate work in English to become a college teacher. As he recalled in his 1964 Amherst interview Wilbur decided to submit additional poems for publication only after a French friend read his manuscripts, "kissed me on both cheeks and said, 'you're a poet.'" In 1947, the year he received his A.M. from Harvard, his first volume of poems, *The Beautiful Changes and Other Poems*, was published.

The Beautiful Changes contains the largest number of poems (forty-two) and the fewest number of translations (three) of any of his collections. Although he began writing his poetry to

relieve boredom while he was in the army, there are actually only seven war poems; and they are more poetic exercises on how to face the problems of disorder and destruction than laments over the losses occasioned by war, as in the traditions of the World War I British poet Wilfred Owen and the World War II American poet Randall Jarrell.

The first of Wilbur's war poems, "Tywater," presents the paradox of the violence illustrated in a Texas corporal's skill in killing the enemy [....] The compassion of Jarrell's war poetry is clearly missing. Instead, there is an ironic detachment somewhat like John Crowe Ransom's but without the meticulous characterization that distinguishes Ransom's best poems: [....]

Another war poem, "First Snow in Alsace," suggests the theme implied by the title of the volume, *The Beautiful Changes* . The beautiful can change man even in times of duress. War is horrible because man permits it in spite of such simple childlike pleasures as a night sentry on being "the first to see the snow." "On the Eyes of an SS Officer" is a poetic exercise on the extremes of fanaticism. Wilbur compares the explorer Roald Amundsen, a victim of the northern ice that he desired to conquer, and a "Bombay saint," blinded by staring at the southern sun, with an SS officer, a villain of the Holocaust. The SS officer in his fanaticism combines what is evident in the eyes of the first two fanatics, ice and fire, for his eyes are "iced or ashen." The persona stays detached and does not explicitly condemn this terrible kind of fanaticism. The poem ends a bit tamely[....]

If there is a prevailing theme in Wilbur's first volume, it is how the power of the beautiful to change can be used as a buttress against disorder. The initial poem, "Cicadas," suggests the necessity for and the beauty of mystery in nature. The song of the *cigales* (better known as the cicada) can change those who hear it, but the reason for the song is beyond the scientist's analytical abilities to explain. It is spontaneous, gratuitous, and consequently a mystery to be appreciated as an aesthetic experience and described by a poet in a spirit of celebration.

"Water Walker" postulates an analogy between man and the caddis flies, or "water walkers," which can live successfully in two elements, air and water. A human equivalent would be the two lives of Saint Paul, described as

"Paulsaul." He serves as an example of a "water walker," a person who was converted from service in the material world to service in the spiritual but who remained capable of living in both. The speaker in this poem desires a similar balance between two worlds, material and spiritual; but he is kept from transcendence, like the larva of the caddis held in the cocoon, by the fear that he might be unable to return to the material world.

In his first book imagination is a creative force necessary to the poet, but Wilbur also touches on an important theme developed more thoroughly in his later poetry, the danger that the imagination may lead to actions based entirely on illusions. His interpretation of Eugène Delacroix's painting, the subject of the poem "The Giaour and the Pacha," seems to be that in his moment of victory the giaour realizes that by killing his enemy he will lose his main purpose in life, which has been based on a single desire that proves valueless and illusory.

Another poem, "Objects," stresses what is to become a dominant theme for Wilbur, the need for contact with the physical world. Unlike the gulls in the poem, the poet cannot be guided by instincts or imagination alone. His imagination requires something more tangible, physical objects from the real world. The poet must be like the Dutch realist painter Pieter de Hooch, who needed real objects for his "devout intransitive eye" to imagine the unreal. It is only through being involved in the real world that the "Cheshire smile" of his imagination sets him "fearfully free." The poet, like the painter, must appreciate the "true textures" of this world before he can imagine their fading away.

One of the best lyrics in the collection is "My Father Paints the Summer." It has an autobiographical basis because Wilbur's father was a painter, but it is not a personal poem. The lyric develops the second meaning implied by the title *The Beautiful Changes*—the existence of change, mutability. It praises the power of the artist to retain a heightened vision in a world of mutability. The last stanza begins with the kind of simple, graceful line that is to become characteristic of Wilbur at his best:[....] Again the concern is balance in the relationship of the imagination and the particulars, the physical things of this world. The imagination needs the particulars of a summer season, but the artist needs his imagination for transcendence of time[....]

The title poem of the volume is also the concluding poem and serves at this stage of Wilbur's poetic career as an example of his growing distrust of Poe-like romantic escapes into illusion and of his preference for a firm grasp of reality enhanced by the imagination. In "The Beautiful Changes" Wilbur gives four examples of how the beautiful can change: the effect of Queen Anne's lace on a fall meadow, the change brought about by the poet's love, a chameleon's change in order to blend in with the green of the forest, and the special beauty that a mantis, resting on a green leaf, has for him. The beautiful changes itself to harmonize with its environment, but it also alters the objects that surround it. The ultimate change described is the total effect of the changes of nature on the beholder, worded in Wilbur's most polished lyric manner: [....]

Wilbur's first volume was generally well received by the reviewers, and it was evident that a new poet of considerable talent had appeared on the postwar scene. Many of his first poems had a common motive, the desire to stress the importance of finding order in a world where war had served as a reminder of disorder and destruction. There were also the first versions of what was to become a recurring theme: the importance of a balance between reality and dream, of things of this world enhanced by imagination.

Wilbur spent three years between the publication of his first volume of poetry in 1947 and the appearance of his second in 1950 as a member of the Society of Fellows at Harvard, working on studies of the dandy and Poe that he never completed. What he did complete, though, was *Ceremony and Other Poems* (1950), continuing his concern with the need for a delicate balance between the material and the spiritual, the real and the ideal. In finding order in a world of disorder, poetry as celebration of nature is a "Ceremony," something aesthetically and humanly necessary. The concept of mutability, secondary in his first volume, is now primary, leading to a consideration of death, both as the ultimate threat of disorder and chaos and as motivation for creating order in the human realm. One of the poems concerned with facing death has come to be among Wilbur's most frequently anthologized poems, "The Death of a Toad." Wilbur finds in the toad a symbol for primal life energies accidentally and absurdly castrated by a tool of modern man, a power mower. The toad patiently and silently awaits his death with his "wide and anti-que eyes" observing this world that has cost him his heart's blood. His antiquity mocks a modern world that is already in decline.

"Year's-End," another poem on the threat of death, even more clearly contrasts the death of natural things, in their readiness to accept it, and the incompleteness and discord that death brings in the human realm[....] This poem demonstrates Wilbur's skill in describing objects but also reveals his sometimes functional, sometimes not, desire to pun....

"Lament" is a poem about death, about expressing regret that the particulars of the world, what is "visible and firm," must vanish. This time a pun is functional:[....] "Still, Citizen Sparrow" is one of Wilbur's best known poems and, along with "Beowulf," introduces a new and important theme: whether heroism is possible in a world of disorder. In "Beowulf" the stress is on the loneliness and isolation of the hero. In "Still, Citizen Sparrow," in contrast to the common citizens (the sparrows), the hero appears as "vulture," a creature the sparrows must learn to appreciate. The poem is tonally complex, beginning as an argument between Citizen Sparrow and the poet over a political leader as a vulture and ending with an argument for seeing the faults of leaders in a broader perspective because they perform essential services, accept the risks of action, and are capable of dominating existence. The "vulture" is regarded as heroic because he is capable of heroic action: he feeds on death, "mocks mutability," and "keeps nature new." Wilbur concludes: "all men are Noah's sons" in that they potentially have the abilities of the hero if they will take the risks.

Another poem, "Driftwood," illustrates what some of Wilbur's early reviewers saw as a possible influence of Marianne Moore: finding a symbol or emblem in something so unexpected that the choice seems whimsical. In this poem the driftwood becomes an emblem for survival with an identity[....] It is isolated but has retained its "ingenerate grain."

In Wilbur's second volume, as in his first, the need for a balance between the real and the ideal that avoids illusions and escapism is a significant theme. In "Grasse: The Olive Trees" the town in its abundance exceeds the normal and symbolizes reaching beyond the usual limits of

reality, the overabundance of the South, that can become enervating and illusionary: [....]

Only the "unearthly pale" of the olive represents the other pole of the reality principle and "Teaches the South it is not paradise."

"La Rose des Vents" is the first dialogue poem for Wilbur, a dialogue between a lady and the poet in a format reminiscent of Wallace Stevens's "Sunday Morning." The lady argues for the sufficiency of accepting the reality of objects, while the poet desires symbols removed from reality. In Wilbur's version the lady has the last word: [....]

"'A World without Objects Is a Sensible Emptiness'" is a poem with perhaps the quintessential Wilbur title. Visions, illusions, and oases are the objects of quests for people in a waste-land world, but the questing spirit, "The tall camels of the spirit," must also have the necessary endurance to turn back to the things of this world as a resource: [....]

Extravagant claims are made for visions that are firmly based on life. A supernova can be seen "burgeoning over the barn,"[....]

In *Ceremony* Wilbur exhibits greater versatility than is evident in his first book. He can now express his major themes in lighter poems, even in epigrams. The importance of a delicate balance between idealism and empiricism, speculation and skepticism, is concisely and wittily expressed in the two couplets of "Epistemology." Samuel Johnson is told to "Kick at the rock" in his rejection of Berkeleyan idealism, but the rock is also a reminder of the molecular mysteries within it:[....] Man's occasional denials of the physical world he so desperately needs are mocked in the second couplet: [....]

With the appearance of his second book of poems, Wilbur was appointed an assistant professor of English at Harvard, where he remained until 1954, living in Lincoln, Massachusetts, with his wife and four children—Ellen Dickinson, Christopher Hayes, Nathan Lord, and Aaron Hammond. He spent the academic year of 1952-1953 in New Mexico on a Guggenheim Fellowship to write a poetic drama. When his attempts at a play did not work out to his satisfaction, he turned to translating Molière's *Le Misanthrope* instead, beginning his distinguished career as translator. A grant of $3,000, the Prix de Rome, permitted Wilbur to live at the American Academy in Rome in 1954. After his return to America his translation, *The Misanthrope* (1955), was published and performed at the Poets' Theatre in Cambridge, Massachusetts.

In 1954 Wilbur was appointed an associate professor of English at Wellesley College, where he taught until 1957. His third volume of poetry, *Things of This World*, was published in 1956. In his September 1956 review of the collection for *Poetry* magazine Donald Hall concluded: "The best poems Wilbur has yet written are in this volume." His judgment was confirmed, as the collection remains Wilbur's most honored book; it received the Edna St. Vincent Millay Memorial Award, the National Book Award, and the Pulitzer Prize. The same year the musical version of Voltaire's *Candide*, with lyrics by Wilbur, book by Lillian Hellman, and a score by Leonard Bernstein, was produced at the Martin Beck Theatre in New York City.

Three poems in *Things of This World* should certainly be ranked among Wilbur's best, "A Baroque Wall-Fountain in the Villa Sciarra," "Love Calls Us to the Things of This World," and "For the New Railway Station in Rome." The last two reveal the influence of his year spent in Rome on a Prix de Rome fellowship. As the title would suggest, there is even a greater stress on the importance of the use of the real in the poems in this volume. If the imagination does create a world independent of objects, it is made clear in "Love Calls Us to the Things of This World" that love always brings one back to the world of objects. Even nuns move away from pure vision back to the impure, "keeping their difficult balance."

It is not always the simpler forms that are the most inspiring. Wilbur remarked in the anthology *Poet's Choice* (1962) that "A Baroque Wall-Fountain in the Villa Sciarra" was based on his daily observation of a "charming sixteenth-or seventeenth-century fountain that appeared to me the very symbol or concretion of Pleasure." The elaborate baroque fountain is described as an artistic embodiment of the pleasure principle. Human aspiration may be more clearly seen in the simpler Maderna fountains[....]

It is indicative of Wilbur's penchant for impersonality that he ends the poem not by indicating the personal delight he feels in the fountain but by imagining what Saint Francis of Assisi might have seen in the fountain:[....]

The final poem in the volume is one of the best, "For the New Railway Station in Rome." The impressive new station becomes a symbol of how man's mind must continually work on things of this world for the imagination to have the power to re-create and to cope with disorder: [....]

Donald Hill has said of Wilbur's early poetry that he has seemingly taken William Carlos Williams's slogan "No ideas but in things" and altered it to "No things but in ideas." Beginning with his third volume, *Things of This World*, Wilbur still recognizes the importance of the imagination, but his emphasis has clearly shifted toward Williams's concept in his stress on the need for things of this world, both for effective endurance in a world of death and disorder and for creativity.

In 1957 Wilbur began a twenty-year tenure as professor of English at Wesleyan University and as adviser for the Wesleyan Poetry Series. He also received a Ford Foundation grant in drama and worked with the Alley Theater in Houston. *Advice to a Prophet and Other Poems*, his fourth book of poetry, was published in 1961. It is a larger volume of poetry than *Things of This World*, with thirty-two poems, including four translations and a passage translated from Molière's *Tartuffe*, as well as "Pangloss's Song" from the comic-opera version of Voltaire's *Candide*. The collection received favorable comments from such critics as Babette Deutsch, Dudley Fitts, M.L. Rosenthal, William Meredith, and Reed Whittemore. But the praise for *Advice to a Prophet* was tempered by criticisms that it had an academic, privileged, even ivory-tower perspective. The title poem is vaguely topical, suggesting the threat of the ultimate atomic holocaust that became a near reality in October 1962 with the Cuban Missile Crisis. Even here Wilbur might be accused of aesthetic detachment: his poem is not humanistic in its concerns but aesthetic and phenomenological, envisioning a world without its familiar objects, without things rather than without people: [....]

Perhaps still showing the influence of Marianne Moore's passion for oddities, Wilbur stresses in this volume what the imagination can do with apparently mundane things. In "Junk" he suggests that intimations of the ideal can be found in the rubbish, the junk of the world, and in "Stop," in the grim everyday objects at a train stop. In "A Hole in the Floor" Wilbur even compares the potentials of his discoveries in the floor with those of a great archeologist:[....]

In "A Grasshopper" Wilbur adds to the poetic bestiary that he had collected in his volume *A Bestiary* (1955). He admires the grasshopper for having achieved a delicate balance between stasis in its pause on a chicory leaf and action in its springs from the leaf. Hall in his *Contemporary American Poetry* (1962) calls the poem "a minor masterpiece," but some reviewers believed that Wilbur seemed too content with "minor masterpieces," both in form and in subject matter. He showed an unwillingness to undertake major experiments in form or to introduce new and socially relevant subject matter at a time when that was becoming expected. To some reviewers and critics, he seemed a poet reluctant to take risks of any sort. In fairness, one must say that Wilbur does experiment with "new" lines in his poetry, such as his use of the Anglo-Saxon alliterative line in "Junk." But in comparison with what such poets as Lowell and John Berryman were then doing, the experimentation is comparatively minor.

Wilbur seemed almost to be writing his poems in a cultural and political vacuum. By the time of the publication of *Advice to a Prophet* the tremendous impact that Lowell had made in *Life Studies* by apparently confessing disorder in his own family life had been felt. Two years after *Life Studies* Wilbur opened his volume with what he intended to be a dramatic poem, "Two Voices in a Meadow," a dialogue between two objects from the world of the mundane, a milkweed and a stone. The drama in this poem and in the title poem, "Advice to a Prophet," seemed humanly insignificant compared to Lowell's more personal approach. Wilbur seemed to fail in his attempts to indicate more dramatically and more positively how order might be restored and what his personal "stays against confusion" are, much as Robinson Jeffers's attempt at a tragic poetry had failed before, because he seems too exclusively concerned with symbolic things rather than with people. Wilbur's message appears to be that when man becomes more familiar with the world's own change, he can deal with his own problems as something related to the reality of things. Wilbur calls those who do not respond to the things of this world, those who prefer their dreams and who move to illusions, "the Undead"—vampires.

In "Shame" Wilbur defines the kind of human behavior that disturbs him—irresoluteness, a failure to deal with reality. He attempts to provide positive examples of heroic behavior, but he fails to create convincing examples as Robert Lowell does with his symbol of the mother skunk, "refusing to scare," in "Skunk Hour." In Wilbur's dialogue poem "The Aspen and the Stream," the aspen is the positive heroic example because it seems to escape its existence by delving into flux, experience—symbolized by the dream—even if the result is only "a few more aspen-leaves."

It was eight years before Wilbur's fifth volume of poetry, *Walking to Sleep*, appeared in 1969. In the interim he published a children's book, *Loudmouse* (1963); his collected poems, *The Poems of Richard Wilbur* (1963); and his translation of Molière's *Tartuffe* (1963), which earned him an award as corecipient of the Bollingen Poetry Translation Prize. The Lincoln Center Repertory Theatre brought his translation of *Tartuffe* to the stage in New York City in 1964. *Walking to Sleep* is a slim collection, with fewer original poems (only twenty-two) and more translations (eleven) than in previous collections. What overall unity there is in the four sections of the volume is suggested by the title: these are poems on the subject of how to "walk"—symbolically, how to live before sleep and death.

As in "Junk," Wilbur experiments with the Anglo-Saxon alliterative line divided by a caesura. In "The Lilacs" the flowers are used as a symbol of the cycle of death and rebirth, the "pure power" of nature perhaps compensating for the "depth" of death....

A kind of balance between life and death may be seen if one can appreciate "the pure power" of life. "In the Field," the title poem of the first section, also suggests that the power in life may be sufficient to compensate for the ultimate disorder, death....

Wilbur also believes that in man's desires lies the answer to his questions. "Running" is, like "In the Field," a longer poem than Wilbur usually writes. It is divided into three parts and describes the act of running at three different times in the poet's life. The poem is intended not only as an affirmative statement about human aspiration but also as an assertion of the ultimate meaning of human activities. Wilbur's running becomes a symbol of aspiration at different stages in life. What keeps man running? It *is* human aspiration: [....]

"Running" is by Wilbur's own admission one of his most personal poems. It also implies the middle-aged poet's belief that his own life is satisfying and worthwhile.

The title poem, "Walking to Sleep," begins with a discussion of going to sleep that soon becomes a meditation on how to live and a warning against a life of illusion. It is also an argument for accepting death without illusions by literally staring it down. This might be regarded as a climactic poem on a major thematic concern. What is recommended is once again a balance, a life in which reality and "strong dream" work together.

One of the few poems in the volume to be almost immediately anthologized, "Playboy" describes the imaginative response of an adolescent stockboy to the impact of a centerfold in *Playboy* showing a beautiful naked woman[....]

Other poems are also atypical of Wilbur's usual themes. He even includes a protest poem addressed to President Lyndon Johnson; the occasion is not the Vietnam War but Johnson's refusing the official portrait painted by the artist Peter Hurd. The protest is more artistic than political. The poem makes a contrast between Johnson and the culture of Thomas Jefferson with his Rotunda and "Palestrina in his head." Although the poems were published in the midst of the Vietnam vortex, Wilbur is once again primarily concerned with maintaining "a difficult balance" between reality and the ideal as the way to personal fulfillment.

Wilbur's sixth volume of poetry, *The Mind-Reader* (1976), contains twenty-seven new poems (nine previously published in *The New Yorker*) and nine translations. The reviews were again mixed, with some reviewers praising his craftsmanship and defending him from what they regarded as unfair attacks on his conservatism as a poet; others found his new volume to be simply more of the same and lamented his not taking risks by seeking new directions. The translations provide new examples of Wilbur's superb ability to translate from the French and the Russian, especially the poems by Andrei Voznesensky.

There are new things in the volume, especially in Wilbur's clearly discernible movement toward simpler diction and more direct poems.

Except for the title poem there are no long poems in this book. Wilbur seems to enjoy working with shorter poems, as in the six-line, three-couplet "To the Etruscan Poets," on the theme of mutability exemplified by the Etruscan poets[....]

Some reviewers found "Cottage Street, 1953" to be provocative. It is an account of Wilbur's meeting a young Sylvia Plath and her mother at the home of his mother-in-law, Edna Ward. A contrast is made between Plath's destructive tendencies and Ward's power of endurance. A few reviewers read the poem as if it were a personal attack on Plath by a poet hostile to confessional poetry. The poem is undoubtedly intended as a variation on Wilbur's theme of a need for balance, which he later came to realize that Plath had always lacked. He opposes love as a principle of order to the "brilliant negative" of Plath in her life. What makes this poem exceptional is that Wilbur is dealing with real people characterized rather brilliantly: [....]

In this poem Wilbur deals with the human problem of survival and death without his usual detachment and with a directness his poems usually lack.

More representative of his usual type of poem is "A Black Birch in Winter." It could have appeared in any of Wilbur's first five volumes. A symbol (the black birch) is found for nature's ability to survive and grow to greater wisdom each year. Except for slightly simpler diction, the poem is a variation on a usual theme, and the conclusion seems a parody of the conclusion of Alfred Tennyson's "Ulysses": [...]

One poem would seem on the surface to be atypical, Wilbur taking the unusual risk of involving his poetry in the political protest against the war in Vietnam. "For the Student Strikers" was written for the Wesleyan *Strike News* at the time of the Kent State shootings. Wilbur's support is not, however, for student protests but for their canvassing programs, house-to-house visits to discuss the student point of view about the war. Typically, he urges dialogue—order—instead of protests—disorder: [....]

There is an evident difference in emotional perspective, in dramatic intensity, and in contemporary relevance between Wilbur in this poem and Lowell in *Notebook 1967-68*.

Whereas Lowell, Anne Sexton, W. D. Snodgrass, Plath, and even James Dickey have told much about their families, until *The Mind-Reader* Wilbur did not mention his family. Two poems about his children mark a change. His son Christopher's wedding is described indirectly in "A Wedding Toast." But "The Writer" is one of Wilbur's most personal poems and perhaps one of his best. As a father and as a writer he empathizes with his daughter's attempts to write a story. He describes her creative struggles [...] and he is reminded of another struggle that he saw before at the same window: [....]

Wilbur's slightly more personal approach is apparent in a few other poems. The engaging persona Wilbur creates in the title poem, "The Mind-Reader," helps that poem achieve more dramatic intensity than is apparent in much of his earlier work. He seems to be seeking even firmer and more affirmative statements of the need for order and responsibility; and his tone in these poems is more confident, as if he is assured that his own artistic life has been worthwhile, that he has himself maintained a balance between reality and imagination. Wilbur's perspective is concisely stated in "C-Minor," a poem about switching off "Beethoven at breakfast" to turn back to the reality of the day: [....]

In 1977 Wilbur moved to Smith College, where he remained as writer-in-residence until his retirement in 1986. While continuing his translating of Molière's work, he also produced translations of John Racine's *Andromache* (1982) and *Phaedra* (1986). In 1987 Wilbur was honored by an appointment as poetry consultant at the Library of Congress and poet laureate.

New and Collected Poems (1988) earned Wilbur the Pulitzer Prize for 1989. The new poems include twenty-six short lyrics and "On Freedom's Ground," the lyrics for a five-part cantata by William Schuman. This long poem was a joint project written to mark the refurbishing of the Statue of Liberty on its centennial in 1987. Wilbur may have had in mind memories of Robert Frost's impromptu reciting of "The Gift Outright" at the John F. Kennedy inauguration, for he offers a variation of Frost's theme that Americans have gradually become worthy of the land: [....]

In several of the newly collected poems Wilbur creates a persona who ruminates on his life and achievement. He clearly has Frost in mind in "The Ride," an extension of "Stopping by Woods on a Snowy Evening" in which the journey of the rider and his horse continues through the night:[....] The poem seems a consummation of a life-journey of creating and drawing on intuitions and dreams that one must believe in or fall victim to the grief that comes from thinking "there was no horse at all." "Leaving" is an indictment of the comforts in modern life. The people at a garden party resemble the stone figures that border the scene. The question raised is whether or not knowledge of the future would have influenced the people's decisions in life: [....]

Auden is a poem written earlier and published only when Wilbur thought it was finished. It is an impressive poem on memory's lost moments as much as a personal lament for Auden: [....]

In "Lying" Wilbur begins by lightly invoking a "dead party," where a white lie "can do no harm" to one's reputation. The poem evolves more seriously as the speaker explores the nature of lying and reality, the imagination and illusionary truth:[....]

He then turns the poem to the ordinary experiences of a summer's day metaphorically likened to all days:[....] The poem concludes by alluding to *The Song of Roland*, implying the superiority of the lie of the romance to the ordinary fact of history[....]

Wilbur's long tenure in academia is still evident in some poems. "A Finished Man" is a portrait, perhaps wryly autobiographical, of a man who has completed his career and is being honored by the university. The enemies, friends, and colleagues who knew his fears and faults now either dead or fading in his memory[....] "Icarium Mare" is clearly an academic poem with arcane references to the mythical figure Icarus, the Greek astronomer Aristarchus of Samos, and St. John the Divine's "geodic skull."

The short poems in the "New Poems" section often seem to be merely sketches, but there is always depth to a Wilbur surface. "Wyeth's Milk Cans" records the lucid simplicity of an N.C. Wyeth scene but at the same time raises doubts about the landscape's beauty. "Shad-Time" examines two events, the spawning of shad and the blooming of the shadblow tree along a river's banks, and raises the old question anew of how to make sense of nature's bounty and waste. The critic Bruce Michelson judges this poem to be proof that Wilbur could produce a postmodernist poem that goes beyond skillful play and raises uncomfortable questions about the self and the world.

Despite Wilbur's achievement as a poet and his many awards, including the gold medal for poetry from the American Academy and Institute of Arts and Letters in 1991, many critics would argue that he has not become the major poet he seemed destined to be when *Things of This World* was so celebrated. Even if this arguable judgment is accepted, Wilbur's poetry alone is not the measure of his significance as a man of letters. For a balanced view of his literary importance it should be acknowledged that he is a discerning critic and an accomplished translator of poetry and drama in verse. Wilbur's view of translating is unquestionably an extension of his poetry writing. Viewing translation as a craft, he has consistently set for himself the goal of authenticity in translating not just the language but the verse forms as well. The importance of including Wilbur's translations in an evaluation of his talents as a poet has been neatly summed up by Raymond Oliver: "His degree of accuracy is almost always very high and his technical skill as a poet is just about equal to that of the people he translates." Wilbur's versions of Molière's works not only read well as verse but have been staged with great success. He has followed success in comedy with highly regarded translations in the 1980s of two of Racine's tragedies.

Wilbur has also had considerable importance as a literary critic. One could contend that he has surpassed, with the possible exceptions of Randall Jarrell and Karl Shapiro, his contemporaries as a poet-critic. He has written perceptively on his poetic opposite, Edgar Allan Poe, and he has delivered a major essay on Emily Dickinson. He has edited the poems of Poe and coedited the poems of William Shakespeare. The sixteen reviews and critical essays collected in *Responses, Prose Pieces: 1953-1976* (1976) and the interviews and conversations in *Conversations with Richard Wilbur* show Wilbur's perception on other writers as well as on his own work. His insights into his own work compare in quality, if not quite in quantity, with James Dickey's attempts in *Self-Interviews* (1970) and *Sorties* (1971) to describe his own creativity.

Certainly, a trenchant defense of Wilbur as a poet is to be made on the grounds that many critics have overlooked the stylistic and tonal complexities of his poetry, much as the New Critic formalists had earlier failed to recognize complexities in Robert Frost, a poet Wilbur has always admired. Wilbur has evidenced a craftsman's interest in a wide variety of poetry—dramatic, lyric, meditation, and light verse. His wit, especially his skillful rhymes and the puns found even in his serious poetry, has not always been treated kindly by critics, but it has often captivated readers. He has been recognized by children's literature specialists for his volumes of light verse—*Loudmouse, Opposites* (1973), *More Opposites* (1991), and *Runaway Opposites* (1995)—all written with grace, wit, and humor.

In John Ciardi's *Mid-Century Poets* (1950) Wilbur identified what has remained his constant goal as a poet, whatever type of poem he has written: "The poem is an effort to articulate relationships not quite seen, to make or discover some pattern in the world. It is conflict with disorder." Wilbur's confrontation with disorder has led him to be satisfied with established patterns and traditional themes, old ways to solve old problems. Consistently a poet of affirmation, he has reacted against the two extremes of disorder: chaos and destruction on the one hand and illusions and escapism on the other. His response as both poet and humanist is to maintain a firm focus on reality as represented by objects, by the things of this world. As a poet he must be modestly heroic, see more, and range further than the ordinary citizen....

Nevertheless, the question raised earlier in Wilbur's career in regard to his development remains in the 1990s: Does his adherence to formalist principles preclude his consideration as a major poet during a postmodernist period in which poets were expected to respond to a changing social and literary landscape?

In *Wilbur's Poetry: Music in a Scattering Time* (1991) Michelson avoids reviving all the old arguments about formalism versus experimentation, closed versus open forms, and academic poetry versus postmodernism, from which Wilbur emerges as a reactionary, if not a heavy. Michelson goes instead directly to the poems to argue not only for evidence of the stylistic range and variety of Wilbur's artistry but also to affirm his sensitivity to the major moral and aesthetic crises of his times. As Lionel Trilling found in Frost, Michelson finds in Wilbur a darker side. He is to be redeemed as not only the acknowledged master of light verse but also of some less acknowledged dark, meditative poems. Michelson does not find Wilbur to be a "terrifying poet" as Trilling did Frost but rather reckons him "a serious artist for an anxious century." He identifies in many of the poems not just "safe creeds and certainties" but, significantly, a tone of "skeptical virtuosity" that has gone largely unrecognized.

If one is satisfied to judge Richard Wilbur in terms of his intentions, he has achieved them well. Nonetheless it is clear he has not been a poet for all decades. In the 1950s his view of poetic creation was compatible with that of the dominant critical view of his generation of emerging poets, the "rage for order view" of creativity promulgated by the formalistic New Criticism. By the 1960s formalism was no longer the dominant critical approach, and man's rage for order was balanced by an interest in man's rage for chaos. In the 1970s modernism had been supplanted by a neo-Romantic postmodernism. Critics discovered the virtues of political correctness by the 1980s and Wilbur seemed relatively lackluster as a poet who was neither politically correct nor notably incorrect.

What Wilbur's critics and his readers must not disregard is his mild irony, sophisticated wit, effective humor, and, as Michelson has appended, his seriousness. His craftsmanship and skill with words and traditional poetic forms should also be considered. Wilbur is a formalist who at his best manages to make formalism seem continually new. For many readers, his poetic art always was, and still is, sufficient.

Source: Richard J. Calhoun, "Richard Wilbur," in *Dictionary of Literary Biography*, Vol. 169, *American Poets Since World War II, Fifth Series*, edited by Joseph Conte, Gale Research, 1996, pp. 297–311.

John Gatta

In the following excerpt, Gatta provides a straightforward interpretation and explication of "Love Calls Us to the Things of This World."

... Wilbur's early classic, "Love Calls us to the Things of this World," remains an essential statement of affective response to this volatile world.

The poem begins, of course, with a homely scene: a man awakens suddenly at the sound of clothesline pulleys to see God's own plenty of laundry flapping outside in the breeze. Yet Wilbur's speaker is no passive observer but a freshly revitalized "soul." Lately "spirited from sleep," he entertains a kind of transcendent vision albeit one tethered firmly in facts of this world. Wind

and the moment's shock of inspiration conspire to turn laundry pieces into spirit bodies:

> Outside the open window
> The morning air is all awash with angels.
>
> Some are in bed-sheets, some are in blouses,
> Some are in smocks: but truly there they are.
> Now they are rising together in calm swells
> Of halcyon feeling, filling whatever they
>   wear
> With the deep joy of their impersonal
>   breathing.

This sudden apprehension of enspirited matter in flow, conveyed poetically with the help of enjambment, initiates the soul's movement toward encounter with a world that is at once volatile and bodily. And yet the speaker's first ecstatic but dazed response—"Oh, let there be nothing on earth but laundry"—is only preliminary. The soul still needs to in-corporate the "deep joy" of this transcendent epiphany within the quotidian light of day, to progress inwardly toward acceptance of a carnal and self-contradictory world. We can even suspect a naive immaturity in the speaker's first impulse to resist the progress of dawn, which he conceives for the moment as a "punctual rape of every blessed day."

But following the sun, which "acknowledges / With a warm look the world's hunks and colors," so also the soul eventually "descends once more in bitter love / To accept the waking body" of self and world. After tasting the "bitter" mystery of incarnational love, the man intones a new word of hortatory blessing:

> "Bring them down from their ruddy
>   gallows;
> Let there be clean linen for the backs of
>   thieves;
> Let lovers go fresh and sweet to be undone,
> And the heaviest nuns walk in a pure
>   floating
> Of dark habits,
>   keeping their difficult balance."

Uttered in a "changed voice" of authority beyond either euphoria or bitterness, this blessing partly "undoes" the previous "rape of every blessed day." It reflects not only an achieved recognition of earthly actualities, of the need to balance claims of the material and spiritual realms, but also something like a divine charity of acceptance and forgiveness for the whole range of characters enacting the human comedy. In its playful aspect, the poem ends up displaying on the same washline, so to speak, a colorfully promiscuous variety of loves—material, erotic, charitable, and sacred.

Within the context of seventeenth-century meditative literature familiar to Wilbur, a soul's final response to the openings of divine love—whether found in scripture tropes or laundry—takes the form of personal colloquy. Such is likewise the case in Wilbur's poem, whose compassionate conclusion registers one soul's answer to the call of Love.

By the same token, Wilbur was clearly affirming the incarnational beauty and necessity of the material world when he insisted in verse of a few years earlier that "A World Without Objects Is a Sensible Emptiness." Here, in fact, the historical moment of a particular barn-birth, haloed with "Lampshine blurred in the steam of beasts," becomes the central paradigm for discovering "the spirit's right / Oasis, light incarnate." And yet, without attending closely to the poem's originative context in Thomas Traherne's *Centuries*, we are not apt to see how much its rejection of ideality has to do with Traherne's own overarching theme of love.

Across the desert landscape of Wilbur's poem, the soul's "tall camels of the spirit" start off walking in pride toward a desolation of thirst and absence. For until this soul descends in loving humility toward a world whose "shinings need to be shaped and borne," it is chasing a cursed mirage. Traherne points out about souls that "till they love they are desolate; without their objects ... but when they shine by Love upon all objects, they are accompanied with them and enlightened by them" (Traherne 80).

In the poem's closing quatrain, then, the true "sight" celebrated is the light of love, which momentarily reveals divine glory in the surrounding trees, creeks, hills, and steaming beasts. If Traherne states that "Life without objects is sensible emptiness," so also he goes on to reflect in the same passage that "Objects without Love are the delusion of life" because "The Objects of Love are its greatest treasures: and without Love it is impossible they should be treasures" (86). Rejecting ideality as a desolating delusion, Wilbur's poem ends up endorsing once again the return to incarnate relation.

Still, the soul's recovery of an illuminative oasis within this world cannot permanently satisfy its longings for the infinite. Restlessness, incompletion, the imperfection of all earthly

loves—these Augustinian motifs have been and remain persistent in Wilbur's writing. As recently as "Hamlen Book," the poet is wondering "How shall I drink all this?" or how carry on the lips that "ache / Nothing can satisfy?" Or as he writes earlier, "The end of thirst exceeds experience" ("A Voice from under the Table"). According to Wilbur, both Traherne and Emily Dickinson had discovered that infinite desire of the soul which, unlike mere appetite, could never rest content in finite satisfactions. This thwarted desire for completion also characterizes a second form of love discernible throughout Wilbur's writing: the love of human beings ...

Source: John Gatta, "Richard Wilbur's Poetry of Love," in *Renascence*, Vol. 45, No. 1–2, September 1992, pp. 3–15.

Frank Littler

In the following article, Littler critiques "Love Calls Us to the Things of This World" from a theological perspective.

In the gospel of St. John, the adjuration to mankind is to "Love not the world, neither the things that are in the world" (1 John 2:15). Man is thus counseled to seek the spiritual directly, avoiding the "things" of this world which presumably would lessen his capacity to exist on a spiritual plane. In Richard Wilbur's poem "Love Calls Us To Things of This World" (*The Poems of Richard Wilbur* [New York: Harcourt, Brace and World, 1963]) however, this biblical notion is examined critically, and the paradoxical notion that man best seeks the spiritual through his participation in the actual or world of the body is put in its place. The poem is not, of course, overtly theological but does make a theological point. Wilbur uses structure and diction to create a highly refined presentation of the contrast between the spiritual and the physical and of the paradox of man's finding the spiritual through the actual—the theme of the poem.

The poem's two part structure is perhaps the most obvious indication of how the contrast of the spiritual and physical is presented. The first part of the poem, running to line seventeen, stresses a fanciful world of spirit, epitomized by the "angels," which to the "soul" are, in the light of false dawn, the transformed clothes hanging on a clothes line. The image of the angels, appearing in the midst of the wholly mundane setting of, perhaps, a tenement district, is a welcome contrast to the real world. Line 17 of the

THE POEM'S TWO PART STRUCTURE CLEARLY INDICATES THE OVERALL CONTRAST INTENDED BETWEEN THE DESIRE FOR THE SPIRITUAL AND THE NECESSITY FOR THE ACCEPTANCE OF THE ACTUAL, BUT THE USE OF INTRICATELY CHOSEN DICTION GIVES CONCRETE FORM AND DEFINITION TO THE CONTRAST."

poem marks a transition point: the soul shrinks back from the actual world and desires to remain in its spiritual world of cleanliness and lightness, though the soul will "descend once more . . . to accept the waking body." This shrinking from the actual and desire for the spiritual is expressed in lines 21 to 23 where the soul wishes for "nothing on earth but laundry, . . . rosy hands in the rising steam / And clear dances done in the sight of heaven." It should be noted, however, that even the content of these lines indicates a movement toward the actual. Instead of the strict personification of laundry as angels, the soul cries for laundry itself and the cleanliness it represents as it is being washed. The rosy hands and rising steam are, though desirable and pleasant to the soul, yet part of the actions of this world, not of the wholly spiritual world of angels.

The contrast is deepened in lines 29 to 34 at which point the soul finally accepts the actual world with its conflicts and paradoxes. This subdivision of the second part of the poem completes the movement from the soul's perception of a spiritual world, through its desiring that that world can remain "unraped" by the descent into the actual, to its final rueful acceptance of the world where, paradoxically, "angels" perform the functions of clothes which in turn are presented in terms of paradox.

The poem's two part structure clearly indicates the overall contrast intended between the desire for the spiritual and the necessity for the acceptance of the actual, but the use of intricately chosen diction gives concrete form and definition to the contrast. The diction is, in fact, so refined and precise that the reader perceives the texture of the two worlds of the poem.

The first part of the poem is dominated, as would be expected, by the use of words which convey a spiritual texture, but part of the poem's complexity is in its natural but intricate selection of words which remind the reader of lightness or airiness, cleanliness especially as related to water, and to laundry itself. In the first stanza, for example, as the "eyes open to a cry of pulleys," the soul is "spirited" from sleep and "hangs" "bodiless." In describing the movement of the angels in the morning air, a number of verbal forms are used which further portray the airiness and lightness of the world of the spirit. The angels are seen as "rising," "filling," "breathing," "flying," and "moving and staying"; all of these word choices denote and connote either free movement or the action of the wind in relation to movement. The laundry is thus "inspired" in the root meaning of that term, that is filled with the breath of spirit. Finally, "swoon" and "nobody" enhance the airy-light texture, denoting respectively a gentle faint and the absence of body.

A second pattern of diction associates the angels with the cleanliness of laundry. In the first part of the poem, the morning air is "awash with angels"; the angels rise together in "calm swells of halcyon feeling," the latter phrasing containing an allusion to the legendary bird who calms wind and waves; the angels move and stay "like white water." In the second part of the poem as the soul longs to remain in its spirit world, the "rosy hands" and the "rising steam" associated with the washing of laundry further establish the cleanliness of the spiritual state. Even more intricate is Wilbur's use of key terms from the common language of laundry to establish the identification of the clothes on the line with the angels the soul sees in the light of false dawn. The air is "awash" with angels which are "in" the literal bed sheets, blouses, and smocks, but "the soul shrinks . . . from the punctual rape of every blessed day." The key term "shrink," denoting as it does the literal shrinking up of washed clothes as well as figuratively a movement away from something unpleasant, thus concretely emphasizing the theme of the soul's desire for a spirit world, the "blessed day," but with this is its realization that the actual will punctually, even violently, intrude on that spirit world.

The diction in the second part of the poem, from line 17 on, though containing several word choices which are akin to the pattern of lightness and cleanliness of the first part, tends to stress the actual. The already mentioned "punctual rape," the "hunks and colors," "the waking body," the "bitter love" with which the soul descends, the "ruddy gallows" are examples of word choices which emphasize the actual world. In the poem's final stanza, however, the diction underscores the paradoxical nature of "this world." As the man "yawns and rises," the angels are to be brought down from "their ruddy gallows." In other words, the angels tinged by the sun are "hung" in the sense of being executed; the clothes line is now a gallows and they have died as angels, have become clothes, and have entered the world of contradiction and paradox, where clean linen covers the "backs of thieves" and lovers put on their finery only to remove it in consummation of their love. In contrast to the traditional symbolism of light and dark, which has been implicit in the first part of the poem, it is the nuns who have the "dark habits" while the thieves wear white linen. In one sense, the "dark habits" are the clothes worn by the nuns, while in another sense, the phrase indicates that nuns too participate in the world's conflict of good and evil. In a final paradox, the nuns, though heavy, still float and retain a balance between things of this world, the work they do in the here and now, and the spiritual world to which they have given allegiance. They particularly need to keep a difficult balance between the things of this world and those of the world of the Spirit.

The carefully expressed paradoxes of the last stanza of the poem are the key to the poem's theme. Wilbur presents an affecting version of the ideal world through his images of angelic laundry, but this world is evanescent, seen only for a moment under the light of false dawn. Though man desires and needs the world of spirit, he must yet descend to the body and accept it in "bitter love" (another apt paradoxical phrase) because this is the world in which man has to live. In contrast to St. John's plea, to avoid the world and the things of it, Wilbur would have us accept them, though we should also retain the capacity to perceive the world of the spirit in the everyday.

Source: Frank Littler, "Wilbur's 'Love Calls Us to Things of This World,'" in *Explicator*, Vol. 40, No. 3, Spring 1982, pp. 53–55.

SOURCES

"1 John 2:15," in *The Holy Bible: King James Version*, Electronic Text Center, University of Virginia, http://etext.lib.virginia.edu/etcbin/toccer-new2?id = KjvlJoh.sgm&images = images/modeng&data = /texts/english/modeng/parsed&tag = public&part = 2&division = div1 (accessed August 31, 2007).

Hill, Donald L., *Richard Wilbur*, Twayne's United States Author Series, No. 117, Twayne Publishers, 1967, p. 122–23.

Michelson, Bruce, *Wilbur's Poetry: Music in a Scattering Time*, University of Michigan Press, 1991, p. 51.

Perloff, Marjorie, *Poetry On & Off the Page*, Northwestern University Press, 1998, p. 85.

Rasula, Jed, *American Poetry Wax Museum: Reality Effects, 1940–1990*, National Council of Teachers of English, 1996, p. 509.

Wilbur, Richard, "Love Calls Us to the Things of This World," in *New and Collected Poems*, Harcourt Brace Jovanovich, 1988, pp. 233–34.

FURTHER READING

Brahm, Jeanne, "A Difficult Balance," in *The Light within the Light*, Godine, 2007, pp. 21–40.
> This chapter of Brahm's short study of major American poets combines a personal look at Wilbur's life with an overview of the critical responses to his work over the years, making it a good starting place for students who are familiarizing themselves with the poet and his work.

Cummins, Paul F., *Richard Wilbur: A Critical Essay*, William B. Eerdmans, 1971.
> Written from a Christian perspective, this short, forty-four-page pamphlet uses the "difficult balance" mentioned in the last line of this poem as a touchstone for examining all of Wilbur's poetry.

Epstein, Daniel Mark, "The Metaphysics of Richard Wilbur," in the *New Criterion*, April 2005, pp. 4–11.
> Epstein's essay, written on the occasion of the publication of Wilbur's *Collected Poems, 1943–2004*, traces the poet's world view over the course of his long career.

Kirsch, Adam, "Get Happy," in the *New Yorker*, November 22, 2004, pp. 94–97.
> Kirsch's overview of Wilbur's career is resplendent with references to other poets, from Randall Jarrell to Sylvia Plath to James Merrill, giving the reader a context in which to place Wilbur's poetic range.

Reibetanz, J. M., "The Reflexive Art in Richard Wilbur," in *University of Toronto Quarterly*, Spring 1998, pp. 592–612.

Reibetanz examines Wilbur's poems, including "Love Calls Us to the Things of This World," for the ways in which the metaphors contained in them reflect Wilbur's ideas about the art of poetry in general.

Stone, Karen, *Image and Spirit: Finding Meaning in Visual Art*, Augsburg Fortress Publishers, 2003.

In the same way that Wilbur finds spirituality in laundry, Stone examines the visual arts and reveals religious implications that are not readily apparent.

Native Guard

NATASHA TRETHEWEY

2006

The title of Natasha Trethewey's Pulitzer Prize-winning collection *Native Guard* (2006) references a regiment of African American soldiers, some of whom were freed slaves, others of whom had enlisted with the Confederate army but had ultimately escaped the rule of white Southerners. This special regiment fought for the Union army during the Civil War, standing guard on Ship Island, off the Mississippi shore, to ensure that Confederate prisoners did not escape.

The title poem of the collection is told in the voice of one of the black soldiers, a freed slave who sees similarity between his role as a soldier and that of a slave. The work is manual labor, just like before, and the rations are also very familiar. The soldier recounts the passage of time as he records his thoughts in a journal-like poem. The poem laments the loss of life, dignity, and freedom. At one point, the poem points out that everyone is a slave to destiny.

AUTHOR BIOGRAPHY

Natasha Trethewey was born in Gulfport, Mississippi, in 1966 to a white father and a black mother. Her father, Eric Trethewey, a poet, and her mother, Gwendolyn Grimmette, a social worker, divorced when Trethewey was six years old. She and her mother then moved to Georgia, where her mother earned a master's degree and

Natasha Trethewey (Logan Mock-Bunting / Getty Images)

later remarried. Trethewey's stepfather murdered her mother several years later, in 1985. Trethewey was nineteen at the time. Trethewey's biracial identity as well as her mother's murder are topics that Trethewey often examines in her poems.

Trethewey earned her bachelor's in English from the University of Georgia; her master's in poetry from Hollins University in Roanoke, Virginia (where her father was a professor); and an MFA in poetry from the University of Massachusetts. Trethewey taught as an assistant professor of English at Auburn University in Alabama before taking on the professorial

position of Phillis Wheatley Distinguished Chair of Poetry at Emory University in Decatur, Georgia.

Trethewey's work has appeared in many different publications, including *The Best American Poetry* (2000 and 2003), *Agni*, *American Poetry Review*, *Callaloo*, *Gettysburg Review*, *Kenyon Review*, *New England Review*, and the *Southern Review*. Trethewey's first collection of poems, *Domestic Work* (2000), won the 2001 Mississippi Institute of Arts and Letters Book Prize and the 2001 Lillian Smith Award for Poetry. Her second collection, *Bellocq's Ophelia* (2002), received the 2003 Mississippi Institute of Arts and Letters Book Prize, was a finalist for the Academy of American Poets' James Laughlin and Lenore Marshall prizes, and was named a 2003 Notable Book by the American Library Association. Her 2006 collection, *Native Guard*, won the 2007 Pulitzer Prize for Poetry.

POEM TEXT

If this war be forgotten, I ask in the name of all things sacred what shall men remember?

Frederick Douglass

November 1862
Truth be told, I do not want to forget
anything of my former life: the landscape's
song of bondage—dirge in the river's throat
where it churns into the Gulf, wind in trees
choked with vines. I thought to carry with me   5
want of freedom though I had been freed,
remembrance not constant recollection.
Yes: I was born a slave, at harvest time,
in the Parish of Ascension; I've reached
thirty-three with history of one younger   10
inscribed upon my back. I now use ink
to keep record, a closed book, not the lure
of memory—flawed, changeful—that dulls the
    lash
for the master, sharpens it for the slave.

December 1862
For the slave, having a master sharpens   15
the bend into work, the way the sergeant
moves us now to perfect battalion drill,
dress parade. Still, we're called supply units
not infantry—and so we dig trenches,
haul burdens for the army no less heavy   20
than before. I heard the colonel call it
nigger work. Half rations make our work
familiar still. We take those things we need
from the Confederates' abandoned homes:
salt, sugar, even this journal, near full   25

with someone else's words, overlapped now,
crosshatched beneath mine. On every page,
his story intersecting with my own.

January 1863

O how history intersects—my own
berth upon a ship called the *Northern Star*   30
and I'm delivered into a new life,
Fort Massachusetts: a great irony—
both path and destination of freedom
I'd not dared to travel. Here, now, I walk
ankle-deep in sand, fly-bitten, nearly   35
smothered by heat, and yet I can look out
upon the Gulf and see the surf breaking,
tossing the ships, the great gunboats bobbing
on the water. And are we not the same,
slaves in the hands of the master, destiny?   40
—night sky red with the promise of fortune,
dawn pink as new flesh: healing, unfettered.

January 1863

Today, dawn red as warning. Unfettered
supplies, stacked on the beach at our landing,
washed away in the storm that rose too fast,   45
caught us unprepared. Later, as we worked,
I joined in the low singing someone raised
to pace us, and felt a bond in labor
I had not known. It was then a dark man
removed his shirt, revealed the scars,
    crosshatched   50
like the lines in this journal, on his back.
It was he who remarked at how the ropes
cracked like whips on the sand, made us take
    note
of the wild dance of a tent loosed by wind.
We watched and learned. Like any shrewd
    master,   55
we know now to tie down what we will keep.

February 1863

We know it is our duty now to keep
white men as prisoners—rebel soldiers,
would-be masters. We're all bondsmen here,
    each
to the other. Freedom has gotten them   60
captivity. For us, a conscription
we have chosen—jailors to those who still
would have us slaves. They are cautious,
    dreading
the sight of us. Some neither read nor write,
are laid too low and have few words to send   65
but those I give them. Still, they are wary
of a negro writing, taking down letters.
X binds them to the page—a mute symbol
like the cross on a grave. I suspect they fear
I'll listen, put something else down in ink.   70

March 1863

I listen, put down in ink what I know
they labor to say between silences
too big for words: worry for beloveds—
My Dearest, how are you getting along—

what has become of their small plots of land—   75
did you harvest enough food to put by?
They long for the comfort of former lives—
I see you as you were, waving goodbye.
Some send photographs—a likeness in case
the body can't return. Others dictate   80
harsh facts of this war: *The hot air carries*
the stench of limbs, rotten in the bone pit.
Flies swarm—a black cloud. We hunger, grow
    weak.
When men die, we eat their share of hardtack.

April 1863

When men die, we eat their share of hardtack   85
trying not to recall their hollow sockets,
the worm-stitch of their cheeks. Today we
    buried
the last of our dead from Pascagoula,
and those who died retreating to our ship—
white sailors in blue firing upon us   90
as if we were the enemy. I'd thought
the fighting over, then watched a man fall
beside me, knees-first as in prayer, then
another, his arms outstretched as if borne
upon the cross. Smoke that rose from each gun   95
seemed a soul departing. The Colonel said:
an unfortunate incident; said:
their names shall deck the page of history.

June 1863

Some names shall deck the page of history
as it is written on stone. Some will not.   100
Yesterday, word came of colored troops, dead
on the battlefield at Port Hudson; how
General Banks was heard to say *I have*
no dead there, and left them, unclaimed. Last
    night,
I dreamt their eyes still open—dim, clouded   105
as the eyes of fish washed ashore, yet fixed—
staring back at me. Still, more come today
eager to enlist. Their bodies—haggard
faces, gaunt limbs—bring news of the mainland.
Starved, they suffer like our prisoners. Dying,   110
they plead for what we do not have to give.
Death makes equals of us all: a fair master.

August 1864

Dumas was a fair master to us all.
He taught me to read and write: I was a man-
servant, if not a man. At my work,   115
I studied natural things—all manner
of plants, birds I draw now in my book: wren,
willet, egret, loon. Tending the gardens,
I thought only to study live things, thought
never to know so much about the dead.   120
Now I tend Ship Island graves, mounds like
    dunes
that shift and disappear. I record names,
send home simple notes, not much more than
    how
and when—an official duty. I'm told
it's best to spare most detail, but I know   125
there are things which must be accounted for.

1865
These are things which must be accounted for:
slaughter under the white flag of surrender—
black massacre at Fort Pillow; our new name,
the Corps d'Afrique—words that take the
    native   130
from our claim; mossbacks and freedmen—
    exiles
in their own homeland; the diseased, the
    maimed,
every lost limb, and what remains: phantom
ache, memory haunting an empty sleeve;
the hog-eaten at Gettysburg, unmarked   135
in their graves; all the dead letters, unanswered;
untold stories of those that time will render
mute. Beneath battlefields, green again,
the dead molder—a scaffolding of bone
we tread upon, forgetting. Truth be told.   140

POEM SUMMARY

November 1862

Trethewey divides her poem "Native Guard" into time frames, beginning with November 1862. In the first stanza, in the voice of an African American soldier, Trethewey provides the background of this soldier, his life prior to enlisting in the army. The soldier reflects on his life as a slave. First Trethewey provides a sense of the physical landscape of a Southern plantation that sits on the side of a river. The Gulf of Mexico is mentioned, setting the scene in one of the gulf states, along the shoreline. The soldier was once a slave, but he mentions that he was already freed earlier in 1862. However, he seems to be so newly freed that he has to remind himself that he is no longer a slave.

The soldier then recounts some of his memories of having been a slave ever since being born into slavery. Marks upon his back, signs of having been whipped, are proof of his history. The soldier makes a reference to Ascension Parish, located in the southeastern part of Louisiana (which has parishes instead of counties). The soldier is thirty-three years old. He compares the marks on his back, which have recorded his history up to now, with the marks he will now make with ink on paper. This is his new form of history taking, as a power that was once the slaveholder's has become his own.

December 1862

A month has passed, and the soldier now mentions a sergeant, comparing the sergeant to a slave master. Both the sergeant and the slave master have their ways of bringing their men around to obeying orders. The soldier and his fellow mates learn to march under the sergeant's drills, but instead of being given guns, the black soldiers are told to dig ditches and work like mules, carrying supplies. The soldier suggests that the top officer over the black soldiers uses derogatory racial slurs when referring to them. In addition to having to listen to the verbal abuse, something they became accustomed to as slaves, the black soldiers are given only half as much food as their white counterparts are granted. This too, the soldier says, is a familiar slave routine. The soldier admits that in order to supplement their supplies, they steal from abandoned homes. This implies that the regiment is not yet on Ship Island, as there are no homes there. Not only do the black soldiers take food from these houses, but also this soldier found in one the paper and ink that he needed to write his journal. The journal this soldier found is already written on, so he crosses out the other person's words (suggesting that these are a white person's writings) and writes his own thoughts over them. This provides an image of the black man rewriting history or possibly just telling it from another perspective.

January 1863

Two sections of this poem have the same date, that of January 1863. In the first section, the soldier mentions a ship that has taken him to Ship Island. The name of the boat and the name of the fort on Ship Island remind the soldier of the North, where many black people live free, the destination of many runaway slaves in the South. This soldier never dared attempt to take that road to freedom, and yet, he is delivered to a place that suggests that journey, at least in name. Though the environment of Ship Island is not easy to endure, as it is too hot and the air is filled with biting insects, the soldier enjoys the open expanse of the horizons, where he can look out across the gulf and dream. On the water he sees the boats that have arrived from the North, filled with Union soldiers who have come to the South to help free the slaves. Then he ponders the question of slavery. Are he and his fellow African Americans the only ones who are slaves? Isn't everyone bound by fate? At this point in the poem, the soldier is considering the equality that everyone is born with as well as the similar patterns that everyone shares in dealing with the world and one's own destiny. He sees the potential for a positive future, a new life that promises to make him feel better as he more fully realizes that he is free.

In the second stanza of January 1863, the soldier is not so hopeful. The dawn of the previous stanza, the one that promised good fortune, is now seen as a warning of danger and trouble. Supplies that were dropped off on the beach were not put in safe storage, and the men were unaware of the possible consequences. A storm came up quickly and washed the supplies away. The supplies needed to be tied down, the soldier now realizes. This image reminds him, once again, of how tied down he had been as a slave. The next day, as the men work, they begin to sing. The rhythm of the song and the sound of their voices brings them together, making them feel as one, buoyed by a sense of community that the soldier had never felt before. A fellow soldier takes off his shirt in the heat and exposes scars on his back that everyone recognizes as the marks of a whip. The ropes that are used to tie down the supplies, the other soldier points out, make sounds similar to that of the whip. This second soldier also points out how their tents blow in the wind, threatening to take off in some wild dance. These are all reminders for the soldier that if he wants to keep something, he must learn to tether it.

February 1863

An irony opens this stanza—the fact that a group of black soldiers is now standing guard over a group of white Confederate soldiers. These white rebels would have been the masters of the black soldiers were it not for the Civil War. Though the white soldiers are prisoners, the soldier comments that they are equal in a strange way; their positions could change so quickly, one taking the other's place. The white soldiers' fight for freedom has led them to be jailed.

The white prisoners are wary of their black captors and try not to look at them. The soldier narrator, realizing that most of the white men are illiterate, senses his own power over them, as he, at least, has the power of words. The white prisoners cannot write letters home except through the skills of the black narrator, who was once their slave. They do not know whether to trust him, however. The soldier thinks that they believe he is writing more than they tell him, but they can only add their signatures, each using no more than an *X*. That is their only power when it comes to the literary process; they are in the black soldier's hands.

March 1863

The narrator details some of the passages from the letters he has written for the white prisoners. They write letters to their wives, asking them how they are doing, how their land is doing, and whether the wives were able to bring in the crop, to provide the family with enough food to last. The soldier narrator mentions that he hears the white prisoners saying more than they are actually telling him; he can read between the lines, such as when the prisoners want to send photographs home so that their wives will remember them should they never return. The prisoners remember their wives waving to them as they left home. The significance of these last images is that the soldiers were departing as if they would be gone for good. Other prisoners talk of more morbid things, like the short supply of food, the oppressive heat, and the smell of death all around them. Their own physical prowess, some of the prisoners tell their families, is failing them.

April 1863

The narrator takes up the theme of death. As the soldiers die, there is more food for the rest of them. There is also mention of a battle at Pascagoula, which is close to the southern shores of Mississippi. In this battle, the black regiment proved that they were capable of fighting. The narrator mentions that many died, and he talks about burying the dead. There is a twist to this story, however. As the black soldiers retreated to their ship, white Union soldiers (who were supposed to be on the black regiment's side) began shooting at them, killing many more. The narrator heard the white colonel in charge of the black regiment make a comment that fell short of describing the way the narrator felt at seeing this senseless killing; the colonel's words described the event as if it were trivial.

June 1863

Two months later, the memorial that was supposed to bear the dead black soldiers's names engraved in stone still does not exist. There are memorials to white soldiers, however. There is mention of another battle, this one at Port Hudson, which is located in Louisiana not far from Baton Rouge, along the Mississippi River. Around 5,000 Union soldiers and some 700 Confederate soldiers died in this battle. Black regiments were involved in this battle, but, according to the poem, the commander in charge, a General Banks, paid little attention to the black soldiers who died there. The narrator remembers them in his mind, imagining a battlefield scene where a black soldier laid unburied.

Despite the prejudice and the dismissal of the sacrifices that the black soldiers are making, more black recruits come to the island, ready to give their lives. They do this because their lives are nothing but suffering anyway. They are starving and are willing to take their chances on the battlefield. The narrator closes this stanza by repeating his earlier claim that whether prisoner or guard, whether white man or black, whether free black or slave, they all share the same lot. They all will soon face their deaths.

August 1864

The name of Francis Dumas is mentioned in the opening lines of this stanza, as the narrator was once a slave of Dumas's. This master—also a black man—was good, the narrator states. Dumas is the one who taught the narrator to read and write, and he also learned about nature from Dumas, who, in other words, helped the narrator to open his mind to other possibilities beyond labor and slavery. The narrator claims that while he lived as a slave, he focused most of his thoughts on life. But his life has drastically changed: Now that he is a free man, all he deals with is death. He buries the dead and tends to their graves, which the wind is constantly disrupting. He writes letters to the wives and families of the men who are dead, keeping the horrid details to himself, though he senses that the families crave more information. He considers that the things the families are not told are like other details about the war that will not be expressed. It is as if the narrator already knows that the black regiments, in particular, will be forgotten.

1865

Possibly a year has passed. The Civil War is either over or at least near its end. The narrator takes the time, then, to list the things that need to be said about the war and his experiences. He wants to be the voice for those things that he has been told not to say. He talks about mass killings and about the maimed. He wonders what will happen to the black soldiers who are now freed but have no homes. He mentions the dead black soldiers who were left on the battlefields to rot or to be eaten by wild animals. Soldiers missing limbs still feel them as if they were still attached, just as the soldiers who were not killed remember those who were. Missing are not just the bodies but also the memories of those soldiers, who, if they were lucky enough to be buried, do not have names on their graves. No one has time to record their stories, so who will remember them? Their bodies have now turned the battlefields green, and traces of their lives have been all but erased.

THEMES

Death

The theme of death permeates Trethewey's poem. Beyond the death that symbolizes the inevitable end that everyone must eventually face, there is also the senseless death that comes from war, prejudice, and negligence. With the setting being the Civil War, one would expect the topic of death to be present, and Trethewey indeed goes far with this theme, talking about massacres and slaughter—huge losses that insinuate overkill. There are men who die on the field of battle as well as men who die of disease because they have been locked up in cells that are unfit for living. The men are cramped into spaces that are poorly ventilated, and they are poorly fed; sanitation is lacking, and the heat is sweltering and suffocating. There are also the deaths of soldiers shot by their own comrades.

A presence of psychological death can also be found in this poem. As Confederate soldiers rot away in prison, they lose hope of ever returning to their families. They write letters home and have visions of their wives while strongly sensing that they will never see them again. Hints of the death of dignity can also be found, as the black soldiers realize that their names will not be remembered because they are discounted as humans, deemed unworthy of even a body count when they fall dead in the fields.

Prejudice

Prejudice as a theme is apparent throughout the poem. The black men in the regiment might be freed slaves, but they have not escaped the prejudice that was partially responsible for their

TOPICS FOR FURTHER STUDY

- To give your classmates a more intimate sense of what it was like to be a slave, find a book with one or more slave narratives—stories told by slaves—and commit a passage or two to memory. Then recite the passages in front of your class, taking on the persona of the person who wrote the narrative.

- Read another black poet's work, choosing someone such as Rita Dove, Lucille Clifton, Maya Angelou, or Nikki Giovanni. Then compare that poet's work with Trethewey's. How do their voices compare or contrast? Are there similarities in the topics that they focus on? Is one poet more personal than the other? What time frames do they write about? What are the social contexts surrounding their lives and their poetry? Write a paper on your findings.

- Read about black soldiers' experiences in the Civil War. List the battles they were involved with and position those battles on a map. Find as many statistics as you can concerning the number of black soldiers in each regiment and the numbers of deaths. Also find out how many medals of honor were won. In what battles were they won? Were any black soldiers dismissed dishonorably? What role did black soldiers play in the Confederate army? Where did they fight? Place as much information as you can on your map and then use the map throughout a presentation as you explain the details that you have uncovered.

- Research the layout of Ship Island during the Civil War. Where were the prisoners kept? Where did the guards sleep and eat? What did Fort Massachusetts look like, and what was it used for? Create a three-dimensional model of the island and its fort. Make the model as realistic as possible to give your fellow students an idea of what life was like during the three years that the Native Guard lived on the island.

being held captive in the first place. They may have been promised freedom, but that freedom came with the price of prejudice. They soon learn that they are the cheap soldiers, the ones who receive less pay and less food than their white counterparts. They work harder, performing all the heavy labor and dirty jobs that need to be done, like tending the dead and their graves, cleaning the toilets, and digging daily wells. They are referred to in derogatory terms not only by the men they work with but also by their supervisors. They remain uncounted and forgotten after they fall. While the white soldiers come and go, stopping on Ship Island only for a few days, the black soldiers are stationed in that unhealthy place for three years. They are mistrusted not because of their deeds or their morals but because of the color of their skin. When given a chance to fight, they prove not only their worthiness but also their valor, volunteering to take the front positions, like pawns in a game of chess. When they turn around and look for cover, they are met by their own fellow Union soldiers shooting at them.

Captivity and Freedom

The double-sided theme of captivity and freedom is played out in the poem in different ways. The narrator of this poem tells the readers that he has spent thirty-three years of his life as a captive. When he is finally given his freedom, he realizes that his freedom is not much different than his captivity, as he is still told what to do and where to go. He still works at very difficult manual labor. He is poorly fed and has the constant fear of death hanging over his head. He might be free, but white people still hate him and treat him like he is less than human. However, he is free in his mind, as his master was an educated black man who taught him to read and write and to study nature. Yet, his body still belongs to the army. The white Confederate prisoners are also caught in this irony. Where once they were free men who had enslaved black men, now they are held captive and are at the mercy of the freed slaves. Thus, the white captives certainly feel they have reason to be wary of the black soldiers. They spent most of their lives belittling black slaves, and now they must depend on black soldiers for their lives. They have lost their freedom to choose whom they want to deal with and whom they can ignore.

Remembrance

As a person comes close to the end of his or her life, there is often a certain question: Will I be remembered? Trethewey wonders about remembrance in "Native Guard". Who will remember this regiment of black soldiers? How many history books skip over this portion of the past and others like it? Trethewey, then, takes up the cause of remembering. She wants to tell the story of the Louisiana Native Guard. Unlike the generals and colonels, she wants to count the heads, inscribe the names, bury the dead, and write about the experiences of at least one soldier who spent three years of his life helping, as best as he was allowed, to fight in the Civil War. What is a life, this poem seems to ask, if it is not remembered? As the narrator of this poem helps the white illiterate soldiers write home to their families, asking their wives and children not to forget them, Trethewey also writes home, in a way, asking her readers not to forget these men. The narrator says that he remembers his youth by the scars on his back, but now that he is thirty-three and a man, he wants to remember in a different way. So he crosses out the writing of a white man and tells a similar story but through a different perspective, a perspective that, if not written down, would never be remembered.

STYLE

Sonnet

"Native Guard" is written in the form of a sonnet sequence. The word *sonnet* comes from the Italian and means "little song." As a poetic form, a sonnet consists of a logical progression of several verses, with a total of fourteen lines.

Traditionally, a sonnet has a rhyming scheme, however, Trethewey's sonnet sequence is unrhymed. Her poem contains ten beats to each line, clustered in two beats per foot, with five feet per line, in what is called iambic pentameter (a scheme often used by Shakespeare). The sonnet was considered an old-fashioned form in the early twentieth century, especially when free verse (which has no rhyming or standard beat) became a recognized form. Free verse, poets argued, was more like normal speech or conversation and was thus appropriate for the confessional type of poetry that was then popular. Since the turn of the twenty-first century, some poets are turning back to the sonnet form, with and without rhyming patterns. Some twentieth-century poets who helped to modernize the sonnet form are Robert Frost, Edna St. Vincent Millay, E. E. Cummings, Jorge Luis Borges, Pablo Neruda, and Seamus Heaney.

Most sonnets are divided into two parts. In the first part, the theme of the poem is provided. It is also in this first part that the poet (or speaker of the poem) raises a question. In the second part of the poem, the speaker attempts to answer that question or at least makes the point of the poem very clear. This transition between the presenting of the problem or question and the subsequent making of a point is called the turn of the sonnet. Such a turn can also be found within a broader sonnet sequence; the turn in Trethewey's sonnet sequence could likely come between the two verses that are both identified as "January 1863." From the beginning of the poem up until the first "January 1863" verse, the speaker talks about his past: what his life was like until he arrived on Ship Island. He mentions his enslavement and then his so-called freedom as a Union soldier. From the second verse called "January 1863" until the end of the poem, the speaker goes into the details of the conditions he faces as a black soldier on the island.

Repetition of Lines

Each verse of Trethewey's poem ends with a line that is then to some degree repeated in the first line of the next verse. Some of the same words or images are used in both lines, thus tying the verses together, carrying over similar themes. At the end of the first verse, she uses the image of a master and a slave and the concept of sharpening, which is again repeated in the first line of the second verse. The lines are not exact replicas of one another, but they are related. The same is true

Capt. Charles Sentmanat, Co. D.
2d Lieut. V. Lavigne, Co. D.   1st Lieut. L. D. Larrieu, Co. A.   2d Lieut. J. L. Montieu, Co. A.   Capt. E. Davis, Co. A.

OUR COLORED TROOPS—THE LINE OFFICERS OF THE FIRST LOUISIANA NATIVE GUARDS.—SKETCHED BY OUR SPECIAL ARTIST.

First Louisiana Native Guard (*Picture Collection, The Branch Libraries, The New York Public Library, Astor, Lenox and Tilden Foundations*)

for each of the following verses. Sometimes the repeated lines are twisted slightly, using similar words but changing the images, thus providing the reader with different interpretations.

Fictional Character as Speaker

The speaker of a poem is not always the same as the voice of the poet. This is obvious in Trethewey's poem, as the fictional speaker confesses that he was once a slave and is now a soldier in the Louisiana Native Guard. Readers gain further knowledge of the speaker as the poem progresses. He is a free man now, one who can read and write. By taking on the persona of such a speaker, the poet can provide more intimate details of what it was like to be a black man on Ship Island, having to watch over the white Confederate soldiers, many of whom used to own slaves. Readers can see the conditions through the speaker's eyes, rather than reading lines that

the poet could only have written through historic accounts. The fact that the speaker is literate and keeps a diary gives the poem vitality and veritableness, as if readers are looking over the man's shoulder and witnessing the writing as well as the experiences that the speaker is recording. If the poet had written from a third-person perspective, as an observer from a distance, the poem might not have been as touching or moving.

HISTORICAL CONTEXT

Ship Island and the Native Guard

Sitting twelve miles off the shores of Mississippi, Ship Island, a barrier island in the Gulf of Mexico, became the site of a Union army presence in the South during the Civil War. Shortly after the Union army lost the first battle of the Civil War,

COMPARE & CONTRAST

- **1860s:** Civil War breaks out in the United States between the North and the South. At stake is the abolition of slavery, the first step toward equality for blacks.

  Today: While inequities still exist among the races, Barack Obama, a black senator, runs for the position of president of the United States in 2008.

- **1860s:** Small numbers of black soldiers fight in the Civil War between the states. Units composed of black soldiers are segregated from white units.

  Today: Black soldiers, both men and women, fight alongside white soldiers in wars in Iraq and Afghanistan.

- **1860s:** Publications by black authors are rare. Frances "Frank" Rollin (1847–1901) writes the first biography of a freeborn African American, *Life and Public Services of Martin R. Delany*, published in 1868.

  Today: Publications by black authors are prevalent. Trethewey, an African American woman, wins the Pulitzer Prize for Poetry in 2007. Other well-known contemporary black authors are Maya Angelou, Toni Morrison, and Edwidge Danticat.

Major General Benjamin F. Butler was given permission to set up a volunteer army based on Ship Island. His plan was to set up a camp there, from where he and his army would then take control of Mobile, Alabama, and eventually New Orleans. Butler brought two regiments with him from the North. Other troops followed; but most of the white regiments came and went in a matter of days or weeks. In contrast, a unit of black soldiers, referred to as the Louisiana Native Guard, assembled on Ship Island and stayed there for three years.

The Native Guard arrived in 1863. The unit was made up of recent slaves and those who had been previously freed. They mostly came from Louisiana, especially the New Orleans area. When the Native Guard moved onto Ship Island, they were met with hostilities from white Union soldiers already stationed there. Noting that the tension between the two groups was counterproductive, the military leaders eventually decided to remove the white Union soldiers to other outposts, leaving the black Native Guard the only army unit there.

The prison situation on Ship Island was first set up in 1862. The prison was used for Confederate prisoners of war as well as for Union soldiers who had committed serious crimes. The number of prisoners on the island peaked in April 1865. By June of that year, all prisoners had been sent to other locations.

Life for the Native Guard soldiers was not easy on Ship Island. They had to endure stifling heat, powerful thunderstorms, mosquitoes, and a lot of blowing sand. Health issues led to the deaths of many of the soldiers, including both prisoners and guards. From among the Confederate prisoners, 153 died; from among the Union side, 232 died on the island. In all, over 180,000 African Americans fought in 163 different units during the Civil War.

At the time of the Civil War, Ship Island was one solid island. However, in 1969, Hurricane Camille, a major storm that hit the Mississippi shore, split the island in two. The islands are now called East Ship Island and West Ship Island. Today, West Ship Island is a tourist attraction. In 2005, Hurricane Katrina caused a thirty-foot wave surge that washed over the island, taking most buildings, notably except Fort Massachusetts, with it.

Fort Massachusetts

Fort Massachusetts, on Ship Island, provides the setting for Trethewey's poem. The fort, a sort of horseshoe-shaped structure, sits on the edge of the water on West Ship Island (formerly the western side of Ship Island). Construction of the fort began in 1859. Two years later, through the work of a hundred-man crew of masons and carpenters, the stone walls stood approximately eight feet high. That same year, Mississippi seceded from the Union, and a band of Confederate militia stormed the island and took over the incomplete fort. A short battle was fought on the island in 1861, when the Union battleship USS *Massachusetts* drew up to the island and exchanged fire with that band of Confederate soldiers, who had brought cannons to the half-built fort. Neither side declared a victory. Shortly afterward, in the middle of September, the Confederate soldiers abandoned the fort and the island completely.

By the middle of 1862 the Union occupied Ship Island and its still half-built fort, with about 18,000 troops stationed there off and on. The U.S. Army Corps of Engineers resumed the construction of the fort at this time and also erected forty other buildings that were used as hospitals, barracks, and a mess hall. The construction on the fort continued until 1866, at which time the fort remained incomplete. It has been assumed that the fort was referred to as Fort Massachusetts in honor of the first Union ship to try to take control of the island, though the name was not officially applied.

Today, Fort Massachusetts is a tourist attraction. With time and saltwater having worn away at the mortar holding the stones together, a restoration project was established in 2001. Although it was completely inundated with water during Hurricane Katrina in 2005, the fort remains a strong reminder of the past.

Major Francis E. Dumas

Major Dumas was one the highest-ranking African American soldiers to see battle in the Civil War. He was an educated man who spoke five languages, including English and French, and a rich plantation owner who had his own slaves. He freed and then enlisted one hundred of his slaves and created his own band in the Native Guard. From January to July 1863, Dumas served on Ship Island. After retiring from the military, Dumas became involved in politics in Louisiana, losing by two votes in seeking his party's nomination to run for governor in 1868.

Overview of African Americans Involved in the Civil War

It has been estimated that by the end of the Civil War, at least 180,000 African Americans were enlisted in the Union army, representing about 10 percent of servicemen. Many of these soldiers served in artillery and infantry like their white counterparts, but the African American soldiers had to cope with the extra burden of prejudice. Their pay was considerably less than that of their white counterparts, with many black soldiers earning only half the pay of the white soldiers. And although they were trained to fight and eventually proved their courage and ability, black soldiers were often given the dirtiest of jobs to complete in camp. Statistics concerning mortalities estimate that one-third of all black soldiers who served during the Civil War lost their lives. African American soldiers were part of almost every major battle between 1863 and 1864. The most famous battle in which black troops fought was the confrontation at Fort Wagner in South Carolina on July 18, 1863. There, a black regiment volunteered to climb the walls of the fort and engage in hours of hand-to-hand combat with Confederate soldiers. Although they were eventually driven back, the black soldiers were highly commended for their bravery. Another impressive battle, one in which fourteen black soldiers received the Medal of Honor, occurred at New Market Heights, Virginia, on September 29, 1864.

Civil War

On December 20, 1860, after Abraham Lincoln was elected president of the United States and declared that the U.S. government could not endure slavery, South Carolina seceded from the Union. Within two months, the states of Mississippi, Florida, Alabama, Georgia, Louisiana, and Texas followed. A few months later, on February 9, 1861, the Confederate States of America was formed, with Jefferson Davis as its president. This act in and of itself did not mark the beginning of the Civil War; that would follow on April 12, 1861, when the Confederates fired cannons on Fort Sumter, off the shores of Charleston, South Carolina, which had previously been controlled by Union forces. Five days later, Virginia also seceded from the Union, as followed by Arkansas, Tennessee, and North Carolina. For four bloody years, battles were fought up and down the East Coast. After casualties of an estimated 360,000 Union soldiers and

258,000 Confederate soldiers, General Robert E. Lee surrendered his Confederate army to General Ulysses S. Grant on April 9, 1865. In a sign of victory for the Union, on April 10, 1865, the American flag was raised over Fort Sumter, where the war began. Lincoln was shot by John Wilkes Boothe at Ford's Theatre, in Washington, D.C., on April 14, 1865.

CRITICAL OVERVIEW

Trethewey's collection *Native Guard* has been critically acclaimed and was awarded the 2007 Pulitzer Prize for Poetry. The collection contains poems about Trethewey's relationship with her mother (who was murdered when Trethewey was a teenager), the poet's biracial experience in Mississippi, and the racial history of Mississippi. The latter topic is explored in the collection's title poem. Donna Seaman, writing in *Booklist*, describes Trethewey's collection as "exacting and resonant." Seaman pays special attention to the title poem and comments on how harrowing some of the images contained in "Native Guard" are. She refers to Trethewey's "bayonet-sharp lyrics" and "loaded phrases and philosophical metaphors."

Ange Mlinko, writing in *Poetry* magazine, states that "Native Guard" attempts to bring together "the racial and the rational, as if to heal the old irrational wound inflicted by the state." This is a reference to the lack of a memorial to recognize the sacrifices that the Native Guard made during the Civil War. Although Mlinko applauds Trethewey's attempts to memorialize the black soldiers, she finds that Trethewey's form becomes a little "too pat" in the process.

David Wojahn, writing in the *Southern Review*, finds that "Native Guard" is "a superbly rendered group of unrhymed sonnets." The *Black Issues Book Review* critic Kelly Norman Ellis in turn describes Trethewey as a "technically sound poet" whose sequence of verses in "Native Guard" demonstrates "a masterful weaving of sound and sense." Ellis concludes with the statement that in Trethewey's poems, "each word, each line represents syllables uttered in the mouths of those silenced by grief, pain and history."

Another reviewer who finds reasons to praise Trethewey's poetry is Darryl Lorenzo Wellington, writing for the *Washington Post*.

Wellington states that the poet "has a gift for squeezing the contradictions of the South into very tightly controlled lines." Regarding the title poem and its sonnet sequence, Wellington remarks, "The graceful form conceals a gritty subject." In conclusion, the reviewer states that Trethewey still has room to improve her written voice, as the poet "may have only scratched the surface of her remarkable talent."

"What matters most in Trethewey's poem," writes the critic Carrie Shipers for the *Prairie Schooner*, "is the muscular eloquence of its first-person speaker." After lauding the poet behind that voice, Shipers states, "In lesser hands, this poem might have allowed the historical information to become a burden instead of an incentive." Trethewey, however, uses restraint, allowing the reader "to experience the speaker's consciousness rather than merely to imagine it." Shipers also finds that "the major stength of these poems is the compelling connections Trethewey makes between personal experience and cultural memory."

CRITICISM

Joyce Hart

Hart is a published author of more than twenty books. In this essay, she examines the various examples of irony that the speaker in "Native Guard" exposes.

In Trethewey's poem "Native Guard," the speaker sometimes implicitly and sometimes explicitly draws attention to the irony of his life and of the situations that he finds himself in. Some of the ironies are simple, some rather complex. Some of them are slightly baffling, while others are downright lethal. The one thing they all have in common is the power to make readers stop and think.

Irony can take various forms. One type of irony can be depicted as the difference between what is said and what is meant. This type of irony is sometimes referred to as sarcasm, occurring, for example, when a speaker tells a person that he or she looks good when it is obvious that the person is ridiculously disheveled. The speaker in this instance did not really mean what he said. Another type of irony can be reflected through the difference between what is expected and what actually occurs. This form is called situational irony, and it is this form

WHAT DO I READ NEXT?

IF HISTORY DOES NOT RECORD TRUTH, WHAT

DOES IT RECORD?"

- In 2002, Trethewey published her second collection of poems, *Bellocq's Ophelia*. The collection is narrated by a light-skinned biracial woman who works as a prostitute in New Orleans prior to World War I.

- Elizabeth Alexander is a poet, playwright, and essayist. Her 2005 collection of poems *American Sublime* was a runner-up for the 2006 Pulitzer Prize. The poems in this collection cover various aspects of African American lives in the nineteenth century.

- Joyce Pettis's *African American Poets: Lives, Works, and Sources* (2002) provides readers with a quick snapshot of poets from the eighteenth century to today. Some of the poets included in this book are Maya Angelou, Paul Laurence Dunbar, Nikki Giovanni, and Jupiter Hammon. The book contains biographical as well as critical material.

- The poet Ai, who describes herself as a mix of African American, Japanese, and Native American, won the National Book Award for her collection of poems *Vice* (1999). In this collection, Ai takes on the voices of famous characters (such as Marilyn Monroe and the legendary comedian Lenny Bruce) as well as lesser-known common criminals.

- *The Classic Slave Narratives* (2002), edited by the renowned scholar Henry Louis Gates, Jr., provides readers with some of the best of the written personal accounts of slavery. Thousands of these narratives have been chronicled; Gates provides four of the most outstanding ones.

that is most prevalent and significant in Trethewey's poem. An example of situational irony might be when a straight-A student fails to pass a final exam in math while an almost-failing student earns the highest grade on that same exam. The math teacher might then state that this outcome is indeed ironic.

Throughout Trethewey's poem, the speaker appears to be constantly amazed at the turns in his life. These turns sometimes send him in a direction 180 degrees different from where he had expected to go. Through these ironic twists of fate, the speaker comes to some interesting conclusions about life. The speaker finds that although on the surface, people can appear to be quite different from one another, everyone faces ironic changes, which can transfer a person from what he was into what he never guessed he would become. In this way, the speaker discovers that on some deeper level, everyone is equal.

The first ironic statement of this poem occurs in the first verse, when the speaker talks of wanting freedom. While one might expect the speaker to be happy to simply enjoy his freedom once he has it, he expresses that he wished to retain that feeling of wanting even after being released from bondage. The memories of having been a slave are so profound that he cannot shake them—but the speaker even says that he does not want to shake them. He wants to remember them all. He is free now, but he is not like other free men who have never been slaves. Free men who have never been enslaved do not even think of themselves as free because they were born that way. Only those who have been released from slavery truly know what it feels like to be free. The speaker's freedom is much more intense because he has known slavery.

In the same first verse is another irony, this one making reference to history. While the speaker was a slave, his history was scrawled across his back, imposed by the whips of his master. The whip was the tool of discipline, the voice of the master, which was imposed upon the slave through torture. After he is freed, however, the speaker voices his new history with a pen and ink. With the markings of the whip, his history was interpreted through symbolism, scars that could arouse sympathy or disgust. That history was imposed by some other voice, one that made the speaker of the poem submissive. With a pen and ink, though, the story can be better represented, in words that tell a story that is closer to the truth, as the speaker conjures them through his own voice. The irony is that the pen, as the speaker clarifies it, helps to dull the marks (and therefore the previous history) of the whip. The master now, who once was the primary voice, is put in a subjugated role because the pen allows the freed slave to find his own voice. If considered in isolation, the whip would seem more powerful or lethal than the pen—but as symbols, the pen, which finally gives the speaker a voice, proves to be the more powerful. This is because the pen tells the truth. People can look at a slave's back and think that the slave was whipped because he did not obey his master or because he had done some dreadful wrong. At the same time, the slave might know that the scars on his back are a sign of injustice. The whip marks, in other words, can be interpreted in many different ways. They are abstractions of events that are not clearly defined. They also are only read when and if the slave removes his shirt, which means that not many people ever see them. But when the slave writes his story down on paper, there is not such a wide margin of interpretation. Words are more specific. If published, they also are communicated to a wider audience. Whereas the whip insinuates that the master is the more powerful, the written story of a slave can tell another side of the story. The slave has feelings. The slave is human and is deserving of civil rights. So with a pen and the knowledge of written language, the slave turns out to have a much more powerful weapon than the master had with his whip.

In the second verse, the speaker points out the irony of his freedom. He has been released from the plantation; but he has found that he is in the hands of yet another master. This one is the army sergeant, who yells and demands that the freed slaves obey him under threat of yet other punishments. How free is he, the speaker wonders, if he must bend himself to the sergeant's demands? And although he is in the army, he is not really a soldier, as he is not given a gun. Instead he is handed a shovel to dig ditches. The irony here is that he is given the title of soldier and yet he is no more than a laborer, as he was before when he was still a slave. In actuality, he has neither more freedom nor more responsibility or trust. His title has switched from slave to soldier, but this changes only the name of things. He is still belittled by derogative words and still discriminated against in terms of food and salary. As the poet ends this verse, Trethewey brings out the fact that the speaker, a black freed slave, has confiscated a Confederate man's journal, writing his story over the white man's. The two lives do not parallel one another, but rather they intersect, barely touching one another, only momentarily crossing. Both men have lives, and they are both human, but they do not seem to share much common ground. An irony here, then, is that the two men do share a degree of common ground, as the rest of the poem will reveal. Their lives are very much the same, especially as the Civil War rages on.

In the third verse, the speaker comments on the irony of his having taken a ship called the *Northern Star*, a ship that transports him to Ship Island, where Fort Massachusetts awaits him. Both the *Northern Star* and Fort Massachusetts remind him of the North of the United States, which stands as a symbol of freedom for slaves. It is the slave's dream to be taken out of bondage and freed in the North, where people supposedly await with open arms, ready to take off the chains and shackles from the slave's feet and hands. But these Northern names do not mean freedom for the speaker. The ship merely transports the speaker from one form of slavery to another. The fort might shelter the speaker from the rain, but it does not remove his shackles. It is at this point in the poem that the speaker sees the irony of life, how all the soldiers, white or black, freed or never enslaved, are all entrapped by their fate and are therefore equal.

Another ironic situation, perhaps the most ironic of all in this poem, is the fact presented in the fifth verse, where the speaker ponders the weird position in which he finds himself—that of guarding former white slave masters. Who would have imagined such a situation just a few years ago? What slave would even have dared to think of it? Added to this ironic situation is the fact that the speaker, a short time ago a slave, is now recording these white soldiers' words and thoughts because he, the former slave, is literate and the white soldiers, his people's former masters, are not. The white prisoners cannot even sign their names. These white men, who not long ago denied the possibility that black people were human, now have to trust that this black soldier will write to their loved ones the personal desires that they are expressing. The white men must learn to trust this man who was once a slave, who was beaten with a whip and treated like a mule, with their most intimate feelings. They must open their hearts before this man, whom they once thought did not even own a heart.

The poem ends on another ironic note. Although the speaker writes letters to the loved ones of the deceased, he is told not to tell them the whole truth. There is an understanding among the military leaders that the details of war should not be shared with those who have not experienced the horrors. If the full truth of war were to be revealed to all, what would happen? Would people become alarmed and upset and demand that no more wars be fought? If they were to learn of the massacres that happened while the soldiers waved the white flag of surrender, would people then declare the war unfair? If they were to know that animals ate the remains of their loved ones, would they demand that laws be made to stop all future wars? Were these the concerns of the generals of this war when they demanded that secrets be kept? Were they saying that war is so brutal that even they cannot admit to the truth? Is the most pointed irony revealed when the poet repeats the poem's final phrase? Is some truth too difficult to be swallowed? If history does not record truth, what does it record?

Source: Joyce Hart, Critical Essay on "Native Guard," in *Poetry for Students*, Gale, Cengage Learning, 2009.

Pearl Amelia McHaney

In the following excerpt from an interview, McHaney and Trethewey discuss the poet's 2007 Pulitzer Prize–winning collection of poetry, Native Guard.

. . . *Trethewey:* When I first started thinking about writing *Native Guard,* it was my interest in the history of the Louisiana Native Guards that got me going. I had gone out to visit my grandmother in Gulfport, right after I started my first job at Auburn University. I took her out to lunch at a restaurant on the beach and I was talking to her about a creative writing assignment that I was going to give my students in which you get them to write about a time when a relative met someone famous. I was telling her that I was going to do this assignment, too, about her

> **I THINK WRITING SOME OF THE ELEGIES AND PERHAPS EVEN THINKING ABOUT MY PLACE IN THE SOUTH HAD A LOT TO DO WITH APPROACHING THE ANNIVERSARY OF MY MOTHER'S DEATH."**

story, about the time her brother, my great-uncle, met Al Capone. Uncle Hubert was a bell-hop at a hotel on the beach, and he shook Al Capone's hand. Al Capone used to go down there when he was running a gambling joint out of the fort at Ship Island. As I am telling my grandmother this, there's a woman who is listening the whole time to our conversation. And I think it is particularly important to mention because of what she said that this is a white woman listening to our conversation. And as she gets up to leave the restaurant, she leans over and she says, "I think there is something else you need to know about Ship Island." It was very much like she was saying, "There's this other history about these black soldiers that you should know as part of your history as well," and so she told me about them. I went right away to the Gulfport Public library to try to look up something about them. And the first thing I found was a small mention in someone's M.A. thesis. And then later on of course I found the full length monograph by James G. Hollandsworth that I mention in the Notes in the book as well as the published diary of the colonel who was stationed there that C. P. Weaver edited. But I was interested in this because I had been going out to that island my whole life and the park rangers don't mention anything about the black presence on the island. There isn't any marker mentioning the Native Guards or their presence the way there is for the Confederate soldiers who were imprisoned there. And that suggested to me a kind of historical erasure from the manmade monumental landscape. I was interested in telling that story, telling a fuller version of our story as Americans in this pivotal moment in history.

McHaney: You said that originally you thought you were working on poems that would lead to two separate books, about the Louisiana Native Guards and then the ones that become the elegies for your mother Gwendolyn Ann Turnbough. When did you realize the confluence of the two projects? When did you realize that these personal poems could successfully frame the public poems about the Louisiana Native Guards?

Trethewey: That took a long time for me to recognize. When I went to Radcliffe on a Bunting Fellowship in 2000, I was still thinking about the soldiers. And I was doing a lot of the research about historical memory, the Civil War, and the idea of what gets memorialized in the form of monuments. It seems to me [it] should have alerted me to something that was on my mind, but it didn't. I was writing, at the same time as these poems, about my mother. Sometimes they would be just a portion of a poem that I wouldn't finish until years later. But I started writing some of them and putting them away in a drawer because I thought, well that's for another thing, another time. I couldn't see how, at the time, they would have anything to do with this larger project that was only about something historical. And maybe because I was coming off the heels of *Bellocq's Ophelia,* still thinking only about a kind of public history, I didn't see the connections, even though what I do in *Bellocq's Ophelia* is to find a way to weave a personal history into what is my imagined history for her.

McHaney: Ophelia moves from in front of the camera, being objectified, to behind the camera, choosing what she takes a picture of, what she sees. It is a similar kind of movement.

Trethewey: Right, the same kind of journey I was taking, but I didn't know that. I did start publishing a lot of those elegies, but I was still thinking they didn't belong. I think I remember at one point feeling that I was coming close to having a new book, and there I was writing all of those things, and I started to think, well, could they go together? But I still didn't know.

McHaney: Didn't know that you would be able to have a first section that were the elegies to your mother and that at the same time they were leading to the Native Guards poems and then that they would be so interwoven by the third section?

Trethewey: Well, I started thinking that a poem like "Miscegenation" and some poems that I was writing about my own personal history as a biracial person growing up in the deep South had a connection to the history of the Native Guards because I saw that the umbrella over them was something about the South. I still

hadn't connected those elegies for my mother. In the meantime, I was living here in Atlanta. Returning to the landscape that was haunted by the tragedy of my mother's death made me write these elegies. I wrote a poem for the book early on called "Graveyard Blues" after jogging through the little Decatur cemetery and being overwhelmed by all the names of the dead. I am one of those people who can't just walk through a graveyard. I feel like I have to read every single name that presents itself to me, and it seemed like a good metaphor for the insistence of history, or for the insistence of people to be heard or their stories to be told, or even their names to be registered or spoken. And so even seeing those names, I was still thinking: this is about history. But the poem I wrote was about the memory of the day we buried my mother. The final image in the poem, the final two lines, reads:

I wander now among names of the dead:
My mother's name, stone pillow for my head.

That's an image of hard, or cold comfort. I might want to lie my head down on my mother's stone and that would be a kind of comfort, but one that was stone and cold. A few months later, I could not, I could not simply deal with the fact that I [had] written those two lines in that poem because I felt that whatever obligation I have to truth was being sacrificed by the poem. So I started writing another poem to undo the lie that I told in "Graveyard Blues." My mother does not have a stone or any marker at all. There's no marker, no memorial at her grave, and so I started writing the poem "Monument" because I wanted to tell the reader that I had lied about this. It was stunning to me when I realized that I had, for the sake of one poem, told a lie and needed to fix it in another one. But it was the realization that I needed to fix the lie that made me realize exactly why those elegies to my mother should be in the same book with the Native Guards. Like them, she had no marker.

McHaney: You arrived at it through a kind of journeying; it evolved in a very natural way. Maybe that is one aspect of your genius, the weavings and stitchings and cross-hatchings all together. That was the work that you had to do.

Trethewey: Well, perhaps it is the genius of poetry. Robert Frost said, "No surprise for the writer, no surprise for the reader." It is absolutely true that I didn't set off knowing exactly what I wanted to say, and when I figured it out, it was because the writing of the poems led me to it. It was stunning for me, too, and painfully so.

McHaney: You dedicate Native Guard *to your mother, in memory, and the book is the elegies for your mother, the weaving together the personal and the public histories, the erasures and the monuments and the memorial. And then, moving backward, you dedicated your second book* Bellocq's Ophelia *to your husband, Brett Gadsden, historian, professor of African American Studies at Emory University. And your first book* Domestic Work, *going back further, you dedicated to your father, Eric Trethewey, a poet, who teaches at Hollins University. In* Domestic Work, *the second section of four is dedicated to your mother's mother, your grandmother: "For Leretta Dixon Turnbough, born June 22, 1916," who is still living. Yet, Rita Dove introduces* Domestic Work *saying, that you "resisted the lure of autobiography ... weaving no less than a tapestry of ancestors." In* Domestic Work, *reading it now again, I see many autobiographical seeds.*

Trethewey: Oh, absolutely.

McHaney: But they are masked just as you said earlier. In "Tableau," for example, the beautiful line "—sees for the first time,/the hairline crack/that has begun to split the bowl in half." And there are poems about your father, your Uncle Son and Aunt Sugar. So what changed? Even though you've explained how Native Guard *came about, what changed even in those jottings and those poems that you would so explicitly write about the private anxieties and grief experienced by your family, so that you were no longer passing, in a sense, when you were addressing your bi-raciality, your grief, the tragedies?*

Trethewey: Rita did a wonderful thing for me in writing what she did about the larger public history that is represented by the poems in *Domestic Work*, particularly the "Domestic Work" ... section. When I started writing those, I really just wanted to write about my grandmother who has lived an extraordinary life. So I thought I was doing a very personal family history. But early on I started placing the events of her life within the context of a particular historical moment. Without understanding the depth of my obsessions, I was already, by using dates or other historical events within the poems, working to blend personal or family stories with collective history. Maybe her taking

note of that helped me to see it as a long term obsession of mine.

McHaney: You said a little bit about how being back here in the physical landscape where the tragedies happened didn't let you escape them. Did your studies at University of Massachusetts, Amherst, influence your shift to the autobiographical?

Trethewey: James Tate once said to me to unburden myself of my mother's death and unburden myself of being black and just write about the situation in Northern Ireland. And I was devastated when he said that. John Edgar Wideman said to me, "You have to write about what you have to write about." But at another point some advice that Tate gave me was to just pour my heart out into the poems, and so by the time I was writing *Native Guard*, I was indeed pouring my heart out into the poems. But I was also not abandoning the very things "I'd been given to write," to use Phil Levine's phrase. I don't know what I would have written if I hadn't written about those things that I have been grappling with my whole adult life.

McHaney: You have also said, "We must identify with the despised parts of ourselves."

Trethewey: I think writing some of the elegies and perhaps even thinking about my place in the South had a lot to do with approaching the anniversary of my mother's death. I was approaching the twentieth anniversary, at the same time approaching my fortieth birthday which was the last age my mother ever was, and so I think those things were heavy on my mind. And perhaps returning to the South after many years in the Northeast made me rethink Southern history, American history, and my place in it, because I can get really angry about my South. Though I love it, it has given me plenty of reason to hate it. And one of the things that I hate, not just about the South but the way Americans remember things, is that so much of that memory is based upon a kind of willed forgetting and there's a lot that gets left out— of the historical record, of textbooks, of public monuments. I wanted to tell a fuller version of what stories I have to add to the historical record.

... McHaney: We've talked a little bit about how your work evolved from the third person to the autobiographical observations to reveal the erasures and to memorialize both personal and public history. Yet, the Pulitzer Prize award has shifted

attention away from those national and regional stories and toward your private stories as we've just been talking about. I'd like to return us to that public story that you started with, the Louisiana Native Guards. Can you tell us a bit about Francis E. Dumas and how you discovered and perhaps identified with him?

Trethewey: He was mentioned in James Hollandsworth's book, and the interesting story that Hollandsworth points out about Major Dumas is that as the son of a white plantation father and a mixed race mother, he inherited his father's slaves and plantation when his father died. Apparently he did not want slaves, didn't believe in slavery, but it was illegal to manumit his slaves in Louisiana at the time, so he had them. When the Union was enlisting men for the Native Guards and he joined, he freed his slaves and encouraged those men of age to join as well. And I found that that was a compelling story because it represented what was perhaps a very personal dilemma for him. He and several other free men of color had actually been part of the Native Guards first when it was a Confederate Regiment. I think Hollandsworth mentions that some of the men felt coerced to join, that they felt like they would lose their property if they did not support Louisiana as Confederate soldiers. Perhaps there were some of them that were so into protecting their own and seeing themselves as so distant from the blacks and the slaves that they didn't care, but Dumas was one who did feel differently about slavery and so became a member again when it was resurrected as a Union Regiment.

McHaney: How do you see these ambiguities of Dumas's and of the other Native Guards that had been slaves but now were not slaves and who found themselves guarding the white Confederates, dying at the guns of their fellow Union soldiers?

Trethewey: I think that what Dumas represents, being of mixed blood, is the larger metaphor of the collection that the cover suggests, and that is the intersections of white and black, north and south, slave and free. I was taken by that idea when I found that Colonel Daniels had confiscated a diary from the home of a Confederate and cross-wrote in it because there was a shortage of paper. That intersection was a gift. *Native Guards* is a book about intersections. Those very intersections are in me, in my very blood, they're in the country, they're in the very nature of history.

McHaney: Tell us about the metaphorical meanings of your title, Native Guard.

Trethewey: The literal is obvious: it is after the Louisiana Native Guards. But, I started thinking about what it means to be a native guardian, of not only personal memory but also of collective memory—and that is certainly what poets are often charged with doing, representing the collective memory of a people. And as a native daughter, a native guardian, that is my charge. To my mother and her memory, preservation.

McHaney: The first O.E.D. definition of "guard," that is said now to be obsolete, is ...

Trethewey: ... "to take care." I knew immediately that the title was going to be *Native Guard*, and I thought it was such a gift that these soldiers were actually named that.

McHaney: What is the relationship between a photograph and a poem? You've pointed out elsewhere that you were the first poet at the Duke University Center for Documentary Studies that usually brings historians and documentary film-makers and photographers together. You said that the director, Tom Rankin, "believes that poetry can do the work of documentary and history." You studied photography and theory of photography at the University of Massachusetts at Amherst. How do you see those two things coming together?

Trethewey: I think again that it is a necessary intersection. I had two quotations. Lewis Hine said, "If I could tell the story in words, I wouldn't lug a camera." But Susan Sontag reminds us that "Nevertheless, the camera's rendering of reality must always hide more than it discloses." What this suggests to me is the need for both photograph and story to work together. What has always interested me about a photograph is that even though it seems to capture and elegize a particular moment, there are all the things that swirl around it, things that are cropped out of the frame, that which was just behind it that we don't see. And there is always a fuller version of the story that needs to be told. I believe the photographic image is a way to focus our attention, and it can be the starting point for a larger exploration of what else is there. As much as a photograph is about seeing what is there, it is equally about seeing what has been left out as it points in some way to what we might know if we are willing to imagine or to think about. What's been cropped out or what's not there—words are like that too.

McHaney: That reminds me how important narrative is within your lyric poems. What do you find that poetry can do when you want to tell a story? Why poetry then, and why not fiction?

Trethewey: Because of those elegant envelopes of form that poems are. Because of the music and lyricism and density and compression, poems can be memorable in a way that a long piece of fiction isn't. Not that the language of the novel or story isn't memorable, but the ease with which we might memorize a poem and carry it with us in our heads is appealing to me. The way a poem has a smaller space to fit into, and because that density and compression of a poem crystallizes and intensifies image, emotion, idea, sound.

McHaney: You have said that writing in form helps to avoid sentimentality, that refrain and repetition allow emotional restraint from excess or provide emphasis. Can you speak of your use of form, the ghazal "Miscegenation," the pantoum "Incident," the villanelle "Scenes from a Documentary History of Mississippi, 1. King Cotton, 1907"?

Trethewey: I had been reading the late Shahid Ali's anthology *Ravishing Disunities: Real Ghazals in English.* The introductory essay is so illuminating about what a ghazal is, the qualities of the ghazal. The particular one is the idea of disunity, the idea that these are closed stanzas that don't necessarily support or aim to support narrative or even linear movement, that they are separate, that in the juxtaposition of one stanza to the next is some sort of tension, and excitement can happen. And movement. And also that it is a form that is a kind of call and response—if the form is done traditionally, audiences know, based on where the rhyme appears, when the refrain comes and they say it with the poet. That is an interesting collective thing happening. Also, that the poet is supposed to invoke her own name in the final stanza is the thing that made that poem get written for me. I was thinking about all these disunified things. They were all connected but they were things that I didn't think I could write about in a straight narrative—my Jesus year or my parents breaking laws in Mississippi. These things are part of the same story, but I couldn't imagine a kind of linear narrative poem being able to put all of it together. So it was the idea of "ravishing disunity" that allowed me to do it.

McHaney: I reread the poem looking at each stanza to have it be its own separate unit as you said, and it does; it works perfectly. What about the pantoum, "Incident."

Trethewey: Oh, I loved figuring out that that poem should be a pantoum and that it was suggesting itself to me. At first, it was an extremely different poem. I showed it to my students at Chapel Hill because I was talking to them about revision. I brought in a copy of two poems. One of them was "Incident," and the other was called "Target," one of its horrible pedestrian titles. I was trying to write about the cross burning, and I was writing bad poems about it because I was focusing on the narrative of it, the story of it, trying to tell the story and then figure out what the story meant. Ultimately I knew that poem wasn't working, and I mined it for what seemed to work of the narrative. In doing so, I got the first four lines:

> We tell the story every year—
> how we peered from the windows, shades drawn—
> though nothing really happened,
> the charred grass now green again.

In those first four lines, I get the scene of us peering from the windows while this cross is being burned, but also the lasting effect that it had on us, that need to retell the story, to keep the memory of this event alive. What is exciting about the pantoum or the villanelle, some of those forms, is the kind of mathematical way that they work. They allow you to see other possibilities. That was exciting. I knew I had to pull out those two lines and place them in the next stanza and then to write around them. It freed me from what can be the trap of linear narrative and it allows the poem to circle back on itself. A lot of the poems in *Native Guard* circle back on themselves. My impulse is to tell a story; it was form that made me do something different with storytelling.

McHaney: What is that trap of linear narrative?

Trethewey: When it is not working well, then that story just goes to an end and that end isn't really anywhere.

McHaney: Just a teleological impulse which is to get to the end, whereas your impulse is to circle back because you get a different view from every edge of the circle?

Trethewey: Yes, and to transform the meaning by circling back.

McHaney: I also read that in a pantoum the poet tells two stories, lines two and four become lines one and three in the subsequent stanza and the first two lines of each stanza build one story or theme and lines three and four another theme. In "Incident" the first two lines are the story, the cross itself, what was seen, and the other story is light, and shedding light and looking for understanding of what that was. So the pantoum was successful in form and in meaning both. What of your villanelle, "Scenes from a Documentary History of Mississippi, 1. King Cotton, 1907"?

Trethewey: When I am using a photograph, I begin describing literally what I can see before I move toward any interpretation. And in that first poem in "Scenes," "1. King Cotton, 1907," I saw the flags and the archway made of bales of cotton; I saw clearly those two things in contrast to each other. And I saw how symbolic this was of that historical moment:

> From every corner of the photograph, flags
> wave down
> the main street in Vicksburg. Stacked to
> form an arch,
> the great bales of cotton rise up from the
> ground

McHaney: You have been writing sonnets and blues poems since your first book; has your use of those forms changed over time?

Trethewey: I admire the sonnet form, little envelopes of small space, ten syllables in fourteen lines. You are forced to get rid of the unnecessary, the things that might try to trick you. There's no room for anything extra. You have to select, and what you select you must infuse with meaning. What is kept has energy, offers the right amount of story. Sonnets are traditionally written in iambic pentameter, the equivalent of the natural English voice, and in rhyme. Somehow, I didn't want to impose such a voice or such rhyme onto the speaker in "Native Guard." I am thinking also about the poems of Agi Mishol and Elizabeth Alexander who write about historical erasures in their cultural experiences. Mishol's poem "Woman Martyr" tells the story of the suicide bomber Andaleeb Takatka, but Mishol says it is not about Takatka, that poetry is always about language.

Rita Dove referred to a "syncopated attitude of the blues" in the poems of *Domestic Work*. I thought that sounded really wonderful and then I realized the real insight of Rita's comment. "Syncopate," in its simplest definition, means to shorten, usually by omitting something, like I described leaving out the unnecessary. But when you talk about syncopation in music, it is putting the stress on the typically unaccented note, putting the accent in an unexpected place, and in poetry, infusing the poems with a syncopated rhythm would be putting emphasis where one would not only not expect it, but would not want it—on the historical erasures, the bi-raciality, the circumstances of the Louisiana Native Guards who could read and write better than their white prisoners . . .

Source: Pearl Amelia McHaney, "An Interview with Natasha Trethewey," in *Five Points: A Journal of Literature and Art*, Vol. 11, No. 3, September 2007, pp. 97–115.

Ange Mlinko

In the following review, Mlinko discusses the three-part structure of Native Guard.

But what of elegiac works that reject the premise of art's enchantment? At barely fifty pages, *Native Guard* nevertheless aspires to monumentality, memorializing both Trethewey's mother, murdered at the hands of her stepfather, and the Louisiana Native Guards, one of the first black Civil War regiments.

Native Guard is structured like a dialectic, in three parts: the autobiographical as thesis, the historical as antithesis, and the intertwining of the personal and the historical as synthesis. First she limns her relationship with her mother, who dies; then she imaginatively reconstructs the experience of the Native Guards in the 1860's; finally, in the strongest section, she combines the personal and the historical in recollections of her childhood in the South in the explosive sixties. The dialectic is used to allegorize her very person: Trethewey is a synthesis of a black mother and white father. Their marriage was illegal in Mississippi, and her birth thereby illegitimate. But the illegitimate daughter refuses to give up her legacy, which encompasses the land and its history, its mess and its murderousness. She comes back again and again, rooted to the source of trauma, and in an act of equal parts reconciliation and defiance, creates a tribute for the Native Guards, whom the state has neglected to memorialize whatsoever.

The story is heroic; the architecture is contained. Between the dialectical structure and the variety of carefully crafted patterns she brings to the matter—blues, ghazal, villanelle, sonnet, and even an ingenious palindrome—Trethewey brings together race and ratio, or the racial and the rational, as if to heal the old irrational wound inflicted by the state. However, the insistence on symmetry and pattern becomes too pat, such as when she sets the book up to begin and end with passages to Gulfport. "Theories of Time and Space," her opener, seems written solely to launch the plot:

> You can get there from here, though
> there's no going home.
> Everywhere you go will be somewhere
> you've never been. Try this:
> head south on Mississippi 49, one-
> by-one mile markers ticking off
> another minute of your life. Follow this
> to its natural conclusion—dead end

Sprezzatura this is not. Like Lowell in *Life Studies* or *For the Union Dead*, Trethewey does some heavy lifting, and taking poetic flight is not an option when you are ruled so fatefully by reality, by facts. Although it is almost unacceptable to say so (*say it!*) monuments are by definition static and therefore risk being staid. Memorial art is of a piece with death, at least if you think, like me, that even representations should be allowed their portion of autonomy. If the poem is simply a vehicle, a means to an end, there's no need to ensure that every line conveys vitality, but only that it communicates its point.

Then again, as a first-generation American who's done my share of bouncing around, what do I know about passionate attachment to a native land? When Trethewey dreams that she is being photographed (in whiteface) with the Fugitive poets and they turn on her with the question, "*You don't hate the South?*" ("Pastoral"), I am moved by the drama's authentic strangeness. Elsewhere, I admire the force of a transverse association: in "Miscegenation" she tells us that her name, Natasha, means "Christmas child" in Russian. A few pages later, the cross that is burned on her lawn one night is "trussed like a Christmas tree" and the whole phantasmagoric scene has the effect of a nightmare version of *The Nutcracker*. There's a lot of portentous symbolism in *Native Guard*, but that unforeseen jeté redeems poems weighed down with message.

I blame Lowell's legacy for the traps that snare Trethewey in a sometimes suffocating elision of closed form, close relations, and closeted history. Trethewey does not match the knowing egocentrism of lines like "I myself am hell" or "I am tired. Everyone's tired of my turmoil." Implicit in her project, though, is Lowell's pinched notion that poetry begins with a psychological "I," piquing prurient curiosity, then elevates that "I" beyond memoir by placing it in a larger context of recovering cultural memory. It's a formula by now, and it wasn't a good idea even when it was new: it reinforces the prejudice against "mere" poetry (lyric, that trivial thing) by requiring that poetry keep memory alive or raise consciousness. If poetry does want to achieve those things, it also has to give us new ways of experiencing pleasure, which, after all, is what makes lyric impossible to ignore.

Source: Ange Mlinko, Review of *Native Guard*, in *Poetry*, Vol. 191, No. 1, October 2007, pp. 59–61.

Carrie Shipers

In the following excerpt, Shipers discusses the power of the past in her review of Trethewey's Native Guard.

"Why the rough edge of beauty?" asks the poem "Photograph: Ice Storm, 1971," in the first section of *Native Guard*, Natasha Trethewey's third collection. The answer offered throughout the book is grief, an emotion explored in permutations ranging from the intensely personal to the historical. The first section of the book takes bereavement, specifically the speaker's loss of her mother, as its subject. In "What the Body Can Say," the speaker considers several familiar gestures—the posture of grief or prayer as well as "the raised thumb / that is both a symbol of agreement and the request / for a ride," the raised fingers of the peace sign—and concludes:

> What matters is context—
> the side of the road, or that my mother
>   wanted
> something I still can't name: what, kneeling,
> my face behind my hands, I might ask of
>   God.

Intertwined with grief for the loss of the mother is grief for loss of an integral part of the self, of one's history, and of the opportunity to better understand who and what we have lost. As in "Theories of Time and Space," the poem that acts as the book's preface, the meditations on grief in the first third of *Native Guard* ask what *home* means after we have left, as well as what happens when our home leaves us or refuses to acknowledge our claim to it.

The question of home is also central to the book's second section, which takes as its epigraph a quote from Nina Simone: "Everybody knows about Mississippi." What the speaker in these poems knows, however, is necessarily partial and subjective. In the poem "Pilgrimage," the speaker spends the night in Vicksburg, a city, like many in the South, that uses Civil War history as a tourist attraction. Trethewey writes, "In my dream, / the ghost of history lies down beside me, / / rolls over, pins me beneath a heavy arm." The subtlety of the speaker's claims resonates throughout this collection: it is the ghost of history, not history itself, that torments her, and it does so in dreams, which speaks to the difficulty of vanquishing such ghosts in waking hours. The specificity with which Trethewey approaches the question of Mississippi history, particularly with regard to race, allows these poems to make claims that might otherwise—and that arguably have been—ignored for many years.

Also contained within this second section is a crown of free-verse sonnets from which the collection takes its title and which commemorates the Louisiana Native Guards, one of the first black regiments to fight for the Union during the Civil War. Notes in the back of the book offer more specific historical information about the experiences of these soldiers, but what matters most in Trethewey's poem is the muscular eloquence of its first-person speaker, a man who records what he sees and thinks in a used journal stolen from a Confederate home, a man who relies on ink rather than "the lure / of memory—flawed, changeful—that dulls the lash / for the master, sharpens it for the slave." In another section of the poem, the speaker recounts how he uses his skill at writing to serve the Union and the other men in his regiment.

... In lesser hands, this poem might have allowed the historical information to become a burden instead of an incentive, but Trethewey's poetic restraint allows us to experience the speaker's consciousness rather than merely to imagine it. The poem's final sentence, "Truth be told" encapsulates the speaker's earnest desire to preserve his understanding of the war, but it also speaks to what Trethewey accomplishes in this poem—she tells a story that matters as only

the truth can. To speak of these things—or to write of them, as do Trethewey and this speaker—does not mitigate the harm of slavery or the hardships suffered by black soldiers at the hands of their white superiors, but it does give voice to an overlooked portion of the historical record.

Many of Trethewey's poems insist that our history is inescapable, even—perhaps especially when—we most want to escape it. The third section of *Native Guard* examines the paradoxical complexities of Mississippi's racial history and how it intertwines with the speaker's personal experiences. In "My Mother Dreams Another Country," Trethewey writes.

... The major strength of these poems is the compelling connections Trethewey makes between personal experience and cultural memory. If these poems are confessional—and I mean that without the implied pejorative often attached to the term—their success lies not only in their specificity but in the enormous control evidenced in their lines. This control extends not only to the poet's use of language, her insistence on using the right word even when it is an ugly one, but also to the variety of forms that are used in the book. Trethewey employs, among others, the pantoum, the villanelle, the ghazal, the blues lyric, and the traditional rhyming quatrain, and she does so while maintaining a sense of precision in every line.

The book's final poem, "South," draws together the book in a poem that is both an elegy for Mississippi's troubled racial history and a personal declaration of defiance...

Source: Carrie Shipers, Review of *Native Guard*, in *Prairie Schooner*, Vol. 80, No. 4, Winter 2006, pp. 199–201.

SOURCES

Ellis, Kelly Norman, Review of *Native Guard*, in *Black Issues Book Review*, Vol. 8, No. 2, March–April 2006, p. 19.

Heidler, David S., and Jeanne T. Heidler, eds., *Encyclopedia of the American Civil War: A Political, Social, and Military History*, Norton, 2000.

Mlinko, Ange, "More Than Meets the I," in *Poetry*, Vol. 191, No. 1, October 2007, pp. 56–72.

Seaman, Donna, Review of *Native Guard*, in *Booklist*, Vol. 102, No. 11, February 1, 2006, p. 22.

Shipers, Carrie, Review of *Native Guard*, in *Prairie Schooner*, Vol. 80, No. 4, Winter 2006, pp. 199–201.

Solomon, Debra, "Native Daughter," in *New York Times Magazine*, May 13, 2007, p. 15.

Trethewey, Natasha, "Native Guard," in *Native Guard*, Houghton Mifflin, 2006, pp. 25–30.

Wellington, Darryl Lorenzo, "My Bondage, My Freedom: In Her Third Collection, a Poet Plumbs Public and Personal Histories," in *Washington Post*, April 16, 2006, p. T4.

Wojahn, David, "History Shaping Selves: Four Poets," in *Southern Review*, Vol. 43, No. 1, Winter 2007, pp. 218–32.

FURTHER READING

Andrews, William, and Henry Louis Gates, Jr., eds. *Slave Narratives*, Library of America, 2000.
> This book includes ten classic slave narratives from such people as Sojourner Truth, Frederick Douglass, and Nat Turner. The material was gathered from stories told from 1772 up until the end of the Civil War.

Berlin, Ira, Joseph P. Reidy, and Leslie S. Rowland, eds., *Freedom's Soldiers: The Black Military Experience in the Civil War*, Cambridge University Press, 1998.
> The editors of this volume researched the National Archives and found letters and eye-witness accounts of black soldiers' experiences in the war. This book invites readers to share the experiences through first-person narratives.

Hollandsworth, James G., Jr., *The Louisiana Native Guards: The Black Military Experience during the Civil War*, Louisiana State University Press, 1998.
> Hollandsworth, through careful research, put together a thorough social and political history of the Native Guard regiments of the Union army.

Rampersad, Arnold, *The Oxford Anthology of African-American Poetry*, Oxford University Press, 2006.
> The material in this collection covers a full range of thoughts and reflections about the African American experience. Some poets in this collection state that it is better to die than grow up black in America, whereas others celebrate their lives.

Ritterhouse, Jennifer, *Growing Up Jim Crow: How Black and White Southern Children Learned Race*, University of North Carolina Press, 2006.
> This book covers the period from shortly after slavery ended in the 1860s to before the Civil Rights Movement of the 1950s began. This era in the South was dominated by Jim Crow laws that were established by whites to continue the subjugation of African Americans living in the South.

The Night Piece: To Julia

ROBERT HERRICK

1648

Robert Herrick's "The Night Piece: To Julia" is a twenty-line lyric poem in which the speaker addresses a woman he desires, imploring her to visit him at night for a love tryst. In the poem, he assures her of the safety of the walk through country fields she would take to reach him. On the surface it is a witty, unassumingly innocent, even childlike song of seduction graced by dainty metrics and musical rhyme, qualities that inform all Herrick's lyrics. "The Night Piece: To Julia" also suggests a spell woven by the poet to ensure not only the physical safety of his mistress on her walk to his quarters but also her moral or spiritual innocence.

"The Night Piece: To Julia" first appeared in 1648 in Herrick's only collection published during his lifetime, *Hesperides; or, The Works Both Humane and Divine of Robert Herrick*, a gathering of some 1,400 of Herrick's secular and religious verses. "The Night Piece: To Julia" also appears in *Selected Poems: Robert Herrick* (2003).

AUTHOR BIOGRAPHY

The exact date of his birth is unknown, but Robert Herrick's baptism was recorded on August 24, 1591. A year later his father, Nicholas, a wealthy goldsmith, committed suicide the day after he wrote his will, declaring his soundness of mind but illness of body. After his father's death, Herrick's mother, Julian, kept

Robert Herrick (*International Portrait Gallery*)

Devon. With the beginning, in 1642, of the English Civil War, which set Parliament against king and Presbyterian Christianity against the more hierarchical and established Anglican Church, Herrick lost his position. He then lived in Westminster, in London, dependent upon his friends and family for support. In London, Herrick occupied himself with his poetry. He issued a collection of verse, *Hesperides; or, The Works Both Humane and Divine of Robert Herrick* (the only collection published in his lifetime), in 1648, dedicating the volume to the Prince of Wales, who became Charles II after the restoration of the monarchy with the fall of the Commonwealth in 1660. Herrick regained the vicarage in Devon in 1662, as appointed by King Charles II. Herrick remained vicar of Dean Prior until his death in October 1674—the exact date is not known—at the age of eighty-three. Herrick never married. He is buried in an unmarked grave in the Dean Prior churchyard; a commemorative tablet and a stained glass window are inscribed to him in the church.

her youngest boy and daughter with her but sent Robert and three of his brothers to live with their uncle William Herrick. The young Robert may have attended the Westminster School as a boy or the Merchant Taylors' School. There is no definitive record, but an early poem, written around 1612 to his brother Thomas, shows the young poet as a well-educated youth. At sixteen he probably became a goldsmith and jeweler's apprentice to his cousin, William Pearson. In 1613, after serving for five years, Herrick left the apprenticeship and entered St. John's College, Cambridge, receiving his BA in 1617 and his MA in 1620. In London, where Herrick was supposed to be studying law, he became associated with a group of lyric poets who frequented taverns, honed their craft, and called themselves the Tribe of Ben because of their admiration for the poet and dramatist Ben Jonson (1572–1637). Herrick, in fact, wrote a number of lyrics celebrating and even sanctifying Jonson.

Politically, Herrick supported King Charles I and opposed his Puritan and parliamentary adversaries. Herrick was ordained deacon and priest in the Church of England in April 1623 and became chaplain to the Duke of Buckingham in 1627. Two years later, after returning from an unsuccessful military expedition with Buckingham, Herrick was made vicar of the parish of Dean Prior in

POEM TEXT

> Her eyes the glow-worm lend thee;
> The shooting stars attend thee;
>   And the elves also,
>   Whose little eyes glow
> Like the sparks of fire, befriend thee.   5
>
> No will-o'-the-wisp mis-light thee;
> Nor snake or slow-worm bite thee;
>   But on, on thy way,
>   Not making a stay,
> Since ghost there's none to affright thee.   10
>
> Let not the dark thee cumber;
> What though the moon does slumber?
>   The stars of the night
>   Will lend thee their light,
> Like tapers clear without number.   15
>
> Then, Julia, let me woo thee,
> Thus, thus to come unto me;
>   And when I shall meet
>   Thy silv'ry feet,
> My soul I'll pour into thee.   20

POEM SUMMARY

Stanza 1

The first of the four stanzas, each with five lines, begins deceptively with a reference to a woman's

MEDIA ADAPTATIONS

- The English composer Roger Quilter (1877–1953) set "The Night Piece: To Julia" to music around 1901. It is available on *Roger Quilter: Songs, Vol. 2* (1995).

eyes. Reasonable expectation, considering that the poem is called "The Night Piece: To Julia," can lead the reader to think that these words refer to Julia's eyes, that the poem is beginning with a conventional tribute to the poet's beloved. By the end of the line, however, it is clear that the first words refer not to Julia's eyes but to the eyes of a glowworm. The extension of the title, "To Julia," indicates not that the poem is dedicated to Julia but that it is addressed to her. The poet wants her to have eyes like a glowworm's so that she can come to him at night and see her way clearly. In addition, he wishes for the sky to be full of shooting stars to illuminate her way and for elves to accompany her, too, as their eyes also give off light.

Stanza 2
After having invoked in the first stanza the good attendants he wishes to accompany his desired Julia on her way to him, in the second, the poet enumerates some of the forces he wishes to be absent. The will-o'-the-wisp is a false and ghostly light sometimes seen at night, usually over swamps or bogs. It is, in folklore, often associated with the devil, and it has the dangerous power to mislead travelers by its false light. Likewise the snake and slowworm—a sluggish reptile that is a sort of long, fat worm with eyes, sonorously contrasted in the poem with the dazzling glowworm—are associated with the devil, who assumed serpentine form when he effected the fall of man from the blissful seat of Eden by tempting Eve to eat of the forbidden tree's fruit. The poet wishes Julia's path free of snakes and false lights. He encourages her to walk without fear and not to linger, not to be afraid of the

night. There will be no ghosts to frighten her, he adds, teasingly as much as reassuringly.

Stanza 3
The third stanza returns to night's fearfulness. The poet tells Julia not to be weighed down, not to be troubled by the darkness. Although the night is moonless, there are stars, which he compares to innumerable candles that will light her way to him. Despite his assurance of ample light from star points, the reader ought to note that the assignation is to take place under cover of full darkness—not only at night but on a moonless night.

Stanza 4
Having shown her that the journey to his door from hers through the night is one she ought not to fear making, the poet implores Julia to allow him to beg her to come to him. Only then does the poet mention one of Julia's attributes. He refers to the color silver and its luminous property in relation to Julia's feet, although the sense of a silver casting, or the lady as an idol, is also suggested. He is alluding to the quality of quickness also attributed to silver, or to mercury, which is called quicksilver. He then suggests their spiritual and physical communion, as well as a lover's worshipful devotion, and again refers to his lady as a goddess.

THEMES

Carpe Diem
Carpe diem is a Latin phrase meaning "seize the day." It is essentially a philosophy whose sole tenet is to enjoy what there is to enjoy in the present, postulating terrestrial experience as valid in itself. It does not, in the manner of Puritanism, consider life on earth as only preparatory for an eternal condition after life that can be attained only through renunciation and suffering. This philosophy runs through much of Herrick's poetry, sometimes pronounced, sometimes submerged. In "The Night Piece: To Julia," it is a governing idea at the root of the entire poem.

Safety and Danger
The theme of safety inside a realm of danger as a practical problem is overt in the poem. Walking at night, in the dark, is hazardous. Dangerous

TOPICS FOR FURTHER STUDY

- Review several poems by the early seventeenth-century poet John Donne, and then write an essay comparing his poetry to Herrick's poetry. Pay particular attention to differences in diction and to the handling of the subject matter.

- Reviewing the several ideological, religious, and political cultures that make up the American landscape, discuss various attitudes and approaches to love and lust presently influencing the nature of American culture, politics, and values. In an essay, compare these circumstances to those in seventeenth-century England.

- Prepare a twenty-minute oral report on the English Civil War. Discuss the conditions that led up to the war, the factions, the issues, the various responses to the issues, and the results of the war, both at the time and afterward.

- Write a song or poem in which you attempt to persuade someone to do something, showing what obstacles may exist to frustrate the desired action and how those obstacles can be overcome.

---

creatures like snakes, or deceptive visions forged in the darkness, may be abroad. Or one may experience the night itself as spooky. On all these points the poet assures Julia to have no fear. Implicitly, the poem suggests by images of snakes and will-o'-the-wisps that Julia may have conscientious objections and not merely practical ones—that her liaison with him may put her in moral danger. It is the problem of sin that the poet addresses by allusions to such emblematic representations of sin as the will-o'-the-wisp and the snake. The will-o'-the-wisp is often assumed to be a work of the devil, an illumination on earth derived from one of hell's burning coals glowing on earth. The snake, in Judeo-Christianity, is a primary representation of the devil, for in

that guise he appeared in Eden to Eve when he tempted her to eat fruit of the forbidden tree and accomplished her expulsion, along with Adam and all mankind, from paradise. The poem is a spell by which the poet banishes such dangers and invokes safety.

Seduction

"The Night Piece: To Julia" is a poem devised to persuade the woman that the poet desires to visit him at night by convincing her that it is not hazardous to come to him. The theme of seduction is implicit, however, rather than overt, since the poet hardly speaks of the lady's qualities or his own. Rather, assuming that her desire is equal to his, the task he sets to in his poem is to encourage her to overcome whatever hesitations she might offer against the liaison, on the surface assuming the hesitations to be practical rather than conscientious.

Sensual Pleasure

"The Night Piece: To Julia" is a poem implicitly celebrating the pursuit of love and sensual pleasure. The nocturnal world of glowworms, will-o'-the-wisps, elves, shooting stars, darkness, ghosts, and the moon surrounds the nocturnal liaison. The sensuous night world constitutes the substance of Herrick's verse and is presented as a palpable presence. Glowworms have eyes that are used to attract other glowworms. Shooting stars flame and vanish, as if emblems in nature of passion aroused and satisfied. Elves have glowing eyes. Snakes bite. Ghosts frighten. The difficulties the poet asks the lady to overcome in her passage to him are all resolved in the sensuous image of her feet, which are silvery perhaps because of silver slippers upon them or because they have the swiftness of quicksilver. The final image of the poet pouring his soul into Julia is obvious in its erotic sensuality. It is an image that yokes the spiritual and the sensual because of the suggestiveness of the word "soul," which is often associated with semen, as it is by Saint Thomas Aquinas in his *Summa Theologica* (written 1265–1274) when he considers, in articles 1 and 2 of question 118, whether the soul is transmitted through the process of sexual insemination.

STYLE

Catalog

"The Night Piece: To Julia" is essentially a catalog, or a list. In it, the poet enumerates the positive phenomena he invokes to accompany Julia, the object of his desire, on her walk to visit him at night as well as the harmful phenomena he wishes to preclude. He lists the glowworm, the stars and shooting stars, and elves as desired companions and the will-o'-the-wisp, the snake, the slowworm, and ghosts as forces he banishes in his poem.

Rhyme Scheme

"The Night Piece: To Julia" is written in a verse whose pastoral innocence belies its more sophisticated, seductive purpose. It has a sing-song lilt in large measure achieved by the *aabba* rhyme scheme in each of its stanzas. The repetitions of the rhymes are not confined to each stanza individually, either. The long *e* sound dominates the rhyming in all but the third stanza. In the last stanza, all five lines end in words with a long *e* sound, including the third and fourth lines, which are otherwise given a variant rhyme.

The pattern of Herrick's verse was given by Ben Jonson in a song, "The Faery Beam upon You" from his 1621 masque, *The Gypsies Metamorphosed*. Like Jonson's lyric, "The Night Piece: To Julia" presents a five line stanza with an a,a,b,b,a rhyme.

Iambic Feet

Like Jonson's lyric, "The Night Piece: To Julia" is composed in verses typically of four essentially iambic feet, with the last truncated, in the first and second lines; three such feet, with one truncated, in the third and fourth lines; and four complete feet in the fifth line. (An iambic foot is a measure of two beats, the first unaccented, the second accented. A truncated foot is one with only one beat; the second beat is cut off, or truncated.) Thus, the first two lines have seven syllables, most often arranged in a pattern where the first syllable is unaccented, the second accented, the third unaccented, and so forth, until the line ends with an incomplete foot, that is, with only an unaccented syllable. The third and fourth lines follow a similar pattern but are one foot shorter. The last line of each stanza is a full four-foot line: there are eight beats and the last foot is complete, giving a sense of resolution.

HISTORICAL CONTEXT

Cavalier Poetry and Metaphysical Poetry

Essentially, two genres, differing considerably from each other, defined what poetry could be during the seventeenth century. Metaphysical poetry, represented most typically by the poetry of John Donne (1572–1631), is a poetry characterized by its intricacy and difficulty, by its psychological depth, and by the complexity of its images and metaphors. Donne, in one of his sonnets, for example, presents the jarring image of the round earth—a recently discovered geographical fact that replaced the idea of a flat earth—along with the older idea of the earth having corners, which can only be imagined, for a globe has no corners.

Cavalier poetry, on the other hand, written by various cavalier poets, of whom Herrick was one of the foremost, attempted to appear to be a casual, even offhand poetry dedicated to celebrating worldly pleasure and elegance in its form and content. The cavalier poets were often courtiers, although Herrick was not, and royalists, or supporters of the monarchy, which Herrick was. They opposed the moral strictness of Puritanism and the Puritan call for political and ecclesiastical reform or even revolution. Cavalier poetry, celebrating the delights of the present world and not sacrificing them for the rewards of a forthcoming existence, is noted for its lyricism, simplicity, and for its concern for easy pleasure and its delight in elegance. Herrick, for example, wrote a gracefully elegant lyric about the graceful elegance and captivating liquidity of Julia's clothes. As the metaphysical poets followed John Donne, the cavalier poets followed Ben Jonson. Donne's is an abstruse and complex poetry of disputation; Jonson's, a poetry of luminosity and songfulness.

The English Civil War

The English Civil War was fought between Royalists, or Cavaliers, those who supported the English monarchy and the Anglican Church, and Parliamentarians, those who supported ecclesiastical reform and the English Parliament in its power struggle with the king; Parliamentarians were also called Roundheads because of their close-cropped haircuts, which distinguished them from the long-haired Cavaliers. The first battles of the war were fought between 1642 and 1646; the second set of battles, in 1648 and 1649; and the third set, between 1649 and 1651, ending

COMPARE
&
CONTRAST

- **1600s:** Cavalier poets write lyrics praising a life of amorous dalliance or lamenting love's disappointments, celebrating fashion and seduction.

  Today: Rock stars and rappers write songs about their experiences of love and rejection, influence fashion, and project larger-than-life personae.

- **1600s:** England is torn by social, religious, and political discord until civil war erupts between opposing factions

  Today: The social unity of the United Kingdom is disrupted by cultural, religious, and political differences between longtime residents and recent immigrants, many from former English colonies.

- **1600s:** Despite the objections and disdain of people who believe that religious authority alone can explain the phenomena of nature, scientific societies develop to explore and disseminate the work of natural scientists.

  Today: Although science is well established as a legitimate mode of inquiry into natural phenomena, some religious fundamentalists still offer resistance to scientific research or to explanations that appear to conflict with theological explanations.

with a decisive victory for the forces of Parliament at the battle of Worcester. King Charles I was beheaded in 1649. A law was passed forbidding his son Charles II from being declared king of England then, although the Parliament of Scotland did proclaim him king. Rather than assume his throne, however, Charles II fled to France with the final defeat of his forces in 1651, to return to England and the throne only in 1660 with the Restoration. Between 1651 and 1660 England became first a Commonwealth and then, in 1653, a Protectorate, ruled by Oliver Cromwell and then by his son Richard. Revolutionary change was religious as well as political, since the exclusive power of the Church of England was terminated and the religion of England was during that period an austere Protestant Puritanism.

The Founding of the Royal Society

The reference to the glowworm in "The Night Piece: To Julia" is noteworthy for the way Herrick easily assumes a knowledge of entomology in his mistress and his readers. The Royal Society of London for the Improvement of Natural Knowledge, dedicated to the study and advancement of science, was founded in 1660 after the Restoration of the English monarchy. Its foundation signaled official recognition and sanction of scientific methodology. Advocates of natural science, observation, and experimentation—that is, advocates of scientific methodology as a way of understanding the natural world—had already formed secret societies for the dissemination of the new discoveries in the natural sciences that were being made and recorded throughout Europe. The reason for early scientific caution resulted from possible conflicts with theological explanations derived from holy writ for natural phenomena. The great scientist Galileo Galilei (1564–1642) was brought before the Catholic Inquisition and, on pain of death, forced to recant his telescopic observations that the earth was not the center of the universe but traveled around the sun.

CRITICAL OVERVIEW

"'Trivial' and 'pagan' are the generic epithets which criticism has habitually hung upon" Herrick, notes S. Musgrove in *The Universe of Robert Herrick*. Such judgment endured beyond the

Illustrated version of Herrick's poem (William L.
Clements Library, University of Michigan)

Magazine in 1875) recognized Herrick's "wonderful art and skill" but found in the poetry an "easy-going callousness of soul" that "makes it impossible for him to feel very deeply." Furthermore, F. R. Leavis, in his essay "English Poetry in the 17th Century," published in 1935 in *Scrutiny* (as cited by Rollin in *"Trust to Good Verses": Herrick Tercentenary Essays*), is less cruel in his rhetoric than Southey or Gosse, calling Herrick's verse "trivially charming."

In spite of these criticisms, Herrick has survived his detractors, and his command of language and meter has long been recognized. Writing in 1804, Nathan Drake, whose "On the Life, Writings and Genius of Robert Herrick" is cited in *"Trust to Good Verses,"* offers one of the earliest serious considerations of Herrick's poetry. Drake calls attention to the unevenness of Herrick's output and to his mastery of the poet's craft. Indeed, Herrick's verse is now admired both by lay readers and by scholars. Rollin, in his introduction to *"Trust to Good Verses,"* calls Herrick "a serious and significant artist rather than a minor if skillful craftsman; ... his *Hesperides* is an encyclopedic and ultimately coherent work rather than a miscellany of charming but trivial poems." Rollin concludes that "many of those poems exhibit patterns of intellectual significance and emotional depth beneath their polished and seemingly simple surfaces."

seventeenth and eighteenth centuries (when hardly any critical attention was paid to Herrick) and into the nineteenth. In fact, a few of Herrick's poems were reintroduced to readers by John Nichols in his *Gentleman's Magazine* in 1796 and 1797, and though they were admired and repeatedly anthologized because of the graceful lyricism of their verse, they were dismissed for the limitations of their subject. A. Leigh DeNeef, in *"This Poetick Liturgie": Robert Herrick's Ceremonial Mode*, cites a particularly virulent attack upon Herrick by the English poet and critic Robert Southey in his 1830 work *An Introductory Essay on the Lives and Works of Our Uneducated Poets*. Southey declares, "We have lately seen the whole of Herrick's poems republished, a coarse-minded and beastly writer, whose dunghill, when the few flowers that grew therein had been transplanted, ought never to have been disturbed." Roger B. Rollin notes in *Robert Herrick* that the famed nineteenth-century critic Edmund Gosse (writing in *Cornhill*

CRITICISM

Neil Heims

Heims is a writer and teacher living in Paris. In the following essay, Heims examines the latent content suggested by the imagery in "The Night Piece: To Julia."

Robert Herrick's "The Night Piece: To Julia," simple as it appears—simple as it really is—contains twenty lines that hardly seem to present any difficulty to a lay reader. The elements of riddle, learning, and song are casually, elegantly, and effortlessly combined to form verse that suggests both poetry and music. (The English composer Roger Quilter [1877–1953], in fact, did set the poem to music.) Because of its hybrid condition, and despite its easily grasped meaning as a verse designed to woo the lady whom the poet desires to visit his chamber at night, there is meaning resonant beneath the surface. Ambiguity arising from a suppressed sense

WHAT DO I READ NEXT?

- *The Diary of Samuel Pepys*, by Samuel Pepys (1633–1703), written between 1660 and 1669, is an honest and clear-eyed account of daily life in seventeenth-century London, focusing on the social, political, and cultural manners and morals of the time.

- "The Ecstasy," by John Donne (1572–1631), first published in 1633, is a poem that describes the emotional excitement of the meeting of two lovers. The poem exhibits a psychological complexity and imaginative richness that exemplifies the difference between metaphysical and cavalier poetry.

- "To His Coy Mistress," by Andrew Marvell (1621–1678), first printed in 1681, is a poem of seduction that mixes the imagistic complexity of metaphysical poetry with the idea of making the most of the present moment. The latter idea is representative of cavalier poetry in general and Herrick's verse in particular.

- *A Masque of the Metamorphosed Gypsies*, by Ben Jonson (1572–1637), performed for King James in 1621, is a courtier's entertainment devised for his sovereign. It is replete with examples of Jonson's lyrical vitality.

---

of sin in the face of a consuming sense of desire governs the rhetoric of "The Night Piece: To Julia." Unspoken though it is in the manifest discourse of the poem, the latent drama or conflict in the poem is conveyed through the imagery of the poem and, because the poem is a poem of seduction, through the attempt to persuade Julia to consent to what must be a clandestine nighttime meeting.

"The Night Piece: To Julia" is a bagatelle, a seeming trifle, a graceful and debonair lyric that appears to be all surface, even if a highly decorated surface carved with images of elves, shooting stars, glowworms, snakes, will-o'-the-wisps,

> AMBIGUITY ARISING FROM A SUPPRESSED SENSE OF SIN IN THE FACE OF A CONSUMING SENSE OF DESIRE GOVERNS THE RHETORIC OF 'THE NIGHT PIECE: TO JULIA.'

---

ghosts, and dainty, scurrying, silver feet. All its content appears manifest, and its meaning appears to be expressed without mediation by symbol or metaphor. Those elves, shooting stars, glowworms, snakes, will-o'-the-wisps, ghosts, and silvery feet, after all, can be read as concrete, nonsymbolic fixtures natural to the rhetorical landscape of the poem and to the geography of the night walk on which the poet is coaxing Julia to set out. But they also suggest underlying meanings for which they are only figures.

"The Night Piece: To Julia" is a lover's attempt to persuade his lady, through assurances of the physical safety of her journey, to visit him at night. Harm, he assures her, will not befall her, in large measure because of his poem, which is not only an invitation to the lady but also a spell, an invocation to aiding forces and an injunction against interfering ones. Noteworthy, and perhaps odd in such a poem of invitation—indeed, of seduction—is the absence of any declaration of the poet's love for the lady or a celebration of her virtues until the final three lines of the poem. Rather than being a declaration of love, a catalog of her charms, or a defense of dalliance, the poem is an assurance to Julia that night presents no obstacle to her coming to his chambers. For that reason, satisfying the desires associated with love should be quite easy and, according to the poet, will present no danger. Precisely that is why she ought to consent to visit him.

In demonstration of the ease and safety of the visit, the poet evokes the landscape of night and subverts night's characteristic properties: darkness and unseen, lurking dangers. He summons glowworms, elves, and stars to guide her. He banishes will-o'-the-wisps, snakes, and ghosts, assuring her that they will not be present to harm her. All these nocturnal phenomena that he conjures or banishes can be read with symbolic as well as unmediated significance, suggesting, therefore, a latent tension apparently absent or ignored in the manifest communication. The poet is not merely or really telling the lady about the natural world but is addressing her conscience. The manifest content must reinforce the latent message of the poem: take the present pleasure. The journey will not imperil the lady, and neither will its purpose. Through reference to the flesh, the poet animadverts to the spirit; but he returns to the flesh having placated the spirit. His song has also become a dance, and the graceful and perfect metrics of his poem suggest the balance he maintains when he enters the realms of passion. He woos formally. He keeps the passion out of his poem, saving it for the lady in the encounter he imagines in the last three lines of his verse.

In his construction of the landscape that Julia must traverse to reach him, the poet mixes light and dark as well as nature and folklore. The glowworm's eyes, the eyes that meet the reader's eyes at the first encounter with the text and that the poet wishes to bestow on Julia for her journey to him, have since at least as long ago as William Shakespeare's time been associated with erotic attraction. In act 3, scene 1, line 171 of *A Midsummer Night's Dream*, Titania instructs her attendant fairies how to tend the peasant weaver, Bottom, upon whom she dotes. She tells her minions to light the waxy thighs of bees at the glowworm's eyes and use them as candles to guide her "love to bed." What natural scientists later ascertained, that glowworms signal each other for mating through bioluminescence, was previously intuited in folk knowledge. The glowworm's eyes, the shooting stars, the elves with their glowing eyes, all suggest the romance of the erotic dance of courtship and the intensity of a passion, like a shooting star, that by its nature blazes gloriously and dissolves in its own incandescence. Elves suggest the friendly forces that are the agencies of achieving wish fulfillment. As much as all these bright phenomena symbolize the evanescent light of passion, they also suggest a counterforce to darkness. Thus these symbols are charged with contrasting but mutually supporting properties: the accumulated, hidden light of passion and the open, flowing light that eases the journey toward the fulfillment of desire. The poet conjures an environment conducive to the escapade he seeks and treats the tryst as an escapade indeed, not as a transgression. Yet it is to take place on a moonless night, cloaked, thereby, despite the stars, in darkness.

As the counter-imagery set beside the images of light suggests, the poet seems to be aware of the element of transgression. In the second stanza, Herrick presents a catalog of quite a different sort from the beneficent one he conjures in the first. In his recapitulation of the phenomena that he wishes to be absent when she makes her way through the night to an assignation with him, the poet lists forces that not only suggest the dangers one may encounter crossing the fields at night but also are emblems of sin and sinfulness. Slowworms replace glowworms, snakes usurp elves, will-o'-the-wisps trump shooting stars, and ghosts can haunt the night, even if only in the thoughts of a silly girl, as the poet implies by the teasing tone that he uses in mentioning ghosts and their absence. In his prayer, all these phenomena are banished, but in the consciousness of the poem's reader, they are present in their absence by their being named. The things one may be relieved from worrying about are, of course, the things that are the sources of concern. As you come to me, the poet assures his mistress, there will be no phantom light to confuse you on your nocturnal path, nor will there be the risk of snake bite or night fright. These assurances of bodily safety suggest spiritual dangers at the same time as they do corporal ones. While a shooting star may suggest the evanescence of passion, with its flare-up and fade-out, the will-o'-the-wisp suggests deception, a light from hell leading the soul in the wrong direction. But sinfulness is not what their liaison is about, the poet thus indirectly assures Julia. The snake itself is the archetypal emblem of diabolical presence and influence, rooted as the snake is in the account of the fall from grace in Eden. Thus the poem addresses and attempts to allay the latent concerns that would be aroused by such a meeting as the poet is beseeching—not anxiety about a tortuous nightscape but anxiety about succumbing to sin. The poet banishes the emblems of sin from their rendezvous.

The irony latent in the poet's overtly focusing on the corporal dangers in his wooing, while apparently overlooking the spiritual ones, is given a final turn in the concluding three lines. The poet pictures himself at Julia's feet, there to perform in reverence to her an act of worship suggesting submission to a deity. Thus his lady is his deity, and by her permission to let him pour his spirit into her, she strips his desire, or its enactment, of any taint of the sin of the

> JULIA IS A SIGNIFYING CHARACTER REPRE-
> SENTATIVE NOT OF JULIA HERRICK DIRECTLY BUT OF
> THE NEED HERRICK SAW FOR THE VINDICATION OF
> THE FEMININE AGAINST THE STRICTURES ENGLISH
> SOCIETY HAD LEVELED AGAINST WOMEN."

intercourse. Indeed, the poem alludes to this sin but has not spoken of it, as the poem's goal is to avoid and banish sin from consideration.

Source: Neil Heims, Critical Essay on "The Night Piece: To Julia," in *Poetry for Students*, Gale, Cengage Learning, 2009.

David Landrum

In the following excerpt, Landrum examines the character of Julia in Herrick's Hesperides.

Robert Herrick wrote hundreds of poems about real or imagined women. It is generally conceded that his "many fresh and fragrant mistresses" were purely imaginary, but understanding how he constructs gender is vital in developing an accurate view of his poetic art. Modern criticism often depicts Herrick as a propagandist for the received standards of his day, yet close examination of his texts reveals that he recognized the ambiguities of gender and the inconsistencies of his era's beliefs pertaining to women, disrupted and interrogated them, and often engaged in outright parodic critique of accepted seventeenth-century gender mores.

The stance Herrick takes in relation to gender issues is rooted in the double-coding of female presence that already existed in the English Renaissance. On one hand stood the traditional Christian idea that women should be subordinate to men—an idea accepted by Protestants and Catholics alike. In Herrick's society, women were viewed "regardless of social rank, as wives and mothers ... and were considered morally evil, intellectually inferior," and "framed by God only for domestic duties" (Dunn, 15). Female submission was considered essential to an ordered, stable society, so that "as wives were subject to their husbands, so women were subject to men, whose authority was sustained

informally through culture, custom and differences in education, and more formally through the law" (Amussen, 3).

Yet within this universally held set of notions about the nature and role of women, hinges, flaws, and contradictions abounded. Neoplatonic thought exalted woman. The cult of the Virgin, Petrarchan love conventions, and the cult of Elizabeth all grew out of this belief in the transcendence of womanhood. And the stringencies of patriarchy, though generally accepted in English society at the time, were qualified by the popular idea of "companionate marriage," which recognized God's grace as operative in women as well as in men and saw this grace as a check against unbridled notions of male superiority and the domination of wives by husbands (McDonald, 260–61).

This contradictory state of affairs was further complicated by the fact that, in contrast to continental Europe, early English society seems to have been exceptional in affording freedoms to women. Many English women were educated and prominent in the period when Herrick wrote his poems, especially at the court of Charles I, where Henrietta Maria "enhanced the status of women by demanding that her courtiers adopt the platonizing attitudes popular at the time in France" (Latt, 40). Herrick would have known the effects of Henrietta Maria's progressive attitude through his contact with the Carolinian court as a chaplain and lyricist before he took up pastoral duties in Devonshire.

Herrick's progressive attitude can be seen in the compositions he addressed not to imaginary mistresses but to real, flesh-and-blood women. His ambiguous attitude, reflecting the uncertainties of his own day, often crops up in these poems. To be sure, women exist as wives and maidens for Herrick, and his attention to them takes the form of sexual attraction in its modified and acceptable version of visual attraction to outward beauty. Yet one often detects an undercurrent of contradictory darkness flowing beneath safe conventions. The women Herrick addresses in his verses are beautiful and fragrant; the poet compares them to goddesses and flowers and lauds them for their good looks and virtue; the imagery he uses suggests the softness and passivity that was also seen as a proper social role for women. But lurking just underneath all of these conventions are the same sorts of "counterplots" that Claude Summers said work to disrupt and undermine Herrick's political poetry (167). While convention operates on the surface of Herrick's poems on women, a great deal of parodic revisionism is simultaneously taking place.

... The verses dedicated to, or dealing with, Julia have been numbered at seventy-seven (Coiro, "Herrick's 'Julia' Poems," 67). One of the Herrick poems frequently anthologized, "Upon Julia's Clothes," is among these numbers. The predominance of poems about her led Gosse to conclude that, while all the other mistresses of *Hesperides* were imaginary, Julia was a real person in Herrick's life, probably a lover in his youth before he went to Devonshire. Gosse picks up on the fact that Julia is the only one of the mistresses for whom we have a physical description.

... He goes on to project an image of her personality gleaned from references to her in Herrick's poetry. His construction of her is worth quoting at length. She is

> an easy, kindly woman ... ready to submit to the fancies of her lyric lover; pleased to have roses on her head, still more pleased to perfume herself with storax, spikenard, galbanum, and all the other rich gums he loved to smell; dowered with so much refinement of mind as was required to play fairly on the lute, and to govern a wayward poet with tact; not so modest or so sensitive as to resent the grossness of his fancy, yet respectable enough and determined enough to curb his license at times. She bore him one daughter, it seems, to whom he addressed of his latest poems one of his tamest. (Gosse, 137)

The poem to which he refers is "My Daughter's Dowry." His remarks suggest Julia is somewhat of a male fantasy to Gosse, a combination of the call girl who willingly acts out Herrick's sexual games and the prudish governess who reigns [sic] him in when he gets too bizarre (and here perhaps we have an image of what Victorian men really wanted when they let their minds roam free).

While most critics reject Gosse's position that she was a real woman with whom Herrick was romantically and sexually involved in his younger days, her position as a literary creation and as symbolic presence in the poetry has been noted and speculated upon. Her name has been associated with Jove. John T. Shawcross notes the connection of her name with both Juno and Venus, and also notes that it is "the feminine form of *Julius,* the name of a Romans gens,

probably resulting from a contraction of *Jovilios,* meaning *pertaining to* or *descending from Jupiter* (as father-god)" (96). This leads him to note the many times religious language is connected with her and to attach salvational significance to her presence in *Hesperides*. This idea of something redemptive or divine in the figure of Julia was taken further by Heather Asals, who connected Julia with Christ through the language of Proverbs. Asals pointed out that Julia is connected with the language found in the Old Testament books generally associated with Solomon—Proverbs, Ecclesiastes, Song of Songs—and that the allegorical figure of Wisdom found in Proverbs was feminine. Asals draws the link between Julia and Jesus Christ, who Paul had called the wisdom of God (I Corinthians 1:24), finding a redemptive element in the persona's relationship to her (368–70).

The connection of Julia to Wisdom should not be overlooked. In a patriarchal society, the embodiment of wisdom as female would be anomalous, and yet the interpretative tradition that saw female Wisdom in the Old Testament as a prefiguration of Christ was well-established. Asals notes that the connection to Julia is forged through intertextual reference and language in the Julia poems that reflects the language of the wisdom literature attributed to Solomon (374).

The most comprehensive study of Julia is by Anne Baynes Coiro. She notes the evolution of Julia's character throughout *Hesperides* from the early poems where Julia is apparently a virgin who is venerated and worshiped by Herrick's persona to a woman who participates in "churching," an Anglican ceremony to be performed after childbirth. As *Hesperides* progresses, Julia assumes much more the role of mother. And Coiro alone notes the connection of Julia with Julia Herrick, Robert Herrick's mother, so named in the poem, "His Tears to Thamasis," H-1028. In extant records she is usually referred to as Julian or Juliana, but is "called simply Julia here in the only surviving mention that Herrick made of her" (Coiro, "Julia," 83). Coiro makes the following observations:

> That Julia, "prime of all," should bear the same name as Herrick's mother seems, at the least, worth noting. Yet the name has never been recognized by any critic of Herrick. The closest acknowledgement of the identical names is elliptical and framed as a warning; F. W. Moorman cautions, "of the poet's relations with [his mother] we know nothing, and

speculation on such a matter is particularly undesirable." The reluctance of critics to cite such an obvious fact as the poet's choice of his mother's name for his most important mistress demonstrates the curious resistance of readers to question or expand the traditional interpretations of Herrick's poetry. (83)

Critics are fastidious about entering the perilous realms of psychosexual speculation. The difficulty with speculating on how Herrick regarded his mother is the same difficulty all critics have felt due to lack of supporting documentation about his life. Reconstructing a psychological profile of Herrick is a perilous venture.

But I would like to suggest a connection between Julia of the mistresses and Julia Herrick. It is not psychological, not a manifestation of oedipal desire projected by the son on to the mother through the creative medium of poetry. Rather, the intent is parodic. Herrick's Julia connects the enterprise of the persona in *Hesperides* with the female-centered environment over which Julia Herrick presided in the days of Robert's childhood. *Hesperides* is authorized by a female muse (mad though she may be) but also given unity by a feminine figure, Julia, whose presence creates unity and whose evolution as a character shapes the dramatic development found throughout the volume. Behind the character of Julia is Julia Herrick, Robert's touchstone, the figure most responsible for his social and psychological development, to whom his loyalty was due, and for whom he would feel a great deal of sympathy and a substantive desire to come to her defense, especially with regard to her place in society. Julia Herrick was restricted and restrained in English society, limited due to her gender, but her namesake knows no such boundaries in *Hesperides*.

. . . The connection between Julia and Julia Herrick is not so much psychological as it is literary and social. It is not fantasy or incest wish fulfillment, it is wish fulfillment projected into the social realm and related to how women should be treated and regarded. Julia Herrick's memory lurks in the questioning of gender roles frequently found in *Hesperides*. Herrick's mother was an exemplar for him in this regard. While we have no direct references to what she might have gone through as a single mother in the time, we know the legal and social status of women then. No doubt some of the less generous terms society dealt to women in early modern England had an impact on Julia Herrick, a thing of which her youngest son would have taken note. In the disruptive landscape of *Hesperides,* Julia is often seen. As Coiro points out, she moves with the persona through the different stages of development in the volume of poetry. She is a constant to which the persona frequently returns. His return to the character of Julia may be understood as a return to questioning, to interrogation, and to parody. Julia is a signifying character representative not of Julia Herrick directly but of the need Herrick saw for the vindication of the feminine against the strictures English society had leveled against women.

Various observations on Julia's presence in the fabric of *Hesperides* exist within Herrick criticism, as we have noted, but in general it can be said that Julia represents, and is a mirror for, the creative response of the persona to the various topics within the poetic volume. Her personality is a rubric of sorts, and through it the speaker of *Hesperides* enters certain spaces of discourse where convention may be challenged and relationships of mutuality between genders explored.

At the most basic level, the character of Julia exists as an object of aesthetic awe and wonder to the persona, a figure regarded through traditional Petrarchan attitude and with attendant terms. Often, the vocabulary of such poetry would anatomize the woman. Nancy J. Vickers argues that since the Diana-Actaeon myth was understood as a *topos* for the encounter of the pursuing lover (Actaeon) with the female love-interest prey (Diana), who unexpectedly unleashes her feminine power against him, an early strategy of Petrarchan love poets was "the neutralization, through descriptive dismemberment, of the threat. He [the poet] transforms the visible totality into scattered words, the body into signs; his description, at one remove from his experience, safely permits and perpetuates his fascination" (273). While I can find no reference to the Actaeon story in *Hesperides,* Herrick does seem to have picked up on this tendency enough that he engages in this same sort of poetic dismemberment of Julia. She is anatomized into "edible or septic pieces" (Schoenfeldt, 143). Her lips, breath, hair, teeth, cheeks, breasts, nipples, sweat, legs, voice, and other body parts are singled out for praise in different poems scattered throughout the secular verses. Herrick's persona can safely approach her in this manner.

But the relationship of Julia and the persona rapidly moves beyond the level of the admiring poet and the edible woman.

Julia and the persona forge a relationship in the book. Unlike the more conventional love poetry that operates around Petrarchan or medieval-romantic paradigms, and in which the remote lover is finally the possession of the pursuing lover, the persona, "Herrick," and Julia interact, even converse at points. This is seen early on in poems such as "His sailing from Julia," H-35. The narrator asks Julia to offer sacrifices to the pagan gods for his safety in his voyage and, for love's sake, to kiss his picture. Rather than the normal protestations of love or admiration of body parts, this poem curiously touches the persona's need for assistance and affirmation.

. . . The emotional tone of this poem, its acknowledgement of fear on the part of the speaker, and his dependence on Julia for his continued identity, are in contrast to the glowing verses about her eyes, breasts, and nipples. Here Julia is not a constructed object of the persona's masculine gaze. The poem contains indications of mutuality. Julia, in fact, assumes the role of priestess and the narrator of communicant, and the narrator is dependent upon her. The phrase embedded in the poem, "mercie and truth live with thee," refers back to an incident recorded in 2 Samuel 15. David flees from his son Absalom, who is trying to kill him. He is surrounded by supporters, including one Ittai, a non-Hebrew dwelling as a foreigner in the land. David tells him he should not take the risk of fleeing with the royal entourage and being killed by Absalom's forces, saying, "return thou . . . mercy and truth be with thee" (v. 20). Ittai, and his people, however, remain loyal and accompany David in his flight from Jerusalem. The narrator hopes to see the same type of loyalty in Julia. This particular section of scripture, too, shows David, the King of Israel, in a state of abjection, often weeping, remorseful, almost certain of his own doom. It is the loyal supporters like Ittai that enable him to survive and eventually to prevail. Perhaps the poem suggests a role reversal similar to what is found in the biblical text. In the biblical text the king becomes the dependent one and his subjects are the active, capable agents in the situation. So with Julia and the persona. The conventions that restrict the female character to being beautiful and desirable give way in this poem to a colloquy of mutuality.

Julia often assumes the role of priestess. In H-539 she is the *Flaminica Dialis,* the Queen Priest, who must make sacrifice for her and the narrator, who have neglected the upkeep of Venus's temple. Here again, the narrator is strangely passive and Julia is the active figure in the situation. She is the one who must put on vestments and burn incense. The speaker begs, "Take then thy Censer; Put in Fire, and thus, / *O Pious-Priestesse! Make a Peace for us."* The entire poem is one of Herrick's curious conflations of Christian and Pagan, for while the worship is to Venus and she is the Roman priestess, the accouterments are reminiscent of a Christian church. The ceremony, on which depends the very lives of the characters in the poem, is entirely in her charge, so that the last words of the poem are a statement to her, *"Redemption comes by Thee."* The narrator assumes a passive role, Julia a religiously active role. The poem is vaguely suggestive of the conventional worship of love, but gender protocol is reversed. Julia is burning male incense.

This condition of equality is found elsewhere. "Herrick" and Julia converse in another poem centered around religious activity. The content of "The Sacrifice, by way of Discourse betwixt himselfe and Julia," H-870, is not particularly remarkable as a poem. What is notable, however, is that the persona and Julia seem to be . . . of equal status. The speaker asks if everything is ready for the sacrifice. Julia replies that all propriety has been observed and all is ready, including the animal "we bring / For our Trespasse-offering." The inclusive plural pronoun appears here, and Julia exhibits relaxed familiarity with the workings and requirements of sacrifice. The persona responds:

> All is well; now next to these
> Put we on pure Surplices;
> And with Chaplets crown'd, we'l rost
> With perfumes the Holocaust:
> And (while we the gods invoke)
> Reade acceptance by the smoake.

Neither of these priests seems to hold rank over the other. Their equality is a startling variance from the accepted roles of men and women in early modern England. By removing the scene to pagan times, Herrick is able to evoke this sort of gender egalitarianism, but references to surplices and chapels, quotations and language from the Bible, and theological words like "transgression," "altar," even "old religion," all give an unquieting sense of modernity to the situations he describes. Julia is on equal footing with narrator, in a removed, artistic environment to be sure, but one that Herrick always manages to link to the tangible world in which his readers lived.

Julia seems, too, intimate enough and important enough to the persona that he frequently shares with her his thoughts and feelings about death, usually his own—though one poem he writes deals with her death. A poem in which the persona considers his demise is "His last request to Julia." The request is, "dearest *Julia* come, / and go with me to chuse my Buriall roome: / My Fates are ended; when thy *Herrick* dyes, / Claspe thou his Book, then close thou up his Eyes." This is not the type of thing a Petrarchan poet would say to the object of his affection. Julia is on a level with the narrator that he can put the deposition of his corpse in her charge, and of his art as well. She is to close his eyes and close his "book" too. The narrator addresses her demise in "To Julia," H-584.

... Julia's death is prefigured by the deaths of the saints to whom the service the narrator reads is commemorative. Currently, however, "we two" sing the service together. This service, unlike the others mentioned up to this point, is a Christian service. Julia, though a woman, co-officiates. At that time, women could not serve in the Anglican Church in any ministerial capacity, yet in this poem she is singing the service with the officiating priest. Here exists not only mutuality but equality of role in an area where gender inequality was strictly enforced.

Like many Renaissance writers, Herrick is not consistently liberating in his attitude toward Julia or his other female subjects. Very often she becomes the object of his gaze, and in this he prefers her naked. At least three poems bring out the voyeur in Herrick's narrator (H-414, H-824, H-939), and he asks her to "Appeare thou to mine eyes / As smooth, and nak't, as she that was / The prime of *Paradice*." Her breasts get a lot of attention, and he talks about them in more than one poem (H-230, H-440, H-491), asking to see them or to caress them. In this, Gordon Braden's observation that *Hesperides,* lacks adult sexuality (223) and that Herrick is a peeping Tom, seems to have more credence than some critics have afforded him (see Rollin,

"Erotics of Criticism"). Yet if indeed something of Julia Herrick is in the character of Julia in *Hesperides,* this distancing would be understandable. With Julia, "prime of all," the narrator wants to see, to touch, but not to consummate. This is not the case with the other mistresses. In a poem addressed to Anthea (H-74) for example, the speaker frankly states his desire to have intercourse with her.

... With Julia he always stops short of consummation. Coiro has observed that "once Julia [Herrick] is recognized, almost simultaneously, as both mother and object of erotic desire, all of the remaining poems in *Hesperides* are poems of purification and sacrifice, with no acknowledgement of her physical attraction" (84). The poems of the two sacrificing together have been mentioned. And Julia does move from the role of a woman whom the persona wants to leer at, delighting in her "nipplets" and getting excited when she slips and he gets a glimpse of her genitals, to a woman who has given birth and goes to a "churching" ceremony (H-898). Through the range of poems she inhabits, she becomes a character who inspires but also disrupts, who is the conventional poetic female figure but then a subversive factor in the volume. Readers must always keep in mind that Herrick speaks through a character he has created and that the voice of the character, even though he is occasionally called "Herrick," is not Herrick himself but an imaginative projection of various psychological and creative dispositions. Much of Herrick is in the persona, but the two are not the same. Similarly, Julia has something of Julia Herrick in her. She is the redemptrix of Herrick's poetry, a salvific figure who comes alongside the persona to save him and his poetry. As Julia Herrick figured in her son's life, so the significance of her namesake in his poetical project is considerable. And due to this connection, she is also a disruptive entity who pushes at the limits of early modern English social conventions. She leads the other mistresses, and the rather large gathering of women, real and imagined, that one finds in *Hesperides,* in a low-key challenge to the historical conditions that Robert Herrick thought inimical to his own mother and to women in general. And what he lacked in understanding on this particular matter he made up for in zeal.

Throughout the text of *Hesperides* (though not in *Noble Numbers*), Herrick moves in directions that challenge accepted gender configurations.

His references to Julia, to the other mistresses, to his muse, his epithalamium poems, his occasional poems addressing both noble and common women, work together to question accepted norms. Trying to understand Herrick's poetry dealing with women without recognizing this subversive, parodic element only leads one into a pathless quagmire as far as interpretation goes. Herrick defies the limits of standard interpretation in his presentation of gender. The subtle directions in his discourse on the matter open up the social text and suggest new possibilities as far as the manner in which women in his time were regarded, going far beyond the limits of poetic traditions, using text and language, using poetic liturgy, as a means by which accepted injustices might be mollified and eventually perhaps even corrected.

Source: David Landrum, "Robert Herrick and the Ambiguities of Gender," in *Texas Studies in Literature and Language*, Vol. 49, No. 2, Summer 2007, pp. 181–207.

Marchette Chute

In the following excerpt, Chute traces the influence that the English poet Ben Jonson had on Herrick's "The Night Piece: To Julia."

... Herrick had admired and imitated Ben Jonson since the days when he was a goldsmith's apprentice, and he knew very well what a privilege it was to be in the great man's company.

Herrick did not possess either Jonson's intellectual vigor or his scholarship, and since he was a wise man he did not try to change himself into something he was not. Herrick gave thanks in the only way a good poet can, by entering the door Jonson had opened to him and making the territory beyond it his own.

For instance, Jonson had once written a song for one of his plays in which he praised the art of "sweet neglect" in a woman's attire. Herrick borrowed both the idea and the metre, and the result is his own brilliantly original lyric, "Delight in Disorder." For Jonson's moral approach he substituted his own pagan sense of play, and he let his imagination flow over the details of a woman's dress with a most affectionate eye for detail.

A winning wave (deserving note)
In the tempestuous petticoat ...

was duly noted by Herrick, who was not only well informed on petticoats but knew how to link them to the most accurate of adjectives.

Once again, some years later, Jonson wrote another poem that Herrick used as the model for a small masterpiece. Jonson wrote some verses on magic and the moon for one of his court masques and used a curious but effective five-line stanza. His good friend Richard Corbet borrowed the metre and in his hands it became doggerel; but when Herrick used it the result was the famous "Night-Piece to Julia."

... Herrick reverenced the art of poetry—what he called "the holy incantation of a verse"—and he reverenced equally the man who had helped him to enter that sacred ground. In Herrick's eyes, Jonson was both priest and saint in an ancient and enchanted land, and he wrote a set of verses that he called "His Prayer to Ben Jonson."

Close as the two men were in their devotion to poetry, there is nothing to indicate that there was a similar closeness in their lives. Herrick was not one of the young protégés whom Jonson took formally under his wing and he was never "sealed of the Tribe of Ben."

... Next to wine and song, Herrick's chief delight was, of course, women, those lovely ladies who flit so amorously through his verses. When he was grey-haired he was still writing about his "fresh and fragrant mistresses," and they fill his poetry with their white arms and their pretty ways—Perilla and Electra, Anthea and Diamene, Lucia, Perenna and over and over again his beloved Julia.

Never were mistresses better suited to a poet, and whether they bore any resemblance to the women Herrick encountered in real life it is impossible to say. With the exception of some young ladies with whom he went junketing up the Thames, none of them seems to exist in London or even in English air. "My girls," as he calls them, were as fragrant as roses and as lovely as daffodils; but none of them is rooted in earth and men seldom encounter such thoroughly satisfactory mistresses except in their dreams.

On the other hand, when Herrick wrote songs to demonstrably real women the tone is not unlike his addresses to Julia. He calls Susan Herrick his "dearest" and compares her to flowers, and when he addresses three poems to his uncle Robert's daughter, Elizabeth Wheeler, she is his "dearest love" and they kiss in the flowery meads. His Valentine to Margaret Falconbrige is also to "my dearest," and the reader would have no way of guessing that Margaret was at the time less than nine years old.

The poems to Julia are more erotic than these, and yet there is no fundamental difference in tone. Herrick is a poet of surfaces, and all beautiful surfaces had a certain resemblance for him. The whiteness of a woman's thigh could stir him to poetry, but so could the sheen of a petticoat or a bough of whitethorn in May, and they all have a kind of innocence that Herrick somehow retains even in his most mischievous verse. If there is a real woman beneath the petticoats he gives no indication of it, and certainly Herrick was no Catullus to report in agonizing reality the progress of an actual love affair.

Herrick's mistresses belong to the lighthearted tradition of Horace with his Chloe and his Lydia, or of Anacreon whose troops of ladies were (he says) as numerous as the waves of the sea. As a poet Herrick was equally willing to bestow his affections wholesale, and he celebrated the pretty things with the same affectionate skill he lavished on violets and primroses. The ladies had reason to be equally grateful to him in return; and the least they could have done, as Herrick once suggested, was to make a yearly pilgrimage to his tomb so that he could cast on his "girls" a final affectionate eye.

Source: Marchette Chute, "Chapter Nineteen," in *Two Gentle Men: The Lives of George Herbert and Robert Herrick*, Secker & Warburg, 1960, pp. 184–91.

SOURCES

Aquinas, Saint Thomas, "Question 118," in *Summa Theologica*, http://www.newadvent.org/summa/1118.htm (accessed February 8, 2008).

DeNeef, A. Leigh, *"This Poetick Liturgie": Robert Herrick's Ceremonial Mode*, Duke University Press, 1974, p. 109.

Herrick, Robert, "The Night Piece: To Julia," in *Seventeenth-Century Prose and Poetry*, 2nd ed., edited by Alexander M. Witherspoon and Frank Warnke, Harcourt, Brace & World, 1963, p. 820.

Jonson, Ben, "The Faery Beam upon You," in *A Masque of the Metamorphosed Gypsies*, in *Ben Jonson: Selected Masques*, edited by Stephen Orgel, Yale University Press, 1975, pp. 211–12.

Musgrove, S., *The Universe of Robert Herrick*, Folcroft Library Editions, 1971, p. 3.

Rollin, Roger B., *Robert Herrick*, Twayne Publishers, 1966, p 207.

Rollin, Roger B., and J. Max Patrick, eds., *"Trust to Good Verses": Herrick Tercentenary Essays*, University of Pittsburgh Press, 1978, pp. 244, 246, 265.

Shakespeare, William, *A Midsummer Night's Dream*, edited by Wolfgang Clemen, New American Library, 1963, p. 77.

FURTHER READING

Chute, Marchette, *Two Gentlemen: The Lives of George Herbert and Robert Herrick*, Dutton, 1959.

    A historically illuminating biography of both Herrick and his contemporary George Herbert. Like Herrick, Herbert was a rural clergyman, but unlike Herrick, he produced verse of greater complexity predominantly concerned with his intensely felt relationship with God.

Herbert, George, "The Agony," in *The Temple*, in *Seventeenth-Century Prose and Poetry*, 2nd ed., edited by Alexander M. Witherspoon and Frank Warnke, Harcourt, Brace & World, 1963, p. 847.

    One of the poems in Herbert's collection The Temple (1633), "The Agony," is about sin and love. But as Herrick's poem to Julia about sin and love is a smooth dismissal of the agonizing aspects of both, Herbert's poem penetrates the depth of Christian agony, the suffering of the crucified Christ, as it defines the experience of both terms.

Milton, John, *Comus: A Masque; Presented at Ludlow Castle*, in *John Milton: Complete Poems and Major Prose*, edited by Merritt Y. Hughes, Odyssey Press, 1957, pp. 90–114.

    Milton explores the forces of love and the struggle between sin and virtue. Unlike Herrick's simple and elegant lyric, Comus (1634) is a complex, baroque drama.

Starkman, Miriam K., "Noble Numbers and the Poetry of Devotion," in *Reason and the Imagination: Studies in the History of Ideas, 1600–1800*, edited by Joseph A. Mazzeo, Columbia University Press, 1962, pp. 1–27.

    Professor Starkman argues that Herrick's verse is actually devotional poetry, a poetry of divine prayer and worship, framed in a domestic and humanistic context.

On Being Brought from Africa to America

PHILLIS WHEATLEY

1773

Phillis Wheatley's poem "On Being Brought from Africa to America" appeared in her 1773 volume *Poems on Various Subjects, Religious and Moral*, the first full-length published work by an African American author. In the poem, she gives thanks for having been brought to America, where she was raised to be a Christian. Wheatley was hailed as a genius, celebrated in Europe and America just as the American Revolution broke out in the colonies. Though a slave when the book was published in England, she was set free based on its success. She had been publishing poems and letters in American newspapers on both religious matters and current topics. She was thus part of the emerging dialogue of the new republic, and her poems to leading public figures in neoclassical couplets, the English version of the heroic meters of the ancient Greek poet Homer, were hailed as masterpieces. Some readers, looking for protests against slavery in her work, have been disenchanted upon instead finding poems like "On Being Brought from Africa to America" to reveal a meek acceptance of her slave fate.

One critical problem has been an incomplete collection of Wheatley's work. In consideration of all her poems and letters, evidence is now available for her own antislavery views. *Phillis Wheatley: Complete Writings* (2001), which includes "On Being Brought from Africa to America," finally gives readers a chance to form their own opinions, as they may consider

this poem against the whole body of Wheatley's poems and letters. In context, it seems she felt that slavery was immoral and that God would deliver her race in time.

AUTHOR BIOGRAPHY

The African slave who would be named Phillis Wheatley and who would gain fame as a Boston poet during the American Revolution arrived in America on a slave ship on July 11, 1761. She was seven or eight years old, did not speak English, and was wrapped in a dirty carpet. She was bought by Susanna Wheatley, the wife of a Boston merchant, and given a name composed from the name of the slave ship, "Phillis," and her master's last name. It is supposed that she was a native of Senegal or nearby, since the ship took slaves from the west coast of Africa. Because she was physically frail, she did light housework in the Wheatley household and was a favorite companion to Susanna. She did not mingle with the other servants but with Boston society, and the Wheatley daughter tutored her in English, Latin, and the Bible. Phillis was known as a prodigy, devouring the literary classics and the poetry of the day. She was baptized a Christian and began publishing her own poetry in her early teens.

Wheatley's mistress encouraged her writing and helped her publish her first pieces in newspapers and pamphlets. She had written her first poem by 1765 and was published in 1767, when she was thirteen or fourteen, in the *Newport Mercury*. These were pre-Revolutionary days, and Wheatley imbibed the excitement of the era, recording the Boston Massacre in a 1770 poem. That same year, an elegy that she wrote upon the death of the Methodist preacher George Whitefield made her famous both in America and in England.

Wheatley's growing fame led Susanna Wheatley to advertise for a subscription to publish a whole book of her poems. This failed due to doubt that a slave could write poetry. Thus, John Wheatley collected a council of prominent and learned men from Boston to testify to Phillis Wheatley's authenticity. The eighteen judges signed a document, which Phillis took to London with her, accompanied by the Wheatley son, Nathaniel, as proof of who she was. In 1773 her *Poems on Various Subjects, Religious and Moral* (which includes "On Being Brought from Africa

Phillis Wheatley (The Library of Congress)

to America") was published by Archibald Bell of London. It was dedicated to the Countess of Huntingdon, a known abolitionist, and it made Phillis a sensation all over Europe. She returned to America riding on that success and was set free by the Wheatleys—a mixed blessing, since it meant she had to support herself.

She was planning a second volume of poems, dedicated to Benjamin Franklin, when the Revolutionary War broke out. The Wheatleys had to flee Boston when the British occupied the city. Phillis lived for a time with the married Wheatley daughter in Providence, but then she married a free black man from Boston, John Peters, in 1778. He deserted Phillis after their third child was born. The first two children died in infancy, and the third died along with Wheatley herself in December 1784 in poverty in a Boston boardinghouse. She had not been able to publish her second volume of poems, and it is thought that Peters sold the manuscript for cash. Some of her poems and letters are lost, but several of the unpublished poems survived and were later found.

A sensation in her own day, Wheatley was all but forgotten until scrutinized under the lens of

African American studies in the twentieth century. Today, a handful of her poems are widely anthologized, but her place in American letters and black studies is still debated. Recent critics looking at the whole body of her work have favorably established the literary quality of her poems and her unique historical achievement.

POEM TEXT

'Twas mercy brought me from my pagan land,
Taught my benighted soul to understand
That there's a God, that there's a Savior too:
Once I redemption neither sought nor knew.
Some view our sable race with scornful eye.   5
"Their color is a diabolic dye."
Remember, Christians, Negroes, black as
      Cain,
May be refined, and join the angelic train.

POEM SUMMARY

Line 1

In line 1 of "On Being Brought from Africa to America," as she does throughout her poems and letters, Wheatley praises the mercy of God for singling her out for redemption. So many in the world do not know God or Christ. How is it that she was saved?

Although she was captured and violently brought across the ocean from the west shores of Africa in a slave boat, a frail and naked child of seven or eight, and nearly dead by the time she arrived in Boston, Wheatley actually hails God's kindness for his delivering her from a heathen land. Here Wheatley seems to agree with the point of view of her captors that Africa is pagan and ignorant of truth and that she was better off leaving there (though in a poem to the Earl of Dartmouth she laments that she was abducted from her sorrowing parents). Here she mentions nothing about having been free in Africa while now being enslaved in America. In fact, the whole thrust of the poem is to prove the paradox that in being enslaved, she was set free in a spiritual sense.

Line 2

Line 2 explains why she considers coming to America to have been good fortune. She was in a sinful and ignorant state, not knowing God or Christ. Many readers today are offended by this line as making Africans sound too dull or brainwashed by religion to realize the severity of their plight in America. It is also pointed out that Wheatley perhaps did not complain of slavery because she was a pampered house servant.

The image of night is used here primarily in a Christian sense to convey ignorance or sin, but it might also suggest skin color, as some readers feel. It seems most likely that Wheatley refers to the sinful quality of any person who has not seen the light of God. From this perspective, Africans were living in darkness. She was instructed in Evangelical Christianity from her arrival and was a devout practicing Christian. Indeed, the idea of anyone, black or white, being in a state of ignorance if not knowing Christ is prominent in her poems and letters. A soul in darkness to Wheatley means someone unconverted. In her poems on atheism and deism she addresses anyone who does not accept Father, Son, and Holy Ghost as a lost soul. Calling herself such a lost soul here indicates her understanding of what she was before being saved by her religion.

Line 3

Line 3 further explains what coming into the light means: knowing God and Savior. William Robinson, in *Phillis Wheatley and Her Writings*, brings up the story that Wheatley remembered of her African mother pouring out water in a sunrise ritual. Susanna Wheatley, her mistress, became a second mother to her, and Wheatley adopted her mistress's religion as her own, thus winning praise in the Boston of her day as being both an intelligent and spiritual being. The definition of *pagan*, as used in line 1, is thus challenged by Wheatley in a sense, as the poem celebrates that the term does not denote a permanent category if a pagan individual can be saved. Wheatley proudly offers herself as proof of that miracle.

Importantly, she mentions that the act of understanding God and Savior comes from the soul. It is not mere doctrine or profession that saves. By making religion a matter between God and the individual soul, an Evangelical belief, she removes the discussion from social opinion or reference. At the same time, she touches on the prejudice many Christians had that heathens had no souls. She wants to inform her readers of the opposite fact—and yet the wording of her confession of faith became proof to later readers that she had sold out, like an Uncle Tom, to her captors' religious propaganda.

Line 4

Line 4 goes on to further illustrate how ignorant Wheatley was before coming to America: she did not even know enough to seek the redemption of her soul. She did not know that she was in a sinful state. This line is meaningful to an Evangelical Christian because one's soul needs to be in a state of grace, or sanctified by Christ, upon leaving the earth. If it is not, one cannot enter eternal bliss in heaven. Thus, she explains the dire situation: she was in danger of losing her soul and salvation. The difficulties she may have encountered in America are nothing to her, compared to possibly having remained unsaved. In this, she asserts her religion as her priority in life; but, as many commentators have pointed out, it does not necessarily follow that she condones slavery, for there is evidence that she did not, in such poems as the one to Dartmouth and in the letter to Samson Occom.

The first four lines of the poem could be interpreted as a justification for enslaving Africans, or as a condoning of such a practice, since the enslaved would at least then have a chance at true religion. This has been a typical reading, especially since the advent of African American criticism and postcolonial criticism. This view sees the slave girl as completely brainwashed by the colonial captors and made to confess her inferiority in order to be accepted. She is grateful for being made a slave, so she can receive the dubious benefits of the civilization into which she has been transplanted. Following fuller scholarly investigation into her complete works, however, many agree that this interpretation is oversimplified and does not do full justice to her awareness of injustice.

Line 5

The last four lines take a surprising turn; suddenly, the reader is made to think. The opening sentiments would have been easily appreciated by Wheatley's contemporary white audience, but the last four lines exhorted them to reflect on their assumptions about the black race. The poet quickly and ably turns into a moral teacher, explaining as to her backward American friends the meaning of their own religion.

Line 5 boldly brings out the fact of racial prejudice in America. The darker races are looked down upon. Wheatley admits this, and in one move, the balance of the poem seems shattered. She separates herself from the audience of white readers as a black person, calling attention to the difference. She thus makes clear that she has praised God rather than the people or country of America for her good fortune. One may wonder, then, why she would be glad to be in such a country that rejects her people.

Line 6

Line 6, in quotations, gives a typical jeer of a white person about black people. The line leads the reader to reflect that Wheatley was not as naive, or as shielded from prejudice, as some have thought. She notes that the black skin color is thought to represent a connection to the devil. The inclusion of the white prejudice in the poem is very effective, for it creates two effects. First, the reader can imagine how it feels to hear a comment like that. Secondly, it describes the deepest Christian indictment of her race: blacks are too sinful to be saved or to be bothered with. While it is true that her very ability to write such a poem defended her race against Jefferson's charge that black people were not intelligent enough to create poetry, an even worse charge for Wheatley would have been the association of the black race with unredeemable evil—the charge that the black race had no souls to save.

Line 7

Line 7 is one of the difficult lines in the poem. She addresses Christians, which in her day would have included most important people in America, in government, education, and the clergy. Some were deists, like Benjamin Franklin, who believed in God but not a divine savior. Wheatley, however, is asking Christians to judge her and her poetry, for she is indeed one of them, if they adhere to the doctrines of their own religion, which preaches Christ's universal message of brotherhood and salvation.

Why, then, does she seem to destroy her argument and admit that the African race is black like Cain, the first murderer in the Bible? This comparison would seem to reinforce the stereotype of evil that she seems anxious to erase. If she had left out the reference to Cain, the poem would simply be asserting that black people, too, can be saved. On the other hand, by bringing up Cain, she confronts the popular European idea that the black race sprang from Cain, who murdered his brother Abel and was punished by having a mark put on him as an outcast. This racial myth and the mention of slavery in the Bible led Europeans to consider it no crime to enslave blacks, for they were apparently a marked and evil race.

Line 8

Wheatley perhaps included the reference to Cain for dramatic effect, to lead into the Christian doctrine of forgiveness, emphasized in line 8. No one is excluded from the Savior's tender mercy—not the worst people whites can think of—not Cain, not blacks. Wheatley may also be using the rhetorical device of bringing up the opponent's worst criticism in order to defuse it. Just as she included a typical racial sneer, she includes the myth of blacks springing from Cain. Judging from a full reading of her poems, it does not seem likely that she herself ever accepted such a charge against her race. There are poems in which she idealizes the African climate as Eden, and she constantly identifies herself in her poems as the Afric muse. She is not ashamed of her origins; only of her past ignorance of Christ. In the last line of this poem, she asserts that the black race may, like any other branch of humanity, be saved and rise to a heavenly fate.

THEMES

Equality

Wheatley explains her humble origins in "On Being Brought from Africa to America" and then promptly turns around to exhort her audience to accept African equality in the realm of spiritual matters, and by implication, in intellectual matters (the poem being in the form of neoclassical couplets). She admits that people are scornful of her race and that she came from a pagan background. The black race itself was thought to stem from the murderer and outcast Cain, of the Bible. Indeed, at the time, blacks were thought to be spiritually evil and thus incapable of salvation because of their skin color. This objection is denied in lines 7 and 8. Skin color, Wheatley asserts, has nothing to do with evil or salvation. The last two lines refer to the equality inherent in Christian doctrine in regard to salvation, for Christ accepted everyone.

TOPICS FOR FURTHER STUDY

- Colonized people living under an imposed culture can have two identities. Look at the poems and letters of Phillis Wheatley, and find evidence of her two voices, African and American. Does she feel a conflict about these two aspects of herself, or has she found an integrated identity? Write an essay and give evidence for your findings from the poems and letters and the history known about her life.

- Read more of Wheatley's poems and write a paper comparing her work to some of the poems of her eighteenth-century model, Alexander Pope. How does Wheatley use a similar moral voice, form, and message to address responsible people in society, thus representing the proper vocation of a classical poet to teach public morals? Give a class presentation on the topic.

- Read Wheatley's poems and letters and compare her concerns, in an essay, to those of other African American authors of any period. How do her concerns differ or converge with other black authors? Do you think that the judgment in the 1970s by black educators that Wheatley does not teach values that are good for African American students has merit today?

- The Quakers were among the first to champion the abolition of slavery. Give a report on the history of Quaker involvement in the antislavery movement. What were their beliefs about slavery?

- Research the history of slavery in America and why it was an important topic for the founders in their planning for the country. What difficulties did they face in considering the abolition of the institution in the formation of the new government? Form two groups and hold a debate on the topic.

Through the argument that she and others of her race can be saved, Wheatley slyly establishes that blacks are equal to whites.

Death and Christian Faith

Religion was the main interest of Wheatley's life, inseparable from her poetry and its themes. Over a third of her poems in the 1773 volume were elegies, or consolations for the death of a loved one. She wrote them for people she knew and for prominent figures, such as for George White-field, the Methodist minister, the elegy that made her famous. The elegy usually has several parts, such as praising the dead, picturing them in heaven, and consoling the mourner with religious meditations. Although most of her religious themes are conventional exhortations against sin and for accepting salvation, there is a refined and beautiful inspiration to her verse that was popular with her audience. It is easy to see the calming influence she must have had on the people who sought her out for her soothing thoughts on the deaths of children, wives, ministers, and public figures, praising their virtues and their happy state in heaven.

In "On Being Brought from Africa to America," Wheatley identifies herself first and foremost as a Christian, rather than as African or American, and asserts everyone's equality in God's sight. The poem uses the principles of Protestant meditation, which include contemplating various Christian themes like one's own death or salvation. Wheatley, however, applies the doctrine of salvation in an unusual way for most of her readers; she broadens it into a political or sociological discussion as well. That is, she applies the doctrine to the black race. She meditates on her specific case of conversion in the first half of the poem and considers her conversion as a general example for her whole race in the second half.

Freedom

Wheatley was in the midst of the historic American Revolution in the Boston of the 1770s. She wrote and published verses to George Washington, the general of the Revolutionary army, saying that he was sure to win with virtue on his side. Washington was pleased and replied to her. Benjamin Franklin visited her. She belonged to a revolutionary family and their circle, and although she had English friends, when the Revolution began, she was on the side of the colonists, reflecting, of course, on the hope of future liberty for her fellow slaves as well.

Those who have contended that Wheatley had no thoughts on slavery have been corrected by such poems as the one to the Earl of Dartmouth, the British secretary of state for North America. Therein, she implores him to right America's wrongs and be a just administrator. She adds that in case he wonders why she loves freedom, it is because she was kidnapped from her native Africa and thinks of the suffering of her parents. This is why she can never love tyranny.

In "On Being Brought from Africa to America," Wheatley asserts religious freedom as an issue of primary importance. In fact, the discussions of religious and political freedom go hand in hand in the poem. The excuse for her race being enslaved is that it is thought to be evil and without a chance for salvation; by asserting that the black race is as competent for and deserving of salvation as any other, the justification for slavery is refuted, for it cannot be right to treat other divine souls as property. In fact, Wheatley's poems and their religious nature were used by abolitionists as proof that Africans were spiritual human beings and should not be treated as cattle.

STYLE

Neoclassical Poetry

Wheatley wrote in neoclassical couplets of iambic pentameter, following the example of the most popular English poet of the times, Alexander Pope. The pair of ten-syllable rhymes—the heroic couplet—was thought to be the closest English equivalent to classical meter. Such couplets were usually closed and full sentences, with parallel structure for both halves.

Neoclassical was a term applied to eighteenth-century literature of the Enlightenment, or Age of Reason, in Europe. This same spirit in literature and philosophy gave rise to the revolutionary ideas of government through human reason, as popularized in the Declaration of Independence. Just as the American founders looked to classical democracy for models of government, American poets attempted to copy the themes and spirit of the classical authors of Greece and Rome. Phillis Wheatley read quite a lot of classical literature, mostly in translation (such as Pope's translations of Homer), but she also read some Latin herself. Her poems have the familiar invocations to the muses (the goddesses of inspiration), references to Greek and Roman gods and stories, like the tragedy of Niobe, and place names like Olympus and Parnassus.

Landing a cargo of black slaves in the American colonies (© *Bettmann* / *CORBIS*)

This style of poetry hardly appeals today because poets adhering to it strove to be objective and used elaborate and decorous language thought to be elevated. The resulting verse sounds pompous and inauthentic to the modern ear, one of the problems that Wheatley has among modern audiences. This could explain why "On Being Brought from Africa to America," also written in neoclassical rhyming couplets but concerning a personal topic, is now her most popular. The power of the poem of heroic couplets is that it builds upon its effect, with each couplet completing a thought, creating the building blocks of a streamlined argument. By writing the poem in couplets, Wheatley helps the reader assimilate one idea at a time. The opening thought is thus easily accepted by a white or possibly hostile audience: that she is glad she came to America to find true religion. This idea sums up a gratitude whites might have expected, or demanded, from a Christian slave. The more thoughtful assertions come later, when she claims her race's equality. Irony is also common in neoclassical poetry, with the building up and then breaking down of expectations, and this occurs in lines 7 and 8.

Puritan Funeral Elegy

With almost a third of her poetry written as elegies on the deaths of various people, Wheatley was probably influenced by the Puritan funeral elegy of colonial America, explains Gregory Rigsby in the *College Language Association Journal*. While Wheatley included some traditional elements of the elegy, or praise for the dead, in "On Being Brought from Africa to America," she primarily combines sermon and meditation techniques in the poem. Many of her elegies meditate on the soul in heaven, as she does briefly here in line 8. Wheatley was a member of the Old South Congregational Church of Boston. The typical funeral sermon delivered by this sect relied on portraits of the deceased and exhortations not to grieve, as well as meditations on salvation. Lines 1 to 4 here represent such a typical meditation, rejoicing in being saved from a life of sin. Generally in her work, Wheatley devotes more attention to the soul's rising heavenward and to consoling and exhorting those left behind than writers of conventional elegies have. As such, though she inherited the Puritan sense of original sin and resignation in death, she focuses on the element of comfort for the bereaved. Her poems thus typically move dramatically in the same direction, from an extreme point of sadness (here, the darkness of the lost soul and the outcast, Cain) to the certainty of the saved joining the angelic host (regardless of the color of their skin). "On Being Brought from Africa to America" finally changes from a meditation to a sermon when Wheatley addresses an audience in her exhortation in the last two lines.

HISTORICAL CONTEXT

Slavery in America

The European colonization of the Americas inspired a desire for cheap labor for the development of the land. The enslavement of Africans in the American colonies grew steadily from the early seventeenth century until by 1860 there were about four million slaves in the United States. Slavery did not become illegal after the Revolution as many had hoped; it was not fully abolished in the United States until the end of the Civil War in 1865.

COMPARE
&
CONTRAST

- **1770s:** Wheatley is the first recognized African American poet. She is a curiosity and a popular phenomenon, in London and Boston alike, and is sought out or commented on by all the great people of the day. Nevertheless, she dies in poverty.

  Today: Oprah Winfrey is the first African American television correspondent; she becomes a global media figure, actress, and philanthropist. Unlike Wheatley, her success continues to increase, and she is one of the richest people in America.

- **1770s:** Both Britain and America make promises to enlist black troops for the war. Washington refuses to use black soldiers, however, until he sees the British recruiting close to 10,000 with the promise of freedom. Most black soldiers on both sides die; few gain the freedom they expected.

  Today: Since the Vietnam War, military service represents one of the equalizing opportunities for blacks to gain education, status, and benefits. An example is the precedent of General Colin Powell, who served as chairman of the Joint Chiefs of Staff during the Gulf War (a post equal to Washington's during the Revolution). During the war in Iraq, black recruitment falls off, in part due to the many more civil career options open to young blacks.

- **1770s:** Thomas Jefferson pronounces the poetry of Phillis Wheatley imitative and states that Africans are unable to produce art.

  Today: African American women are regularly winners of the highest literary prizes; for instance, Toni Morrison won the 1993 Nobel Prize for Literature, and Suzan-Lori Parks won the 2002 Pulitzer Prize for Drama.

- **1770s:** Most African Americans are enslaved and uneducated. Wheatley is unusual in being literate and able to participate in white society.

  Today: African Americans are educated and hold political office, even becoming serious contenders for the office of president of the United States.

Africans were brought over on slave ships, as was Wheatley, having been kidnapped or sold by other Africans, and were used for field labor or as household workers. Later generations of slaves were born into captivity. Most of the slaves were held on the southern plantations, but blacks were house servants in the North, and most wealthy families were expected to have them. The prosperous Wheatley family of Boston had several slaves, but the poet was treated from the beginning as a companion to the family and above the other servants.

The Puritan attitude toward slaves was somewhat liberal, as slaves were considered part of the family and were often educated so that they could be converted to Christianity. In the South, masters frequently forbade slaves to learn to read or gather in groups to worship or convert other slaves, as literacy and Christianity were potent equalizing forces. Later rebellions in the South were often fostered by black Christian ministers, a tradition that was epitomized by Dr. Martin Luther King, Jr.'s civil rights movement. Slaves felt that Christianity validated their equality with their masters. The masters, on the other hand, claimed that the Bible recorded and condoned the practice of slavery.

Wheatley was bought as a starving child and transformed into a prodigy in a few short years of training. She did light housework because of her frailty and often visited and conversed in the social circles of Boston, the pride of her masters. She was the first African American to publish a full book, although other slave authors, such as

Lucy Terry and Jupiter Hammon, had printed individual poems before her.

The American Revolution

Against the unlikely backdrop of the institution of slavery, ideas of liberty were taking hold in colonial America, circulating for many years in intellectual circles before war with Britain actually broke out. This was the legacy of philosophers such as John Locke who argued against absolute monarchy, saying that government should be a social contract with the people; if the people are not being served, they have a right to rebel. These ideas of freedom and the natural rights of human beings were so potent that they were seized by all minorities and ethnic groups in the ensuing years and applied to their own cases. Even before the Revolution, black slaves in Massachusetts were making legal petitions for their freedom on the basis of their natural rights. These documents are often anthologized along with the Declaration of Independence as proof, as Wheatley herself said to the Native American preacher Samson Occom, that freedom is an innate right.

Revolutionary Boston

Wheatley lived in the middle of the passionate controversies of the times, herself a celebrated cause and mover of events. The Wheatley home was not far from Revolutionary scenes such as the Boston Massacre and the Boston Tea Party. While she had Loyalist friends and British patrons, Wheatley sympathized with the rebels, not only because her owners were of that persuasion, but also because many slaves believed that they would gain their freedom with the cause of the Revolution.

Henry Louis Gates, Jr., claims in *The Trials of Phillis Wheatley* that Boston contained about a thousand African Americans out of a population of 15,520. Only eighteen of the African Americans were free. This condition ironically coexisted with strong antislavery sentiment among the Christian Evangelical and Whig populations of the city, such as the Wheatleys, who themselves were slaveholders. In fact, the Wheatleys introduced Phillis to their circle of Evangelical antislavery friends. John Hancock, one of Wheatley's examiners in her trial of literacy and one of the founders of the United States, was also a slaveholder, as were Washington and Jefferson.

There were public debates on slavery, as well as on other liberal ideas, and Wheatley was no doubt present at many of these discussions, as references to them show up in her poems and letters, addressed to such notable revolutionaries as George Washington, the Countess of Huntingdon, the Earl of Dartmouth, English antislavery advocates, the Reverend Samuel Cooper, and James Bowdoin. Her praise of these people and what they stood for was printed in the newspapers, making her voice part of the public forum in America.

The question of slavery weighed heavily on the revolutionaries, for it ran counter to the principles of government that they were fighting for. The justification was given that the participants in a republican government must possess the faculty of reason, and it was widely believed that Africans were not fully human or in possession of adequate reason. Proof consisted in their inability to understand mathematics or philosophy or to produce art. Into this arena Phillis Wheatley appeared with her proposal to publish her book of poems, at the encouragement of her mistress, Susanna Wheatley. She was about twenty years old, black, and a woman.

The collection was such an astonishing testimony to the intelligence of her race that John Wheatley had to assemble a group of eighteen prominent citizens of Boston to attest to the poet's competency. They signed their names to a document, and on that basis Wheatley was able to publish in London, though not in Boston. She was so celebrated and famous in her day that she was entertained in London by nobility and moved among intellectuals with respect. Her published book, *Poems on Various Subjects, Religious and Moral* (1773), might have propelled her to greater prominence, but the Revolutionary War interrupted her momentum, and Wheatley, set free by her master, suddenly had to support herself. It is supremely ironic and tragic that she died in poverty and neglect in the city of Boston; yet she left as her legacy the proof of what she asserts in her poems, that she was a free spirit who could speak with authority and equality, regardless of origins or social constraints.

CRITICAL OVERVIEW

From the 1770s, when Phillis Wheatley first began to publish her poems, until the present day, criticism has been heated over whether she was a genius or an imitator, a cultural heroine or a pathetic victim, a woman of letters or an item of curiosity. The early reviews, often written by people who had met her, refer to her as a genius. William Robinson provides the diverse early

Frontpiece and title page from Phillis Wheatley's Poems on Various Subjects, Religious and Moral

(Copyright © The Pierpont Morgan Library / Art Resource NY. Reproduced by permission)

assessments in his edited volume *Critical Essays on Phillis Wheatley.* Wheatley's English publisher, Archibald Bell, for instance, advertised that Wheatley was "one of the greatest instances of pure, unassisted Genius, that the world ever produced." Benjamin Rush, a prominent abolitionist, holds that Wheatley's "singular genius and accomplishments are such as not only do honor to her sex, but to human nature." Abolitionists like Rush used Wheatley as proof for the argument of black humanity, an issue then debated by philosophers. According to Robinson, the *Gentleman's Magazine* of London and the *London Monthly Review* disagreed on the quality of the poems but agreed on the ingeniousness of the author, pointing out the shame that she was a slave in a freedom-loving city like Boston. From the start, critics have had difficulty disentangling the racial and literary issues.

Thomas Jefferson's scorn (reported by Robinson), however, famously articulates the common low opinion of African capability: "Religion, indeed, has produced a Phillis Whately, but it could not produce a poet. The compositions published under her name are below the dignity of criticism." On the other hand, Gilbert Imlay, a writer and diplomat, disagreed with Jefferson, holding Wheatley's genius to be superior to Jefferson's. As cited by Robinson, he wonders, "What white person upon this continent has written more beautiful lines?"

A resurgence of interest in Wheatley during the 1960s and 1970s, with the rise of African American studies, led again to mixed opinions, this time among black readers. Eleanor Smith, in her 1974 article in the *Journal of Negro Education*, pronounces Wheatley too white in her values to be of any use to black people. Carole A. Parks, writing in *Black World* that same year, describes a Mississippi poetry festival where Wheatley's poetry was read in a way that made her "Blacker." Henry Louis Gates, Jr., in *The Trials of Phillis Wheatley: America's First Black Poet and Her Encounters with the Founding Fathers* (2003), contends that Wheatley's reputation as a whitewashed black poet rests almost entirely on interpretations of "On Being Brought from Africa to America," which he calls "the most reviled poem in African-American literature." The reception became such because the poem does not explicitly challenge slavery and almost seems to subtly approve of it, in that it brought about the poet's Christianity.

Recently, critics like James Levernier have tried to provide a more balanced view of Wheatley's achievement by studying her style within its historical context. Levernier considers Wheatley predominantly in view of her unique position as a black poet in Revolutionary white America. This position called for a strategy by which she cleverly empowered herself with moral authority through irony, the critic claims in a *Style* article. The debate continues, and it has become more informed, as based on the complete collections of Wheatley's writings and on more scholarly investigations of her background.

CRITICISM

Susan Andersen

Andersen holds a PhD in literature and teaches literature and writing. In the following essay on "On Being Brought from Africa to America," she focuses on Phillis Wheatley's self-styled persona

WHAT DO I READ NEXT?

- *The Interesting Narrative of the Life of Olaudah Equiano, or Gustavus Vassa, the African,* by Olaudah Equiano, was first published in 1789, causing a sensation in British antislavery circles. His patroness was the Countess of Huntingdon, Wheatley's patron. This first slave narrative by an African writer furthered the abolitionist cause.

- *The Black Presence in the Era of the American Revolution* (1989), by Sidney Kaplan and Emma N. Kaplan, gives details of the lives of black soldiers, women, preachers, writers, artists, and legal petitioners for freedom in the Revolutionary period. It includes an account of Wheatley, putting her in context with other significant black contributors to the Revolution.

- Mary Beth Norton presents documents from before and after the war in *Liberty's Daughters: The Revolutionary Experience of American Women, 1750–1800* (1996). She includes the experiences of different classes and races.

- *The Collected Writings of Samson Occom, Mohegan: Literature and Leadership in Eighteenth-Century Native America* (2006) contains Samson Occom's personal narrative and his letters, lending another view of the Revolutionary period. Like Wheatley, he went to England for support, finding Christianity to be a great equalizer, and Wheatley wrote one of her most famous letters to him about freedom. Also like Wheatley, he published his writings in newspapers during his life.

and its relation to American history, as well as to popular perceptions of the poet herself.

Though lauded in her own day for overcoming the then unimaginable boundaries of race, slavery, and gender, by the twentieth century

> NEVERTHELESS, WHEATLEY WAS A LEGITIMATE WOMAN OF LEARNING AND LETTERS WHO CONSCIOUSLY PARTICIPATED IN THE PUBLIC DISCUSSION OF THE DAY, IN A VOICE REPRESENTING THE LIVING TRUTH OF WHAT AMERICA CLAIMED IT STOOD FOR—WHETHER OR NOT THE SLAVE-OWNING CITIZENS WERE PREPARED TO ACCEPT IT."

Wheatley was vilified, primarily for her poem "On Being Brought from Africa to America." Both black and white critics have wrestled with placing her properly in either American studies or African American studies. If allowances have finally been made for her difficult position as a slave in Revolutionary Boston, black readers and critics still have not forgiven her the literary sin of writing to white patrons in neoclassical couplets.

Providing a comprehensive and inspiring perspective in *The Trials of Phillis Wheatley: America's First Black Poet and Her Encounters with the Founding Fathers*, Henry Louis Gates, Jr., remarks on the irony that "Wheatley, having been pain-stakingly authenticated in her own time, now stands as a symbol of falsity, artificiality, of spiritless and rote convention." Gates documents the history of the critique of her poetry, noting that African Americans in the nineteenth century, following the trends of Frederick Douglass and the numerous slave narratives, created a different trajectory for black literature, separate from the white tradition that Wheatley emulated; even before the twentieth century, then, she was being scorned by other black writers for not mirroring black experience in her poems. In effect, she was attempting a degree of integration into Western culture not open to, and perhaps not even desired by, many African Americans.

Of course, Wheatley's poetry does document a black experience in America, namely, Wheatley's alone, in her unique and complex position as slave, Christian, American, African, and woman of letters. "On Being Brought from Africa to America" is a statement of pride and comfort in who she is, though she gives the credit to God for the blessing. Arthur P. Davis, writing in *Critical Essays on Phillis Wheatley*, comments that far from avoiding her black identity, Wheatley uses that identity to advantage in her poems and letters through "racial underscoring," often referring to herself as an "Ethiop" or "Afric." As her poem indicates, with the help of God, she has overcome, and she exhorts others that they may do the same. She places everyone on the same footing, in spite of any polite protestations related to racial origins.

In fact, although the lines of the first quatrain in "On Being Brought from Africa to America" are usually interpreted as celebrating the mercy of her white captors, they are more accurately read as celebrating the mercy of God for delivering her from sin. Her being saved was not truly the whites' doing, for they were but instruments, and she admonishes them in the second quatrain for being too cocky. Notably, it was likely that Wheatley, like many slaves, had been sold by her own countrymen. Wheatley does not reflect on this complicity except to see Africa as a land, however beautiful and Eden-like, devoid of the truth. To a Christian, it would seem that the hand of divine Providence led to her deliverance; God lifted her forcibly and dramatically out of that ignorance. The world as an awe-inspiring reflection of God's will, rather than human will, was a Christian doctrine that Wheatley saw in evidence around her and was the reason why, despite the current suffering of her race, she could hope for a heavenly future.

The impact of the racial problems in Revolutionary America on Wheatley's reputation should not be underrated. Even Washington was reluctant to use black soldiers, as William H. Robinson points out in *Phillis Wheatley and Her Writings*. In fact, blacks fought on both sides of the Revolutionary War, hoping to gain their freedom in the outcome. Indeed, racial issues in Wheatley's day were of primary importance as the new nation sought to shape its identity. Could the United States be a land of freedom and condone slavery? This question was discussed by the Founding Fathers and the first American citizens as well as by people in Europe. Wheatley's identity was therefore somehow bound up with the country's in a visible way, and that is why from that day to this, her case has stood out, placing not only her views on

trial but the emerging country's as well, as Gates points out.

While Wheatley's poetry gave fuel to abolitionists who argued that blacks were rational and human and therefore ought not be treated as beasts, Thomas Jefferson found Wheatley's poems imitative and beneath notice. Jefferson, a Founding Father and thinker of the new Republic, felt that blacks were too inferior to be citizens. Although he, as well as many other prominent men, condemned slavery as an unjust practice for the country, he nevertheless held slaves, as did many abolitionists. This discrepancy between the rhetoric of freedom and the fact of slavery was often remarked upon in Europe.

In *A Mixed Race: Ethnicity in Early America*, Betsy Erkkila explores Wheatley's "double voice" in "On Being Brought from Africa to America." She notes that the poem is "split between Africa and America, embodying the poet's own split consciousness as African American." Given this challenge, Wheatley managed, Erkkila points out, to "merge" the vocabularies of various strands of her experience—from the biblical and Protestant Evangelical to the revolutionary political ideas of the day—consequently creating "a visionary poetics that imagines the deliverance of her people" in the total change that was happening in the world.

Erkkila's insight into Wheatley's dualistic voice, which allowed her to blend various points of view, is validated both by a reading of her complete works and by the contemporary model of early transatlantic black literature, which enlarges the boundaries of reference for her achievement. Vincent Carretta and Philip Gould explain such a model in their introduction to *Genius in Bondage: Literature of the Early Black Atlantic*. Reading Wheatley not just as an African American author but as a transatlantic black author, like Ignatius Sancho and Olaudah Equiano, the critics demonstrate that early African writers who wrote in English represent "a diasporic model of racial identity" moving between the cultures of Africa, Europe, and the Americas. Carretta and Gould note the problems of being a literate black in the eighteenth century, having more than one culture or language. Such a person did not fit any known stereotype or category. Western notions of race were still evolving. No wonder, then, that thinkers as great as Jefferson professed to be puzzled by Wheatley's poetry.

There was no precedent for it. Nevertheless, Wheatley was a legitimate woman of learning and letters who consciously participated in the public discussion of the day, in a voice representing the living truth of what America claimed it stood for—whether or not the slave-owning citizens were prepared to accept it.

The need for a postcolonial criticism arose in the twentieth century, as centuries of European political domination of foreign lands were coming to a close. Postcolonial criticism began to account for the experience and alienation of indigenous peoples who were colonized and changed by a controlling culture. Such authors as Wheatley can now be understood better by postcolonial critics, who see the same hybrid or double references in every displaced black author who had to find or make a new identity. Wheatley calls herself an adventurous Afric, and so she was, mastering the materials given to her to create with. In *Jackson State Review*, the African American author and feminist Alice Walker makes a similar remark about her own mother, and about the creative black woman in general: "Whatever rocky soil she landed on, she turned into a garden."

Source: Susan Andersen, Critical Essay on "On Being Brought from Africa to America," in *Poetry for Students*, Gale, Cengage Learning, 2009.

Mary McAleer Balkun

In the following excerpt, Balkun analyzes "On Being Brought from Africa to America" and asserts that Wheatley uses the rhetoric of white culture to manipulate her audience.

... Wheatley's cultural awareness is even more evident in the poem "On Being Brought From Africa to America," written the year after the Harvard poem in 1768. The later poem exhibits an even greater level of complexity and authorial control, with Wheatley manipulating her audience by even more covert means. Rather than a direct appeal to a specific group, one with which the audience is asked to identify, this short poem is a meditation on being black and Christian in colonial America. As did "To the University of Cambridge," this poem begins with the sentiment that the speaker's removal from Africa was an act of "mercy," but in this context it becomes Wheatley's version of the "fortunate fall"; the speaker's removal to the colonies, despite the circumstances, is perceived as a blessing. She does not, however, stipulate exactly

> HERS IS AN INCLUSIONARY RHETORIC, REINFORCING THE SIMILARITIES BETWEEN THE AUDIENCE AND THE SPEAKER OF THE POEM, INDEED ALL 'CHRISTIANS.' ..."

whose act of mercy it was that saved her, God's or man's. One result is that, from the outset, Wheatley allows the audience to be positioned in the role of benefactor as opposed to oppressor, creating an avenue for the ideological reversal the poem enacts. Hers is a seemingly conservative statement that becomes highly ambiguous upon analysis, transgressive rather than compliant.

While the use of italics for *"Pagan"* and *"Savior"* may have been a printer's decision rather than Wheatley's, the words are also connected through their position in their respective lines and through metric emphasis. (Thus, anyone hearing the poem read aloud would also have been aware of the implied connection.) In lieu of an open declaration connecting the Savior of all men and the African American population, one which might cause an adverse reaction in the yet-to-be-persuaded, Wheatley relies on indirection and the principle of association. This strategy is also evident in her use of the word *benighted* to describe the state of her soul (2). While it suggests the darkness of her African skin, it also resonates with the state of all those living in sin, including her audience. To be "benighted" is to be in moral or spiritual darkness as a result of ignorance or lack of enlightenment, certainly a description with which many of Wheatley's audience would have agreed. But, in addition, the word sets up the ideological enlightenment that Wheatley hopes will occur in the second stanza, when the speaker turns the tables on the audience. The idea that the speaker was brought to America by some force beyond her power to fight it (a sentiment reiterated from "To the University of Cambridge") once more puts her in an authoritative position. She is both in America and actively seeking redemption because God himself has willed it. Chosen by Him, the speaker is again thrust into the role of preacher, one with a mission to save others. Like them (the line seems to suggest), "Once *I* redemption neither sought nor knew" (4; my emphasis). However, in the speaker's case, the reason for this failure was a simple lack of awareness. In the case of her readers, such failure is more likely the result of the erroneous belief that they have been saved already. On this note, the speaker segues into the second stanza, having laid out her ("Christian") position and established the source of her rhetorical authority.

She now offers readers an opportunity to participate in their own salvation:

Some view our sable race with scornful eye,
"Their colour is a diabolic die."
Remember, *Christians, Negroes,* black as *Cain,*
May be refin'd, and join th' angelic train. (5–8)

The speaker, carefully aligning herself with those readers who will understand the subtlety of her allusions and references, creates a space wherein she and they are joined against a common antagonist: the "some" who "view our sable race with scornful eye" (5). The members of this group are not only guilty of the sin of reviling others (which Wheatley addressed in the Harvard poem) but also guilty for failing to acknowledge God's work in saving "Negroes." The result is that those who would cast black Christians as other have now been placed in a like position. The audience must therefore make a decision: Be part of the group that acknowledges the Christianity of blacks, including the speaker of the poem, or be part of the anonymous "some" who refuse to acknowledge a portion of God's creation. The word *Some* also introduces a more critical tone on the part of the speaker, as does the word *Remember,* which becomes an admonition to those who call themselves "Christians" but do not act as such. Adding insult to injury, Wheatley co-opts the rhetoric of this group—those who say of blacks that "'Their colour is a diabolic die'" (6)—using their own words against them. Betsy Erkkila describes this strategy as "a form of *mimesis* that mimics and mocks in the act of repeating" ("Revolutionary" 206). The effect is to place the "some" in a degraded position, one they have created for themselves through their un-Christian hypocrisy.

Suddenly, the audience is given an opportunity to view racism from a new perspective, and

to either accept or reject this new ideological position. Further, because the membership of the "some" is not specified (aside from their common attitude), the audience is not automatically classified as belonging with them. Nor does Wheatley construct this group as specifically white, so that once again she resists antagonizing her white readers. Her refusal to assign blame, while it has often led critics to describe her as uncritical of slavery, is an important element in Wheatley's rhetorical strategy and certainly one of the reasons her poetry was published in the first place. Hers is an inclusionary rhetoric, reinforcing the similarities between the audience and the speaker of the poem, indeed all "Christians," in an effort to expand the parameters of that word in the minds of her readers. Rather than creating distinctions, the speaker actually collapses those which the "some" have worked so hard to create and maintain, the source of their dwindling authority (at least within the precincts of the poem).

Wheatley's shift from first to third person in the first and second stanzas is part of this approach. Although her intended audience is not black, she still refers to "our sable race." Her choice of pronoun might be a subtle allusion to ownership of black slaves by whites, but it also implies "ownership" in a more communal and spiritual sense. This phrase can be read as Wheatley's effort to have her privileged white audience understand for just a moment what it is like to be singled out as "diabolic." When the un-Christian speak of "'their color,'" they might just as easily be pointing to the white members of the audience who have accepted the invitation into Wheatley's circle. Her rhetoric has the effect of merging the female with the male, the white with the black, the Christian with the Pagan. The very distinctions that the "some" have created now work against them. They have become, within the parameters of the poem at least, what they once abhorred—benighted, ignorant, lost in moral darkness, unenlightened—because they are unable to accept the redemption of Africans. It is the racist posing as a Christian who has become diabolical.

The reversal of inside and outside, black and white has further significance because the unredeemed have also become the enslaved, although they are slaves to sin rather than to an earthly master. Wheatley continues her stratagem by reminding the audience of more universal truths than those uttered by the "some." For example, while the word *die* is clearly meant to refer to skin pigmentation, it also suggests the ultimate fate that awaits all people, regardless of color or race. It is no accident that what follows in the final lines is a warning about the rewards for the redeemed after death when they "join th' angelic train" (8). In addition, Wheatley's language consistently emphasizes the worth of black Christians. For instance, the use of the word *sable* to describe the skin color of her race imparts a suggestion of rarity and richness that also makes affiliation with the group of which she is a part something to be desired and even sought after. The multiple meanings of the line "Remember, *Christians*, *Negroes* black as *Cain*" (7), with its ambiguous punctuation and double entendres, have become a critical commonplace in analyses of the poem. It has been variously read as a direct address to Christians, Wheatley's declaration that both the supposed Christians in her audience and the Negroes are as "black as Cain," and her way of indicating that the terms *Christians* and *Negroes* are synonymous. In fact, all three readings operate simultaneously to support Wheatley's argument. Following her previous rhetorical clues, the only ones who can accept the title of "Christian" are those who have made the decision not to be part of the "some" and to admit that "*Negroes* . . . / May be refin'd and join th' angelic train" (7–8). They must also accede to the equality of black Christians and their own sinful nature.

Once again, Wheatley co-opts the rhetoric of the other. In this instance, however, she uses the very argument that has been used to justify the existence of black slavery to argue against it: the connection between Africans and Cain, the murderer of Abel. The line in which the reference appears also conflates Christians and Negroes, making the mark of Cain a reference to any who are unredeemed. Thus, in order to participate fully in the meaning of the poem, the audience must reject the false authority of the "some," an authority now associated with racism and hypocrisy, and accept instead the authority that the speaker represents, an authority based on the tenets of Christianity. The speaker's declared salvation and the righteous anger that seems barely contained in her "reprimand" in the penultimate line are reminiscent of the rhetoric of revivalist preachers.

In the event that what is at stake has not been made evident enough, Wheatley becomes most explicit in the concluding lines. While ostensibly about the fate of those black Christians who see the light and are saved, the final line in "On Being Brought From Africa to America" is also a reminder to the members of her audience about their own fate should they choose unwisely. It is not only *"Negroes"* who "may" get to join "th' angelic train" (7–8), but also those who truly deserve the label *Christian* as demonstrated by their behavior toward all of God's creatures. "*May* be refined" can be read either as synonymous for 'can' or as a warning: No one, neither Christians nor Negroes, should take salvation for granted. To the extent that the audience responds affirmatively to the statements and situations Wheatley has set forth in the poem, that is the extent to which they are authorized to use the classification "Christian." Ironically, this authorization occurs through the agency of a black female slave.

Starting deliberately from the position of the "other," Wheatley manages to alter the very terms of otherness, creating a new space for herself as both poet and African American Christian. The final and highly ironic demonstration of otherness, of course, would be one's failure to understand the very poem that enacts this strategy. Through her rhetoric of performed ideology, Wheatley revises the implied meaning of the word *Christian* to include African Americans. Her strategy relies on images, references, and a narrative position that would have been strikingly familiar to her audience. The "authentic" Christian is the one who "gets" the puns and double entendres and ironies, the one who is able to participate fully in Wheatley's rhetorical performance. In effect, both poems serve as litmus tests for true Christianity while purporting to affirm her redemption. For the unenlightened reader, the poems may well seem to be hackneyed and pedestrian pleas for acceptance; for the true Christian, they become a validation of one's status as a member of the elect, regardless of race . . .

Source: Mary McAleer Balkun, "Phillis Wheatley's Construction of Otherness and the Rhetoric of Performed Ideology," in *African American Review*, Vol. 36, No. 1, 2002, pp. 121–35.

William J. Scheick

In the following essay, Scheick argues that in "On Being Brought from Africa to America," Wheatley

SHE ALSO INDICATES, APROPOS HER POINT ABOUT SPIRITUAL CHANGE, THAT THE CHRISTIAN SENSE OF ORIGINAL SIN APPLIES EQUALLY TO BOTH RACES. BOTH RACES INHERIT THE BARBARIC BLACKNESS OF SIN."

relies on biblical allusions to erase the difference between the races.

"On Being Brought from Africa to America" (1773) has been read as Phillis Wheatley's repudiation of her African heritage of paganism, but not necessarily of her African identity as a member of the black race (e.g., Isani 65). Derived from the surface of Wheatley's work, this appropriate reading has generally been sensitive to her political message and, at the same time, critically negligent concerning her artistic embodiment of this message in the language and execution of her poem. In this verse, however, Wheatley has adeptly managed biblical allusions to do more than serve as authorizations for her writing; as finally managed in her poem, these allusions also become sites where this license is transformed into an artistry that in effect becomes exemplarily self-authorized.

... In this poem Wheatley finds various ways to defeat assertions alleging distinctions between the black and the white races (O'Neale). She does more here than remark that representatives of the black race may be refined into angelic matter—made, as it were, spiritually white through redemptive Christianizing. She also indicates, apropos her point about spiritual change, that the Christian sense of Original Sin applies equally to both races. Both races inherit the barbaric blackness of sin.

Particularly apt is the clever syntax of the last two lines of the poem: "Remember, *Christians,Negros,* black as *Cain* / May be refin'd." These lines can be read to say that Christians—Wheatley uses the term *Christians* to refer to the white race—should remember that the black race is also a recipient of spiritual refinement; but these same lines can also be read to suggest that Christians should remember that in a

spiritual sense both white and black people are the sin-darkened descendants of Cain. This latter point refutes the notion, held by many of Wheatley's contemporaries, that Cain, marked by God, is the progenitor of the black race only. Wheatley's revision of this myth possibly emerges in part as a result of her indicative use of italics, which equates *Christians,Negros,* and *Cain* (Levernier, "Wheatley's"); it is even more likely that this revisionary sense emerges as a result of the positioning of the comma after the word *Negros.* Albeit grammatically correct, this comma creates a trace of syntactic ambiguity that quietly instates both Christians and Negroes as the mutual offspring of Cain who are subject to refinement by divine grace.

In short, both races share a common heritage of Cain-like barbaric and criminal blackness, a "benighted soul," to which the poet refers in the second line of her poem. In spiritual terms *both* white and black people are a "sable race," whose common Adamic heritage is darkened by a "diabolic die," by the indelible stain of original sin. In this sense, white and black people are utterly equal before God, whose authority transcends the paltry earthly authorities who have argued for the inequality of the two races.

The poet needs some extrinsic warrant for making this point in the artistic maneuvers of her verse. This legitimation is implied when in the last line of the poem Wheatley tells her readers to remember that sinners "May be refin'd and join th' angelic train." To instruct her readers to *remember* indicates that the poet is at this point (apparently) only deferring to a prior authority available to her outside her own poem, an authority in fact licensing her poem. Specifically, Wheatley deftly manages two biblical allusions in her last line, both to Isaiah. That Wheatley sometimes applied biblical language and allusions to undercut colonial assumptions about race has been documented (O'Neale), and that she had a special fondness for the Old Testament prophecies of Isaiah is intimated by her verse paraphrase entitled "Isaiah LXIII. 1–8" (Mason 75–76).

The first allusion occurs in the word *refin'd.* Speaking for God, the prophet at one point says, "Behold, I have refined thee, but not with silver; I have chosen thee in the furnace of affliction" (Isaiah 48:10). As placed in Wheatley's poem, this allusion can be read to say that being white (silver) is no *sign* of privilege (spiritually or culturally) because God's chosen are refined (purified, made spiritually white) through the afflictions that Christians and Negroes have in common, as mutually benighted descendants of Cain. Wheatley may also cleverly suggest that the slaves' affliction includes their work in making dyes and in refining sugarcane (Levernier, "Wheatley's"), but in any event her biblical allusion subtly validates her argument against those individuals who attribute the notion of a "diabolic die" to Africans only. This allusion to Isaiah authorizes the sort of artistic play on words and on syntax we have noted in her poem.

A second biblical allusion occurs in the word *train*. Speaking of one of his visions, the prophet observes, "I saw also the Lord sitting upon a throne high and lifted up, and his train filled the temple" (Isaiah 6:1). The Lord's attendant *train* is the retinue of the chosen referred to in the preceding allusion to Isaiah in Wheatley's poem. And, as we have seen, Wheatley claims that this angel-like following will be composed of the progeny of Cain that has been refined, made spiritually bright and pure.

As the final word of this very brief poem, *train* is situated to draw more than average attention to itself. This word functions not only as a biblical allusion, but also as an echo of the opening two lines of the poem: "'Twas mercy brought me from my *Pagan* land, / Taught my benighted soul to understand." The final word *train* not only refers to the retinue of the divinely chosen but also to how these chosen are trained, "Taught ... to understand." In returning the reader circularly to the beginning of the poem, this word transforms its biblical authorization into a form of exemplary self-authorization. At this point, the poem displaces its biblical legitimation by drawing attention to its own achievement, as inherent testimony to its argument. In effect, the reader is invited to return to the start of the poem and judge whether, on the basis of the work itself, the poet has proven her point about the equality of the two races in the matter of *cultural* well as spiritual refinement.

For Wheatley's management of the concept of refinement is doubly nuanced in her poem. The refinement the poet invites the reader to assess is not merely the one referred to by Isaiah, the spiritual refinement through affliction. She also means the aesthetic refinement that likewise (evidently in her mind at least) may accompany spiritual refinement. Wheatley's verse generally reveals this conscious concern with poetic grace, particularly in terms of certain eighteenth-century models (Davis; Scruggs). Nevertheless, in her association of spiritual and aesthetic refinement, she also participates in an extensive tradition of religious poets, like George Herbert and Edward Taylor, who fantasized about the correspondence between their spiritual reconstruction and the aesthetic grace of their poetry. And indeed, Wheatley's use of the expression "angelic train" probably refers to more than the divinely chosen, who are biblically identified as celestial bodies, especially stars (Daniel 12:13); this biblical allusion to Isaiah may also echo a long history of poetic usage of similar language, typified in Milton's identification of the "gems of heaven" as the night's "starry train" (*Paradise Lost* 4:646). If Wheatley's image of "angelic train" participates in the heritage of such poetic discourse, then it also suggests her integration of aesthetic authority and biblical authority at this final moment of her poem.

Among her tests for aesthetic refinement, Wheatley doubtless had in mind her careful management of metrics and rhyme in "On Being Brought from Africa to America." Surely, too, she must have had in mind the clever use of syntax in the penultimate line of her poem, as well as her argument, conducted by means of imagery and nuance, for the equality of both races in terms of their mutually "benighted soul." And she must have had in mind her subtle use of biblical allusions, which may also contain aesthetic allusions. The two allusions to Isaiah in particular initially serve to authorize her poem; then, in their circular reflexivity apropos the poem itself, they metamorphose into a form of self-authorization. Like many Christian poets before her, Wheatley's poem also conducts its religious argument through its aesthetic attainment. As Wheatley pertinently wrote in "On Imagination" (1773), which similarly mingles religious and aesthetic refinements, she aimed to embody "blooming graces" in the "triumph of [her] song" (Mason 78).

If the "angelic train" of her song actually enacts or performs her argument—that an African-American can be trained (taught to understand) the refinements of religion and art—it carries a still more subtle suggestion of self-authorization. In this poem Wheatley gives her white readers argumentative and artistic proof; and she gives her black readers an example of how to appropriate biblical ground to self-empower their similar development of religious and cultural refinement. That there was an audience for her work is beyond question; the white response to her poetry was mixed (Robinson 39–46), and certain black responses were dramatic (Huddleston; Jamison). In appealing to these two audiences, Wheatley's persona assumes a dogmatic ministerial voice.

This voice is an important feature of her poem. In alluding to the two passages from Isaiah, she intimates certain racial implications that are hardly conventional interpretations of these passages. The liberty she takes here exceeds her additions to the biblical narrative paraphrased in her verse "Isaiah LXIII. 1–8." In "On Being Brought from Africa to America" Wheatley alludes twice to Isaiah to refute stereotypical readings of skin color; she interprets these passages to refer to the mutual spiritual benightedness of both races, as equal diabolically-dyed descendants of Cain. In thusly alluding to Isaiah, Wheatley initially seems to defer to scriptural authority, then transforms this legitimation into a form of artistic self-empowerment, and finally appropriates this biblical authority through an interpreting ministerial voice.

When we consider how Wheatley manages these biblical allusions, particularly how she interprets them, we witness the extent to which she has become self-authorized as a result of her *training* and *refinement*. Perhaps her sense of self in this instance demonstrates the degree to which she took to heart Enlightenment theories concerning personal liberty as an innate human right; these theories were especially linked to the abolitionist arguments advanced by the New England clergy with whom she had contact (Levernier, "Phillis"). Nevertheless, that an eighteenth-century woman (who was not a Quaker) should take on this traditionally male role is one surprise of Wheatley's poem. That this self-validating woman was a black slave makes this confiscation of ministerial role even more singular. Either of these implications would have profoundly disturbed the members of the Old South Congregational Church in Boston, which Wheatley joined in 1771, had they detected her "ministerial" appropriation of the authority of scripture. Accordingly, Wheatley's persona in "On Being Brought from Africa to America" qualifies the critical complaints that her poetry is imitative, inadequate, and unmilitant (e.g., Collins; Richmond 54–66); her persona resists the conclusion that her poetry shows a resort

to scripture in lieu of imagination (Ogude); and her persona suggests that her religious poetry may be compatible with her political writings (e.g., Akers; Burroughs). In this regard, one might pertinently note that Wheatley's voice in this poem anticipates the ministerial role unwittingly assumed by an African-American woman in the twenty-third chapter of Harriet Beecher Stowe's *The Minister's Wooing* (1859), in which Candace's hortatory words intrinsically reveal what male ministers have failed to teach about life and love.

In these ways, then, the biblical and aesthetic subtleties of Wheatley's poem make her case about refinement. She demonstrates in the course of her art that she is no barbarian from a "*Pagan* land" who raises Cain (in the double sense of transgressing God and humanity). Her biblically authorized claim that the offspring of Cain "may be refin'd" to "join th' angelic train" transmutes into her self-authorized artistry, in which her desire to raise Cain about the prejudices against her race is refined into the ministerial "angelic train" (the biblical and artistic train of thought) of her poem. This poetic demonstration of refinement, of "blooming graces" in both a spiritual and a cultural sense, is the "triumph in [her] song" entitled "On Being Brought from Africa to America."

Source: William J. Scheick, "Phillis Wheatley's Appropriation of Isaiah," in *Early American Literature*, Vol. 27, 1992, pp. 135–40.

SOURCES

Carretta, Vincent, and Philip Gould, Introduction, in *Genius in Bondage: Literature of the Early Black Atlantic*, edited by Vincent Carretta and Philip Gould, University Press of Kentucky, 2001, pp. 1–13.

Davis, Arthur P., "The Personal Elements in the Poetry of Phillis Wheatley," in *Critical Essays on Phillis Wheatley*, edited by William H. Robinson, G. K. Hall, 1982, p. 95.

Erkkila, Betsy, "Phillis Wheatley and the Black American Revolution," in *A Mixed Race: Ethnicity in Early America*, edited by Frank Shuffelton, Oxford University Press, 1993, pp. 233, 237.

Gates, Henry Louis, Jr., *The Trials of Phillis Wheatley: America's First Black Poet and Her Encounters with the Founding Fathers*, Basic Civitas Books, 2003, pp. 18, 33, 71, 82, 89–90.

Levernier, James, "Style as Process in the Poetry of Phillis Wheatley," in *Style*, Vol. 27, No. 2, Summer 1993, pp. 172–93.

Parks, Carole A., "Phillis Wheatley Comes Home," in *Black World*, Vo. 23, No. 4, 1974, p. 95.

Rigsby, Gregory, "Form and Content in Phillis Wheatley's Elegies," in *College Language Association Journal*, Vol. 19, No. 2, December 1975, pp. 248–57.

Robinson, William H., *Phillis Wheatley and Her Writings*, Garland, 1984, pp. 92–93, 97, 101, 115.

———, ed., *Critical Essays on Phillis Wheatley*, G. K. Hall, 1982, pp. 24, 27–31, 33, 36, 42–43, 47.

Shields, John C., "Phillis Wheatley and the Sublime," in *Critical Essays on Phillis Wheatley*, edited by William H. Robinson, G. K. Hall, 1982, pp. 189, 193.

Smith, Eleanor, "Phillis Wheatley: A Black Perspective," in *Journal of Negro Education*, Vol. 43, No. 3, 1974, pp. 103–104.

Walker, Alice, "In Search of Our Mothers' Gardens: Honoring the Creativity of the Black Woman," in *Jackson State Review*, Vol. 61, 1974, pp. 49, 52.

Wheatley, Phillis, *Complete Writings*, edited by Vincent Carretta, Penguin Books, 2001.

———, "On Being Brought from Africa to America," in *The Norton Anthology of American Literature*, Vol. 1, edited by Nina Baym, Norton, 1998, p. 825.

FURTHER READING

Baker, Houston A., Jr., *Workings of the Spirit: The Poetics of Afro-American Women's Writing*, University of Chicago Press, 1991.

>   Baker offers readings of such authors as Zora Neale Hurston, Toni Morrison, and Ntozake Shange as examples of his theoretical framework, explaining that African American women's literature is concerned with a search for spiritual identity.

Gates, Henry Louis, Jr., "Phillis Wheatley and the Nature of the Negro," in *Critical Essays on Phillis Wheatley*, edited by William H. Robinson, G. K. Hall, 1982, pp. 215–33.

>   In this essay, Gates explores the philosophical discussions of race in the eighteenth century, summarizing arguments of David Hume, John Locke, and Thomas Jefferson on the nature of "the Negro," and how they affected the reception of Wheatley's poetry.

Shockley, Ann Allen, *Afro-American Women Writers, 1746–1933: An Anthology and Critical Guide*, G. K. Hall, 1988.

>   This is a chronological anthology of black women writers from the colonial era through the Civil War and Reconstruction and into the early twentieth century. Both well-known and unknown writers are represented through biography, journals, essays, poems, and fiction.

Shuffelton, Frank, "Thomas Jefferson: Race, Culture, and the Failure of Anthropological Method," in *A Mixed Race: Ethnicity in Early America*, edited by Frank Shuffelton, Oxford University Press, 1993, pp. 257–77.

>   This essay investigates Jefferson's scientific inquiry into racial differences and his conclusions that Native Americans are intelligent and that African Americans are not. Shuffelton also surmises why Native American cultural production was prized while black cultural objects were not.

Pantoun for Chinese Women

SHIRLEY GEOK-LIN LIM

1985

"Pantoun for Chinese Women" was first published in Shirley Geok-lin Lim's third poetry collection, *No Man's Grove, and Other Poems*, which was published in 1985. "Pantoun for Chinese Women" is one of Lim's most frequently discussed poems, in part because of its stark description of murder. The poem personifies the epigraph, which describes the increase in female infanticide in 1980s China, by providing a singular example of female infanticide. Readers are thus forced to confront a social reality that is too often hidden away. They are also exposed to the helplessness experienced by Chinese women who must accept a tradition that values sons and devalues daughters. The ambivalence of the mother who agrees to the murder of her infant daughter is a powerful image that forces Lim's readers to consider the complexity of motherhood and marriage in such a culture.

The *pantoun* style, also spelled *pantun*, is a Malaysian technique that involves a very intricate repetition of lines. In Lim's poem, the tight construction of the pantoun, with its iterations, creates a greater emphasis on the injustice and oppression that Chinese women face. Lim weaves themes of infanticide, motherhood, and the implications of long-established cultural tradition into a poem that turns a statistic into a very real vision. Lim's poem reveals the injustice and oppression that women face and the effect this culture has on women's lives in China. "Pantoun for Chinese Women" has been reprinted in

the anthology *The Forbidden Stitch: An Asian American Women's Anthology*, published in 1989, and in Lim's *Monsoon History: Selected Poems*, published in 1995.

AUTHOR BIOGRAPHY

Shirley Geok-lin Lim was born in Malacca (later Malaya), Malaysia on December 27, 1944. Lim's father named her Shirley, after the movie star Shirley Temple, but he raised his only daughter as a culturally traditional Chinese woman. Lim, her father, Chin Som, her mother, Chye Neo Ang, and her brothers all lived with her paternal grandfather and her grandfather's other children and grandchildren until she was five years old. When she was five, her father opened a shoe store, and the family finally moved into their own home. Lim was eight years old when her mother abandoned the family.

Malaysia was a British colony, and so Lim received a British colonial education. English was her primary language as a child, and she was educated at a British Catholic convent school. In 1967, she received a BA with first-class honors in English from the University of Malaya in Kuala Lumpur, where she continued with graduate studies until 1969. Lim received a Fulbright Scholarship in 1969 and moved to the United States, where she entered Brandeis University, just outside Boston, Massachusetts. She completed an MA in 1971 and a PhD in 1973, both in English and American literature. While still in graduate school, Lim married Charles Bazerman, who had been a fellow graduate student at Brandeis. During her time in graduate school, Lim worked as a teaching assistant at Brandeis and at Queen's College, in New York City. After graduation, she took a position as an assistant professor at Hostos Community College, of the City University of New York. In 1976, Lim left Hostos and began teaching at Westchester Community College, part of the State University of New York.

Lim's first collection of poems, *Crossing the Peninsula, and Other Poems*, was published in Kuala Lumpur in 1980. Her first book to be published in the United States was a collection of short stories, *Another Country, and Other Stories*, published in 1982. Another book of poetry, *No Man's Grove, and Other Poems*, which includes the poem "Pantoun for Chinese Women," followed in 1985. In 1989, Lim served as one of the editors for the first anthology of Asian American women's poetry ever published, *The Forbidden Stitch: An Asian American Women's Anthology*. That same year, she published another collection of poetry, *Modern Secrets: New and Selected Poems*. Since 1994, Lim has published several additional books, including poetry, short stories, the memoir *Among the White Moon Faces: An Asian-American Memoir of Homelands* (1996), and the two novels *Joss and Gold* (2001) and *Sister Swing* (2006). She has also edited a lengthy list of journals and literary texts and has published dozens of articles and chapters in other books. Since 1991, Lim has been a professor at the University of California at Santa Barbara.

POEM TEXT

At present, the phenomena of butchering, drowning and leaving to die female infants have been very serious.

The People's Daily, Peking, March 3rd, 1983

They say a child with two mouths is no good.
In the slippery wet, a hollow space,
Smooth, gumming, echoing wide for food.
No wonder my man is not here at his place.

In the slippery wet, a hollow space,   5
A slit narrowly sheathed within its hood.
No wonder my man is not here at his place:
He is digging for the dragon jar of soot.

That slit narrowly sheathed within its hood!
His mother, squatting, coughs by the fire's
    blaze   10
While he digs for the dragon jar of soot.
We had saved ashes for a hundred days.

His mother, squatting, coughs by the fire's blaze.
The child kicks against me mewing like a flute.
We had saved ashes for a hundred days,   15
Knowing, if the time came, that we would.

The child kicks against me crying like a flute
Through its two weak mouths. His mother
    prays
Knowing when the time comes that we would,   20
For broken clay is never set in glaze.

Through her two weak mouths his mother
    prays.
She will not pluck the rooster nor serve its
    blood,
For broken clay is never set in glaze:
Women are made of river sand and wood.

She will not pluck the rooster nor serve its
    blood.   25
My husband frowns, pretending in his haste
Women are made of river sand and wood.

Milk soaks the bedding. I cannot bear the
waste.

My husband frowns, pretending in his haste.
Oh, clean the girl, dress her in ashy soot!   30
Milk soaks our bedding, I cannot bear the
waste.
They say a child with two mouths is no good.

POEM SUMMARY

Epigraph

The epigraph that opens "Pantoun for Chinese
Women" is a simple statement from a Peking
newspaper. The single sentence reports that
there is a serious problem of infanticide directed
toward female babies. These children are being
drowned, left outside to die, or murdered in
other ways. The epigraph suggests to the reader
that the content of the poem will relate to this
newspaper reference.

Stanza 1

The first stanza of Lim's poem makes clear that
female infants are devalued. In fact, a daughter is
no good for a family hoping for a male child. The
mother, who narrates the poem, places the
blame for her child's worthlessness on those
who have established a tradition in which female
children are considered useless. Lim uses the
subjective personal pronoun *they* as a vague
reference to unknown people who are not identified. The blame is clearly placed on traditions
that claim that girls have no value in this society.

Readers are reminded that the newborn
baby girl is just an extra mouth to feed. She
needs to be fed, and her mouth opens wide,
searching for her mother's breast and nourish-
ment. The child's hunger is another reminder
that the female child will take from the family
but will not give anything back when she is older.
This stanza ends with the mother's observation
that her husband is not at her bedside to celebrate the birth of a son. There is no blame
directed toward the husband because of his
absence. In fact, the mother understands that
there is no reason to celebrate this birth and no
reason for her husband to be proud, so she is not
surprised that he is absent. In this first stanza the
mother's acceptance of her husband's disappointment makes clear that she understands

and accepts the lack of value that accompanies
the birth of a female infant.

Stanza 2

As is customary for the pantoun format, the
second and fourth lines of the preceding stanza
are repeated as the first and third lines of the
following stanza. Accordingly, this stanza opens
with the line from stanza 1 that refers to the
smooth empty space of the baby girl's mouth.
This, again, is the reason why the baby's father is
not there beside his wife. The wife knows that he
is busy retrieving ashes that had been buried
during her pregnancy. As the poem reveals only
through an allusion, the ashes will be used to
suffocate the baby. Even in this stanza, there is
no suggestion that the mother intends to protect
her child. There is only regret that the child is not
the hoped-for son. If the child had been a boy,
the father would not need to dig up the ashes that
they had buried.

Stanza 3

Because the mother's pregnancy now has no
value, her husband's mother squats down by
the fire and does not celebrate her new grand-
child. Instead of proudly cooing over the new
baby, this grandmother sits apart, away from the
mother and child, waiting for her son to dig up
the jar of ashes. Readers are told in the fourth
line of this stanza that these are ashes that the
family saved for the past three months of the
pregnancy. That is, as the mother's belly grew
large with child, the husband, his wife, and his
mother planned for the murder of the infant if a
girl were to be born. Presumably, the child will
be placed in a box, with ashes that will be used to
smother her face.

Stanza 4

The opening line again tells readers that the husband's mother is by the fire. She remains separate
from her daughter-in-law and granddaughter
while she waits for her son to return with the
ashes. While the two mothers wait, the child lies
against her mother's body. Her mother feels each
tiny squirm and movement and is perhaps
reminded of the same movements that this baby
made when still inside her womb. The baby's
small sounds must remind the mother that the
infant is alive and needs to be fed.

The last two lines of this stanza remind the
reader of how the family saved ashes in prepara-
tion for this moment. They hoped for a son but

prepared for a daughter. If the desired son had been born, the father would not have needed to dig up the jar of ashes. In the final line of this stanza, the poet makes clear that the family, including the mother, has been prepared to do what would be necessary. Thus, her pregnancy was not just a time of planning and joyous celebration, as it was also a time of planning for the possibility that they would murder the child. The mother knows that murdering the baby is what the family will do; she has no doubt of the outcome, even though her words are tinged with regret.

Stanza 5

The opening line of this stanza reminds readers that the child is alive, as she makes small noises and moves against her mother. The kicks and noises remind the mother of the child's existence—but she is a girl, and her fate has been determined. The infant is powerless against a tradition that renders girls valueless. The mother-in-law prays, perhaps for the child, who is not unloved, just unwanted. The husband's mother is not without feeling, but she, too, a female herself, knows that a baby girl has no value.

The poet repeats the line from the previous stanza explaining that the family has always known what they must do and has been prepared to do it, but this time, the line is a continuation of the grandmother's prayer. The husband's mother has always known what must be done, just as her daughter-in-law has known. Thus, in this stanza readers may imagine that the grandmother is also filled with regret that the child must die. The baby girl is compared to a clay pot that breaks before it has been fired. There is no point in finishing the pot; it is worthless. For many Chinese families—particularly those in poverty—there may likewise be no point in letting a baby girl grow to become a child, a teenager, or an adult, as she simply cannot be afforded. She is essentially "broken," as she has no value and must be thrown out.

Stanza 6

The mother-in-law is also an ineffectual female. In a sense, the husband's mother is as helpless and has as little value as her newborn granddaughter. She uses her powerless mouth to pray; whether her prayers are intended to save her granddaughter, perhaps, or to change the traditions and culture that place no value on the life of a girl is open to interpretation. The

grandmother is defenseless against this tradition. She will not prepare a feast to celebrate, and the rooster will not be killed. The rooster has particular importance in Chinese culture, as it is one of the twelve zodiac signs, and rooster blood is thought to represent good fortune and to signify a strong life. Roosters also provide good meat, and so having a rooster slaughtered to eat and for blood to drink would be an important celebration for the birth of a boy. Since there is nothing to celebrate with the birth of a girl, the rooster's life is spared—while the life of the baby girl will be forfeit.

The third line of this stanza again tells readers that a baby girl is like a clay pot that is broken and never completed. This time the line ends with a colon, and so the following line builds upon a phrase that in the previous stanza made clear that a baby girl is as unfinished and worthless as a broken pot. Here, women are compared to wood and sand from a river, both of which are bendable and malleable. River sand constantly shifts and reforms to redirect the river's flow. Wood is porous and easily bent, but it is also easily repaired because it is supple and flexible. Thus, perhaps, unlike the rigid traditions that place no value on females, women are pliable and can adapt when called upon to do so. On the other hand, the reference to sand and wood can also be understood to mean that even adult women are perceived as less than human—as no more than the sum of the clay used to make the pot and the wood burned to fire it.

Stanza 7

The opening line of this stanza reminds readers that there will be no celebration at the birth of the baby girl. The husband is in a hurry, now. He has the ashes and is ready to kill the baby, but he frowns. This is perhaps meant to assuage his wife's misery, or, as would be indicated by the way the second line continues into the third line, he may be frowning because he is unhappy to be doing what he is doing; in order to do what he believes he must do, he must pretend that he believes that women are of so little value that the killing of an infant daughter is justified. Meanwhile, the mother's milk has dampened the bed. The nuzzling of the infant against her mother and the soft sounds of hunger caused the mother's breast milk to flow, but the child is not receiving that milk. The poet laments the waste—the waste of nurturing milk and, with the child about to be killed or already killed, the waste of the child's life.

Stanza 8

In the final stanza, the husband continues to frown, as he continues to pretend to believe that his daughter has no value, that he is doing the right thing. The mother expresses her wish for the child to be cleaned, then also asks that the girl be dressed in sooty ashes. The mother perhaps wants to honor the child by washing her even though she will be smothered in ashes afterward. The line could also be understood to mean that the mother considers the act of dressing the girl in ashes to be an act of final cleansing, in that the daughter will be cleansed of her life. The poet next repeats the line from the previous stanza that refers to the lost milk and the death of the newborn as a waste. The mother's milk has gone unused, a reminder that no child will be nursing at the mother's breast. As is customary for the pantoun format, the final line of the poem repeats the opening line. A female child is useless; she is just an extra mouth to feed. As was the case before, the blame is placed on traditions, or on some traditional persons, that hold that girls have no value in this society. When this line opened the poem, it was a statement of history, culture, and tradition. When it reappears as the final line, it reads more as a lament for what this family has had to do—for the daughter who is no more—and for what cannot be changed.

THEMES

Cultural Traditions

The sentence that opens "Pantoun for Chinese Women" is a vague reference to the traditions that govern this new mother's life. The very first word is a subjective personal pronoun that refers to a collective group of people. These unnamed people, whose values have determined that a girl's life has no meaning, are the people who are responsible for the family's choice to murder the child. The reader learns from the mother of her own acceptance of the family's choice. She mentions that she knew ahead of time that if the baby were to be a girl, she would have to be killed. The narrator uses the possessive pronoun *we* to include herself in this planning. Thus, she is helping to continue the traditions of a culture that places so little value on girls that the killing of female babies is routinely practiced and even planned for during pregnancy.

TOPICS FOR FURTHER STUDY

- Choose a brief sentence from a newspaper and use it as the basis for a poem, just as Lim has done with "Pantoun for Chinese Women." In writing your poem, try to mimic the pantoun style, with its specific repetitions of sentences. When you have completed your poem, write a brief evaluation of your work, comparing it to Lim's poem. In your written critique of your poem, consider what you learned about the difficulty of writing a poem in the pantoun style.

- Research infanticide in China and in India, two countries where the birth of a girl is traditionally not valued. After you have gathered enough information, create a poster that compares these two countries' female infanticide rates as well as any efforts that are being made to halt the practice.

- Poetry should create images and pictures in the reader's mind. Draw or illustrate one of the images from Lim's poem. You can also use photography if you choose. Then write an essay that explains how you chose and produced your image and what you think your image adds to your understanding of Lim's poem.

- The epigraph that Lim uses to begin her poem tells readers about the murder of female infants. It does not tell readers anything about the mothers of those infants. Research the lives of women in China and write an essay in which you discuss your findings. While focusing on motherhood, also research what is known about marriage in China and how marriage changes women's lives.

The Role of the Father

The one demonstrably unsympathetic person in this poem is the narrator's husband. The narrator relates that he is not there with her, even though she has just given birth to his child.

Presumably, rather than comforting his wife, he left as soon as he discovered that his new baby is a daughter. The new mother is not surprised that her husband has gone, as they had already planned for what was to be done in the event that the child was a girl. The narrator paints an ambiguous picture of her husband, who performs his tasks hastily, as if eager to kill the baby, but who frowns and pretends that he values women as little as his culture values them. As the narrator describes it, the frown can be understood to be not real; perhaps he is only pretending to be sad that he must kill his child. From this perspective, his rushing to complete the deed before either his wife or mother changes her mind reveals his true nature: He is in such a hurry to commit murder that his display of grief is no more than a frown. He cannot even show sympathy or understanding for the loss his wife might feel, as his mind is fixated only on the son that his wife failed to give him. From another perspective, the fact that he must pretend not to care indicates that he does what he does against even his own heart's wishes. Nevertheless, there can be little doubt that, whatever his emotional state, he performs the horrific deed that supposedly must be performed.

Infanticide

The author's choice to write a poem about infanticide calls attention to the issue. The epigraph tells readers that female infanticide is a very serious problem in China. As the reader studies the poem, it becomes clear that the poem is about the fate that awaits a newborn baby girl. Lim makes infanticide personal by making the mother the narrator, such that the mother's voice relates the details of the events that follow the girl's birth. Although the mother has helped to plan for this possibility, she is ambivalent about having to kill her baby. Lim makes the mother-narrator regretful over the waste of milk that will not nourish the infant and over the human life that will be wasted because the child is not the desired son. Since the reader sees infanticide from the mother's point of view, there is a greater impact on readers, who are compelled to see the problem in a more personal way.

Maternity and Motherhood

There are two mothers in Lim's poem. The new mother narrates the poem, and so readers see the events from her point of view. The baby's body is snuggled against her mother, who feels the child move against her, just as the child moved in her womb only the day before. The mother's milk flows, an involuntary acknowledgement of her role as nourishing mother to this baby girl. The milk is a reminder that this mother's role is to care for her baby; to kill her child is the antithesis of motherhood. The mother knows in her mind that she will have to kill her newborn, but her body remembers the child and longs to feed her. The mother-in-law is also a mother, one who once felt her own son kick inside her womb and who once felt her breast milk flow, as well. Initially, the narrator describes the mother-in-law as distant. She stays away from the new mother and infant, squatting down next to the fire. When the narrator explains that her husband's mother is praying, however, the reader suddenly sees her in a more sympathetic light. The killing of this child cannot be easy for her, either. The two mothers are forced to do what their culture tells them is their obligation, even though motherhood is about giving life, not taking life. The ambivalence of both mothers regarding what lies ahead is clearly established in the story the narrator tells.

STYLE

Asian American Women's Poetry

The phrase "Asian American women's poetry" is a broad term that refers to many different traditions, none of which are easily defined. Thus, the term really refers to a multicultural tradition of women writing largely about topics that, according to Lim, have "too long been forbidden to Asian American women." In her introduction to the anthology *The Forbidden Stitch*, Lim describes Asian American women's poetry as capable of increasing readers' awareness of cultural difference. Although Asian American women poets represent a diverse multicultural background, they also tend to reflect a distinctly Asian voice, whether speaking of their countries of origin or of their adopted American country. Their poetry is often marked by emphases on culture, kinship, and family relationships. Lim's poem reflects such an emphasis on culture and family dynamics. "Pantoun for Chinese Women" narrates a story that is not usually the subject of poetry, and it is a story that is not often discussed. The issue of female infanticide in China is a distinctly Asian issue that reflects concerns about kinship, family, and cultural values.

Epigraph

An epigraph is generally known as an inscription used to mark a burial. Originally epigraphs were used to mark Egyptian tombs. The Greeks and Romans wrote epigraphs to celebrate their generals, but they also wrote epigraphs that celebrated the lives of their wives and children. An epigraph is also a quotation placed at the beginning of a literary work to serve as a sort of introduction to the topic. The use of the epigraph to begin Lim's poem correlates with its purpose as a way to mark a tomb. "Pantoun for Chinese Women" is in a sense a funeral ode for a newborn child, and the epigraph serves as the tombstone that explains that this child is only one of many who have died for the same reason—because the child was a girl.

Pantoun

The *pantoun* poem, which is sometimes also spelled *pantoum* or *pantun*, originated in Malaysia during the fifteenth century. The poem consists of several four-line stanzas; the number of stanzas has no designated limit, and so the poem can be any length. The structure is very rigid, however. The second and fourth lines of every stanza are repeated as the first and third lines in the following stanza. The first line of the poem is also repeated as the final line of the poem. Thus, almost every line in a pantoun is repeated once. Typically, the first two lines of each stanza create an image, while the final two lines provide the thematic meaning. One of the most interesting aspects of a pantoun is how the meaning can be changed when the lines are repeated. Lim does this with subtle changes in wording and punctuation. For example, in the fifth stanza, the narrator describes her baby's two feeble mouths and her mother-in-law praying; when the line is repeated in the sixth stanza, the mother-in-law is the one said to have two feeble mouths. This indicates that the mother-in-law has little more power than her newborn granddaughter.

Social Awareness Poetry

Poetry can be used to increase social awareness of injustice. Poetry that focuses on social issues can give voice to topics that are important but are not often discussed. Poems of protest can be used to seek an end to war, as they were during the Vietnam War, and they can be used to create social change. The emotional impact of a poem can spur readers to action; Lim's poem, for example, may inspire readers to investigate infanticide and work to eliminate the practice. Lim's use of the mother as narrator makes the poem more personal and the impact of infanticide more dramatic, thus making the poem itself more influential.

HISTORICAL CONTEXT

History of Infanticide

Lim's poem "Pantoun for Chinese Women" puts a personal face on the story of infanticide in China. Lim shows only one family's decision to kill their infant girl, but the problem, of course, extends far beyond that single family. The history of infanticide is quite long. Female infanticide was practiced by the Greeks during their golden age and has been practiced by almost every civilized country since then. Many victims of infanticide have been children with physical handicaps or female infants. Often, population control and economics have been motivating factors for infanticide. In times of food shortages, infants may be killed to preserve the supply of food, but female infanticide in particular reveals a preference for male children. Infanticide may have been a serious problem in Arabia, as well, since the Koran includes laws against female infanticide. Indeed, the historical evidence regarding such laws tends to suggest that infanticide must have been enough of a problem to create a need to outlaw the practice. In Victorian England, infanticide was frequent enough to become the subject of novels, such as those written by Charles Dickens and George Eliot. Infanticide is even a problem in the United States, which has one of the highest levels of infant murder among developed countries. In fact, historical evidence suggests that at the end of the 1970s, female infanticide was no more frequent in China than in many European countries. For children under one year of age, the murderer is most often the mother. Historically, in fact, the parent who most frequently commits infanticide is the mother.

Infanticide in China

As is the case for nearly all countries, in China infanticide has a long history, but after the formation of the People's Republic of China in 1949,

COMPARE
&
CONTRAST

- **1980s:** In 1981, the United Nations adopts the Declaration on the Elimination of Discrimination against Women. This is the only international statement guaranteeing women's human rights.

  Today: In 2005, a United Nations statement by Secretary-General Kofi Annan calls violence against women a global issue. He cites infanticide, genital mutilations, and dowry-based violence as some of the most common instances of violence directed toward women.

- **1980s:** Because of China's one-child rule, the number of abandoned children increases dramatically. The majority of these children are girls. The orphanages in which they are placed are so poorly run that mortality rates are between 50 and 90 percent in some areas of China, according to the organization Human Rights Watch. It is estimated that most of the abandoned children never even reach orphanages, dying on the streets instead.

  Today: In 2007, the U.N. General Assembly establishes the post of special representative of the secretary-general on violence against children. The position is created as part of the effort to eliminate the hidden and often socially approved violence against children that occurs in many nations.

- **1980s:** China dismantles collective farming and allows farmers the freedom to run their farms as private enterprises. Farmers expect that this change will allow them more economic freedom and a greater ability to support their families.

  Today: In 2005, there are more than 87,000 protests by farmers and workers, who complain about the economic instability and disparities that have led to greater poverty in rural areas (where the government has artificially depressed wages). Many families are living in extreme poverty.

---

the practice fell into disfavor; infanticide was outlawed, and as a result, infanticides dropped significantly. The increase in infanticides in the mid-1980s is most often attributed to the one-child policy adopted by the Chinese government in 1979. Under this policy, families having more than one child are economically penalized. Parents who have more than one child might be subjected to monetary fines, or husbands could lose their jobs. Rural families are permitted two children, but only if the first child is a girl. With the practical limit of a single child, the preferred choice is most often to have a son. The preference for boys is based upon cultural traditions. Boys carry on the family name, and they are expected to work in business or on the farm and thus support the family. In addition, sons are the designated caregivers of elderly parents.

When girls marry, they essentially then belong to their husband's family. Thus, girls are of no lasting benefit to their parents. To increase the possibility of having a male child, prenatal testing has become quite common; if the fetus is a girl, the mother may have an elective abortion. This practice, too, has been outlawed, but it still continues outside the law. In areas where sex-selective abortion is not an option, female infanticide becomes more common. The killing of infants is also against the law but still continues. Many girls are abandoned, while some are turned over to adoption agencies. Indeed, the children in China's adoption agencies are overwhelmingly female, and in many cases the orphanages are where girls are sent to die. A September 1995 report in the *South China Morning Post* revealed that in many orphanages, girls die of neglect in record numbers. Infanticide and sex-selective abortions have created a significant disparity in the numbers of girls and boys in China. Some estimates suggest that anywhere from 80 to 110 million men in China will be unable to marry due to a shortage of women. Regardless of the social and economic problems caused by infanticide, the cultural desire for sons has resulted in a veritable genocide of China's daughters.

CRITICAL OVERVIEW

Shirley Geok-lin Lim is a prolific writer. In addition to her novels, her memoir, and her many collections of poems and short stories, she has edited several anthologies and has published more than 130 articles or chapters in books. To be in such demand suggests that Lim's work is much admired. Yet, in spite of her copious output, her poetry has received "little critical attention," as Andrew Ng notes in his 2007 article in *Women: A Cultural Review*. Ng notes that "Lim's poems provide profound insights into Malaysia," where she was born. Her poems also address "the problematic social spaces of women." One poem that has received more critical attention and that addresses the social space of women is "Pantoun for Chinese Women." Ng refers to this poem as "one of Lim's most powerful poems." One element to the poem that Ng suggests is particularly impressive is Lim's use of the pantoun format. The repetition of lines in the pantoun works to reenact the trauma that victims of abuse feel when they constantly relive a traumatic event. Thus, the use of the pantoun, according to Ng, creates a poem that is "stylistically sensitive to a traumatic experience that cannot be expressed directly." Since for the mother, "mere words fail to convey her suffering," the choice to construct this poem as a pantoun allows the poet to create a work "stylistically sensitive" to that suffering. Overall, then, the repetition of lines and the subtle changes that Lim makes in punctuation help to create a more profound image of feminine grief.

In a 1986 review of *No Man's Grove*, the collection in which "Pantoun for Chinese Women" appears, Bernard Gadd is especially enthusiastic about Lim's poetry. In his review, which was printed in *World Literature Today*, Gadd says of Lim that this collection "confirms her as a writer of verse that is not only perceptive and intelligent but also enjoyable." Lim's poetry is compared favorably with the English romantic tradition, and in particular her use of imagery is described as being "lush." Gadd refers to Lim's writing as "quick with

intelligence." Although Lim's literary work has not received as much attention as one might expect, the attention she has received has been largely positive.

CRITICISM

Sheri Metzger Karmiol

Karmiol has a doctorate in English Renaissance literature and teaches literature and drama at the University of New Mexico, where she is a lecturer in the university honors program. She is also a professional writer and the author of several reference texts on poetry and drama. In this essay, Karmiol discusses Lim's use of imagery in "Pantoun for Chinese Women."

Poetry can provide readers with a way to view ideas, history, and customs that might otherwise never be experienced. Poetry illuminates a world that readers have never seen, never visited, and in some cases, never knew existed. Poetry educates and inspires, and it changes the world by illuminating injustice and by showing readers that the world needs to be changed. Poetry creates an emotional response that can make it difficult for readers to simply walk away from suffering. Most importantly, poetry clarifies the injustices of bias and discrimination and educates readers about the need for change. In "Pantoun for Chinese Women," Shirley Lim uses analogy and imagery to create a picture of helplessness and oppression in women's lives.

Poetry uses language to create meaning, but not in the same way that prose creates meaning. Poetic meaning is derived from the reader's own experience, which in part depends on the analogies created by the poet. For instance, in Maxine Hong Kingston's memoir *The Woman Warrior: Memoirs of a Girlhood among Ghosts*, the narrator tells the story of her mother, who was a midwife in their village. In one instance, her mother delivered a baby who was born without an anus and who was subsequently left outside in the outhouse to die. The narrator uses this story as an example to suggest that her mother was not one of those midwives who would "prepare a box of clean ashes beside the birth bed in case of a girl." In such cases, if the baby was a girl, the baby's face would be buried in the ashes. The narrator's mother said of the act of smothering the baby, "It was very easy." While this dramatic episode is designed to get the reader's attention, it does not function in the same way as a poetic

WHAT DO I READ NEXT?

- *Among the White Moon Faces: An Asian-American Memoir of Homelands* (2000) is Lim's memoir. It includes her memories of life in Malaysia and of life after immigrating to the United States.

- Lim's second novel, *Sister Swing* (2006), is the story of three sisters whose Chinese ancestry continues to become the focus of their new lives in the United States.

- *Transnational Asia Pacific: Gender, Culture, and the Public Sphere* (1999), edited by Shirley Geok-lin Lim, Larry E. Smith, and Wimal Dissanayake, is a collection of essays that explore the ways in which globalization influences culture and society, especially the ways in which women's identities are impacted.

- *Home to Stay: Asian American Women's Fiction* (1990), edited by Sylvia Watanabe and Carol Bruchac, is a collection of short stories by twenty-nine different Asian American women writers.

- *An Interethnic Companion to Asian American Literature* (1997), edited by King-Kok Cheung, offers writings that explore the cultural identity of Asian American writers. The collection of eleven essays explores gender, immigration, and critical theory as well as other topics that contribute to an understanding of the cultural context of Asian American poetry.

rendering of the same situation. In her poem, Lim describes the pregnant mother-to-be, her husband, and his mother saving ashes for three months, so that if the baby was a girl, they would know what to do. The image is incomplete, such that it requires that the reader understand the unspoken meaning of the ashes. The three months of saving ashes are the last trimester of the wife's pregnancy. This is a time when the

> LIM'S USE OF IMAGERY IN 'PANTOUN FOR CHINESE WOMEN' CREATES AND ENRICHES THE MEANINGS THAT ARE HIDDEN WITHIN THE POEM."

baby is fully formed; he or she is growing and moving in the mother's womb. All of this is implied but not stated, as the poet only alludes to the possible interpretations through an image. It is up to the reader to fill in the details. Poetry, then, is typically not as easy as prose. Kingston leaves no room for misinterpretation, as she does not require that the reader create his or her own meaning.

Kingston's memoir presents another example of how a daughter can be eliminated from the household, when she depicts an episode that occurs in the marketplace. The narrator describes her mother walking through the Canton markets and coming upon a scene where parents are selling their daughters to be slaves. These were "the sellers of little girls." Sometimes there was only a father selling his daughter, but other times "there were fathers and mothers selling their daughters, whom they pushed forward" as potential buyers walked by them. The implication in these descriptions is clear. Girls can be assigned so little value as to be sold like merchandise, a commodity to be disposed of like vegetables from the garden or furniture marketed for sale. Lim also creates an image of girls as valueless or as useless members of the family, but her description has hidden meanings and depth not available to prose writers. Lim describes a girl as a child with two mouths, a child who is no good. The child with two mouths is a child that is doubly wasteful. No infant contributes productivity to a household, but a boy will grow up to help on the farm or in the business. He will care for his parents in their old age, but a girl contributes nothing. She just eats food and needs clothing and wastes resources. She will marry and then belong to her husband's family. The value assigned to girls is made clear in Kingston's image of parents selling their daughters; but Lim's image of two mouths carries meaning that must be deciphered, and every person who reads the poem finds different meaning in it.

It is the reader who creates and re-creates meaning with every reading of a poem. Kristie S. Fleckenstein argues in her essay in *College English* that images do not just exist. Instead, "an image evolves when we shape a reality based on the logic of analogy." That is, readers create meaning from the imagery that the poet creates, and they shape the image based on analogies with which they are familiar. Another example of how imagery enriches "Pantoun for Chinese Women" is found in Lim's use of language to describe the mother's flowing breast milk. This foundational image creates multiple supplementary images. In the most common analogy attached to the image of breast milk, the milk signifies the maternity of the mother and her readiness to nurse her new baby. But in Lim's poem, the breast milk soaks the mother's bedding and goes to waste. It soaks the bedding because the baby is being killed, and all that the mother can do is mourn the waste. She grieves for the waste of the baby, as well as for the waste of the milk. The image of wasted breast milk suggests multiple meanings of loss and suffering, of a mother denied the opportunity to nurse her baby and a baby denied her life. As Fleckenstein observes, "An image is never just one thing; it is many different things at the same time." The poem has more power, then, by virtue of the multifaceted image that the poet creates of wasted milk. Once again, it is the reader's interpretation of that imagery that infuses the poem with meaning. Because poetry requires that the reader seek out meaning and work for understanding, some readers conclude that poetry is just too difficult to read—and prose ends up being the more privileged literature. According to Fleckenstein, "Historically, language has overshadowed image, preventing us from recognizing the essential role of imagery in meaning." If readers privilege the imagery, they emerge from a reading of "Pantoun for Chinese Women" with a greater understanding of the helplessness of women's lives in China.

Imagery is especially important in understanding the cultural context of "Pantoun for Chinese Women." In his essay in *Women: A Cultural Review*, Andrew Ng points out that Lim's poetry reflects a cultural context that positions Chinese women as both victimized and silenced, such that their suffering has not been given voice. While the husband in "Pantoun for Chinese Women" goes outside to dig up the ashes that he will need to kill his newborn daughter, his wife and mother can only remain silently in the house. The new mother holds her baby close to her, while the husband's mother squats by the fire and prays. She prays, but her prayers only emerge from her own weak mouth. Neither woman objects to the murder of the baby girl; in fact, they have participated in saving the ashes and have always been prepared to do what they know must be done. Ng argues that "Lim's poems imaginatively recreate moments of" the suffering endured by Chinese women; where these women have had no voice and thus no history, her poems "reposition them back into 'history' through a different discursive strategy (poetry instead of official history record)." If history has not recorded the suffering of women who are undervalued or even valueless, then Lim can give them value by articulating their pain and suffering. Female infants—the primary victims of infanticide—have even less voice, but Lim manages in "Pantoun for Chinese Women" to take these invisible and silenced infants and make them visible. She even gives them a voice, when she has the infant cry against her mother's body. The baby, who nuzzles against her mother's body and whose movements remind both the mother and Lim's readers that this child should live, becomes real. This is not an abstract statistic, as the newspaper quoted in the epigraph might have provided; this is a living child, a baby whose birth would have been celebrated if only "she" had been a "he."

In the world of "Pantoun for Chinese Women," males are the honored members of society. They have the advantages and the opportunities denied to females; however, it is the women who people Lim's poems. These female protagonists are drawn from what Ng observes is "a distinct cultural background which privileges the male." According to Ng, Lim's poetry, "in a sense, can be seen as a means by which these repressed voices can be reinstated into a public space of discourse." In "Pantoun for Chinese Women," the husband's voice is mediated by his wife's narration. He is silenced, with only his actions and mannerisms described. This is an example of Lim's choice to give voice to the mother's point of view. Ng remarks that in Lim's poetry, "It is often the women's viewpoint that is privileged," and that is certainly the case in this poem.

Lim's use of imagery in "Pantoun for Chinese Women" creates and enriches the meanings that are hidden within the poem. In each reading of Lim's poem, readers find something new hidden within the images. In this poem, what emerges is the voice of a woman who has not been given any other way to express her pain. The brief newspaper reference from the epigraph does not tell a story of suffering and anguish; it tells of a serious social problem, but the scope of loss is not articulated. That task is for the poet to perform. Ng asserts that "Lim's poems, by re-imagining the lives of marginalized women, effectively return these forgotten victims to contemporaneity, and directly articulate their suffering and trauma." To ignore these women's voices is to ignore social history. Lim is not about to let that happen.

Source: Sheri Metzger Karmiol, Critical Essay on "Pantoun for Chinese Women," in *Poetry for Students*, Gale, Cengage Learning, 2009.

Mohammed A. Quayam

In the following excerpt from an interview, Lim contrasts writing poetry with academic writing and discusses her Malaysian-Chinese heritage.

. . . [Mohammed A. Quayum:] Why do you write? Is it for the sheer joy of writing—the joy of telling a story, for example—or because you have some ideas to convey, some instructions perhaps? Is writing an obsessive, compulsive activity for you or is it a way of solving problems, private or societal?

[Shirley Geok-lin Lim:] When I was much younger I might have replied that I wrote for the "sheer joy" of writing, but this has not been the case for a long time. That I feel driven to write is clear. That writing provides me with a deeply satisfying sense of coming to who I am, becoming who I believe myself to be, is also clear. But I am less certain now that "joy" has anything to do with it.

More often than not, writing means long hours and days of loneliness, isolation, doubt. And more and more I feel the absence of time for the kind of writing I want to do. Working on this interview with you, for example, means losing time for writing. Entire months and even years go by with very little time for the kind of writing you are asking me about.

Writing is surely no way to go about solving problems. I would like to think that my poems and prose works offer symbolic action and so participate in a significant way in the social world—in a political public sphere, but that is a

> I FEEL PROFOUNDLY THAT I HAVE NOT BECOME THE WRITER I MAY HAVE BEEN IF I HAD TAKEN THE RISK TO LEAVE ACADEMIA."

faint hope and as easily winked out even during my lucid moments.

Is writing obsessive for me? Not in the psycho-neurotic sense, the way an obsessive-compulsive has no rational control over her actions. My sense of duty, my work ethic, is very strong, and I spend most of my life devoted to my salaried profession as a university teacher and citizen. Social responsibilities take up an enormous amount of my energy, whether they were/are childcare, housekeeping chores or community services. If I did not have to work for a living, I would probably have devoted myself to the work of poetry and fiction and be a different kind of writer.

MAQ: You had a difficult childhood and adolescence I understand. How have those early experiences helped to shape the writer you are?

SL: It is perhaps those early years that have made it so difficult for me to disengage from the academic profession, which offers steady employment and social respect, to enter fully into the life of writing. In that way, those years have made me a discontinuous writer. I am always amazed to hear anyone say that I am a "prolific" writer. Compared with prose authors such as Charles Dickens, Mark Twain, George Eliot, Virginia Woolf, or, in our time, Doris Lessing, Salman Rushdie, Anita Desai, or poets such as Adrienne Rich—and I do not mean to claim equal standing with them, merely use them as known figures for illustrative purpose—my literary output is meagre. All these figures lived their lives professionally and socially as writers. I have not.

I feel profoundly that I have not become the writer I may have been if I had taken the risk to leave academia. But then, knowing how difficult if not impossible it is to make a living out of selling one's books, I might have been tempted to write to please the market. My writing has remained quirky, not attuned to a popular readership, really "minor," "deterritorialized," in the way that Deleuze and Guattari used these terms, as a form of "flight from territorialization." Childhood misery, of course, has also provided some of the materials and themes in my writing, particularly in the poems and the memoir. More significant I think is the ideological weight that bears on most of my thinking—the leftward leaning perspective, the sympathy for the weaker, poorer, the outsider.

MAQ: You are both a poet and a fiction writer, and an academic to boot. How important is it for a writer/writer-academic to keep abreast with the global developments in writing and criticism? Does the theoretical awareness, or awareness of criticism and literary scholarship, interfere with the process of writing which I believe is largely a spontaneous/ unconscious activity?

SL: A scholar and teacher in a top research university is by the very nature of the institution expected to be part of the leading edge in her discipline; and as you know, disciplines are now shaped within globally circulating discourses. Air travel, the Internet (which has practically made faxes unnecessary!), even the development of English as a global language for the science, technology, and infotainment industries, signify that this academic must be a global worker as well.

But a writer is not or not always an academic. I do not believe that a poet or even a novelist needs to know what is happening in the next village, not to say in "global developments in writing and criticism." A sense of history for a writer may even shirk a sense of the global contemporary, which in its speed and transitoriness may be only so much ineffectual noise for the writer.

This is not to say that there is one prescriptive mode for a writer to process his materials. Doris Lessing is as different socio-politically and stylistically from Jane Austen as a woman writer can be, and yet one may trace certain similarities of social engagement in their novels. "Theoretical awareness" may be so much useless twaddle for some writers and catalytic for others. Writers are as varied as the fruits of nature and they produce in many kinds of climates. Only totalitarian absoluteness can silence them, and not for long.

MAQ: Would you elaborate on the way you write? Are there any idiosyncrasies associated with your writing such as gulping down a big cup

of coffee as, for example, Hemingway did every time he sat down to write?

SL: I write best given huge chunks of time. Being away from familiar ground helps. Being alone helps. Having other writers to talk to and engage with helps; and if this appears to contradict the statement before, that can't be helped. Not having to worry about laundry and meals and public appearance helps. In short, I have found that living like a pampered hermit, the way that Thoreau did when he wrote of being alone at Walden Pond while all the while he was going off for meals every evening with the Emersons and others down the road, helps. I would live in a writers' retreat, in the lap of a social privilege that provides tranquil hours and a supportive community when needed.

Alas, absent these conditions, I write in between chores, on weekends and teaching breaks and very occasional fellowships, after I have completed some research project. My memoir and novel were written under such conditions. I write long journal entries on plane rides. As for poems, they usually arrive late at night and more and more rarely as my nighttime energy level declines with age.

MAQ: In what way does teaching influence your own work?

SL: My immediate response is very little. Perhaps if I spend more time pondering on this question I may come up with a better answer. My immediate response, however, is that the time taken up teaching is time away from writing. In that way, teaching may have saved the public from more books by me.

MAQ: How is writing a poem different for you from writing a short story, or for that matter an academic essay?

SL: A poem is an intense writing experience. I have hardly ever written a poem in cold blood, that is, as an exercise with no emotional occasion attached. The heat of the feelings that move me to the act of composing or that accompany that composition, to my mind, is what produces, cooks, the rhythm, the pulse that gives rise to lines of words. Such feelings become "embodied" for me in the poetic form, in its sounds and rhythms.

Poetry does not sprawl for me—it is no extravagant exhibition of language, rather an extravagant exhibition of intensity, the form the words take, their lines, images, rhythms, rhymes, alliterative force, shaping an inward sense that is the radical opposite of "emoting." I dislike poems that emote, the way I dislike make-up on a woman for deceiving appearance. More and more I am trying to discover an organic form that is true to the particular moment of the particular poem, the simple plain inwardness of that moment. A short story also possesses intensity but that quality is more carefully and deliberately rather than "spontaneously" wrought. One must take care not to be writing poetry when writing a short story, even as rhythmic and figurative language plays a major part in how a story evokes meaning and feeling. Prose has its own hard-won pleasures from poetry, a different pacing and staging for irony, ideas, and insights, a compulsory insistence on separate voices of characters, their separate values and actions. Michel Bakhtin is correct in noting that the novel (and the short story) comes from a dialogic imagination that incorporates heteroglossic and carnivalesque features, while poetry—especially lyric poetry—tends to work in a more monological manner.

As for academic writing, it belongs to a very different universe of discourse. The imperatives for citation, rigorous evidentiary argument, some form of logical clarity, despite what appears to be humanism's total surrender to the poststructuralist dogmas of undecidability, indeterminacy, and contingency, all impose a closed conventional structure where even writing something differently becomes framed as playing against such discursivity, that is, becomes part of academic writing.

MAQ: Is California or Kuala Lumpur your home turf? You left Malaysia to take up residence in America more than thirty years ago but you still seem to be "writing home"—narrating Malaysian life and experiences in many of your stories, including your first novel Joss and Gold, *which is partly set in Malaysia and deals mostly with Malaysian characters.*

SL: Kuala Lumpur is definitely not MY home turf; I am not delusionary. But neither is California. As I had said earlier, my work is deterritorialized, an ironic prior property for a writer to whom "home" has been such a first-order question and thematic.

Much of my imagination has been and continues to be located in my earlier experiences as a Malaysian. After all, not only was I about 24 years old when I left Kuala Lumpur for Boston, but I return home frequently to visit my numerous brothers, relatives, and friends. The prospect of spending a good part of my later years in Malaysia is very much a possibility.

But I am a US citizen with an American family. This is not to say that I have no home turf or two. Imagination is a tricky power; it refuses to stay in one or even two places.

My recent two years as Chair Professor of English at the University of Hong Kong resulted in a number of poems that, for the first time, explore the question of a Chinese identity in my individual and collective history. However, more and more I find myself wanting to explore what having lived in America, as you note, for over thirty years means imaginatively.

MAQ: Really moving from Kuala Lumpur to California has not changed your circumstances all that much—it is like moving from one margin to another, from being a Malaysian Chinese to an Asian American, right?

SL: Your assumption is incorrect. The status of a Malaysian Chinese is nothing like that of an Asian American, because the two states have very different constitutions and institutional structures. What you imply, I think, is that both identities are marginal. But they are identities embedded in very different socio-political economies and rights. Asian Americans do not face a constitutional restriction on their rights as citizens. Prejudice and racism are as present in the United States as they are anywhere, but actions proven to arise from these evils are legally prohibited. The rights of minorities are protected by the constitution, and although there is no utopia here, no internal security act bans struggles for a more equal and just union. Of course the ISA applies equally to ALL Malaysians, regardless of ethnicity. As a US citizen, I can open my big mouth, and I sometimes do, without fear of losing my job, losing a promotion, or losing my liberty.

However, Chinese Malaysians are not a marginal community in Kuala Lumpur as they are here in California. While Chinese Malaysians are not the majority community, neither are they marginal to the nation, its history, culture, and economy the way that Asian Americans still are in the United States.

That is, my circumstances as an equal national citizen here make me part of the American mainstream, whereas in Malaysia, I would be a marginalized citizen. But my ethnic position here makes me part of a very marginal ethnic cultural community whereas in Malaysia I would remain part of a visible and vital cultural community. Citizenship rights versus ethnic community vitality: perhaps that is the dilemma in US assimilation for Asians coming to America.

MAQ: What are the distractions of a modern writer? Do you think literature could survive the current technological onslaught or is it becoming increasingly "obsolete"—"finished," as some would suggest?

SL: You are not the first to put forward the death of literature. When the Internet first came into popular use, as distinct from its use by university researchers, there was a great deal of talk about the disappearance of print—no more newspapers, journal publications, books. But e-books have not taken off, and e-publishing still suffers from an excessive ephemerality, even in the context of the relative short lives of journals.

Instead, more and more people world-wide have taken to literacy, especially in English, as they engage in writing e-mail, memos, interactions in chat rooms. That is, more and more of contemporary human reality is transpiring as written text. Current technology is turning humans in a massive manner into cyborgs of the written (word-processing).

Thus, I do not see "literature" as becoming obsolete but as being transformed where it interfaces with technology, but also maintaining its ancient pleasures of narrative and song. The amount of poetry and its accessibility over the Internet is amazing. As for distractions facing the modern writer, when were distractions, be they the insistent necessities of livelihood and family or decadent corruptions of drink and play, ever absent for writers?

MAQ: How is present internationalism/globalism important to the writer and literature?

SL: I had intimated earlier that present globalism may have different emphases for different writers. As part of a global cultural industry, publishing has been affected by the tastes and purchasing habits particularly of profitable markets in the West. Writers who are also national intellectuals are inevitably influenced by ideas and practices from outside their local sphere. The Bengali Nobel Laureate Rabindranath Tagore was as much influenced by Western philosophical values of modernity as by Hindu-based philosophy. Lu Xun, the preeminent

Chinese writer for the first part of the twentieth century, studied medicine in Japan, itself undertaking reform with European models as guides. Gao Xingjian, the first Nobel Laureate from China, now lives in France. Abdullah bin Abdul Kadir Munshi's *Hikayat Abdullah* (1849) would not have been written without the instruction received from Middle Eastern Islamic thought and the influence of British colonialism. In this way, "internationalism" whether as colonialism or as individually undertaken study, has had a profound influence on writers from Asia for centuries.

Is this openness of writers to external intellectual forces important and continuing today? I hope so . . .

Source: Mohammed A. Quayam, "Shirley Geok-lin Lim: An Interview," in *MELUS*, Vol. 28, No. 4, Winter 2003, pp. 83–99.

Kirpal Singh

In the following excerpt from an interview, Lim speaks of herself as a poet and a woman.

. . . [Kirpal Singh:] More and more your poems appear to adopt a very strong "women's" voice. Do you think that there is a need still for women to "band" together? Has there not been, in your opinion, a real change so that poets like yourself can now put behind you women's issues and write for and about everyone?

[Shirley Geok-lin Lim:] I am not certain how to respond to this question, as I reject almost all its premises. First, I do not see that women "band" together. Some women are activists and organize politically to achieve social justice. Many others live individual, separate lives, identifying with their husbands and families or communities. Also, I do not write poems in order to express women's issues, nor poems directed only to women. I write about what is important to me emotionally, and about what I find beautiful or mysterious. The notion that I can now put something behind me because of "real" social change in women's positions in the world is nonsense. I don't write polemical or political tracts. Should a man stop writing about his feelings for his father once his father is dead or about how trees are mysterious once the United Nations passes a world ban against illegal timber clearing?

When Crossing The Peninsula won the Commonwealth Poetry Prize [1980], did you feel that you had arrived? What does "arrival" mean to you

> ALSO, I DO NOT WRITE POEMS IN ORDER TO EXPRESS WOMEN'S ISSUES, NOR POEMS DIRECTED ONLY TO WOMEN. I WRITE ABOUT WHAT IS IMPORTANT TO ME EMOTIONALLY...."

as a writer? Would being put in an anthology which is then widely used in schools, colleges, and universities signal a sense of arrival with which you are comfortable?

As I wrote in my memoir, I was surprised when *Crossing the Peninsula* won the Commonwealth Prize. And no, I did not feel then that I had "arrived," perhaps because the prize appeared so illusory to me. I did not go to London to accept the Prize and did no publicity for it. I was nursing my newborn infant, and literary awards were very far from my mind then. I am not sure what "arrival" means, as this is not a word that I use. If being in a popular college anthology signals arrival, then I had arrived a while ago. The strange thing is that it never occurs to me that I have or have not arrived. What presses on my consciousness is all those poems, those stories, those books I have not yet written.

Obviously your subjects have changed, though I suspect your themes have remained the same. Do you think that more than 25 years of living in the US have made it hard for you to write powerfully about subjects Malaysian-Singaporean still? Does your childhood, for instance, still return with the same intensity as that felt in your first volume of poems?

My subjects have changed. I have moved on psychologically and geographically. I don't write from contemporary Singaporean-Malaysian settings. In my first novel, still unpublished, large parts are set in the Kuala Lumpur of 1969 and the Singapore of 1982 or so—historical periods when I was resident in those two places. Very few readers question V. S. Naipaul's or Paul Theroux's claim to write of places and people that they are little acquainted with except through very brief visits; and often, reviewers praise such writers for the power of their portrayals. But my residence in the US seems to lead to questions as to my ability to write from an Asian location or with Asian settings. Yet I return frequently to Asia, to Malaysia and Singapore, and I have a very large family still in both states. In July 1999, I will be taking up a two-year appointment as Chair and Professor of English at the University of Hong Kong. I do not think that my writing identity is so clearly restricted to prescribed national boundaries.

When you deal with the theme of sexuality, I detect there are two broad categories: woman-to-man, and woman-to-woman—would you agree? And would you agree that your woman-to-woman poems are somehow more personal, more intense, more painful?

I am not sure what your question is asking. It may be that some of my poems appear to address men and others women. But I would not therefore conclude that these poems are equally "about sexuality," whatever that means. Some are love poems, with their own tinctures of passion, confusion, memory, and so forth. Some are sister poems, offering shared experiences of life. I had thought that my earlier "love" poems, if such emotions could be easily identified as "love," were, to use your terms again, personal, intense, and painful.

You have spoken about your education and the way this instilled in you a love for English Literature. When did you begin to value non-British literature written in English? Who influenced you to stress the crucial importance of postcolonial, non-canonical writings in English?

My reading of American literature, much of which is, of course, canonical in the United States, opened my eyes radically to a different cultural production of "great writing." I remember reading Wallace Stevens, William Carlos Williams, h.d., Edna St. Vincent Millay, Henry James, and so forth, and finding this an utterly different and distinctive literature. Then, when Lloyd Fernando taught the "Commonwealth Literature" course at the University of Malaya in 1966, we read Chinua Achebe, George Lamming, Ee Tiang Hong, and others, and suddenly I glimpsed what it was to write out of—both in the sense of grounded in but also at a place away from—the British tradition. Much later, in my thirties and forties, I read works in translation. The Latin American writers—Borges, Marquez, and especially Neruda—were such wonderful original visionaries.

As a scholar-critic who is also a vibrant writer, do you feel that sometimes scholars/critics tend to over-value the "surface" of creative works while somehow missing the essential "artistic" qualities? Do you enjoy detailed analyses of your poems in terms of their stylistic experiments, or do you prefer to have your works read in terms of their larger social/political/cultural content and voice?*

I do not see how scholar-critics ever over-value the surface of creative works. That is a failure I find in my undergraduate students whose theoretical apparatus is weak. You may mean something else by that word than I do. I do not separate the qualities of a work into "surface" and "artistic," as surface is art polished, and art is manifested through surface as well. I seldom read critical works on my writing, although recently I have been receiving quite a few articles, chapters of dissertations and books that treat my writing. I cannot say I "enjoy" such reading. It makes me happy when a reader finds something valuable about my work, but after reading the chapter or article, I move on and do not re-read it.

Why have you not written more fiction? Are you more comfortable writing poetry? Or are the kinds of experiences you wish to share and express more readily voiced through poetry rather than through prose?

Oddly enough, I believe that it is factually correct to say that I have written much more prose than I have poetry. I am working on a second novel. If all goes well, the first novel may yet be published. I have written probably too many critical articles and books. My memoir has brought me more critical and popular attention than any of my books of poetry. I agree that I have not written that many short stories. I have all kinds of stories in my head, but unfortunately I have only one life and 24 hours in a day. Most of that life is spent as an academic, a critic, scholar, and housekeeper. Poems are much more difficult to voice than fiction or other prose genres. It takes a lot of time and space for a poem to emerge, if at all, which explains why I have not written that much poetry.

By the standard of recent autobiographies, yours is considered by many to be "tame," "safe." Would you apply these labels yourself? There are so many hints at more urgent matters that crave expression in your memoir. Were you overly "self-conscious" and therefore unnecessarily censorious? Looking back at it now, do you think there were things you could/would have stated differently?

I am not sure who these "many" are who consider my memoir to be tame and safe. A critically astute scholar said to me that he considered the portrayal of the daughter-father relationship risqué. Others have talked about my courage and so forth. Perhaps among academic women, the frankness of my discussion of emergent sexuality may be considered not so safe. What are you comparing my memoir to? To Sybil Kathigasu's *No Dram of Mercy* or Janet Lim's *Sold for Silver* or Maxine Hong Kingston's *The Woman Warrior*? I did not write the memoir to shock but to inscribe a history of a community and a particular experience of gender and colonial education, as well as to produce a work that would "stand" on its use of language, a contribution to the long line of other literary productions recognized as memoirs, but with its insistent inflection on the Malaysian gendered, colonial, and immigrant subject.

With age comes mellowness in some cases. In your case your poems and stories reveal a maturity in excess of your age when you wrote them. Is this because of the suffering you yourself endured from a very early age? Did your relationships with your parents emphasize a stance which you have since found wanting in terms of what your writing demands?

I assume that you are complimenting me on early maturity in my writing. I do not think that "literary" maturity has anything to do with "suffering." One is in language, the other in life experience. If suffering resulted in literary maturity, then our greatest writers should come from the poor, dispossessed, diseased, and so forth. As to the second part of your question, you seem to express criticism of what you call "a stance" in my writing. Do you mean that the relationship to father and mother that my writing sometimes constructs has resulted in a "stance" that leads to an inadequacy in my writing? I am not certain what kinds of dynamics are being suggested here. Of course, as my first novel shows, I am capable of imagining other forms of these relationships. But I am careful not to confuse what you may see as "real" or autobiographical relationships with relationships imagined in texts, be they poems or stories. I could, if I wanted to, valorize mothers and fathers—and I have read very loving poems that do exactly this. But this is not what I wish to say or explore. I wish to explore the fierce complexities, contradictions, and ambivalences at the heart of all relationships—not to celebrate but to intimate that fearful intimacy.

What do you think of women (or men for that matter) telling all? Would you say even when there are big battles to be fought there are good reasons why a writer must not go beyond certain time-honored boundaries of telling, of revealing?

Is it ever possible to tell all? One person's all may very well be another's nothing or trifle. The boundaries that concern me are not the trivialities of whether we use the "f" word or describe degrees of wet or dry, but boundaries of how stories work, how language and form work, how cultural and deeply psychic understandings halt and how we can break out of such haltings.

What are you working on now? Are you going to follow up with another memoir?

I am working on a second novel. At the same time, I am preparing three edited and co-edited scholarly and literary volumes for publication this year, another two for publication in the year 2000, and a critical book. All this leaves me no time for poetry.

As the world shrinks and we move away from issues of national/cultural identities to larger questions of technological imperatives, do you think it behooves writers to enter more the world of science, the world of technology?

Of course it behooves us all, writers and non-writers, to enter the world of science and technology. My son is in the school of engineering, studying Computer Science. He is fully in this world. Yet he reads postmodern authors such as Thomas Pynchon and Don DeLillo, adores dramatists such as Samuel Beckett and Tom Stoppard, and writes deliciously witty postmodern plays himself, one of which was performed by the Drama Department of the University of California (Santa Barbara) when he was sixteen years old. He is at home in both the Arts and the Sciences; his creativity is impressive. In comparison, I find myself limited, still struggling with ancient questions of identity, subjectivity, and the literary.

Would you say that in the final count being recognized as a truly international writer, while being very, very good, is still smaller than that wonderful recognition given us by those we love and who say, "You are a good human being"?

I love it that you say I am a good human being. That is important to me, for it validates my struggle to be a decent person, to be sensitive to those poorer, weaker, and less able. As a colonized child, I was also poor, weak, and powerless, and my identification with that condition is primary. But I do not see this desire for validation as a good human being as on the same plane as recognition for one's writing. The good thing about recognition is that it may bring you readers and perhaps improved conditions for more writing. But whether one is recognized as a good person or recognized as a good writer—these are very different domains.

Source: Kirpal Singh, "An Interview with Shirley Geoklin Lim," in *Ariel: A Review of International English Literature*, Vol. 30, No. 4, October 1999, pp. 135–41.

Brinda Bose

In the following review, Bose evaluates the poetry in Lim's collection Monsoon History.

Laurel Means, in her introduction to Shirley Geoklin Lim's selected poems, *Monsoon History*, accords her a "rightful place" in postcolonial Malaysian writing in English, yielding her also a legitimate claim within the Chinese American canon. It is befitting that Means concludes her introduction with a discussion of Lim's "place" and "claim" within the English literary canon, because it is apparent that location, identity, and language—in their various complex interrelations—are the overriding concerns of Lim's writing. To this extent, the organization of this selection of her poems "in six sections more or less chronologically aligned with [her] personal history" manages to convey a vivid sense of Lim's life and visions; many of her particular concerns are further explicated in the short essay "Tongue and Root: Language in Exile" that is reproduced as an afterword to the selection of poems.

Clearly, Lim is a typical product of the postcolonial migrant generation, whose diasporic experience has been, in her own evaluation, empowering even while being somewhat disquieting. The biographical details of her life—growing up in British Malacca, being educated in the English medium in a convent school, going on to a "first class Honours English" B.A. degree from the University of Malaya, and then coming to America for graduate studies and staying on to work and live there—may read like a case study of any of the millions of the diasporic elite in twentieth-century America; but in fact they hold the key to understanding, and appreciating, much of Lim's creative (and, in fact, critical) work.

The English language, by her own admission (if not in so many words), is Lim's primary, almost obsessive, concern, and there is no doubt that she employs it well. The foreword to *Monsoon History*, in the form of a poem, sums up the dislocations and the relocations that English has engineered in her life: "It was like learning / to let go and to hold on: / a slow braking, shifting / gears ... carrying the child / to foreign countries." Fittingly enough, the first section traces a return to the land of origin, as an adult, with all the adult burdens of memory and guilt and exhilaration that are born out of the yoking of two worlds. Upon her return, the second section locates her within her "Malay-ness," an essence that she struggles to retrieve in order that she may evaluate her history. Understandably, it is difficult for her to find a stable point of reference in the world of her childhood, long abandoned. The third section witnesses another crossing, this time to her adopted homeland. Lim poignantly expresses in her poetry the complexities of diasporic identity entwined with her disappointment with the present-day politics of her original homeland. The subsequent three sections record her responses to those ideas and issues which crowd and confront her adult existence: Western art, literature and culture, elements of the natural world, and women.

Although Lim's poetry is sensitive to the problematics of her place in history, there is a tendency to oversimplify the solution to diasporic fracturing by privileging the English language, adorning it with near-divine powers of unity and healing. It appears that to justify her "voluntary exile," Lim transcends the realities of location and space to find her "calling" in a language: "I make my living teaching it to native speakers, I clean up the grammar of English professors, I dream in its rhythms ... Reading it and writing it is the closest experience I have ever had to feeling infinity in my presence." One wonders whether the native speakers themselves might squirm in the face of such devotion!

Source: Brinda Bose, Review of *Monsoon History*, in *World Literature Today*, Vol. 70, No. 4, Fall 1996, pp. 1033–34.

SOURCES

Chow, Zoe, "The Dying Room," in *South China Morning Post*; reprinted in *World Press Review*, September 1995, p. 39.

Fleckenstein, Kristie S., "Words Made Flesh: Fusing Imagery and Language in a Polymorphic Literacy," in *College English*, Vol. 66, No. 6, July 2004, pp. 612–31.

Gadd, Bernard, Review of *No Man's Grove*, in *World Literature Today*, Vol. 60, Summer 1986, p. 523.

Gittings, John, "Growing Sex Imbalance Shocks China," in *Guardian*, May 13, 2002, http://www.guardian.co.uk/international/story/0,3604,714412,00.html (accessed February 11, 2008).

Holmgren, J., "Myth, Fantasy or Scholarship: Images of the Status of Women in Traditional China," in *Australian Journal of Chinese Affairs*, No. 6, July 1981, pp. 147–70.

Kingston, Maxine Hong, *The Woman Warrior: Memoirs of a Girlhood among Ghosts*, Vintage, 1976, pp. 79, 86.

Lim, Shirley Geok-lin, Introduction, in *The Forbidden Stitch: An Asian American Women's Anthology*, edited by Shirley Geok-lin Lim, Mayumi Tsutakawa, and Margarita Donnelly, Calyx Books, 1989. p. 11.

———, "Pantoun for Chinese Women," in *The Forbidden Stitch: An Asian American Women's Anthology*, edited by Shirley Geok-lin Lim, Mayumi Tsutakawa, and Margarita Donnelly, Calyx Books, 1989, pp. 204–205.

Ng, Andrew, "The Maternal Imagination in the Poetry of Shirley Lim," in *Women: A Cultural Review*, Vol. 18, No. 2, 2007, pp. 162–81.

Rummel, R. J., *Death by Government*, Transactions Publishers, 1994, pp. 65–66.

Sandis, Eva E., "United Nations Measures to Stop Violence against Women," in *Annals of the New York Academy of Sciences*, Vol. 1087, November 2006, pp. 370–83.

FURTHER READING

De Bary, William Theodore, and Irene Bloom, eds., *Sources of Chinese Tradition*, 2 Vols., Columbia University Press, 1999–2000.
    These texts are a good resource for information about Chinese philosophy and religion as well as Chinese culture in general.

Johnson, Kay Ann, *Wanting a Daughter, Needing a Son: Abandonment, Adoption, and Orphanage Care in China*, Yeong & Yeong, 2004.
    This book explores the interaction between China's efforts at population control and the country's social practices, which place greater value on the birth of a son.

Morton, W. Scott, and Charlton M. Lewis, *China: Its History and Culture*, 4th ed., McGraw-Hill, 2005.
    This text details China's history from the Neolithic period to the modern period, including the country's scientific, political, and economic history.

Schwartz, Lita Linzer, and Natalie K. Isser, *Endangered Children: Neonaticide, Infanticide, Filicide*, CRC Press, 2000.

This book focuses on the sociological, philosophical, and criminal aspects of why parents murder their children and includes a focus on the psychological and psychiatric defenses that are offered.

Sen, Mala, *Death by Fire: Sati, Dowry, Death, and Female Infanticide in Modern India*, Rutgers University Press, 2002.

Female infanticide occurs in both India and China. This book examines three personal stories that illustrate how females are devalued in modern India.

Thorp, Robert L., and Richard Ellis Vinograd, *Chinese Art and Culture*, Prentice Hall, 2003.

This book includes more than 350 illustrations. The authors incorporate political, social, and economic contexts in their discussion of the art they showcase.

Poem in Which My Legs Are Accepted

KATHLEEN FRASER

1968

Kathleen Fraser's "Poem in Which My Legs Are Accepted" was first published in 1968 in *The Young American Poets*, an anthology edited by Paul Carroll. It is one of Fraser's early poems, appearing in print only two years after her first volume of verse, *Change of Address, and Other Poems* (1966). She later included this poem in her book of collected and new poetry *What I Want* (1974), which is still available. "Poem in Which My Legs Are Accepted" was reprinted in the anthology *In Her Own Image: Women Working in the Arts* (1980), which is also still available.

"Poem in Which My Legs Are Accepted" is about growth: from adolescence to womanhood, from awkward embarrassment over the flaws of one's body to confidence and acceptance. Fraser's long career as an experimental and feminist poet spans more than forty years. "Poem in Which My Legs Are Accepted" is less experimental in form than Fraser's later work, focusing instead on the intimate and important theme of loving one's body.

AUTHOR BIOGRAPHY

Kathleen Joy Fraser was born in Tulsa, Oklahoma, on March 22, 1935 (some sources say 1937), to Marjorie (Axtell) Fraser and James Fraser II. She was the eldest of four siblings. Fraser inherited a love of words and language from her father, who often recited nonsense

Kathleen Fraser (*Photograph by A. K. Bierman*)

verse and sang silly songs. She majored first in philosophy and then in English literature at Occidental College in California, graduating with a bachelor's degree in 1959.

Fraser's path to becoming a poet was not easy. She was discouraged early on by grade-school teachers who presented a limited, traditional viewpoint on writing and reading verse. In college, she discovered the works of Walt Whitman, E. E. Cummings, and William Carlos Williams and began to write her own poetry. After graduation, Fraser moved to New York City, where she worked at *Mademoiselle* magazine and took poetry writing classes with Stanley Kunitz and Kenneth Koch. Fraser met her first husband, Jack Mitchell, in one of these classes; they married in 1960. The next decade was crucial for Fraser's emerging poetic voice. She struggled to cast off the oppressive hand of her formal education, a battle she was aided in by friends and teachers such as Kenneth Koch, Barbara Guest, and Frank O'Hara.

Change of Address, Fraser's first book of poetry, was published in 1966; her son David was born later that year. Fraser and Mitchell

abruptly moved across the country to San Francisco in 1967 after their apartment in New York City was burgled. The couple divorced in 1970, and in a short time, after teaching at the Iowa Writers' Workshop (1969–1971) and as writer-in-residence at Reed College in Portland, Oregon (1971–1972), Fraser found that her calling lay in education. She subsequently became Director of The Poetry Center (1972–1976) at San Francisco State University, where she continued to teach as a Professor of Creative Writing in the MFA graduate program until 1992.

During these years, Fraser was the recipient of numerous awards. She received both the Discovery Award from the YMHA Poetry Center, NYC, and the Frank O'Hara Poetry Award (for innovation in poetry) from The New School, NYC, in 1964. She received the "Young Writers Discovery Award" from the National Endowment for the Arts (1971–1972) and was awarded a National Endowment for the Arts Fellowship (1978). A few years later, she was awarded the Guggenheim Fellowship in Poetry (1980–1981).

What I Want was published in 1974 and collects much of Fraser's previously published work, including "Poem in Which My Legs Are Accepted," which originally appeared in Paul Carroll's influential anthology *The Young American Poets* (1968). Fraser, who loved to play with language all her life, was drawn toward experimental form and syntax. As a feminist, experimental forms also gave her the unique opportunity to challenge patriarchy at the basic level of communication. Frustrated with the preponderance of male editors and lack of other experimental women writers being published, Fraser founded *HOW(ever)*, a journal serving feminist experimental writers. She served as managing editor from 1983–1989; the journal ceased publication in 1992 but was revived in 1999 as *HOW2*, for which Fraser serves as publisher.

Fraser met her second husband, the photographer A. K. Berman, at San Francisco State University in the 1970s, and they were married in 1985. The couple began spending winters in Rome, Italy, which afforded Fraser the opportunity to explore further linguistic experiments in her work, such as seen in her chapbook of an unusual collage poem, *hi dde violeth i dde violet* (2004). Fraser has been Visiting Writer at California College of the Arts from 2002 to 2008. As of 2008, Fraser split her time between San Francisco and Rome, teaching, writing, and translating, having published fifteen book collections or chapbooks of poetry, with numerous other publications featuring her work.

POEM TEXT

Legs!
How we have suffered each other,
never meeting the standards of magazines
    or official measurements.

I have hung you from trapezes,   5
    sat you on wooden rollers,
        pulled and pushed you
        with the anxiety of taffy,
and still, you are yourselves!

Most obvious imperfection, blight on my
    fantasy life,   10
strong,
plump,
never to be skinny
or even hinting of the svelte beauties in history
    books
            or Sears catalogues.   15
Here you are—solid, fleshy and
white as when I first noticed you, sitting on the
    toilet,
        spread softly over the wooden seat,

having been with me only twelve years,
        yet   20
as obvious as the legs of my thirty-year-old
    gym teacher.

Legs!
Oh that was the year we did acrobatics in the
    annual gym show.
How you split for me!
        One-handed cartwheels   25
        from this end of the gymnasium to the
            other,
        ending in double splits,
legs you flashed in blue rayon slacks my mother
    bought for the
            occasion   30
and though you were confidently swinging
    along,
the rest of me blushed at the sound of clapping.

Legs!
How I have worried about you, not able to hide
    you,
embarrassed at beaches, in high school   35
    when the cheerleaders' slim brown legs
            spread all over
            the sand
            with the perfection
            of bamboo.   40
I hated you, and still you have never given out
    on me.

With you
I have risen to the top of blue waves,
with you
I have carried food home as a loving gift   45
        when my arms began un-
        jelling like madrilène.
Legs, you are a pillow,
white and plentiful with feathers for his wild
    head.
You are the endless scenery   50
behind the tense sinewy elegance of his two
    dark legs.
You welcome him joyfully
and dance.
And you will be the locks in a new canal
    between continents.
        The ship of life will push out of you   55
        and rejoice
            in the whiteness,

            in the first floating and rising of
                water.

POEM SUMMARY

Stanza 1

"Poem in Which My Legs Are Accepted" opens with an exclamation about legs, which are quickly revealed to be the narrator's own legs. Whether good or not, it is clear from the first line that her legs elicit strong emotion. This emotion is clarified when the narrator declares the anguish she and her legs have caused each other. She is unhappy with their imperfection, and the text implies that her legs—so strong and confident—are themselves let down by the lack of self-esteem exhibited by their owner. This misery is measured by the failure of her legs to meet the perfection of legs seen in magazines, and worse, their failure even to be average.

Stanza 2

In the second stanza, the narrator recounts the efforts she made to force those unsightly legs to endure various strenuous and athletic activities, such as hanging from trapeze and rowing. They may not be beautiful, but her legs are not deficient in any other way. In lines 7 and 8, she figuratively describes trying to stretch her legs into a different shape. She worries, but to no effect. This culminates in the frustration in line 9 that, despite all her efforts, these legs remain the same. All of this exercise has not changed her physiology, it has not made her slim and lovely. Her legs remain strong—and large.

Stanza 3

In stanza 3, the narrator deplores her legs for their deficiency in not being skinny and sexy, again mentioning beautiful models seen in books and magazines as the standard against which she evaluates herself. It is a painful comparison because it is both unrealistic for many people and unreasonable for the narrator to be so hard on herself. The narrator becomes even more intimate with her readers in lines 17 and 18 when she describes her pasty legs as seen spread ingloriously against a toilet seat, a setting inherently unflattering to any person. She describes this as the moment when she first became aware of her legs, as if, again, they were an entity separate from herself. Interestingly, this separation of her legs from the rest of her body affords her the opportunity to blame them without necessarily blaming herself. The narrator reveals this to be the adolescent angst of a twelve-year-old girl, even as she compares her young, strong, but large legs to those of her much older gym teacher. It is an irrational comparison for a teenage girl, but she *is* comparing herself to an athletic adult and not to someone who is overweight or misshapen.

Stanza 4

As with the first stanza, the narrator opens the fourth stanza with an exclamation, overcome with the emotions she feels concerning her legs. Here she remembers, with a mixture of embarrassment and pride, the acrobatic feats those twelve-year-old legs performed for a school program. She knows she did an excellent job, but her memory of the day is colored by embarrassment at the applause she received, perhaps because her legs were on display to an audience as sheathed in shiny new pants. Again, her legs are their own creature, confident and unabashed. The mention of the applause in the final line may refer both to the audience's approval and to the sound her pants could make as they slap together, making themselves even more conspicuous in her mind.

Stanza 5

The exclamation repeats for a third time at the beginning of stanza 5, heralding another emotional outburst. The tone of this stanza is more apologetic. The narrator painfully recalls high school and beaches, two places where a teenager's self-image is vulnerable. Here she is a little older, fifteen to eighteen years old, and embarrassment has turned to hate for her legs. She cannot hide them, and she cannot change them—but she recognizes that no matter how much she despises this physical feature of her body, her legs have always been there for her, strong and unfailing. In fact, she is embarrassed by this hatred of her own body but still has difficulty letting go of her self-loathing.

Stanza 6

The tone of the poem changes significantly in stanza 6. The narrator, almost reluctantly or perhaps sheepishly, yields to a celebration of the strength in her legs. She is an adult and the focus of importance has shifted from unrealistic magazine standards to real life. Her legs swim, walk home, make love. In lines 46 and 47, she suggests that her legs have more stamina than her arms. This comparison, pitting one part of her body against another, is humorous. In line 48 she directly addresses her legs, but more calmly than in lines 1, 22, and 33, without the exclamation points. She compares her legs to pillows, which can be read as a reference to their plumpness but also as a description of comfort provided to other people. Line 50 implies that her legs are vast, but again she directs this description toward the positive in line 51, where her legs are a backdrop to the contrasting beauty of a man's legs. Lines 52 and 53 mention dancing, a euphemism for sex. The calm joy and serene attitude of these lines are a far cry from the embarrassment of her twelve-year-old girlhood.

At the end of stanza 6, the narrator goes beyond herself and beyond all other activities. Her legs have a place not only in her life but also in the lives of others. In lines 54 and 55, the narrator uses highly figurative language to describe another important stage in life in which her legs play an important role: childbirth. The verse is joyful, anticipatory, and even reverent of the legs she often maligned. She likens her legs to canal locks, an acclimatizing passage through which this child will pass on its way to join the world.

Stanza 7

Stanza 7 is very brief, only two lines long. They describe the new life she has created, born with the help of her strong legs, the infant rising up to meet the world.

THEMES

Self-Esteem

The primary theme of "Poem in Which My Legs Are Accepted" is self-esteem, or belief in one's own abilities and characteristics. People with self-esteem are poised and confident, which gives them charisma, or likability, and can lead to success simply through perception rather than mere skill. In this poem, Fraser, as a young teenager, struggles with self-esteem, as many teenagers do. She encapsulates her problem in her legs, which are plump instead of slim. She is painfully aware, through magazines and books, that her legs do not fit the cultural ideal, and she sees her legs as having more in common with her gym teacher's than with those of her cheerleader classmates. At the same time, this teenager is amazed at the strength in her legs, which swim, tumble, and do splits with agility.

As the poet grows older, her lack of esteem for her legs gives way to appreciation. As she has gained self-esteem in other areas of her life, her childish worries over the suitability of her legs have faded. Her legs, in fact, have never failed her. At the end of the poem, the poet celebrates her legs as a gateway to new life. With her legs she makes love to a man she loves. Later these legs will help to deliver the child the two have made together. The end of the poem is the beginning of a new life.

The narrator's lack of confidence in her legs largely stems from her comparison against what she has been taught to perceive as beautiful or, at least, typical. In the United States during Fraser's childhood in the late 1940s and early 1950s, as in the early twenty-first century, slim figures were favored over fuller ones, although the line between what is attractive and healthy and what is not is highly subjective, sometimes contradictory, and constantly shifting, generally toward skinnier and skinnier extremes. Many people who do not fit the media-advertised ideal of feminine appeal go on to have happy and fulfilled lives as adults, whether or not they are ever able to physically replicate the ideal. What these people realize, as does Fraser at the end of her poem when she is grown up, is that self-fulfillment has little to do with these purported ideals of physical beauty.

Physical Activity

In "Poem in Which My Legs Are Accepted," the narrator as a teenager despairs about the acceptability of her thick legs despite all the physical activities she can engage in: hanging from trapeze, rowing, and cartwheels, for instance. She is clearly a healthy young woman, despite her lack of confidence. As an adult, she continues to be active, through swimming, walking, sex, and childbirth. Any perceived deficiency with her legs is all in her mind, but the mind exerts considerable influence over physical well-being. The narrator survives her teenage years healthy and intact because, although she dislikes her heavy legs, they are still strong, capable legs that carry her confidently through many activities and achievements. Through physical activity, the adolescent narrator's legs exhibited the confidence she herself never felt.

As a teenager in the early 1950s, Fraser as the poem's narrator confronts her perceived deficiency with physical activity, hoping that her legs will slim down and be tanned instead of pasty white; however, she does not condone self-abuse or dieting. It is not part of the consciousness that created this poem. "Poem in Which My Legs Are Accepted" was written in the mid-1960s, at the cusp of the second wave of feminism, when women were casting off patriarchal roles and expectations such as the model-perfect body.

TOPICS FOR FURTHER STUDY

- Fraser is an experimental poet. Read her 2004 collage poem *hi dde violeth i dde violet*, available from Nomados Press. What is it about? How did it make you feel? Using Fraser's creative expression as inspiration, compose your own experimental poem and present it to your class.

- Models and celebrities have a profound influence on perceived ideas of beauty and health. Assemble a visual aid comparing images of models (male and female) to images of ordinary people. For extra credit, also make a historical comparison. What characterizes beauty in the Western world? Be specific about different physical features such as height, weight, hair, and skin. Are models healthy? Why or why not? What constitutes a healthy body? What are parents, doctors, and educators doing to give young people healthy self-images and balance the extreme ideas of beauty represented in popular media? Present your findings to the class.

- In the United States, five million people suffer from eating disorders, such as bulimia and anorexia. Of those afflicted, four million are women. Choose an eating disorder, either one of the two listed here or another, and write an in-depth research paper about it. Who tends to be affected? What causes the disorder? How is it treated or cured? What can friends and family do to help, either directly or indirectly?

- Fraser was influenced as a young poet by the New York School, an informal group of poets contemporary to, but distinct from, the Beat poets. Read a selection of five to ten poems from both the New York School poets and the Beat poets. Which poems do you like better? What characterizes the two groups? How are they different? How are they similar? Do you see connections with either of these groups to Fraser's work? Discuss the topic in an essay.

- Word play is very important to Fraser's creative process. Spend fifteen minutes brainstorming unusual word combinations, with related or unrelated contexts. Select the best combinations and use them in a finished piece such as a poem, essay, or story. For inspiration, also look to the work of the American writer Gertrude Stein, whose work was known for inventive word play.

This new self-awareness is evident in the final two stanzas, where the narrator, still physically active, embraces the capabilities of her legs, including the fundamental ability to participate in reproducing.

STYLE

Free Verse and Experimental Line Breaks

Fraser used free verse for the composition of "Poem in Which My Legs Are Accepted." Free verse is a poetic form that does not use formal rhyme or meter, leaving the category wide open to interpretation. Fraser, an avant-garde poet, also experiments with line breaks in the tradition of E. E. Cummings and other modern poets. Experimental line breaks happen in unusual places, such as in the middles of sentences, clauses, and words. Lines are also begun in unusual places, such as the middle or the right side of the page. Fraser's use of experimental line breaks is relatively restrained in this poem. Although she breaks lines in the middles of sentences and clauses and starts lines in places other than the left side of the page, she does not alter syntax, break lines in the middle of words, or otherwise play with the sense of the language that the poem was written in, as she is known to do in later works. Free verse and experimental line breaks give the poet deeper control over the cadence of language and the importance imparted to specific words.

Evolving Tone

The tone or emotional state of Fraser's poem is anguish that later turns to joy. In the first three stanzas, the poet, as narrator, remembers her teenage years, when she tormented herself about her less-than-perfect legs. She uses exclamation points and frequently broken lines, which can read like sobs, hiccups, or shy hesitations. The latter half of the poem shares how Fraser came to terms with her disappointment at not having model-perfect legs. As an adult, the exclamation points melt away, and the lines break less erratically. Fraser has realized that her legs have always been there for her, strong and confident. Her voice becomes more confident, too, and the tone of the poem turns to joy as Fraser contemplates the strength in her legs for lovemaking and childbirth.

HISTORICAL CONTEXT

Sexual Revolution

The sexual revolution was a sociohistorical change in attitudes toward sex within the Western world. This revolution, which has no firmly defined beginning or end, was concentrated in the 1960s and 1970s, although the ideas emerged after World War II, possibly in response to the increased economic and social freedoms that women experienced at this time. Some argue that the sexual revolution dates back to the bohemians of the Victorian era. In truth, radical social ideas toward sex have not been uncommon throughout human history.

In 1967 in America, counterculture youths known as hippies converged on a San Francisco neighborhood to live together and share their ideas in an event known as the Summer of Love, though it actually lasted all year. The Summer of Love brought national attention to radical beliefs embraced by hippies, such as "free love" (a term for open sexual relationships), homosexuality, bisexuality, and celibacy. Hippies believed that sex is a natural act and that people should not be ashamed of sex or the human body. They also believed that monogamy, a relationship between only two people, is a restrictive and unnatural approach to physical intimacy. Sexuality was not the only concern hippies had, and many embraced celibacy, or refraining from sex, while they turned their attention toward spirituality and social aid.

The birth-control pill was also made available in the 1960s, which had a radical effect on the sexual liberation of women, who were until then largely expected to marry before having sex because of the risk of pregnancy. The oral contraceptive Enovid was approved by the U.S. Food and Drug Administration in 1957 for menstrual disorders and in 1960 for contraception. By 1972, various laws were overturned to make oral contraceptives available to all women regardless of where they lived or whether or not they were married.

The sexual revolution of the 1960s and 1970s was brought to an abrupt halt in the early 1980s when AIDS (Acquired Immune Deficiency Syndrome) was identified by the U.S. Centers for Disease Control. The spread of this fatal virus is attributed to the exchange of bodily fluids, such as occurs during unprotected sexual activity.

Second-Wave Feminism

Feminism is the promotion of women's rights based on the belief that women should be equal to men economically, socially, and politically. Feminism has a long history, beginning in the modern era with the first-wave feminists of the nineteenth and early twentieth centuries. Second-wave feminism emerged around 1963, when Betty Friedan published her seminal book *The Feminine Mystique*. This book made public Friedan's findings that women were not fulfilled in their roles as mothers and homemakers. This unspoken unhappiness became widely discussed, and women began to seek out new approaches to success in life. Also in 1963, the Presidential Commission on the Status of Women, chaired by Eleanor Roosevelt, released a report that documented pervasive discrimination against women in the United States. Harvard University began to merge with its female counterpart, Radcliffe College, in 1963, forming the first coeducational university in the United States. Many other universities and colleges followed this pattern over the next two decades. Some prominent all-female colleges, such as Mount Holyoke, Smith, and Bryn Mawr, decided against coeducation to preserve a focus on quality education for women.

COMPARE
&
CONTRAST

- **1960s:** Organized sports for girls are practically nonexistent at U.S. high schools. Physical activities are limited to gymnastics, cheerleading, and sometimes volleyball.

  Today: Girls' sports are as varied as boys' sports in U.S. high schools. In making it illegal to discriminate on the basis of sex in schools, Title IX of the Educational Amendments of 1972 ensured not only equal opportunity to play football or to cheerlead but also the equal funding of girls' and boys' sports.

- **1960s:** Female fashion models and celebrities of the decade include Twiggy, Sofia Loren, and Jane Fonda. On average, they are five feet six inches tall, and weigh 120 pounds.

  Today: Female models and celebrities are typically taller and thinner than they once were, averaging five feet ten inches tall, and weighing 110 pounds. Models of this era include Gisele Bündchen, Tyra Banks, and Heidi Klum.

- **1960s:** Popular poets publishing in English include John Ashbery, Denise Levertov, and Robert Lowell. Stream of consciousness, featuring long, unbroken thoughts, is a popular form of composition.

  Today: Formal rhyme and meter are making a comeback in contemporary poetry, while experimental forms continue to be produced as well. Popular poets include Billy Collins, Yusef Komunyakaa, and Nikki Giovanni.

In 1964, the Civil Rights Act was passed, which was significant for women because Title VII makes discrimination against women in the workplace illegal. The National Organization of Women (NOW) was founded in 1966, with Betty Friedan as the first president. NOW was, and still is, a powerful advocate for women's issues. The first legal victory for minor girls came in 1972 with the passing of the Educational Amendments, including Title IX, which forbade inequalities in school sports between boys and girls. In 1973, the U.S. Supreme Court handed down its decision in *Roe v. Wade*, effectively granting women, instead of the state, the right to choose whether or not a pregnancy would be carried to term.

Second-wave feminism slowed down in the late 1980s, when third-wave, or postmodern, feminism emerged. Third-wave feminism has focused on race and on definitions of gender, femininity, and sexuality. These waves, different in their motives and ideas, have run concurrently, rather than one replacing the other.

CRITICAL OVERVIEW

Kathleen Fraser entered into her career as a poet uncertain of her place in an arena that was still largely formal and masculine. Encouraged by friends, such as the avant-garde poet Barbara Guest, and mentors like Kenneth Koch, Fraser developed her unique experimental style and feminist voice. Her poetry was published in major magazines like the *New Yorker* and *Harper's*, but it bothered her that nearly all the editors of such periodicals were men, and women (especially the avant-garde women writers) were underrepresented in magazines and anthologies. In her extensive *Contemporary Literature* essay about Fraser's work, Linda A. Taylor writes, "With her first book of poetry, *Change of Address* (1967), Kathleen Fraser joined other feminist poets in the mid 1960s whose works challenged poetic convention by openly speaking in women's voices about women's experiences." In the 1970s, Taylor adds, "the hostility directed toward her avant-garde practice caused Fraser to feel doubly marginalized—as a women and as an experimental writer." In response to this lack of venue for experimental feminist writers, Fraser founded the avant-garde feminist journal *HOW(ever)* in the early 1980s.

Fraser's career as a poet, editor, and educator spans more than forty years. Although her experimental forms and feminist themes are not popular with every reader and editor, she has a solid following and (as of 2008) continues to write, publish, and receive positive reviews. Carol Muske, reviewing Fraser's poetry collection *When New Time Folds Up* for the *New York Times Book Review* in 1994, writes, "Her poems are exhilarating and daring, bringing her longtime love of words as objects into play with provocative ideas." Fraser's 1997 collection of old and new poems, *il cuore: the heart*, garnered praise from David Clippinger, writing in the *Chicago Review*. He states that "the 'heart' of Fraser's poetry remains here—a heart that through its mastery of language and perception is more than capable of generating and deepening our pathos." Clippinger also notes, "Fraser's task as a poet is archeological ... in that she engages in the act of excavating history in order to discover (or rediscover) the matrix of meaning or meanings."

Fraser's work in the early 2000s has continued to push boundaries. A fan of painting and visual arts, Fraser most recently experimented with combining her writing with visual presentations. For example, her 2004 book, *hi dde violeth i dde violet*, was composed as a collage of verse on the walls of her studio in Rome.

CRITICISM

Carol Ullmann

Ullmann is a freelance writer and editor. In the following essay, Ullmann examines Fraser's use of experimental form and feminist voice in "Poem in Which My Legs Are Accepted." Ullmann argues that as an early example of Fraser's work, this poem is not very experimental in form but is surprisingly avant-garde in its message.

In Kathleen Fraser's "Poem in Which My Legs Are Accepted," a young teenage girl is tormented by her supposedly imperfect body; many teenagers experience this with differing levels of anxiety and scrutiny. Fraser's poem is told from the point of view of the girl as an adult, an adult who has come to accept and even rejoice

WHAT DO I READ NEXT?

- *The Feminine Mystique* (1963), by Betty Friedan, heralded the second wave of the feminist movement in challenging the commonly held notion that women were content to be housewives.

- *The Art of Love* (1975) is a famous collection of poetry by Kenneth Koch. Koch was Fraser's teacher and was famous for his exuberance and silliness, which inspired Fraser to play with language.

- *Tender Buttons: Objects, Food, Rooms* (1914), by Gertrude Stein, is a novel about lesbian sexuality, an unusual topic at the time it was first published. Stein enjoyed juxtaposing unlike words to elicit new meanings, and the language of this novel is very experimental. Stein, like Koch, influenced Fraser's writing.

- *Selected Poems* (1995), by Barbara Guest, gives a good overview of the work of one of Fraser's oldest friends. Guest's attention to language was an inspiration to Fraser.

- One of Fraser's experimental works is *hi dde violeth i dde violet* (2004). It is a poem that was collaged together on the wall of Fraser's studio in Rome. She wrote it for a friend who had a stroke and could no longer speak or write.

- *Of Being Numerous* (1968), by George Oppen, won the Pulitzer Prize for Poetry in 1969. Oppen was a friend of Fraser's and was well known for taking part in the "objectivist" poetry movement, an outgrowth of Ezra Pound's imagism.

- H.D., also known as Hilda Doolittle, was a prominent feminist and avant-garde American writer in the early twentieth century. Her work, such as offered in her *Collected Poems, 1912–1944* (1986), had a great impact on Fraser as a young poet.

> THE NARRATOR, AS AN ADULT LOOKING BACK AT HER ADOLESCENCE, EMBRACES THE STRENGTH AND FERTILITY OF HER BODY, WHATEVER ITS SHAPE, AND THROWS OFF THE EXPECTATIONS OF ATTRACTIVENESS THAT SHE LEARNED AS A CHILD."

in the strength of her legs, despite her inability to make them slim, brown, and flawless, in accord with social and cultural dictates. Fraser is known as an avant-garde and feminist poet, with both qualities informing each other as she seeks to break away from patriarchal modes of communication. "Poem in Which My Legs Are Accepted" is among Fraser's earliest works and provides an interesting blend of experimentation and convention in her use of form and voice.

Avant-garde is a French term that means "leading edge." It does not refer to a specific style of expression in the arts; the avant-garde, by definition, is constantly changing. As soon as something becomes convention and something else emerges as new and radical, the idea of what is avant-garde shifts. Fraser has consistently pushed the edges of what is expected or acceptable, marking her as an avant-garde, experimental poet. "Poem in Which My Legs Are Accepted" is unusual, however, because it is not as stylistically and linguistically adventurous as her later work, nor is it as risky as the work of other experimentalists writing in the mid-1960s. At that time, Fraser was still maturing as a writer. Stylistically, the unconventional line breaks and line lengths were not radical enough to be considered experimental when this poem was published in the late 1960s. Fraser maintained sentence structure and syntax in her line breaks and also preserved a linear narrative throughout the poem, qualities that keep this verse firmly in the mainstream.

The line structure in "Poem in Which My Legs Are Accepted" is designed not merely to dress the page and fill it up but more importantly to communicate disquiet and awkwardness through its staggering and breaking. This uneasiness is especially evident in the first part of the poem, lines 1 through 41, when Fraser's

narrator is remembering her adolescence. Her emotional awkwardness is belied by the fact that her legs are actually athletic and powerful. The abrupt line breaks and deep indentations provide Fraser the opportunity to deliver her verse with cadence, pauses, and emphases, as readers are used to experiencing in more formal poetry with rigid rhyme and meter. An example of Fraser's experimentation with cadence and emphases comes in the description in lines 11 through 13, where the narrator describes her legs with a few sharp, quick words, which are quick thrusts at a sore wound. In lines 37 to 40, the narrator describes the cheerleaders' legs as looking like bamboo, while the physical arrangement of these lines on the page resembles horizontal stalks of bamboo and/or legs.

The end of "Poem in Which My Legs Are Accepted," lines 55 to 59, is more experimental than the rest of the poem because here the words are visually walking away from the poem. This takes the author's use of form from an abstract conducting of cadence to actual experimentation of the synergy between form and function. At the end of the poem, the narrator has documented her acceptance of her legs, even celebrated them, and now she prepares to give birth. It is an event she looks forward to with joy. She is finished with the pain of her adolescence and wishes to leave it behind. The single word on line 59, the last line of the poem, is at the furthest edge of the page, pushing its way toward the future. This line structure is symbolic both for the narrator of the poem and for the child the narrator is anticipating. In this poem, Fraser's experimental elements are subtle but present, as is her feminist voice.

Feminism is the advocacy of women's rights and issues. The feminist message in "Poem in Which My Legs Are Accepted" is not surprising considering the virulent era of social reform from which it arose. The narrator, as an adult looking back at her adolescence, embraces the strength and fertility of her body, whatever its shape, and throws off the expectations of attractiveness that she learned as a child. This unabashed love of self and enjoyment of sex typifies the women's liberation movement of the 1960s and 1970s. Women left homemaking to start careers; they threw out their bras; they had open, uncommitted relationships with multiple partners. In Fraser's poem, the narrator comes to accept her strong, plump legs and to love them for what they can do. Placing this revelation in the context of the liberation movement, the critic Lynn Keller notes in a 2001 *differences* essay, "While Fraser's poetic personas have freed themselves from the traditional position of passive object defined by the male gaze, they are rarely able to deviate from the decade's 'normal' gender roles." That is, "Poem in Which My Legs Are Accepted" ends with a heterosexual relationship between the narrator and a man and with anticipation of childbirth as a result of their physical union. In light of the strong feminist voice of the 1960s, calling women to cast off cultural roles such as spouse, mother, and homemaker, Fraser's narrator has not gone beyond the traditional roles of femininity at the conclusion of this poem. She has abandoned her preoccupation with body image for motherhood, which some second-wave feminists see as a concession to established gender roles.

The second wave of feminism was an important movement because during this period, women earned rights equal to those of men in the workplace and in education, rights that are supported by law. Third-wave feminism emerged in the late 1980s as a response to the failures of and backlash against second-wave advances. The third wave is primarily concerned with definitions of gender, race, femininity, and sexuality and puts less emphasis on an us-versus-them mentality, often evident in arguments for equal rights between men and women. The third wave also directly challenges the second wave concerning what is good for women, what women want, and how to go about fulfilling women's needs. This opens up a dialogue for women who are feminists as well as homemakers, for example.

The historical context of this piece is that Fraser, at the time she wrote "Poem in Which My Legs Are Accepted," was publishing her first book of poetry (a creation that needs stewardship) and, even more significantly, was becoming a mother for the first time. *Change of Address* was published in early 1966; her son David was born in December 1966; and "Poem in Which My Legs Are Accepted" first appeared in a 1968 anthology. As Keller argues, there may be a temptation to read the end of this poem as something less than liberation, but actually it is a very personal poem. Fraser's social, feminist commentary is secondary here to the joy she feels at giving up the myths of bodily perfection and

embracing the real power of her physiology: the ability to reproduce.

Fraser's "Poem in Which My Legs Are Accepted," as interpreted from a third-wave point of view, is not a failed feminist's concession to her biological role but instead an anthem of a woman who has found confidence in her body, fulfillment with a partner, and joy in the child their union will produce. In a modest salute to feminism, Fraser is underlining an activity that she and her legs can accomplish which no man can: childbirth. Fraser's choice of title for her "Poem in Which My Legs Are Accepted" is another salute to feminism. Her narrator is not merely speaking of her own forgiveness of herself, or she might call it "Poem in Which *I* Accept *My* Legs." Fraser's poem title thus pays quiet homage to the women's liberation movement and sexual revolution occurring when the poem was written: because of advances in social tolerance, the narrator's legs are acceptable to society; she is permitted to decide for herself if she is attractive, rather than accept what is portrayed in magazines. The title may also refer to the implicit (or explicit) acceptance of her legs by her male partner. At peace with herself, legs included, the adult woman narrator ends the poem as much happier and more stable than the girl of the beginning. In "Poem in Which My Legs Are Accepted," Fraser seems to have inadvertently written a poem that has a very avant-garde feminist message for the 1960s but is only mildly experimental in its structure.

Source: Carol Ullmann, Critical Essay on "Poem in Which My Legs Are Accepted," in *Poetry for Students*, Gale, Cengage Learning, 2009.

Lynn Keller

In the following excerpt, Keller examines Fraser's experimentation with both poetic form and content.

... I will begin with Kathleen Fraser, who from the start straddled divergent poetic camps. The first writing workshop she took, while pursuing a career in journalism by writing for *Mademoiselle* magazine, was taught by Stanley Kunitz. From him she learned to admire the work of Elizabeth Bishop, and through both Kunitz and Robert Lowell she began to hear of Sylvia Plath. "In the summer of 1962 we were listening to her poems," Fraser recalls. "[B]y 1963, she was dead. Plath was my first female role model in poetry" (*Translating the Unspeakable* 28). Also in the early sixties, Fraser first

> YET THE POEMS REVEAL HOW FRASER'S INVESTMENT IN HETEROSEXUAL EROTICISM BECOMES A POINT OF RETREAT FROM NEW KINDS OF SELF-CREATION."

encountered some "wonderfully intelligent poems" by Adrienne Rich. But her next important teacher, in 1963, represented a very different aesthetic: that was Kenneth Koch, who in turn introduced her to Frank O'Hara, who led her to Barbara Guest. Looking back at that time, Fraser has recalled "shuttl[ing] back and forth" between readings by uptown and downtown poets,

> listening to Bishop and Rich uptown, and the next night reading with my friends Joe Ceravolo and Hannah Weiner downtown. Each "family" had a poetics that prohibited, via witty or arrogant dismissal, any interest in the work of what was seen as a rival or wrong-minded group. People couldn't seem to function in the literary world without asserting and then defending their own agenda. This territorial attitude meant that poets could neither mingle with ease nor appreciate each other's work.

But, she goes on: "I didn't want to have to choose—FOR one and AGAINST another—in order to feel comfortable in a particular writing community. So I didn't" ("Eavan Boland and Kathleen Fraser" 393–94).

For Fraser, that nonchoosing seems to have been particularly important in relation to women poets. It enabled Adrienne Rich and Barbara Guest to function side by side, and not necessarily in conflict, as her models. Recalling the beginnings of her desire to locate a female poetics, Fraser has said, "For me, the awakening began out of some combination of Simone de Beauvoir's call to consciousness in *The Second Sex,* Adrienne Rich's grave and alarming poem 'The Roofwalker,' and Barbara Guest's tenacious insistence on the primacy of reinventing language structures in order to catch one's own at-oddness with the presumed superiority of the central mainstream vision" (*Translating the Unspeakable* 31). In this period when women writers had to wait to be taken up by male

editors or stars who would launch their careers, Fraser found women generally reluctant to help each other. Adrienne Rich, Fraser recalls, was an exception:

> She was wonderfully generous to me at that time. She was eager to talk and to exchange ideas and, even though her work didn't provide a model that I followed in terms of the way I wanted to write, certainly her generosity as an older woman to a woman of my generation made a difference in my ability to sustain a serious work process. Barbara Guest was also such a person. I was fortunate to meet these women in the mid-sixties, just as I was formulating my own poetics. Guest ... made me feel that what I was thinking about poetically mattered, and my love of painting was heightened and refined by my discussions with her. ("An Interview" 12–13)

In this interview statement from 1996, Fraser carefully distances herself from Rich's mode of writing. Elsewhere, and perhaps somewhat contradictorily, she has dismissed her early work as "girlish, Plath-fed lyrics" (Perloff 121). But such retrospective denials and dismissals seem to me distortions, both because they obscure the diversity of lineages and examples feeding Fraser's sixties poetics, and because they impose on the sixties divisions that were not firmly in place until the seventies. Before the seventies, a woman writer could at least partially suspend the divisions of the anthology wars in order to make headway in issues related to gender: she could find liberating and even courageously innovative models in work that gave direct expression to women's experience *as well as* in mysteriously oblique, disjunctive, and visually attuned work like Guests's. Fraser's poems of the mid-sixties themselves suggest that she did not then choose between then—and I mean not only the mentoring friendships but also the poetic examples of the feminist who uses language instrumentally and the linguistically innovative one.

The title poem of Fraser's 1967 collection *Change of Address and Other Poems* (published by Kayak) challenges the reader not to pigeonhole Fraser or her writing. The two ways of reading a "Change of Address" suggest a shift in location (with all the social implications that can have) and an alteration in one's form of verbal communication. The title thereby invites us to understand the speaker's refusal to be trapped in roles and mistaken identities as the poet's refusal of neat and fixed aesthetic categories. The zestful speaker has great fun leading us on, encouraging us to imagine her roles in such sensuous detail that we're at least momentarily taken in by them.

... If you did, you were mistaken, the poem implies—as you were if you thought the speaker could be identified with the roles, based on expressionist paintings, vividly depicted in the second stanza. The third and final stanza reads:

> You can tear up your lecture notes now,
>   erase every phone number
> under my name and go shopping in someone
>   else's suitcase.
> I've changed my address again. And don't
>   waste your money
> on bilingual road maps. After a six-day
>   ocean voyage,
> a train ride and three Metro transfers you'd
>   only find nights
> where the breath churns to snow after dark
> and a bench with a man making blankets of
>   his arms, his wife
> in her black wool nightgown and a three-
>   legged cat
> in her lap. And then would you know me?

As the figure of the quick-change artist suggests, Fraser's work of the mid- and late-sixties offers a good deal of variety: celebratory exclamations within everyday routine recall O'Hara's poetry; visually exotic and often comically inventive metaphors recall Guest or Wallace Stevens; sometimes raw emotion with an edge of desperation recalls Plath; elsewhere carefully pared lines and plain diction echo Creeley, and so on. Yet, from today's perspective, there are clear limits to the work's daring or range on the levels of both form and content. While the female speakers struggle against conventional roles without really breaking free of them, the poet pushes against the conventional lyric envelope only to a limited degree. Venturing toward the extreme, they nonetheless find resolution within the normal.

Take, for instance, "Poem in Which My Legs are Accepted." The speaker of this poem proclaims her acceptance of what has been her "most obvious imperfection," her embarrassingly unglamorous, plump legs that have always fallen so far short of conventional standards of female beauty. Stepping free of that hegemonic perspective, she now celebrates her legs for their wondrous functionality: they have performed gymnastic feats, they have enabled her to swim to the top of blue waves, etc. Yet, reading on to

the poem's close, we find she values her legs most for the support they give her in performing socially approved gender roles.

... In lovemaking, her fleshy white legs may dance, but they also become mere background, setting off the dark elegance of the man's limbs. It is through their sexual enhancement of the man and their ability to bring forth his progeny that her appendages attain their greatest worth. To a post-sixties reader, the limits of such sexual liberation are obvious. Formally, too, one perceives the limits of the poem's challenge to the norm: the appearance of the page suggests Charles Olson's composition by field, with its shifting margins and uneven line lengths, but most of the line breaks respect syntactic units, and the poem is composed entirely in unambiguous, logically contiguous sentences, all addressed to the legs. Fraser's poem looks more daring than it is.

Like "Poem in Which My Legs Are Accepted," many poems in Fraser's sixties collections celebrate the speakers' sexuality and sensuality; this was an important personal freedom women seized in the 1960s, and we must be wary of taking that achievement for granted now. Yet the poems reveal how Fraser's investment in heterosexual eroticism becomes a point of retreat from new kinds of self-creation. While Fraser's poetic personas have freed themselves from the traditional position of passive object defined by the male gaze, they are rarely able to deviate from the decade's "normal" gender roles—any more than Fraser herself is able to push the lyric beyond the free-verse possibilities opened by the generation of Rich and Creeley.

How might we account for this correlation between what happens on the level of feminist content and what happens on the level of form? An answer is suggested by a phrase Fraser has recently used to characterize lyric: "the lyric vise" ("An Interview" 16). It is as if her speakers have been locked into particular conventional gender roles partly by the inherited conventions of lyric itself. Rachel Blau DuPlessis, in her essay "'Corpses of Poesie,'" has usefully clarified that "a cluster of foundational materials with a gender cast are built into the heart of the lyric" (71). Those foundational materials tend to silence the woman, identify her with nature, frame her in terms of the male gaze, and position her within masculine narratives of romance or of poetic inspiration. The beauties of poetry are bound up with the beauties of women, which are the proper possession of men. It is not surprising, then, that expectations associated with lyric—involving, for instance, closure, coherence, the potential range of tone and voice, lyric cadence, and lyric beauty—even in the less rule-bound forms common in the sixties, would still work against impulses to radically reposition women and female subjectivities within the genre. I do not claim that the traditions behind lyric prohibit *all* women from exploring alternative notions of subjectivity within the genre, but Kathleen Fraser seems to have been among those who found herself unworkably constrained within that form.

Fraser did gradually free herself from this vise. And part of what made the beautiful seamless lyric less and less available, pushing her toward the more fragmented experiments of the decades to follow, was the experience of motherhood, in her case single motherhood—that life of interruption and others' constant demands that Rich would describe in her landmark essay "When We Dead Awaken." (Looking ahead, it is worth noting that Fanny Howe—who had three children within four years—has also observed that the domestic duties that constrained her to write "only in fits and starts" profoundly affected her style and contributed to her work becoming more eccentric, disjunctive, and generically hybrid.) The final Fraser poem I will consider is one that confronts the frustrations of a mother's broken-up time and the strain of existing between the roles of mother and poet. Not coincidentally, I believe, in its structure, syntax, and language, this poem is one of the most unconventional of her works of the sixties.

As Peter Quartermain and others have noted, the title "In Defiance (of the Rains)" deliberately puns: kingly reigns and the reins that control horses are as pertinent here as soggy rains. The poem concerns a woman's struggle to maintain a sense of herself and to be a writer in the face of patriarchal demands epitomized by a "he" who seems to be her young son but who could easily represent male demands more generally. It is built of paratactically arranged, disjunct stanzas ranging in length from one to a dozen lines. The first stanza, suggesting the influences of Creeley and Plath at once, begins with a terse description of the self she projects: strong and capable, the rock of domesticity. But as early as the fourth line, a sense of passionate needs unmet, of entrapment, and conflict around domestic love begins to emerge.

... The short second stanza presents one source of her frustration, the imperative desires of the child: "he brings me a dandelion gone to seed / and wants me to blow it and wants his way." As I read it, the next stanza presents the decorum of sincerity as insufficient to this situation, invoking as alternatives more defiant rhetorical strategies that tear at the fabric of literary—perhaps lyric—tradition. Then we have a report, at once whimsical and sobering, of how the public perceives a woman in terms of the men who desire and thereby validate her: "They said when the diamond merchant loved me / my skin sparkled authentically." Semantic and syntactic uncertainties abound here, but as I read the penultimate stanza, the speaker explores similarities between herself and her son, who is creating a painting.

... Just as he watches his hand place the paint (defying societal convention or parental authority in not following the approved method of application), anticipating the dramatic effect of added color, she attends to the cluster of words that lie under her awareness, hoping that they will "explode. / All the new flash." In the poem's last line, "He wanted her pen to write poems in the grass," the boy attempts to claim the privileges traditionally allotted to the male artist: he would take away her writing implement so that he can produce his own poems. "In Defiance (of the Rains)" ends without revealing whether the mother/poet will hand over the pen, enabling the boy's creativity, or insist that the pen is hers to control. With its keen non-formulaic exploration of a woman's conflicted situation, its inventive metaphors, wit, multiple perspectives, and syntactic variety, the poem points toward Fraser's wonderfully ranging explorations of an experimental feminist poetics that would follow in the seventies and eighties...

Source: Lynn Keller, "'Just one of / the girls:—/ normal in the extreme': Experimentalists-To-Be Starting Out in the 1960s," in *differences: A Journal of Feminist Cultural Studies*, Vol. 12, No. 2, 2001, pp. 47–69.

Peter Quartermain

In the following excerpt, Quartermain gives a critical analysis of Fraser's work.

As director of the Poetry Center at San Francisco State University from 1973 through 1975, founder of the American Poetry Archives (possibly the largest collection of audio- and

" SUCH WRITING IS MARKED BY OVERT RISK-
TAKING, BY AN ACUTELY PAINFUL HONESTY OF REVE-
LATION AND DETAIL OF DIALOGUE AND RESPONSE, OF
THOUGHT AND DESIRE, OF ANGER AND DELIGHT."

videotape recordings by contemporary poets in North America), and founding editor of *HOW(ever)* (1983-1991), a much-imitated radical journal of women's innovative poetry, Kathleen Fraser has had an important influence on American poetry and poetics for a quarter century. That her work nevertheless remains little recognized is at least in part a direct result of her own decision, after the publication of *New Shoes* by Harper and Row in 1978, to withhold all her future work from major New York trade publishing companies in favor of little magazines and small private presses. Her earliest work appeared in such well-established and prestigious journals as *Poetry* (Chicago), *The New Yorker*, *The Hudson Review*, *The Nation*, and *Mademoiselle*. Since the mid 1970s, however, Fraser has chosen to publish almost exclusively in little magazines such as *TemblorHambone-ConjunctionsSulfur*, and *Avec*.

Nevertheless, Fraser's poetic output shows remarkable consistency. Though she seems in the early years to have concentrated on and excelled at writing the "well-made" expressionist lyrical poem, grounded in clearly identifiable personal experience, and in her later years to show clear and even compelling affinities with the work of the language writers, deliberately foregrounding language as material object, criticizing habits of meaning by defamiliarizing customary language patterns, her work has, throughout its shift from a publishing career to a writing career, been marked by a delight in rhetorical forms and strategies and what one reviewer, Peter Scheldahl, has called "an eager and uncomplicated impulse toward love and friendship." Fraser's work is notable for the immediacy and directness of both the sensual and the emotional, while avoiding the pitfalls of display to which confessional poetry is so prone. At heart, it is a poetry of exploration and of zest. It is remarkably accessible yet by no means conventional.

The eldest of four children (one boy, three girls), Kathleen Joy Fraser was born in Tulsa, Oklahoma, on 22 March 1935 to Marjorie Joy (Axtell) Fraser and James Ian Fraser II. One year after beginning his practice as an architect, her father—a graduate of the University of Tulsa School of Architecture—reached the decision to change professions and entered the Union Theological Seminary in Chicago to prepare for the Presbyterian ministry, a calling which he followed until his death from a head-on car crash in 1966. In several essays Fraser recalls with affection her father's inveterate habit of reciting nonsense verse and singing silly songs—a practice that, coupled with his highly vocal love for the rhetorical orotundity of the King James Bible, would have a lasting and in some respects problematic effect on her poetry. After a childhood in which she spent three years (from grades six through nine) in the high mountains of Glenwood Springs, Colorado, and finally settled in Covina, California, where she lived until graduating from high school, Fraser knew by heart "great chunks" of the Bible, as well as a great deal of English nonsense verse. She also acquired from her father an irrepressible delight in the sounds of words.

... perhaps, one can see the seeds of Fraser's lifelong struggle—a struggle she came to feel was shared by many women, whether writers or not—against her education. By the time she reached high school Fraser found herself essentially well trained to fear poetry. Alienated by its refusal to yield meanings other than those few handed down by her teachers, Fraser had, like countless others, learned not to take classes that foregrounded poetry[....]

Much later, teaching creative writing at San Francisco State in the 1970s, Fraser came to believe that this particular problem of meaning is gender related. As she observed in the introduction to her 1984 anthology of student writing, *Feminist Poetics*: "there is an expectation in [women students themselves] of failure, of not doing it right and never being quite sure they understand what right means, when they've been told that the materials, feelings and structures of many of their poems are inappropriate to the professional world of poetry." In the case of her own development as a poet, Fraser found that the persistence of the rhythms and sounds and attitudes, the mindset encapsulated and embodied in the grand English tradition, was a serious inhibition in the development of her own poetic, imposing as it did a mellifluous sonorous continuity on a life that she felt, as a woman, to be essentially discontinuous, fragmented, marginalized, and multiple. Her need to escape a grand tradition to which she felt strongly attracted came to constitute in complex ways a form of almost self-inflicted intimidation, which influenced her decision to major in philosophy when she entered Occidental College in Los Angeles as a sophomore in 1954.

Yet in her senior year Fraser switched to an English literature major, thereby postponing graduation until January 1959. This change was partly a result of what she learned in a humanities/classics two-year, required course, where she read Herman Melville and Walt Whitman as well as standard English classics, but it was mainly the result of browsing in the library or bookstores—where she discovered works such as Virginia Woolf's *The Waves* (1931). Through intense college friendships she was introduced to the work of writers such as E. E. Cummings, James Joyce, and William Carlos Williams, and she began scribbling poetry[....] For her birthday her college friends joined together to give her T. S. Eliot's *Collected Poems* (1936), Williams's *Journey to Love* (1955), and Cummings's *i: six nonlectures* (1953)—works that, along with the writings of Dylan Thomas, became models for her early verse. Cummings was especially attractive because his radical breaking of normative syntax and grammar spoke directly [to Fraser's internal struggle]. This struggle within and against her education came to inform Fraser's whole career as a writer, a writing life perpetually venturing into what she called, in *HOW(ever)* in 1982, "the tentative regions of the untried."

On graduating from college in 1959 Fraser left an increasingly incompatible southern California for New York City, where she began work writing copy for the fashion magazine *Mademoiselle*. By this time committed to a life of writing poetry, she felt she knew virtually nothing of the contemporary writing scene: at college she had never in class been introduced to the work of any living writers (other than perhaps William Faulkner or Ernest Hemingway), though she had attended a reading at Occidental by Robert Lowell. She had never read or even come across such major women modernists as H. D. (Hilda Doolittle), Marianne Moore, or Gertrude Stein. Hungry for news, she found herself excited by everything she read—Pablo Neruda, César Vallejo, Paul Célan, Giuseppe Ungaretti, Eugenio Montale—but with no basis for comparison. She found herself perpetually learning, unlearning, and then learning to do things differently.... It was some years before she could evolve a poetic philosophy and technique commensurate with her experience, but her hunger for writing news was such that almost immediately on her arrival in New York she took a poetry course offered by poet Stanley Kunitz at the Ninety-second Street Young Men's Hebrew Association (YMHA), enrolling in his workshop in the fall of 1959 and again in the following semester. Fraser was "thrilled," she would later say, by Kunitz's "Yeatsian language and passionate metaphysical vision," and she learned through him to admire the work of Elizabeth Bishop. Kunitz, a generous and sympathetic teacher, was at this time still strongly traditionalist in his own verse, which was strictly formal in structure and lofty in theme. (It was only in the 1960s, for instance, that Kunitz began some of his lines with lower-case letters.) "A high style," he said, "wants to be fed exclusively on high sentiments." Such an approach to poetry could not satisfy for long someone of Fraser's immediacy and passion. For by instructing Fraser to cast herself and her experience as representative—and to think of her condition as writer as both universal and transcendent, unaffected by the world, free of such quotidian distractions as race or gender—Kunitz made an icon of the lyric poetic self, elevating it to a position superior to that of the reader by installing its own power as seer, transformer, and possessor of meaning. In thus subordinating the reader to the role of witness seeking to "understand" the poem, rather than participant in the construction of meaning, it perpetuated the very condition Fraser had found so crippling as a student in school.

In Kunitz's workshop Fraser met the young poet Jack Marshall. In 1960 he became her first husband. Their conversations opened up for Fraser the world of poetry and painting: he took her to see the work of Willem de Kooning, Franz Kline, Jackson Pollock, and Sam Francis.... She began to meet other New York writers—having been drawn almost from her arrival in New York to Greenwich Village and to the "downtown" poets, including Robert Kelly, Paul Blackburn, Jerome Rothenberg, Armand Schwerner, Carol

Berge, and Diane Wakoski; to Black Mountain writers such as Robert Creeley, Robert Duncan, Denise Levertov, and Charles Olson; and to the New York School poets Frank O'Hara, Kenward Elmslie, Edwin Denby, James Schuyler, and especially Barbara Guest. Such avant-garde writers on the margin were, whether they knew it or not, Fraser's teachers. In her mind they made up her literary family.

During this same period she came across the work of Wallace Stevens, hearing two young men recite his work at a party in Greenwich Village. As she recounts the story in "Things that do not exist without words," she was transported into an "untranslatable elation." The next day she bought his poems, which she read, "transfixed," every day in the office at lunch hour. For Fraser, Stevens was the great "unloosener"[....] Stevens thus became the first of several figures who drew Fraser away from poetry as she had learned it in school, who drew her back toward the poetry of her childhood.

Fraser's reading fed into her increasing dissatisfaction with her own writing situation and thus drew her in the summer of 1964 to enroll in Daisy Alden's two-week course at Wagner College. Because Alden was ill, Kenneth Koch taught the course instead. Koch, famously imaginative and strong-minded as a teacher, gave silly nonsense-writing assignments that restored to Fraser the playful attitude toward poetic language she had acquired from her father in her childhood. Koch's hostility in class toward any sign of high seriousness or emotional vulnerability, whether in the writing or in the individual, and his disdain for sentimental poetic retreads were crucial for Fraser at this stage in her career, when she felt in need of liberation from older forms and inhibitions. Soon after, through Frank O'Hara, Fraser met Barbara Guest, whose intensely disciplined attention to the accuracy of her language [...] would have a pervasive and lasting effect. Guest's sense of language as a prison, her sense that language is inadequate to the writing event itself, had its kinship with the work of the New York painters about whom she wrote so brilliantly.

During these years Stevens and Guest became Fraser's great exemplars and inspirations; finally, hearing George Oppen read his work early in 1967 firmly secured her sense of her own difference from the mainstream. Striking Fraser as wholly without posture, modest yet severe in its unflinching attention to detail and nuance, Oppen's work appealed to her as a new kind of attentiveness, speaking to some neglected level of gravity. Oppen joined Stevens and Guest as prime constituents of Fraser's writing life. Fraser's personal life, meanwhile, had not been without its troubles. In 1965 her father was killed in a head-on car crash. Later, in 1969, her sister Mary died. A mezzo-soprano, she too appears in Fraser's writings. Christmas of 1966 saw the birth of her son, David, on 26 December. The New York neighborhood in which Fraser lived was becoming increasingly the site of drug trafficking and consumption; in September 1967 she and Marshall returned home from walking their son to find their apartment completely trashed and everything portable (including typewriters, stereo, and tape recorder) stolen. Within the week they left for San Francisco, with one month's rent and few prospects.

The move to San Francisco proved extremely fortunate. George and Mary Oppen became close friends, George reading (and advising her about) her poems. As a writer Fraser found the atmosphere of the Bay Area congenial, contrasting sharply with the flash and dazzle of writing performance characteristic of so many New York poets. Fraser's first book, *Change of Address & Other Poems* (1966), had already been published in San Francisco by George Hitchcock's Kayak Press; in 1968 the prestigious publishing house Atheneum brought out *Stilts, Somersaults, and Headstands*, a book of poems for children. Much of the energy for this book no doubt came from Fraser's work caring for her son, but the childlike directness of the language and the simplicity of the sound patterns so prominent in these verses for children carry over into Fraser's subsequent work, most directly in the poems gathered in *In Defiance of the Rains* (1969), again published by Hitchcock.

The title of Fraser's first book, *Change of Address*, suggests the extent to which her poetry is drawn directly from her immediate daily experience in a physical world. The poems themselves, often centering on an "I" or a readily imaginable "you," investigate different relations in and of speech and exploit some of the puns implicit in the title. The poems in *In Defiance of the Rains* explore line breaks, punctuation, and sentence pattern in their construction of sound[....]

Some of the poems play with context and reader expectation, at the same time punning the alphabet, as in the epistolary "Letters: to him," "to her," and "to Barbara," and the title of the collection itself can be read as a punning and coded resistance to another's rule. These two Kayak books are Fraser's initial steps toward exploring the physicality of language as experience: while they clearly and emphatically deal with the apparent trivia of daily life, especially in its domesticity (a focus in later years to be closely identified with feminist writing), they certainly do not regard language as a clear glass through which to regard the world. These poems, later gathered in *What I Want*, are intensely personal and intimate, paying astonishingly close attention to the physical, the immediate materiality of experience.

On a visit to San Francisco in late spring 1969 George Starbuck, director of the Iowa Writers' Workshop, offered Fraser and Marshall teaching posts at the workshop, where Fraser taught from 1969 to 1971. The following year she was writer-in-residence at Reed College in Portland, Oregon. (The couple was divorced in 1970.) Teaching turned out to be Fraser's vocation, and at Reed her latent feminism began to emerge into informal classes on Stein and H. D. held at her house. At that time the notion that the modernist women writers had any relevance to feminism was unfashionable in feminist politics, where a more commonly spoken language was virtually de rigueur for any woman who wanted acceptance in the women's writing community.

From Portland, Fraser moved to San Francisco, where she directed the San Francisco Poetry Center (1973-1976) and taught creative writing at San Francisco State University. In 1985 she began to spend up to five months of each year working and living in Rome, where, that same year, she married the philosopher A. K. Bierman, whom she had met during her first year at San Francisco State. Her experience in Italy afforded radical linguistic and cultural challenges that significantly informed and colored the poems gathered in *Notes Preceding Trust* (1987) and later collections. She retired from San Francisco State as a full professor in 1993, having converted her position from full- to part-time a few years earlier. Concurrent with her first years in San Francisco, Fraser got to know women writers whose work seemed generatively close to her own[....] In 1974 Harper and Row published *What I Want*, which consists mainly of work gathered from her previous collections, with some new poems that show an intensifying commitment to syntactical experiment and unconventional form.

The first major indication, however, of Fraser's increasing alignment with experimental and even avant-garde writing is *Magritte Series* (1977), published by Lyn Hejinian as number six in her Tuumba series of chapbooks. (Other writers appearing in that "First Series" include Dick Higgins, Susan Howe, and Kenneth Irby, as well as Hejinian herself.) In *Magritte Series*—to an even greater extent than in "The History of My Feeling" and "Six Uneasy Songs" at the close of *What I Want*—it becomes clear that the writing is creating the situation to which it refers, a mode no conventional reader can comfortably accept, since reference is at a minimum. The poems of *Magritte Series* wittily and disturbingly play familiar ordinary syntax with the grotesque, thereby constituting a stylistic equivalent to the paintings of René Magritte, to which the poems seek to be companions.

These poems were later collected in *New Shoes* (1978), Fraser's last book with a major New York trade publisher. The wit and the cultivation of the bizarre function as controlling devices to keep the reader distant from—but at the same time intensely aware of—the controlled but never hidden high emotional charge of these intensely personal poems. "One of the Chapters," for instance, tempers the poet's sheer outrage at the preposterous difficulties of living in a university town (where the men make up the universe) through a carefully controlled comic ironic tone, coupled with the important news that the poem draws on someone else's text. Yet Peter Schjeldahl, reviewing this book in *The New York Times Book Review* (13 August 1978), praised Fraser's "delight in rhetorical forms and ... sense of what words mean" but nevertheless concluded—perhaps with the deliberate grotesques of the *Magritte Series* specifically in mind—that, "lushly synesthetic" and "full of appeal to the senses," the work is at times "self-absorbed to (and sometimes over) the brink of solipsism and incoherence." *What I Want* and *New Shoes* reveal the extent to which Fraser has learned to trust rather than bully the reader—no mean feat when the poems are full of scorn or anguish. The poems are remarkably skillful, with Fraser firmly in control of the meaning, which is transmitted with great emotional impact to the reader.

By the late 1970s Fraser found herself increasingly reluctant to submit her work to male editors and no longer found it possible to accept their well-meaning but patronizing "corrections" of her work. Some of her difficulties and a great deal of her passion as a writer came in her eyes to have an increasingly gendered origin, a theme she would explore with remarkable and indeed devastating effectiveness in *Each Next: Narratives* (1980). This book marks the great turning point in Fraser's career.

Since the title declines the label *fiction*, for example, there is no means to tell whether these largely prose works are fictions or not; they bear the stamp of direct and immediate autobiography. A passionate defense of nontraditional writing by women, the narratives were written exactly at the time when Fraser felt isolated as a writer in San Francisco, unable to "submit" her work to male editors and finding precious few if any feminist journals prepared to publish stylistically innovative heterosexual work. The book was also published exactly at the time when Fraser, Beverly Dahlen, and Frances Jaffer were embarking on a series of conversations and investigations that would result in the founding two years later of Fraser's important journal *HOW(ever)*. Adapting Olson's famous dictum that "one perception must immediately and directly lead to a further perception"—already a feature of some of the poems in *New Shoes* and before—Fraser finds, especially in "Talking to Myself Talking to You," a fierce narrative drive to push the writing headlong from discovery to discovery; multiple and complex feelings and responses suggest the fragmenting of daily life and self so alien to the discourse of male power, at times fragmenting syntax, continuity, and image. At the same time, these prose poems erase conventional narrative concepts such as point of view in an ironic melange of fragments, and they dissolve generic boundaries. All the poems in *Each Next* are "about" writing (and necessarily then about reading) as a woman, and the reader, forced by the linguistic play into the active construction rather than the passive reception of meaning, finds procedural and even methodological clues. The narratives of *Each Next* pave the way to discovery by participating in it and moving the reader into such participation:[....]

Such writing is marked by overt risk-taking, by an acutely painful honesty of revelation and detail of dialogue and response, of thought and desire, of anger and delight. These are powerful poems of desire, interrogating the beloved, interrogating the very nature of "other," and—by means of the comments others reportedly make in these stories—interrogating the self, or selves:[....] The poems also interrogate, then, their own writing and invite the reader into the act.

The formal and especially thematic achievement of *Each Next* is to dissolve generic contrasts between "prose" and "verse" and the boundaries between "fact" and "fiction," rendering such distinctions not only irrelevant but intrusive. Fraser's next books, *Something (even human voices) in the foreground, a lake* (1984) and *Boundayr*, written some three years later but not published until 1988, are a devastating assault on the possession of meaning, on the social and intellectual certainties implicated in hegemonic and institutionalized powers. They do so by destabilizing the text and by flattening out the voice. Some of the poems in *Something* abandon referentiality almost completely; those in *Boundayr* cultivate error as compositional principle. These writings are intimately connected with Fraser's founding of *HOW(ever)*, which she edited from 1983 to 1991, with guest editors in 1990.

As editor of *HOW(ever)*, Fraser created a place where women could "focus attention on language and ... discover what [could] be written in other than traditional syntactical or prosodic structures." The magazine gave women an immensely important opportunity to publish experimental work that would call into question conventional models of language usage and the social institutions that enforce those conventions. A groundbreaking enterprise, the project shared many of the goals of the language writers, who deliberately foreground language as material object and seek to criticize habits of meaning by defamiliarizing customary language patterns. Its most important features were its openness to new writers of whatever persuasion and its refusal to adopt a partisan feminist position:[....] At the same time the magazine undertook the important work of retrieving work by forgotten women modernists such as Mary Butts, Mina Loy, Lorine Niedecker, and others, and it became the model for *f(lip)* magazine in Vancouver and *6ix* magazine in Philadelphia.

The great work of editing *HOW(ever)*, so closely linked as it was with Fraser's own writing, set the pattern for her future books, each of which deliberately pursues a course of discovery implicit in her earlier work—and each of which is formally innovative. Thus, the work in *Boundayr* freed Fraser to write poems such as *Giotto: Arena*, first published as an entire issue of *Abacus* (15 November 1991) and collected in *When New Time Folds Up* (1993). As Meredith Quartermain observed in an important review (*West Coast Line*, Winter 1994-1995), the title poem affords the reader a remarkable complex of manifold relations and voices, formally invoking and interrogating the tradition of which it declares itself a part. Carol Muske, in a judicious but nevertheless enthusiastic review in *The New York Times Book Review* (6 February 1994), called Fraser a maverick who "belongs to no school" and commented that through her "voracious desire" to enter and deconstruct language Fraser "demonstrates how thinking evolves, how we think what we see and vice versa," remarking that the poems are to a great extent the harvest of her rich early work (influenced by poets as diverse as Frank O'Hara and George Oppen) and her subsequent language experiments. Rachel Blau DuPlessis, writing in *Sulfur* (Spring 1994) on "the rich tinctures of multifarious webbings" in these poems, pointed to Fraser's use of II. D. "for the pensive, illuminating reading and rereading on signs (a play with repetition and recirculation most striking in the final, and title poem)" and of Virginia Woolf for "the delicate, determined 'deliberate burdens through the temporal.'"

Despite its extraordinary technical sophistication and capacity to disturb the reader, the work in *When New Time Folds Up* and Fraser's more recent books is completely unintimidating. Drawing on a great range of resources, including graphics—and in *Wing* (1995) playing with great charm and indeed passion with the visual shape of the poem—Fraser's work has become more and more playful and less and less dogmatic, while at the same time cultivating a meditative and cogitative stance and habit that continually cultivate and exploit the random and the accidental. ... Reading through Fraser's work in chronological order makes one see clearly that her whole career has been a move away from certainty and into discovery. Overall, it reflects a great generosity of spirit, a necessary corollary to a deep and abiding curiosity. The chief characteristic of her work, persisting through its abiding lyrical intensity and condensation and love of color and the sheer body-ness of the

language and the vision, is its stubborn and courageous refusal to rest satisfied with any sort of status quo, a determination to find a language adequate to the writing occasion of which it is witness: the perturbability of the writer....

The essay [...] "This Phrasing Unreliable Except As Here" (published in *Talisman*, 1995), could well serve as a motto for the collected work, obedient as each poem is to the writing occasion itself.

Source: Peter Quartermain, "Kathleen Fraser," in *Dictionary of Literary Biography*, Vol. 169, *American Poets Since World War II, Fifth Series*, edited by Joseph Conte, Gale Research, 1996, pp. 106–15.

SOURCES

Clippinger, David, Review of *il cuore: the heart; Selected Poems (1970–1995)*, in *Chicago Review*, Vol. 43, No. 4, Fall 1997, pp. 162–65.

Fraser, Kathleen, "Poem in Which My Legs Are Accepted," in *What I Want*, Harper & Row, 1974, pp. 25–27.

Keller, Lynn, "'Just one of / the girls:– / normal in the extreme': Experimentalists-to-Be Starting Out in the 1960s," in *differences*, Vol. 12, No. 2, Summer 2001, p. 55.

Muske, Carol, "Outside the Fence, Three Renegade Stylists," in *New York Times Book Review*, February 6, 1994, p. 32.

Taylor, Linda A., "'A Seizure of Voice': Language Innovation and a Feminist Poetics in the Works of Kathleen Fraser," in *Contemporary Literature*, Vol. 33, No. 2, Summer 1992, pp. 337–72.

FURTHER READING

Banes, Sally, *Greenwich Village 1963: Avant-Garde Performance and the Effervescent Body*, Duke University Press, 1993.
> Avant-garde art and literature rose in popularity during the 1960s. In this book, Banes chronicles the people and events that constituted this creative movement.

Faludi, Susan, *Backlash: The Undeclared War against American Women*, Crown, 1991.
> Faludi reveals the second-wave backlash that especially affected women seeking careers in the 1980s. This book won the National Book Critics Circle Award.

Fraser, Kathleen, *Translating the Unspeakable: Poetry and the Innovative Necessity; Essays*, University of Alabama Press, 2000.

> This book is a collection of essays written by Fraser from 1979 to 1998, blending criticism and autobiography.

Frost, Elisabeth A., *The Feminist Avant-Garde in American Poetry*, University of Iowa Press, 2003.

> Frost examines the feminist avant-garde movement from 1910 through 1990, including detailed examinations of poets such as Gertrude Stein and Sonia Sanchez.

Hogue, Cynthia, "An Interview with Kathleen Fraser," in *Contemporary Literature*, Vol. 39, No. 1, Spring 1998, pp. 1–26.

> In this interview, Hogue and Fraser discuss Fraser's writing process, her editorship of *HOW(ever)*, and the motivation behind her projects.

St. Roach

MURIEL RUKEYSER
1976

Over the course of a poetic career that kept her in the international spotlight for more than forty years, Muriel Rukeyser established a reputation for concern about social justice. This concern is evident in "St. Roach," which was published in her final book, *The Gates*, in 1976. On its surface, this poem is about the ways in which the poet was taught to view cockroaches with disgust and hatred, thinking of them only to plan ways to kill them. Not far below the surface, however, is a message about racial enmity or hostility. In the end, the poem offers a solution when the speaker looks at the cockroach and notices what is noble and beautiful about it.

While Rukeyser has not been considered a major poet by critics, her work remains just shy of the distinction and has nevertheless garnered a lasting critical respect. In the years since her death in 1980, various collections of Rukeyser's poems have gone in and out of print. "St. Roach" can now be found in *The Collected Poems of Muriel Rukeyser* (2005).

AUTHOR BIOGRAPHY

Muriel Rukeyser was born in New York, New York, on December 15, 1913. Her father, Lawrence, was a concrete salesman, and her mother, Myra, was a housewife who had been a bookkeeper. Rukeyser attended high school at a

Muriel Rukeyser (AP Images)

private school in the Bronx, the Fieldston School, and then went to Vassar College in Poughkeepsie before moving back to New York City to attend Columbia University. After finishing college, she returned to Poughkeepsie, and her passion for progressive politics began to show. Rukeyser, along with Elizabeth Bishop, Mary McCarthy, and Eleanor Clark, created a new literary magazine, *Student Review*, to compete with the mainstream *Vassar Review*. In 1932 Rukeyser traveled south as a reporter for *Student Review* to cover the trial of nine black men in Scottsboro, Alabama, who were accused of raping two white women in what was to become one of the most famous civil rights cases in the country's history. For the rest of her life, Rukeyser was committed to social issues, giving her vocal and financial support to the underdogs and dissidents in causes ranging from the Spanish Civil War of the 1930s to the Vietnam War in the 1970s. She wrote columns for the *Daily Worker*, a newspaper published by the American Communist Party. She also wrote extensively about feminism and Judaism. Because of her strong political beliefs and her willingness to stand up for what she believed, Rukeyser was a divisive figure, often criticized by those on all sides of the political spectrum.

Her career as a poet started with acclaim when her first collection, *Theory of Flight*, won the Yale Younger Poets Prize and was then published by Yale University Press. Over the next forty-one years she wrote constantly, publishing poems, novels, translations, television scripts, biographies, and essays. Her notable works include the poetry collections *U.S. One* (1938), *Elegies* (1949), and *The Speed of Darkness* (1968) as well as the novel *The Orgy* (1965) and several unpublished plays. Almost all of her work reflected her social concerns and political situations of the times they were written in. She supported herself, first with office jobs and then, as her career developed, by teaching at Sarah Lawrence College in Bronxville, New York. Over the years, her writing won several prestigious awards, including the Harriet Monroe Poetry Award in 1941 and the Levinson Prize for poetry in 1947. She also received a National Institute of Arts and Letters grant in 1942 and fellowships from the Guggenheim Foundation and the American Council of Learned Societies.

Rukeyser suffered a stroke in 1964, at the age of fifty-one. The event did little to inhibit her writing or political activism, however, as she went on to travel to Hanoi during the Vietnam War and to South Korea to protest the planned execution of the poet Kim Chi-Ha. That visit, in 1975, inspired the poems in Rukeyser's collection *The Gates*, in which "St. Roach" was published. Rukeyser suffered another stroke in 1978 and was permanently disabled by it. She died in New York City in 1980.

POEM SUMMARY

"St. Roach" comprises three stanzas of varying lengths; at twenty-two lines, the first stanza is by far the longest, followed by the five-line second stanza and the four-line third stanza.

Stanza 1

The poem begins with a form of address that implies that readers are joining the speaker in the middle of an ongoing conversation. The actual subject being addressed is not even identified within the poem, such that it must be assumed to be the roach, or cockroach, mentioned in the title.

The first two lines of the poem use negative observations to draw attention to how little the speaker has been taught about the cockroach.

MEDIA ADAPTATIONS

- Rukeyser reads from *The Gates* and talks about her life in a 1978 film called *Muriel Rukeyser*, produced by Perspective Films and available from Coronet/MTI Film and Video.

- "St. Roach" is read by Rukeyser on *The Poetry and Voice of Muriel Rukeyser*. Originally released in 1977 by Caedmon on an LP album, it is also available on audio cassette.

Both of these lines start with what could be positive associations, to know the cockroach and to touch it. However, they each end with the negative associations that were taught to the speaker as she was growing up: that the roach is to be dreaded and that it is filth. The third line does not have the split positive/negative feelings of the first two, instead going for one straightforward, extreme point. The speaker has been taught not to dislike or distrust the cockroach but to despise it—and not just certain elements about it but everything about it.

The poem's fourth line begins with the same words that begin the first two lines. It diverts from the pattern established by them, however, by extending the observation to a full line rather than a half. This line goes far to confuse the identity of the subject of the poem: while cockroaches can be unknown and untouched and despised, as in the previous lines, wars are usually fought between people. Readers are therefore given a clear indicator that, even as it speaks of attitudes toward cockroaches, this poem is hinting at human relations as well.

The speaker's response to observing the war on the cockroach is given in line 5, which repeats the poem's first idea of basic unfamiliarity. This line, according to the pattern, is connected to line 4, and its thought is also carried over into line 6, which explains the unfamiliarity as stemming from the speaker's childhood, lived in places that were kept clear of cockroaches.

Lines 7 through 9 contain one continuous thought. This thought is centered around the violent imagery of line 8, which uses the poem's most explicit language and images. Line 7 leads into this violence with the ironic reference to people meeting the subject, as if the acts that are to follow are going to be friendly actions. Line 9 completes the idea of pouring boiling water and then goes on to pair it with flushing cockroaches down toilets, keeping all of the water imagery on one line.

The idea of being unable to distinguish cockroaches from one another is brought up for the third time in line 10, using almost the same wording that was used in line 5. The following lines expand upon the idea that the poem is perhaps talking about cockroaches but is perhaps also talking about people. While the three words used to describe the cockroach in line 11 do describe insects, Rukeyser also indulges in humanizing them. The personification is even more pronounced in line 12, in which the poet draws a comparison between the physique of the cockroach and her own build. The fact that a person is built differently than a cockroach is obvious, but the perceived differences between members of one ethnic or racial group and another are worth giving some consideration. The poet's awareness of how she differs from her subject is only significant if her subject is another human being.

In the poem's center lines (lines 13 through 19), the personification of the cockroach is made unequivocally clear. Insects do not have poems, sayings, or language, but Rukeyser attributes all of these to the poem's subject. By this point, then, there is no way to avoid the conclusion that Rukeyser is actually writing about people. What is not made explicitly clear, however, is the identity of the people she is writing about. They are presumably a social group, a culture that would share the same language, sayings, and songs. As line 11 explains, they are dark, slender, and fast on their feet. These characteristics can describe many different peoples around the globe, and the poet does nothing to pinpoint any in particular. By leaving the identity of the group vague, Rukeyser indicates that the target of this poem is prejudice in general.

The question of how prejudice continues is brought up in lines 17 through 20. Previously, the speaker has focused on the fact that she was not taught to understand or appreciate the cultures of others. In line 17, she notes that she passes along the same insular worldview to children of the next generation. In noting what she fails to expose children to from the subject's culture, the speaker uses examples from the preceding lines—poems, from line 13, and songs, from line 16—but also adds a new, more essential element in talking about the food of the other culture.

In the last two lines of the first stanza, the speaker changes to using the first-person plural. She herself is thus presented more as an innocent party, a victim of her culture who was raised to know no better than the common prejudices, from earlier lines. However, her use of the pronoun *we* indicates that she has internalized the narrow-mindedness. This is particularly significant when line 21 is compared to line 2: In the earlier line, the speaker says that she was told of the filthiness of the people being discussed, while in line 21 she is one of those who is saying these derogatory things.

Stanza 2

In the second stanza, Rukeyser shows how the prejudice that was drilled into her finally began to dissolve. What is more important is that she is putting aside the habit of seeing others, whether they are humans or insects, as a group, to instead pay particular attention to individual members of the group. In this instance, rather than approaching the subject with the preconceived notions that she was taught from her childhood, she let the evidence of her own senses tell her about the person she was observing. The high significance of this act is emphasized by the way Rukeyser says almost the same thing in two lines close together, lines 23 and 26.

In lines 24 and 25, the poem focuses on the issue of color in relation to prejudice. Having mentioned in line 11 that the other, the mysterious one that she had been trained to fear and loathe, was dark, she notes upon observing one particular example of cockroach or person that this one is not as dark as those that have been observed from afar. Line 25 makes a point of noting that this lightness is meaningless. A point of this poem is to show how distinctions such as those made by color or race are arbitrary; to say that darkness is better or that darkness is worse would contradict that point.

Line 26 repeats the same idea that was expressed three lines earlier, in line 23, giving emphasis to the speaker's amazement at how unaware of this aspect of her world she has

been up to this point. In line 27, the speaker attributes complex mental processes to the one she is observing, far beyond the capabilities of a cockroach. If this poem were read as speaking strictly about cockroaches, as the title indicates it is, then it would be projecting human attributes onto a creature with an insect's intellectual capacity. If it is read as a metaphor for human relations, then the recognition that the subject is troubled and witty represents a willingness to accept the truth of other people's humanity.

Stanza 3

While much prejudice is overcome by looking at the other, there is still much more progress to be made through actual physical contact, an act of intimacy. These things happen in stages in the poem. For the poem's speaker, who has been taught that the other cockroach or person carries filth and disease, touching the thing she has been taught to hate is a bold step.

After physical contact is made, the associations are all positive; the other is compared to a dancer. Rukeyser admits to a sense of wonderment that overwhelms the fears that dominated the earlier part of the poem. As the poem says in its last line, this represents the beginning of a relationship. Though it took much for the poet to get herself to initiate this contact with an other, there is still much more understanding to be gained before she will really know that other.

THEMES

Prejudice

The relationship between the speaker of this poem and the cockroach being discussed is the same one that many people have with people of other cultures. The poet identifies ways in which she was taught to fear the cockroach: she had no firsthand knowledge of it, having grown up in a place kept free of insects, but was told by others of its dangers. Her experience with cockroaches has been limited to seeing them killed, leaving the impression that their deaths are necessary. Her hatred of cockroaches, like all prejudices, is allowed by a lack of familiarity.

The fact that Rukeyser is dealing with human prejudice here is not in the least hidden. Although she identifies her subject as a cockroach in the poem's title, she does not use that word in the poem itself. What she does do is talk

TOPICS FOR FURTHER STUDY

- Choose an insect or animal that you do not like and research it. Afterwards, identify the attributes that you find admirable, and write a poem about the creature.

- Research the Catholic Church's criteria for sainthood. In a class presentation, explain how the standards that must be met could be applied to the cockroach.

- This poem references the cockroach's songs and language. Present a diagram of cockroach anatomy to your class and explain how cockroaches communicate.

- According to legend, cockroaches will survive long after mankind is destroyed by atomic radiation. Write a report that explains how this myth started and its basis in reality.

- Make a list of the strange things that people from outside your culture, race, or gender believe or might believe about the people in your culture, race, or gender. If possible, note why and how these beliefs could have come into being.

about human elements, such as the songs and the language of the subject. Very few readers would miss the point that the things she says about cockroaches echo the things that people say about other races and cultures.

To make the comparison to human prejudice complete, Rukeyser brings up the issue of color in a few places. In line 11, she says that her ignorance of the other is limited to recognizing its darkness. Most cockroaches are in fact dark, but heightened awareness of skin tone is also a standard of racial prejudice around the world; thus, the darkness together with the fear and anger that she was taught to view the cockroach match elements of racial prejudice perfectly. In line 24 she says that upon paying attention to individual cockroaches for the first time in her life, she notes a difference in skin tone from one to another. She is overcoming the tendencies to

group all members of a race or culture together and to assume that they will all act the same and all have the same wants and needs, which are at the core of prejudice.

Mysteriousness of the Unknown

Perhaps the fact that the poet grew up in a place without cockroaches, or without people from different ethnic or racial backgrounds, enables her to push on beyond the prejudices she has been taught simply in expanding her world. While other people raised in the same circumstances might remain in place, carry on with the same narrow views, and pass them along to their children, this poem shows a person who views something or someone unfamiliar to her as a mystery to be explored.

The poem begins with the speaker's admission that she does not know the subject that she is talking about, and for about three-fourths of its length she lists things about this other that are not familiar to her. The climax of this catalog of mysteries occurs when, in line 21, she expands her ignorance to include all of those in her social class by switching the subject to *we*, the plural. As soon as she acknowledges that her whole group, not just herself, finds the others a mystery, she sets about in line 23 to correct the situation by demystifying the cockroach. For the most part, this is a poem about a speaker who recognizes what she does not know and feels drawn to what is unfamiliar, even though she has been told it is dangerous.

Seeking Insight

By the end of the poem, Rukeyser's speaker has not gained any real insight into the life of the cockroach that has captured her attention. The insight that she has gained by the last line is about how much knowledge she lacks. Having been fooled by her prejudices for most of her life into believing that she knew all that she needed to know about others, she is just beginning the process of breaking through the wall of ignorance that surrounds her.

Just as the speaker of the poem starts to pay serious attention to others, the poem ends. Readers are not told anything about the specific observations she makes regarding cockroaches or regarding people from different races or cultures. The insight is not about what she learns: it is about the need to learn. Over the course of the poem she has gained enough insight to know better than to view the world the way she has all her life.

STYLE

Anthropomorphism

Anthropomorphism is the practice in literature of giving human qualities to nonhuman objects. It is often used in children's tales, as in familiar animated films about talking lions or dancing brooms. In this poem, anthropomorphism is seen in the way that Rukeyser talks about the language, songs, and food of what are understood to be cockroaches and in the way that she describes the cockroach as humorous and compares its movements to those of a dancer. Of course, cockroaches have not developed any of these aspects of culture, but speaking as if they have allows the poem to make readers draw certain conclusions. Just as an anthropomorphized car might invite its audience to think about the ways in which a car's grille is like a human's teeth and its headlights are like eyes, so, too, does the anthropomorphic cockroach draw attention to the ways that a person might dismiss another category of people as if they were bugs.

Extended Metaphor

A *metaphor* is a figure of speech that uses one idea to bring another to mind. The comparison made by a metaphor is implied and not stated. In "St. Roach," for instance, Rukeyser does not state that she looked upon people of other cultures as if they were cockroaches; instead, she talks about cockroaches and lets her readers imagine how much the things said about cockroaches match the things people say about cultures they do not know.

The power of the metaphor lies in its transferring some of the thought process to the reader. When the comparison is not stated explicitly, readers are forced to look beneath the surface of the words to determine why the writer is talking about two things at once. An example might be if someone referred to another person as "a rock": the person hearing this expression is forced to determine which qualities of a rock—density? steadfastness? weight?—might apply to the person called one. They would have to think about the context in which the word was used, and they would therefore be active in making meaning of an expression that might not otherwise make sense.

The implied comparison used in "St. Roach" is an *extended metaphor*. Rukeyser does not just imply the relationship between how one treats unfamiliar races and how one treats cockroaches once, but

further she repeats the comparison in several different places. She refers in one place to color, in another to food, in another to language, in another to songs, and so on. This range of implied comparisons makes readers look at the metaphor from different angles. With the many associations that are implied here, Rukeyser is able to show that the problem of seeing other people in unjust ways is deeply ingrained in social attitudes.

Repetition

Lines 1, 2, 4, 6, 7, 10, and 13 start with the same two words. This pattern is repeated with a slight variation in lines 14 through 17 and then with yet another slight variation in lines 21 and 22. Starting so many of the poem's lines with one of these three similar phrases gives "St. Roach" the feel of an incantation, as if the speaker is trying to summon mysterious forces, when in fact she is trying to understand her own conflicting emotions—often a mysterious process. The repetition also lends coherence to a poem that does not use traditional poetic devices such as rhyme or meter to give structure to its ideas.

Archaic Diction

Rukeyser begins this poem by phrasing her observations in a stilted, unnatural way, using a style of inverted sentences that she repeats in line after line. Her diction resembles the sort of grandiloquence that readers might associate with a royal pronouncement or even a passage of biblical verse. By addressing the subject, understood to be a common cockroach, this way, the poem elevates the terms of the discussion. The speaker uses language that shows her awareness that her ignorance and prejudice are as significant in scale as the most serious observations ever set down in poetry. Readers may feel uplifted, even though the details given in the poem are fairly mundane, because the burgeoning revelation at the end of the poem thus framed by the archaic diction is indeed a grand one.

HISTORICAL CONTEXT

Shifting Cultural Awareness from the 1950s through the 1970s

In the 1970s, American culture was at the height of a movement away from established preconceptions toward a recognition of the diversity in society. The roots of this shift can be traced back

COMPARE
&
CONTRAST

- **1970s:** The traditional literature taught in schools is mostly written by Caucasian men.

  Today: School reading lists reflect greater cultural diversity.

- **1970s:** The foods of many different cultures are considered exotic and may only be available, if at all, in specialty restaurants.

  Today: Advanced transportation and refrigeration techniques have made exotic foods

and ingredients readily available. Magazines and television shows frequently feature recipes from a variety of cultures.

- **1970s:** Cockroaches are thought to carry germs and spread disease.

  Today: It has been shown that cockroaches give off an allergen that is one of the most severe triggers of asthma in children.

---

to the civil rights movement of the 1950s and 1960s. With nearly a century having passed since the end of the Civil War, it became more and more difficult to justify the "separate but equal" doctrine that the U.S. Supreme Court had established in 1896. Under this standard, blacks and whites could be kept separated in social situations because they would, at least in theory, be given equal opportunities in their own areas. This resulted in segregated housing, travel accommodations, and educational facilities, down to separate movie theaters and drinking fountains for "whites" and for "coloreds." What this policy did not establish was a standard for equality; usually, the opportunities for African Americans were far below those available for their white counterparts. The unfairness of this situation was brought to the nation's attention in the 1950s, when several factors converged: Southern blacks who had served in Europe in World War II had seen the balance of racial equality in other countries; young whites, unhampered by the economic depression and war that had occupied the country for decades, traveled to the southern states to challenge the fairness of separatist doctrines; television brought awareness of the fight for civil rights to those who lived in areas where there was no racial diversity; and civil rights groups such as Dr. Martin Luther King, Jr.'s Southern Christian Leadership Conference pursued the problem with diligence. The result was heightened

awareness of the nation's racial differences and of the racial inequality of American society that grew throughout the 1950s and 1960s. By the 1970s, the civil rights movement had made tremendous gains, from Rosa Parks's refusal to vacate her seat for a white person on a bus in Montgomery, Alabama, in 1955 to the Civil Rights Acts passed by Congress in 1957, 1964, and 1968.

As the country grew to recognize the ways in which African American rights had been suppressed, increased awareness spread to other social groups. The late 1960s saw the rise of the women's rights movement, culminating in the passage in Congress of the Equal Rights Amendment in 1972. This proposed amendment to the Constitution, which had been introduced to every session of Congress since 1923, was intended to guarantee gender equality, but it failed to become law when only thirty-five of the needed thirty-eight state legislatures agreed to ratify it.

From these two pillars of social awareness arose other struggles for social recognition among those traditionally excluded from American society. Native American, Hispanic, and Asian American groups fought the stereotypes that had been assigned to them over the centuries by the dominant culture. Homosexuals fought for their right to be recognized, as did persons with disabilities. While the 1980s would witness a backlash from people who resented what they saw as enforced "political correctness," the

---

changes that occurred in the 1960s and 1970s helped many Americans feel, for the first time, that they were truly a part of the society in which they lived.

Kim Chi-Ha

The collection that "St. Roach" comes from, *The Gates*, was written after Rukeyser traveled to South Korea to protest the imprisonment and scheduled execution of the poet Kim Chi-Ha. In 1974, Kim was arrested after the publication of his collection *Cry of the People, and Other Poems*. The poems constituted an angry tirade against the government, calling upon students to stand up and fight against the existing order. The government of President Park Chung Hee detained Kim with sedation and sentenced him to death.

South Korea had declared itself an independent nation in 1948. During the Korean War (1950–1953), it fought for its independence from North Korea, a struggle which left the two nations as separate political entities but which also left South Korea suffering, with a damaged economy. The corrupt government was overthrown in a coup led by Park Chung Hee in 1961, and in 1963 Park assumed the powers of a civilian president. His policies helped stabilize the economy and made South Korea competitive on the world stage, but domestically he relied on strong-arm, repressive tactics to control citizens.

Rukeyser became involved in the case of the poet Kim as the president of International PEN, an organization devoted to supporting writers and their rights to freedom of expression. When she traveled to South Korea in 1975, Kim had been accused of infiltrating the Catholic Church for the Communist party and had signed a confession that he later explained was coerced. After pressure from International PEN and other groups, his execution was commuted, though he was sentenced to life in prison in 1976.

In 1979, Park Chung Hee was assassinated during a coup in which the head of the Korean Central Intelligence Committee assumed power. Kim Chi-Ha's sentence was commuted, and he was released from prison in 1980.

CRITICAL OVERVIEW

Muriel Rukeyser's poetry has always been closely associated with her political activism.

While most critics have lauded her writing for its heartfelt passion, some have questioned whether that passion is matched with technical skill. Although the poet was recognized early in her career, she was never grouped with the highest ranks of her peers in literature. Critical acclaim for her work has tended to vary, often depending on how much a particular reviewer felt Rukeyser's social conscience to be an integral part of her literary accomplishments.

In a 1995 *Ploughshares* article, the famed literary critic M. L. Rosenthal addresses the issue of Rukeyser's reputation as a writer. After making it clear that he is delighted over the reissue of her work in *A Muriel Rukeyser Reader*, Rosenthal explains how the poet's particular skills "have a special place in our poetry," going on to explain that she "was a driven artistic experimenter." He later declares that "Rukeyser was, indeed, a true poet." David Orr, discussing the 2004 release of *Muriel Rukeyser: Selected Poems* in *Poetry* magazine, makes the same point about critical handling of Rukeyser's reputation. Indeed, Orr's own assessment is split: "At its best, Rukeyser's work can be open, energetic, and well constructed, if a little enamored of its own goody-goodness." He goes on to note, "At its worst, her work has the campy, creepy tone of someone soliciting for the International Union of Absolutely Good People."

CRITICISM

David Kelly

Kelly is a writer and an instructor of creative writing and literature at two colleges in Illinois. In the following essay on "St. Roach," Kelly explains that even if the poem's social impact has diminished over the years, its understated structural control makes it worth continuing study.

Muriel Rukeyser's "St. Roach" is the sort of poem that is likely to be described by readers as straightforward. As a description, this is often meant as a positive critique, indicating that the poet has allowed the poem's message to speak for itself, plainly and simply. The straightforwardness of this poem is twofold. First, there is its lack of poetic technique. "St Roach" is predominantly written in free verse. It does not follow any standard poetic form, and it does not create a standard for itself by sticking to

WHAT DO I READ NEXT?

- Marion Copeland's book *Cockroach* (2004) includes an examination of artistic works that, like this poem, present the insect as a symbol of different things, all having to do with revulsion and endurance.

- *The Invisible Elephant: Exploring Cultural Awareness* (2006), by Tom Verghese—a Malaysian writer living in Australia, gives readers an idea of how to experience unfamiliar cultures with respect and attention.

- In 1915, Franz Kafka published "The Metamorphosis," a work of short fiction about a traveling salesman who wakes up one morning to find that he has been transformed into a gigantic insect (with most interpretations identifying the insect as a cockroach). The story is about what it feels like to be alienated in the modern world and is considered to be a part of the Western literary canon.

- In *How Shall We Tell Each Other of the Poet? The Life and Writing of Muriel Rukeyser* (1999), the editors Anne F. Herzog and Janet E. Kaufman bring together thoughts and reminiscences about Rukeyser and her works. Essays written by friends, critics, students, and other poets communicate the overall effect of Rukeyser's career.

- First published in 1949, Rukeyser's *The Life of Poetry* is a meditation on what poetry is, what it is good for, and what it should do. The poet's theories, though they did not fit in with the standards set by most literary critics, did not change much over time.

- The poet Anne Sexton, a friend of Rukeyser's, wrote her well-known antiwar poem "The Firebombers" (1968) under the influence of Rukeyser's strident views regarding poetry as political activism. It is available in *The Complete Poems: Anne Sexton* (2000).

> BUT NOW THAT THE STRANGLEHOLD OF TRADITIONAL WHITE CULTURE, WHICH PREVAILED INTO THE 1970S, HAS BEEN BROKEN, THE OBVIOUS QUESTION ARISES: WHO WOULD APPROVE OF EQUATING OPPRESSED MINORITIES WITH COCKROACHES?"

any consistent rhyme scheme, meter, line length, or stanza structure.

In the absence of any stylistic flourishes, the poem's message becomes central. There is nothing too mysterious about what "St. Roach" wants to tell readers. Starting with the title, it is fairly clear that what she is saying isn't meant to be taken literally: though she might make a case for being more attentive to what the cockroach has to offer, no one would seriously imagine that she is nominating the insect for sainthood. With a tendency for exaggeration established, readers can hardly fail to see how the references to human culture that are attributed to cockroaches eventually stop being applicable to any creatures but humans. The cultural aspects that she talks about, specifically songs, poems, and food, imply that she is talking about human beings. References to darkness further indicate that the poem is about the feelings that separate the races, not really the distrust between humans and insects at all. This message resides fairly close to the surface of the poem, so that few could fail to understand it after sufficient study.

Ironically, what may have once been the poem's chief virtue—that it confronts race relations directly, with very little artifice for readers to dig through—has come to be its downfall over the course of time, obscuring what is good about it. Readers of the twenty-first century still understand the message it offers, but times have changed. The children or even grandchildren of Rukeyser's original audience do not live in a world where there is racial equality, but nor do they live in a world where race relations are defined by mystery. Multiculturalism is an idea that has caught on. People of all backgrounds run for political offices, control the destinies of their employees, and are familiar to readers of magazines from *Forbes* to *People*. Of course, there are people who live in prejudice, who view others practically like cockroaches, but the wrongness of this is so universally accepted that a poem that stands up to that kind of prejudice can seem patronizing and self-congratulatory.

In the context of modern race relations, Rukeyser's poem actually serves to promote the sort of narrowed thinking that it is trying to fight. The problem stems from the poet's audacity in speaking up for the disenfranchised: in 1976, that might have been a good and necessary strategy, but more and more over the decades society has learned to let those who have been denied a voice tell their own fascinating stories and speak from their own perspectives. In fact, this can be read as a victory for the position taken in "St. Roach," since it is a sign that people have overcome fears of other races and are interested in paying attention to those who are unfamiliar. But now that the stranglehold of traditional white culture, which prevailed into the 1970s, has been broken, the obvious question arises: Who would approve of equating oppressed minorities with cockroaches? Certainly members of those oppressed minorities would not.

So it may seem that time has drained "St. Roach" of its relevance. It is indeed less culturally significant than it was when Rukeyser was calling for white culture to heed, not fear, the stories of others; her argument is already generally accepted. But there still is the structure to consider. "St. Roach" is a poem, and its argument is therefore put on the page in a specific form. Although the poem steers away from the formal elements already listed, that does not mean that it does not have a structure, only that it has a structure that is unique unto itself. As it lays on the page, the poem seems to lack order, with new ideas being introduced according to the author's whim. Looking at elements out of order, though, makes Rukeyser's design a little more evident.

The clearest shift in focus takes place in line 23. Up to this point, "St. Roach" has been an expression of a situation—an attitude, expressed in general terms with a few specific details tossed in here and there. As soon as Rukeyser mentions a specific point in time, however, the poem turns into a story of particular events happening in particular places at particular times. This story even has progression, as good stories do. First it talks about what happened yesterday, and then it tells about today. Instead of simply feeling

sorry about the circumstances as they exist, as they have been made to do in the first part, readers are drawn into the narrative. They are invited to free themselves of their learned prejudices by watching what happens when the poet does just that. The poem ends on an uplifting note, with a triumphant act of self-liberation on the part of the speaker.

This last section, from line 23 to line 31, spans nine lines—just under one-third of the poem. This could just be the amount of space Rukeyser wished to devote to completing this train of thought, but it could also be a sign of the poem's overall structure. If this one-third is part of consistent design, then the remaining two-thirds should divide equally, or nearly equally, into sections of one-third each.

That in fact turns out to be the case. The first part of the poem, starting with the first line, maintains a consistency of style and theme until line 11. In this part, the lines are long, so much so that over half are divided by commas. The long lines are necessary because this introductory section deals with the complexities of the speaker's feelings. The tone is one of anger or resentment, set by the use of powerful words.

The second third of the poem, from lines 13 to 22, is marked by a different tone and a different style. The subject matter remains the speaker's dismay at having been made to think that those unlike her are her enemies, but the focus here is on what she has missed out on, the aspects of other cultures that she has been taught to ignore. The tone is one of sadness and regret. To show this, the lines are not nearly as complex; for the most part, they are short and direct. When Rukeyser does see fit to extend a thought, she breaks it apart so that each clause is a separate line, as in lines 17 through 20. This section of the poem, again roughly a third of its length, has its own identity, as much as the other two sections have.

This subtle three-part structure is significant for readers who might be inclined to think too little of Rukeyser's skill as an artist. The emphasis of her work has always been the message conveyed; the human aspect is given precedence over literary device or wordplay. A poet's being so often associated with the messages of her poems should be seen as a credit to her skills as a poet, such as with Rukeyser. But because of this, there is the temptation, when studying a poem like "St. Roach," to feel that the work's value is only in its faded, timeworn message. That Rukeyser uses such a deceptively simple yet effective structure to convey her message, however, points to an altogether different conclusion.

Source: David Kelly, Critical Essay on "St. Roach," in *Poetry for Students*, Gale, Cengage Learning, 2009.

Michele S. Ware

In the following review, Ware critiques the representative poems from all periods of the poet's life and work.

The resurgence in the last decade of critical attention to Muriel Rukeyser and her important place in twentieth-century American poetry alone warrants the publication of this new annotated scholarly edition of *The Collected Poems of Muriel Rukeyser*. Yet this impressive collection makes Rukeyser's extensive body of work available and accessible, for the first time in years, to the general reader as well. Long out of print, the 1978 *Collected Poems,* published by McGraw-Hill, suffered from serious omissions and errors, which Kaufman and Herzog correct in this volume. The result is a welcome and necessary contribution to contemporary Rukeyser scholarship that reveals the poet's persistent, career-long dedication to the poetry of witness, her wide-ranging intellectual curiosity, and her powerful, inclusive, and generous vision.

Of particular interest are Rukeyser's numerous translations and the full text of *Wake Island* (1942), inexplicably omitted from the 1978 *Collected Poems*. By using Rukeyser's individual volumes of poetry as their copy texts, the editors have restored her important translations of Octavio Paz to the poems in *The Green Wave* (1948) and *Body of Waking* (1958). Rukeyser's affinity with Paz is obvious in these beautiful lyric poems, and the textual notes and annotations, including Rukeyser's original notes and commentary from 1978, offer a glimpse of the poet's process. Her passion for translation demonstrates the "vast reach" of her poetic explorations, extending to such disparate sources as Northern/Eskimo poems and *rari* love-chants, among many others. Kaufman and Herzog speculate in their "Editors' Notes" that limited space may have been the rationale for excluding such an integral part of Rukeyser's oeuvre, but the omission of *Wake Island* is more suspicious, especially since its critical reception was so negative and cruel. This long poem celebrating the heroism of embattled and doomed Marines in

the Pacific was mistakenly perceived as Rukeyser's naïve and nationalistic endorsement of American military will during World War II, for which she was attacked both personally and professionally. The poem's significance, however, according to James Brock (in "The Perils of a 'Poster Girl': Muriel Rukeyser, *Partisan Review,* and *Wake Island*"), lies in its function as an early example of Rukeyser's global political preoccupations. Here again, the editors offer several plausible explanations for the poem's earlier exclusion (Rukeyser's failing health, self-censorship) and wisely include it. *Wake Island* is somewhat uneven, but as Kaufman and Herzog note, "it is consistent with her lifelong vision that poetry should respond to questions of social justice and freedom, as well as to the historical moment, not only within her own country but globally."

In many ways, the new *Collected Poems* is a sensitive and thoughtful work of restoration, a concerted effort on the editors' part to discern Rukeyser's artistic sensibilities and intentions and at the same time do justice to a complex and massive body of work, a difficult task when the poet's intentions are unclear or contradictory. For example, Rukeyser resisted breaking up *One Life,* her experimental biography of Wendell Willkie, to excerpt poems for the 1978 *Collected Poems*. "The arrangement is the life" (xxvi), she insisted. Yet the selections she made from *One Life* to include in that volume are "virtually inscrutable taken out of the context." To correct the problem, the editors have here reduced the excerpts to eighteen poems later chosen by Rukeyser for publication in *Body of Waking,* thus fulfilling their purpose (to collect all the poems) while respecting the integrity of Rukeyser's art. She was intensely vigilant about the order, spacing, and punctuation of her poems in their published forms, and Kaufman and Herzog have taken care to attend to these matters. For example, they based their decision to reorder into a single unit Rukeyser's elegies, a series of ten related poems that originally appeared in three different volumes of poetry, on her later publication of *Elegies* (1949) and the poet's own reordering of the elegies in subsequent collections. While they are rather too gentle in their criticism of the error-ridden 1978 *Collected Poems,* it is clear why Kaufman and Herzog returned to the original volumes of poems for their definitive texts. All corrections, deviations, and alternate versions are meticulously described in the "Annotations" and "Textual Notes." Such precision not only corrects the flaws of the earlier *Collected Poems;* it also takes into consideration Rukeyser's own later critical reassessment of her work.

By including a selection of Rukeyser's juvenilia—seventeen poems she wrote as an adolescent at Vassar and the Ethical Culture and Fieldston schools—Kaufman and Herzog make Rukeyser's earliest work available, revealing the poet's fledgling experimentation with form and development of an aesthetic and a voice that were remarkably consistent throughout Rukeyser's long career. The editors close the volume with the last known published poem that appeared after the 1978 *Collected Poems* and before Rukeyser's death in 1980. According to Rukeyser, "An Unborn Poet," written for Alice Walker (Rukeyser's student at Sarah Lawrence College), refers not to Walker but to Rukeyser herself. A meditation on teaching, the connections between the past and the present, between old poets and new, and the inspiration that comes from the questioning creativity of youth, this poem moves between memory and possibility and signals a rekindling of Rukeyser's poetic power: "Alice, landscaper of grief, love, anger, bring me to birth, / bring back my poems. No. Bring me my next poem!" It is comforting and satisfying to know that Rukeyser ended her life as a poet with the same generous and optimistic vision with which she began it.

For Rukeyser scholars, Kaufman and Herzog have opened another door, as they did with their 1999 critical collection, *"How Shall We Tell Each Other of the Poet?": The Life and Writing of Muriel Rukeyser.* Their thorough and thought-provoking editorial annotations and explanations, drawing on biography with the help of Jan Heller Levi, literary criticism, interviews, and the fullness of Rukeyser's own genre-defying body of work, make *The Collected Poems of Muriel Rukeyser* a rich mine of resources for future study of a poet of unquestionable importance and value to twentieth-century American literature.

Source: Michele S. Ware, Review of *The Collected Poems of Muriel Rukeyser*, in *College Literature*, Vol. 33, No. 2, Spring 2006, pp. 199–201.

Ted Solotaroff

In the following essay, written in memory of Rukeyser, Solotaroff calls "St. Roach" one of Rukeyser's best poems.

> IN HER BODY AND IN HER MIND, IN HER LIFE AND IN HER ART, SHE FOUGHT AGAINST NUMBNESS."

When I first and best knew Muriel, five or six years ago, she was a large, somewhat top-heavy woman in her early 60s with a broad, crafty Russian face—the kind you might see behind the counter of a Jewish deli—an infirm walk and a full heart. She was one of those people who come across immediately, which I remember thinking was surprising in a poet as famous as she was. Fame, at least literary fame, tends to make people cagey, not to mention the conflicts that maintain them as poets and make them, in person, usually wear a sleeve on their hearts.

Not Muriel. She arrived before you on a wave of feeling each time you saw her, a bit disheveled from the ride. At least that's how I remember our meetings. What brought us together was a matter of literary politics. A faction at P.E.N. needed someone to stand for president at the last moment. It doesn't pay to go into the reasons, which I'm not nearly as convinced of now as I was then, but anyway we felt we needed a writer who was not only renowned but also one whose career would immediately have a commanding appropriateness for the post: a veteran literary freedom fighter. Some of us were also hoping for an activist who might get American P.E.N. off the dime of a certain dated genteelness on which we felt it had been languishing and make it a center of literary community in New York.

For both jobs Muriel seemed a terrific choice. She was one of the few literary radicals from the 1930s who hadn't lost faith in her social conscience: that special blend of outrage and tenderness which was always on tap in her poetry—"the desperate music/poverty makes." Her radicalism still prompted her active engagement with the causes and movements of the 1960s and early 1970s as it had in Spain and in the coal-belt factory and mining towns and in the Deep South thirty years ago. At the same time, she was already a kind of one-woman center of energy and community for poetry. She was a mainstay of the Translation Center, an organization that was trying to reclaim this wasteland sector of American letters. She was also a force for good in the 92nd Street YMHA poetry program, which was in several ways a model for what we wanted to do with American P.E.N. Muriel had a special workshop going there; instead of teaching poetry writing, as her peers did, she taught poetry reading. When her friend, Louise Bernikow, once asked her what she did besides writing, Muriel said she was "mainly reading poems with people: undergraduates; 2 year olds; dropouts; the old; the blind, etc." She was also reading a lot of poems by young poets; she was a rarity in that way too, a "name" who took the manuscripts that were thrust at her at readings and meetings, who tried hard to get the good ones published. She was so approachable: that warm, steady look that took you in in the way you liked to be seen, that smile which gave you welcome, one which could easily be taken for the smile of Fortune.

At the time we approached her on the P.E.N. matter, Muriel was recovering from a heart attack, the latest of her cardiovascular problems, and looked it. Listening to her breathing, I wondered whether we were asking too much of her. Sitting there in her studio loft in the artists' housing project known as Westbeth (where else would she live?), surrounded and protected by the tools and arrangements and icons of a working literary life, what did she need us and our thorny issue and airy plans for? But she listened to us intently and then, I think, she held up her hand and said, "All right, I know what needs to be done now. I'll do it if you'll help me."

And so she did and so we did. The bureaucracy of P.E.N. at the time didn't know what to make of her and gave her a hard time. She didn't go through channels and agendas very well; as Grace Paley says, "Muriel was like the ocean instead of a stream or a puddle." There was a poet, Kim Chi Ha, in prison in South Korea. Instead of sending letters and cables to Seoul, Muriel sent herself. She went to see the authorities and when they wouldn't let her visit Kim Chi Ha in his cell, she went to the prison anyway and stood outside in the mud and rain and bore witness. Back home at the executive board meetings, she also poured herself out. Somewhat indifferent to the housekeeping problems—to which her standard response was a wily "What

is the board's pleasure?"—she pressed on to the heavy issues such as decentralizing P.E.N. through regional centers and creating programs for writers in the New York area. Her pet project was a conference on "the life of the writer," a topic that had a kind of numinous meaning for her but remained somewhat vague to the rest of us. Without much support, she persisted and brought it off in Washington, D.C. In her public actions, as in her poetry, she trusted her visionary gleam, a trust that made her, in the fullest sense of the word, undiscourageable.

Gallant Muriel. The final few years beggar description. Her health, which had always been precarious, was devastated by a serious stroke, by cataracts, and by her longtime nemesis, diabetes, "the Caligula of diseases," as Richard Selzer puts it. Still, as always, she did what she could, writing poetry and bringing out her *Collected Poems,* going her appointed rounds of literary panels and juries and conferences and keeping up her readings. As Grace Schulman tells it, "Whenever poetry was being celebrated, Muriel would somehow get there." At one such event, a group of poets was assembled on a stage; Muriel arrived and then, walker and all, virtually blind, she somehow hoisted herself up on that stage, for that was where she belonged.

In one of her late poems, "Facing Sentencing" (she was about to go to jail for protesting the war on the steps of the Senate), these lines appear:

> But fear is not to be feared
> Numbness is To stand before my judge
> Not knowing what I mean

Muriel was not a measured poet. Like Whitman, a powerful early influence, she was a sayer rather than a maker. Her mind ranged and ranged, from aviation to zoology, from the mines of West Virginia to the sacred caves of India, from the writings of Akiba to the speeches of Wendell Willkie. In her *Collected Poems,* there is a series of portraits of the early physicist Willard Gibbs, the painter Albert Ryder, the aristocratic man of letters John Jay Chapman, the labor organizer Ann Burlack and the composer Charles Ives. Her verse is typically open, notational, even documentary; its rhythm comes from the onrushing movement in her mind of the experience, from the flow of her passion for the object. There are transcripts of trials in her poems, the minutes of Congressional hearings, detailed descriptions of silicosis.

Her experiments tended to be on the side of plenitude rather than restriction, of inclusiveness rather than exclusiveness. For she had much to clarify, much to keep alive. In her body and in her mind, in her life and in her art, she fought against numbness.

Muriel had a peculiar habit. She never said goodbye. You would call her up, an animated conversation would ensue, reach a conclusion and then suddenly she would be gone. Now she's hung up for good, leaving her poems, as she hoped they would, to speak from her silence to ours. One of the best ones, "St. Roach," seems to me pure Muriel.

Source: Ted Solotaroff, "Rukeyser: Poet of Plenitude," in *Nation*, March 8, 1980, pp. 277–78.

SOURCES

Orr, David, Review of *Muriel Rukeyser: Selected Poems*, edited by Adrienne Rich, in *Poetry*, Vol. 187, No. 3, December 2005, pp. 242–43.

Rosenthal, M. L., Review of *A Muriel Rukeyser Reader*, in *Ploughshares*, Vol. 21, No. 1, Spring 1995, pp. 198–200.

Rukeyser, Muriel, "St. Roach," in *The Collected Poems of Muriel Rukeyser*, McGraw-Hill, 1982, p. 593.

FURTHER READING

Gordon, David G., *The Compleat Cockroach: A Comprehensive Guide to the Most Despised (and Least Understood) Creature on Earth*, Ten Speed Press, 1996.

Gordon's book provides all of the facts that a reader could want regarding the history and physical abilities of the cockroach. This book follows the spirit of Rukeyser's poem in taking an unflinching look at the feared and reviled insects.

Kertesz, Louise, *The Poetic Vision of Muriel Rukeyser*, Louisiana State University Press, 1980.

This overview of Rukeyser's life and career is broken down by decades. Thusly, readers can see the historical context in which Rukeyser was writing.

Rukeyser, Muriel, "The Education of a Poet," in *The Writer on Her Work*, edited by Janet Sternburg, Norton, 1980, pp. 217–30.

This essay is an adaptation of a talk that Rukeyser gave for the American Academy of Poets in 1976, the same year "St. Roach" was published. In the essay, Rukeyser addresses how she came to take up poetry as a profession.

Ware, Michele S., "Opening *The Gates*: Muriel Rukeyser and the Poetry of Witness," in *Women's Studies*, Vol. 22, No. 3, June 1993, pp. 297–309.

Ware gives a detailed examination of *The Gates*, focusing on the social context of Rukeyser's work.

When We Two Parted

Lord George Gordon Byron's "When We Two Parted" is a short lyric poem written in the middle phase of Byron's poetic career. Like many of his poems, it contains biographical references, which the poet attempts to conceal. A key figure in the Romantic movement (an eighteenth- and nineteenth-century philosophical, literary, and artistic movement with a variety of interpretations generally focusing on the love of nature, and the importance of individualism, independence, and imagination), Byron is often lauded more for his political satire and his longer narrative poems and plays than for poems such as "When We Two Parted." Indeed, his short lyric verses are often either critically ignored or only briefly acknowledged as simplistic and intensely autobiographical. Originally published in 1816 in *Poems, 1816* by John Murray (the reprinted volume is available through Woodstock Books, 1990), the poem is falsely attributed by Byron as having been written in 1808. Byron's later correspondence indicates that he made this false attribution in order to protect the name and reputation of the poem's subject, Lady Frances Wedderburn Webster. The poem is available in *The Poetical Works of Byron*, edited by Robert F. Gleckner, published in 1975, and more recently, in *Lord Byron: The Major Works*, edited by Jerome J. McGann, and published in 2000.

"When We Two Parted" recounts the narrator's feelings of grief, betrayal, and regret

LORD GEORGE GORDON BYRON

1816

Lord (George Gordon) Byron (The Library of Congress)

following the end of a clandestine romantic relationship. The poem exemplifies the typical romantic lyric prevalent at this point in Byron's career in that it is deeply introspective and expresses intense personal feelings. It is rooted in the pathos of human nature, rather than in the poet's experience with Nature. The latter is a common characteristic of the lyrical works of Byron's Romantic contemporaries, and thus the poet's work is somewhat atypical for its time.

AUTHOR BIOGRAPHY

Born on January 22, 1788, in London, George Gordon Byron was the son of a Scottish heiress, Catherine Gordon of Gight, and Captain John Byron, also known as "Mad Jack." The Captain was an English fortune hunter who also had a daughter, Augusta, with another woman, and who had before long relieved his wife Catherine of her inheritance. The marriage dissolved not long after the birth of George, for which Captain Byron was not present. In 1789, Mrs. Byron returned to Scotland with her son, residing in Aberdeen. Two years later, Captain Byron died, leaving Mrs. Byron and her young son to

manage on an income that was decidedly lower middle class. At the age of six, Byron began attending Aberdeen Grammar School. Several years later, in 1798, Byron and his mother discovered that Byron had inherited the barony, and his family's estates. They subsequently moved to England to their new home at Newstead Abbey, near Nottingham. The estate was in serious disrepair and had to be rented out in order to help pay for renovations, as well as for Byron's education at Harrow; Byron attended the school from 1801 through 1805. He was skilled as an orator, and began writing verse at this time. From Harrow, he went on to Trinity College, in Cambridge, earning a master's degree in 1808.

In addition to the formal education Byron received during these years, he also was sexually initiated by his maid. As a young man he formed strong sexual attractions to both young men and women. He also excelled at going into debt at Cambridge, spending large amounts of money with his friends and going to the theater. In 1806, Byron collected the early writings from his youth into a selection of verses called *Fugitive Pieces*, which he had privately printed. The following year he revised the anthology and changed the title to *Pieces on Various Occasions*, also self-published and intended primarily for those individuals who were the subjects of the poems. Byron edited the selection again and toned down the eroticism of the love poems and published a new version of the collection, now titled *Hours of Idleness* in 1807. The following winter, in February 1808, the collection was derided as self-indulgent and derivative by the *Edinburgh Review*. Byron answered in 1809 with the scathing satire *English Bards and Scotch Reviewers*, which won him favorable critical reviews.

In 1809, Byron and his friend John Hobhouse toured Europe. Byron began writing the first cantos (divisions of long narrative poems) of *Childe Harold's Pilgrimage* at this time. The narrative verse was destined to be regarded as Byron's best work. He returned to England in 1811. His mother and a close friend died that same year. In 1812, John Murray published the first two cantos of *Childe Harold's Pilgrimage*. Byron was suddenly famous; the poem was wildly successful. By the end of 1813, Byron had a series of relationships with various women and had begun corresponding with, and likely having an affair with his half-sister Augusta. He also had a flirtation with Lady Frances Wedderburn

Webster, during this time; she is the subject of "When We Two Parted." It has been speculated that he wrote the verse in 1813, although it is more widely held that Byron wrote the piece the year it was published, in 1816 (*Poems, 1816*). Throughout the ensuing months, Byron corresponded with Anne Isabella Milbanke, who had previously rejected an earlier marriage proposal by Byron. In 1814, he proposed again and she accepted. The marriage produced a daughter, Augusta Ada, but ended in 1816 due to Anne Isabella's accusations of Byron's violent outbursts and her suspicions of an incestuous relationship between Byron and his half-sister Augusta. These details were the subject of much gossip and public speculation. Byron left England in 1816, never to return.

Arriving in Geneva, Byron met up with fellow poet Percy Bysshe Shelley and his wife Mary Godwin Shelley. The year was a productive one for Byron; he penned the third canto of *Childe Harold's Pilgrimage*, "The Prisoner of Chillon," and shorter verses, all of which were published later that year, as was "When We Two Parted." The following year Byron settled in Italy where he continued to write *Childe Harold's Pilgrimage*. Here he also wrote the satirical narrative verse *Don Juan*. Byron increasingly became involved in Venetian politics and also with the Greek struggle for independence from Turkey. He joined the fight in Greece in 1823. The following year, Byron succumbed to a fever and died in Mesolonghi, Greece, on April 19, 1824.

POEM TEXT

> When we two parted
>   In silence and tears,
> Half broken-hearted
>   To sever for years,
> Pale grew thy cheek and cold,   5
>   Colder thy kiss;
> Truly that hour foretold
>   Sorrow to this.
>
> The dew of the morning
>   Sunk chill on my brow—   10
> It felt like the warning
>   Of what I feel now.
> Thy vows are all broken,
>   And light is thy fame;
> I hear thy name spoken,   15
>   And share in its shame.
>
> They name thee before me,
>   A knell to mine ear;

MEDIA ADAPTATIONS

- *The Poetry of Lord Byron* is an unabridged audiobook, read by Linus Roache, and was published by HarperCollins AudioBooks in 1997.

> A shudder comes o'er me—
>   Why wert thou so dear?   20
> They know not I knew thee,
>   Who knew thee too well:—
> Long, long shall I rue thee,
>   Too deeply to tell.
>
> In secret we met—   25
>   In silence I grieve
> That thy heart could forget,
>   Thy spirit deceive.
> If I should meet thee
>   After long years,   30
> How should I greet thee?—
>   With silence and tears.

POEM SUMMARY

Stanza 1

A brief lyric consisting of four short stanzas, "When We Two Parted" is a poem about grief and regret in which the first-person speaker mourns not only the loss of a romantic relationship, but also a loss of innocence. From the present tense, the poem looks back in time, to when the affair was ended. It also predicts the results of a possible future meeting of the two former lovers. In the first stanza, the speaker describes the pain of the ending of the romance. The tone in this stanza and throughout the poem is dark and bleak, with words and images that evoke feelings of depression and emptiness: the woman's pale cheek and cold kiss presage the depression now felt by the speaker.

Stanza 2

In the second stanza, the cold imagery is reinforced with the chilly dew foretelling of the narrator's future feelings of sorrow. Mention is made of the woman's broken promises, and the tarnishing of her reputation. In a letter from 1823, Byron refers to this poem and its relation to his 1813 flirtation with Lady Frances Wedderburn Webster. In 1816, when many scholars believe the poem was written, Lady Frances was scandalously linked with the Duke of Wellington. Byron had written earlier sentimental sonnets to Lady Frances and in "When We Two Parted" he appears pained to hear of her entanglement with the Duke. When he speaks of the vows she has broken it is possible that he is referring either to her wedding vows to her husband that Lady Frances has betrayed with her affair, or alternatively, promises she may have made to Lord Byron. He discusses as well the shame he feels. This could be viewed as an empathetic response to what his former sweetheart is going through. It could also be interpreted as a judgment upon her. The relationship between Lady Frances and Lord Byron was rumored to not have been consummated sexually, and perhaps the poet is, in his way, scolding her for having actually gone through with an adulterous affair.

Stanza 3

The third stanza speaks of the secretive nature of the affair, how others did not know of the narrator's relationship with the woman. Again the tone is dark, he hears her name as a "knell," an ominous toll typically associated with death. The speaker reveals the depth of his regret and predicts he is likely to retain such feelings indefinitely. "Why wert thou so dear?", a key line in this stanza, offers the only indication of the nature of the speaker's relationship to the woman. He has not even spoken of loving her; in fact the word love does not appear at all in the poem. But this question "Why wert thou so dear?" is the singular suggestion in the poem of the warm and positive connection the two people had shared.

Stanza 4

In the fourth and final stanza, the narrator once again refers to the clandestine nature of the affair and his grief at what he perceives to be the woman's betrayal. The future is once more referred to, with the portent that a future meeting with the woman would bring the speaker to tears, and would result in his continued silence. By this he refers not only to the fact that he no longer

communicates with his former lover, but to the fact that he has never discussed their secret relationship and he will continue to keep his silence on the matter. This emphasizes the fact that while she may have defamed herself by being caught in another affair, he at least has handled himself like a gentleman by not revealing the truth about their own relationship with one another. The speaker expresses his grief that his lover has forgotten him, and emphasizing his betrayal with the lines "That thy heart could forget, / Thy spirit deceive." It seems unlikely that Byron is speaking of Lady Frances deceiving her husband. Rather, his betrayal stems from the fact that when Lady Frances did choose to commit adultery it was with another man, the Duke of Wellington, and not with him. The final stanza ends with a reiteration of the "silence and tears" phrase from the first stanza, emphasizing the speaker's sense of being frozen in this moment of betrayal and heartbreak.

THEMES

Betrayal

In "When We Two Parted," the poet speaks often of his sorrow and pain. He recalls the tears shed when the relationship was severed, of being broken-hearted, of how his sorrow has not abated over the years. The cause of such pain is more than the simple fact of the relationship's termination. Promises have been broken. The speaker may be referring to promises the woman made to him, or perhaps to the fact that she has broken her own marriage vows to her husband when she had an affair with another man, as was the case with Lady Frances. Presumably, the woman is the subject of gossip: the poet speaks of her celebrity in the poem's second stanza ("light is thy fame"). From this we can infer that she is now being discussed lightly, no longer taken seriously. Hearing her name results in the poet's own shame. It is unclear whether he is embarrassed *for* her, or is himself ashamed for having himself been another man she'd once had a flirtation with. Perhaps more telling of the poet's feeling of betrayal, more than his many mentions of his sorrow, is his statement in the final stanza: "That thy heart could forget / thy spirit deceive." The speaker is positively wounded to have been cast aside, to have his affections replaced by those of another man.

TOPICS FOR FURTHER STUDY

- Byron was known for his rebellious spirit and for his liberal politics. He fought on the side of the Greeks during their war for independence from Turkey, which was waged from 1821 through 1832. Why were the Turks invading Greece? Were other nations involved in the war? What could have motivated Byron to become involved in a foreign nation's struggle for sovereignty? Write a report on the Greek War of Independence and include a discussion of Great Britain's role in the war and its resolution.

- "When We Two Parted" centers on the end of a romantic relationship and the far-reaching emotional conflicts that follow. Write a poem about a personal, painful event that has happened in the past; attempt to duplicate the rhythm and rhyme scheme of "When We Two Parted."

- Read Byron's "Fare Thee Well," which he composed in 1816 when his separation from his wife became final. How is this poem similar to "When We Two Parted"? How do the poems differ in tone and sentiment? How do biographical facts inform your reading of the poem? Write an essay on your comparison.

- Byron, Percy Bysshe Shelley, and John Keats were all writing Romantic lyrics in the early 1800s. Compare the form, content, and style of "When We Two Parted" with Shelley's "Stanzas" and Keats's "I Cry Your Mercy." Both, like Byron's poem, express longing for a woman's love. How do the modes of expression differ? Which do you prefer and why? Give a class presentation on this topic and a dramatic reading of your favorite of the three poems. Be sure to discuss the reasons for your preference.

According to biographers and to Byron's 1823 correspondence, he is dismayed at the notion of Lady Frances having become entangled with the Duke of Wellington. She married her husband, Sir James Wedderburn Webster, in 1810, and Byron, a friend of Sir James's, fell in love with Frances in 1813; she was already out of reach, so to speak, although Byron's affairs with apparently unavailable women were numerous. While some biographers have contended that Byron's relationship with Lady Frances was romantic but not physical, his feelings for her were strong enough for him to still feel the pain of betrayal at a married woman's dalliance with another man.

Remorse and Regret

The betrayal the speaker feels has lead him to bitterly regret that he had ever had feelings for the woman in the poem. "When We Two Parted" is brimming with notes of despair, sadness, and especially remorse. Almost nothing is said about the woman that would indicate the speaker is glad to have known her and at least to have shared the intimacies that they had. He wonders "Why wert thou so dear?" This question, itself imbued with a sense of regret, provides a tiny glimpse into the terminated relationship, suggesting warmth, and affection. The word "dear" is the only positive notion in a collection of stanzas filled with such negative images as pale cheeks, cold kisses, silence, tears, chilly dew, broken promises, shudders of pain, and long years of regret. Aside from this single reminder of the poet's love, he speaks primarily of his past, present, and future sorrow, and predicts that the regret he feels at having allowed himself to love and be hurt by the woman will only deepen over time. The reader is reminded of this at every turn. In the first stanza, the pain felt at the moment of the break up was a prophesy of the current suffering of the speaker. In the second stanza, the chilly, wet morning served as a warning for what the poet now feels. At the end of the third stanza, the speaker again transitions from past ("They know not I knew thee / Who knew thee too well") to the future ("Long, long shall I rue thee"). The final stanza reiterates the duration of his agony from the past, secret meetings to the current silence in which he grieves, and through to the future: "If I should meet thee / After long years, / How should I greet thee?— / With silence and tears." The poem repeats the phrase "silence and tears," in the first and last stanzas, emphasizing the progressive accumulation of pain and regret from the termination of the affair through the present and into the future as well. At the same time, the repetition of that phrase encapsulates the entire poem, emphasizing the sense that the speaker is in a way frozen within his own bitter emotions. While his pain has intensified over the years, the fact of the pain itself seems static: he was, is, and will be remorseful.

STYLE

Lyric Form

"When We Two Parted" is written as a short, romantic lyric. Lyrics are designed to be expressions of the poet's thoughts and feelings, rather than a narration of a story, and are typically subjective and meditative. Often, romantic lyrics are written in ballad form, with a rhyme pattern of *abcb*. Byron however chooses a longer, eight-line stanza, with a correspondingly extended rhyme pattern of *ababcdcd*, thereby distancing his work from the standard form. The octave, or eight-line stanza, is used often by Lord Byron but with a different rhyme pattern *abababcc*; this type of octave, written in iambic pentameter, is known as *ottava rima*, and is often used for narrative verse and for sonnets. The lines in "When We Two Parted" are shorter than in the *ottava rima* form, consisting primarily of two accented syllables, or metrical feet, per line; this keeps the work a concise, flowing lyric, and at the same time, the use of long stanzas emphasizes the tangled and complicated nature of the emotions the speaker is experiencing.

Romantic Sensibilities

In this poem, the reader hears the first-person speaker's thoughts as he ruminates over his former romantic entanglement. The grief and regret are feelings the poet speaks of having experienced at the time of the break up, and at the time the poem was written; he projects these feelings into his future as well. The collective weight of these emotions colors the entire poem in dark, foreboding terms. It is tangibly oppressive in its depiction of the effects of lost love on the speaker. Byron's lyrics differ stylistically from those of other Romantic poets, such as William Wordsworth, in that Byron often uses his poetry as a means of coping with emotional difficulties, whereas other Romantic poets frequently discuss, in their lyrics, their relationship with nature, or their place in the universe. Indeed, they often take a more philosophic,

Portrait of Annabella Anne Isabella known as Lady Byron or Lady Noel Byron (née Milbanke), estranged wife of the English poet (© *Lebrecht Music and Arts Photo Library | Alamy*)

rather than personally emotional stance. In later, longer works, Byron would skillfully combine the personal and the philosophical, as in *Childe Harold's Pilgrimage*.

HISTORICAL CONTEXT

The French Revolution

Byron was writing during the burgeoning of the Romantic movements in literature, art, and philosophy. The specifics of romanticism differed for each subject area. Romantic poetry generally included a reverence for nature, intimate self-revelations, and expressions of intense personal emotions. Romanticism is also associated with other characteristic traits, including individualism, spontaneity, subjectivity, a freedom from rules, and the elevation of imagination above reason. The Romantic movements were generated to some degree by the social changes taking

COMPARE & CONTRAST

- **1800s:** From 1821 through 1832, Greeks within the Ottoman Empire battle Turkish forces for their independence. Greek rebels declare their independence in 1822. Three separate invasions by the Turks follow; their numbers are reinforced by Egyptian forces. Europe's intervention results in an end to the hostilities. In 1832, at a conference in London, Greece is declared an independent monarchy.

  Today: Greece is now a republic that emulates western democracies. They joined NATO in 1952 and the European Union in 1981. Greece is led by Prime Minister Konstandinos Karamanlis.

- **1800s:** In 1812 Byron gives a speech to the House of Lords regarding the exploitation of workers in the hosiery trade. Luddism—the destruction of production machinery intended to cheaply manufacture goods and eliminate the need for skilled craftsmen—is a tool that is becoming increasingly popular among workers to draw attention to their cause. It is proposed by conservative nobles that this practice become a capital felony, that is, punishable by death. In his speech, Byron argues vehemently against this proposal.

  Today: Britain faces an enormous influx of foreign workers whose rights, like those of native-born citizens, must be protected. The government has expanded programs that allow temporary foreign workers the right to British employment. Many British workers fear losing employment opportunities to foreign workers.

- **1800s:** As a handsome, flirtatious nobleman with a successful literary career, Byron is among Britain's first true celebrities. Many of his indiscretions are ignored due to his fame, and they only fuel his intriguing reputation as a rebel. But when his peers and the public perceive that he has gone too far—having had too many well-publicized extramarital affairs, and having pursued a scandalous affair with his half-sister—Byron falls out of public favor. Due to this vehement reaction against him, he is forced to permanently leave the country.

  Today: Modern British male celebrities include actors such as Daniel Radcliffe, sports figures such as David Beckham, and royals such as Princes William and Harry. The public's appetite for information on such figures is fed, and fueled by, tabloid magazines reporting on all aspects of celebrities' lives. Modern fans are fickle in their tastes, but often more forgiving than the media when a celebrity fails to live up to the idealized images that fans have created.

- **1800s:** Great Britain plays an active role in European politics. British forces fight against, and eventually defeat, the French military dictator Napoleon Bonaparte. Following a period of military conservatism, British statesmen approve efforts to aid the Greeks and are instrumental in securing peace in the region. Political power shifts between the Tory and Whig political parties.

  Today: Great Britain maintains a strong presence in international politics, but incurs the disdain of many European nations for former Prime Minister Tony Blair's support of American President George W. Bush's invasion of, and sustained military presence in, Iraq.

place in Europe during the late 1700s and the early- to mid-1800s. In particular, the French Revolution, which began in 1789, resulted in the dissolution of class barriers and the destruction of royal power in France. Byron's mother had been a fervent supporter of the French

Revolution and Byron inherited his mother's liberal politics. The early British romantic poets, Byron's predecessors and older contemporaries, including William Blake, William Wordsworth, Samuel Taylor Coleridge, Robert Southey, Charles Lamb, and William Hazlitt, were all sympathetic toward the cause of the French Revolution, but in general, they gradually grew more conservative in their views.

The Industrial Revolution

Concurrently, in England, the Industrial Revolution was drastically changing the way goods were produced. Hand made products created by skilled craftsman were replaced by mass produced goods generated by machines in factories. While this did create a working middle class, it also resulted in the exploitation of individuals whose rights were deemed less important than the rapid production of cheap goods for the profit of factory owners. Byron attempted to use his position within the House of Lords to speak out in favor of exploited workers.

Nineteenth-Century British Foreign Policy

As time went on, the moderate revolutionary party in France lost their power to a more extreme radical group, and in 1799, Napoleon Bonaparte seized control of the French government and established a military dictatorship. He abdicated in 1814, only to gain power again, briefly in 1815, until he was finally defeated later that year by the Duke of Wellington—the same Duke of Wellington with whom Byron's one-time love, Lady Frances, became entangled. From the rubble of the revolution and its aftermath rose, once again, a monarchy. King Louis XVIII of France and his counterparts in Russia, Prussia, and Austria formed an alliance that suppressed liberalism throughout Europe. Byron and his friend Percy Bysshe Shelley, among other liberals, who were typically associated with the Whig political party, spoke out strongly against the conservative, or Tory, British statesmen who initially cooperated with these oppressive policies. In Italy, Byron experienced firsthand the injustice of the Austrian rule over Venice; he participated in political resistance against Austrian rule there. By 1822, British foreign policy tended toward more liberal politics and supported, for example, Greece's revolt against Turkey. In the last years of his life, Byron fought on the side of the Greeks in this cause,

and lost his life as part of the Greek resistance. Romanticism became associated with the liberal ideal of personal and political freedom largely due to Byron's devotion to the Greek cause.

CRITICAL OVERVIEW

By the time "When We Two Parted" was published in 1816, Byron's earlier work had been fairly well received by the public and critics alike. He and his poetry had also been bitterly attacked by one journal in particular, the *Edinburgh Review*. Due to governmental fears of a revolution similar to the one that had been raging in France, a country now lead by the military dictator Napoleon Bonaparte, poetry produced in England during this time was expected to be somewhat patriotic. Conservative critics were fierce in their suspicions and attacks on liberal poets. But Byron, despite his own liberal politics, had managed to secure the backing of a conservative publisher, John Murray, and so managed to keep his writing available for public consumption. Following the success of the first cantos of *Childe Harold's Pilgrimage*, Byron's literary reputation suffered due to the scandals regarding his personal life; that is, his separation from his wife and the rumors of an incestuous affair with his half-sister. Critics refused to distinguish between Byron's poetry and his personal affairs and acted on their moral and religious outrage at his behavior by cooling their responses to his poetic efforts. His work, including later cantos of *Childe Harold's Pilgrimage*, came to be viewed as self-indulgent. Other poems from this time period were derided for metrical irregularities and grammatical carelessness. In general, despite some dissenting voices praising Byron's experimentation with form, subject, and genre, his work was not critically reappraised until after his death.

Modern critics have lauded the narrative poem *Childe Harold's Pilgrimage* as Byron's best work, but his lyric poetry is often undervalued, ignored all together, or studied primarily for biographical insights. Discussing romantic lyric poetry in his 1971 *Natural Supernaturalism: Tradition and Revolution in Romantic Literature*, M. H. Abrams omits any analysis of Byron's work, stating: "Byron I omit altogether; not because I think him a lesser poet than the others

Newstead Abbey in Nottinghamshire, England, the family estate of Lord Byron (© Ian Francis / Alamy)

but because in his greatest work he speaks with an ironic counter-voice and deliberately opens up a satirical perspective on the vatic [prophetic] stance of his Romantic contemporaries." In a 1954 introduction to Byron's poetry, however, A. S. B. Glover remarks that "When We Two Parted" "had all the qualities of his best work" in the lyric form. Glover also observes that the poem "is quite simple both in thought and expression, but beneath the quiet rhythm there is a strong current of feeling." Nevertheless, Byron's biographer Leslie Marchand discusses "When We Two Parted," in a 1957 biography and in a 1965 introduction to Byron's work, but the poem is only discussed in its relation to Byron's private life.

James Soderholm, in a 1994 essay in *Studies in English Literature, 1500–1900*, offers an explanation as to why Byron's lyrics in general are largely ignored, arguing that Byron's lyrics do not fit the conventional lyric mode as established by earlier Romantics such as Wordsworth. In particular, Soderholm notes, the confessional tone of Wordsworth's lyrics is characteristically English, while Byron's confessional tone relies more on the French notion of sincerity. English sincerity is predicated only on the speaker not being deceitful, whereas French sincerity involves being truthful "about oneself to oneself and to others." Other critics speak more generally about how Byron's earlier poetry relates to his later writing. Byron's work is often divided into that which he wrote before he left England in 1816, and the poetry he wrote during his self-exile. Because it was published during that first year of exile, during a period of transition, "When We Two Parted" is a poem as much about isolation as the works written following Byron's departure. Yet, some critics reject the notion that there is a clear difference between Byron's earlier and later work. Mark Phillipson, in a 2000 *Studies in Romanticism* essay challenges critics who suggest that Byron's later work repudiates the poetry from his youth. Phillipson contends that the themes of isolation and self-exile are already present in Byron's poetry before he left England, and that this feature, as well as other stylistic elements present in both early and late poetry, emphasize the continuity of Byron's work.

WHAT
DO I READ
NEXT?

- *Childe Harold's Pilgrimage*, written by Byron over a period of several years and published by the canto from 1812 through 1818, is widely considered to be his best work. The narrative poem is inspired by Byron's travels throughout Europe, and the persona of the narrator is often indistinguishable from Byron himself. It is an emotionally intense quest poem, the object of the quest being a kind of natural spirituality, a sense of moral and intellectual certitude.

- *Lord Byron at Harrow School: Speaking Out, Talking Back, Acting Up, Bowing Out* (2000), by Paul Elledge, is a book-length biographical account of Byron's years at Harrow. The study offers insights into how the school curriculum and atmosphere helped shaped Byron's poetry and his public persona.

- *Byron: A Self-Portrait: Letters and Diaries, 1798–1824* (1990), edited by Peter Quennell, includes a full reprinting of Byron's journals. The book also pieces together a biography of Byron through a selection of his correspondence.

- *Prometheus Unbound* was written by Percy Bysshe Shelley and published in 1820. Shelley was Byron's friend and traveling companion in Europe, and they had in common the fact that they were both exiled from England due to sexual scandals. Shelley's closet drama (meaning that it was never intended to be performed) concerns the mythical Prometheus and an abstract, idealized notion of revolution.

- *The Greek War of Independence: The Struggle for Freedom from Ottoman Oppression and the Birth of the Modern Greek Nation* (2003), by David Brewer, focuses on the cause that Lord Byron died for: Greek Independence. Brewer draws analogies between modern political and military conflicts and describes the military campaigns and political factors that shaped the outcome of the war. The book includes an examination of the key role played by England, France, and Russia in forcing the Ottomans to end the war and accept Greek independence.

CRITICISM

Catherine Dominic

Dominic is an author and freelance editor. In this essay, Dominic analyzes Byron's Genevra sonnets (which feature Lady Frances Wedderburn Webster as their subject) as a means of accessing and understanding the complex array of emotions present in "When We Two Parted." She asserts that an understanding of these sonnets is essential to a full appreciation of "When We Two Parted."

Byron's "When We Two Parted," is an achingly beautiful poem, at once tender and pessimistic. Like many of his autobiographical lyrics, it is often critically disregarded as a self-indulgent set of stanzas, dashed off as a means of purging despair and disappointment.

Byron writes in "Sonnet, to Genevra," and "Sonnet, to the Same," of his feelings for a woman known through Byron's personal correspondence to be Lady Frances Wedderburn Webster, the wife of Byron's friend, Sir James Wedderburn Webster. Biographers have suggested that the relationship between Lady Frances and Byron was an infatuation, but was never a physical affair. In his 1965 *Byron's Poetry: A Critical Introduction*, Leslie Marchand describes Lady Frances as "the woman who got away or whom [Byron] 'spared.'" Marchand also observes that in the sonnets Byron composed to Lady Frances, Byron was moved by her innocence. In the first of the sonnets, the poet speaks lovingly of the lady's blue eyes, her fair hair, her soft, serene appearance. He goes on to observe

THE BITTER TONE IN 'WHEN WE TWO PARTED'
FITTINGLY UNDERSCORES BYRON'S SENSE OF
BETRAYAL."

an air of sadness about the woman. The speaker then refers to a painting by Guido Reni, titled "The Penitent Magdalen," and compares the sorrowful, remorseful but lovely subject of the poem, the biblical Mary Magdalen, with his love, the subject of the poem. The poet is quick to assert that she, however, unlike Mary Magdalen, the bible's famous whore, "hast nothing to repent." Emphasizing the woman's unimpeachable virtue, the poet seems to be confirming what biographers suspect: that Byron's relationship with Lady Frances was an intense emotional affair, but one that left her vows to her husband intact.

The second of the sonnets also includes a brief litany of the subject's beautiful physical traits, her lovely complexion, her "deep-blue eyes," her "long dark lashes." Clearly the speaker is completely enamored with the woman in the poem. As in the first sonnet, the poet refers to the woman's sadness, a sense of melancholy about her. Biographers have suggested that Lady Frances's marriage to Sir James was one of convenience, as she sought to escape an unpleasant family situation, while he was eager to marry the daughter of an Earl. Perhaps the sadness the poet observes is the woman's struggle between her sense of duty to her husband and her feelings for the poet. The sonnet ends with the poet expressing his adoration and love for the woman.

The depth of feeling in these sonnets illuminates the pain and regret expressed about the same woman in "When We Two Parted." In that poem, the speaker focuses heavily on his deep, enduring sadness but offers few glimpses into the relationship itself, and what specifically he misses about the woman. The reader knows little about what made the poet love the woman while they were together. After studying the Genevra sonnets, the pain embedded in the question "why wert thou so dear?" in "When We Two Parted" becomes amplified, clarified. Now, the reader has a better understanding of the

connection between Byron and Lady Frances. The poet was perpetually moved by her beauty, by her palpable sorrow, by her sweetness and innocence. Knowing the events of 1816, how Lady Frances had a scandalous affair with the war hero, the Duke of Wellington, illuminates the heavy notes of regret in "When We Two Parted." Lady Frances had chosen, after she and Byron had terminated their relationship, to have an affair, finally breaking her marriage vows to Sir James. This perhaps explains the intensity of the poet's sorrow in "When We Two Parted": Byron was not the man Lady Frances chose to have an affair with. Not only did she cast aside her much-admired (in the Genevra sonnets) innocence, but the affair became public knowledge due to the indiscretion of Lady Frances and the Duke of Wellington. "Thy vows are all broken," the poet states in "When We Two Parted," "and light is thy fame."

The bitter tone in "When We Two Parted" fittingly underscores Byron's sense of betrayal. He hears the name of the woman he loved and he "share[s] in its shame," feeling perhaps nearly as humiliated as the woman's husband. Marchand, in his 1957 biography of Lord Byron, explains that Byron's publisher, John Murray, wrote to Byron to inform him that Sir Wedderburn Webster had won a libel law suit against a publication which had written of the Lady Frances-Duke of Wellington affair. Given the highly publicized nature of Lady Frances's association with the Duke, the poet recalls his own relationship with an unnamed woman in the Genevra sonnets and in "When We Two Parted," commenting that others knew not of their flirtation; they, at least, had managed to be discreet about their feelings toward one another. He emphasizes more than once the secretive nature of their meetings. With the object of his affection involved with another man, the speaker of "When We Two Parted" wonders that the woman could forget him, and deceive him the way she has. The Genevra sonnets reveal the woman's power and potential to wound the poet; the sonnets explicate the virtues that the poet does not speak of in "When We Two Parted" but that he held dear and regrets the loss of. Byron thought he knew Lady Frances; he perceived her to be virtuous, and innocent. He presumed, perhaps, that his adoration of her was mutual. Yet although the biographical subject of the Genevra poems and "When We Two Parted" is the same woman, she has changed drastically from when the sonnets were written to when Byron penned "When We Two Parted." She has traded her innocence for a reputation as an adulteress; she has transferred her affections from one man to another. It is this transformation that so shocks and dismays the poet of "When We Two Parted."

Byron himself was well-known for his affairs with married women, and once he was married, he certainly participated in his own indiscretions, including scandalous homosexual relationships as well as his affair with his half-sister. It may well be argued that it was unreasonable of Lord Byron to presume that Lady Frances would remain physically faithful to her husband, and emotionally faithful to Byron. Despite the hypocrisy of Byron's apparent expectations, the love he expresses for Lady Frances in the Genevra poems and the pain at having truly lost her—his idealized notion of her—in "When We Two Parted" are conveyed with both insight and sincerity. His pessimism about the future is more easily understood when one has analyzed the poet's feelings toward Lady Frances in the Genevra poems and the sorrow and pain he feels now that she has become involved with someone else. He presumes that a meeting with her again, even after still more time has passed, would only result in more sadness. In a sense, he remains faithful to her. Despite the grief she has caused him, he continues to keep their affair confidential. Indeed, when the poem was published in 1816, shortly after Byron had learned from his publisher about Sir Wedderburn Webster's successful lawsuit, Byron included a false date of 1808, in order to remain true to the secret he and Lady Frances shared. Byron was rumored to often be callous in his treatment of his lovers, but Lady Frances was treated like a lady, at least in this regard.

Source: Catherine Dominic, Critical Essay on "When We Two Parted," in *Poetry for Students*, Gale, Cengage Learning, 2009.

Mark Phillipson

In the following excerpt, Phillipson notes that some critics feel that Byron's later poetry rejects the modes of his earlier works. However, Phillipson feels that Byron's late poems and early poems actually exhibit an underappreciated continuity.

Before he left England in a flurry of scandal, and before he created that most disillusioned of expatriates, Childe Harold, Lord Byron was irresistibly drawn to self-exile. In particular he

> AS SUCH, BYRON'S CANON, HOWEVER IT MAY SEEM TO REPUDIATE ITSELF, STAYS FAITHFUL TO HIS EARLY INSIGHT THAT THE UNSETTLING PASSAGE AWAY FROM THE FAMILIAR, FROM A POINT OF ORIGIN, GIVES RISE TO UNCANNY EMERGENCE OF WHAT HAS BEEN LEFT BEHIND."

paid close attention to the example of Shakespeare's misanthropic exile, Timon of Athens. Not only did Byron fashion Harold in the mold of Timon, arranging for his character to escape, like the disillusioned Athenian, from the "heartless parasites of present cheer" (Canto I, line 75); three years before the splashy publication of *Childe Harold's Pilgrimage* Cantos I & II (1812), the young Lord Byron was looking in the mirror and seeing Timon. "Weary of love, of life, devour'd with spleen, / I rest a perfect Timon, not nineteen," Byron wrote in Childish Recollections (1806)—though, perhaps to his credit, he later canceled the line. Thanks to the tumultuous events of his life, Byron, like Timon, indeed became an "archetype of all towering persons whose stature forces a severance from their community." But years before his actual departure from England, Byron's verse followed Shakespeare's king in discovering, within the process of self-exile, displaced relics of the past.

Timon, digging for roots in the woods, instead unearths gold, which he hails ironically as the "visible god, / That solder'st close impossibilities / And mak'st them kiss" (Timon, of Athens IV.iii.391–93). As an improbable reminder of the power and corruption he fled from in Athens, Timon's new gold is a glitteringly paradoxical discovery: a disruptive presence, at once a return of the past and a measure of its displacement. As such, it acts as a ghostly incarnation of Timon's past, a "revenant" as defined by Jacques Derrida in his study of 'hauntology'; "There is something disappeared, departed in the apparition itself as reapparition of the departed." Byron's verse likewise embraces departure only to be haunted by ghosts, who recall the past even as they embody its disruption.

At the similarly tender age of twenty, in another poem entitled "To a Lady, on being asked my reasons for quitting England in the spring," Byron set the double movement of banishment—its charged, liminal, past-and-present interchange—into the fundamental terms of Genesis: "When man expell'd from Eden's bowers, / A moment linger'd near the gate, / Each scene recall'd the vanish'd hours..." Such lingering would actually last much longer than a minute for Byron; one only has to recall the gate-shadowed action of *Cain* (1821), taking place in "The land without Paradise," to realize the constancy of this setting in his canon—after thirteen years still giving rise to "melancholy yearnings o'er the past," (III.i.36) still prompting spectral walk-ons. Cain's lingering by "the inhibited walls" (I.i.80) of Eden attracts Lucifer, the slippery "Master of Spirits," (I.i.98) whose proud alienation ("I dwell apart; but I am great" [I.i.308]) evokes a long line of scowling and once wildly popular Byronic heroes. Such figures, whose impact had faded to cliche long before Cain, nonetheless prove surprisingly trenchant haunters of Byron's later verse, liable at any time to come back from the world of spirits. Selim, doomed hero of *The Bride of Abydos* (1813), specifically waits to reemerge on the shoreline of his lover's cypress grove: "And there by night, reclin'd, 'tis said, / Is seen a ghastly turban'd head—/ And hence extended by the billow, / 'Tis named the 'Pirate-phantom's pillow'!" (II.725–28).

Even before he was cast aside by his author, left to haunt Byron's later verse as the relic of an abandoned mode, the Byronic hero had been more phantom than man. In the series of narratives often referred to as Byron's Eastern Tales— best-sellers dashed off during his London Years of Fame (1812–1816)—this breed of hero lives and dies amid unsettling recollections of what has vanished; expelled by force or temperament from his homeland, he moves within a purgatory of specters. His world is an uncomfortable blend of spectral disenchantment: *Childe Harold*'s death-in-life Greece ("In all save form alone, how changed!" he observes of a land populated by "Shades of the Helots" (II.711, 726) defines the general climate of the Tales. *The Giaour* (1813), the first Eastern Tale, is set in the same dead Greece ("'T is Greece, but living Greece no more! / So coldly sweet, so deadly fair, / We start, for soul is wanting there" [91–93]); like *Childe Harold*, the *Giaour* wends through this wasteland bereft of love, of soul, constantly nostalgic, and doomed by a curse to origin-haunting

displacement ("on earth as Vampire sent, / Thy course shall from its tomb be rent: / Then ghastly haunt thy native place, / And suck the blood of all thy race" [755–58]). Byron's later texts, even as they take sharp turns away from the Eastern Tales in format and tone, build on this early obsession with perpetual dislocation and its attendant hauntings; they teem with corrupted settings and uprooted evocations of a figure who, from the beginning, had been presented to the reader as irretrievably alienated.

As such, Byron's canon, however it may seem to repudiate itself, stays faithful to his early insight that the unsettling passage away from the familiar, from a point of origin, gives rise to uncanny emergence of what has been left behind. Stocking his later texts with references to outmoded protagonists, Byron was not mocking his earlier career, or even ironically "exploit[ing] a winning formula." Instead he was preserving a sense of disrupted origins that, ultimately, drives the vast carnival of displacement comprising *Don Juan* (1818–24): the open-ended unhousing emblematic of what Edward Said has called "interpretive series." The movement of Byron's career is from vortexes of disenchantment into the paradoxical vision that was already apparent to him as a youth on the brink of Eden's bowers: the improbable rise of close impossibilities. In later texts, Byron's exilic haunting gives rise to double visions important and sustaining enough to exemplify what Michael G. Cooke has called "the force of coincidentia oppositorum, an identification or interpresence between phenomena that seem to deny each other." The awareness of displacement blooms into particularly charged acts of binding in Byron's work as his canon turns back on itself: continual confrontations of the past with what is replacing, even repudiating it.

Paul Elledge has characterized the promiscuity of *Beppo* (1818)—its digressive presentation of an adulterous affair—as "a strategy by which departure need not entail division, or separation necessarily forfeit attachment."We can push that formula further: Byron's embrace of exile was commitment to a strategy of writing whereby departure multiplies possibilities, division leads to unlikely reemergence. The confrontation of a (nostalgic) present with an (uprooted) past is bristling and unpredictable; the anachronism alone (in Derrida's terms, "a dis-located time of the present ... the joining of a radically dis-jointed time, without certain conjunction" is a disruptive challenge to the haunted work. By attuning his later verse to evocations of the Byronic Hero, Byron avidly pursued such disruption—a power beyond control, a roiling adjacency of the past that operates despite and because of banishment.

I emphasize continuity in Byron's poetic career, an essential interactivity between late and early in his canon, in order to counter the standard characterization of Byron's later verse as a revolutionary repudiation of his past work. This late mode of Byron's—sometimes termed the Don Juan "manner" or "effect"—is usually said to be test-driven by the playful *Beppo*, which anticipates *Don Juan*'s ottava rima form, insouciant narrator, and digressive tendencies. Jerome McGann's commentary to CPW stands as the authoritative characterization of a crucial turn in Byron's poetry:

> *Beppo* is one of the most important poems in the canon because it inaugurates the verse project which was to reach fulfillment in *Don Juan*. Like the latter, *Beppo* was written in conscious reaction to the "monotony and mannerism' (BLJ vi.25) of his own earlier Romantic work, and to the 'wrong revolutionary poetical system—or systems' of the entire Romantic Movement (BLJ v.265–66).

McGann thus follows a long tradition that reads the conversational, digressive, satirical ottava rima stanzas of *Beppo* and *Don Juan* as not only turning the gloomy vortexes of the Eastern Tales inside out, but also signaling Byron's decisive break with his past success. Despite the fact that the writing of Beppo was an extremely brief interlude during the much larger project of finishing *Childe Harold*, this initial forage into the Don Juan manner has come to signal a "process of disengagement" in Byron's canon, a repudiation of pre-exile modes and themes. The division of McGann's influential studies of Byron reflects an abiding fissure: *Don Juan* finds no real place in the fairly comprehensive *Fiery Dust*; it is held apart instead for the later *Don Juan in Context*. Ironically enough, the latter study's valuable insight that "DJ is a poem that is, in fact, always in transition"—shuttling between engagements with biography, history, forms of rhetoric, and its own plot—seems purchased by isolation of the poem from the rest of Byron's canon. It is an isolation that opens up real explanatory gaps in studies that build on McGann's characterization

of *Don Juan* as an "assault upon the degenerate poetical manners of his day," an "attack upon [the] romantic stylistic revolution," and "Byron's practical illustration of the sort of critical stance romantic poetry ought to take toward itself" (McGann, *Don Juan in Context* 63, 73, 107). One sifts in vain through Jerome Christensen's ever-resourceful *Lord Byron's Strength*, for example, to find an indication of exactly why Byron would buck the system that had marketed him so well, why he would launch the "revolutionary text" (215) of Don Juan—a postmodern shakeup of "Byronism" and its "cultural monopoly" (220) that appears in Christensen's pages as suddenly as a rock through a shop window.

The division of Byron's work and pre- and post- *Don Juan* is often justified by his letters from Venice, such as the one specifically quoted by McGann, signaling the poet's disengagement from the "wrong revolutionary poetical system." Byron was clearly taken with this disavowal of a past revolution, repeating it several times, yet doing little to define a new program, a better revolution. In 1818 he would distance himself again from the "wrong poetical system"—a phrase so broad it could refer to the Byronic Hero as well as Wordsworth's *Excursion*; "I mean all (Lakers included)," Byron wrote to the also-implicated poet Thomas Moore. And yet, as usual, the longer Byron continues his repudiation, the more a complicating nostalgia enters into his writing. "'Us youth' were on the wrong tack," Byron elaborates, "But I never did say that we did not sail well." As Peter Manning has pertinently observed, the buried reference to Falstaff in Byron's letter could easily signal ulterior tactics, and certainly muddles the letter as a statement of intent. The next modulations of the letter to Moore suggest a simultaneous flightiness and persistence:

> The next generation (from the quantity and facility of imitation) will tumble and break their necks off our Pegasus, who runs away with us . . . Talking of horses, I not only get a row in my gondola, but a spanking gallop of some mile daily along a firm & solitary beach. (Feb. 2, 1818; BLJ 6.10)

Byron's prose here plunges wildly from the nautical to the equestrian, from post-revolutionary sobriety to nostalgic pride, from poetic manifesto to the merest biographical detail which, nevertheless, refers right back to the entrance of that most hardened of early Byronic heroes, the *Giaour*:

Who thundering comes on blackest steed,
With slacken'd bit and hoof of speed?
Beneath the clattering iron's sound
The cavern'd echoes wake around
In lash for lash, and bound for bound;
The foam that streaks the courser's side
Seems gather'd from the ocean-tide.
Though weary waves are sunk to rest,
There's none within his rider's breast;
And though to-morrow's tempest lower,
'Tis calmer than thy heart, young Giaour!
(180–90)

Ultimately, the challenge to Moore and any reader of Byron's "revolutionary" letter of 1818 lies in accounting for its waking echoes, the reemergence of what had seemed to be swept away.

Such evocation at the very moment of renunciation is typical of the way Byron vexes his reader with the interplay of fiction and life; it lures even critics who insist, like T. S. Eliot, that they are "not concerned" with the poet's life into scanning his writing for "honesty" or "genuine self-revelation.["] It comes as no surprise that Leslie Marchand, still Byron's best biographer, characterizes the revolution of the *Don Juan* manner as a sudden turn to self-representation: "With one stroke he freed himself from the fetters of British propriety and the *Childe Harold* manner, and something of the careless and relaxed realism of his letters invaded his verse. Let the critics cavil; he would be himself" (Marchand). But often in Byron's writing even in supposedly direct self-representations, such as the 1818 letter—the invasion runs just the other way: verse invades his letters, and the originating self is unsettled by the specter of fictional models. The Byronic hero's persistent cameo in the very statement which implies his demise should lead us to regard even the most seemingly direct pronouncement in Byron as stalked by the fiction it supposedly controls...

Source: Mark Phillipson, "Byron's Revisited Haunts," in *Studies in Romanticism*, Vol. 39, No. 2, Summer 2000, 10 pp.

SOURCES

Abrams, M. H., Preface, in *Natural Supernaturalism: Tradition and Revolution in Romantic Literature*, W. W. Norton, 1971, pp. 11–16.

Byron, Lord George Gordon, "Sonnet, To Genevra," in *Poetical Works*, edited by Frederick Page, new edition revised by John Jump, Oxford University Press, 1989, p. 71.

———, "Sonnet, To The Same," in *Poetical Works*, edited by Frederick Page, new edition revised by John Jump, Oxford University Press, 1989, p. 71.

———, "When We Two Parted," in *The Poetical Works of Byron*, Cambridge Edition, edited by Robert F. Gleckner, Houghton Mifflin, 1975, p. 151.

Franklin, Caroline, "Criticism," in *Byron*, Routledge, 2007, pp. 84–122.

———, "Life and Contexts," in *Byron*, Routledge, 2007, pp. 1–30.

Gatton, John Spalding, "George Gordon Byron," in *Dictionary of Literary Biography, Vol. 96: British Romantic Poets, 1789–1832, Second Series*, edited by John R. Greenfield, Gale Research, 1990, pp. 18–69.

Glover, A. S. B., Introduction, in *Byron*, Penguin Books, 1954, pp. 7–16.

Marchand, Leslie A., "1816: The Separation," in *Byron: A Biography*, Vol. 2, Alfred A. Knopf, 1957, pp. 563–608.

———, "Shorter Romantic Poems," in *Byron's Poetry: A Critical Introduction*, Houghton Mifflin, 1965, pp. 117–35.

Perkins, David, "General Introduction," in *English Romantic Writers*, Harcourt Brace Jovanovich, 1967, pp. 1–24.

Phillipson, Mark, "Byron's Haunts Revisited," in *Studies in Romanticism*, Vol. 39, No. 2, Summer 2000, p. 303–24.

Soderholm, James, "Byron's Ludic Lyrics," in *Studies in English Literature, 1500–1900*, Vol. 34, No. 4, Autumn 1994, pp. 739–52.

FURTHER READING

Eldridge, Richard, *The Persistence of Romanticism: Essays in Philosophy and Literature*, Cambridge University Press, 2001.

> Eldridge offers a philosophical defense of Romanticism's ethics and ideals and traces the literary legacy of the philosophical movement of Romanticism.

Elfenbein, Andrew, "Byronism and the Work of Homosexual Performance in Early Victorian England," in *Modern Language Quarterly*, Vol. 54, No. 4, December 1993, pp. 535–67.

> Elfenbein analyzes the perceptions that early Victorians had regarding Byron's scandalous sexual behavior. Elfenbein also emphasizes the relationship between his celebrity and his homosexuality.

Fletcher, Christopher, "Lord Byron: Unrecorded Autograph Poems," in *Notes and Queries*, Vol. 43, No. 4, December 1996, pp. 425–29.

Fletcher discusses five autographed poems by Byron, discovered in the papers belonging to Sara Sophia Fane, Fifth Countess of Jersey. The poems were inscribed privately to Lady Jersey. Other versions of the poems were later published.

MacDonald, D. L., "Childhood Abuse as Romantic Reality: The Case of Lord Byron," in *Literature and Psychology*, Vol. 40, No. 1–2, Spring–Summer 1994, pp. 24–48.

In discussing the sexual abuse that Byron suffered at the hands of his maid when he was a youngster (ages nine through eleven), MacDonald assesses the effects of the abuse on Byron's poetry, observing that Byron's frequent return to the subject of premature aging sprang from these experiences.

McGann, Jerome J., Introduction, in *Lord Byron: The Major Works*, Oxford University Press, 2000.

McGann offers a concise overview of Byron's life, major works, and critical reception.

Glossary of Literary Terms

A

Abstract: Used as a noun, the term refers to a short summary or outline of a longer work. As an adjective applied to writing or literary works, abstract refers to words or phrases that name things not knowable through the five senses.

Accent: The emphasis or stress placed on a syllable in poetry. Traditional poetry commonly uses patterns of accented and unaccented syllables (known as feet) that create distinct rhythms. Much modern poetry uses less formal arrangements that create a sense of freedom and spontaneity.

Aestheticism: A literary and artistic movement of the nineteenth century. Followers of the movement believed that art should not be mixed with social, political, or moral teaching. The statement "art for art's sake" is a good summary of aestheticism. The movement had its roots in France, but it gained widespread importance in England in the last half of the nineteenth century, where it helped change the Victorian practice of including moral lessons in literature.

Affective Fallacy: An error in judging the merits or faults of a work of literature. The "error" results from stressing the importance of the work's effect upon the reader—that is, how it makes a reader "feel" emotionally, what it does as a literary work—instead of stressing its inner qualities as a created object, or what it "is."

Age of Johnson: The period in English literature between 1750 and 1798, named after the most prominent literary figure of the age, Samuel Johnson. Works written during this time are noted for their emphasis on "sensibility," or emotional quality. These works formed a transition between the rational works of the Age of Reason, or Neoclassical period, and the emphasis on individual feelings and responses of the Romantic period.

Age of Reason: See *Neoclassicism*

Age of Sensibility: See *Age of Johnson*

Agrarians: A group of Southern American writers of the 1930s and 1940s who fostered an economic and cultural program for the South based on agriculture, in opposition to the industrial society of the North. The term can refer to any group that promotes the value of farm life and agricultural society.

Alexandrine Meter: See *Meter*

Allegory: A narrative technique in which characters representing things or abstract ideas are used to convey a message or teach a lesson. Allegory is typically used to teach moral, ethical, or religious lessons but is sometimes used for satiric or political purposes.

Alliteration: A poetic device where the first consonant sounds or any vowel sounds in words or syllables are repeated.

Allusion: A reference to a familiar literary or historical person or event, used to make an idea more easily understood.

Amerind Literature: The writing and oral traditions of Native Americans. Native American literature was originally passed on by word of mouth, so it consisted largely of stories and events that were easily memorized. Amerind prose is often rhythmic like poetry because it was recited to the beat of a ceremonial drum.

Analogy: A comparison of two things made to explain something unfamiliar through its similarities to something familiar, or to prove one point based on the acceptedness of another. Similes and metaphors are types of analogies.

Anapest: See *Foot*

Angry Young Men: A group of British writers of the 1950s whose work expressed bitterness and disillusionment with society. Common to their work is an anti-hero who rebels against a corrupt social order and strives for personal integrity.

Anthropomorphism: The presentation of animals or objects in human shape or with human characteristics. The term is derived from the Greek word for "human form."

Antimasque: See *Masque*

Antithesis: The antithesis of something is its direct opposite. In literature, the use of antithesis as a figure of speech results in two statements that show a contrast through the balancing of two opposite ideas. Technically, it is the second portion of the statement that is defined as the "antithesis"; the first portion is the "thesis."

Apocrypha: Writings tentatively attributed to an author but not proven or universally accepted to be their works. The term was originally applied to certain books of the Bible that were not considered inspired and so were not included in the "sacred canon."

Apollonian and Dionysian: The two impulses believed to guide authors of dramatic tragedy. The Apollonian impulse is named after Apollo, the Greek god of light and beauty and the symbol of intellectual order. The Dionysian impulse is named after Dionysus, the Greek god of wine and the symbol of the unrestrained forces of nature. The Apollonian impulse is to create a rational, harmonious world, while the Dionysian is to express the irrational forces of personality.

Apostrophe: A statement, question, or request addressed to an inanimate object or concept or to a nonexistent or absent person.

Archetype: The word archetype is commonly used to describe an original pattern or model from which all other things of the same kind are made. This term was introduced to literary criticism from the psychology of Carl Jung. It expresses Jung's theory that behind every person's "unconscious," or repressed memories of the past, lies the "collective unconscious" of the human race: memories of the countless typical experiences of our ancestors. These memories are said to prompt illogical associations that trigger powerful emotions in the reader. Often, the emotional process is primitive, even primordial. Archetypes are the literary images that grow out of the "collective unconscious." They appear in literature as incidents and plots that repeat basic patterns of life. They may also appear as stereotyped characters.

Argument: The argument of a work is the author's subject matter or principal idea.

Art for Art's Sake: See *Aestheticism*

Assonance: The repetition of similar vowel sounds in poetry.

Audience: The people for whom a piece of literature is written. Authors usually write with a certain audience in mind, for example, children, members of a religious or ethnic group, or colleagues in a professional field. The term "audience" also applies to the people who gather to see or hear any performance, including plays, poetry readings, speeches, and concerts.

Automatic Writing: Writing carried out without a preconceived plan in an effort to capture every random thought. Authors who engage in automatic writing typically do not revise their work, preferring instead to preserve the revealed truth and beauty of spontaneous expression.

Avant-garde: A French term meaning "vanguard." It is used in literary criticism to describe new writing that rejects traditional approaches to literature in favor of innovations in style or content.

B

Ballad: A short poem that tells a simple story and has a repeated refrain. Ballads were originally intended to be sung. Early ballads, known as folk ballads, were passed down through generations, so their authors are often unknown. Later ballads composed by known authors are called literary ballads.

Baroque: A term used in literary criticism to describe literature that is complex or ornate in style or diction. Baroque works typically express tension, anxiety, and violent emotion. The term "Baroque Age" designates a period in Western European literature beginning in the late sixteenth century and ending about one hundred years later. Works of this period often mirror the qualities of works more generally associated with the label "baroque" and sometimes feature elaborate conceits.

Baroque Age: See *Baroque*

Baroque Period: See *Baroque*

Beat Generation: See *Beat Movement*

Beat Movement: A period featuring a group of American poets and novelists of the 1950s and 1960s—including Jack Kerouac, Allen Ginsberg, Gregory Corso, William S. Burroughs, and Lawrence Ferlinghetti—who rejected established social and literary values. Using such techniques as stream of consciousness writing and jazz-influenced free verse and focusing on unusual or abnormal states of mind—generated by religious ecstasy or the use of drugs—the Beat writers aimed to create works that were unconventional in both form and subject matter.

Beat Poets: See *Beat Movement*

Beats, The: See *Beat Movement*

Belles- lettres: A French term meaning "fine letters" or "beautiful writing." It is often used as a synonym for literature, typically referring to imaginative and artistic rather than scientific or expository writing. Current usage sometimes restricts the meaning to light or humorous writing and appreciative essays about literature.

Black Aesthetic Movement: A period of artistic and literary development among African Americans in the 1960s and early 1970s. This was the first major African-American artistic movement since the Harlem Renaissance and was closely paralleled by the civil rights and black power movements. The black aesthetic writers attempted to produce works of art that would be meaningful to the black masses. Key figures in black aesthetics included one of its founders, poet and playwright Amiri Baraka, formerly known as LeRoi Jones; poet and essayist Haki R. Madhubuti, formerly Don L. Lee; poet and playwright Sonia Sanchez; and dramatist Ed Bullins.

Black Arts Movement: See *Black Aesthetic Movement*

Black Comedy: See *Black Humor*

Black Humor: Writing that places grotesque elements side by side with humorous ones in an attempt to shock the reader, forcing him or her to laugh at the horrifying reality of a disordered world.

Black Mountain School: Black Mountain College and three of its instructors—Robert Creeley, Robert Duncan, and Charles Olson—were all influential in projective verse, so poets working in projective verse are now referred as members of the Black Mountain school.

Blank Verse: Loosely, any unrhymed poetry, but more generally, unrhymed iambic pentameter verse (composed of lines of five two-syllable feet with the first syllable accented, the second unaccented). Blank verse has been used by poets since the Renaissance for its flexibility and its graceful, dignified tone.

Bloomsbury Group: A group of English writers, artists, and intellectuals who held informal artistic and philosophical discussions in Bloomsbury, a district of London, from around 1907 to the early 1930s. The Bloomsbury Group held no uniform philosophical beliefs but did commonly express an aversion to moral prudery and a desire for greater social tolerance.

Bon Mot: A French term meaning "good word." A *bon mot* is a witty remark or clever observation.

Breath Verse: See *Projective Verse*

Burlesque: Any literary work that uses exaggeration to make its subject appear ridiculous, either by treating a trivial subject with profound seriousness or by treating a dignified subject frivolously. The word "burlesque" may also be used as an adjective, as in "burlesque show," to mean "striptease act."

C

Cadence: The natural rhythm of language caused by the alternation of accented and unaccented syllables. Much modern poetry—notably free verse—deliberately manipulates cadence to create complex rhythmic effects.

Caesura: A pause in a line of poetry, usually occurring near the middle. It typically corresponds to a break in the natural rhythm or sense of the line but is sometimes shifted to create special meanings or rhythmic effects.

Canzone: A short Italian or Provencal lyric poem, commonly about love and often set to music. The *canzone* has no set form but typically contains five or six stanzas made up of seven to twenty lines of eleven syllables each. A shorter, five- to ten-line "envoy," or concluding stanza, completes the poem.

Carpe Diem: A Latin term meaning "seize the day." This is a traditional theme of poetry, especially lyrics. A *carpe diem* poem advises the reader or the person it addresses to live for today and enjoy the pleasures of the moment.

Catharsis: The release or purging of unwanted emotions—specifically fear and pity—brought about by exposure to art. The term was first used by the Greek philosopher Aristotle in his *Poetics* to refer to the desired effect of tragedy on spectators.

Celtic Renaissance: A period of Irish literary and cultural history at the end of the nineteenth century. Followers of the movement aimed to create a romantic vision of Celtic myth and legend. The most significant works of the Celtic Renaissance typically present a dreamy, unreal world, usually in reaction against the reality of contemporary problems.

Celtic Twilight: See *Celtic Renaissance*

Character: Broadly speaking, a person in a literary work. The actions of characters are what constitute the plot of a story, novel, or poem. There are numerous types of characters, ranging from simple, stereotypical figures to intricate, multifaceted ones. In the techniques of anthropomorphism and personification, animals—and even places or things—can assume aspects of character. "Characterization" is the process by which an author creates vivid, believable characters in a work of art. This may be done in a variety of ways, including (1) direct description of the character by the narrator; (2) the direct presentation of the speech, thoughts, or actions of the character; and (3) the responses of other characters to the character. The term "character" also refers to a form originated by the ancient Greek writer Theophrastus that later became popular in the seventeenth and eighteenth centuries. It is a short essay or sketch of a person who prominently displays a specific attribute or quality, such as miserliness or ambition.

Characterization: See *Character*

Classical: In its strictest definition in literary criticism, classicism refers to works of ancient Greek or Roman literature. The term may also be used to describe a literary work of recognized importance (a "classic") from any time period or literature that exhibits the traits of classicism.

Classicism: A term used in literary criticism to describe critical doctrines that have their roots in ancient Greek and Roman literature, philosophy, and art. Works associated with classicism typically exhibit restraint on the part of the author, unity of design and purpose, clarity, simplicity, logical organization, and respect for tradition.

Colloquialism: A word, phrase, or form of pronunciation that is acceptable in casual conversation but not in formal, written communication. It is considered more acceptable than slang.

Complaint: A lyric poem, popular in the Renaissance, in which the speaker expresses sorrow about his or her condition. Typically, the speaker's sadness is caused by an unresponsive lover, but some complaints cite other sources of unhappiness, such as poverty or fate.

Conceit: A clever and fanciful metaphor, usually expressed through elaborate and extended comparison, that presents a striking parallel between two seemingly dissimilar things—for example, elaborately comparing a beautiful woman to an object like a garden or the sun. The conceit was a popular device throughout the Elizabethan Age and Baroque Age and was the principal technique of the seventeenth-century English metaphysical poets. This usage of the word conceit is unrelated to the best-known definition of conceit as an arrogant attitude or behavior.

Concrete: Concrete is the opposite of abstract, and refers to a thing that actually exists or a description that allows the reader to experience an object or concept with the senses.

Concrete Poetry: Poetry in which visual elements play a large part in the poetic effect. Punctuation marks, letters, or words are arranged on a page to form a visual design: a cross, for example, or a bumblebee.

Confessional Poetry: A form of poetry in which the poet reveals very personal, intimate, sometimes shocking information about himself or herself.

Connotation: The impression that a word gives beyond its defined meaning. Connotations may be universally understood or may be significant only to a certain group.

Consonance: Consonance occurs in poetry when words appearing at the ends of two or more verses have similar final consonant sounds but have final vowel sounds that differ, as with "stuff" and "off."

Convention: Any widely accepted literary device, style, or form.

Corrido: A Mexican ballad.

Couplet: Two lines of poetry with the same rhyme and meter, often expressing a complete and self-contained thought.

Criticism: The systematic study and evaluation of literary works, usually based on a specific method or set of principles. An important part of literary studies since ancient times, the practice of criticism has given rise to numerous theories, methods, and "schools," sometimes producing conflicting, even contradictory, interpretations of literature in general as well as of individual works. Even such basic issues as what constitutes a poem or a novel have been the subject of much criticism over the centuries.

D

Dactyl: See *Foot*

Dadaism: A protest movement in art and literature founded by Tristan Tzara in 1916. Followers of the movement expressed their outrage at the destruction brought about by World War I by revolting against numerous forms of social convention. The Dadaists presented works marked by calculated madness and flamboyant nonsense. They stressed total freedom of expression, commonly through primitive displays of emotion and illogical, often senseless,

poetry. The movement ended shortly after the war, when it was replaced by surrealism.

Decadent: See *Decadents*

Decadents: The followers of a nineteenth-century literary movement that had its beginnings in French aestheticism. Decadent literature displays a fascination with perverse and morbid states; a search for novelty and sensation—the "new thrill"; a preoccupation with mysticism; and a belief in the senselessness of human existence. The movement is closely associated with the doctrine Art for Art's Sake. The term "decadence" is sometimes used to denote a decline in the quality of art or literature following a period of greatness.

Deconstruction: A method of literary criticism developed by Jacques Derrida and characterized by multiple conflicting interpretations of a given work. Deconstructionists consider the impact of the language of a work and suggest that the true meaning of the work is not necessarily the meaning that the author intended.

Deduction: The process of reaching a conclusion through reasoning from general premises to a specific premise.

Denotation: The definition of a word, apart from the impressions or feelings it creates in the reader.

Diction: The selection and arrangement of words in a literary work. Either or both may vary depending on the desired effect. There are four general types of diction: "formal," used in scholarly or lofty writing; "informal," used in relaxed but educated conversation; "colloquial," used in everyday speech; and "slang," containing newly coined words and other terms not accepted in formal usage.

Didactic: A term used to describe works of literature that aim to teach some moral, religious, political, or practical lesson. Although didactic elements are often found in artistically pleasing works, the term "didactic" usually refers to literature in which the message is more important than the form. The term may also be used to criticize a work that the critic finds "overly didactic," that is, heavy-handed in its delivery of a lesson.

Dimeter: See *Meter*

Dionysian: See *Apollonian and Dionysian*

Discordia concurs: A Latin phrase meaning "discord in harmony." The term was coined by the eighteenth-century English writer Samuel Johnson to describe "a combination of dissimilar images or discovery of occult resemblances in things apparently unlike." Johnson created the expression by reversing a phrase by the Latin poet Horace.

Dissonance: A combination of harsh or jarring sounds, especially in poetry. Although such combinations may be accidental, poets sometimes intentionally make them to achieve particular effects. Dissonance is also sometimes used to refer to close but not identical rhymes. When this is the case, the word functions as a synonym for consonance.

Double Entendre: A corruption of a French phrase meaning "double meaning." The term is used to indicate a word or phrase that is deliberately ambiguous, especially when one of the meanings is risque or improper.

Draft: Any preliminary version of a written work. An author may write dozens of drafts which are revised to form the final work, or he or she may write only one, with few or no revisions.

Dramatic Monologue: See *Monologue*

Dramatic Poetry: Any lyric work that employs elements of drama such as dialogue, conflict, or characterization, but excluding works that are intended for stage presentation.

Dream Allegory: See *Dream Vision*

Dream Vision: A literary convention, chiefly of the Middle Ages. In a dream vision a story is presented as a literal dream of the narrator. This device was commonly used to teach moral and religious lessons.

E

Eclogue: In classical literature, a poem featuring rural themes and structured as a dialogue among shepherds. Eclogues often took specific poetic forms, such as elegies or love poems. Some were written as the soliloquy of a shepherd. In later centuries, "eclogue" came to refer to any poem that was in the pastoral tradition or that had a dialogue or monologue structure.

Edwardian: Describes cultural conventions identified with the period of the reign of Edward VII of England (1901-1910). Writers of the Edwardian Age typically displayed a strong reaction against the propriety and conservatism of the Victorian Age. Their work often exhibits distrust of authority in religion, politics, and art and expresses strong doubts about the soundness of conventional values.

Edwardian Age: See *Edwardian*

Electra Complex: A daughter's amorous obsession with her father.

Elegy: A lyric poem that laments the death of a person or the eventual death of all people. In a conventional elegy, set in a classical world, the poet and subject are spoken of as shepherds. In modern criticism, the word elegy is often used to refer to a poem that is melancholy or mournfully contemplative.

Elizabethan Age: A period of great economic growth, religious controversy, and nationalism closely associated with the reign of Elizabeth I of England (1558-1603). The Elizabethan Age is considered a part of the general renaissance—that is, the flowering of arts and literature—that took place in Europe during the fourteenth through sixteenth centuries. The era is considered the golden age of English literature. The most important dramas in English and a great deal of lyric poetry were produced during this period, and modern English criticism began around this time.

Empathy: A sense of shared experience, including emotional and physical feelings, with someone or something other than oneself. Empathy is often used to describe the response of a reader to a literary character.

English Sonnet: See *Sonnet*

Enjambment: The running over of the sense and structure of a line of verse or a couplet into the following verse or couplet.

Enlightenment, The: An eighteenth-century philosophical movement. It began in France but had a wide impact throughout Europe and America. Thinkers of the Enlightenment valued reason and believed that both the individual and society could achieve a state of perfection. Corresponding to this essentially humanist vision was a resistance to religious authority.

Epic: A long narrative poem about the adventures of a hero of great historic or legendary importance. The setting is vast and the action is often given cosmic significance through the intervention of supernatural forces such as gods, angels, or demons. Epics are typically written in a classical style of grand simplicity with elaborate metaphors and allusions that enhance the symbolic importance of a hero's adventures.

Epic Simile: See *Homeric Simile*

Epigram: A saying that makes the speaker's point quickly and concisely.

Epilogue: A concluding statement or section of a literary work. In dramas, particularly those of the seventeenth and eighteenth centuries, the epilogue is a closing speech, often in verse, delivered by an actor at the end of a play and spoken directly to the audience.

Epiphany: A sudden revelation of truth inspired by a seemingly trivial incident.

Epitaph: An inscription on a tomb or tombstone, or a verse written on the occasion of a person's death. Epitaphs may be serious or humorous.

Epithalamion: A song or poem written to honor and commemorate a marriage ceremony.

Epithalamium: See *Epithalamion*

Epithet: A word or phrase, often disparaging or abusive, that expresses a character trait of someone or something.

Erziehungsroman: See *Bildungsroman*

Essay: A prose composition with a focused subject of discussion. The term was coined by Michel de Montaigne to describe his 1580 collection of brief, informal reflections on himself and on various topics relating to human nature. An essay can also be a long, systematic discourse.

Existentialism: A predominantly twentieth-century philosophy concerned with the nature and perception of human existence. There are two major strains of existentialist thought: atheistic and Christian. Followers of atheistic existentialism believe that the individual is alone in a godless universe and that the basic human condition is one of suffering and loneliness. Nevertheless, because there are no fixed values, individuals can create their own characters—indeed, they can shape themselves—through the exercise of free will. The atheistic strain culminates in and is popularly associated with the works of Jean-Paul Sartre. The Christian existentialists, on the other hand, believe that only in God may people find freedom from life's anguish. The two strains hold certain beliefs in common: that existence cannot be fully understood or described through empirical effort; that anguish is a universal element of life; that individuals must bear responsibility for their actions; and that there is no common standard of behavior or perception for religious and ethical matters.

Expatriates: See *Expatriatism*

Expatriatism: The practice of leaving one's country to live for an extended period in another country.

Exposition: Writing intended to explain the nature of an idea, thing, or theme. Expository writing is often combined with description, narration, or argument. In dramatic writing, the exposition is the introductory material which presents the characters, setting, and tone of the play.

Expressionism: An indistinct literary term, originally used to describe an early twentieth-century school of German painting. The term applies to almost any mode of unconventional, highly subjective writing that distorts reality in some way.

Extended Monologue: See *Monologue*

F

Feet: See *Foot*

Feminine Rhyme: See *Rhyme*

Fiction: Any story that is the product of imagination rather than a documentation of fact. Characters and events in such narratives may be based in real life but their ultimate form and configuration is a creation of the author.

Figurative Language: A technique in writing in which the author temporarily interrupts the order, construction, or meaning of the writing for a particular effect. This interruption takes the form of one or more figures of speech such as hyperbole, irony, or simile. Figurative language is the opposite of literal language, in which every word is truthful, accurate, and free of exaggeration or embellishment.

Figures of Speech: Writing that differs from customary conventions for construction, meaning, order, or significance for the purpose of a special meaning or effect. There are two major types of figures of speech: rhetorical figures, which do not make changes in the meaning of the words, and tropes, which do.

Fin de siecle: A French term meaning "end of the century." The term is used to denote the last decade of the nineteenth century, a transition period when writers and other artists abandoned old conventions and looked for new techniques and objectives.

First Person: See *Point of View*

Folk Ballad: See *Ballad*

Folklore: Traditions and myths preserved in a culture or group of people. Typically, these are passed on by word of mouth in various forms—such as legends, songs, and proverbs—or preserved in customs and ceremonies. This term was first used by W. J. Thoms in 1846.

Folktale: A story originating in oral tradition. Folktales fall into a variety of categories, including legends, ghost stories, fairy tales, fables, and anecdotes based on historical figures and events.

Foot: The smallest unit of rhythm in a line of poetry. In English-language poetry, a foot is typically one accented syllable combined with one or two unaccented syllables.

Form: The pattern or construction of a work which identifies its genre and distinguishes it from other genres.

Formalism: In literary criticism, the belief that literature should follow prescribed rules of construction, such as those that govern the sonnet form.

Fourteener Meter: See *Meter*

Free Verse: Poetry that lacks regular metrical and rhyme patterns but that tries to capture the cadences of everyday speech. The form allows a poet to exploit a variety of rhythmical effects within a single poem.

Futurism: A flamboyant literary and artistic movement that developed in France, Italy, and Russia from 1908 through the 1920s. Futurist theater and poetry abandoned traditional literary forms. In their place, followers of the movement attempted to achieve total freedom of expression through bizarre imagery and deformed or newly invented words. The Futurists were self-consciously modern artists who attempted to incorporate the appearances and sounds of modern life into their work.

G

Genre: A category of literary work. In critical theory, genre may refer to both the content of a given work—tragedy, comedy, pastoral—and to its form, such as poetry, novel, or drama.

Genteel Tradition: A term coined by critic George Santayana to describe the literary practice of certain late nineteenth- century American writers, especially New Englanders. Followers of the Genteel Tradition emphasized conventionality in social, religious, moral, and literary standards.

Georgian Age: See *Georgian Poets*

Georgian Period: See *Georgian Poets*

Georgian Poets: A loose grouping of English poets during the years 1912-1922. The Georgians reacted against certain literary schools and practices, especially Victorian wordiness, turn-of-the-century aestheticism, and contemporary urban realism. In their place, the Georgians embraced the nineteenth-century poetic practices of William Wordsworth and the other Lake Poets.

Georgic: A poem about farming and the farmer's way of life, named from Virgil's *Georgics*.

Gilded Age: A period in American history during the 1870s characterized by political corruption and materialism. A number of important novels of social and political criticism were written during this time.

Gothic: See *Gothicism*

Gothicism: In literary criticism, works characterized by a taste for the medieval or morbidly attractive. A gothic novel prominently features elements of horror, the supernatural, gloom, and violence: clanking chains, terror, charnel houses, ghosts, medieval castles, and mysteriously slamming doors. The term "gothic novel" is also applied to novels that lack elements of the traditional Gothic setting but that create a similar atmosphere of terror or dread.

Graveyard School: A group of eighteenth-century English poets who wrote long, picturesque meditations on death. Their works were designed to cause the reader to ponder immortality.

Great Chain of Being: The belief that all things and creatures in nature are organized in a hierarchy from inanimate objects at the bottom to God at the top. This system of belief was popular in the seventeenth and eighteenth centuries.

Grotesque: In literary criticism, the subject matter of a work or a style of expression characterized by exaggeration, deformity, freakishness, and disorder. The grotesque often includes an element of comic absurdity.

H

Haiku: The shortest form of Japanese poetry, constructed in three lines of five, seven, and five syllables respectively. The message of a *haiku* poem usually centers on some aspect of spirituality and provokes an emotional response in the reader.

Half Rhyme: See *Consonance*

Harlem Renaissance: The Harlem Renaissance of the 1920s is generally considered the first significant movement of black writers and artists in the United States. During this period, new and established black writers published more fiction and poetry than ever before, the first influential black literary journals were established, and black authors and artists received their first widespread recognition and serious critical appraisal. Among the major writers associated with this period are Claude McKay, Jean Toomer, Countee Cullen, Langston Hughes, Arna Bontemps, Nella Larsen, and Zora Neale Hurston.

Hellenism: Imitation of ancient Greek thought or styles. Also, an approach to life that focuses on the growth and development of the intellect. "Hellenism" is sometimes used to refer to the belief that reason can be applied to examine all human experience.

Heptameter: See *Meter*

Hero/Heroine: The principal sympathetic character (male or female) in a literary work. Heroes and heroines typically exhibit admirable traits: idealism, courage, and integrity, for example.

Heroic Couplet: A rhyming couplet written in iambic pentameter (a verse with five iambic feet).

Heroic Line: The meter and length of a line of verse in epic or heroic poetry. This varies by language and time period.

Heroine: See *Hero/Heroine*

Hexameter: See *Meter*

Historical Criticism: The study of a work based on its impact on the world of the time period in which it was written.

Hokku: See *Haiku*

Holocaust: See *Holocaust Literature*

Holocaust Literature: Literature influenced by or written about the Holocaust of World War II. Such literature includes true stories of survival in concentration camps, escape, and life after the war, as well as fictional works and poetry.

Homeric Simile: An elaborate, detailed comparison written as a simile many lines in length.

Horatian Satire: See *Satire*

Humanism: A philosophy that places faith in the dignity of humankind and rejects the medieval perception of the individual as a weak, fallen creature. "Humanists" typically believe in the perfectibility of human nature and view reason and education as the means to that end.

Humors: Mentions of the humors refer to the ancient Greek theory that a person's health and personality were determined by the balance of four basic fluids in the body: blood, phlegm, yellow bile, and black bile. A dominance of any fluid would cause extremes in behavior. An excess of blood created a sanguine person who was joyful, aggressive, and passionate; a phlegmatic person was shy, fearful, and sluggish; too much yellow bile led to a choleric temperament characterized by impatience, anger, bitterness, and stubbornness; and excessive black bile created melancholy, a state of laziness, gluttony, and lack of motivation.

Humours: See *Humors*

Hyperbole: In literary criticism, deliberate exaggeration used to achieve an effect.

I

Iamb: See *Foot*

Idiom: A word construction or verbal expression closely associated with a given language.

Image: A concrete representation of an object or sensory experience. Typically, such a representation helps evoke the feelings associated with the object or experience itself. Images are either "literal" or "figurative." Literal images are especially concrete and involve little or no extension of the obvious meaning of the words used to express them. Figurative images do not follow the literal meaning of the words exactly. Images in literature are usually visual, but the term "image" can also refer to the representation of any sensory experience.

Imagery: The array of images in a literary work. Also, figurative language.

Imagism: An English and American poetry movement that flourished between 1908 and 1917. The Imagists used precise, clearly presented images in their works. They also used common, everyday speech and aimed for conciseness, concrete imagery, and the creation of new rhythms.

In medias res: A Latin term meaning "in the middle of things." It refers to the technique of beginning a story at its midpoint and then using various flashback devices to reveal previous action.

Induction: The process of reaching a conclusion by reasoning from specific premises to form a general premise. Also, an introductory portion of a work of literature, especially a play.

Intentional Fallacy: The belief that judgments of a literary work based solely on an author's stated or implied intentions are false and misleading. Critics who believe in the concept of the intentional fallacy typically argue that the work itself is sufficient matter for interpretation, even though they may concede that an author's statement of purpose can be useful.

Interior Monologue: A narrative technique in which characters' thoughts are revealed in a way that appears to be uncontrolled by the author. The interior monologue typically aims to reveal the inner self of a character. It portrays emotional experiences as they occur at both a conscious and unconscious level. Images are often used to represent sensations or emotions.

Internal Rhyme: Rhyme that occurs within a single line of verse.

Irish Literary Renaissance: A late nineteenth- and early twentieth-century movement in Irish literature. Members of the movement aimed to reduce the influence of British culture in Ireland and create an Irish national literature.

Irony: In literary criticism, the effect of language in which the intended meaning is the opposite of what is stated.

Italian Sonnet: See *Sonnet*

J

Jacobean Age: The period of the reign of James I of England (1603-1625). The early literature of this period reflected the worldview of the Elizabethan Age, but a darker, more cynical attitude steadily grew in the art and literature of the Jacobean Age. This was an important time for English drama and poetry.

Jargon: Language that is used or understood only by a select group of people. Jargon may refer to terminology used in a certain profession, such as computer jargon, or it may refer to any nonsensical language that is not understood by most people.

Journalism: Writing intended for publication in a newspaper or magazine, or for broadcast on a radio or television program featuring news, sports, entertainment, or other timely material.

K

Knickerbocker Group: A somewhat indistinct group of New York writers of the first half of the nineteenth century. Members of the group were linked only by location and a common theme: New York life.

Kunstlerroman: See *Bildungsroman*

L

Lais: See *Lay*

Lake Poets: See *Lake School*

Lake School: These poets all lived in the Lake District of England at the turn of the nineteenth century. As a group, they followed no single "school" of thought or literary practice, although their works were uniformly disparaged by the *Edinburgh Review*.

Lay: A song or simple narrative poem. The form originated in medieval France. Early French *lais* were often based on the Celtic legends and other tales sung by Breton minstrels—thus the name of the "Breton lay." In fourteenth-century England, the term "lay" was used to describe short narratives written in imitation of the Breton lays.

Leitmotiv: See *Motif*

Literal Language: An author uses literal language when he or she writes without exaggerating or embellishing the subject matter and without any tools of figurative language.

Literary Ballad: See *Ballad*

Literature: Literature is broadly defined as any written or spoken material, but the term most often refers to creative works.

Lost Generation: A term first used by Gertrude Stein to describe the post-World War I generation of American writers: men and women haunted by a sense of betrayal and emptiness brought about by the destructiveness of the war.

Lyric Poetry: A poem expressing the subjective feelings and personal emotions of the poet. Such poetry is melodic, since it was originally accompanied by a lyre in recitals. Most Western poetry in the twentieth century may be classified as lyrical.

M

Mannerism: Exaggerated, artificial adherence to a literary manner or style. Also, a popular style of the visual arts of late sixteenth-century Europe that was marked by elongation of the human form and by intentional spatial distortion. Literary works that are self-consciously high-toned and artistic are often said to be "mannered."

Masculine Rhyme: See *Rhyme*

Measure: The foot, verse, or time sequence used in a literary work, especially a poem. Measure is often used somewhat incorrectly as a synonym for meter.

Metaphor: A figure of speech that expresses an idea through the image of another object. Metaphors suggest the essence of the first object by identifying it with certain qualities of the second object.

Metaphysical Conceit: See *Conceit*

Metaphysical Poetry: The body of poetry produced by a group of seventeenth-century English writers called the "Metaphysical Poets." The group includes John Donne and Andrew Marvell. The Metaphysical Poets made use of everyday speech, intellectual analysis, and unique imagery. They aimed to portray the ordinary conflicts and contradictions of life. Their poems often took the form of an argument, and many of them emphasize physical and religious love as well as the fleeting nature of life. Elaborate conceits are typical in metaphysical poetry.

Metaphysical Poets: See *Metaphysical Poetry*

Meter: In literary criticism, the repetition of sound patterns that creates a rhythm in poetry. The patterns are based on the number of syllables and the presence and absence of accents. The unit of rhythm in a line is called a foot. Types of meter are classified according to the number of feet in a line. These are the standard English lines: Monometer, one foot; Dimeter, two feet; Trimeter, three feet; Tetrameter, four feet; Pentameter, five feet; Hexameter, six feet (also called the Alexandrine); Heptameter, seven feet (also called the "Fourteener" when the feet are iambic).

Modernism: Modern literary practices. Also, the principles of a literary school that lasted from roughly the beginning of the twentieth century until the end of World War II. Modernism is defined by its rejection of the literary conventions of the nineteenth century and by its opposition to conventional morality, taste, traditions, and economic values.

Monologue: A composition, written or oral, by a single individual. More specifically, a speech given by a single individual in a drama or other public entertainment. It has no set length, although it is usually several or more lines long.

Monometer: See *Meter*

Mood: The prevailing emotions of a work or of the author in his or her creation of the work. The mood of a work is not always what might be expected based on its subject matter.

Motif: A theme, character type, image, metaphor, or other verbal element that recurs throughout a single work of literature or occurs in a number of different works over a period of time.

Motiv: See *Motif*

Muckrakers: An early twentieth-century group of American writers. Typically, their works exposed the wrongdoings of big business and government in the United States.

Muses: Nine Greek mythological goddesses, the daughters of Zeus and Mnemosyne (Memory). Each muse patronized a specific area of the liberal arts and sciences. Calliope presided over epic poetry, Clio over history, Erato over love poetry, Euterpe over music or lyric poetry, Melpomene over tragedy, Polyhymnia over hymns to the gods, Terpsichore over dance, Thalia over comedy, and Urania over astronomy. Poets and writers traditionally made appeals to the Muses for inspiration in their work.

Myth: An anonymous tale emerging from the traditional beliefs of a culture or social unit. Myths use supernatural explanations for natural phenomena. They may also explain cosmic issues like creation and death. Collections of myths, known as mythologies, are common to all cultures and nations, but the best-known myths belong to the Norse, Roman, and Greek mythologies.

N

Narration: The telling of a series of events, real or invented. A narration may be either a simple narrative, in which the events are recounted chronologically, or a narrative with a plot, in which the account is given in a style reflecting the author's artistic concept of the story. Narration is sometimes used as a synonym for "storyline."

Narrative: A verse or prose accounting of an event or sequence of events, real or invented. The term is also used as an adjective in the sense "method of narration." For example, in literary criticism, the expression "narrative technique" usually refers to the way the author structures and presents his or her story.

Narrative Poetry: A nondramatic poem in which the author tells a story. Such poems may be of any length or level of complexity.

Narrator: The teller of a story. The narrator may be the author or a character in the story through whom the author speaks.

Naturalism: A literary movement of the late nineteenth and early twentieth centuries. The movement's major theorist, French novelist Emile Zola, envisioned a type of fiction that would examine human life with the objectivity of scientific inquiry. The Naturalists typically viewed human beings as either the products of "biological determinism," ruled by hereditary instincts and engaged in an endless struggle for survival, or as the products of "socioeconomic determinism," ruled by social and economic forces beyond their control. In their works, the Naturalists generally ignored the highest levels of society and focused on degradation: poverty, alcoholism, prostitution, insanity, and disease.

Negritude: A literary movement based on the concept of a shared cultural bond on the part of black Africans, wherever they may be in the world. It traces its origins to the former French colonies of Africa and the Caribbean. Negritude poets, novelists, and essayists generally stress four points in their writings: One, black alienation from traditional African culture can lead to feelings of inferiority. Two, European colonialism and Western education should be resisted. Three, black Africans should seek to affirm and define their own identity. Four, African culture can and should be reclaimed. Many Negritude writers also claim that blacks can make unique contributions to the world, based on a heightened appreciation of nature, rhythm, and human emotions—aspects of life they say are not so highly valued in the materialistic and rationalistic West.

Negro Renaissance: See *Harlem Renaissance*

Neoclassical Period: See *Neoclassicism*

Neoclassicism: In literary criticism, this term refers to the revival of the attitudes and styles of expression of classical literature. It is generally used to describe a period in European history beginning in the late seventeenth century and lasting until about 1800. In its purest form, Neoclassicism marked a return to order, proportion, restraint, logic, accuracy, and decorum. In England, where Neoclassicism perhaps was most popular, it reflected the influence of seventeenth-century French writers, especially dramatists. Neoclassical writers typically reacted against the intensity and enthusiasm of the Renaissance period. They wrote works that appealed to the intellect, using elevated language and classical literary forms such as satire and the ode. Neoclassical works were often governed by the classical goal of instruction.

Neoclassicists: See *Neoclassicism*

New Criticism: A movement in literary criticism, dating from the late 1920s, that stressed close textual analysis in the interpretation of works of literature. The New Critics saw little merit in historical and biographical analysis. Rather, they aimed to examine the text alone, free from the question of how external events—biographical or otherwise—may have helped shape it.

New Journalism: A type of writing in which the journalist presents factual information in a form usually used in fiction. New journalism emphasizes description, narration, and character development to bring readers closer to the human element of the story, and is often used in personality profiles and in-depth feature articles. It is not compatible with "straight" or "hard" newswriting, which is generally composed in a brief, fact-based style.

New Journalists: See *New Journalism*

New Negro Movement: See *Harlem Renaissance*

Noble Savage: The idea that primitive man is noble and good but becomes evil and corrupted as he becomes civilized. The concept of the noble savage originated in the Renaissance period but is more closely identified with such later writers as Jean-Jacques Rousseau and Aphra Behn.

O

Objective Correlative: An outward set of objects, a situation, or a chain of events corresponding to an inward experience and evoking this experience in the reader. The term frequently appears in modern criticism in discussions of authors' intended effects on the emotional responses of readers.

Objectivity: A quality in writing characterized by the absence of the author's opinion or feeling about the subject matter. Objectivity is an important factor in criticism.

Occasional Verse: poetry written on the occasion of a significant historical or personal event. *Vers de societe* is sometimes called occasional verse although it is of a less serious nature.

Octave: A poem or stanza composed of eight lines. The term octave most often represents the first eight lines of a Petrarchan sonnet.

Ode: Name given to an extended lyric poem characterized by exalted emotion and dignified style. An ode usually concerns a single, serious theme. Most odes, but not all, are addressed to an object or individual. Odes are distinguished from other lyric poetic forms by their complex rhythmic and stanzaic patterns.

Oedipus Complex: A son's amorous obsession with his mother. The phrase is derived from the story of the ancient Theban hero Oedipus, who unknowingly killed his father and married his mother.

Omniscience: See *Point of View*

Onomatopoeia: The use of words whose sounds express or suggest their meaning. In its simplest sense, onomatopoeia may be represented by words that mimic the sounds they denote such as "hiss" or "meow." At a more subtle level, the pattern and rhythm of sounds and rhymes of a line or poem may be onomatopoeic.

Oral Tradition: See *Oral Transmission*

Oral Transmission: A process by which songs, ballads, folklore, and other material are transmitted by word of mouth. The tradition of oral transmission predates the written record systems of literate society. Oral transmission preserves material sometimes over generations, although often with variations. Memory plays a large part in the recitation and preservation of orally transmitted material.

Ottava Rima: An eight-line stanza of poetry composed in iambic pentameter (a five-foot line in which each foot consists of an unaccented syllable followed by an accented syllable), following the abababcc rhyme scheme.

Oxymoron: A phrase combining two contradictory terms. Oxymorons may be intentional or unintentional.

P

Pantheism: The idea that all things are both a manifestation or revelation of God and a part of God at the same time. Pantheism was a common attitude in the early societies of Egypt, India, and Greece the term derives from the Greek *pan* meaning "all" and *theos* meaning "deity." It later became a significant part of the Christian faith.

Parable: A story intended to teach a moral lesson or answer an ethical question.

Paradox: A statement that appears illogical or contradictory at first, but may actually point to an underlying truth.

Parallelism: A method of comparison of two ideas in which each is developed in the same grammatical structure.

Parnassianism: A mid nineteenth-century movement in French literature. Followers of the movement stressed adherence to well-defined artistic forms as a reaction against the often chaotic expression of the artist's ego that dominated the work of the Romantics. The Parnassians also rejected the moral, ethical, and social themes exhibited in the works of French Romantics such as Victor Hugo. The aesthetic doctrines of the Parnassians strongly influenced the later symbolist and decadent movements.

Parody: In literary criticism, this term refers to an imitation of a serious literary work or the signature style of a particular author in a ridiculous manner. A typical parody adopts the style of the original and applies it to an inappropriate subject for humorous effect. Parody is a form of satire and could be considered the literary equivalent of a caricature or cartoon.

Pastoral: A term derived from the Latin word "pastor," meaning shepherd. A pastoral is a literary composition on a rural theme. The conventions of the pastoral were originated by the third-century Greek poet Theocritus, who wrote about the experiences, love affairs, and pastimes of Sicilian shepherds. In a pastoral, characters and language of a courtly nature are often placed in a simple setting. The term pastoral is also used to classify dramas, elegies, and lyrics that exhibit the use of country settings and shepherd characters.

Pathetic Fallacy: A term coined by English critic John Ruskin to identify writing that falsely endows nonhuman things with human intentions and feelings, such as "angry clouds" and "sad trees."

Pen Name: See *Pseudonym*

Pentameter: See *Meter*

Persona: A Latin term meaning "mask." *Personae* are the characters in a fictional work of literature. The *persona* generally functions as a mask through which the author tells a story in a voice other than his or her own. A *persona* is usually either a character in a story who acts as a narrator or an "implied author," a voice created by the author to act as the narrator for himself or herself.

Personae: See *Persona*

Personal Point of View: See *Point of View*

Personification: A figure of speech that gives human qualities to abstract ideas, animals, and inanimate objects.

Petrarchan Sonnet: See *Sonnet*

Phenomenology: A method of literary criticism based on the belief that things have no existence outside of human consciousness or awareness. Proponents of this theory believe that art is a process that takes place in the mind of the observer as he or she contemplates an object rather than a quality of the object itself.

Plagiarism: Claiming another person's written material as one's own. Plagiarism can take the form of direct, word-for-word copying or the theft of the substance or idea of the work.

Platonic Criticism: A form of criticism that stresses an artistic work's usefulness as an agent of social engineering rather than any quality or value of the work itself.

Platonism: The embracing of the doctrines of the philosopher Plato, popular among the poets of the Renaissance and the Romantic period. Platonism is more flexible than Aristotelian Criticism and places more emphasis on the supernatural and unknown aspects of life.

Plot: In literary criticism, this term refers to the pattern of events in a narrative or drama. In its simplest sense, the plot guides the author in composing the work and helps the reader follow the work. Typically, plots exhibit causality and unity and have a beginning, a middle, and an end. Sometimes, however, a plot may consist of a series of disconnected events, in which case it is known as an "episodic plot."

Poem: In its broadest sense, a composition utilizing rhyme, meter, concrete detail, and expressive language to create a literary experience with emotional and aesthetic appeal.

Poet: An author who writes poetry or verse. The term is also used to refer to an artist or writer who has an exceptional gift for expression, imagination, and energy in the making of art in any form.

Poete maudit: A term derived from Paul Verlaine's *Les poetes maudits* (*The Accursed Poets*), a collection of essays on the French symbolist writers Stephane Mallarme, Arthur Rimbaud, and Tristan Corbiere. In the sense intended by Verlaine, the poet is "accursed" for choosing to explore extremes of human experience outside of middle-class society.

Poetic Fallacy: See *Pathetic Fallacy*

Poetic Justice: An outcome in a literary work, not necessarily a poem, in which the good are rewarded and the evil are punished, especially in ways that particularly fit their virtues or crimes.

Poetic License: Distortions of fact and literary convention made by a writer—not always a poet—for the sake of the effect gained. Poetic license is closely related to the concept of "artistic freedom."

Poetics: This term has two closely related meanings. It denotes (1) an aesthetic theory in literary criticism about the essence of poetry or (2) rules prescribing the proper methods, content, style, or diction of poetry. The term poetics may also refer to theories about literature in general, not just poetry.

Poetry: In its broadest sense, writing that aims to present ideas and evoke an emotional experience in the reader through the use of meter, imagery, connotative and concrete words, and a carefully constructed structure based on rhythmic patterns. Poetry typically relies on words and expressions that have several layers of meaning. It also makes use of the effects of regular rhythm on the ear and may make a strong appeal to the senses through the use of imagery.

Point of View: The narrative perspective from which a literary work is presented to the reader. There are four traditional points of view. The "third person omniscient" gives the reader a "godlike" perspective, unrestricted by time or place, from which to see actions and look into the minds of characters. This allows the author to comment openly on characters and events in the work. The "third person" point of view presents the events of the story from outside of any single character's perception, much like the omniscient point of view, but the reader must understand the action as it takes place and without any special insight into characters' minds or motivations. The "first person" or "personal" point of view relates events as they are perceived by a single character. The main character "tells" the story and may offer opinions about the action and characters which differ from those of the author. Much less common than omniscient, third person, and first person is the "second person" point of view, wherein the author tells the story as if it is happening to the reader.

Polemic: A work in which the author takes a stand on a controversial subject, such as abortion or religion. Such works are often extremely argumentative or provocative.

Pornography: Writing intended to provoke feelings of lust in the reader. Such works are often condemned by critics and teachers, but those which can be shown to have literary value are viewed less harshly.

Post-Aesthetic Movement: An artistic response made by African Americans to the black aesthetic movement of the 1960s and early '70s. Writers since that time have adopted a somewhat different tone in their work, with less emphasis placed on the disparity between black and white in the United States. In the words of post-aesthetic authors such as Toni Morrison, John Edgar Wideman, and Kristin Hunter, African Americans are portrayed as looking inward for answers to their own questions, rather than always looking to the outside world.

Postmodernism: Writing from the 1960s forward characterized by experimentation and continuing to apply some of the fundamentals of modernism, which included existentialism and alienation. Postmodernists have gone a step further in the rejection of tradition begun with the modernists by also rejecting traditional forms, preferring the anti-novel over the novel and the anti-hero over the hero.

Pre-Raphaelites: A circle of writers and artists in mid nineteenth-century England. Valuing the pre-Renaissance artistic qualities of religious symbolism, lavish pictorialism, and natural sensuousness, the Pre-Raphaelites cultivated a sense of mystery and melancholy that influenced later writers associated with the Symbolist and Decadent movements.

Primitivism: The belief that primitive peoples were nobler and less flawed than civilized peoples because they had not been subjected to the tainting influence of society.

Projective Verse: A form of free verse in which the poet's breathing pattern determines the lines of the poem. Poets who advocate projective verse are against all formal structures in writing, including meter and form.

Prologue: An introductory section of a literary work. It often contains information establishing the situation of the characters or presents information about the setting, time period, or action. In drama, the prologue is spoken by a chorus or by one of the principal characters.

Prose: A literary medium that attempts to mirror the language of everyday speech. It is distinguished from poetry by its use of unmetered, unrhymed language consisting of logically related sentences. Prose is usually grouped into paragraphs that form a cohesive whole such as an essay or a novel.

Prosopopoeia: See *Personification*

Protagonist: The central character of a story who serves as a focus for its themes and incidents and as the principal rationale for its development. The protagonist is sometimes referred to in discussions of modern literature as the hero or anti-hero.

Proverb: A brief, sage saying that expresses a truth about life in a striking manner.

Pseudonym: A name assumed by a writer, most often intended to prevent his or her identification as the author of a work. Two or more authors may work together under one pseudonym, or an author may use a different name for each genre he or she publishes in. Some publishing companies maintain "house pseudonyms," under which any number of authors may write installations in a series. Some authors also choose a pseudonym over their real names the way an actor may use a stage name.

Pun: A play on words that have similar sounds but different meanings.

Pure Poetry: poetry written without instructional intent or moral purpose that aims only to please a reader by its imagery or musical flow. The term pure poetry is used as the antonym of the term "didacticism."

Q

Quatrain: A four-line stanza of a poem or an entire poem consisting of four lines.

R

Realism: A nineteenth-century European literary movement that sought to portray familiar characters, situations, and settings in a realistic manner. This was done primarily by using an objective narrative point of view and through the buildup of accurate detail. The standard for success of any realistic work depends on how faithfully it transfers common experience into fictional forms. The realistic method may be altered or extended, as in stream of consciousness writing, to record highly subjective experience.

Refrain: A phrase repeated at intervals throughout a poem. A refrain may appear at the end of each stanza or at less regular intervals. It may be altered slightly at each appearance.

Renaissance: The period in European history that marked the end of the Middle Ages. It began in Italy in the late fourteenth century. In broad terms, it is usually seen as spanning the fourteenth, fifteenth, and sixteenth centuries, although it did not reach Great Britain, for example, until the 1480s or so. The Renaissance saw an awakening in almost every sphere of human activity, especially science, philosophy, and the arts. The period is best defined by the emergence of a general philosophy that emphasized the importance of the intellect, the individual, and world affairs. It contrasts strongly with the medieval worldview, characterized by the dominant concerns of faith, the social collective, and spiritual salvation.

Repartee: Conversation featuring snappy retorts and witticisms.

Restoration: See *Restoration Age*

Restoration Age: A period in English literature beginning with the crowning of Charles II in 1660 and running to about 1700. The era, which was characterized by a reaction against Puritanism, was the first great age of the comedy of manners. The finest literature of the era is typically witty and urbane, and often lewd.

Rhetoric: In literary criticism, this term denotes the art of ethical persuasion. In its strictest sense, rhetoric adheres to various principles developed since classical times for arranging facts and ideas in a clear, persuasive, appealing manner. The term is also used to refer to effective prose in general and theories of or methods for composing effective prose.

Rhetorical Question: A question intended to provoke thought, but not an expressed answer, in the reader. It is most commonly used in oratory and other persuasive genres.

Rhyme: When used as a noun in literary criticism, this term generally refers to a poem in which words sound identical or very similar and appear in parallel positions in two or more lines. Rhymes are classified into different types according to where they fall in a line or stanza or according to the degree of similarity they exhibit in their spellings and sounds. Some major types of rhyme are "masculine" rhyme, "feminine" rhyme, and "triple" rhyme. In a masculine rhyme, the rhyming sound falls in a single accented syllable, as with "heat" and "eat." Feminine rhyme is a rhyme of two syllables, one stressed and one unstressed, as with "merry" and "tarry." Triple rhyme matches the sound of the accented syllable and the two unaccented syllables that follow: "narrative" and "declarative."

Rhyme Royal: A stanza of seven lines composed in iambic pentameter and rhymed *ababbcc*. The name is said to be a tribute to King James 1 of Scotland, who made much use of the form in his poetry.

Rhyme Scheme: See *Rhyme*

Rhythm: A regular pattern of sound, time intervals, or events occurring in writing, most often and most discernably in poetry. Regular, reliable rhythm is known to be soothing to humans, while interrupted, unpredictable, or rapidly changing rhythm is disturbing. These effects are known to authors, who use them to produce a desired reaction in the reader.

Rococo: A style of European architecture that flourished in the eighteenth century, especially in France. The most notable features of *rococo* are its extensive use of ornamentation and its themes of lightness, gaiety, and intimacy. In literary criticism, the term is often used disparagingly to refer to a decadent or over-ornamental style.

Romance: A broad term, usually denoting a narrative with exotic, exaggerated, often idealized characters, scenes, and themes.

Romantic Age: See *Romanticism*

Romanticism: This term has two widely accepted meanings. In historical criticism, it refers to a European intellectual and artistic movement of the late eighteenth and early nineteenth centuries that sought greater freedom of personal expression than that allowed by the strict rules of literary form and logic of the eighteenth-century neoclassicists. The Romantics preferred emotional and imaginative expression to rational analysis. They considered the individual to be at the center of all experience and so placed him or her at the center of their art. The Romantics believed that the creative imagination reveals nobler truths—unique feelings and attitudes—than those that could be discovered by logic or by scientific examination. Both the natural world and the state of childhood were important sources for revelations of "eternal truths." "Romanticism" is also used as a general term to refer to a type of sensibility found in all periods of literary history and usually considered to be in opposition to the principles of classicism. In this sense, Romanticism signifies any work or philosophy in which the exotic or dreamlike figure strongly, or that is devoted to individualistic expression, self-analysis, or a pursuit of a higher realm of knowledge than can be discovered by human reason.

Romantics: See *Romanticism*

Russian Symbolism: A Russian poetic movement, derived from French symbolism, that flourished between 1894 and 1910. While some Russian Symbolists continued in the French tradition, stressing aestheticism and the importance of suggestion above didactic intent, others saw their craft as a form of mystical worship, and themselves as mediators between the supernatural and the mundane.

S

Satire: A work that uses ridicule, humor, and wit to criticize and provoke change in human nature and institutions. There are two major types of satire: "formal" or "direct" satire speaks directly to the reader or to a character in the work; "indirect" satire relies upon the ridiculous behavior of its characters to make its point. Formal satire is further divided into two manners: the "Horatian," which ridicules gently, and the "Juvenalian," which derides its subjects harshly and bitterly.

Scansion: The analysis or "scanning" of a poem to determine its meter and often its rhyme scheme. The most common system of scansion uses accents (slanted lines drawn above syllables) to show stressed syllables, breves (curved lines drawn above syllables) to show unstressed syllables, and vertical lines to separate each foot.

Second Person: See *Point of View*

Semiotics: The study of how literary forms and conventions affect the meaning of language.

Sestet: Any six-line poem or stanza.

Setting: The time, place, and culture in which the action of a narrative takes place. The elements of setting may include geographic location, characters' physical and mental environments, prevailing cultural attitudes, or the historical time in which the action takes place.

Shakespearean Sonnet: See *Sonnet*

Signifying Monkey: A popular trickster figure in black folklore, with hundreds of tales about this character documented since the 19th century.

Simile: A comparison, usually using "like" or "as", of two essentially dissimilar things, as in "coffee as cold as ice" or "He sounded like a broken record."

Slang: A type of informal verbal communication that is generally unacceptable for formal writing. Slang words and phrases are often colorful exaggerations used to emphasize the speaker's point; they may also be shortened versions of an often-used word or phrase.

Slant Rhyme: See *Consonance*

Slave Narrative: Autobiographical accounts of American slave life as told by escaped slaves. These works first appeared during the abolition movement of the 1830s through the 1850s.

Social Realism: See *Socialist Realism*

Socialist Realism: The Socialist Realism school of literary theory was proposed by Maxim Gorky and established as a dogma by the first Soviet Congress of Writers. It demanded adherence to a communist worldview in works of literature. Its doctrines required an objective viewpoint comprehensible to the working classes and themes of social struggle featuring strong proletarian heroes.

Soliloquy: A monologue in a drama used to give the audience information and to develop the speaker's character. It is typically a projection of the speaker's innermost thoughts. Usually delivered while the speaker is alone on stage, a soliloquy is intended to present an illusion of unspoken reflection.

Sonnet: A fourteen-line poem, usually composed in iambic pentameter, employing one of several rhyme schemes. There are three major types of sonnets, upon which all other variations of the form are based: the "Petrarchan" or "Italian" sonnet, the "Shakespearean" or "English" sonnet, and the "Spenserian" sonnet. A Petrarchan sonnet consists of an octave rhymed *abbaabba* and a "sestet" rhymed either *cdecde, cdccdc,* or *cdedce*. The octave poses a question or problem, relates a narrative, or puts forth a proposition; the sestet presents a solution to the problem, comments upon the narrative, or applies the proposition put forth in the octave. The Shakespearean sonnet is divided into three quatrains and a couplet rhymed *abab cdcd efef gg*. The couplet provides an epigrammatic comment on the narrative or problem put forth in the quatrains. The Spenserian sonnet uses three quatrains and a couplet like the Shakespearean, but links their three rhyme schemes in this way: *abab bcbc cdcd ee*. The Spenserian sonnet develops its theme in two parts like the Petrarchan, its final six lines resolving a problem, analyzing a narrative, or applying a proposition put forth in its first eight lines.

Spenserian Sonnet: See *Sonnet*

Spenserian Stanza: A nine-line stanza having eight verses in iambic pentameter, its ninth verse in iambic hexameter, and the rhyme scheme ababbcbcc.

Spondee: In poetry meter, a foot consisting of two long or stressed syllables occurring together. This form is quite rare in English verse, and is usually composed of two monosyllabic words.

Sprung Rhythm: Versification using a specific number of accented syllables per line but disregarding the number of unaccented syllables that fall in each line, producing an irregular rhythm in the poem.

Stanza: A subdivision of a poem consisting of lines grouped together, often in recurring patterns of rhyme, line length, and meter. Stanzas may also serve as units of thought in a poem much like paragraphs in prose.

Stereotype: A stereotype was originally the name for a duplication made during the printing process; this led to its modern definition as a person or thing that is (or is assumed to be) the same as all others of its type.

Stream of Consciousness: A narrative technique for rendering the inward experience of a character. This technique is designed to give the impression of an ever-changing series of thoughts, emotions, images, and memories in the spontaneous and seemingly illogical order that they occur in life.

Structuralism: A twentieth-century movement in literary criticism that examines how literary texts arrive at their meanings, rather than the meanings themselves. There are two major types of structuralist analysis: one examines the way patterns of linguistic structures unify a specific text and emphasize certain elements of that text, and the other interprets the way literary forms and conventions affect the meaning of language itself.

Structure: The form taken by a piece of literature. The structure may be made obvious for ease of understanding, as in nonfiction works, or may obscured for artistic purposes, as in some poetry or seemingly "unstructured" prose.

Sturm und Drang: A German term meaning "storm and stress." It refers to a German literary movement of the 1770s and 1780s that reacted against the order and rationalism of the enlightenment, focusing instead on the intense experience of extraordinary individuals.

Style: A writer's distinctive manner of arranging words to suit his or her ideas and purpose in writing. The unique imprint of the author's personality upon his or her writing, style is the product of an author's way of arranging ideas and his or her use of diction, different sentence structures, rhythm, figures of speech, rhetorical principles, and other elements of composition.

Subject: The person, event, or theme at the center of a work of literature. A work may have one or more subjects of each type, with shorter works tending to have fewer and longer works tending to have more.

Subjectivity: Writing that expresses the author's personal feelings about his subject, and which may or may not include factual information about the subject.

Surrealism: A term introduced to criticism by Guillaume Apollinaire and later adopted by Andre Breton. It refers to a French literary and artistic movement founded in the 1920s. The Surrealists sought to express unconscious thoughts and feelings in their works. The best-known technique used for achieving this aim was automatic writing— transcriptions of spontaneous outpourings from the unconscious. The Surrealists

proposed to unify the contrary levels of conscious and unconscious, dream and reality, objectivity and subjectivity into a new level of "super-realism."

Suspense: A literary device in which the author maintains the audience's attention through the buildup of events, the outcome of which will soon be revealed.

Syllogism: A method of presenting a logical argument. In its most basic form, the syllogism consists of a major premise, a minor premise, and a conclusion.

Symbol: Something that suggests or stands for something else without losing its original identity. In literature, symbols combine their literal meaning with the suggestion of an abstract concept. Literary symbols are of two types: those that carry complex associations of meaning no matter what their contexts, and those that derive their suggestive meaning from their functions in specific literary works.

Symbolism: This term has two widely accepted meanings. In historical criticism, it denotes an early modernist literary movement initiated in France during the nineteenth century that reacted against the prevailing standards of realism. Writers in this movement aimed to evoke, indirectly and symbolically, an order of being beyond the material world of the five senses. Poetic expression of personal emotion figured strongly in the movement, typically by means of a private set of symbols uniquely identifiable with the individual poet. The principal aim of the Symbolists was to express in words the highly complex feelings that grew out of everyday contact with the world. In a broader sense, the term "symbolism" refers to the use of one object to represent another.

Symbolist: See *Symbolism*

Symbolist Movement: See *Symbolism*

Sympathetic Fallacy: See *Affective Fallacy*

T

Tanka: A form of Japanese poetry similar to *haiku*. A *tanka* is five lines long, with the lines containing five, seven, five, seven, and seven syllables respectively.

Terza Rima: A three-line stanza form in poetry in which the rhymes are made on the last word of each line in the following manner: the first and third lines of the first stanza, then the second line of the first stanza and the first and third lines of the second stanza, and so on with the middle line of any stanza rhyming with the first and third lines of the following stanza.

Tetrameter: See *Meter*

Textual Criticism: A branch of literary criticism that seeks to establish the authoritative text of a literary work. Textual critics typically compare all known manuscripts or printings of a single work in order to assess the meanings of differences and revisions. This procedure allows them to arrive at a definitive version that (supposedly) corresponds to the author's original intention.

Theme: The main point of a work of literature. The term is used interchangeably with thesis.

Thesis: A thesis is both an essay and the point argued in the essay. Thesis novels and thesis plays share the quality of containing a thesis which is supported through the action of the story.

Third Person: See *Point of View*

Tone: The author's attitude toward his or her audience may be deduced from the tone of the work. A formal tone may create distance or convey politeness, while an informal tone may encourage a friendly, intimate, or intrusive feeling in the reader. The author's attitude toward his or her subject matter may also be deduced from the tone of the words he or she uses in discussing it.

Tragedy: A drama in prose or poetry about a noble, courageous hero of excellent character who, because of some tragic character flaw or *hamartia*, brings ruin upon him- or herself. Tragedy treats its subjects in a dignified and serious manner, using poetic language to help evoke pity and fear and bring about catharsis, a purging of these emotions. The tragic form was practiced extensively by the ancient Greeks. In the Middle Ages, when classical works were virtually unknown, tragedy came to denote any works about the fall of persons from exalted to low conditions due to any reason: fate, vice, weakness, etc. According to the classical definition of tragedy, such works present the "pathetic"—that which evokes pity—rather than the tragic. The classical form of tragedy was revived in the sixteenth century; it flourished especially on the Elizabethan stage. In

modern times, dramatists have attempted to adapt the form to the needs of modern society by drawing their heroes from the ranks of ordinary men and women and defining the nobility of these heroes in terms of spirit rather than exalted social standing.

Tragic Flaw: In a tragedy, the quality within the hero or heroine which leads to his or her downfall.

Transcendentalism: An American philosophical and religious movement, based in New England from around 1835 until the Civil War. Transcendentalism was a form of American romanticism that had its roots abroad in the works of Thomas Carlyle, Samuel Coleridge, and Johann Wolfgang von Goethe. The Transcendentalists stressed the importance of intuition and subjective experience in communication with God. They rejected religious dogma and texts in favor of mysticism and scientific naturalism. They pursued truths that lie beyond the "colorless" realms perceived by reason and the senses and were active social reformers in public education, women's rights, and the abolition of slavery.

Trickster: A character or figure common in Native American and African literature who uses his ingenuity to defeat enemies and escape difficult situations. Tricksters are most often animals, such as the spider, hare, or coyote, although they may take the form of humans as well.

Trimeter: See *Meter*

Triple Rhyme: See *Rhyme*

Trochee: See *Foot*

U

Understatement: See *Irony*

Unities: Strict rules of dramatic structure, formulated by Italian and French critics of the Renaissance and based loosely on the principles of drama discussed by Aristotle in his *Poetics*. Foremost among these rules were the three unities of action, time, and place that compelled a dramatist to: (1) construct a single plot with a beginning, middle, and end that details the causal relationships of action and character; (2) restrict the action to the events of a single day; and (3) limit the scene to a single place or city. The unities were observed faithfully by continental European writers until the Romantic Age, but they were never regularly observed in English drama. Modern dramatists are typically more concerned with a unity of impression or emotional effect than with any of the classical unities.

Urban Realism: A branch of realist writing that attempts to accurately reflect the often harsh facts of modern urban existence.

Utopia: A fictional perfect place, such as "paradise" or "heaven."

Utopian: See *Utopia*

Utopianism: See *Utopia*

V

Verisimilitude: Literally, the appearance of truth. In literary criticism, the term refers to aspects of a work of literature that seem true to the reader.

Vers de societe: See *Occasional Verse*

Vers libre: See *Free Verse*

Verse: A line of metered language, a line of a poem, or any work written in verse.

Versification: The writing of verse. Versification may also refer to the meter, rhyme, and other mechanical components of a poem.

Victorian: Refers broadly to the reign of Queen Victoria of England (1837-1901) and to anything with qualities typical of that era. For example, the qualities of smug narrowmindedness, bourgeois materialism, faith in social progress, and priggish morality are often considered Victorian. This stereotype is contradicted by such dramatic intellectual developments as the theories of Charles Darwin, Karl Marx, and Sigmund Freud (which stirred strong debates in England) and the critical attitudes of serious Victorian writers like Charles Dickens and George Eliot. In literature, the Victorian Period was the great age of the English novel, and the latter part of the era saw the rise of movements such as decadence and symbolism.

Victorian Age: See *Victorian*

Victorian Period: See *Victorian*

W

Weltanschauung: A German term referring to a person's worldview or philosophy.

Weltschmerz: A German term meaning "world pain." It describes a sense of anguish about the nature of existence, usually associated with a melancholy, pessimistic attitude.

Z

Zarzuela: A type of Spanish operetta.

Zeitgeist: A German term meaning "spirit of the time." It refers to the moral and intellectual trends of a given era.

Cumulative
Author/Title Index

Cumulative
Nationality/Ethnicity Index

Subject/Theme Index

Cumulative Index of First Lines

She sang beyond the genius of the sea. (The Idea of Order at Key West) V13:164

She walks in beauty, like the night (She Walks in Beauty) V14:268

She was my grandfather's second wife. Coming late (My Grandmother's Plot in the Family Cemetery) V27:154

Side by side, their faces blurred, (An Arundel Tomb) V12:17

Since the professional wars— (Midnight) V2:130

Since then, I work at night. (Ten Years after Your Deliberate Drowning) V21:240

S'io credesse che mia risposta fosse (The Love Song of J. Alfred Prufrock) V1:97

Sky black (Duration) V18:93

Sleepless as Prospero back in his bedroom (Darwin in 1881) V13:83

so much depends (The Red Wheelbarrow) V1:219

So the man spread his blanket on the field (A Tall Man Executes a Jig) V12:228

So the sky wounded you, jagged at the heart, (Daylights) V13:101

Softly, in the dark, a woman is singing to me (Piano) V6:145

Some say it's in the reptilian dance (The Greatest Grandeur) V18:119

Some say the world will end in fire (Fire and Ice) V7:57

Something there is that doesn't love a wall (Mending Wall) V5:231

Sometimes walking late at night (Butcher Shop) V7:43

Sometimes, a lion with a prophet's beard (For An Assyrian Frieze) V9:120

Sometimes, in the middle of the lesson (Music Lessons) V8:117

somewhere i have never travelled,gladly beyond (somewhere i have never travelled,gladly beyond) V19:265

South of the bridge on Seventeenth (Fifteen) V2:78

Stop all the clocks, cut off the telephone, (Funeral Blues) V10:139

Strong Men, riding horses. In the West (Strong Men, Riding Horses) V4:209

Such places are too still for history, (Deep Woods) V14:138

Sundays too my father got up early (Those Winter Sundays) V1:300

Sweet day, so cool, so calm, so bright, (Virtue) V25:263

Swing low sweet chariot (Swing Low Sweet Chariot) V1:283

T

Take heart, monsieur, four-fifths of this province (For Jean Vincent D'abbadie, Baron St.-Castin) V12:78

Take sheds and stalls from Billingsgate, (The War Correspondent) V26:235

Tears, idle tears, I know not what they mean (Tears, Idle Tears) V4:220

Tell me not, in mournful numbers (A Psalm of Life) V7:165

Temple bells die out. (Temple Bells Die Out) V18:210

That is no country for old men. The young (Sailing to Byzantium) V2:207

That negligible bit of sand which slides (Variations on Nothing) V20:234

That time of drought the embered air (Drought Year) V8:78

That's my last Duchess painted on the wall (My Last Duchess) V1:165

The apparition of these faces in the crowd (In a Station of the Metro) V2:116

The Assyrian came down like the wolf on the fold (The Destruction of Sennacherib) V1:38

The bored child at the auction (The Wings) V28:242

The broken pillar of the wing jags from the clotted shoulder (Hurt Hawks) V3:138

The bud (Saint Francis and the Sow) V9:222

The Bustle in a House (The Bustle in a House) V10:62

The buzz saw snarled and rattled in the yard (Out, Out—) V10:212

The couple on the left of me (Walk Your Body Down) V26:219

The courage that my mother had (The Courage that My Mother Had) V3:79

The Curfew tolls the knell of parting day (Elegy Written in a Country Churchyard) V9:73

The fiddler crab fiddles, glides and dithers, (Fiddler Crab) V23:111–112

The force that through the green fuse drives the flower (The Force That Through the Green Fuse Drives the Flower) V8:101

The grasses are light brown (September) V23:258–259

The green lamp flares on the table (This Life) V1:293

The house is crammed: tier beyond tier they grin ("Blighters") V28:3

The ills I sorrow at (Any Human to Another) V3:2

The instructor said (Theme for English B) V6:194

The king sits in Dumferling toune (Sir Patrick Spens) V4:177

The land was overmuch like scenery (Beowulf) V11:2

The last time I saw it was 1968. (The Hiding Place) V10:152

The Lord is my shepherd; I shall not want (Psalm 23) V4:103

The man who sold his lawn to standard oil (The War Against the Trees) V11:215

The moon glows the same (The Moon Glows the Same) V7:152

The old South Boston Aquarium stands (For the Union Dead) V7:67

The others bent their heads and started in ("Trouble with Math in a One-Room Country School") V9:238

The pale nuns of St. Joseph are here (Island of Three Marias) V11:79

The Phoenix comes of flame and dust (The Phoenix) V10:226

The plants of the lake (Two Poems for T.) V20:218

The rain set early in to-night: (Porphyria's Lover) V15:151

The river brought down (How We Heard the Name) V10:167

The rusty spigot (Onomatopoeia) V6:133

The sea is calm tonight (Dover Beach) V2:52

The sea sounds insincere (The Milkfish Gatherers) V11:111

The slow overture of rain, (Mind) V17:145

The Soul selects her own Society— (The Soul Selects Her Own Society) V1:259

The time you won your town the race (To an Athlete Dying Young) V7:230

The way sorrow enters the bone (The Blue Rim of Memory) V17:38

When the world was created wasn't it like this? (Anniversary) V15:2

When they said *Carrickfergus* I could hear (The Singer's House) V17:205

When we two parted (When We Two Parted) V29:297

When you consider the radiance, that it does not withhold (The City Limits) V19:78

When you look through the window in Sag Harbor and see (View) V25:246–247

When, in disgrace with Fortune and men's eyes (Sonnet 29) V8:198

Whenever Richard Cory went down town (Richard Cory) V4:116

While I was gone a war began. (While I Was Gone a War Began) V21:253–254

While my hair was still cut straight across my forehead (The River-Merchant's Wife: A Letter) V8:164

While the long grain is softening (Early in the Morning) V17:75

While this America settles in the mould of its vulgarity, heavily thickening to empire (Shine, Perishing Republic) V4:161

While you are preparing for sleep, brushing your teeth, (The Afterlife) V18:39

Who has ever stopped to think of the divinity of Lamont Cranston? (In Memory of Radio) V9:144

Whose woods these are I think I know (Stopping by Woods on a Snowy Evening) V1:272

Whoso list to hunt: I know where is an hind. (Whoso List to Hunt) V25:286

Why should I let the toad *work* (Toads) V4:244

Y

You are small and intense (To a Child Running With Out-stretched Arms in Canyon de Chelly) V11:173

You can't hear? Everything here is changing. (The River Mumma Wants Out) V25:191

You do not have to be good. (Wild Geese) V15:207

You should lie down now and remember the forest, (The Forest) V22:36–37

You stood thigh-deep in water and green light glanced (Lake) V23:158

You were never told, Mother, how old Illya was drunk (The Czar's Last Christmas Letter) V12:44

Cumulative
Index of Last Lines

And makes me end where I begun (A Valediction: Forbidding Mourning) V11:202

And 'midst the stars inscribe Belinda's name. (The Rape of the Lock) V12:209

And miles to go before I sleep (Stopping by Woods on a Snowy Evening) V1:272

and my father saying things. (My Father's Song) V16:102

And no birds sing. (La Belle Dame sans Merci) V17:18

And not waving but drowning (Not Waving but Drowning) V3:216

And oh, 'tis true, 'tis true (When I Was One-and-Twenty) V4:268

And reach for your scalping knife. (For Jean Vincent D'abbadie, Baron St.-Castin) V12:78

and retreating, always retreating, behind it (Brazil, January 1, 1502) V6:16

And settled upon his eyes in a black soot ("More Light! More Light!") V6:120

And shuts his eyes. (Darwin in 1881) V13: 84

And so live ever—or else swoon to death (Bright Star! Would I Were Steadfast as Thou Art) V9:44

and strange and loud was the dingoes' cry (Drought Year) V8:78

and stride out. (Courage) V14:126

and sweat and fat and greed. (Anorexic) V12:3

And that has made all the difference (The Road Not Taken) V2:195

And the deep river ran on (As I Walked Out One Evening) V4:16

And the midnight message of Paul Revere (Paul Revere's Ride) V2:180

And the mome raths outgrabe (Jabberwocky) V11:91

And the Salvation Army singing God loves us. . . . (Hopeis a Tattered Flag) V12:120

and these the last verses that I write for her (Tonight I Can Write) V11:187

and thickly wooded country; the moon. (The Art of the Novel) V23:29

And those roads in South Dakota that feel around in the darkness . . . (Come with Me) V6:31

and to know she will stay in the field till you die? (Landscape with Tractor) V10:183

and two blankets embroidered with smallpox (Meeting the British) V7:138

and waving, shouting, *Welcome back*. (Elegy for My Father, Who Is Not Dead) V14:154

And—which is more—you'll be a Man, my son! (If) V22:54–55

and whose skin is made dusky by stars. (September) V23:258–259

And wild for to hold, though I seem tame.' (Whoso List to Hunt) V25:286

And would suffice (Fire and Ice) V7:57

And yet God has not said a word! (Porphyria's Lover) V15:151

and you spread un the thin halo of night mist. (Ways to Live) V16:229

And Zero at the Bone— (A Narrow Fellow in the Grass) V11:127

(answer with a tower of birds) (Duration) V18:93

Around us already perhaps future moons, suns and stars blaze in a fiery wreath. (But Perhaps God Needs the Longing) V20:41

As any She belied with false compare (Sonnet 130) V1:248

As ever in my great Task-Master's eye. (On His Having Arrived at the Age of Twenty-Three) V17:160

As far as Cho-fu-Sa (The River-Merchant's Wife: A Letter) V8:165

as it has disappeared. (The Wings) V28:244

As the contagion of those molten eyes (For An Assyrian Frieze) V9:120

As they lean over the beans in their rented back room that is full of beads and receipts and dolls and clothes, tobacco crumbs, vases and fringes (The Bean Eaters) V2:16

aspired to become lighter than air (Blood Oranges) V13:34

at home in the fish's fallen heaven (Birch Canoe) V5:31

away, pedaling hard, rocket and pilot. (His Speed and Strength) V19:96

B

Back to the play of constant give and change (The Missing) V9:158

Before it was quite unsheathed from reality (Hurt Hawks) V3:138

before we're even able to name them. (Station) V21:226–227

behind us and all our shining ambivalent love airborne there before us. (Our Side) V24:177

Black like me. (Dream Variations) V15:42

Bless me (Hunger in New York City) V4:79

bombs scandalizing the sanctity of night. (While I Was Gone a War Began) V21:253–254

But, baby, where are you?" (Ballad of Birmingham) V5:17

But be (Ars Poetica) V5:3

but it works every time (Siren Song) V7:196

but the truth is, it is, lost to us now. (The Forest) V22:36–37

But there is no joy in Mudville— mighty Casey has "Struck Out." (Casey at the Bat) V5:58

But we hold our course, and the wind is with us. (On Freedom's Ground) V12:187

by a beeswax candle pooling beside their dinnerware. (Portrait of a Couple at Century's End) V24:214–215

by good fortune (The Horizons of Rooms) V15:80

C

Calls through the valleys of Hall. (Song of the Chattahoochee) V14:284

chickens (The Red Wheelbarrow) V1:219

clear water dashes (Onomatopoeia) V6:133

Columbia. (Kindness) V24:84–85

come to life and burn? (Bidwell Ghost) V14:2

Comin' for to carry me home (Swing Low Sweet Chariot) V1:284

cool as from underground springs and pure enough to drink. (The Man-Moth) V27:135

crossed the water. (All It Takes) V23:15

D

Dare frame thy fearful symmetry? (The Tyger) V2:263

"Dead," was all he answered (The Death of the Hired Man) V4:44

deep in the deepest one, tributaries burn. (For Jennifer, 6, on the Teton) V17:86

Delicate, delicate, delicate, delicate—now! (The Base Stealer) V12:30

Die soon (We Real Cool) V6:242

Do what you are going to do, I will tell about it. (I go Back to May 1937) V17:113

down from the sky (Russian Letter) V26:181

Down in the flood of remembrance, I weep like a child for the past (Piano) V6:145

Downward to darkness, on extended wings. (Sunday Morning) V16:190

Driving around, I will waste more time. (Driving to Town Late to Mail a Letter) V17:63

dry wells that fill so easily now (The Exhibit) V9:107

dust rises in many myriads of grains. (Not like a Cypress) V24:135

dusty as miners, into the restored volumes. (Bonnard's Garden) V25:33

E

endless worlds is the great meeting of children. (60) V18:3

Eternal, unchanging creator of earth. Amen (The Seafarer) V8:178

Eternity of your arms around my neck. (Death Sentences) V22:23

even as it vanishes—were not our life. (The Litany) V24:101–102

every branch traced with the ghost writing of snow. (The Afterlife) V18:39

F

fall upon us, the dwellers in shadow (In the Land of Shinar) V7:84

Fallen cold and dead (O Captain! My Captain!) V2:147

filled, never. (The Greatest Grandeur) V18:119

Firewood, iron-ware, and cheap tin trays (Cargoes) V5:44

Fled is that music:—Do I wake or sleep? (Ode to a Nightingale) V3:229

For I'm sick at the heart, and I fain wad lie down." (Lord Randal) V6:105

For nothing now can ever come to any good. (Funeral Blues) V10:139

For the love of God they buried his cold corpse. (The Bronze Horseman) V28:31

forget me as fast as you can. (Last Request) V14:231

from one kiss (A Rebirth) V21:193–194

G

garish for a while and burned. (One of the Smallest) V26:142

going where? Where? (Childhood) V19:29

H

Had anything been wrong, we should certainly have heard (The Unknown Citizen) V3:303

Had somewhere to get to and sailed calmly on (Mus'e des Beaux Arts) V1:148

half eaten by the moon. (Dear Reader) V10:85

hand over hungry hand. (Climbing) V14:113

Happen on a red tongue (Small Town with One Road) V7:207

hard as mine with another man? (An Attempt at Jealousy) V29:24

Has no more need of, and I have (The Courage that My Mother Had) V3:80

Has set me softly down beside you. The Poem is you (Paradoxes and Oxymorons) V11:162

Hath melted like snow in the glance of the Lord! (The Destruction of Sennacherib) V1:39

He rose the morrow morn (The Rime of the Ancient Mariner) V4:132

He says again, "Good fences make good neighbors." (Mending Wall) V5:232

He writes down something that he crosses out. (The Boy) V19:14

here; passion will save you. (Air for Mercury) V20:2–3

History theirs whose languages is the sun. (An Elementary School Classroom in a Slum) V23:88–89

How at my sheet goes the same crooked worm (The Force That Through the Green Fuse Drives the Flower) V8:101

How can I turn from Africa and live? (A Far Cry from Africa) V6:61

How sad then is even the marvelous! (An African Elegy) V13:4

I

I am a true Russian! (Babii Yar) V29:38

I am black. (The Song of the Smoke) V13:197

I am going to keep things like this (Hawk Roosting) V4:55

I am not brave at all (Strong Men, Riding Horses) V4:209

I could not see to see— (I Heard a Fly Buzz—When I Died—) V5:140

I cremated Sam McGee (The Cremation of Sam McGee) V10:76

I didn't want to put them down. (And What If I Spoke of Despair) V19:2

I have just come down from my father (The Hospital Window) V11:58

I hear it in the deep heart's core. (The Lake Isle of Innisfree) V15:121

I never writ, nor no man ever loved (Sonnet 116) V3:288

I romp with joy in the bookish dark (Eating Poetry) V9:61

I see Mike's painting, called SARDINES (Why I Am Not a Painter) V8:259

I shall but love thee better after death (Sonnet 43) V2:236

I should be glad of another death (Journey of the Magi) V7:110

I stand up (Miss Rosie) V1:133

I stood there, fifteen (Fifteen) V2:78

I take it you are he? (Incident in a Rose Garden) V14:191

I turned aside and bowed my head and wept (The Tropics in New York) V4:255

If Winter comes, can Spring be far behind? (Ode to the West Wind) V2:163

I'll be gone from here. (The Cobweb) V17:51

I'll dig with it (Digging) V5:71

In a convulsive misery (The Milkfish Gatherers) V11:112

In balance with this life, this death (An Irish Airman Foresees His Death) V1:76

in earth's gasp, ocean's yawn. (Lake) V23:158

In Flanders fields (In Flanders Fields) V5:155

In ghostlier demarcations, keener sounds. (The Idea of Order at Key West) V13:164

In hearts at peace, under an English heaven (The Soldier) V7:218

In her tomb by the side of the sea (Annabel Lee) V9:14

in the family of things. (Wild Geese) V15:208

in the grit gray light of day. (Daylights) V13:102

In the rear-view mirrors of the passing cars (The War Against the Trees) V11:216

In these Chicago avenues. (A Thirst Against) V20:205

in this bastion of culture. (To an Unknown Poet) V18:221

in your unsteady, opening hand. (What the Poets Could Have Been) V26:262

iness (l(a) V1:85

Into blossom (A Blessing) V7:24

Is Come, my love is come to me. (A Birthday) V10:34

is love—that's all. (Two Poems for T.) V20:218

is safe is what you said. (Practice) V23:240

is still warm (Lament for the Dorsets) V5:191

It asked a crumb—of Me (Hope Is the Thing with Feathers) V3:123

It had no mirrors. I no longer needed mirrors. (I, I, I) V26:97

It is our god. (Fiddler Crab) V23:111–112

it is the bell to awaken God that we've heard ringing. (The Garden Shukkei-en) V18:107

it over my face and mouth. (An Anthem) V26:34

It rains as I write this. Mad heart, be brave. (The Country Without a Post Office) V18:64

It was your resting place." (Ah, Are You Digging on My Grave?) V4:2

it's always ourselves we find in the sea (maggie & milly & molly & may) V12:150

its bright, unequivocal eye. (Having it Out with Melancholy) V17:99

It's the fall through wind lifting white leaves. (Rapture) V21:181

its youth. The sea grows old in it. (The Fish) V14:172

J

Judge tenderly—of Me (This Is My Letter to the World) V4:233

Just imagine it (Inventors) V7:97

L

Laughing the stormy, husky, brawling laughter of Youth, half-naked, sweating, proud to be Hog Butcher, Tool Maker, Stacker of Wheat, Player with Railroads and Freight Handler to the Nation (Chicago) V3:61

Learn to labor and to wait (A Psalm of Life) V7:165

Leashed in my throat (Midnight) V2:131

Leaving thine outgrown shell by life's un-resting sea (The Chambered Nautilus) V24:52–53

Let my people go (Go Down, Moses) V11:43

Let the water come. (America, America) V29:4

life, our life and its forgetting. (For a New Citizen of These United States) V15:55

Life to Victory (Always) V24:15

like a bird in the sky … (Ego-Tripping) V28:113

like a shadow or a friend. *Colombia.* (Kindness) V24:84–85

Like Stone— (The Soul Selects Her Own Society) V1:259

Little Lamb, God bless thee. (The Lamb) V12:135

Look'd up in perfect silence at the stars. (When I Heard the Learn'd Astronomer) V22:244

love (The Toni Morrison Dreams) V22:202–203

Luck was rid of its clover. (Yet we insist that life is full of happy chance) V27:292

M

'Make a wish, Tom, make a wish.' (Drifters) V10: 98

make it seem to change (The Moon Glows the Same) V7:152

May be refined, and join the angelic train. (On Being Brought from Africa to America) V29:223

midnight-oiled in the metric laws? (A Farewell to English) V10:126

Monkey business (Business) V16:2

More dear, both for themselves and for thy sake! (Tintern Abbey) V2:250

My foe outstretchd beneath the tree. (A Poison Tree) V24:195–196

My love shall in my verse ever live young (Sonnet 19) V9:211

My soul has grown deep like the rivers. (The Negro Speaks of Rivers) V10:198

My soul I'll pour into thee. (The Night Piece: To Julia) V29:206

N

never to waken in that world again (Starlight) V8:213

newness comes into the world (Daughter-Mother-Maya-Seeta) V25:83

Nirvana is here, nine times out of ten. (Spring-Watching Pavilion) V18:198

No, she's brushing a boy's hair (Facing It) V5:110

no—tell them no— (The Hiding Place) V10:153

Noble six hundred! (The Charge of the Light Brigade) V1:3

nobody,not even the rain,has such small hands (somewhere i have never travelled,gladly beyond) V19:265

Nor swim under the terrible eyes of prison ships. (The Drunken Boat) V28:84

Not a roof but a field of stars. (Rent) V25:164

not be seeing you, for you have no insurance. (The River Mumma Wants Out) V25:191

Not even the blisters. Look. (What Belongs to Us) V15:196

Not of itself, but thee. (Song: To Celia) V23:270–271

Nothing, and is nowhere, and is endless (High Windows) V3:108

Nothing gold can stay (Nothing Gold Can Stay) V3:203

Now! (Alabama Centennial) V10:2

nursing the tough skin of figs (This Life) V1:293

O

O Death in Life, the days that are no more! (Tears, Idle Tears) V4:220

O Lord our Lord, how excellent is thy name in all the earth! (Psalm 8) V9:182

O Roger, Mackerel, Riley, Ned, Nellie, Chester, Lady Ghost (Names of Horses) V8:142

o, walk your body down, don't let it go it alone. (Walk Your Body Down) V26:219

Of all our joys, this must be the deepest. (Drinking Alone Beneath the Moon) V20:59–60

of blood and ignorance. (Art Thou the Thing I Wanted) V25:2–3

of gentleness (To a Sad Daughter) V8:231

of love's austere and lonely offices? (Those Winter Sundays) V1:300

of peaches (The Weight of
    Sweetness) V11:230

Of the camellia (Falling Upon Earth)
    V2:64

Of the Creator. And he waits for the
    world to begin (Leviathan)
    V5:204

Of what is past, or passing, or to
    come (Sailing to Byzantium)
    V2:207

Oh that was the garden of
    abundance, seeing you. (Seeing
    You) V24:244–245

Old Ryan, not yours (The
    Constellation Orion) V8:53

On the dark distant flurry (Angle of
    Geese) V2:2

on the frosty autumn air. (The
    Cossacks) V25:70

On the look of Death— (There's a
    Certain Slant of Light) V6:212

On your head like a crown (Any
    Human to Another) V3:2

One could do worse that be a swinger
    of birches. (Birches) V13:15

"Only the Lonely," trying his best to
    sound like Elvis. (The Women
    Who Loved Elvis All Their
    Lives) V28:274

Or does it explode? (Harlem) V1:63

Or help to half-a-crown." (The Man
    He Killed) V3:167

or last time, we look. (In Particular)
    V20:125

Or might not have lain dormant
    forever. (Mastectomy) V26:123

or nothing (Queen-Ann's-Lace)
    V6:179

or the one red leaf the snow releases
    in March. (ThreeTimes My Life
    Has Opened) V16:213

    ORANGE forever. (Ballad of
    Orange and Grape) V10:18

our every corpuscle become an elf.
    (Moreover, the Moon) V20:153

outside. (it was New York and
    beautifully, snowing . . . (i was
    sitting in mcsorley's) V13:152

owing old (old age sticks) V3:246

P

patient in mind remembers the time.
    (Fading Light) V21:49

Perhaps he will fall. (Wilderness
    Gothic) V12:242

Petals on a wet, black bough (In a
    Station of the Metro) V2:116

*Plaiting a dark red love-knot into her
    long black hair* (The
    Highwayman) V4:68

Powerless, I drown. (Maternity)
    V21:142–143

Práise him. (Pied Beauty) V26:161

Pro patria mori. (Dulce et Decorum
    Est) V10:110

R

Rage, rage against the dying of the
    light (Do Not Go Gentle into
    that Good Night) V1:51

Raise it again, man. We still believe
    what we hear. (The Singer's
    House) V17:206

Remember the Giver fading off the lip
    (A Drink of Water) V8:66

Ride me. (Witness) V26:285

rise & walk away like a panther. (Ode
    to a Drum) V20:172–173

Rises toward her day after day, like a
    terrible fish (Mirror) V1:116

S

Shall be lifted—nevermore! (The
    Raven) V1:202

Shantih shantih shantih (The Waste
    Land) V20:248–252

share my shivering bed. (Chorale)
    V25:51

Show an affirming flame.
    (September 1, 1939) V27:235

Shuddering with rain, coming down
    around me. (Omen) V22:107

Simply melted into the perfect light.
    (Perfect Light) V19:187

Singing of him what they could
    understand (Beowulf) V11:3

Singing with open mouths their
    strong melodious songs (I Hear
    America Singing) V3:152

Sister, one of those who never
    married. (My Grandmother's
    Plot in the Family Cemetery)
    V27:155

slides by on grease (For the Union
    Dead) V7:67

Slouches towards Bethlehem to be
    born? (The Second Coming)
    V7:179

So long lives this, and this gives life
    to thee (Sonnet 18) V2:222

So prick my skin. (Pine)
    V23:223–224

Somebody loves us all. (Filling
    Station) V12:57

Speak through my words and my
    blood. (The Heights of Macchu
    Picchu) V28:141

spill darker kissmarks on that dark.
    (Ten Years after Your
    Deliberate Drowning) V21:240

Stand still, yet we will make him run
    (To His Coy Mistress) V5:277

startled into eternity (Four
    Mountain Wolves) V9:132

Still clinging to your shirt (My
    Papa's Waltz) V3:192

Stood up, coiled above his head,
    transforming all. (A Tall Man
    Executes a Jig) V12:229

strangers ask. *Originally?* And I
    hesitate. (Originally)
    V25:146–147

Surely goodness and mercy shall
    follow me all the days of my life:
    and I will dwell in the house of
    the Lord for ever (Psalm 23)
    V4:103

syllables of an old order. (A Grafted
    Tongue) V12:93

T

Take any streetful of people buying
    clothes and groceries, cheering
    a hero or throwing confetti and
    blowing tin horns . . . tell me if
    the lovers are losers . . . tell me if
    any get more than the lovers . . .
    in the dust . . . in the cool tombs
    (Cool Tombs) V6:46

Than from everything else life
    promised that you could do?
    (Paradiso) V20:190–191

Than that you should remember and
    be sad. (Remember) V14:255

that does not see you. You must
    change your life. (Archaic
    Torso of Apollo) V27:3

That then I scorn to change my state
    with Kings (Sonnet 29) V8:198

that there is more to know, that one
    day you will know it.
    (Knowledge) V25:113

That when we live no more, we may
    live ever (To My Dear and
    Loving Husband) V6:228

That's the word. (Black Zodiac)
    V10:47

the bigger it gets. (Smart and Final
    Iris) V15:183

The bosom of his Father and his God
    (Elegy Written in a Country
    Churchyard) V9:74

the bow toward torrents of *veyz mir.*
    (Three To's and an Oi) V24:264

The crime was in Granada, his
    Granada. (The Crime Was in
    Granada) V23:55–56

The dance is sure (Overture to a
    Dance of Locomotives)
    V11:143